Integrated Management of Networked Systems

Concepts, Architectures, and Their Operational Application

The Morgan Kaufmann Series in Networking

Series Editor, Dave Clark

Integrated Management of Networked Systems

Concepts, Architectures, and Their Operational Application

Heinz-Gerd Hegering
University of Munich

Sebastian Abeck
University of Karlsruhe

Bernhard Neumair
DeTeSystem GmbH

GOVERNORS STATE UNIVERSITY
UNIVERSITY PARK
IL 60466

Morgan Kaufmann Publishers
San Francisco, California

Senior Editor: Jennifer Mann
Editorial Assistant: Karyn Johnson
Director of Production & Manufacturing: Yonie Overton
Production Editor: Sarah Burgundy
Cover Design: Wall-to-Wall Studios, Pittsburgh, PA
Cover Image: © A. Child/The Stock Solution
Text Design: Rebecca Evans and Associates
Illustration: Dartmouth Publishing, Inc.
Composition: Ed Sznyter, Babel Press
Copyeditor: Robert Fiske
Proofreader: Jennifer McClain
Indexer: Steve Rath
Printer: Courier Corporation

Morgan Kaufmann Publishers, Inc.
Editorial and Sales Office
340 Pine Street, Sixth Floor
San Francisco, CA 94104-3205
USA

Telephone	415/392-2665
Facsimile	415/982-2665
Email	*mkp@mkp.com*
WWW	*http://www.mkp.com*

Order toll free   800/745-7323

Copyright © 1998 by dpunkt-Verlag für digitale Technologie
Title of German original: Integriertes Management vernetzter Systeme

ISBN: 3-932588-16-9

Translation Copyright © 1999 by Morgan Kaufmann Publishers, Inc.
All rights reserved
Printed in the United States of America
03   02   01   00   99   5   4   3   2   1

Library of Congress Cataloging-in-Publication Data

Hegering, Heinz-Gerd, 1943–
　　[Integriertes Management vernetzter Systeme. English]
　　Integrated management of networked systems: concepts, architectures, and their operational application / Heinz-Gerd Hegering, Sebastian Abeck, Bernhard Neumair
　　　　p.　　cm. — (Morgan Kaufmann series in networking)
　　Includes bibliographical references and index.
　　ISBN 1-55860-571-1
　　1. Computer networks—Management. 2. Computer network architectures.
I. Abeck, Sebastian. II. Neumair, Bernhard. III. Title. IV. Series.
TK5105.5.H43313 1999
　　004.6—dc21   99-35160
　　　　　　　　　　　　　　　　　　　　　　　　　　　　　　　　　　CIP

Contents

PART II
Management Architectures   101

PART V
The Outlook   595

Preface

Networked systems are indispensable infrastructures in the environment of a global economy based on a distribution of workload; for corporate success, it is essential that these systems offer secure and speedy functions. Reliable communication services and distributed applications are also vital for science as well as for society. The function of technical management is to ensure that networked systems operate with the efficiency and effectiveness predefined in the quality of service parameters.

The title of this book highlights the importance of viewing the management of networked systems in its entirety: network, system, applications, and enterprise management represent only separate aspects of networked system management. An integrated view is a must for anyone who wants to confront the vast complexity of the management of distributed heterogeneous systems that is a result of the growing integration of networks and refinement of workload distribution. Management applications are themselves distributed applications that evolve from operational objectives and processes. Coping with heterogeneity means working with standardized management architectures with management systems that can be used as a platform for interoperable and portable or reusable management solutions.

Audience

The aim of this book is to present a clear analysis of existing methods and concepts for the effective and efficient management of heterogeneous distributed systems. In the authors' view, it is more important to focus on principles and background rather than on the short-lived or random features of different products so that the reader is provided with a basis for the evaluation of products and management solutions.

The book is mainly a textbook, but it is also a reference work (in the sense of providing an overview rather than being a dictionary) on state-of-the-art technology in this field. It is therefore equally suitable for network and system planners, users and system administrators who work in the field, and students of computer science and commercial informatics.

Contents

Organized into five parts, the book presents a clear overview of these issues and looks at existing approaches to solutions; each part begins with a separate introduction followed by chapters that cover different aspects of the relevant technology.

Part I focuses on the signifance of management against the background of the current trends in networked systems. Networked systems form the basis for many mission-critical solutions that are designed in a distributed cooperative manner. Since resources and services of networked systems are the objects of management, it is essential that the fundamental aspects of networks, distributed systems, and services be introduced. Part I therefore deals with basic concepts and fundamental architectures, with components, and with services.

Integrated management in distributed heterogeneous environments requires specifications that apply across systems and are not dependent on any particular manufacturer. These frameworks are called management architectures. Part II familiarizes the reader with the most important open management architectures. These include OSI management, telecommunications management network (TMN), Internet management, common object request broker architecture (CORBA), desktop management architecture (DMTF-DMI), and Web-based management, as well as the issues that arise in relationship to the gateways between the management architectures. The book does not cover proprietary architectures; this would go far beyond its scope.

Part III is devoted to management tools and techniques. In addition to learning about isolated (autonomous) tools, the reader is presented with information on management platforms as architecture-related carrier systems for management solutions, integrating tools such as trouble ticket systems, management development tools, and tools for specialized applications scenarios.

Part IV of the book consciously looks at integrated management technologies and tools from a different angle: Tools are always only "a means to an end," and the purpose of management tools is to make the operation of networked systems more reliable, easier, and more efficient. Therefore, the operating processes must be analyzed from the standpoint of what kind of technical tool support an operator wants or requires for a particular operational situation. Even though there is a clear demand for this kind of approach by operators, in other words, by the users of the management tools, until now there have not been any universally accepted procedures that address the needs of the operator and provide the necessary management tools. Therefore, some of the solutions presented in this part are still the subject of research.

Lastly, Part V looks at recognizable trends and describes the management scenarios and solutions that should be available in the future but for which reliable information is not yet available or for which no standards have yet been passed and no products yet exist. Since this part studies the prospects for the future, of necessity it contains subjective assessments of the technologies.

Acknowledgments

This book did not originate from an ivory tower. The authors have had many years of experience working in concrete environments and on projects for industry. Together with their research teams, the Munich Network Management Team (MNM Team) and the Cooperation & Management (C & M) research group, they have been actively involved in the standardization and development of management procedures and in the conceptualization, implementation, and application of tools.

Hundreds of degree theses, numerous doctoral dissertations, a close working relationship with industry, and international contacts with other developers and researchers all contribute to the mosaic that forms this book. The authors want to give special thanks to the two teams mentioned for their productive review of the manuscript as it has evolved. We particularly want to mention the contributions made by two informatics specialists: Christian Mayerl (sections 17.2, 18.4, 18.5) and Robert Scholderer (section 19.4). We express our gratitude to Mrs. Annette Kostelezky for her role in producing many of the illustrations. Our appreciation also goes to Jennifer Mann and Karyn Johnson from Morgan Kaufmann Publishers for their excellent role in the realization process for the book and to the production editor Sarah Burgundy. We are also grateful to Hedwig Jourdan von Schmöger, who had the difficult task of translating the German manuscript. We want to thank Michael Barabas from Dpunkt Verlag in Germany as well for establishing the contact to Morgan Kaufmann. Finally, we are indebted to Lisa Phifer,

Adarsh Sethi, Adrian Tang, and Jeff Konz for carefully reviewing the English manuscript and giving valuable comments and suggestions.

We also want to thank our families and friends for their tremendous patience.

Munich and Karlsruhe, February 1999
Heinz-Gerd Hegering
Sebastian Abeck
Bernhard Neumair

Part I

Introduction and Fundamentals

Defined in general terms, the *management of networked systems* comprises all the measures necessary to ensure the effective and efficient operation of a system and its resources pursuant to an organization's goals. The aim of management is to provide the services and applications of a networked system with the desired level of quality and to guarantee availability and a rapid, flexible deployment of networked resources. If the priority is management of the communications network and its components, the term used is *network management*; if emphasis is on the end systems, the reference is to *system management*. *Applications management* is responsible for applications and services that are provided on a distributed basis.

To appreciate the problems and approaches to solutions that are relevant to management tasks, we first have to have a common understanding of the fundamental characteristics of networks, network components, end systems, and applications and to establish a framework for the aspects encompassed within the overall complex of management. Part I therefore introduces the reader to the relevant terminology, provides an overview of the current network technologies and system services, and presents the first classification of management tasks.

Using new trends in cooperative processing and network development, the availability of modern communications services, the advances being made in software technology, and changes in managerial organizational forms as a basis, Chapter 1 explains why an *integrated management* approach should be applied to the entire networked system. The *definition of fundamental concepts* such as management architecture and management platform lays the foundation for the subsequent parts of the book and is the motivation for its structure.

The *fundamental structures of networked systems* are discussed in Chapter 2. This chapter outlines the architectures of communications systems and distributed systems and the characteristics of resources such as transmission media; LAN, WAN, and Internet components; network services; end system resources; and system services.

Using representatively selected scenarios, Chapter 3 tries to convey to the reader just how complex management tasks can be. From these scenarios, we derive *different classifications* that can be used for dividing the overall complex of management into subtasks. The chapter introduces a functional classification for the areas of configuration, fault, performance, accounting, and security management and describes the organizational and time-related aspects of management.

The Management of Networked Systems: Task Definition

Modern IT supply structures are being shaped more and more by cooperative networked systems (Figure 1.1). *Cooperative processing* means that a task is performed in a distributed way, that is, the subtasks constituting the overall task are carried out in different systems but in a coordinated, goal-oriented manner. Cooperative processing enables a high degree of flexibility in the allocation of the modules of a distributed application to the components of a distributed system. It favors a deliberate dedication of functions to appropriately configured carrier systems or platforms, thereby supporting company-specific system solutions (customizing). Client–server computing is only one example of cooperative processing. Initially, client–server computing or cooperative processing gives no suggestion of the type or size of the participating systems or about the type of underlying networking. Instead, it indicates only that tasks are defined according to certain rules of cooperation in a distributed but coordinated mode of operation. Therefore, the object of supporting management is the distributed application itself, the participating systems, and the network that connects them.

Cooperative processing

There are a number of reasons why cooperative processing has recently become a popular option—in fact, even essential—in certain application areas.

Reasons for the development of cooperative information processing

Network development. Fast networks are a prerequisite for highly transparent link networks between the function-dedicated components of a distributed cooperative supply structure. The development of transmission techniques, including protocol hierarchies and coupling components for very high transmission rates (e.g., Gigabit-Ethernet, ATM, SONET, WDM), has provided an excellent foundation in the local network and long-distance traffic areas (MAN, WAN). Standardization

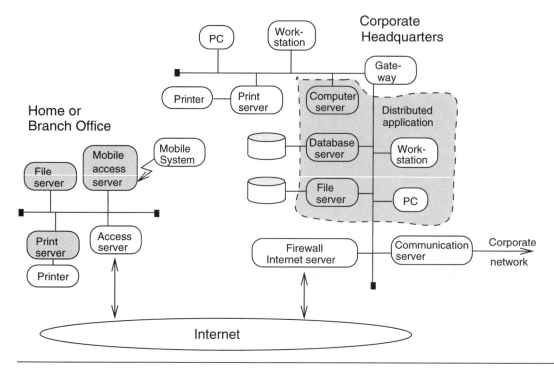

Figure 1.1
Environment for a cooperative IT infrastructure

in transport systems (e.g., Internet protocols) is a contributory factor, as is the merging of data communications and telecommunications (integration of PBX systems, multimedia mail, Internet telephony, video-conferencing). The new technologies are promoting and, at the same time, enabling the flexible configuration of communication structures. The network thereby becomes more than just a connection structure; it is like a market, like an independent system offering services that can be flexibly configured and negotiated (service management, trader systems) in dynamic communications relationships. Individual communication and mass communication begin to become one and the same: Classical point-to-point communication is supplemented by individually controllable 1:m, n:1, or m:n relationships—in other words, by general information and invocation services, distribution services, and conferences. The relevant keywords are virtual workgroups, Centrix, virtual LANs (VLANs), virtual private networks (VPNs), intelligent networks (INs), and interactive service-on-demand networks [ISS98].

Use of new communications services: There is a long way to go before the opportunities offered by services that have already been introduced are fully exploited and integrated into all operating and business processes; these services include email, Faxserver, WWW, conferencing, and multimedia services. Networked systems, however, support distributed cooperative work approaches. The operative concepts include computer-supported cooperative work (CSCW), workflow management systems, telecooperation, teleworking, tele-engineering, and applications sharing. Of course, there is a great interest in having all these services available on a universal corporatewide basis. Universality does not stand only for uniform exchange formats but also for uniform service access interfaces, as well as for standardized name and address concepts. This includes merging all the relevant data, such as all addresses, into a corporate directory. End users of cooperative distributed systems should have as much transparency as possible when determining which technical subsystem of an IT supply structure is providing their communications services. They should have the option to select or be able to change to the service that is most suitable for each respective work step in the business process.

Advances in software technology: The development of open programming environments, of modularization concepts, service interfaces, object orientation, client–server and CORBA concepts, and of Java applets, all of which will be covered in detail later in the book, results in the availability of applications and system services based on distributed system networks. These networks allow the data, processing, and representation modules of a distributed application to be separated logically and these modules to be distributed on a function-dedicated and usage-dependent basis to appropriate physically separate systems. If standardized programming interfaces, so-called open application programming interfaces (APIs), and standardized protocols are used between modules, then an appropriate "rightsizing" using even heterogeneous computer systems is possible. Networked systems even enable the formation of virtual computing structures over significant physical distances (*metacomputing*). An example of this is the use of large numbers of networked high-performance workstations as virtual parallel systems for tasks requiring extensive computing and storage space. The possibilities even extend to the creation of virtual computer centers.

Changes in organizational forms: Cooperative IT supply structures support the implementation of flexible organizational forms, and in fact are a prerequisite for them. None of the following would be possible if a supporting distributed and networked IT structure did not exist: decentralization and outsourcing of IT functions, intranets and extranets, cooperating independent business units, function dedication (that is, division of labor over physical distances) and just-in-time supplier relationships, workgroups and workflow management, market globalization, and new management structures.

Corporate networks as a prerequisite for cooperative computing

Corporate networks, that is, corporatewide unifying communication structures, form the basis for cooperative IT supply structures. They require the following:

- Creation in the local area of a flexible future-oriented cabling structure that is preferably not dependent on any particular network technology and can also cope with the bandwidth requirements of new services and increasing traffic volumes.

- Creation of a uniform protocol structure for the transport system to ensure interconnectivity and interoperability between different LANs, proprietary networks, and public data networks.

- Integration of voice and data networks and associated services.

- Availability of comprehensive, corporatewide communications services, service access interfaces, name and address spaces, directories, and so forth.

- Creation of protected gateway points to the global Internet, other public service networks, or other corporate networks using integrated security concepts.

- Uniform management concept.

IT management comprises a number of management levels that have to be compatible with one another in terms of corporate policy

Not only the corporate network but the entire cooperative distributed IT infrastructure complete with the services and distributed applications provided by it must be subordinated to a preferably integrated management structure. By *management* in this context, we mean *all measures ensuring the effective and efficient operation of a system with its resources in accordance with corporate goals.* Management is therefore responsible for providing, ensuring the availability, and maintaining the services and applications of the distributed system. Viewed in general terms, the management of distributed systems encompasses personnel, procedures, and programs as well as the technical systems (tools), and affects different levels of objects (e.g., resources, services) that are managed (Figure 1.2). The emphasis of *network management* is on the management of communication services and network components, whereas *systems management* relates to the resources of end systems and networked systems. *Applications management* is responsible for distributed applications and services available on a dispersed basis. However, if a service is a general "system service," then the distinction between system and applications management can be unclear. If services are implemented by distributed

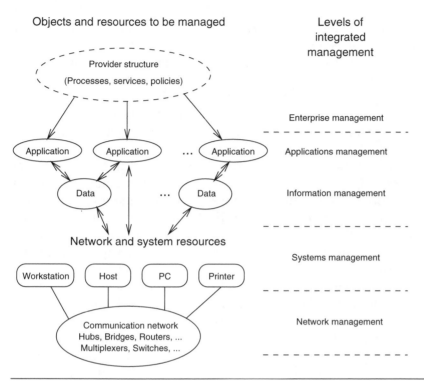

Objects and resources to be managed

Levels of
integrated
management

Provider structure
(Processes, services, policies)

Enterprise management

Application   Application   ...   Application   Applications management

Data   ...   Data   Information management

Network and system resources

Workstation   Host   PC   Printer

Systems management

Communication network
Hubs, Bridges, Routers, ...
Multiplexers, Switches, ...

Network management

Figure 1.2
Levels of integrated management

applications (e.g., value-added services in voice communication, mail or directory services, WWW services) and offered to the internal and external customers of an enterprise, then these services must be managed so that they can be processed, provisioned, and administered in a customer-oriented way with respect to possible service level agreements. This means that a *service and customer management* level is to be inserted above applications management. Of course, all layers provide services, but in this context we mean an enterprise user-delivered service.

Objects of network management include lines, transmission, and switching equipment (switches, bridges, routers, hubs, multiplexers), as well as protocol entities. Objects of system management include CPUs, memory, disk peripheral devices, processes, servers, users, contingents, logs, file systems, and software modules. Examples of system management services include data storage, software distribution, license control, load distribution, spooling, accounting, alarm forwarding, and state management, the last two also being services of network management. Examples of objects of applications management include email, directories, documents, performance reports, trouble tickets, invoices, service level agreements, bookkeeping, and purchasing.

Information management deals with the design and maintenance of corporatewide data, and—if it is used on a distributed basis—ensuring that this data is consistent and fully accessible.

Enterprise management or business management combines the tasks of financial, personnel, technology, and production management from the standpoint of corporatewide aspects (areas of business, business processes) and establishes policies covering IT infrastructure, operating processes, associated services, and data. The policies of enterprise management produce the conditions for creating the management layers below it. This book concentrates on network and system management; in Part IV, however, we will also look at ways to realize and implement enterprise management. We will use case studies to discuss the necessary steps for deriving requirements for service, system, and network management from enterprise management goals.

IT management is itself a distributed application that must be carefully conceptualized and related to a specific environment

Different aspects play a role in differentiating distributed system environments from one another: objectives (services and service quality), communication characteristics (quantitative and time distribution of interactions and traffic relationships), underlying topology, protocol hierarchies, and the organizational and operational structure that exists for the operators and users of the distributed system. Furthermore, the complexity of management in concrete IT structures is determined by the number and the variety of the objects being managed, the heterogeneity of the components, physical distribution, the number of participating organizational units, the depth of service integration, and the number of subnets involved. What is obvious is that there cannot be only *one* management system and only *one* management solution to suit all situations and that a scenario-specific customizing process is essential. Figure 1.3 illustrates the degree to which the dimensions of management-relevant aspects can vary. Yet only a few aspects of the technical management of distributed systems have been mentioned. There has not even been any reference to the economic, legal, or organizational aspects.

We will refer to some of the dimensions of technical management again in Chapter 3 when we cover general requirements for the management of distributed systems, particularly at the network and system management levels.

Through its distribution of the objects that are being managed, management itself is obviously represented as a distributed application. Network and system management in large networked systems can therefore be implemented only through the means of network support.

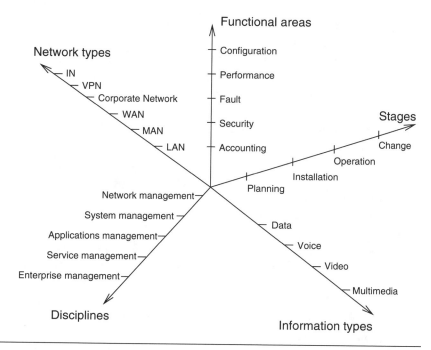

Figure 1.3
Some of the dimensions of technical management

The goal must be an *integrated management* that uses standardized concepts for global management databases, permits an integral approach to different management aspects, includes organizational aspects (e.g., domain concept), supports heterogeneous systems, and offers open programming and user interfaces. Management concepts become "integrated" the easier it is to apply them to more than one management layer. In an integrated management environment, all management-relevant system components cooperate on the basis of shared interoperability standards. An aim of this book is to emphasize the aspect of integrated management. Integrated management therefore requires the specification of a goal-oriented operating concept. The definition of domains, interfaces, and sequences in the management process, as outlined in detail in Part IV of this book, are a prerequisite for the implementation of this concept. The tool functionality requirements can then be established accordingly. This kind of integrated network and system management also requires that the resources being managed in a heterogeneous environment provide sufficient management-relevant information. The information should be capable of interpretation on a vendor-independent basis and be made accessible over well-defined interfaces and protocols. An understand-

Integrated management concepts make goal-oriented management solutions easier to achieve

ing of the principles of distributed systems, the subject of Chapter 2, is imperative for this purpose.

The framework for management-relevant standards is called *management architecture*. The information model for this architecture describes the possibilities that exist on a syntactical and a semantic basis for modeling and describing resources and information in a management-relevant and vendor-independent way. The communications model defines access to management objects and management protocols. The function model organizes the complex task "management" into manageable units and defines the generic management functions. This provides the basis for a building-block system of modular management solutions or for management by delegation. Lastly, the organization model defines roles, cooperation models, and domains.

Part II of this book deals with management architectures. A detailed discussion of basic concepts and submodels of management architectures (Chapter 4) is followed by a presentation of the key management architectures; the emphasis is on vendor-independent management architectures (Chapters 5 to 9) and the possible gateways between management architectures (Chapter 10).

Management architectures, of course, serve only as a framework, which means that the specification of a management architecture by no means implies a uniform implementation. Implementations of management architectures using standardized programming and service interfaces, the so-called open application programming interfaces (APIs), are called *management platforms*. Platforms are carrier systems for management solutions, so they represent the infrastructure for the usually distributed application network and system management. Currently, there is still a gap between management architectures and implementations.

But platforms are not the only tools that exist in the management environment. Measurement tools, documentation systems, trouble ticket systems, workflow management systems, along with special tools for certain application scenarios, are also used to support the IT manager and in some situations must interact with the platform—for instance, through appropriate data transfer mechanisms. We cover the subject of management tools and techniques in Part III.

Cooperative networked systems used as IT infrastructures offer flexibility for a great freedom of scope in rightsizing and downsizing for all different kinds of organizational and operational structures and information processing scenarios. In some circumstances, this can substantially increase effectiveness in the workplace and of business processes (this is covered in detail in Part IV). The price to be paid in

---

Standards are indispensable for the management of heterogeneous environments

Platforms implement architectures and provide integrated tools

It is essential that management tools be integrated into the processes

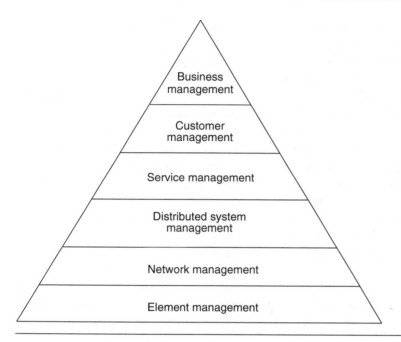

Figure 1.4
Management pyramid

return is complex management that should be as transparent to the user as possible. Management is controllable and affordable only if the underlying concepts here too are structured and flexible and based on an integrated approach. Of course, in a distributed environment a more highly qualified staff that is able to think in "integrated" and "networked" terms is also needed both for management and operations.

Who is affected by management? End users of distributed systems are interested only in results and not in the methods used. They want applications and services to be reliable, flexible, secure, effective, and inexpensive. Quality of service targets and expectations serve as the basis for specifiying the requirements of these technical management processes. From the standpoint of business management, technical management encompasses only a part of the total management pyramid (Figure 1.4, which is an extension of ITU-T Recommendation M.3010. Figure 1.2 is a particular shaping of Figure 1.4).

It is clear that most real management systems do not operate at all the levels of the pyramid, although this would be desirable from the standpoint of integrated management. But what does become immediately obvious is that the economic success of management is primarily manifested in the top end of the pyramid with the lower levels acting as the "enablers." Generally, level N cannot be managed effectively if level N−1 is not operating effectively.

On the other hand, IT managers expect a technical management system to provide everything. They are the ones wedged between the end users and business management for whom the system is essentially only a cost center. The direct users of a management system and of management tools are usually network and system administrators, help desk personnel, customer care centers, network planners, operators, inventory staff, and documentation centers.

Corporate management or those with responsibility for the management of the higher layers of the pyramid are usually interested only in cost and company-related or layer-relevant benchmarks for monitoring and control that are obtainable through the tools of the lower layers.

An integrated management concept is expected to support all the groups mentioned with appropriate tools and as much uniformity as possible with respect to management information and workflow.

Fundamental Structures of Networked Systems

This chapter presents an overview of the fundamentals of networked systems. The content of the chapter is essential as background information for developing an understanding of the relevant management issues that are dealt with in subsequent discussions throughout the book. The architectures of communication systems (OSI model, Internet model) and distributed systems (DCE, CORBA, ODP, and TINA) are presented, along with definitions and brief descriptions of relevant protocols and services. Because these are implemented through the use of resources (media, network, and system components) that are frequently technology specific, the resources are also described briefly. The discussion in this chapter focuses on the definition of functional aspects, whereas the management-relevant aspects are dealt with in later chapters. Readers who have a firm grounding in networked systems have the option of skipping this chapter. The subject treatment in the following sections is presented with varying degrees of detail because the relevant examples that appear in later chapters also vary in detail.

2.1 Terminology

A study of the subject of management, thus networked systems, is required before attention can be given to the management of distributed systems. Generally speaking, a *distributed system* is a system in which a range of individual functional units interconnected over a transport system interact in the execution or implementation of distributed applications. If the functional units comprise data terminal equipment (such as hosts, servers, workstations, PCs, and terminals), the designation *data communications networks* is also often used. If the functional units are telephones, branch exchanges, fax machines,

The terms *distributed system*, *communications network*, and *transport system* have no strict delineation

and telecommunications servers, then the appropriate reference is to *telecommunications networks*. Functional units can, of course, also be software modules or processes within end systems. Of course, it should be mentioned that the distinction between data networks and telecommunications networks is increasingly blurred (e.g., voice-over IP).

A *transport system* consists of transmission media (e.g., electrical conductors, optical fiber, radio paths, virtual channels) and transmission or switching components (e.g., modems, multiplexers, bridges, routers, switches). It can also be made up of several subnetworks (LANs, MANs, WANs, private networks, public networks). The components and services worlds in data and telecommunications networks still differ from each other when it comes down to certain details, although an integration of the two worlds is gradually taking place. However, many similarities exist when it comes to management, therefore obviating any major differentiation where architectures and techniques are concerned. The umbrella terminology we use will simply be *networks* and *communications systems*. The terms *data communications networks* and *computer networks* will be used interchangeably.

In the literature, the terms *communications system*, *network*, and *distributed system* still often relate to the degree of transparency with which services are provided to end users by networked systems. If there is a (network) operating system coordinating the processing steps required to run an application on different systems in a network (distributed application) in such a way that users do not have to be concerned about where the individual steps are executed, then we prefer to refer to the systems network as a distributed system. If the systems network incorporates a visible connectivity structure, in other words, the end systems in the network and the distributed applications processes are contactable over addresses, then the preferred term is *communications network*, with the connection structures often also called *transport networks* (connection networks, transport systems). Where this distinction is not as critical, we often talk about *networked systems* to emphasize that both aspects, the system and the networking, are more or less equal in importance. The (distributed) operating system kernel of a distributed system is of course run on a communications network. The term *distributed system* also tends to be used in the product world if the transparency described is provided only partially or only with certain functions (e.g., virtual global file systems).

Networked systems are generally identified by the following characteristics: physical separation of the cooperating systems, autonomy of the different systems, and heterogeneity. Autonomy means that all the different systems and components operate independently of one another on the basis of an unconfirmed knowledge of the current status of the other components or of the overall system. Heterogeneity refers to the incompatibility that exists in terms of hardware, interfaces, operating systems, communications protocols, formats, and data. These are the characteristics that need to be considered in the communications mechanisms of a distributed system.

Networked systems and communications networks are in this book assumed to be heterogeneous systems

Networked systems are described on the basis of two key structures, namely, physical structure and logical structure. The physical structure describes the actual user systems, the means of transmission (media, topology), and the transmission and switching components. The logical structure describes the structure of the communicating processes as well as of the data being exchanged and the rules of information exchange (i.e., protocols and protocol hierarchies). There can be many logical structures for the same set of physical resources.

A basic knowledge of the structural elements of a distributed system is essential for dealing with the problems of management. Consequently, a brief description of the key architectures and resources for communications networks and distributed systems is given here. Many sources cover these topics in detail, including [HAL96, KER95, STA97, TAN96].

Key concepts for the logical structure of distributed systems are described in architectures that generally model communications processes, make recommendations for a functional analysis of these processes, and provide the basis for resource descriptions and protocol definitions. Protocols stipulate the conventions for the controlled exchange of information for a particular communications service within a cooperation model.

We have limited our discussion to open architectures, in other words, those designed to be multivendor architectures and standardized by consortia or standardization bodies. Since the management architectures discussed later in Part II are based on the architectures for distributed systems and communications networks, we will provide some background information about them. The following sections deal with the architecture for ISO (OSI, including the ITU's TMN) and IETF (Internet) communications systems as well as the architecture for OSF (DCE) and OMG (CORBA) distributed systems. ODP and TINA are sketched, too.

2.2   Communication Architectures

Communication architectures are, in general, characterized by a layered set of protocols that define a functional decomposition of the overall commuications task. Of course, there are several possibilities of specifying the borderlines (interfaces) between the layers. The following sections explain the structuring principles for communication architectures, deal with general protocol functions, and discuss the two most important open (i.e., standardized) communication architectures, namely, the OSI and the Internet architecture.

2.2.1   Structuring Principles, General Protocol Functions

Architectures provide the basis for a common understanding of the communications processes in a heterogeneous environment. This is the prerequisite for providing a precise definition of network services and protocols and creates a vendor-neutral reference world.

Structuring principles for communication architectures

The structuring principle used with most communication architectures involves modeling the behavior of cooperating entities by specifying interaction interfaces at the boundaries of the entities (Figure 2.1). The architectural model originates from the fact that this principle is applied in three ways:

The system, service, and protocol interfaces characterize the communication architecture

- The *system interface* defines the discrete systems between which communication is to take place. It differentiates between the end system, transit system, and transmission medium. A transit system can be a computer or a computer network, which means that system interfaces can be defined more than once depending on the need for abstraction.

- The specification of *service interfaces* breaks down communications processes functionally into (delegatable) subprocesses, ultimately leading to the creation of functional layers. The layering is designed so that functions that resemble each other are allocated to the same layer and independent subprocesses to different layers. Enough flexibility must be built in to allow layers to be implemented on different hardware components or through the use of different techniques, if necessary. Service interfaces therefore define virtual communication machines, which as service providers offer their communication services to entities of the next highest layer at *service access points* (SAPs). Communication at the service access points, therefore between the layers within a system, takes

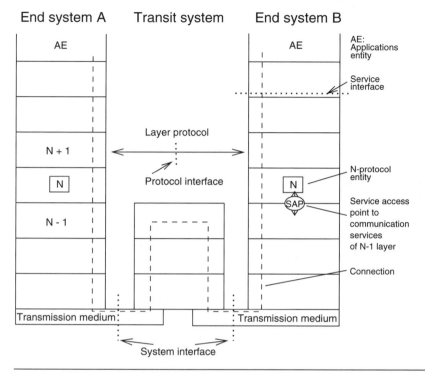

Figure 2.1
Architectural model and defined interfaces

place over *service primitives* (i.e., service requests). Although the significance of these conceptual service requests has to be defined uniformly, the concrete implementation of them can be on a fully system-specific basis (such as through procedural calls or system commands or in separate processes). Service interfaces therefore produce "vertical" communication within a system.

- The *protocol interface* defines how a service specified by a service interface can be provided by the entities of a layer that are located in physically dispersed systems. Whereas service interfaces define virtual communication systems, protocol interfaces consider their implementation by separate autonomous systems. The communication rules and data formats required are defined in *layer protocols* that control the layer connections in partner entities. A whole protocol hierarchy therefore exists on which the connection between application entities can be established, depending on the function layers and services selected.

Entities (processes, programs, stations) in the same layer in different systems are able to communicate with one another ("horizontal" communication) if they use the same layer protocol. If the underlying communication hierarchies are not compatible, then appropriate mapping functions are required between the protocol hierarchies of the different systems.

The different standardized (e.g., ISO, Internet) and proprietary (e.g., SNA) communication architectures used in practice differ from one another in number of layers, the definition of the layer boundaries (service layers), and consequently, the protocol definition. Protocol mapping between the architectures using so-called gateways is usually necessary when these systems are supposed to work together.

A fundamental understanding of the protocol mechanisms is essential for network management

- *Protocols* are a precise specification (in syntactical, procedural, and semantic terms) of the regulations and rules governing information exchange between two or more partners at the same level of functional layering in a communications system. Some typical protocol functions that keep recurring in actual protocols are listed next with no dependence on any particular layer. The functions and the language used in concrete environments vary according to the specific protocols. The linguistic aspect is reflected in the *protocol data units* (PDU), which contain the syntax specified for the protocol-specific information unit (frame, block, packet). Typically, each PDU divides into two logical parts: one part that contains the text and user data to be transported and one part that notifies the partner entity of the protocol functions to be executed (control information, protocol control information PCI, header).

- *Protocol functions for connection management:* These include all the elements that request, reject, or acknowledge connection establishment and connection termination. They also include multiplexing and splitting functions, therefore, the mapping of layer N connections onto N−1 connections. Protocol selection, the capability of being able to negotiate protocol subsets and parameters at the point a connection is being established, is also included among these connection management functions.

- *Protocol functions for data transfer:* (N)-PDUs, which are protocol data units of the layer N protocol, are actually transported by the next lower layer through the use of (N−1)-PDUs. If the format sizes do not match, segmentation and blocking or concatenation of the PDUs is sometimes indicated. This is, of course, also reflected in the protocol control information (PCI) and corresponding control information for the service primitives. The layer N user data, which is transported from layer (N−1) across an (N−1) connection and delivered to the destination system of layer N, is referred to as (N−1) service data units (SDUs). The size of all data units, of course, depends on the resources of the respective system (data terminal equipment, network components) and thus becomes a subject of network management. In some architectures, the control data is also transported separately from the user data (e.g., ISDN). However, this does not affect the applicability of the other considerations.

- *Procotol functions for flow control and routing:* Protocols must contain elements for *flow control* to prevent an inundation of data at the receiver (e.g., adapt sending rate or avoid excessive retransmission in the event of failure). Flow control should not be confused with congestion control; the latter relates to the overload control of entire (sub)networks and not to connections. Protocol elements for *routing* are sometimes also necessary.

- *Protocol functions for error handling:* Falsification, loss, duplication, and mix-ups are typically the kinds of problems that can occur during transmission. Protocol functions for error detection and handling comprise consecutive message numbering (sequence numbers), checksumming (parity, block check characters, frame check sequences), acknowledgments, time outs, error notifications, and test functions as well as reset mechanisms. All these functions are reflected in the PDUs through the appropriate control information and in the operating characteristics of the protocol entities.

- *Connectionless and connection-oriented communication:*
Connection-oriented communication (CO) is based on three phases: connection setup, data transfer, and connection termination. Characteristically, the communication entities store status variables for the connection as well as for the transmitted data and in some cases are able to reserve resources implicitly or explicitly for the entire communications process. This is, of course, reflected in the PDUs of a connection-oriented protocol. Connection-oriented communication is suitable, for example, for applications such as dialog and file transfer, in other words, for cooperative relationships that involve a large volume of transfer or are of long duration or require a guarantee that the correct sequence will be maintained when data is exchanged; it is also suitable for telephony and video-conferencing. For certain communications relationships (e.g., the interchange of short messages that do not need acknowledgment),

it is too complicated to set up and terminate connections and provide status management. This is a case when connectionless communication (connectionless mode, CL, datagram service) is appropriate. A characteristic of this type of service is that each individual data unit is treated independently and no connection status is maintained.

2.2.2   OSI Layers

What makes the ISO reference model with the architectural model so important is that the ISO has created a standardized reference world for communication systems. In practice, the OSI model has found some application in telecommunications networks and hardly at all in computer networks. But OSI upper layer and applications protocols (like X.500) are not uncommon in data networks; the architecture itself has wider applicability as a framework for emergent technologies (ATM, FR, SONET, ISDN, etc.). With respect to later chapters, it is nevertheless useful to include a brief introduction to the OSI model since it is related to the OSI management architecture.

The OSI reference model defines seven main layers plus sublayers for some of the layers (Figure 2.2). We will examine these layers in detail. Most of the information provided does not only apply to OSI but essentially also to the Internet world.

Physical layer (layer 1)   The *physical layer* is responsible for the transparent transmission of bit sequences over different media. The specifications for this layer take into account the different mechanical (e.g., pin layout and pin configuration), physical (electrical, electromagnetic, acoustic, optical), and functional (e.g., the meaning of pin signals) characteristics of transmission media and interfaces. The different types of transmission (such as analog-digital, synchronous-asynchronous) and modulation and coding procedures are constituent parts of this layer.

Medium access layer (MAC layer, layer 2a)   The *datalink layer* can be divided into two sublayers. The *medium access layer* comes into play when the transmission medium is not dedicated to two communicating partners and—for example, in the case of LANs or with wireless communication—a large number of potential communications partners (stations) use the same medium. The MAC layer then regulates the allocation of the shared resources, that is, the transmission medium, on the basis of a fixed scheme (e.g., time multiplexing, frequency multiplexing) or dynamically through so-called multiple-access protocols (reservation procedures, stochastic access procedures). The CSMA/CD procedure (IEEE 802.3), on which

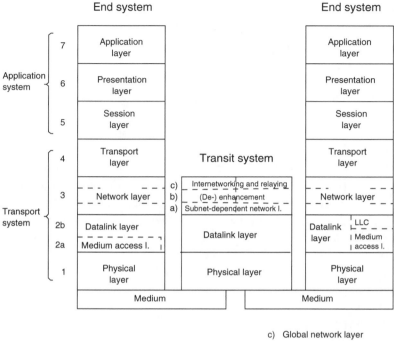

c)   Global network layer
b)   Network adaptation layer
a)   Subnetwork network layer

Figure 2.2
OSI layer model

Ethernet is based, belongs to the category of stochastic procedures. Another access method is token passing, which is used with Token Ring (IEEE 802.5), token bus (IEEE 802.4), and FDDI (ANSI X.3T9.5, ISO 9314). DQDB (IEEE 802.6), which is a reservation procedure used in MAN networks such as Datex-M, also merits mention.

If a transmission medium has been assigned to a communication by the MAC layer, *the logical link layer* (LLC, layer 2b, corresponds to the original datalink layer in ISO/OSI) can be used to provide the security mechanisms for the medium and transmission technique. Layer 2b is responsible for framing, that is, mapping physical signals to data framed for transmission, grouping bit sequences into blocks (bytes, frames), synchronizing the blocks, detecting errors at the block or frame level, and in some cases, executing error recovery. Its goal is to provide the reliable transport of characters or bit sequences, that is, to improve unprotected system connections across physical lines through the detection and correction of errors from the physical layer. The supervisory and control mechanisms and procedures for error

Logical link layer
(layer 2b)

handling are still media dependent, but the network layer is supplied with a service interface that is not media dependent or contingent on the transmission technology used. The protocols normally used in layer 2b are LLC in accordance with IEEE 802.2 or HDLC (ISO 3309).

Network layer (layer 3)

The *network layer* is by and large responsible for switching the paths for logical connections across the network. This action requires so-called transit systems (relay systems, switching systems, node computers). Layer 3 is therefore concerned with routing and switching. If a network consists of a complex of subnetworks, then, of course, the task of routing and switching takes place twice: once in each subnetwork (layer 3a) and once in the network complex (internetworking, layer 3c). Since the layer 3 procedures used in layers 3a and 3c can vary considerably, the network services may sometimes have to be adapted, and this adaptation (called a subnetwork convergence function, SNCF) takes place in layer 3b. X.25 packet layer protocol (ISO 8208) and the connectionless ISO Internet protocol ISO-IP (ISO 8473) are OSI-conformant layer 3 protocols (connection oriented and connectionless, respectively).

Transport layer (layer 4)

The *transport layer* provides a network-independent transport service between two end systems (end to end). It maps the different network services of the network layer to the transport service using the appropriate transport protocols. Transport protocols are oriented toward end systems and ensure that messages between end users are transported end to end and per requirements. "As required" means allowing the higher-ranking layer the possibility of selecting the quality parameters for throughput, delay, availability, residual error rate, and so on. Multiplexing and splitting user (applications entity) connections also fall within the layer's functions, as does flow control (i.e., the "breaking function" between sender and receiver). Layers 1 to 4 represent the *transport system* and evolved from a systematic and functional expansion of the characteristics of the transmission media and switching components. The interface between layer 4 and layer 5 delineates the transport system from the applications-oriented layers, the *applications system*. OSI has defined a connection-oriented (ISO 8073 with five categories of transport protocols) and a connectionless (ISO 8602) transport service used by applications systems to access the transport system.

Session layer (layer 5)

The *session layer* supports the establishment, structuring, and control of sessions. Sessions, which are logical connections of level 5 entities, are temporary cooperative relationships set up for applications processes. The session layer provides services for context management (protocol selection of so-called high-level protocols for applications systems, also context switching), interaction management (control and structuring sessions into segments, granting authorization for specific actions during a session), and synchronization (definition of checkpoints, such as restart and reset functions). What becomes obvious is that the data transport elements above layer 4 are replaced in importance by the applications-oriented communications aspects (ISO 8327 connection oriented, ISO 9548 connectionless).

A prerequisite for communication is that all parties are "speaking the same language." It is therefore essential that all parties agree to a common "presentation context" (a syntax defined by abstract data types) and communicate with one another using a common representation of the data being exchanged (transfer syntax). The coding agreements and mapping that apply to the syntax are the responsibility of the *presentation layer*. This layer provides the services that enable an application to interpret interchanged data; in particular, these are description services for a globally uniform display and interpretation of information. They allow system-specific coding of data structures and data displays in heterogeneous environments to be converted to a data transfer syntax that can be understood by different partners (ISO 9576, ISO 8823, ISO 8824, ISO 8825). It is useful to apply a programming analogy—just as languages like C++ have defined abstract data types (int, char) independent of storage, application protocols are defined with abstract syntax notation (ASN.1, ISO 8823). The presentation layer converts these to a data transfer syntax by applying encoding rules.

Presentation layer (layer 6)

The *application layer* contains applications in the narrower sense, in other words, the processes that account for the actual semantic content of a communication. Architecturally, these processes are not prejudiced by the lower layers. In other words, communication layers 1 to 6 should be able to provide distributed applications with as few restrictions as possible in the same way as a universal operating system is able to support a large variety of applications software on a computer. Of course, this means that having only one layer 7 protocol would not suffice. Consequently, OSI developed a number of applications-relevant standards, for example:

Application layer (layer 7)

- Association control service elements (ACSE, ISO 8649/50), which is a basic service for setting up and administering cooperative relationships (associations) between application entities. An application entity (AE) is the part of an application process responsible for communication and an association as an application layer "connection" between AEs.

- Remote operation service elements (ROSE, ISO 9072), a general RPC mechanism (see section 2.3.1) used to coordinate requests and replies between application processes.

- Reliable transfer service elements (RTSE), a reliable transport service for application PDUs.

- Message handling system (MHS, ITU X.400), an easy-to-use general mail protocol.

- Directory (ITU X.500, ISO 9594), a comprehensive and flexible directory service.

- File transfer, access, and management (FTAM, ISO 8571), a virtual file system, including file transfer.

- Distributed transaction processing (DTP, ISO 10026), a framework for coordinating and synchronizing distributed application processing.

Refer to [KER95, HEB93] for more detailed information.

2.2.3 Internet Communication Architecture

The Internet architecture now plays a dominant role in computer networks. The global Internet as a network of subnetworks and even many intranets, a modern version of corporate networks, are based on an Internet protocol hierarchy.

The easiest way to describe the Internet reference model is by comparing it to OSI, as shown in Figure 2.3.

The basic tasks of the different layers are the same. Layers 1, 2a, and 2b are directly comparable to OSI. They implement the network access. The transport system consisting of layers 3 and 4 links hosts (i.e., end systems) across intermediate nodes (routers) and sometimes even across subnets. At layer boundary 3/2, the last router on the path to the destination host must implement the mapping of the Internet address, the unique identification for a host in the Internet, to the connection-specific layer 2 address of the host (e.g., to the MAC address of the LAN in which the host is located).

Internet merges the applications system into one layer

What we see is that the Internet model does not incorporate any explicit layers 5 and 6. The corresponding layer tasks, of course, still have to be carried out even in an Internet communication, but this is effected in a specific way in the respective application protocol.

Figure 2.4 presents a selection of Internet protocols, some of which we will discuss briefly. Detailed explanations for the Internet world can

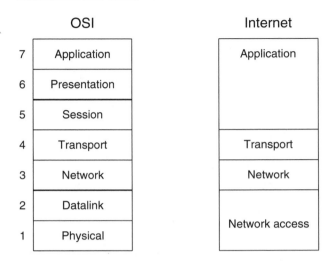

Figure 2.3
Comparison of Internet and OSI communication architectures

be found in [STE94, WRS95, STE96, COS95, COM98, COS97]. Adaptation protocols that map IP, the layer 3 protocol, to specific types of networks (Ethernet, frame relay, FDDI, X.25, ATM, SerialLines SLIP, etc.) are used below layer 3. The datalink protocol PPP (RFC 1171) for bidirectional transmission of multiprotocol datagrams over point-to-point channels also deserves mention in this context. The address resolution protocol (ARP, RFC 826) and reverse address resolution protocol (RARP, RFC 906) are used for mapping between an Internet address and a physical address, such as a MAC address.

The best-known and most important protocol is the Internet protocol (IP) in layer 3. IP (RFC 1883, RFC 791) implements a datagram-oriented network service based on the store-and-forward principle between end or intermediate systems, which can even be located in different networks (internetworking). The routing always takes place in network nodes (IP routers) that are addressed over IP addresses. Internet control message protocol (ICMP, RFC 792) is an IP-supporting protocol for the transmission of control information and error messages. Internet group management protocol (IGMP, RFC 1112) is also a layer 3 auxiliary protocol that is integrated into all computers supporting the IP protocol in multicast. This protocol is used, for example, by open shortest path first (OSPF, RFC 1583) and TIME. OSPF and the routing information protocol (RIP, RFCs 1721–24) are management protocols for exchanging routing information between routers within an Internet domain; the border gateway protocol (BGP, RFC 1771) does

The network layer forms the heart of the Internet

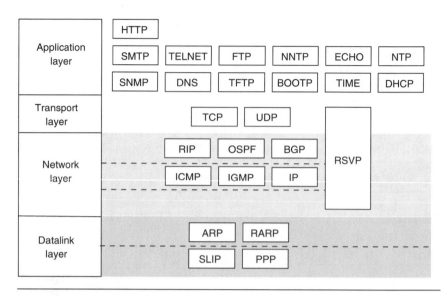

Figure 2.4
Selection of Internet protocols

the same thing between routers of different domains. Resource reservation protocol (RSVP, RFC 2205) allows future applications (e.g., for interactive voice and video transmission) to request certain resources in the router (e.g., guaranteed bit rates, priorities) for their data streams.

The most important protocols in the transport layer are the transmission control protocol (TCP, RFCs 793, 1122, and 1323), a connection-oriented protocol comparable to OSI protocol TP4, and the user datagram protocol (UDP, RFC 768), a datagram service comparable to OSI connectionless transport.

A large number of application protocols are available. The most
Internet RFCs popular ones are the dialog protocol TELNET (RFC 854), file transfer
have defined protocol (FTP, RFC 959), and simple mail transfer protocol (SMTP,
many application RFC 821), for electronic mail. The protocols that are of interest in the
protocols context of management are TIME (RFC 868, supplies time information), ECHO (RFC 862, returns everything that has been received), domain name system (DNS, RFCs 1034, 1035, and 1183, a directory service for mapping the names of end systems to IP addresses), dynamic host configuration protocol (DHCP, RFC 1541, a boot and configuration protocol), and lastly, the actual Internet management protocol, namely, simple network management protocol (SNMP, RFC 1157 and successor RFCs). This last-mentioned protocol will be dealt with extensively in Chapter 6. Network news transfer protocol (NNTP, RFC 977) controls the way in which newsgroups, thus discussion forums, are set up

in the Internet and corresponding messages exchanged. Hypertext transport protocol (HTTP, RFCs 1945 and 2068), which is based on TCP, is a communication protocol for the transport of WWW pages, thus of hypertexts that have been produced using the document description language HTML. The client (i.e., the Web browser) uses HTTP to refer to the WWW server. HTTP is without doubt one of the dominant application protocols in the Internet. Secure HTTP is a variation of the protocol and offers different levels of confidentiality and authentication. The reliance of application protocols on the transport protocols, of course, depends on the requirements of the application layer. Thus, for example, BOOTP, DHCP, SNMP, DNS, and TFTP are often based on UDP. TCP forms the basis for TELNET, FTP, SMTP, NMTP, and HTTP. Both options are available to ECHO and TIME. Whereas SNMP is almost exclusively deployed over UDP, the RFCs define mappings to both TCP and UDP. The drawings of the protocol boxes in Figure 2.4 do not imply a layering or relationships of the protocols within (e.g., the application layer or datalink layer).

2.3   Architectures for Distributed Systems

Architectures for distributed systems define a modular structure for platforms that are especially designed to support distributed applications. Typical concepts that are specified in such an architecture concern the cooperation scheme (e.g., client–server RPC, or ORB), a shared virtual file concept, common distributed system services, a global naming structure, and so forth. In the following sections we will discuss four architectures for distributed systems, namely, DCE, CORBA, ODP, and TINA.

2.3.1   Distributed Computing Environment (DCE)

DCE [LOC94, OSF92] is an initiative of the Open Software Foundation and provides a framework for the cooperation between open systems. The consortia OSF and X/Open have now joined to form the Open Group (*http://www.opengroup.org*). DCE is a definition of the services and tools that support the creation, use, and administration of distributed applications in heterogeneous computer environments. DCE considerations played an important role in the emergence of client–server computing. DCE is based on three concepts of distributed computing:

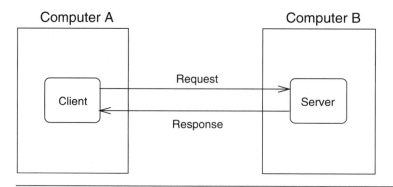

Figure 2.5
Client–server model

- The *client–server model* is used to define a method for structuring distributed applications.

- The principle of *remote procedure call* (RPC) offers a mechanism for direct communication between the individual components (subprocesses) of a distributed application run on different systems.

- The concept of *shared data storage* enables the processing of data in a distributed environment. The individual components of a distributed application communicate indirectly using common globally available data.

The client–server principle establishes an unsymmetrical cooperation model

With the *client–server model* (see Figure 2.5), a distributed application is split into a minimum of two components (processes) that are usually run on different computers. In an asymmetric communications relationship, the client submits a job (request) that is processed by the server and replied to with a response. This is conceptually similar to OSI ROSE, with important differences in protocol and implementation consequences.

The terms *client* and *server* describe the relative roles of the communication partners in a given job request. For the sake of simplicity, the words *client* and *server* not only refer to the components of a distributed application but also to the computers on which these components are run. The DCE architecture, however, obviously allows any combination of clients and servers to be run on a computer.

Aspects of client–server computing

The client–server model recommends that computer systems have specialized functions and interact with each other based on a division of workload along the lines of "distributed processing." Servers are then designed so that the services offered are generally available to a previously unknown large number of clients. This has an effect on the SW and data organization on the servers and on the coordination of access to the servers (authorization, consistency). The allocation of services to servers therefore usually depends on the type of service involved because of greatly differing requirements. The result is that servers specialize in specific functions and frequently are also even localized to different computers. Examples include:

- Servers for the shared use of resources (file servers, disk servers, print servers, compute servers)
- Servers for specific applications (electronic mail servers, fax servers, database servers, calendar servers)
- Servers for shared system services (name servers, time servers, authentication servers, network monitors, network access servers)

Consequently, the organization of client–server systems is generally affected as follows:

- Most of the processing in a distributed application is usually carried out by a server. Consequently, most of the software required is located on the server. Furthermore, servers frequently specialize in the provision of a single task.
- The software required for a specific service (i.e., for an outsourced function) is available only on the server. In comparison, computers with clients are more generally configured (often as workstations) because user applications (e.g., an information service) are able to rely on more than one distributed service (e.g., name servers, file servers, and accounting servers) to carry out a task.
- The server side is frequently implemented as a process (daemon), whereas the client side is usually available as a library for the application programmer.

DCE services are themselves examples of distributed applications based on the client–server model that uses RPC. This is a concept that enables applications to carry out the communication required to perform their tasks. From the standpoint of the developer, an RPC is similar to a normal procedure call. The only difference is that the "procedure" is transferred to another process, which in practice, is often even run on a different computer, the server.

Because the implementation is on a distributed basis:

- An RPC call initiates a new process or contacts another process that is already being run. For the RPC client and the RPC server, this

Implementation of an RPC call

inevitably produces different life spans that not only differ in length but can also be staggered in relationship to one another.

■ In general, a server must be able to cope with overlapping requests from different clients.

■ A client is usually blocked when an RPC procedure is being processed, which produces synchronous call behavior.

■ Clients and servers work in different operating environments with different areas of variables.

■ A server's RPC procedures must therefore be familiarized with a special mechanism of the RPC runtime system on the client (see the list that follows).

■ Furthermore, only values can be used as parameters (call by value).

The processing of an RPC procedure involves the following steps:

■ The client executes an action that looks like a procedure call.

■ The parameters supplied during the call are transmitted over the network to the server by the RPC mechanism (request).

■ The server receives the request, including the related data, carries out the desired "procedure," and produces the appropriate response.

■ Lastly, the RPC mechanism again ensures that the result data is transmitted to the client (response) and delivers it there as a result of the "procedure."

Figure 2.6 juxtaposes the relationships between the different components of an RPC system. The client stub and the server stub are program blocks that implement the connection to the modules of the RPC runtime system for the programmer. These segments of the source code are generated by a corresponding compiler from specifications that are written in a special language to describe the interfaces (*interface definition language*, or IDL).

Owing to the distributed processing triggered by the RPC mechanism, complications can arise when faults occur:

■ What should be done in the client when a fault occurs (in the network, in the client computer, or in the client itself) before completion of the RPC procedure?

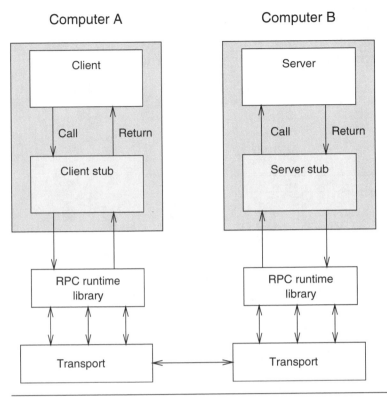

Figure 2.6
Structure of an RPC system

- How can a client find out how far the server has progressed with the execution of an RPC procedure and where the fault is located if a fault does occur?

- Which semantics should be used to execute RPC procedures (i.e., what should the RPC runtime system do when a fault occurs)? Should faults be ignored ("maybe" semantics)? Should the call be repeated until it has been successfully completed ("at least once" semantics)? Should there be a maximum of one execution ("at most once" semantics)? Is it necessary for the call to be executed just once ("exactly once" semantics)?

DCE Architecture and Components

Distributed applications can be based on the DCE, which in turn can be based on the local operating system and the network. DCE thereby provides applications with services that allow heterogeneous computers, operating systems, and networks to give the impression

DCE as a carrier architecture for distributed applications

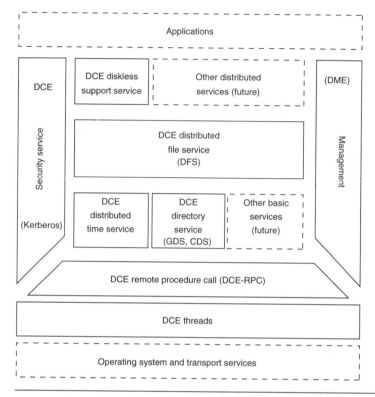

Figure 2.7
Architecture of DCE

of being one big single system. Figure 2.7 illustrates the individual components of DCE architecture along with their relationships to each other, to the operating environment, and to placeholders for future services. A brief description of DCE components is provided next.

DCE threads

DCE enables a number of parallel "*threads*" to be generated, managed, and synchronized within a single process. This type of concept is required because a server should be able to accommodate several clients. The operating system, computer architecture, local configuration, configuration of the hardware, and porting of the DCE threads help determine whether the logically parallel threads are really being processed at the same time.

DCE threads are required by all DCE services and conceptually are part of the layer below it, the "operating system." In the reference implementation of DCE, this mechanism is offered in the form of a user library. However, if a corresponding mechanism already exists in the local operating system, then two other alternatives are available for the porting: Either the DCE threads are completely replaced in the source code by the local mechanism or the DCE threads continue to be used as an interface (although internally they rely on the local version).

The *DCE-RPC* consists of a development environment and a runtime system. The development environment is a compiler for a language that supports the development of distributed applications based on the client–server model. Code is produced that automatically transfers procedure calls as messages. The runtime system implements the protocol that is used in the communication between client and server. Lastly, the DCE-RPC also contains a tool for producing unique identifiers (e.g., for the identification of interfaces and resources). It should be mentioned here that DCE-RPC is a service of the application layer, and it is defined independent from the underlying communication system. Thus it can make use of both OSI and Internet application protocols.

The *DCE directory service* manages information on the resources of distributed systems (e.g., user, computer, RPC-based services). It includes an information unit that consists of the name of the resource and the corresponding attributes (e.g., a user's home directory). The DCE directory service consists of a number of components:

Directory service

- The *cell directory service* (CDS) manages the information on a group of computers described as a DCE cell. CDS is a general name service that can be used to achieve local transparency for servers within a cell.

- The *global directory service* implements the OSI directory (ISO 9594 or X.500), thereby providing a global name space that integrates the local DCE cell into a worldwide hierarchy.

- The *global directory agent* represents the link between the cell directory service and the global directory service. It also supports the DNS service of Internet.

- The X/Open directory service API is used as a programming interface for the cell directory service and the global directory service.

The *DCE distributed time service* synchronizes the computer to "coordinated universal time."

The *DCE security service* utilizes the following components to ensure the protection of communication in distributed environments. The authentication service based on Kerberos (RFCs 1411 and 1510) is used to provide positive identification of individual users or services. Appropriate procedures within the DCE-RPC guarantee secure communication

Security through Kerberos

(e.g., confidentiality and protection from alteration through coding). Access protection is provided on the basis of access control lists and authorization within the framework of the *privilege service*. The *login facility* initializes a secure user environment; the *registry service* manages all information relating to the security database.

DCE-DFS makes physical file storage transparent

The *DCE distributed file service* (DFS) is a distributed file system. Files are organized in a global name space that is totally transparent from the standpoint of its physical storage location. The cell directory service is used to ensure consistency in the name space. Caching on the local system improves performance and at the same time reduces network traffic. Supplementary functions also provide handy backup support and the possibility of ensuring the consistency of replicas held on different servers. The distributed file service also includes the *DCE local file system* with additional features that are useful in a distributed environment. These include possibilities for replicating data and achieving a rapid recovery, data administration support, and a possibility of providing access control lists for files and directories.

The *DCE diskless support service* provides services that can be used in the operation of computers that lack local disks. The *management* component in Figure 2.7 does not relate to an integrated tool but to the corresponding components of the individual DCE services that enable administration via the network. In addition, some DCE services are used in their entirety for the management function (e.g., in the administration of users in the security service and in the registration of the addresses of servers in the directory service).

It should also be mentioned that, to supplement DCE, OSF has designed its own object-oriented management architecture, distributed management environment (DME), as the basis for distributed management applications. DME is based substantially on DCE services (RPC, directory services, security services). By the use of special adapter objects, it provides the possibility to embrace both OSI and Internet management. The specifications for a number of the management services are also based on OSF. However, DME has not succeeded in making its mark in the market; for management purposes, OSF has adopted CORBA and the concepts of the Object Management Group (section 2.3.2 and Chapter 7) to supplement DCE. DME will therefore not be covered in this book.

2.3.2   Common Object Request Broker Architecture (CORBA)

The *Object Management Group* (OMG) is promoting the global interoperability of universal distributed applications and is encouraging the use of object-oriented technologies. Boasting more than 800 member firms, OMG is probably the largest consortium in the world involved in IT standardization. It has defined the *Object Management Architecture* (OMA), which is designed to support communication and cooperation between objects in open heterogeneous environments. This architecture provides the basic framework for the development of the relevant middleware. A number of specifications for subareas have been drawn up within this framework during the last few years. The most important one of these specifications is the *common object request broker architecture* (CORBA), which contains fundamental mechanisms for communication between objects through the use of a so-called *object request broker* (ORB). Building on this concept, *CORBAservices* offer additional services that are required for the efficient implementation of object-oriented distributed applications. A detailed discussion of CORBA will be given in Chapter 7.

CORBA as a platform architecture for distributed applications

There are three key differences compared to DCE:

- The client–server model is expanded considerably and offers more flexibility due to the introduction of a broker.
- Communicating partners are equal-ranking objects (i.e., a symmetrical cooperation model is used as the basis).
- The specification of the communicating modules is object oriented with the usual characteristics of an object model, in other words, with data abstraction, encapsulation, inheritance, and polymorphism. These simplify the modeling process and allow a reuse of the object specifications.

CORBA as an extension of the client–server principle

In traditional client–server models, clients and servers generally have precisely defined m:1 relationships for certain jobs and the clients usually have to address the server in the RPC. OMG has expanded this traditional client–server model by introducing a broker (Figure 2.8).

The broker is an intermediary between client and server; it has the capability of selecting the server that is best suited to fulfilling the requirements of the client. It separates the interface that the client can see from the server implementation. The client is therefore unaware of the number of servers available, the changes made to implementation (e.g., new version), the number of changes made, and which server was

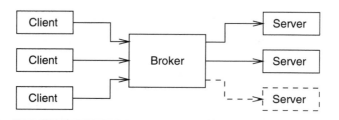

Figure 2.8
Communication over a broker

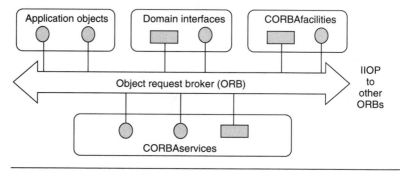

Figure 2.9
The components of OMA

used. The idea of the broker was specified by OMG through CORBA. CORBA defines the ORB that has been introduced into OMA and is the communication system for Object Management Architecture (Figure 2.9). Again, CORBA will be treated in great detail in Chapter 7.

The ORB implements the procedure that communicates location-transparent requests for methods between objects of the same system or of different systems. ORB is generally implemented as a distributed service, and it operates like a cross-system software bus.

CORBA comprises:

- An object-oriented interface definition language (IDL).
- Specifications for an interface repository (IR) containing the interface definitions of all static and dynamic objects, including a registration of objects.
- Specifications for object adapters that separate the details relevant to an implementation from details relevant to the communication.
- Measures for (de)activating and invoking objects, for creating objects and object references, for allocating resources to objects, and for authentication during access to objects.

Further details about CORBA and OMA and source references are provided in Chapter 7, which also presents an analysis of the importance of OMA as the basis for a management architecture. Recommendations on the coexistence of DCE and CORBA (DCE/CORBA interworking specification) are also defined by OSF and can be of significance to heterogeneous system worlds. CORBA middleware is available for use on most computing platforms, but they may be supplied by a third party (Expersoft, etc.)—CORBA is not quite a platform component like TPC yet.

2.3.3 Open Distributed Processing (ODP)

The reference model for open distributed processing (RM-ODP) is a joint standardization activity by both ISO and ITU-T. The goal of RM-ODP is to enable the development of standards that allow the benefits of distribution of information processing services to be realized in an environment of heterogeneous IT resources and multiple organizational domains (see ISO/IEC 10746 or ITU-T X.901–X.904). It does not itself prescribe particular standards but provides concepts and terminology to enable the development of specific standards. RM-ODP can therefore be considered a "meta-standard" for open distributed processing (see, e.g., [BLS 97]).

Object Model

RM-ODP adopts an object-oriented approach for the specification of distributed systems. The RM-ODP object model defines the concept of objects that encapsulate details of their implementation and provide an abstract view of their behavior. Objects are accessed through one or more interfaces, each of them providing one abstract view of the object.

ODP object model

Objects are defined in terms of templates that contain a complete description of the object at a given level of abstraction and can be used to instantiate new objects. RM-ODP introduces the concepts of *type* and *class*. A type is a predicate defined over the environment of objects. A class is then the set of objects satisfying this predicate at a given time. RM-ODP also defines the notions *subtype* and *subclass*. Finally, the object model supports the concept of a *composite object* (i.e., a configuration of interacting objects that offer a composite behavior at one or more interfaces).

Viewpoints and Viewpoint Models

A major problem in open distributed processing is its wide scope and inherent complexity. Therefore, a complete specification of a distributed system has to address, for example, the flows of information in an organization, the information itself, the design of systems that support these flows, the development of supporting applications, and the technologies used in this process. The RM-ODP addresses these aspects through the introduction of the concepts of *viewpoints* that partition a specification into a number of different components.

ODP viewpoints

RM-ODP defines five viewpoints, namely, the enterprise, information, computational, engineering, and technology viewpoints, each with a corresponding viewpoint model. These models are called *viewpoint languages* and provide a basic terminology required to model the concerns of a given viewpoint. However, the languages do not prescribe a particular syntax or detailed semantics and can therefore be considered as "metalanguages" that can be instantiated with particular notations.

The *enterprise viewpoint* considers the role, the scope, and the objectives of the distributed system in an enterprise. Its main concept is that of a contract expressing the obligations of the different participants in the enterprise.

The *information viewpoint* considers a distributed system from the perspective of the information content (i.e., the various information elements in an enterprise), the flow of this information, and its processing. The corresponding model enables the specification of information schemas over objects, namely, invariant schemas that describe relationships that must always be true, static schemas that describe assertions that must be true at a single point in time, and dynamic schemas, which define how the system should evolve.

The *computational viewpoint* considers the functional decomposition of a system into objects that interact at interfaces. However, this decomposition does not imply any particular realization such as mapping to nodes or address spaces. Three types of interfaces are defined: operation interfaces (supporting the invocation of operations and the return of results), stream interfaces (supporting continuous media interactions), and signal interfaces (supporting realtime processing). Additional concepts include environmental contracts—that is, sets of constraints on the underlying implementation, including the required level of distribution transparency and the quality of service offered and required by the interface.

The *engineering viewpoint* considers the mechanisms and functions required to support distributed interactions between objects. The engineering model defines a basic set of abstract concepts to model communications and end system resources. Regarding communications, the model defines the concept of a channel consisting of a configuration of stubs, binders, and protocol objects. Regarding end system resources, the model defines the notions of nodes (e.g., physical machines), capsules (execution environments for objects) and clusters (migratable sets of objects).

The *technology viewpoint* considers the development of a distributed system from the perspective of the specific hardware or software technologies that are used to realize the system.

Distribution Transparency

Distribution transparency is the ability to mask the problems occurring in a distributed environment. The higher the level of distribution transparency, the less a programmer has to be aware of the distributed nature of a system. The approach in RM-ODP is to support selective transparency whereby the programmer can elect for a given level of transparency. A number of distribution transparencies are defined in RM-ODP:

ODP distribution transparency

- Access transparency masks differences in access methods when interworking between objects.

- Location transparency hides the physical location of the object in the environments.

- Failure transparency hides the occurrence of a failure from other objects.

- Migration transparency hides the fact that a system might decide to move an object to another location.

- Replication transparency hides the fact that a given object is replicated at several locations in a distributed system.

- Further transparencies include relocation, persistence, and transaction transparency.

Hint: The CORBA object model can be considered (with some restrictions) an instantiation of the ODP object model. IDL defines the interface of objects, so it can be related to the computational viewpoint and can be considered computational language. Several concepts of the engineering viewpoint are implemented in CORBA (stubs, etc.).

2.3.4   Telecommunications Information Networking Architecture (TINA)

TINA as a framework for future telco networks

The telecommunications information networking architecture (TINA) is a development of the TINA Consortium (see *http://www.tinac.com*). The goal of TINA is to provide a framework for the development of future telecommunications networks. It was developed to support improved interoperability, to be able to reuse software as well as technical specifications, and to add flexibility to the design and deployment of the distributed applications that can be found in a telecommunications network. Furthermore, it was designed to integrate existing telecommunications architectures like IN (see [MAP96]) and TMN (see section 5.6). The architecture is based on the RM-ODP, but has been specialized to meet the specific requirements of the telecommunications domain. It can be seen as an example of applying the principles of RM-ODP.

The overall architecture consists of four building blocks, namely, the distributed processing environment (DPE), the network resource architecture, the service architecture, and the management architecture. We will have a look at each of these blocks.

According to TINA, the heart of an information networking architecture is the *distributed processing environment* (DPE). This DPE provides a homogeneous platform for the execution and deployment of the various distributed applications that compose a telecommunications network. DPE is specified using the RM-ODP computational and engineering models. The TINA Consortium decided to use CORBA as the technology of choice to serve as the basis for the TINA DPE. Objects and interfaces are described using the so-called TINA object definition language (ODL), which is an extension of the OMG IDL (see section 7.2) that allows description of an object as a collection of interfaces and to associate attributes with objects. DPE forms the execution environment that is used by the other three blocks.

The *network resource architecture* defines concepts for the description and control of transport networks. It includes a network resource information model that defines notions of network elements and connections that are independent of any particular transmission or switching technology. Based on these notions, a generic network architecture is given that describes how the individual elements in a network are related and interconnected and how they can be configured to provide an end-to-end communication path. The connection management framework specifies generic components for the control of these end-to-end communication paths.

The *service architecture* defines concepts and basic classes that are useful for the design, deployment, operation, and management of information services in a TINA environment. Concepts and classes include user agents, service and communication sessions, and mediation services.

The *management architecture* provides a set of generic management principles and concepts for the TINA service and network architecture and the DPE. The architecture covers two main areas, namely, management of end systems and telecommunications management. The latter is based primarily on OSI management and TMN standards and principles (see Chapter 5). In particular, it adopts the TMN functional layers and focuses primarily on the network element, network, and service management layer.

2.4   Communication Network Resources

Sections 2.4 and 2.5 provide an overview of the resources of distributed systems. We start with the resources of communications networks, in other words, transmission media and components. The resources then still required for distributed systems are the end systems and the servers (section 2.5). The services provided characteristically represent the resource requirements for servers.

Resources are objects of management

The functionality of these resources forms the centerpiece of the following discussion since an awareness of the functionality is an important prerequisite for understanding the management aspects (management information and management functions) described in detail in later chapters.

We restrict ourselves to the description of resources that are objects of network and system management. But it should have become clear from Chapter 1 that there are also resources that are typical for the higher layers in the management pyramid (e.g., the business/service management layer). Examples of domain or business resources are service level agreements, trouble tickets, performance reports, inventory documentation, accounts, invoices, and so on. Business- and service-related resources will be treated when we talk about management solutions.

The purpose of a communication network is to provide a transport system and therefore also to support certain communication services. This goal must also, of course, be supported by network management. Therefore, the relevant managed objects are the modules of the transport system (i.e., transmission media and the network components,

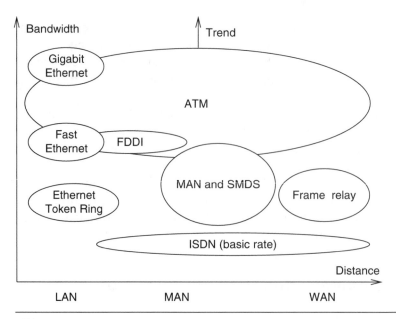

Figure 2.10
Network technologies (based on [BLA97])

both of which we discuss in this section) as well as the supervisory and control parameters necessary to guarantee the required quality of service.

Network components are the main resources of a communications network because, with the assistance of the media used, they are what enables communication in the transport system. This explains why network components are of such importance to network management.

A striking characteristic of network components is the variety of different types and versions. A distinction particularly has to be made here between a number of different network architectures and network technologies, each of which represents its own network component world (Figure 2.10).

Coping with a vast variety of components is one of the main priorities of any integrated management approach. Integrated management is based on an overall concept that allows an integration of all network architectures. Companies that use architectures from one vendor only are increasingly recognizing the importance of this integration and already developing migration strategies to standardized open architectures. The following discussion on network components is limited to standardized network architectures because this is where integrated management approaches are concentrated.

Media and network components are resources of communications networks. The components implement the protocol hierarchies

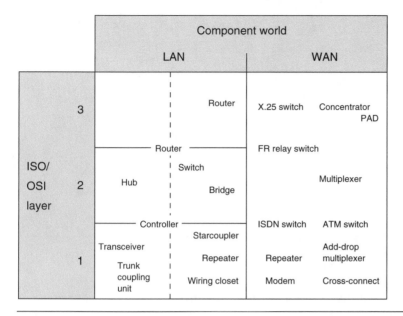

Figure 2.11
Classification of network components

An initial classification identifies two major historic component worlds:

1. The *LAN and Internet world*, which is essentially defined by the IEEE 802.X standards and Internet RFCs
2. The *WAN and public data network (PDN) world*, which is described by the recommendations of the ITU and ISO

This classification, of course, should not give the impression of a close coupling of Internet world to LANs since Internet technologies are used in LAN and WAN areas. On the other hand, the ITU and the ISO define network technologies that are not used in the LAN area.

A rough classification of components from the LAN and WAN worlds to the lower layers of the ISO/OSI reference model produces the breakdown shown in Figure 2.11. The classification into layers reflects the users' view of technology, which can sometimes differ from that of the provider. Some of these components will be covered in more detail later.

The breakdown presented, of course, represents only one of various conceivable possibilities; another approach would be to separate the components into those for data communications and those for tele-communications because historically these two worlds of services and

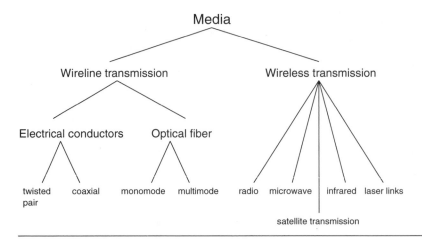

Figure 2.12
Classification of transmission media

networks and their components were initially developed separately. A classification of components based on network technologies associated with LAN, MAN, and WAN bandwidth requirements is presented in Figure 2.10.

2.4.1   Transmission Media

In order for messages to be exchanged, they must first be coded into signal sequences. Signals are a physical representation of information or of information elements dictated by the type of transmission medium being used. Major differences exist between the different media (Figure 2.12) from the standpoint of *transmission* and *operational* aspects.

The transmission aspects include:

- Maximum achievable transmission rates
- Spannable distances
- Medium-specific characteristics such as impedance with electrical conductors and refractive indices with optical fiber
- Medium-specific interference such as attenuation, electromagnetic emission, crosstalk, reflection, skin effects, mode dispersion, and weather conditions

The operational aspects to be considered include:

- Laying characteristics of a medium (e.g., tensile strength, load capacity, permitted laying radius)
- Fireproofing, outer/inner cables
- Availability of network components (interfaces) that support a particular medium
- Cost
- Future prospects

Instead of providing detailed descriptions of the different media, we refer you to the relevant literature. However, a brief survey of the uses of the different media follows.

Today, electrical cable is being used almost exclusively only in the access area ("last mile") of telecommunications networks and in LANs with data networks. Twisted cable and broadband coaxial cable are used in telecommunications networks, the latter particularly in cable distribution networks (Cable TV, CATV). These access networks were not originally designed for data transfer, in other words, for high data rates or symmetric traffic. Recent developments in telephone access networks through the use of efficient modulation and multiplexing methods for digital subscriber lines (e.g., ADSL, HDSL, SDSL, VDSL, IDSL; sometimes combined under xDSL) and a different frequency band segmentation for CATV networks are also permitting data rates of up to several Mbps in the existing access networks of telecommunications systems.

Electrical conductors

In LANs, electrical conductors are used as twisted-pair cable, baseband coaxial cable (e.g., in conventional Ethernet), or occasionally, as broadband coaxial cable. Standard recommendations such as EIA/TIA 568 (Commercial Building Telecommunications Standard), which apply to modern building cabling structures, essentially stipulate that electrical conductors should be used in the tertiary area only (floor and room cabling). Category 5 and 6 cables are recommended to ensure that future applications with high transmission requirements can be accommodated. This involves using shielded twisted-pair (STP) cable with a supplementary screen, referred to as screened STP (S-STP). This low-loss LAN cable guarantees high transmission rates of 100 or 625 Mbps over 100 meters and supports the different network technologies in compliance with IEEE 802.X as well as with FDDI and voice transmission. Of course, the lower categories of cable suffice for low transmission rate requirements.

Electrical conductors in the LAN area

Optical fiber is normally used in the primary and secondary areas (campus and building supply) of structured LAN cabling, and because

Optical fiber in the LAN and WAN areas

of the somewhat less expensive optical transmitters and receivers, it is often used as multimode fiber. Only monomode fiber is used in the WAN area because of the clearly superior broadband-length product. It will soon be possible to achieve several 100 Gbps using optical fiber cable. Complete fiber optic networks no longer requiring an optoelectric conversion of the network components will also become a cost-effective option in the near future. A deployment of WDM (wavelength-division multiplexing) techniques will even allow the transmission capacity of a single fiber to be multiplexed. Because of the inability of a single transmission channel to utilize fully the high capacity of fiber optic cable, multiplexing techniques (such as SONET, SDH; compare section 2.4.3) based on flexible multiplexing hierarchies are being used for remote transmission.

Possibilities offered by wireless transmission

Radio (10^4–10^8 Hz), microwave (10^8–10^{11} Hz), infrared (10^{12}–10^{14} Hz), and visible light (around 10^{14}–10^{15} Hz) are the frequency subbands that are suitable for wireless transmission in the electromagnetic frequency spectrum. Radio waves and microwaves are normally used for remote transmission in telecommunications networks, infrared in wireless LANs, and visible light in the form of laser links, for example, as a wireless link between high buildings when distances range up to a few kilometers. Satellite systems (stationary as well as those that will soon be orbiting) operate in the GHz area and are generally used for individual communication and for mass communication (distribution communication) over large distances between stations, supporting both stationary and mobile end systems. The long signal propagation times in satellite communication often present a problem for interactive and realtime-critical communication services. The different wavelengths for wireless transmission have different characteristics from the standpoint of the penetrability of material (e.g., building, walls), absorption (by rain, fog), propagation behavior, and trunking. These characteristics not only determine the area of use but also the requirements of components such as transmitters, receivers, and amplifiers.

2.4.2   LAN and Internet Components

The dominant network components for LANS and the Internet world are primarily specified by IEEE 802 standards and FDDI definitions for layers 1 and 2. At layer 3, routers are then responsible for routing and message transport through IP forwarding. Although ATM is also deployed in LANs, it is described in the next section on WAN components because it was originally specified mainly for use in WANs.

Attachment Components

Layer 1 standards comprise media characteristics, definitions of transmission codes and rates, interchanges of relevant control information, and messages (e.g., code violations). In LANs, a medium will often be shared by a number of different stations, in which case a medium access procedure is required. IEEE 802.3 defines the carrier sense multiple access with collision detect (CSMA/CD) procedure used with Ethernet. A token passing procedure (defined by IEEE 802.4/5, ANSI X3T9.5) is used with token bus, Token Ring, and fiber distributed data interface (FDDI). The access protocol defined by IEEE 802.6 is the reservation procedure distributed queue dual bus (DQDB). Attachment components implement the different types of LAN/MAN *attachment unit interfaces* (AUIs) to the user. According to the architectural model based on IEEE 802, an attachment component is implemented as an integrated module (e.g., slide-in card) or as several separate modules (*transceivers, controllers*) with explicit AUI cabling. The classic Ethernet with its bus structures is being replaced more and more by Switched Ethernet, in which star topologies and Ethernet hubs and switches dominate. This particularly applies to the very fast Ethernet versions Fast Ethernet (100 Mbps) and Gigabit Ethernet. With these networks, stations are connected to a hub or a switch over a point-to-point connection (usually S-STP).

Attachment components are usually layer 1 and layer 2a components

Compared to Ethernet, coupling a station to a Token Ring is active (i.e., the information running around the ring passes the connection point of each attached station). A *trunk coupling unit* enables the attachment of a terminal with a built-in *Token Ring controller*. The trunk coupling unit is designed so that the information transported on the ring bypasses a terminal that is switched off (bypass state).

In terms of media and attachment components, we have so far looked only at those resources that are required for building individual LAN segments. LAN coupling components that can be used to couple LANs to different layers of the OSI/ISO reference model are described later.

LAN coupling components exist on layers 1, 2a, and 3

Repeaters

The function of a repeater (Figure 2.13) is to couple two segments of the same LAN type while eliminating the existing length restrictions of the segments caused by signal amplification. To do so, a repeater

Repeaters are level 1 coupling components

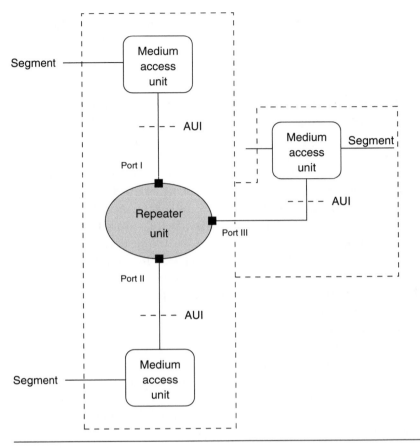

Figure 2.13
Organization of a repeater set

regenerates and repeats all the signals of each segment and passes them on to the other segment. The functions of an Ethernet repeater include:

- Listening in channels (carrier sense)
- Collision detection
- Generating collision signals (JAM signals)
- Producing the preamble of the Ethernet blocks
- Extending block fragments to a minimum of 96 bits
- Providing clocked signal regeneration and, in some cases, recoding
- Adhering to delay conditions
- Supporting "monitor mode" operating mode

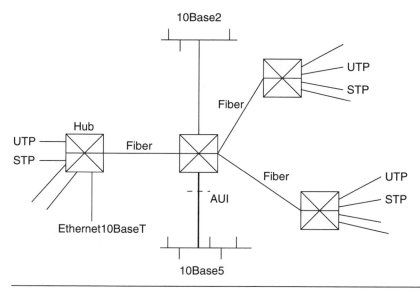

Figure 2.14
Ethernet configuration with hubs

■ Removing faulty segments (e.g., when continuous collisions occur due to the lack of a terminating resistor)

Repeaters can be implemented either as devices (local repeater) or as remote repeaters linked over fiber optics. Because repeaters are layer 1 components, networks consisting of segments connected by Ethernet repeaters operate as one collision domain with respect to the CSMA/CD procedure.

Star Couplers, Hubs

If a repeater set is extended to support several ports to which different media within a LAN topology can be attached, then topologies similar to the one shown in Figure 2.14 are configured. The central components in this kind of cascaded network are *star distributors, star couplers*, and *hubs*. Hubs at layer 1 carry out amplification and signal conversion.

Star-coupled components have the task of distributing the signals received at a port to all the other ports, with all attached stations able to listen in on all the messages sent on the segment. Collisions can therefore occur in the same way as they do with "classic" Ethernet. Collisions are resolved in compliance with the Ethernet standard based on CSMA/CD.

Hubs are multiport repeaters with media-adaptation functions

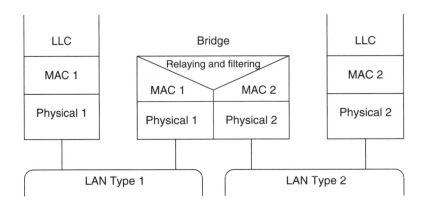

Figure 2.15
Structure of a MAC bridge

Whole star-coupled hierarchies can be formed, thereby creating a "tree of star structures." Similar to Ethernet, the depth of this tree is restricted because of the maximum signal propagation time allowed (i.e., there is a limit to the number of star couplers that can be cascaded).

Hubs act as a key point of concentration, a so-called *wiring concentrator*, particularly in connection with structured (i.e., star-shaped) cabling. A wiring concentrator for Token Ring can therefore also be seen as a hub.

We have already mentioned that the hub concept is now no longer limited to layer 1 functionality (see the following for more discussion).

Bridges

Bridges are LAN layer 2 coupling elements. They enable two or more LAN subnetworks to be coupled (in some cases using a wide area network line). Because bridges implement the coupling of LAN subnetworks at layer 2a, the medium access control (MAC) layer, they are also referred to as MAC-level bridges or, in short, MAC bridges.

Figure 2.15 shows the entities that appear in a MAC bridge: the MAC entity and the MAC relay entity. MAC entities can differ depending on the type of subnetworks being coupled (Ethernet, Token Ring, FDDI). MAC relay entities undertake the conversion of one MAC level to another MAC level. In the event that the MAC entities support different types of networks, the MAC relay entity must carry out a protocol conversion (e.g., a frame conversion with regard to frame size, header syntax, and priority bits).

Bridges are couplers from level 2. They serve to separate the MAC segments

Two important issues that arise in connection with networks coupled with bridges are the extent to which the coupling structure (number, position, and addresses of bridges) should be made known to the end user (station, host) and how the bridges should be made aware of the existence of the hosts because the bridges ultimately have to initiate a conversion of their ports to MAC addresses. Two types of bridges exist: transparent bridges (used with Ethernet) and source routing bridges (used with Token Ring).

With *transparent bridges*, users are not aware that the bridges exist, so none of the MAC addresses is known to them either. A backward-learning algorithm enables the bridges to find out which stations are located in which LAN. Initially, they send all the frames to all the attached LANs and set up a hash table based on the sender and receiver addresses. This table is then used later in frame forwarding. The actual topology is superimposed by a logical tree structure that is calculated using the familiar spanning tree algorithm; this algorithm ensures that endless loops do not occur because of redundant bridges when multiple paths exist. The spanning tree then serves as the basis for the routing in frame forwarding (i.e., message forwarding). Bridges that function this way are therefore fully transparent to the host; the network configuration is updated automatically, forwarding is connectionless, and the bridges deal with errors on layers 1 and 2a. Bridges can be added and removed without the awareness of the stations on the network.

Transparent bridges

With *source routing bridges*, hosts are aware of the coupling structure. Each LAN in the group and each bridge within a LAN has a unique identification. Each source host sends a search frame (broadcast) across the entire network to the destination host. The bridges add their identification to the response so that the transmitter is aware of all the possible routes and is able to select the best one. It includes this information with the next transmittal to the destination. Source routing theoretically offers the possibility of selecting an optimal path, whereas a transparent bridge is restricted by the spanning tree. On the other hand, faults and errors are more difficult to deal with in source routing. Furthermore, it is always the hosts that are affected because they store the routes, send discovery frames, and copy the path information in each MAC frame.

Source routing bridges

From the standpoint of management, both types of bridges offer advantages because they can be used in structuring integrated networks.

Bridges enable a separation of traffic and filtering

- The coupling is carried out independently of media and access procedures since MAC bridges work on the MAC layer. Bridges also provide fault isolation up to level 2a, which means there is no fault propagation over bridges.

- Local LAN traffic is not propagated beyond the bridges. This automatically separates the traffic load.

- Because bridges work on the store-and-forward principle, filter mechanisms can also prove effective with the underlying frame structure. This means, for example, that certain types of frames, addresses, or higher types of protocols can be excluded from the forwarding, which thereby allows protective functions to be incorporated into bridges. Other management functionality can also be combined with bridges, but this will be dealt with later.

Similar to the repeaters discussed earlier, there are remote bridges and multiport bridges as well as simple local bridges. Hubs now often offer bridge functions.

Switches

Switches pro-
duce fast port-
to-port connec-
tions with a high
throughput rate

Switches are used in LANs to enhance the performance of the coupling elements. Although they are similar to efficient multiport bridges, switches are able to maintain a number of communications relationships between different LAN segments simultaneously. This allows stations to have dedicated connections between each other without a restriction in bandwidth, which can result in an increase in overall throughput compared to bridges. The switch assumes the function of an almost delay-free "through connection" of data packets (frames) from the input location to the output location (frame switching). *Cut-through switches* forward a frame directly upon recognition of the destination address. *Store-and-forward switches* first examine the entire packet, which enables them to detect FCS errors, whereas *near-cut-through switches* seek a middle course using a configurable forwarding process. The various switches available on the market differ from one another by type of switching fabric (crosspoint matrix, shared memory, shared high-speed backplane), cumulative bandwidth, internal data format (frames or cells), buffering or overload behavior, number and type of supported ports, and supported management options.

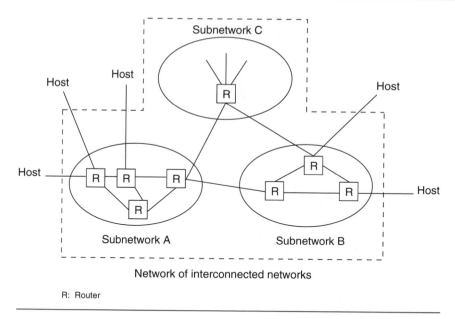

Network of interconnected networks

R: Router

Figure 2.16
Subnetworks and integrated networks

Routers

The last components we will deal with before leaving IEEE 802 standards are routers that implement LAN (and WAN) coupling at layer 3 of the ISO/OSI reference model.

Even if bridges play a key role in network coupling in the LAN area, routers remain the classic network components for coupling subnetworks. Yet the development of router technology was not started in the LAN area and instead dates back to the switching systems used to construct WANs.

The key layer 3 tasks are switching and routing. Switching is the logical path switching between end systems (hosts) through the use of transit systems. Basically, this kind of task can additionally exist on other layers, for example, the application layer (application gateway), the transport layer (transport gateway), or even the lowest layers (such as in ATM). The switching technology can be store and forward, packet switching, or circuit switching. Switching requires the availability of the appropriate routing in the event that more than one path leads to the same destination. Static (fixed) and dynamic (adaptive) routing procedures are available.

Looking at Figure 2.16, it is obvious that the layer 3 task occurs twice: in the individual subnetworks and, when there is a need to

Routers handle routing and switching on layer 3. They serve as the basis for internetworking

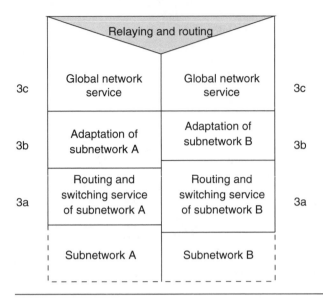

Figure 2.17
Organization of router functionality

switch beyond these, in the network of interconnected subnetworks. If the subnetworks are using different layer 3 procedures, this can increase the complexity of the router functionality. With a more exact classification of routers in the layer model, it becomes obvious that the sublayers of layer 3 must also be taken into consideration (Figure 2.17).

The network layer is divided into three sublayers because, when different types of subnetworks exist, a separation has to be made between subnetwork-specific tasks in layer 3a (e.g., intranetworking routing) and in layer 3c (e.g., internetworking routing), thereby sometimes requiring an adaptation of services in layer 3b.

The network layer must be familiar with the internal structure of a subnetwork (i.e., the routers) to enable it to select suitable paths. Therefore, in contrast to bridges, packets that are to be processed by a router must be addressed directly to the router. Upon the arrival of a packet, the router must first determine which protocol world it originates from and select the corresponding protocol stack. This selection is made on the basis of the network address contained in the received packet. Once this is done, the *routing* is carried out. A routing table is used to determine what happens next to the packet: either the packet has reached its destination (i.e., the router is able to transfer it to a local subnetwork) or the next node on the path to the destination has been established. In this way, the packet is usually switched from router to router (hop by hop).

Providing and adapting routing information using an appropriate cost function is a management task

The routing table is an important element in the context of router functionality. It can play a key role in ensuring that the resources of a network are used to maximum efficiency and cost-effectiveness.

Routing tables are updated either statically by the network manager or dynamically through configuration modifications that are automatically noticed by the routers. Developments in router management, of course, have to include automation with adequate monitoring and access available in a suitable form to the network manager. We will return to this topic later.

Routing in the Internet [COM95] is based on the IP addressing scheme. This scheme recognizes network IDs and host IDs in three different categories of addresses, with subnet masks used within the space of the host ID to provide further structuring within a network. Each host is identified by an IP address that is located in a particular subnet of the network. Routing is carried out on the basis of the current routing table. Adaptive routing methods are used (i.e., the routing tables are updated to reflect any configuration changes in the subnets or in the integrated network). The interchange protocols used are RIP or OSPF for routing information within subnets and exterior gateway protocols (EGP, RFCs 890 and 904) between subnets. BGP is representative of the EGP category (compare section 2.2.3) between subnets of separate routing domains. Destination routers also map the IP address of the destination host to the MAC address of the destination host using ARP.

Smart Hubs, Intelligent Hubs

Intelligent hubs are the node points of the different LAN technologies. These hubs are hybrid devices in the sense that they are hubs with the functionality of repeaters, bridges, or routers. In addition, they support all the popular management systems. Intelligent hubs offer the option of being fit with a variety of modules in the same chassis with shared and often redundantly designed power supply (e.g., UPS). Internal backplane buses form the heart of these hubs. Some of the buses are based on LAN technology, in which case the allocation conforms to MAC procedures to enable the coexistence of different LANs (represented by the different slide-in cards with their ports) in the same chassis. Communication between different hub modules can also take place over system buses, thus allowing the option of multiprotocol bridging or routing.

Intelligent hubs are comparatively expensive and vendor specific, and in a certain way, they are also a "single point of failure." On the

Intelligent hubs are hybrid coupling components

other hand, they are flexible multiprotocol nodes with a uniformly consistent operating and management interface.

Distribution cabinets are comparatively important components for structured cabling (Figure 2.18) and the management thereof. They contain distribution frames for the different media and are used for the acceptance of the network components described earlier. Distribution cabinets constitute the heart for the maintenance and configuration of the physical cabling structure. For security reasons, they should be supplied with sufficient power, UPS, and ventilation and be lockable.

2.4.3   WAN Components

Data communication networks that operate on the basis of ITU-T standards (formerly CCITT) are generally referred to as *wide area networks* (WANs). This book does not cover pure voice networks (POTS or mobile telephony).

Components in WANs strongly rely on the network technologies used. These include SONET/SDH, ISDN, DQDB, ATM, frame relay, and X.25. Switched multi-megabit data service (SMDS), which is referred to in Europe as connectionless broadband data service (CBDS), also requires mention in this context. This is a cell-oriented, connectionless public high-speed data service for anisochronous LAN–LAN connections with E1/E3 and T1/T3 transfer rates. SMDS is a service and does not define any transport platforms, so it can be implemented across technically different networks (e.g., DQDB and ATM). It defines a network access protocol for variable packet lengths and different access speeds. In Germany, Datex-M uses DQDB for its SMDS service.

The different network technologies are used in different areas of application (compare Figure 2.10). It would not be possible to list all the available network technologies in this book, so we refer you to the literature (e.g., [BLA97, STA95]). We will limit our discussion to a brief description of SONET/SDH, frame relay, and ATM and refer you to [BOC96, HOP95] for information about ISDN.

Synchronous Digital Hierarchy (SDH)/Synchronous Optical Network (SONET)

SONET/SDH is the basis for the flexible utilization of high transmission capacities

SONET/SDH [CSS96, GOR97] designates a digital high-speed multiplex transmission technology for fiber optic remote lines that can be used in the provision of transparent channels for diverse underlying network technologies (e.g., trunked telephone traffic, ATM, frame relay). It also enables different network providers to share the same physical fiber

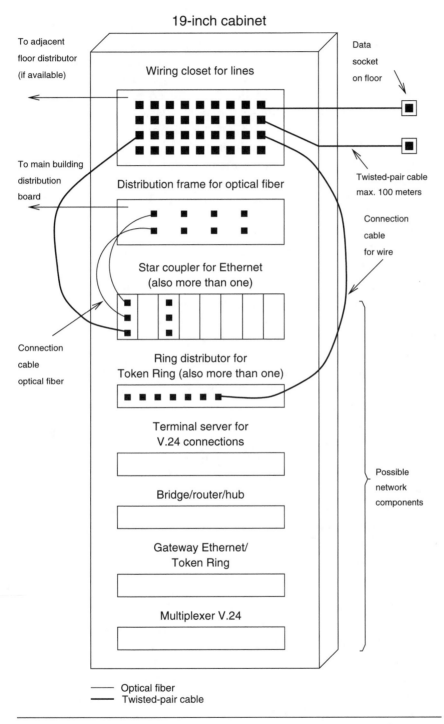

Figure 2.18
Layout of a distribution cabinet

optic cable. SONET was originally developed by Bellcore in the USA; SDH was standardized by the ITU-T in the G.707/8/9 recommendations. SONET/SDH therefore concerns the specifications within OSI layer 1. Very few differences exist between SONET and SDH: For example, in SONET, the basic channel STS-1 (electrical) or OC-1 (optical) has a rate of 51.84 Mbps; whereas the optical basic channel in SDH has 155.52 Mbps (i.e., STM-1=STS-3 or OC-3). The multiplexing levels up to STM-64 are defined. Special multiplexers are required to incorporate channels with low transfer rates, such as PCM channels (64 kbps) and E1 (2048 kbps) or T1 (1544 kbps), into a basic SONET/SDH channel. SDH components multiplex by bytes. Figure 2.19 illustrates the basic components of a SONET/SDH system.

The terminal is normally itself a multiplexer that produces basic SONET/SDH frames. ADM is an add-drop multiplexer that utilizes the fact that subframes from lower stages in the hierarchy can be directly decoupled through a clever pointer structure in the basic SONET/SDH frame without the need for complete demultiplexing across all the levels of the hierarchy. Digital cross-connect system (DCS) is a channel group cross-connector, in other words, a component that allows whole groups of user data channels to be switched to other transmission paths without the need to run through the entire multiplex hierarchy. This can occur, for example, with faults or overloading, or when new channel groups are established. In this case, the management information of the operator of the SONET/SDH system is analyzed and not the control information of the end user, as occurs in routing. Each basic SONET frame (9×90 bytes) contains 9×3 bytes of overhead for system management purposes and bytes for section, line, and path management.

Sections are the links between directly neighboring components and repeaters, lines are the links between hubs (ADM, DCS), and paths can be the links between terminals (source, destination) or switches. Repeaters can be used between all components.

Frame Relay (FR)

Frame relay has proven itself with LAN coupling over WAN

Frame relay (FR) networks [BLA95a, SMI93] are the successors to X.25 networks. The error-handling mechanisms in FR were improved from X.25 in order to achieve higher data rates. The multiplexing takes place at level 2 instead of level 3; therefore, FR relates to ISO layers 2 and 3. Typically, FR networks are used for LAN–LAN coupling over WANs and are equipped to handle bursty traffic. Figure 2.20 presents the components of an FR network. Routers with FR cards or special adapter

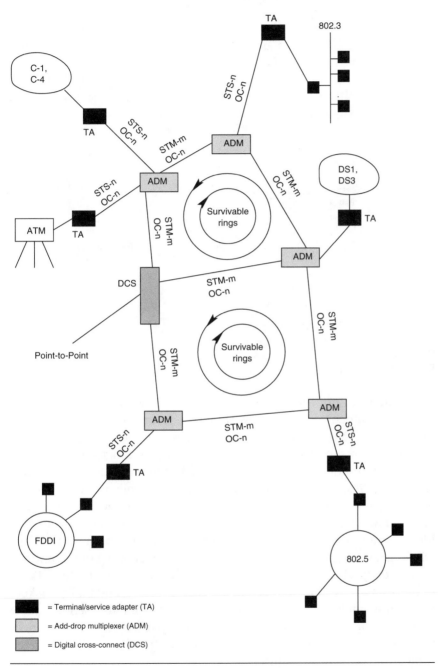

Figure 2.19
Basic components of a SONET/SDH system (based on [BLA97])

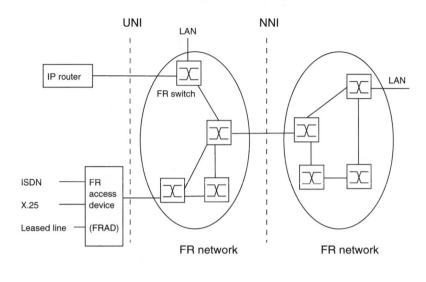

FR: Frame relay
UNI: User-to-network interface
NNI: Network-to-network interface

Figure 2.20
Frame relay network

components (frame relay access devices, or FRAD), which map the LAN or other protocols to the network access interface (user-to-network interface, or UNI), are usually used as access components.

FR networks are packet oriented with variable-length packets; they support permanent and switched virtual connections. The transfer rates range from 64 kbps to 2.048 kbps (theoretically up to 45 Mbps). Signaling and user data transport are separate (outband signaling) and are similar in this respect to the control plane in ISDN. Instead of identifying a user over a level 3 virtual circuit number, as is the case with X.25, FR implements this through a datalink connection identifier (DLCI) of level 2, which also supports the multiplex streams. Error detection is essentially reduced to checksums (FCS), and faulty packets are immediately discarded and rerequested from the sender. Flow control is implicit (back pressure). As with all packet-oriented networks with variable packet lengths, there is no guarantee of transmission delay time or the prevention of jitter.

ATM Networks

Asynchronous transfer mode (ATM) [KYA95, BLA97, GIN98, HHS98] defines a non-media-related transmission, multiplex, and switching technology that strives for high data rates with very low transmission delays. This technology enables the support of different types of information such as data, interactive voice, and video. ATM is suitable for LAN and WAN use, particularly also for voice-integrated data networks and multimedia applications. Computers, routers, LANs, private branch exchanges (PBXs), multimedia stations, and video systems are all appropriate for attachment to ATM networks (Figure 2.21). Public ATM networks require an adherence to the standardized access interface public UNI, private UNI defines the interface between a user and a private ATM switch, and network-to-network interface (NNI) is used between ATM nodes.

ATM is a service-integrating technology. It is suitable for data as well as isochronous traffic for LANs and WANs

ATM comprises layer 1 and part of layer 2 in the OSI layer model. (In [TAN 96], ATM is even incorporated into layers 3 and 4.) In an ATM switch, cells with a fixed length of 53 bytes are always switched over the same path between source and destination in a connection-oriented mode similar to packet switching. ATM connections are identified by two identifiers: Virtual channel identifiers (VCIs) refer to channels between switches or between switches and users, and virtual path identifiers (VPIs) describe the virtual path between user stations across an ATM network. VPs are able to accept more than one VC (multiplexing). Two types of ATM switching units are differentiated: those for path switching (cross-connect, VP switches) and those for channel switching (ATM switches, VC-connect). With cross-connect, the paths end and are switched to another path, with no affect on the channels. With ATM switches, the channels as well as the paths end and are always rerouted to other ones. The high transmission rates (currently available up to 2488 Mbps) place heavy demands on the switching fabric within a switch. The actual ATM layer does not transmit the cells synchronously, which accounts for the "A" (asynchronous) in its name. The mapping of ATM cell transmission to the bit plane can be implemented in different ways. In LAN environments, the cell transmission (cell-based physical layer) is usually effected directly on the medium; in WAN environments, the mapping is often onto SONET/SDH frames.

The ATM adaptation layer maps user data (payload) to the transparently transmitted cells. The adaptation layer recognizes different classes of service with different attributes for the quality of service parameters bit rate (constant, variable), connection mode (CO, CL), and timing conditions between transmitter and receiver (whether it is

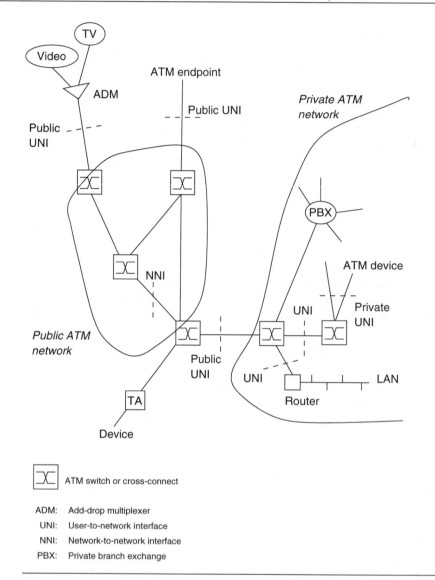

Figure 2.21
ATM network

required or not). For example, voice transmission would be characterized by the connection orientation, the fixed bit rate (e.g., 64 kbps),
and the well-known constraint with respect to delay and jitter.

There are various approaches, such as LAN emulation (LANE),
classical IP, and MPOA (multiprotocol over ATM), to mapping the
Internet and LANs to ATM networks. A number of ATM components
are available for the LAN environment. ATM signaling and the ATM

service spectrum are frequently proprietary, so it is not always possible to couple directly to public ATM networks due to nonconformance to the NNI interface.

Integrated or autonomous terminal adapters (TAs) are used to adapt non-ATM conformant components. Add-drop multiplexers (ADMs) can also be connected as adaptation devices for devices with lower channel rates.

2.4.4 Network Services

The resources we discussed in the previous sections have been different components of transport systems of various network technologies in the LAN and WAN areas. Configuring, managing, and operating these resources failure-free on a continuous and efficient basis is the task of network management. However, the communication services and essential auxiliary services carried out by the transport network are also objects of network management because they generally offer an option of choice and scope when it comes to service functionality (service features) and quality of service. Examples of network services include:

Services are also objects of management

- Electronic mail (SMTP deploying, e.g., the protocols POP or IMAP, X.400)
- Multimedia mail, voice mail. Multipurpose Internet mail extensions (MIME, RFCs 1521–24) also deserve mention in this context
- Conversion of email/fax/voice mail
- Conferencing (newsgroups, Internet relay chat (IRC))
- Videoconferencing
- Internet telephony (voice over IP)
- Value-added services with voice communication (ISDN service features), value-added services with intelligent networks (IN capability sets) [FGK97, MAP96]
- File transfer (FTP, FTAM)
- Directory services (X.500 using, e.g., lightweight directory access protocol (LDAP) or DNS together with DNS protocol)
- Distribution services (e.g., Mbone)
- Demand services (video-on-demand, telelearning)
- Retrieval services (e.g., WWW using the protocols HTTP or SHTTP)
- Cooperative services (distributed editor, whiteboard, telemarker/telepointer, application sharing, telepresence services [FWO95])

- Dialup services (access server, modem server, callback services) using, for example, the protocols PPP or SLIP and RADIUS access control
- Encryption services, authentication services, certification services
- Web hosting
- Firewall operation
- VPN services
- Umbrella management for voice and data services

The management of these services includes service provisioning, user administration, authentication, selection of concrete service features, adherence to service level agreements (SLAs), and accounting. From the standpoint of the service provider, services are resources and, consequently, managed objects.

We are not including a detailed description of the network services listed but will be covering certain related management aspects in later sections of this book.

2.5   Resources of Distributed Systems

The term *system management* has established itself as the concept that relates to the management of the resources of distributed systems (see Figure 1.2). It therefore applies to the end systems and servers, the networked system (distributed system in a narrow sense), and the services these provide.

2.5.1   System Resources

System resources are usually the resources of the end systems in a network

By *systems*, we mean user systems attached to a communications network. These can be workstations, PCs, mainframes, or servers; the term *host* is sometimes used as a collective term. Hosts are autonomous computer systems that supply local resources (in contrast to network resources) to the applications that are run on them. These local resources are usually managed by the local system administrator with the help of operating system functions. In distributed systems, you frequently find that individual systems are operated remotely (through remote operating, remote monitoring, or remote controlling) or managed by a network service created through the interaction of several systems. This then also requires (in some cases, even in heterogeneous environments) a capability for describing the characteristic resources of the system. Examples of system resources and system parameters include:

- Processors (available, in use)
- Memory (types of memory such as main memory, cache, disk storage, and virtual memory; information about capacity, use, and partitioning required)
- Input–output devices (keyboards, printers, displays, tape units, mouses, modems, etc.)
- Network interface cards (network technology, protocols, transmission rates)
- Installed software (product, version, dependencies)
- File systems (available/occupied space, record size, mount status, etc.)
- Processes (maximum number, status, allocation)
- Applications

The system parameters listed can be used to describe the characteristic values of system resources, but this information is not sufficient for the purposes of management, as we will see later.

2.5.2   System Services

In distributed systems, particularly in client–server structures, it is often not the local resources that are at the center of management but the services that have been supplied by the servers or the network system. These, of course, depend on the specific scenario or application, and therefore, it would be impossible to provide a complete list of these services. It should also be mentioned that, dependent on the view, the distinction between network service and system service is not always that sharp. If communication is the focus, we tend to enumerate the service as network service; if (distributed) processing is the focus, the notion of system service is preferred. Examples of server services are:

System services, too, are management objects

- *File service.* This is generally viewed as the most important service in a distributed system and offers the possibility of a globally transparent file system and (long-term) data storage.
- *Print service, spool service.* This service provides the shared use of printing resources or other output devices.

- *Process service.* This is a service that creates and carries out processes through a server that distributes the process jobs appropriately to individual systems.

- *Boot service.* This service is designed for booting a system.

- *Terminal service.* This service is for attaching terminals over a terminal server that serves as a concentrator and sometimes provides functions for the adaptation of terminals.

- *Name service, directory service.* This is used for localizing addressable units within a distributed system through the input of names. It also maps names to addresses.

- *Mail service.* The mail service is used to exchange messages between users. Processes sometimes also use this service for the notification of users.

- *Time service.* This provides uniform time information in distributed systems; the service is also used to synchronize clocks in distributed systems.

- *Gateway service.* This service must be used when communication is with a remote system (i.e., a system that is not part of the distributed system) and a protocol conversion is required by the corresponding gateway server.

- *Security service.* This service executes various security requirements, including the protection of communication (coding) and provision of user identification through appropriate authentication procedures.

- *Accounting service.* This calculates the use of the resources in distributed systems.

- *Software distribution service, licensing control.* These services are responsible for the corporate wide distribution and installation of software packages as well as the control of the licensing of installed SW products.

The file, print, process, and boot services are regarded as the "classic" server services. The goal of these services is to make the (virtual) local system resources of other systems accessible.

The services that specifically deal with distribution problems and contribute to their resolution are the name, mail, time, and gateway services. The third category comprises those services that are already handling the management aspects of distributed systems; these services include security, software distribution, and accounting services.

We will be covering the management aspects of some of the aforementioned services in later sections of this book.

2.6   Chapter Summary

The object of the management under discussion is networked systems and the services they offer. Networked systems are based on end systems and network components and the media that link them. The functional and communicative interaction between these different modules is provided by standardized frameworks in the form of communication architectures and architectures for distributed systems. These architectures specify cooperation procedures, layers, and protocols. The result is different technologies that determine the structure and functionality of network and system components. A knowledge of these technologies is essential to enable administrators to monitor and to control components on the basis of predetermined goals and policies. Chapter 2 has provided a relevant introductory overview.

The most prevalent standardized communication architectures are the OSI model and the Internet model. The basic architectural approach is similar in both models although the Internet application system is not divided further into explicit layers. Despite certain similarities between the two models, the resulting layer protocols in the transport system are different.

The different protocols and areas of application (e.g., LAN, MAN, WAN) have resulted in the creation of different network technologies (Ethernet, Token Ring, SONET/SDH, ATM, ISDN, FR), with each technology having developed its own component world (e.g., attachment units, adapters, add-drop multiplexers, hubs, bridges, cross-connectors, switches, and routers). The functioning of these components is characterized by different internal algorithms that can be monitored and controlled from external locations through the appropriate management information. We cover characteristic information about resources relevant to management later under the concept of managed object; the information about architectures and resources in earlier sections is a prerequisite for the discussion on managed objects.

The same applies to the treatment of distributed applications in communication networks. The architectures DCE, CORBA, and TINA serve as the basis for the discussion on distributed systems. DCE supports an asymmetrical cooperation scheme (client–server using DCE-RPC), whereas CORBA supports a symmetrical (transparent object-oriented communications using an ORB) scheme.

The network and system services provided by networked systems are likewise the object of management and therefore have been outlined in the overview presented in Chapter 2.

Requirements of the Management of Networked Systems

We will start by presenting sample scenarios from a variety of different application areas and with completely different levels of abstraction to outline some of the requirements of management. What we find is that the requirements vary. It therefore appears sensible to consider whether the management functions as a whole could be structured in some way. The following discussion considers this possibility and looks at the complex "management" from the standpoint of functional areas, lifecycles, and organizational consequences.

3.1 Management Scenarios

The scenarios presented in this section comprise customer network management requirements, management requirements of distributed data storage, central graphics archive, as well as shared document systems. Another scenario deals with help desk support systems and related management problems. Nomadic systems and domain name services make quite different demands on management. Finally, management requirements of backup and archiving systems are discussed.

Scenario 1: Customer Network Management

Figure 3.1 presents a diagram of the national communications infrastructure (B-WIN) of German scientific institutions, in other words, the public corporate network for the universities and research institutes.

Scenario 1: Customer Network Management

   The example shows the following customer–provider relationships, which also typify other corporate networks:

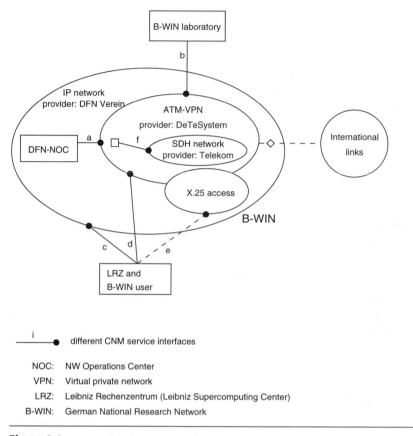

Figure 3.1
German scientific network

1. Provider: Deutsche Telekom; Customer: DeTeSystem; Service: Provision of physical line capacity (SDH hierarchy).

2. Provider: DeTeSystem; Customer: DFN Verein; Service: Provision of a virtual network (ATM-VPN) with access capacities of 34 Mbit/s and 155 Mbit/s as individual or group access rates with the following types of service: available bit rate, PVC constant bit rate, SVC being planned.

3. Provider: DFN Verein; Customer: Scientific facility (the one in the example is the Leibniz Supercomputer Center LCC); Service: IP service (Internet access) and ATM-PVC. DFN Verein provides the mentioned services with the aid of three physically separate groups—the DFN business office, the DFN-NOC (network center), and the DFN laboratory (performance and quality of service monitoring).

4. Provider: LRZ; Customer: Universities in Munich, technical departments (each having its own local networks) with a total of more than 100,000 end users; Service: IP service, directory services, Web hosting, access to diverse special-purpose computers (including supercomputers), and databases; operation from access servers (several hundred telephone-dialed access points, analog/ISDN).

As the example shows, an entire customer–provider hierarchy exists in which the contractual hierarchy and the service hierarchy with its associated technical implementation have different interfaces. The IP service as well as the ATM-PVC service are therefore available to the university end user or LRZ. Contractually, both are provided by DFN Verein; technically, the first one is provided by DFN, the second by DeTeSystem. Management information from a number of lower sources is required for use of a service, the generation of fault reports, performance supervision, and management of the services that are made available to the next highest "level" in the user–provider chain.

The scenario given is a complex one, but it provides an insight into a whole range of different management requirements:

- First of all, each provider must manage its own network. An integral part of this task is component management, which concerns the supervision of the availability, capacity utilization, security, and fault-free operation of the individual components. Added to this is the functioning of the network as a whole. This requires management tasks such as routing and switching, multiplexing data streams, and monitoring logical paths and channels.

- At the access to a network, all providers offer their customers services with a certain quality of service (QoS) based on a service level agreement (SLA). The constant monitoring of service quality is a management task. The management of the customer–provider interface also includes procedures for fault reporting and for service adaptation or service provisioning (e.g., ordering the establishment of an ATM-PVC).

- In a scenario like the preceding one, it is essential that customers have access to specific management information (e.g., service quality, service availability) because this is the information they need if they themselves want to develop added value and other new services based on the network services they are already using. For customers, it is the service-related information based on the customer SLA that is generally interesting rather than the "raw data" from the component management of their providers.

Customer network management stands for the transition from a component-oriented management to a service-related management. Customer and service-relevant criteria are provided

Customer network management (CNM) or *customer service management* (CSM) is first and foremost a controlled transfer of information by the provider of a communications service to its customers. CNM enables customers to see the relevant part of a usually public network, therefore their VPN (represented through the management information), as a part of their own network structure. This makes the public network more transparent to customers so that they no longer perceive it as a "black box." Ideally, customers are informed immediately of any problems in the network and can be saved the time of making long and difficult phone calls to find out what is causing a failure.

The CNM-MIB must reflect services and SLAs

First of all, a data model for the implementation of the CNM management information base (CNM-MIB) must be defined for the scenario described. The data comprises user and accounting information, statistics and measurement results, and fault reports as well as breakdown messages and is derived from many different sources. Furthermore, a process model must be defined that describes the data flows and operation processes involved in obtaining and forwarding information. Lastly, a specification of the CNM service interfaces that provide access to the CNM-MIB is required. In Figure 3.1, individual lowercase letters are used to indicate the different CNM service interfaces. We refer you to [LLN98] for other versions.

Scenario 2: Distributed Data Storage

Scenario 2: Distributed Data Storage

A company's data is stored in many places—on PCs, workstations, servers, and special-purpose computers, in computer centers and in departments, within the intranet, and externally with suppliers and dealers.

Systems that are part of a data complex should have universal concepts for structuring file systems and allowing data access. One possible principle is to compartmentalize individual file systems and databases using explicit security barriers such as firewalls; another concept would be to create global virtualization with locally transparent access.

If a network consists of systems with different architectures or supplied by different vendors (as shown, for example, in Figure 3.2), there will usually be a number of details (such as different system parameters) that the network operator will first have to settle through management. A network structure must be able to cope with many different version states of the products involved. Data confidentiality and integrity must also be considered.

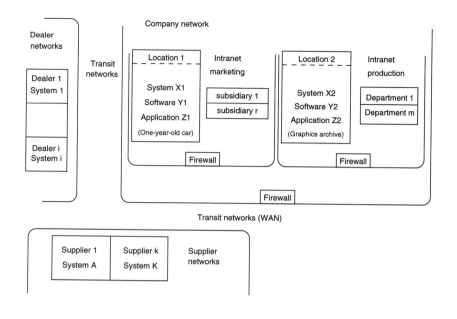

Figure 3.2
Corporate network

If transparency is wanted, then a location-dependent global name space is required: Users always want to be able to find their data over the same access route regardless of which computers they happen to be using.

If security is wanted, then domain concepts that allow areas of accountability and security to be specified are useful. Policies that control the access filtering and authentication mechanisms and initiate messages and event handling when security breaches occur must be specified for access systems.

The security aspect is also responsible for data consistency in redundant data storage with replication, for data backup to prevent short-term loss, and for long-term data storage in the form of archiving. Because some of the data is often stored in different locations at different storage hierarchy levels, policies have to be defined for migrating to these levels.

Scenario 3: Central Graphics Archive

Another search system provides a totally different management task. An automobile manufacturer that has operations all over the world has

Scenario 3: Central Graphics Archive

a central digital graphics archive for every type of design (of products as well as of production plants). Access to this archive should be available to designers, maintenance personnel, dealers, and suppliers anywhere in the world. The management task consisted of the following:

- Setting up an appropriate directory structure, including directory services.

- Making available a level of fast cache servers for the central archive, which consists of several archive servers.

- Integrating cache strategies and allowing them to be changed.

- Defining and operating a platform-independent access procedure.

- Guaranteeing security through suitable authorization, authentication, and encryption procedures.

- Protecting the different intranets from one another using firewalls or other suitable privacy methods.

Scenario 4: Shared Document System

Scenario 4: Shared
Document System

The patent examiners in one particular patent office use a multilevel search procedure comprising around 20 million documents in the form of image information (pixel images) (8 TBytes as 300-dpi documents, 4 TBytes as 150-dpi documents); in addition, 600,000 documents are available for full-text search. Figure 3.3 illustrates a possible system for this purpose.

Based on the service level agreement, the system is to provide:

- Availability: 98 percent during main hours of work
- Search times for 60 parallel queries and up to 100,000 hits: 3 seconds per query without trunking, 4–20 seconds per query with trunking
- Viewing time: 0.7 second within and 1.5 seconds between documents

The management tasks from this scenario comprise:

- Monitoring quality of service (QoS) parameters in accordance with SLA requirements
- Applications management (software distribution, parameter provision and search system updates, operation of distributed "search" applications)

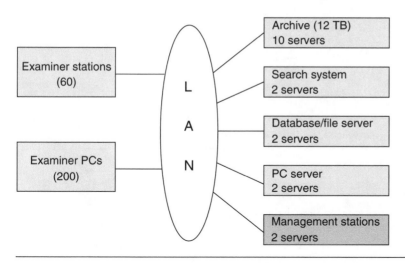

Figure 3.3
Search system

- Network and system management: security of infrastructure operations (network and end systems), data backup
- User administration, cost compilation
- Reports, message services in regard to QoS

Scenario 5: Help Desk Support

Fault tracking is a difficult and time-consuming process due to the increasing complexity of distributed systems and communication services. Providers of large infrastructures frequently offer their customers fault notification procedures in which a help desk, a hotline, or a call center serves as the central coordinating point. A variety of different tools are available to a help desk: active tools that can be used to monitor or control a distributed system and passive tools that support a call center. These include documentation systems (inventory registers, cabling plans, system documentation, user and SLA directories) and in some cases trouble ticket systems (TTSs). A TTS is a system in which fault reports are administered as documents, or trouble tickets (TTs), from the time a fault is recorded to when a diagnosis is made and the fault is then corrected.

Scenario 5: Help Desk Support

The following case study (compare Figure 3.4) is a very simplified example of a typical fault handling procedure and highlights the tasks of a TTS:

Course of fault repair processing

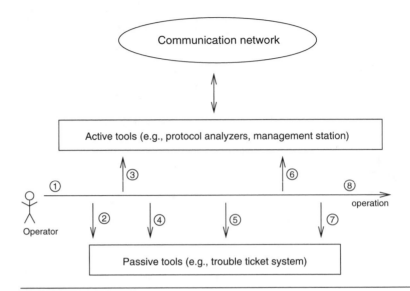

Figure 3.4
Trouble ticket systems are used in the fault repair process

1. A user who wants to access centralized archive data in a computer center from the PC at his workstation is unable to make a connection. This is reported to the network operator in the computer center.

2. The network operator searches the TTS to check whether a similar problem has already been reported. If another TT cannot be found, the operator records the current fault and provides the user with a fault identification number, the TT ID. This number enables the user to check at any time on the progress being made with diagnosing or repairing the fault.

3. The operator checks network component availability from a management station but is unable to detect any faults. He documents his actions, including his findings, in the TTS, and transfers the task of dealing with the fault to the relevant expert.

4. The expert receives the appropriate message (e.g., via email) and accesses the appropriate TT for details and any previous actions undertaken. He then searches the TTS for similar fault cases that have already been resolved. The results of the search query indicate that in similar cases the defective configuration of a network component was usually the cause of the fault.

5. The expert checks the network documentation system to find out about any recent modifications that have been carried out and locates an appropriate entry.

6. A configuration tool is used to verify the pocket of a component (e.g., a router) and possibly shows that a defective packet filter exists that is preventing access by the user to the archive. The configuration is modified, and the component is reloaded.

7. The expert documents the actions taken, including information about the source of the fault in the TTS, and completes his part of the process.

8. A message that is generated automatically by the TTS informs the user that the fault has been corrected.

This is, of course, only a simple case scenario and omits a whole range of integrated management issues, only a small number of which are presented here:

- Direct coupling of a TTS to active management tools.

- Integration of a TTS into a workflow management system to control the overall fault handling process.

- Generation of intelligent front ends for TT creation, such as by guiding users through the process of fault localization. The basic idea is to allow users themselves—transparently using predetermined decision trees—to perform diagnostics and to query databases. Through these actions, the information needed by the experts to solve a problem is collected and formally entered into a TT.

- Accompanying support of help desks through the availability of appropriate telephone systems (computer-telephony-integration [CTI], automatic call distribution [ACD], uniform collective calling numbers).

- Intelligent use of TT databases as case study databases and analysis based on appropriate information methods (TT correlation, case-based reasoning).

On this basis (also compare Figure 3.5), TTSs can evolve into integrating tools because they are sometimes coupled with the active network and system components and with customer support systems. They also trigger and monitor actions. This subject will be addressed again in Chapter 14.

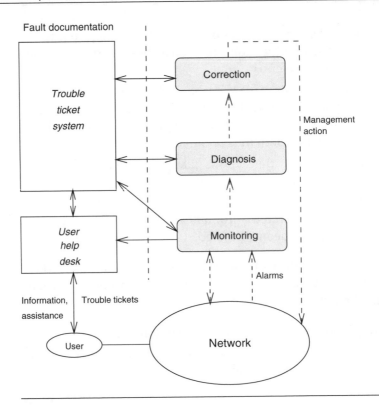

Figure 3.5
TTS system as a tool in the management environment

Scenario 6: Nomadic Systems

Scenario 6:
Nomadic Systems

Imagine a situation involving several intranets of cooperating companies linked over a WAN but separated by firewalls, in other words, security components with access filter functions before a subnet. Within the framework of the cooperation, employees take their mobile computers (laptops, notebooks) to the premises of one of the partner firms to work temporarily in another department. Staff, of course, want to "take along" their familiar data processing (DP) work environments. The issues that arise in this connection are:

- How do the IP addresses "travel"? This is not only significant in terms of routing. There are a number of applications for which the fixed IP address of a computer is important, such as in the configuration of databases, in licensing control, and in the security area. Fixed IP addresses are also important for Internet telephony and in videoconferencing because they are treated as though they uniquely identify a user.

- How is authorization for certain resources such as printers and some servers granted on a short-term basis or transferred to the other intranet?

- How is the accounting handled (e.g., how are accounts and account numbers transferred or new ones set up, how are the costs allocated)?

Addressing these issues is the challenge facing successful deployment and management of virtual private networks.

Scenario 7: DNS Management

DNS is one of the elementary Internet services and is used to translate names to IP addresses and vice versa. For both mappings, the DNS information is divided into two independent hierarchical and worldwide unique name spaces: one for IP addresses and another for domain names. The DNS service consists of a DNS client in each terminal, a resolver, and primary and secondary DNS servers. The particularly noteworthy servers are the so-called root servers that are principally used as the first starting point for each query sent by the interconnected DNS servers. Because DNS is realized as a worldwide distributed system, the fault situations that can occur are very complex. A management solution addresses the conceptional and operational aspects, with the conceptional aspects including:

Scenario 7: DNS Management

- Definition of naming conventions
- Division of the name spaces into appropriate subspaces
- Name server structuring
- Mapping parts of the name space to zones (delegation)
- Definition of the resolver hierarchy

The operational aspects include:

- Configuration of the resolvers in the terminals (hosts)
- Configuration and operation of the name server, updating the data of the zones in the name server, caching query results obtained by each server
- Assurance of the consistency of both address and domain name spaces
- All measures relating to fault management

The organizational issues arising in relationship to the updating and coordination of the internal name server complex are particularly complicated when corporatewide DNS servers are used in large firms with several hundred zones. Ultimately, the DNS relies on administration by a central authority called the Inter NIC and fault-free configuration and operation of root servers.

Scenario 8: Backup and Archiving System

Scenario 8: Backup and Archiving System

The example relates to a large organization with many quite autonomous organizational operating units (such as a university with all its departments and institutes). The basic data processing equipment for the operating units is provided on an autonomous decentralized basis. High-speed computers, overflow capacity, and certain central services, which can include a backup and archiving system, are available centrally. Because the operating units compute on all sorts of different distributed and central systems and, furthermore, are physically dispersed, a distributed file system (e.g., DCE/DFS; see Chapter 2) is installed for security reasons and to provide the local transparency required. What are the management requirements of a backup and archiving system? We have listed a number of these requirements here, some of which will be familiar from the previous scenarios.

Examples of management requirements

- Domains: It is essential that the administration of managed data can be delegated on a hierarchical basis. The technical partitioning of an entire archive should not have a direct effect on the administration; instead, it should be possible to set up a large archive that technically is a coupling of a number of smaller archives, and vice versa, to file data in an archive independently of the areas administered. If a domain structure exists beyond the archive application, then a relationship should exist between the domain structure within and outside the archive; it could be obstructive to force a 1:1 representation in each case.

- Name spaces: Distributed file systems such as DCE/DFS must be mappable to the name spaces of the backup and archive system. In particular, a file that can be viewed on different computers cannot give the archive system the impression of consisting of several different files.

- Security techniques: If a special security technique (e.g., use of shadow files with DCE/DFS to force consistency) exists for a file system, then the security system of the backup system should not undermine this technique.

- Backup strategies: It should be possible to specify the backup strategies a user requires (frequency, life of backed-up data) as well as the operational conditions (certain times of the day for backup) to the automated system.

- Allocation of resources: Control over the resources used must remain with the administrators.

- Access control: Authorized users must be able to access their own files as well as those to which they have been expressly granted access rights, but not the files of other users. Administrators must be allowed to operate on behalf of the users they administer. There must be a way of controlling the extent to which users are allowed to undertake actions on their own that are normally carried out for them by the administrator (e.g., regular backups). The authorization model for archived and backed-up data should be compatible with the authorization model for online data (e.g., data accessible through DCE-DFS); under no circumstances should it undermine any of the security measures.

- Integration into more global management structures: If an enterprise management tool is used in an operation, then appropriate modules must be available to control and supervise the backup and archive system using the same resources. Conversely, this process should not be contingent on the use of a specific tool.

- Software distribution: A backup and archive system has client software that is distributed a hundred or a thousand times. Mechanisms are required for automating the distribution of new versions of client software.

- Performance (e.g., management): A system must be able to cope with large quantities of files (e.g., up to a billion) and corresponding large databases for registering the archive files. With some applications in the high-speed computing area, transfer rates also play a major role. If different media are used within an archive, then there should be a way of controlling the distribution of data over this media to achieve optimal performance.

The scenarios presented serve only as examples that can be extended and expanded in any number of ways. They relate to the levels of network, system, and application management. More and more importance is being attached to distributed systems and the management

Importance of management to the business processes

of them because the competition is increasingly being based on the processing and exchange of information—often in place of real values or things (e.g., the stock market, money transfer, ordering goods, along with simulation, virtual reality). Many companies are in the process of using "business engineering" to adapt their business processes to this information-based competition.

However, distributed systems create management barriers: These relate to system complexity, change flexibility, service availability, and cost of ownership. System complexity is a product of the variety of technologies and conceivable solutions (see Figure 1.3) and the different levels of approach available (Figure 1.2). Added to this is the fact that a form of distribution can exist at every level. The complexity of the systems being managed is also reflected in the complexity of the management system, and this in turn translates into a requirement for more highly trained staff.

Change flexibility is essential because products and services have to adapt to a fast-changing market. Business processes and the operating processes for the information processing infrastructure derived from them are compelled to follow the market; lastly, the management solutions must be adaptable as well. However, management systems need to be flexible to deal with the consequences of change in the upper part of the management pyramid (Figure 1.4) and to cope with location moves, adaptations to new hardware and software visions, adaptations to processing load changes, and so forth.

Distributed systems are not an end in themselves, but they should provide services (see sections 2.4.4 and 2.5.2). Services are provided by a manager in accordance with a service level agreement. But it is not enough to describe services only from the standpoint of functionality. An "operable" interface is required to allow services to be invoked and evaluated. Being evaluated means that it should be possible to assess the quality of service (QoS) achieved. QoS assesses the quality of a service as a whole as well as the quality of the security of the service and its customer service. Quality of service is typical interface information between service provider and service user. The task of monitoring it falls to performance management. We will return to this topic in the next section.

3.2　Management Functions

The scenarios presented in section 3.1 gave an indication of the variety of management tasks possible. Because the solution to a management task for distributed systems is itself a distributed application, it should also be possible to describe the modules used. In heterogeneous system environments, this even has to be an "open," in other words, multivendor, approach. Moreover, not all management requirements will be the same in each concrete scenario. It is therefore useful to classify the total task "management" into functional areas and then to describe the management functions that are typical for each specific area.

Even this line of approach will fundamentally produce all different kinds of classifications. We will first concentrate on the five functional areas defined in the functional model of the OSI management architecture (more on this in Chapter 5): fault management, configuration management, accounting management, performance management, security management. When relating to these functional areas, often the abbreviation FCAPS is used in the literature. We will describe typical management tasks based on these five areas. For didactic reasons, we will describe FCAPS in a different order. Later on, we will also discuss how the OSI areas could be extended.

It should be emphasized that in principle the functional areas apply to all object types (i.e., the classification of function areas is orthogonal to the classification of the levels of Figure 2.2).

3.2.1 Configuration Management

As stated in [HEI97], the term *configuration* frequently has different meanings (depending on the immediate context). A configuration can be:

The term *configuration* can have different meanings

- A *description* of a distributed system based on the physical and geographical arrangement of resources (i.e., media, network components, systems or hosts, software), including how these resources are actually interconnected, and information about their logical relationships. This description of a configuration can be abstracted from the physical arrangement of the resources based on different views, such as organizational, geographical, administrative, or security-related aspects.

- The *process* of configuration as an activity or as a manipulation of the structure of distributed systems, therefore, setting and changing the parameters that control the normal operation of a system and establishing the system environment required for this normal operation.

- The *result* of a configuration process, therefore, the generated system in the sense of a set of certain parameter values that are characteristic for the normal operation of a resource.

The context will generally indicate which meaning is appropriate for the term *configuration.* Where necessary, we differentiate between a configuration description, which is frequently also reflected in the appropriate documentation systems, a configuration result, or generated system, and the configuration process, also known as configuration or system generation.

Configuration is an adaptation of systems to operating environments and includes installing new software, expanding old software, attaching devices, or making changes to network topology or to traffic load. Although configuration also encompasses aspects of physical installation, it is usually carried out through a software-controlled generation and setting of parameters; these include function-selection parameters, authorization parameters, protocol parameters (message lengths, windows, timers, priorities), attachment parameters (type and class of device, procedure, bit rate, parity), entries in routing tables, name servers, directories, as well as filter parameters for bridges (addresses, types of protocols, integration), spanning tree parameters for a bridge (priority of bridge or port), parameters for the connecting paths of routers (interfaces, speed, flow control procedures), maximum file size, computing times, and services allowed.

The following issues arise in relationship to operation and communication:

There are different evaluation criteria for configuration tools

- *Location of configuration:* The system being configured for (target system) is not always compatible with the system on which the configuration is being performed. This can be due to technical reasons such as a requirement for editors and macroprocessors that are not available on the target system. But there can also be security or organizational reasons for the problem, especially when configuration data can be loaded remotely. A configuration can take place on a component for the component itself, on each component for any other component, or at a selected station (network management station) for all components.

- *Storage of a configuration:* Different solutions exist in this area also. If data is stored in NVRAM or on disks or on the hard disk in the component, a configuration can be changed easily and quickly through an exchange of the disks or a reloading over the network. However, this does not work when storing with EPROMs.

Moreover, the scope of the configuration parameters can be lower due to capacity limitations, which can also reduce flexibility. A configuration can also be stored on a boot server and called up through appropriate load protocols.

- *Validity of a configuration:* A static configuration is one in which each reconfiguration is coupled with an interruption to operations. Dynamic configuration, on the other hand, allows changes to be made to configuration data during running operations. Thus the events that signal the validity of new operating parameters can be the reloading of a component, the restart of a component, or the restart of one of the affected component ports.

- *User interface of the configurator:* The quality of a user interface depends, on one hand, to what extent individual parameters can quickly be changed and, on the other hand, to what extent the network administrator can be relieved of dealing with the individual parameters of a large number of devices. This can be addressed through the definition of different options, device profiles, or versions of configurations and the use of configuration macros to include entire groups of devices. It is also convenient to have corresponding documentation on the configuration data that at the same time lends itself to the support of network control. It should also be mentioned that the configurator and the configuration files must be protected against unauthorized use. The variations of access protection range from dispensing with passwords to breaking down the areas responsible for a configuration through a separation of network-global, component-global, and function-specific passwords. Another approach is securing the management protocols used to carry out configuration.

Configuration management therefore encompasses setting parameters, defining threshold values, setting filters, allocating names to managed objects—loading configuration data, if necessary—providing documentation of configuration changes, and actively changing configurations. The tool functionality that is assigned to configuration management (this will be dealt with again later) covers:

Tools for configuration management

- Autotopology and autodiscovery, thus the ability to extrapolate a description of a configuration from the concrete actual system environment

- Systems for documenting descriptions of configurations, master databases

- Tools for generating network maps for the visualization of configuration data
- Tools for activating backup systems to detach missing components and so forth
- Tools for setting and invoking configuration parameters and system status
- Tools for software distribution and licensing control
- Tools for supervising and controlling authorization

3.2.2   Fault Management

Fault management deals with the detection, isolation, and elimination of abnormal system behavior. Identifying and tracking faults is a major operational problem with all data processing systems. Compared to nonnetworked, localized systems, fault management in computer networks and distributed systems is more difficult for a variety of reasons. These include the large number of components involved, the wide physical distribution of the resources, the heterogeneity of the hardware and software components, and the different domains components fall under (e.g., personnel of different organizational units).

Faults are target/performance deviations in the behavior of resources. Fault management comprises reactive and proactive measures

A fault can be defined as a deviation from the set operating goals, system functions, or services. Messages about faults are usually conveyed by the components themselves or by the users of the system. Some of the sources of faults are data transmission paths (e.g., transceiver cable, twisted-pair cable, optical fiber, leased lines, virtual channels), network components (e.g., transceivers, repeaters, bridges, star couplers, server computers, data terminals), end systems, software for components, inadequate interface descriptions (indirectly), or even incorrect operation.

Fault management tasks

The function of fault management is to detect and correct faults quickly to ensure that a high level of availability of a distributed system and the services it provides is maintained. The tasks that have evolved from this objective include (compare with Figure 3.5):

- Monitoring network and system state
- Responding and reacting to alarms
- Diagnosing fault causes (i.e., fault isolation and root cause analysis)
- Establishing error propagation
- Introducing and checking error recovery measures (i.e., testing and verification)

- Operating trouble ticket systems
- Providing assistance to users (user help desk)

The following technical capabilities can assist in fault analysis:

Important aids for fault management

- Self-identification of system components
- Separate testability of components
- Trace facility (i.e., keeping records of switched message traffic or labeling messages for the purpose of traceability or special compatability reports)
- Error log
- Message echos at all protocol layers (i.e., at transmission links and on an end-to-end basis such as "heartbeat" or "keep alive" messages that detect failure)
- Retrieval possibilities for memory dumps
- Measures for purposely generating errors in defined system environments
- Start possibilities (which can also be initiated and monitored centrally) for self-test routines and the transmission of test texts to specific ports (loop test, remote test, problem file) as well as reachability tests such as ICMP packets for ping and trace route analysis of network reachability
- Setting options for threshold values
- Triggering of planned resets and restarts (directed to specific ports, port groups, and components)
- Availability of special test systems (oscilloscopes, time-domain reflectometers, interface checkers, protocol analyzers, hardware monitors for line supervision)
- Support of filter mechanisms for fault messages or alarms and event correlation for reducing the number of relevant events and for root cause analysis
- Interfaces of fault management tools to trouble ticket systems and help desks (e.g., for automated propagation of fault notifications and corrections)

3.2.3 Performance Management

In terms of its objectives, performance management could be seen as a systematic continuation of fault management. Whereas fault management is responsible for ensuring that a communications network or a distributed system just operates, this is not enough to satisfy the objectives of performance management, which wants the overall system to perform well. It is this "performing well" that signals the first problem that has to be resolved by performance management, namely, the definition of quality of service.

The starting point for performance management is the guarantee of quality of service

Quality of service is a typical mechanism for conveying interface information between provider (i.e., the one responsible for a communications network or for the IT infrastructure) and customer, thus the service user. Its importance increases as more customer–provider relationships are involved in the implementation of corporate networks or distributed systems. The service interface is defined as follows:

- Specification of the service and service type (e.g., deterministic, statistic, best possible)

- Description of relevant QoS parameters (with quantifiable values; this includes usage value, mean value, limit value)

- Specification of the monitoring operations (information regarding measurement method, measuring points, and measurement values; specification of measurement report)

- Description of reactions to changes of the QoS parameters mentioned earlier

It is very difficult to provide uniform guarantees in a layered and distributed system

The crux, however, is that it is very difficult and not always possible to provide a complete definition of a service interface on the basis of the aforementioned. The following problems tend to arise:

- Vertical QoS mapping problems: Because communication systems are layered systems, the layer-specific QoS parameters of layer N have to be mapped onto the QoS parameters of layers (N=1) or (N-1) at the respective layer boundaries, for example, applications-oriented QoS (e.g., speech quality) to network-dependent QoS (e.g., jitter). QoS hierarchies have not yet been definitively defined for all services and protocol hierarchies. This problem is exacerbated when services of different layers are provided by different carriers or providers.

- Horizontal QoS mapping problems: If more than one carrier is incorporated into a corporate network, the result can be a concatenation of the different subnets or trunk sections that are used to provide services with a uniform quality of service for end user to end user communication. This assumes that the different carriers have implemented the same quality of service features or else are using standardized QoS negotiating protocols, resource reservation protocols, or management protocols. The more complex the service is, the less often this requirement is met. You just have to think about the voice service and the noncompatible proprietary signaling protocols of telecommunications systems and the fact that quadrature signaling (QSIG) is used.

- Measurement methods: The optimal way to assess quality of service would be to apply measurement methods based on visible quantities at the service interface rather than to use an analysis of the technology supplied by the provider. The latter can change quickly, and furthermore, the quantities measured are often of no interest to the customer who first has to convert them into QoS parameters.

Performance management therefore encompasses all the measures required for ensuring that the quality of service conforms to the service level agreement. It includes:

Performance management measures

- Establishing quality of service parameters and metrics
- Monitoring all resources for performance bottlenecks and threshold crossings
- Carrying out measurements and trend analysis to predict failure before it occurs
- Evaluating history logs (i.e, records on system activity, error files)
- Processing measurement data and compiling performance reports
- Carrying out performance and capacity planning. This entails providing analytical or simulative prediction models that are used to check the results of new applications, tuning measures, and configuration changes

Monitors, protocol analyzers, statistics packets, report generators, and modeling tools are some of the typical tool functionalities in this area.

3.2.4   Accounting Management, User Administration

User administration comprises tasks such as name and address administration, including the related directory services, authorization granting the right to use resources, and finally, the accounting services.

User administration as a basis for authentication, authorization, and customization

There are costs involved in providing communication and server services that must be allocated to the users of the respective service (e.g., access charges and utilization charges). The strategies and procedures for cost allocation cannot and should not be rigidly established by an accounting system; it is the subject of accounting policy. It is therefore important that accounting management is able to configure this following the guidelines of accounting policy.

Accounting management includes compiling usage data (resource usage or sevice usage accounting based on monitoring and metering), defining accountable units, keeping settlement accounts and accounting logs, allocating costs to these accounts, assigning and monitoring quotas, maintaining statistics on usage, and lastly, defining accounting policies and tariffs, which leads to billing and charging. If several providers are involved to support a service, usage reconciliation also belongs to accounting management. The settlement of the reconciliation between two providers can be done using either an accounting revenue division procedure, a flat rate procedure, or a traffic unit price procedure.

How an accounting system is implemented, which approach will be used in compiling accounting parameters and how costs will be allocated, is a management decision. This decision can be influenced by company policy because of the need to balance the ratio between the cost of compiling the costs and the benefits derived.

Once the fixed and variable costs of all the components (e.g., cabling systems, network components, connection paths, servers, system services) to be included in the calculation have been compiled, the costs must be allocated to the appropriate user. There are all sorts of ingenious ways of compiling and then passing on these costs. The more subtle the approach, the more complicated and cost intensive is the accounting procedure. This means that usage accounting services need to be cost-justified in the same way as any other service.

The underlying usage parameters of a cost compilation include number of transmitted packets or bytes, duration and time of day/week of a connection, bandwidth and QoS of the connection, location of other communications partners (e.g., when public networks are used), conversion costs for gateway services, use of resources in the server, and use of software products (licensing control). In addition to variable costs, fixed costs are also taken into account (cost of office space, maintenance charges, depreciation).

To sum up, the accounting management functions comprise at least usage management functions (usage generation, usage edits and validation of call events or service requests, usage error correction, usage accumulation, usage correlation, usage aggregation, usage distribution), accounting process functions (usage testing, usage surveillance,

Accounting is extremely important for telcos

management of usage stream, administration of usage data collection), control functions (tariff administration, tariff system change control, record generation control, data transfer control, data storage control), and charging functions (charge generation, bill production, payment processing, debt collection, external reconciliation, contract processing). Many of the mentioned functions are especially important for public telco providers. In such environments, services are often multi-network services (i.e., multiple network nodes, different providers, or mobile subscribers may be involved). So, accounting management must address distributed collection of usage data, improved performance requirements for usage collection and report generation (in near real time), and multiple charging strategies.

The administration data needed for user administration and accounting management includes [VAR94]: subscriber details (demographic data, contract ID, credit information, subscriber history), contract information services covered, contract validity, authorized users, quotas, service level agreements, billing and payment details, tariff information, usage information, and administration system parameters.

From this nonexhaustive list, it should become obvious that accounting management bears a very close relationship to service and business management layers.

3.2.5 Security Management

This term is not used to refer to the security of management (i.e., ensuring management is performed securely), but to the management of security in distributed systems. The starting point for the discussion is the resources of a company that are worth protecting. Information, IT infrastructures, services, and production represent values that are exposed to threats of attack or improper use. Security measures that reflect the results of threat analyses or security risk analyses are needed to prevent damage and loss. Typical *threats* are created by:

Security management requires a threat analysis

- Passive attacks: eavesdropping on information; producing a user profile or an undesirable traffic flow analysis or theft of information (passwords, etc.)

- Active attacks: masquerades (i.e., users pretending to be someone else, or spoofing); manipulating message sequences by changing the sequence, inadmissible repeating, giving priority to or delaying messages; modifying messages; manipulating resources through overloading, reconfiguration, reprogramming, and so forth (unauthorized access, viruses, Trojan horses, denial-of-service attacks)

- Malfunctioning of resources
- Faulty or inappropriate behavior and incorrect response operation

Breakdown of security management tasks

Security requirements and goals are established on the basis of threat analyses and the values (resources and services) needing protection. The security policies defined ultimately identify the security requirements. Examples of security policies are "Passwords have to be changed every three weeks"; "Only second-line managers have access to personnel data"; "All attacks on security have to be recorded and followed up on." These policies serve as the framework for the security services needed and consequently implemented. Security management therefore comprises:

- Conducting threat analyses
- Defining and enforcing security policies
- Checking identity (authentication based on signatures, notarization, or certification)
- Carrying out and enforcing access controls
- Guaranteeing confidentiality (encryption)
- Ensuring data integrity (message authentication)
- Monitoring systems to prevent threats to security
- Reporting on security status and violations or attempted violations

It can be assumed that a reliable set of recognized security procedures, which for the most part are already available as public domain software, exists in the security management area.

The main problem is finding the right way to embed these procedures into management architectures and to control them in a uniform way within the framework of a security policy.

3.2.6 Other Approaches to Classifying Management Functions

Business and service management yield other functional areas

Until now, we have chosen to use the OSI management functional areas as the examples in our presentation of management functions. The literature [HUN98, MCC96, TER95] even mentions other areas such as inventory/asset management, problem management, systems administration, change management, and service level agreements.

According to [TER95], *inventory management* comprises functions that have to do with inventory, archiving, backup, change services, and ordering. Activities of the directory services are also included. If we disregard the ordering area, we see that we have subsumed the other functions under configuration management. Inventory management is the updating of documentation systems (e.g., network databases, directories of all components). We have also included these management functions under configuration management. A documentation system is without doubt the heart of all management procedures. We will come back to this again in our coverage of tools (Chapters 12 and 16). *Asset management* differs from inventory management in that it also incorporates an economic assessment that helps to provide more reliable information about the "cost of ownership" of IT infrastructures.

Problem management refers to facilities provided in the environment of help desks, hotlines, and trouble ticket systems. These have been presented as components of fault management.

Service level agreements (SLAs) are part of performance management within our interpretation of it. They can also be interpreted as a component of service management from the standpoint of the management pyramid (Figure 1.4). This often happens in the telecommunications network area where a distinction is made within service management of the stages service creation, service provisioning, service subscribing, and service operation. The SLA would then particularly apply to the two last stages.

In a narrower interpretation, *change management* can be viewed as part of configuration management. On the other hand, it can also be seen as a process that transcends all functional areas (the "management building" shown in Figure 3.6). It is in this context that we deal with change management in detail in Chapter 19.

According to [TER95], *administration* is responsible for updating user profiles, providing software services, including the monitoring of versions, and distributing software. We added the first area to user administration and the last two to configuration management. [HUN98] describes administration as being system management along the lines of Figure 1.2.

We could also take the tack of dissecting the complex management according to the layering in Figures 1.2 and 1.4 to arrive at a description and classification of management functions. This approach is, however, orthogonal to the one we have selected. The functional areas we have selected break down types of tasks; the layering breaks down objects of management.

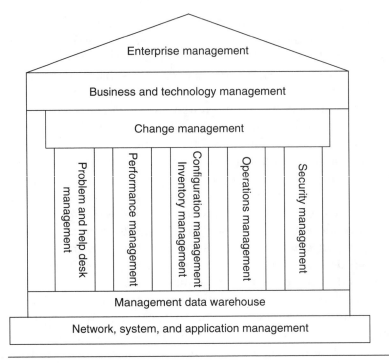

Figure 3.6
The management building

3.3 Organizational Aspects of Management

Integrated manage-
ment must consider
organizational
aspects

The management of IT infrastructures should not only be considered from a technical standpoint; an integrated solution must always also be analyzed in its entirety. On the one hand, an integrated approach involves slotting the solution into the management pyramid (Figure 1.4), but it also means adapting management to the corporate operational and organizational structure. This entails:

- Defining the management processes that support the business processes. A definition of the different roles involved is also required.

- Defining the *domains* to which specific management policies and procedures apply.

- Specifying interfaces between domains to enable the exchange of management information and the invocation of management actions.

- Planning and establishing a management infrastructure. This planning entails defining procedures for implementing the management processes and specifying the tool functionality required.

- Establishing an operational and organizational structure for carrying out management. This includes specifying job specifications for workplaces in areas such as operating, administration, planning, analysis, and help desks. The qualifications of required staff vary according to the assignment of duties. [TER92] lists examples of job specifications.

We will examine aspects of this operational conversion in detail in Part IV. There the term *operating concept* is used to refer to the specification of conditions for technical management in a concrete environment. The operating concept defines the distributed application "management" as something that defines services, tasks, job allocations to organizational units, procedures, and information flows. This concept is therefore the prerequisite for the selection and operation of management systems, procedures, and tools.

IT infrastructures can also be structured into domains (logical subdomains) based on:

Criteria for defining domains

- Different organizations or companies that are part of the management environment: carriers, Internet service providers, outsourcers, suppliers of management tools, user organizations.

- Organizational structure of a particular company (teams, groups, departments, operating areas).

- Geographical conditions (country, location, campus, building, floor, room).

- Business areas.

- Data processing–related aspects (e.g., LAN/WAN, central/distributed DP, systems of a specific vendor).

- Types of resources: hardware, system software, applications software, data, operating materials, premises, technical infrastructure.

Establishing domains also always means forming groups of managed objects. These groups of managed objects are assigned different jobs such as planning, selection, procurement, provisioning and implementation, operation, maintenance, and adaptation.

When an organizational definition of management is provided, it also includes a distribution of responsibility, in other words, a domain-related assignment of jobs and responsibilities. This distribution of responsibility essentially plays a key role in determining the extent of management-relevant communication required as well as the complexity of the security concept needed by management. In Chapter 4, we will present some basic models showing distribution of responsibility (centralized, hierarchical, distributed management). In addition to the subareas and activities mentioned earlier, the distribution of responsibility can also be oriented toward the management function areas presented in section 3.2. It has an influence on the positioning of management systems and tools, the development of procedures, and the definition of name spaces.

3.4   Time Aspects of Management

The factor time is an issue that occurs in different places. Similar to what happens with objects that are the subject of management, the consideration of the time factor in the implementation of management tasks leads to the lifecycle phases planning, provisioning, operating, and change. This applies as much to the framework for the operating concept as it does to an individual management application or a management tool.

Planning as a stage in the lifecycle requires a number of accompanying analyses

Although the planning phase is not dealt with as a single block below, many references are made to planning aspects. Planning itself is another process that consists of different steps, including:

- *Application analysis*: This determines which services are to be provided. The services for their part are characterized by the definitions of functionality and quality of service.

- *Demand priority analysis*: This analysis establishes how the users and resources of a distributed system are physically distributed and serves as a basis for topology studies and an analysis of traffic relationships.

- *Demand size analysis*: This deals with determining the distribution of transactions and exchanged data from the standpoint of time and volume.

- *Component analysis*: Component analysis establishes the type and quantity of components to be taken into account in a distributed system, including interface characteristics and software.

- *Analysis of other conditions*: Other conditions that can affect planning or product selection include protection of current investments (e.g., compatibility requirements for software versions, interfaces,

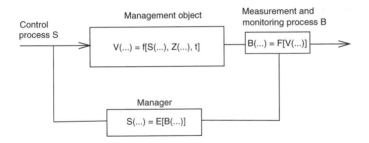

B: Control result
F: Measurement and analysis rules for monitoring
E: Decision-making for management operation
S: Control process as a management operation
Z: State of management object before intervention and change context
V: Behavior of management object due to intervention
 t: Time

Figure 3.7
Time behavior of managed objects as a feedback result

and services), availability of MTBF/(MTBF+MTTR) with MTBF meaning "meantime between failure" and MTTR meaning "meantime to repair," data protection requirements, capacity reserves, expansion capabilities, cost restrictions, implementation costs, technological developments, market trends, and standardization.

- *Planning the introduction of a system*: This includes (at the very least) the following: checking operational procedures (operating concepts), adapting organizational charts, planning the physical installations, making plans for training, and making plans for delivery and installation.

The adaptation phase mentioned earlier generally also impinges on the planning phase. This observation of feedback applies in general and can also be applied within each phase. The time behavior of managed objects can be seen as a feedback loop result (Figure 3.7).

Resources are controlled or manipulated through parameter changes resulting from management intervention (control). The effect of this intervention is apparent later and is monitored at the appropriate location. The results of this measurement are evaluated by the manager or management system (e.g., event analysis, threshold analysis) and can sometimes initiate new management actions.

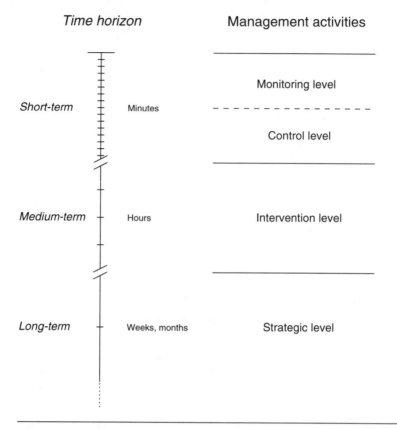

Figure 3.8
Time horizons and management activities

The different management activities that take place during the operating phase can in turn be assigned to different time horizons according to Figure 3.8.

- *Short-term horizon:* Short-term management tasks comprise those measures that have to be implemented within seconds or minutes. These include a whole area of monitoring tasks that involve determining in a short time, therefore in seconds or in minutes, whether certain operating goals, such as availability and security, are being endangered. Other examples of short-term actions include executing fault messages and replacing resources that have failed with automated standbys.

- *Medium-term horizon:* Medium-term tasks are carried out within a period of hours. Whereas short-term tasks have to be completely automated in the management system because of the short time frame allowed, medium-term tasks are usually undertaken in conjunction with a human expert. An example of a medium-term task is the diagnosis of a fault by an expert with the help of a diagnostic or trouble ticket system. Other examples include carrying out tests, generating configuration changes, activating and deactivating, and collecting and evaluating short-term measurement data.

- *Long-term horizon:* In this case the time horizon relates to weeks or even months. The goal of long-term tasks is to use the experience from day-to-day network operations to improve operations for the future. Planning is therefore a key aspect here. An example of a long-term management task is the maintenance of statistics on failures to help in selecting the right vendor for the procurement of new network components in the future. Relevant terms in this context are trend analysis and capacity planning.

The services at the *monitoring level* must be able to detect all types of faults short term, and services at the *intervention level* must reproduce the required state in the medium term. However, certain kinds of faults must be corrected immediately. A *control level* is introduced between the monitoring level and the intervention level for the relevant services. As has already been mentioned, long-term services incorporate planning aspects. To delineate conceptually from the tasks of the planning phase, we refer to the level of long-term services as the *strategic level.*

The time horizon does not only identify activities but is also important for the generation of tools and databases. Therefore, for many monitoring tasks, the monitoring interval must be stipulated as a frame of reference. This frame of reference determines the resolution granularity with many benchmarks and consequently has an effect on counter sizes, buffer sizes, measurement frequency, measurement accuracy, and analysis procedures. It also affects the distribution and communication aspects of relevant management information. Time aspects also affect management-relevant data storage. Thus, for example, contractual conditions require that accounting information should be kept for a minimal period; data protection laws dictate how long data has to be stored for the purposes of furnishing proof of individual charges, traffic matrices, and so forth. The storage of system history data and different versions of configurations is essential for tracking faults and resetting configurations.

The time horizon affects how resources are interpreted for management purposes

3.5   Chapter Summary

The scenarios presented in section 3.1 provide an insight into the management tasks that occur in actual areas of application. We have made a deliberate effort to keep the examples as general as possible. They show a wide variety of management tasks with evidence of a repetition of some of the functions. The questions therefore arise as to whether management tasks on the whole can be relegated to application areas and whether typical management functions can be identified within these areas.

There are several approaches to classifying management tasks. The best-known approach is the FCAPS one from ISO, which organizes areas into fault, configuration, accounting, performance, and security management. These are introduced in section 3.2. The FCAPS classification is particularly suitable for network and system management and widely used in that area. Other types of classifications, presented in section 3.2.6, are more appropriate when it comes to business or service management. The basis here is an orientation toward business and IT processes.

Section 3.3 emphasizes that not only technical aspects but also organizational conditions (such as local distribution, organizational structure, cooperation with other companies) must be considered in the management of IT infrastructures and IT services.

Section 3.4 illustrates the importance of the aspect of time. It emphasizes the necessity of establishing whether the effectiveness of management actions should be geared to the short, medium, or long term. The time aspect is also important when it comes to reversing to previous states and versions, to tracking error and account data, or to carrying out trend analyses and capacity planning. Management functions that are typical for individual phases in the lifecycle of services and resources also exist.

Management Architectures

S pecifications that have a cross-system and multivendor orientation are the prerequisites for integrated management in distributed, heterogeneous environments, the importance of which was highlighted in Part I. A framework that consists of all the necessary specifications is called a management architecture. A management architecture provides the basis for different manufacturers to develop interoperable management solutions largely independent of one another.

Part II concentrates on *management architectures*. It first discusses in general terms the specifications that a management architecture must incorporate and illustrates which fundamental submodels should be used in its structure. This descriptive framework is used to introduce the different manufacturer-neutral architectures prevalent today.

Chapter 4 takes the various forms of architecture in which different management tools can communicate and cooperate and extrapolates from them the requirements for a *management architecture* with its *submodels*. It introduces the four submodels: information, organization, communication, and function.

The management architecture that most successfully incorporates these four submodels from a conceptional standpoint is *OSI management* of the ISO and ITU-T, which also represents the basis for the *telecommunications management network* (TMN). OSI is therefore highlighted in Chapter 5 and is given precedence over all other approaches by being the first concrete architecture to be described, even though it is more widely used in the telecommunications environment and does not have a significant role in data communications.

The *Internet management architecture*, often also referred to by the management protocol as *SNMP management*, currently forms the basis for most cross-vendor management solutions in the data communications area. One of the reasons for its success is its design, which has purposely been kept simple and is described in Chapter 6.

Along with these two architectures that have been developed exclusively for the management of networked systems, *CORBA* has recently been making an impact on the management environment. This OMG middleware architecture is not particularly oriented toward management applications but has been developed to provide general support to distributed applications. Today, it is being used more and more as the basis for management solutions. The architecture itself and approaches for its adaptation for management purposes are the subject of Chapter 7.

Today, the majority of all components in distributed data processing infrastructures are used in networked workstation computers (e.g., PCs and Unix workstations). The Desktop Management Task Force (DMTF) consequently developed its own management architecture that directly addresses the requirements of these components. Chapter 8 describes the relevant architecture, called desktop management architecture, the chief component of which is the *desktop management interface* (DMI).

The widespread growth of intranets and Web-based applications in the corporate world has also led to an interest in using the underlying technologies for management purposes (e.g., using Web browsers as management consoles). In addition to the proprietary approaches that exist, several management architectures have been defined recently that are specifically geared to the use of Web technology in integrated management, so-called *Web-based management*. The two architectures playing a particularly important role in this area, namely, Web-Based Enterprise Management (WBEM) and Java Management API (JMAPI), are outlined in Chapter 9.

Integrated management in today's environments, in which more than one of the management architectures mentioned can usually be found, can be successfully realized only if gateways exist between these architectures. Chapter 10 describes different versions of these *gateways* and then focuses on *management gateways*, in particular the efforts of the IIMC and JIDM initiatives, whose concerns are gateways between OSI, SNMP, and CORBA.

4

Management Architectures and Their Submodels

Management platforms are host systems for management solutions and therefore provide the infrastructure for the distributed application "management." Different approaches with varying degrees of integration exist for management platforms (section 4.1). For integrated management in a heterogeneous network and system environment, it is essential that the resources being managed supply adequate information that can be interpreted on a manufacturer-independent basis and is accessible through well-defined interfaces and protocols. The framework for management-relevant standards is referred to as a *management architecture*.

A management architecture generally consists of four groups of standards, referred to here as submodels. The information model (section 4.2) is concerned with the modeling and specification of management information, whereas the organization model (section 4.3) deals with the specification of roles and cooperation forms between managing entity and managed entity. The communication model (section 4.4) specifies the possibilities for the communication of management information, and the function model (section 4.5) defines the possibilities for breaking down the complex task "management."

This chapter looks at submodels from a general standpoint, not in conjunction with specific management architectures. This makes it easier for us to understand the different versions and shapings of the submodels when the individual architectures are described later on (Chapters 5 to 9). Yet we will also discover that not all the submodels are defined for each architecture.

4.1   Architectures as the Prerequisite for Open Platforms

It should be obvious from the requirements outlined for the management of distributed systems presented in Chapter 3 that management solutions have to be computer and network supported. Three fundamental approaches to tool support (see Figure 4.1) are described separately later. In practice, the transitions between the approaches can sometimes be fluid, and in concrete management environments, approaches are frequently used side by side.

With an *isolated approach*, isolated tools are created for each management problem. Tools work independently of one another, usually on the basis of independent data and user interfaces. Against the backdrop of a complex, heterogeneous, and highly distributed network and system landscape, isolated management—isolated in terms of vendor, functional areas, management discipline, and approach—is not technically viable or tenable from the standpoint of personnel. Not even the organizational measure that would enable physically different operating stations for the various tools to be concentrated in one place will make a difference. The approach basically remains an isolated one, even if the operating stations are integrated to allow the still isolated tools to be controlled by separate windows on a monitor from one physical operating location.

> An isolated tool approach is inadequate for integrated management

With a *coordinated approach*, the management tools that are still isolated in the way they provide a function are coordinated in their use (i.e., the tools complement each other in different ways). This means that a result that has been achieved with one tool can serve as the input for another tool. On this basis, scripts can also be produced for programming the interaction between different tools.

> A coordinated approach is supported by a user interface integration of tools

In surface integration or user interface integration within a coordinated approach (not to be confused with integrated approach), the different management applications and tools are operated and controlled over a *common* user interface (e.g., common GUI). This is, of course, based on the assumption that the isolated tools that exist as they did before have recourse to certain "communalities." This could be a common interface between the interface process and the management applications. If one exists, then, for example, a uniform display of the network topology or of a menu system for selecting different applications will also be available on the operator's console. The coordinated approach allows certain processes to be coordinated and user interfaces to be standardized, yet this does not mean that there is any

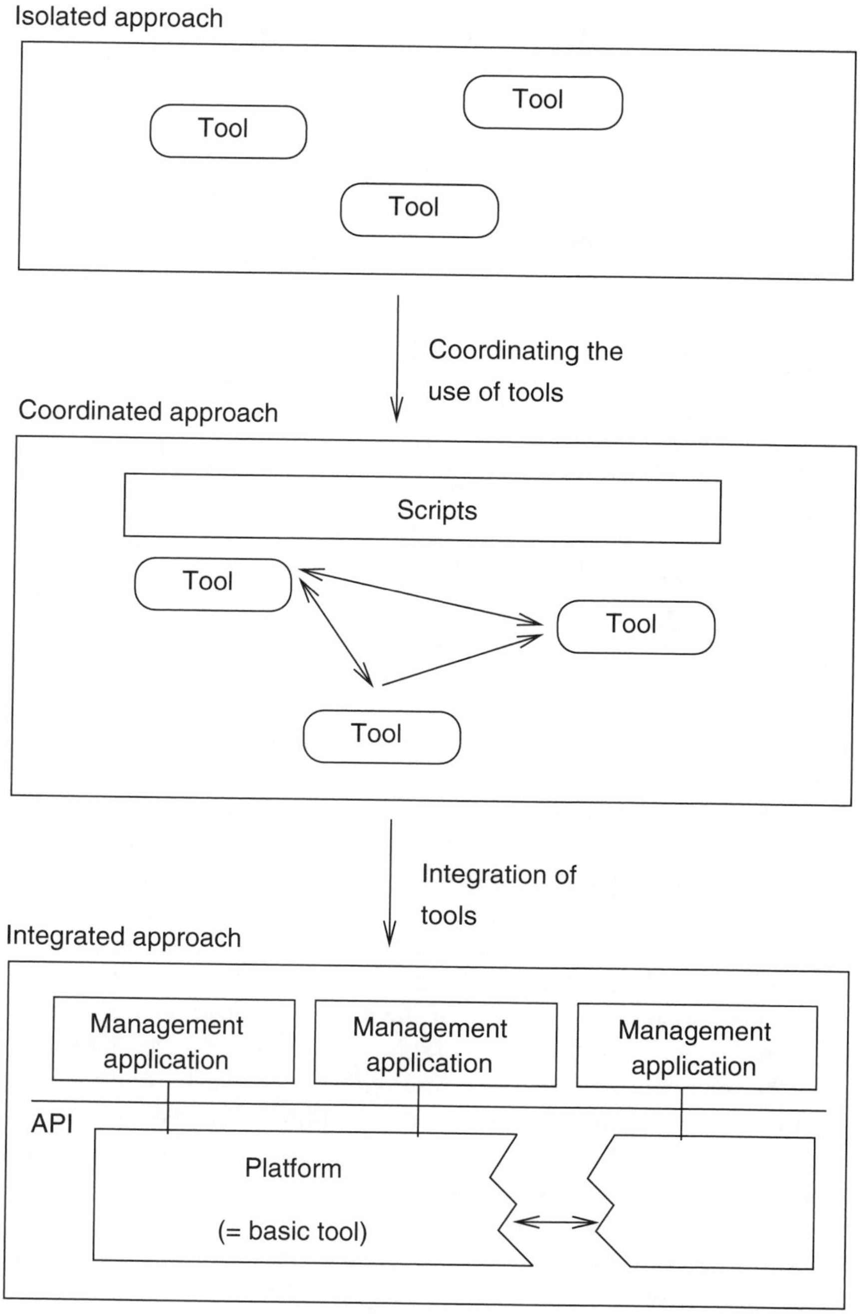
Isolated approach
Tool
Tool
Tool
Coordinating the use of tools
Coordinated approach
Scripts
Tool
Tool
Tool
Integration of tools
Integrated approach
Management application
Management application
Management application
API
Platform
(= basic tool)

Figure 4.1
Approaches to implementing management solutions

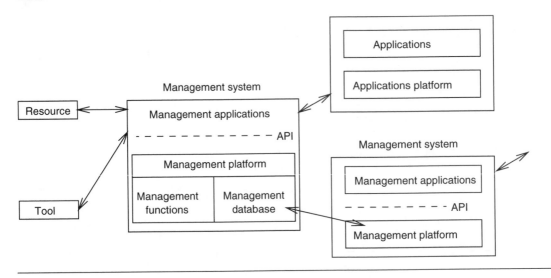

Figure 4.2
Platforms as open carrier systems for management applications

uniformity in the data or in the functions of individual applications and tools.

Open platforms
serve as the basis
for an integrated
approach

With the coordinated approach, the isolated tools or management access systems to different resources have already been placed in a common context, but the concept of integration has been avoided. We speak of an *integrated approach* if the components being managed in a heterogeneous environment are able to supply information that can be interpreted in a non-vendor-dependent way. Furthermore, this information must be accessible over well-defined interfaces and protocols. (Note: distinction between the coordinated and integrated approach is not sharp; the different terms should emphasize the different rationale behind the concepts. Surely vendor-dependent information can be integrated even if not mediated into a standard format.) As we will explain later, the management platform offers this kind of basic functionality by providing an open carrier system for applications (see Figure 4.2). It is also desirable if network, system, and applications management are merged conceptionally because the same activities arise with many management functions independently of the managed objects, and a difference in terminology often does not seem appropriate to the user. You just have to consider the many basic functions from the different functional areas that are shared and that are related organizational procedures, shared resources, and shared data. Platforms also provide the right basis for this kind of integration of management applications.

Open management platforms provide the basis for an integrated approach. Platforms are carrier systems for management applications, which in turn make use of other management systems, tools, or resources that need to be managed. If a management platform is to be used for integrated management in a heterogeneous environment, then the following aspects must be specified on a multivendor basis:

- Description of managed objects (information model)
- Treatment and support of organization aspects, roles, and cooperation forms (organization model)
- Description of communication processes for management purposes (communication model)
- Structuring of management functionality (function model)

A framework for management-relevant standards with respect to the four aspects mentioned is called *management architecture*. Management architectures are a prerequisite for the design of management systems (platforms) in heterogeneous environments.

Distributed system environments can vary greatly with respect to structure, size, and orientation. This is why, as was mentioned earlier, it is not possible to have one management solution that will work with all networked systems. The goal of a management architecture is to define a framework within which a Lego-like "building box" of modules (which by all means can also be partial solutions from different vendors) can be created; it should be possible to combine the parts of the "box" that deal with the individual management problem areas with a maximum of flexibility and interoperability (preferably in a plug-and-play manner), thereby enabling an optimal management solution to be produced for each environment.

It is already being claimed that this complex set of tasks can result in different forms of management architectures; the most important ones are presented in Chapters 5 to 9. Didactically, they will always be presented on the basis of the submodels mentioned in this book. The following sections therefore examine which fundamental issues and approaches can be concealed behind the submodels, thereby facilitating the categorization of the actual specifications for individual architectures.

4.2   Information Model

The information model controls the methods used for modeling and describing management objects

In heterogeneous environments, there is no a priori common understanding of which information needs to be interchanged to solve management tasks or how resources should be characterized. The information model that is ultimately the heart of each management architecture specifies a description framework for managed resources. From the management view, knowledge of the entire structure or of all the internal processes of resources such as bridges, protocol entities, and file systems is not necessary. It is only the parameters relevant to management (e.g., configuration and tuning parameters and functions such as start, stop, and activate data backup) that have to be modeled. The management view can therefore be interpreted as a model (abstraction) of the actual hardware or software resources for management purposes.

Managed objects represent (an abstraction of) the characteristics of the resources on which management operates. Consequently, the information model must provide the possibility of specifying how the object can be identified, what it consists of, how it behaves, how it can be manipulated (e.g., through operation, actions, or invocation of a method), which relationships exist to other managed objects, and how it can be operated on through the management protocol. Managing in the view of a management architecture therefore means access to a managed object (MO) through the use of management commands that are transmitted by management protocols to the managed entity (e.g., agent) responsible for the managed object. Monitoring would constitute read access to the representation of an MO; controlling would be a write access to an MO (Figure 4.3). The effects of the access would have to be described in the specification of the MOs (definition of operation semantics). For instance, the fan of a component could be described by a Boolean value, and a setting to "TRUE" could stand for switching it on. The slide-in cards for a board could be modeled through the use of a sequence of tables with the table columns containing the characteristic values of an interface, such as transmission rate (e.g., integer values), byte counters, and operating state (e.g., 0 = inactive, 1 = normal operation, 2 = error). The mapping of an MO to the concrete resource represented by that MO is a local matter (i.e., not relevant from the standpoint of standardization because MIB access is already standardized). In general terms, the notion *management information base* (MIB) describes the set of managed objects managed by a manager or an agent system, although in concrete architectures MIB can have a slightly different meaning.

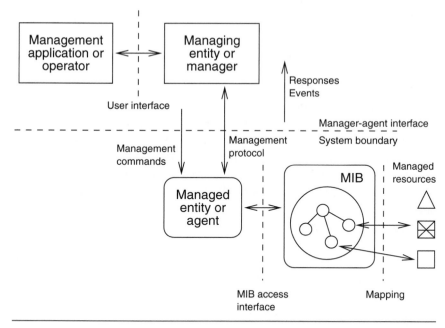

Figure 4.3
Management through MIB access

The information model of a management architecture defines the modeling approach (e.g., entity relationship, data type approach, or object orientation) and a unique notation for describing the management information. The ISO and the OMG have therefore selected an object-oriented approach to modeling, the IAB a data type approach. The ISO and the IAB/IETF use subsets of the description language ASN.1 but define different description templates; OMG is using IDL and programming language data types within CORBA.

If management interoperability is to be guaranteed, heterogeneous networked systems must have the capability of interacting in a meaningful way for management purposes. For this to happen, it is necessary for the objects of management to be selected from the start and for their characteristics to be identified as well as described on the basis of state models, operations, or messages. The choice of modeled characteristics of the resources also inevitably restricts the possible scope of the functions of the management applications operating on the managed objects. The type of modeling and the degree of abstraction also have an effect on the complexity of the applications. The way in which actual management information is specified in the form of managed objects and (in the case of an object-oriented approach) appropriate

Standardized MO definitions are a prerequisite for management interoperability

attributes, operations, and messages is therefore of central importance for management.

Management information is specified from different perspectives: resources, procedures, vendors, operators, and customers. The bottom-up approach attempts to derive management-relevant abstraction from the prescribed protocols, components, and products (question: which information is available?). The top-down approach tries to derive the management information from the requirements for management applications (measurement methods, accounting procedures, algorithms), users (information needs, SLAs), or operators (organizational information, inventories, versions) (question: which information is needed?). In practice, a big gap sometimes exists between the objects defined through each of these two approaches.

The managed object concept should not be interpreted too narrowly. Of course, network components as outlined in section 2.4.1, or system resources as indicated in section 2.4.2, have to be describable as MOs. Managed objects can also be dynamic objects (ATM-SVC, TCP connections), administrative objects (contact person, installation location of a resource, trouble ticket, user record, price table), utility and control objects (log file, filter, discriminator), generic management functions (such as measurement methods), policies, or domains. However, not all architectures provide a mechanism for describing these kinds of complex or composite MOs.

4.3   Organizational Model

Management architectures should not be allowed to prejudice the organizational and operational structures of operators of networked systems, but instead, they must support the variety of conceivable forms that characterize organizations by providing suitable options for adaptation. This means that the architecture should enable a description of forms of cooperation, roles, the way groups are organized, and so forth.

Figure 4.4 shows a variety of different topological and functional arrangements that exist for management systems. With central management, one management system is responsible for all tasks. With multipoint control, resources are combined into groups (domains) according to certain aspects (topological, functional, organizational), and a manager is assigned to each group. If you want to coordinate the managers from the multipoint control approach, then, depending on the cooperation schema, this produces either multicenter control or

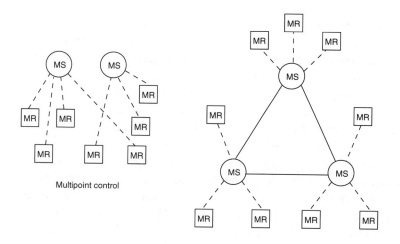

Multipoint control

Multicenter control

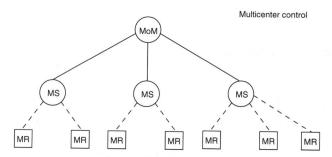

Hierarchical management

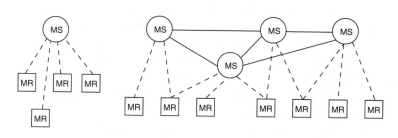

Central management   Network of managers

MoM: Manager of managers
MS: Management system
MR: Managed resource

Figure 4.4
Different relationships between management systems and managed resources

hierarchical management. The latter is not only restricted to two hierarchy levels. The most complex form is a network of managers in which there is no clear-cut allocation of resources to management systems. The type of allocation depends on many factors. For instance, the same resources can be allocated to several managers if, say, one manager is responsible for security management and the other one for performance management. If the management systems in a hierarchical or networked scheme do not all employ the same management architecture, an intermediary manager is required as the *management gateway* (mediation system, proxy). The aim is to map management service, but in essence a proxy maps management architectures to one another. This, in particular, produces a mapping of the MO representations (information model) and the management protocols (communication model). Intermediate managers can also handle preprocessing tasks such as the collection and evaluation of monitoring data, threshold analyses, and event filtering or correlation. This permits a suitable distribution of management functionality and relieves the network of management information traffic.

Management architectures reflect two cooperation models: manager–agent and peer to peer

The organization model of a management architecture defines the actors, their roles, and the fundamental principles of their cooperation. There are currently two different forms of cooperation for management. The manager–agent model with its *asymmetrical–hierarchical* cooperation form assumes a customer–provider relationship for its cooperation and is therefore similar to the familiar client–server model. The manager (client) instructs the agent (server) to execute a specific operation or to provide information. The agent then responds with the result of the operation or the requested information. All in all, this represents an m:n relationship because the manager can instruct more than one agent to carry out its actions, and an agent usually serves more than one manager. The assignment of roles to the actors is often not static, and the roles can change dynamically depending on the task. This is the most popular cooperation form currently used in the management area. OSI management and Internet management use this form.

There has recently been a trend toward a completely *symmetrical cooperation form* that emanates from the communication and cooperation of basically equal objects. This form offers a flexible and reciprocal job relationship and exchange of information in both directions and is referred to as a peer-to-peer approach. CORBA uses this kind of a cooperation model.

An interest often exists in characterizing subsets of resources separately, for instance, to group them into domains for organizational reasons in order to implement different (management) views. If an organizational model provides a domain concept, it must specify how such groups can be formed, how responsibilities can be assigned to these domains, and how these assignments can be modified dynamically. Depending on how the domains are formed, one and the same system in the network plays out different roles. Even with permanent roles, it may be desirable to vary the job allocation with respect to the management application, depending, for example, on the "intelligence" of a component or the workload of the manager. If a management architecture is to incorporate this characteristic, the conditions for this type of "management by delegation" (description, transport, and effectiveness of management scripts) would have to be formulated in the organizational model.

Domains define management views of groups of resources

The concept of *policy* is closely related to the concept of domains. Policies are prescribed courses of action derived from corporate objectives or IT processes for those with responsibility for IT or for technical management. Examples of policies include "A backup run is to be carried out on Monday evening"; "The passwords are to be changed every four weeks at the latest"; "All data transfer for the personnel department is to be coded"; "User-oriented accounting is applicable only to outside users." Domain formation offers a possibility for structuring resources according to policy aspects [STW94, MOF94, WIE95]. Domains and policies in turn are themselves objects of management and can therefore be interpreted as managed objects.

Policies define domain-specific management rules

4.4   Communication Model

Management is the monitoring and control of potentially physically dispersed resources. An intrinsic part of this process is the exchange of management information. The communication model of a management architecture defines the concepts for this exchange of information between the actors. Depending on the respective goals, communication takes place:

Remote monitoring and control require management protocols

- Through an exchange of the control information that should have an influence on a resource or the managed object that represents the resource (controlling). The management system usually takes the initiative in this case.

- Through status requests (monitoring). These, too, are mainly triggered by the manager.

- Through asynchronous event messages that are initiated by the system in which the resource is located.

Consequently, the communication model must deal with the following aspects:

- Specify the communicating partners.
- Specify the communication mechanism for the three communication goals mentioned (i.e., specification of services and protocols for the exchange of management information). Mechanisms for forming subsets (profiles) should also be provided.
- Define the syntax and semantics for the communicative data structures (exchange formats).
- Embed management protocols into the service architecture or protocol hierarchy of the underlying communications architecture. This likewise affects the interfaces to the usual (nonmanagement) protocol entities, applications processes, and local operating system processes. The embedding of the protocols can be inband or outband. With the inband approach, management communication takes place on the same transport network as normal managed communication; with the outband approach, a logical autonomous network exists for the management communication. For example, in the case of TMN architecture (compare section 5.6), a physically or logically separate network for management information flow may be provided for the management of the TC networks.

4.5   Functional Model

The functional model of a management architecture dissects the whole complex of management into management function areas (e.g., configuration management, fault management, accounting management) and attempts to specify generic management functions (some related to specific areas). The functional model therefore provides the basis for the management building-block box referred to earlier; it serves as the basis for libraries of partial management solutions and for the delegation of management functionality to agents. The expected functionality and services along with the managed objects required for implementing this functionality must therefore be defined in the functional model for the individual functional areas. The managed objects that belong to the management functions, of course, have to be

The function model provides the basis for "building blocks" of management functions

described according to the conventions of the associated information model. The invocation conventions for management functions also require specification. This includes designing and specifying APIs and internal interfaces for managers as the basis for open platforms as well as internal interfaces for agents as the basis for expandable or intelligent agents. The definition and implementation of functionality, which has widespread application, can be flexibly configured, and is delegatable, is extremely important for the efficient management of large DP infrastructures, especially for management scalability.

The approach to the development of function and service modules is based on the principle "stepwise refinement." Management aspects are considered (e.g., state management) from the standpoint of function areas (e.g., configuration management). An attempt is then made to develop as comprehensive a model as possible to incorporate these aspects. An example would be a state model that is familiar with administrative states (unlocked, shutting down, locked) and operating states (disabled, enabled, active, busy) as well as perhaps other information about state (under repair, in test, not installed). The state model should, of course, reflect those states that, in reality, also occur with actual resources; in other words, an abstraction that applies to all managed objects should exist. The model also includes a definition of the state transitions. This approach provides a general basis for the generic specification of functions, services, and associated managed objects that can be accessed in the sense of a program library of management functions in an actual implementation. Figure 4.5 presents the state model of OSI management as an example. The fundamental procedure described for the development of functional modules is, of course, not subject to any concrete management architecture.

Another example of a model that is used to create a generic management function is presented in Figure 4.6 and shows the modules (objects, subjects, relationships) of an accounting activity (a) and the related information flow (b) i.e., the data structures and their interrelationships).

If generic functional models are to be used to describe resource utilization in performance management, then three levels in a model can be selected to represent resource utilization, resource demand rate, and inquiry rejection rate. Threshold values can be defined at each level, such as for a maximum value and for several warning stages and their resolution. It should then be possible to write a management application that uses this utilization measurement function and, depending on the threshold value achieved, initiates events or triggers corrective actions.

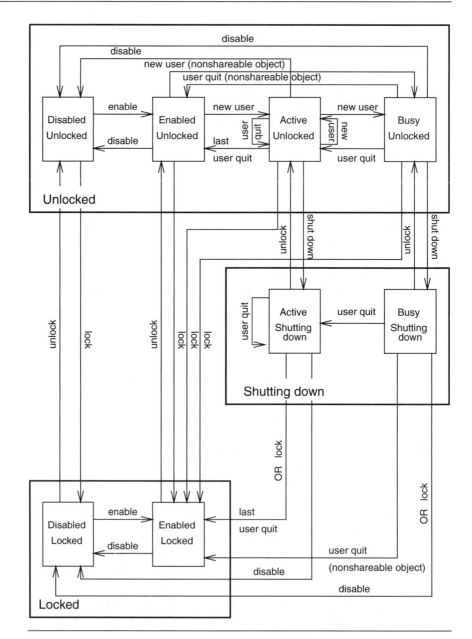

Figure 4.5
State model (ITU X 732)

(a)

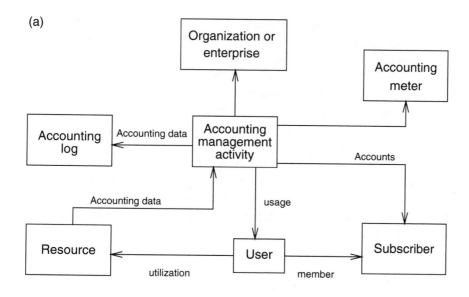

(b)

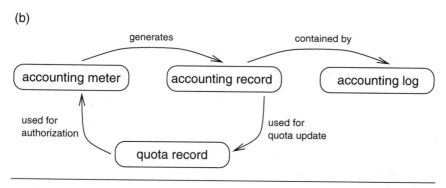

Figure 4.6
Model for accounting management

A new development affecting both the organizational model and the functional model is called *management by delegation*. Figure 4.4 illustrates different ways in which management functionality can be distributed over a system. For the most part, this allocation is static (i.e., the apportionment of management functionality to resources, components, intermediate managers, and manager of managers is devised beforehand during the planning of management solutions). This approach does not have the scalability or necessary flexibility to cope with rapidly growing large networks or considerably changing management requirements.

Management by delegation supports flexibility and scalability of management

The idea is to remove the static characteristic of function allocation through the possibility of dynamic function delegation [GYE95]. Management components in distributed systems thereby become flexible agents [MOU97] if they provide a runtime environment that allows the acceptance of suitably defined dynamic functionality. The execution can be language dependent on universally available interpreters (e.g., for Java or Telescript), or the interpreter can also be included in the delegation. The delegation can be user or event controlled; its validity can be nonrecurrent, permanent, or event controlled. A breakdown of the overall management task into the parameterized and standardized functional blocks described earlier can be helpful in resolving the question of what should be delegated and how the delegatable functionality can be described in concrete terms.

4.6   Chapter Summary

The framework for management-relevant standards is called a *management architecture*. The information model of such an architecture specifies the syntactic and semantic possibilities that exist for modeling and describing resources and information from a management-relevant standpoint and for *open* architectures on a manufacturer-independent basis. The communication model defines access to managed objects and management protocols. The function model separates the complex "management" into manageable units and defines generic management functions. These modules thereby provide the basis for a building-block system of modular management solutions or for management by delegation. Lastly, the organization model defines roles, cooperation models, and domains.

Management architectures, of course, serve only as frameworks, meaning that their specification does not necessarily entail a uniform implementation. The implementation of a management architecture using standardized programming and service interfaces, thus so-called open application programming interfaces (API), is called a *management platform*. Platforms are carrier systems for management solutions and therefore represent the infrastructure for the application "network and systems management," which is usually a distributed application.

Platforms provide a truly integrated approach to the implementation of management solutions. The coordinated approach represents a weaker form of integration that generally allows only separate applications and tools to be controlled over a common user interface.

Note: There is a growing tendency to prevent the details of submodels from being explicitly visible to the applications. Instead, the emphasis in new management architectures is on standardizing the programming interfaces between management applications and management platforms, referred to as *management API* (compare Figures 4.1 and 4.2). This is the case with Web-based approaches (Chapter 9) and the DMTF desktop management interface (Chapter 8). Even then the reference is frequently made to management architectures. The described submodels are then hidden implicitly in the API and explicitly in the virtual machine that is implemented by the platforms and their cooperation. Specifications for the submodels are also needed in this situation. Management APIs are also dealt with in Chapter 15.

OSI Management and TMN

This chapter looks at the OSI management architecture that was standardized by ISO. It also provides a description of the telecommunications management network (TMN), a management architecture for telecommunications networks based on the OSI management architecture. Section 5.1 presents an overview for the entire chapter. Sections 5.2 to 5.5 describe the different submodels of the OSI management architecture. TMN is presented in section 5.6.

5.1 Overview

Although there are other management architectures that in practice play a more important role in the data communications environment, OSI management is an interesting one to study for a number of reasons. First, OSI management serves as the basis for TMN, an architecture for the distributed management of telecommunications (TC) networks. Second, OSI management is the first architecture that has created all four submodels and can therefore be used as a kind of architectural reference. Compared to Internet management (Chapter 6), OSI management is more complex but, on the other hand, offers more effective options for modeling managed objects.

With OSI management all four submodels are developed

The *management framework* is described as addendum 4 of the ISO's OSI reference model (ISO 7498-4). It incorporates fundamental concepts and terminology that are then refined in a number of other documents. OSI management is viewed as communications oriented, which means that the management function is realized through the cooperation of open systems (i.e., those complying with the OSI standard).

The *information model* (section 5.2) systematically uses an object-oriented approach in the abstraction of management-relevant resources. This produces an extensive repertoire for structuring the management information base (MIB). For OSI, an MIB is the collection of management information made visible by a managed system.

The *organizational model* (section 5.3) is based on a distributed cooperative management in a network of open systems. Roles (managers, agents) are differentiated with systems able to adopt different roles with respect to certain resources.

The underlying communications architecture is the OSI layer model. The *communication model* (see section 5.4) of the OSI-NM architecture is based on this and incorporates three mechanisms for the exchange of management information: communication between layer 7 management applications processes (*systems management*), communication between layer-specific management entities (*layer management*), and management communication between normal protocol entities (*layer operation*).

The *functional model* (section 5.5) subdivides the entire management system into five functional areas (fault, configuration, accounting, performance, and security) and is concerned with the derivation of generic management functions that support one or more functional areas.

Telecommunications management network (TMN) is based on OSI management concepts

We will present the architecture for TMN in section 5.6. This is a reference architecture for the distributed management of TC networks and allows networks that were previously managed separately to be integrated into a standardized form for management purposes and management information to be exchanged between different network operators.

TMN is based on OSI management concepts (i.e., communications protocols, functions, and information modeling standards). Although the level of abstraction of the OSI management model is very high (compared to Internet management), the OSI approach is better suited to the requirements of operators that run large heterogeneous networks with complex and expensive components. The object-oriented approach that incorporates multiple inheritance and allomorphism; a separation of inheritance, containment, and registration hierarchies; flexible control options over discriminators and filter mechanisms; as well as semantically complex systems management functions offers designers of management systems extensive freedom of scope. This is one reason why OSI approaches have been particulary proven popular in the public network area. Besides technical advantages there are, of course, other business drivers that motivate telcos to employ TMN and therefore OSI, including international origin, regulatory and government policies requiring use of standards, and existence of third-party conformance testing organizations. (Note: This same group of network operators is also turning toward other complex management architectures such as TINA or CORBA, which is discussed in Chapter 7.)

An advantage of the OSI information model is that it not only promotes a bottom-up approach to specifying management information but also supports the use of generic "higher" managed objects through its object-oriented approach. This brings us closer to the top-down approach needed for complex management applications. This is also evident in the systematic attempt by the ISO to "extract" management functions in the form of generic objects and generic functions from different applications areas to enable their reuse by all management applications. This idea of permitting categories of objects irrespective of the technology to be available to all applications areas is being adopted in the newer approaches to architecture in Web-based management (e.g., in the common information model of DMTF; see section 9.3).

5.2   OSI Information Model

The ISO applies a totally object-oriented approach to its very complex information model, called the *structure of management information* (SMI) (ISO 10165x). Managed objects (MOs) are instantiations of managed object classes (MOCs) whose externally visible properties are described on the so-called *managed object boundary* according to the respective class. This managed object boundary encompasses attributes, defined operations, notifications, and descriptions of behavior. The boundary therefore implements an abstraction of the resources from the management view (i.e., a "black-box" approach). Just how the attribute values and operations are actually mapped onto the real resource based on a description of behavior is a "local matter" and not of interest from the view of the standardized abstraction. OSI attributes can be simple, structured, or set-valued types of data.

The OSI information model also incorporates the principle of *inheritance* from the object-oriented approaches. A managed object class can be defined as a subclass of one or more superclasses, thereby inheriting all the properties of the superclass(es). These properties can only be refined or expanded. Thus strict and multiple inheritance exists. An example of an inheritance hierarchy is device, printing device, printer, laser printer, HP LaserJet. Usually, the further the class hierarchy is refined, the more specific the modeling of the managed resources can be. Support of allomorphic behavior (called *allomorphism* here) is optional. This means that a concrete resource (to be more precise, the MO representing it) can be seen as an MO, or an instantiation of

Modeling of managed objects

different MOCs in the inheritance hierarchy. It would thus be possible to manage a concrete laser printer as an entity of the "laser printer" class or as an entity of the "output device" class. Another example is upwardly compatible software packages. Allomorphism can therefore simplify the formulation of management algorithms because it allows resources to be divided into groups that in the view of management should be dealt with similarly. This comes close to the way of thinking of system administrators. The advantages of allomorphism are even more pragmatic than explained so far. Allomorphism also allows new versions to be extended but managed by older tools; it allows vendor extensions for value-added features and promotes interoperability without rigid adherence to standard object class definitions.

Definition of managed objects

A simple template metalanguage (ISO 10165-4), which is defined on the basis of the ASN.1 macromechanism [HEB93] (ISO 8824), is used to describe MO classes. The metalanguage is described in *Guidelines for the Definition of Managed Objects* (GDMO) (ISO 10165-4); this document specifies a format for and contains guidelines on MOC definitions. In the template definitions, reference can be made to other template definitions. Each template reference can be replaced "inline" (macro expansion) by the corresponding template definition. References to ASN.1 definitions use the ASN.1 external type/value reference syntax.

OSI-SMI currently uses the following generic template structures: managed object class, package, parameter, attribute, attribute group, behavior, action, notification, and name-binding; other template definitions for extending the concepts are at the discussion stage. The template *managed object class* is at the highest level, so to speak; the other templates can be used to define it more accurately with stepwise decomposition (e.g., class composed of packages, packages composed of attributes, notifications, behaviors, and parameters; see Figures 5.1 and 5.2). In terms of the reusability of specifications, the OSI information model is therefore "highly granular" because it not only allows the reuse of MOC definitions but also of each template specification.

Components of an MO class description

The description structure of an MO class comprises the following:

- The *attributes* that are visible on the MO boundary and characterize the properties and the status of the managed object. The attribute types used depend on the object being modeled. Attributes may be associated with any ASN.1 types or may be derived from a generic attribute such as counters, gauges, thresholds, names, timers, as well as more complex types defined in (ISO 10165-2 or X.721). Permissible values and operations are specified for each attribute,

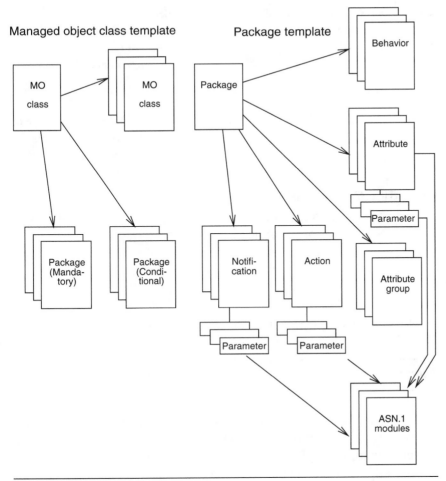

Figure 5.1
Specification of object classes using templates

thereby allowing value ranges to be restricted and write protection to be applied. Attribute templates are used to describe attributes. A group template enables attributes to be combined into groups that can be accessed (retrieved or set to default) through the use of a single command. The attribute-related operations provided are get (reading an attribute value), replace (writing an attribute value), replace-with-default, add (adding a value to set-valued attributes), remove (removing an attribute value from a set), set-by-create (assigning a value only when an MO is being created), and no-modify (prevents refinement by subclassing).

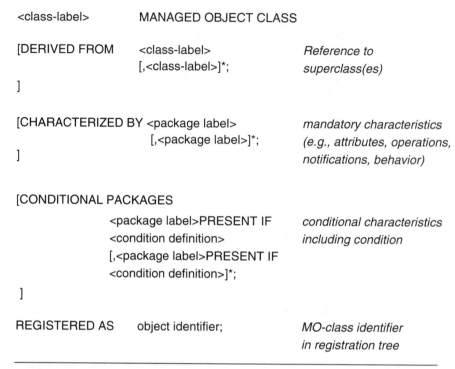

<class-label>   MANAGED OBJECT CLASS

[DERIVED FROM   <class-label>   *Reference to*
                   [,<class-label>]*;   *superclass(es)*

]

[CHARACTERIZED BY <package label>   *mandatory characteristics*
                  [,<package label>]*;   *(e.g., attributes, operations,*
]   *notifications, behavior)*

[CONDITIONAL PACKAGES
                  <package label>PRESENT IF *conditional characteristics*
                  <condition definition>   *including condition*
                  [,<package label>PRESENT IF
                  <condition definition>]*;

]

REGISTERED AS   object identifier;   *MO-class identifier*
                                             in registration tree

Figure 5.2
Templates that define an MO class

- A set of *actions*. Actions are complex operations that affect not only an attribute but the entire MO. They can be defined to be MO specific; an example is the action "reset MO." An action template is used to specify actions. Whereas actions enable MO-specific operations to be freely defined, there are two other operations predefined by the standard that always affect the entire MO: create MO (dynamic instantiation) and delete MO.

- A set of *notifications*. MOs can usually also be autonomous resources in which asynchronous events may occur. Notifications are mechanisms for signaling events that can be initiated by an MO without previously having received a request from the management system. The notification template is used in describing the notifications that can (but need not) be specific to an MO.

- The respective *behavior* that is specified in the behavior template. This template records the semantics of attributes, operations, and notifications, and indicates relationships to other MOs, side effects, and so forth. Behavior is usually described informally using normal language. But a number of approaches that incorporate formal description techniques (FDTs) for describing behavior exist already; these include specification and description language (SDL, ITU-T Z.100) and Z, which recently became an amendment to the ISO 10165 series of standards. However, these required standardization of an extension to the GDMO language (GDMO+).

- *Conditional packages* to incorporate variants of certain properties and functions. When an MO is instantiated, a decision is taken based on the if-conditions in the MOC definition on whether a conditional package will become an integral component of the MO (i.e., the conditional statement in the class template specifies when the package will or will not be present in an instance of that class). This can make it easier to map an MO to a real resource. Conditional packages offer a high level of flexibility in specification because of "late binding."

- The position of a class in the MOC inheritance hierarchy is indicated by reference to the superclasses from which specifications for MO properties are inherited.

It is useful at this point to refer to the three different tree structures used in the OSI information model. The common *registration tree* of both ISO and ITU is a directory structure in which, along with other contents (compare Figure 6.3), all OSI documents and all pre-defined template specifications are filed (Figures 5.2 and 5.4). These specifications can then be reused in MOC definitions. Using a natural approach, the inheritance principle induces an *inheritance tree* that contains MOC definitions and shows how these are related to each other through the use of inheritance principles. The tree itself develops through references to the superclasses. What still needs to be mentioned is the *containment tree* that shows the actual MIB structure of a system, the so-called *management information tree* (MIT). As we will see again, this tree is also used in the unique naming of managed objects. The root of each containment tree is ROOT; the root of the inheritance tree is designated a TOP; and the root of the registration tree is unnamed. (When we study the Internet information model later on, we will see that it only has a registration tree and that none of the other structuring tools are available.) Figure 5.3 shows the three trees in coexistence.

A number of generic MOCs that can be reused as superclasses have been predefined. Examples include LOG RECORD (superclass of different records), DISCRIMINATOR and SCHEDULER (parents of MOCs used to control management functions, e.g., event reporting

Three trees are used for structuring management information

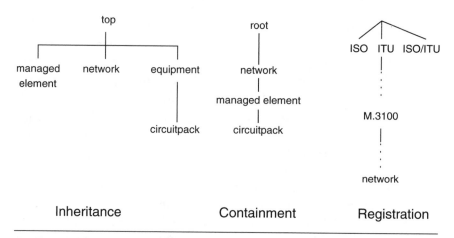

Inheritance	Containment	Registration

Figure 5.3
Trees related to the OSI information model

[ISO 10165-2]). A number of protocol entities have also been modeled with GDMO, such as the "transport connection" entity (ISO 10165-5 and ISO 10737) and MOs from the applications system (ISO 10165-8) and the systems management protocol environment (ISO 10165-9).

MOC examples from the telecom-munications world
Other MOCs that merit mention are those in the TMN *generic network information model* (ITU-T M.3100) and include network frag-ment, managed element fragment, termination point fragment, trans-mission fragment, cross-connection fragment, and functional area fragment. In general, fragments are collections of MOCs that describe management functions. Since the OSI information model serves as the basis for TMN (see section 5.6), an extensive selection of prede-fined MOC, attribute, and notification catalogs are available for the telecommunications network environment. Different working groups (SG4, SG11, SG15) under the ITU defined management information for the management of SDH and ATM networks, for ISDN support, for the TMN-X interface (compare section 5.6), for a cross-connection model, for circuits and paths, and for different TMN management functions.

The *cross-connection model* in turn contains MOCs for switching fabric, cross-connection, group termination point, termination point (TP), and TP pool. The operations supported in the model include add/remove TP to/from group TP, add/remove TP to/from pool, con-nect to create one or more cross-connections, disconnect to delete cross-connection, trace connectivity, create preprovi-sioned cross-connection, trace connectivity, create preprovi-sioned cross-connection in a certain state. This generic model is also applied in conjunction with SDH (G.774.x).

The *circuit MOC*, the circuit modeling recommended by the NM Forum [NMF006], contains the following attribute types, some of which are optional: Name, Administrative State, A-Endpoint Name, Circuit Bandwidth, Component Names, Transmission Direction, Operational State, Z-Endpoint Name, Circuit Type, Circuit Group Type, Contact Names, Customer Names, Facility Names, Network Names, Provider Name, Service Name. Again it is obvious that technical as well as organizational information is relevant to the management of resources.

A number of abstract attribute types have also been predefined as reusable generic definitions; these include counter, gauge, threshold, and tide mark. The definitions specify the structure of the attribute values, allowable operations, inherent properties, relationships to other attributes, and application properties (e.g., in the case of counters, the event counted and counting frequency). A number of notifications are also predefined (e.g., for attribute and status changes, for reporting creation of MOs, and for alarms).

All predefined MOC and other template descriptions that are available for reuse are filed in the ISO registration tree, a general directory structure (see also Figures 5.2 to 5.4). In addition to the ISO and the ITU, other consortia, including the IEEE, the NM Forum, ETSI, NIST, and ANSI, have defined catalogs that build on the OSI information model. MOCs defined by these organizations are registered in branches of the same registration tree.

From the management angle, real resources can be elementary or *composite*. For example, a hub network component can have more than one interface card in some circumstances; the latter in turn can have several ports. Resources modeled by MOs must therefore also be able to mirror this fact. This can be done through name-binding templates that are used to create the containment hierarchies. Composite MOs contain other MOs. The former are superior MOs to the latter, which are subordinate to them (Figure 5.4).

> Forming containment hierarchies using name-binding

A mandatory attribute in each MOC definition is an attribute that lends itself to naming. The value of this attribute, the actual name, is not bound until a managed object is created. The assumption is that each MO of an OSI system is incorporated into a containment hierarchy. Each system has a local root (can be more than one), subordinate to a global *management information tree* (MIT) that ultimately starts with the global root (see [ISO 10165-1]). This containment hierarchy by nature produces a name tree that generates globally unique names. For instance, if the object IF, an entity of the interface card class, is allocated through name-binding to the objects H1 and H2 of the hub class, then the names H1.IF and H2.IF are globally unique because H1

Hub   MANAGED OBJECT CLASS
           DERIVED FROM ISO/IEC 10165-2: Top;
           CHARACTERIZED BY:
               BEHAVIOR   ....
               ATTRIBUTES   HubID GET
                                       NumberOfRelays GET,
                                       RelayActive GET,
                                       TimeSinceHubSystemReset GET,
                                       HubResetTimeStamp GET,
                                       HubHealth GET,
                                       GroupMap GET;
               ACTIONS   ResetHubSystemAction,
                                       RelayChangeoverAction;
               NOTIFICATIONS   HubHealth,
                                       GroupRelayConfigChange,
                                       ProprietaryExtensionAlarm;
           REGISTERED AS   iso(1)std(0)iso8802(8802)csma(3)hubmgt(18)objectclass(0)
                           hubobjectclass(X)

HubName   NAME-BINDING
               SUBORDINATE OBJECT CLASS   Hub;
               NAMED BY SUPERIOR OBJECT CLASS   ISO/IEC 10165-
                                                  2:System;
               WITH ATTRIBUTE   HubID;
               BEHAVIOR   HubBehavior
           REGISTERED AS   iso(1)std(0)iso8802(8802)csma(3)hubmgt(18)namebinding
                           (3)hubname(X);

HubID ATTRIBUTE
           WITH ATTRIBUTE SYNTAX   IEEE802CommonDefinitions.uniqueIdentifier,
           MATCHES FOR   Equality
           BEHAVIOR   HubIDBehavior,
           REGISTERED AS   iso(1)std(0)iso8802(8802)csma(3)hubmgt(18)attribute(4)h
                           ubid(X);

Remark: TOP is superclass in the inheritance tree
           Object of class SYSTEM is superior object in the containment tree, above hub

---

Figure 5.4
Hub-object class definition (from IEEE 802.3)

and H2 are OSI systems. Had the objects P1 and P2 of the port class been bound to IF, then H1.IF.P2 would designate the second port of an interface card in hub H1. Each level's label in the MIT is known as the *relative distinguished name* (RDN). Concatenating the RDNs of a tree leads the full identifier of an MO instance, which is known as a *distinguished name* (DN) because it allows the completely unambiguous identification of an MO throughout the hierarchy. This procedure is reminiscent of the information model for the X.500 directory service. An MO is "added" to a local unique name in the name tree through a so-called *name-binding template*. The inheritance hierarchy and the containment hierarchy are therefore two mutually independent structurings of the MIB. Inheritance relates classes, containment relates instances.

MOs do not stand on their own and have to be viewed in context. Attribute types can be part of a relationship, for example, a counter and the corresponding threshold value. The attributes of an MO can point to other MOs (e.g., `is-owned-by`, `is-backed-by`). Furthermore, as just mentioned, name-binding can place MOs in a containment relationship to one another. Relationships could basically also be described in behavior templates, but ISO offers even another possibility: modeling relationships between MOs through a separate relationship MO. A general relationship model (GRM) was developed in (ISO 10165-7 and ITU-X.725) that permits a "managed relationship" to be described as an MOC. The operations in this class include `bind` (adding an MO to an existing relationship) and `unbind`, `establish` (establishing a relationship) and `terminate`, `query` (obtaining information about relationships) and `notify`. Roles and cardinalities can be included in the class definition. The first applications of this standard (September 1996) are found in the TMN environment where it is being used in modeling the network level.

Relationships between MOs

5.3 OSI Organizational Model

OSI management (ISO 10040) incorporates two roles for systems: a manager role and an agent role. Figure 5.5 shows the interaction between the two roles. Basically, OSI systems can assume both roles, even simultaneously. The role assignment can change dynamically depending on the individual management communication processes. With ISO management MOs are considered "active" in the sense that they are autonomously able to trigger asynchronous event notifications. (Actually, it is the agent implementing the MO that is responsible for generating potential event reports; the resource itself may be passive.) As the illustration shows, an asymmetric cooperation model is used.

OSI provides an extensive and flexible *domain concept* (Figure 5.6) in which a distinction is made between organizational and administrative domains. *Organizational domains* are MOs grouped for the following purposes:

- MOs grouped according to function (e.g., for security management, accounting management)

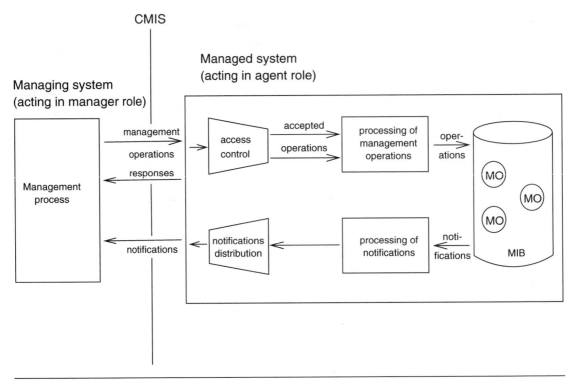

Figure 5.5
Interaction between manager and agent

- MOs grouped within a function area to enable the pursuit of a common policy (management procedure class)
- Temporary assignment of manager and agent roles

Administrative domains are management domains in which all managed objects are subject to exactly one administrative authority. These domains are used to:

- Create and manipulate organizational domains
- Control the action flow between (possibly overlapping) domains

Administrative management domains (ADMDs) and private management domains (PRMDs) familiar from X.400 are examples of administrative domains.

Domains themselves are the objects of management decisions and hence also managed objects that in turn can be described by an MOC specification. A specifiable and also changeable group criterion is used to group MOs into domains. (The criteria for creating domains

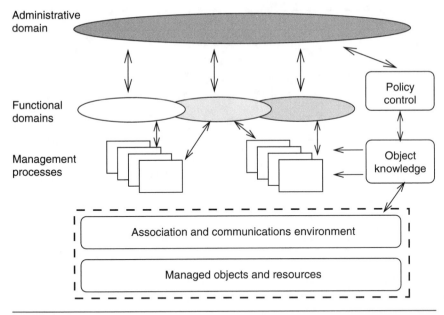

Administrative domain

Functional domains

Management processes

Policy control

Object knowledge

Association and communications environment

Managed objects and resources

Figure 5.6
Organizational and administrative domains

were discussed in Chapter 4.) A management policy specified as a set of rules can be assigned to a domain. These rules can restrict the behavior of the MOs concerned but are not allowed to contradict the MO behavior. Policies themselves are changeable and dynamic MOs. Domains and policies are administered with the support of corresponding management functions from the function model.

In order to cooperate effectively, systems must be familiar with the management-relevant functionality of the other systems. The term *management knowledge* encompasses the knowledge that manager and agents must have as a basis for distributed management applications; this includes protocol knowledge (e.g., applications context), functional knowledge (e.g., supported functional units, systems management functions), and MO knowledge (defined MOCs, MO entities). Because many concrete versions of management knowledge can exist, it would be helpful if some predefined "profiles" were available. The *international standard profiles* (ISPs) merit mention in this connection; the profiles with the codes AOM1xx and AOM2xx define specifications for management communication, management functions, and managed objects.

Management knowledge

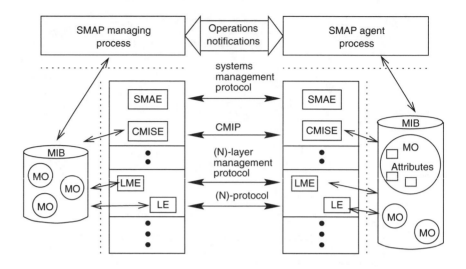

MO: Managed object

MIB: Management information base

LE: Layer entity

LME: Layer management entity

CMISE: Common management information service entity

CMIP: Common management information protocol

SMAE: Systems management application entity

SMAP: Systems management application process

Figure 5.7
OSI communication model

5.4   OSI Communication Model

The whole idea of management is to supervise and control resources according to operational objectives. This includes the possibility of exchanging management information between cooperating open systems. The OSI communication model incorporates three different categories of management: *systems management* (SM), *layer management* (LM), and *protocol management* (layer operation). These terms are clarified in Figure 5.7. The ISO management architecture does not define how the three categories of management interact with one another, nor does it describe the type of interaction that exists with local management (e.g., operating system). This is understandable from the standpoint of the communication model (i.e., the standardization), but not so from the standpoint of the implementation. All categories of management have access to the information in the MIB.

5.4.1   Systems Management

Systems management concerns the overall management behavior of cooperating systems. It is evident in *systems management applica-tions* (SMA) that involve the cooperation of corresponding application processes (*systems management application processes*, SMAP). Management induces asymmetrical relationships, which explains why an SMAP can assume the role of either manager or agent for a specific application. The role can change, and in an OSI system it is possible for SMAPs with different roles to coexist.

Systems management

    The communications-relevant part of a management application is the *systems management applications entity* (SMAE), which, using the appropriate *systems management protocols*, exchanges management information with the SMAEs of other systems. This type of management communication is the norm in the OSI-NM architecture and often requires that a system have full OSI functionality (all seven layers). But it must be mentioned that various short stack approaches have also been defined to support OSI systems management, including CMIP over LLC and CMIP over SONET ECC.

    The OSI management architecture designates that management information that is exchanged between the application processes over the SMAE (see Figure 5.7) can be based [ISO 9595, ISO 9596] on specif-ically designed services, called *common management information ser-vices* (CMIS), and the corresponding associated management protocol, *common management information protocol* (CMIP). CMIS is used for access to and manipulation of (remote) MOs, permitting operations to be carried out on the entire information tree (containment tree) of the MIB, called the *management information tree* (MIT). CMIS is a connection-oriented service that uses the association control service element (ACSE) for the connection management of services and ROSE for the transmission of management operations. CMIS incorporates the following service groups:

CMIP/CMIS

- Association management: Initializing, terminating, and abort-ing CMIP connections is performed by just using ACSE services.

- Execution of operations: M-GET (to read MO attributes), M-SET (to set or modify MO attributes), M-ACTION (to initiate an MO action), M-CREATE (for dynamic creation of an MO), M-DELETE (to delete an MO), M-CANCEL-GET (to cancel a GET operation that has been requested previously).

- Event notification: M-EVENT-REPORT (to transmit an MO notification).

Some services are confirmed services, others can be unconfirmed services, and some can be either confirmed or unconfirmed. It would be beyond the scope of this book to provide individual explanations of the many parameters of the services. Some will be mentioned later in this section. CMIS service primitives are passed to the CMIP protocol machine, and provided they are not part of association management, they are used to form CMIP-PDUs, which are then embedded within ROSE services according to the OSI standards. It should be mentioned at this point that CMIP can be based on several underlying protocol stacks. There exist CMIP over OSI stack, CMIP over TCP (the most common stack deployed, ref RFC 1006), or CMIP over short stacks (as mentioned in section 5.1).

Scoping and filtering

The choice of MOs and passing of parameters to MOs provided by CMIS/CMIP as well as the structure of the protocol data units (CMIP-PDUs) are, of course, closely related to the OSI information model and incorporate its flexibility and capabilities. The mechanisms used in the selection of managed objects are interesting. Objects are identified by name with the containment hierarchy stipulating (name-binding) that the objects are arranged logically in hierarchical order according to their names in the form of a tree (management information tree) in the MIB. For every service, CMIS provides:

- A set of MOs potentially relevant to this service call as a subtree with a specified depth (Figure 5.8) within the containment tree. This facility is called *scoping*. All services identify at least one MO class and instance; some services permit multiple object selection with a "scope" parameter. In these services, the base object refers to the managed object that is to be used as the starting point for the scoping selection. The scope parameter specifies the position in the object hierarchy. Some possible sets of MOs are "base object only," "*n*th level below base object," "base object and all subordinate objects up to the *n*th level," and "base object and complete subordinate subtree." Scoping also makes it easy to reset, for example, "each fifth port of the interface cards" or "all the ports of a card" using a single CMIS operation.

- The possibility to select certain objects from this set (result set of scoping) through filtering. A filter consists of one or more statements

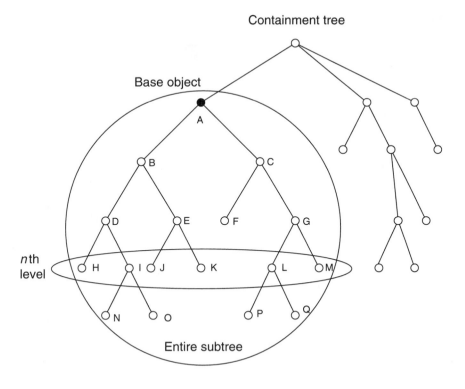

Base object = A
Base + whole subtree = A...Q
3rd level = H...M

Figure 5.8
Selection of MOs in the object hierarchy (scoping)

about the existence or value of MO attributes. The filter is specified in the CMIS filter parameters and is therefore used in attribute-related object selection. Taking the example mentioned a step further, you could use filtering to express that, of the ports listed, only those ports that support the HDLC interface and have a connection rate of 64 kbps should be reset. (We are assuming that the interface and the connection rate are attributes of the port class.)

- Appropriate synchronization conditions (atomic, best effort) that can be requested when more than one MO is being accessed. In the first case (atomic), a check would be made beforehand to ensure that the operation is executable for all target objects.

Parameter	EVENT-REPORT Req Ind	EVENT-REPORT Rsp Conf	GET Req Ind	GET Rsp Conf	SET Req Ind	SET Rsp Conf	ACTION Req Ind	ACTION Rsp Conf	CREATE Req Ind	CREATE Rsp Conf	DELETE Req Ind	DELETE Rsp Conf	CANCEL-GET Req Ind	CANCEL-GET Rsp Conf
Invoke identifier	M	M(=)	M	M	M	M	M	M	M	M(=)	M	M	M	M(=)
Linked identifier	-	-	-	C	-	C	-	C	-	-	-	C	-	-
Mode	M	-	-	-	M	-	M	-	-	-	-	-	-	-
Base object class	-	-	M	-	M	-	M	-	-	-	M	-	-	-
Base object instance	-	-	M	-	M	-	M	-	-	-	M	-	-	-
Scope	-	-	U	-	U	-	U	-	-	-	U	-	-	-
Filter	-	-	U	-	U	-	U	-	-	-	U	-	-	-
Managed object class	M	U	-	C	-	C	-	C	M	C	-	C	-	-
Managed object instance	M	U	-	C	-	C	-	C	U	C	-	C	-	-
Access control	-	-	U	-	U	-	U	-	U	-	U	-	-	-
Synchronization	-	-	U	-	U	-	U	-	-	-	U	-	-	-
Attribute identifier list	-	-	U	-	-	-	-	-	-	-	-	-	-	-
Modification list	-	-	-	-	M	-	-	-	-	-	-	-	-	-
Get invoke identifier	-	-	-	-	-	-	-	-	-	-	-	-	M	-
Action type	-	-	-	-	-	-	M	C(=)	-	-	-	-	-	-
Action information	-	-	-	-	-	-	U	-	-	-	-	-	-	-
Reference object instance	-	-	-	-	-	-	-	-	U	-	-	-	-	-
Superior object instance	-	-	-	-	-	-	-	-	U	-	-	-	-	-
Attribute list	-	-	-	C	-	U	-	-	U	C	-	-	-	-
Current time	-	U	-	U	-	U	-	U	-	U	-	U	-	-
Action reply	-	-	-	-	-	-	-	C	-	-	-	-	-	-
Event type	M	C(=)	-	-	-	-	-	-	-	-	-	-	-	-
Event time	U	-	-	-	-	-	-	-	-	-	-	-	-	-
Event information	U	-	-	-	-	-	-	-	-	-	-	-	-	-
Event reply	-	C	-	-	-	-	-	-	-	-	-	-	-	-
Errors	-	C	-	C	-	C	-	C	-	C	-	C	-	C

M : mandatory
C : conditional
U : user option
- : not applicable

Figure 5.9
CMIS primitives and their parameters

As is usually the case with complex OSI services, CMIS also allows subsets to be grouped into *functional units* (FUs) that always describe a certain functionality. This permits the configuration of the power of a CMIS/CMIP entity. The kernel FU initially offers CMIS services without scoping, filtering, or synchronization. If these supplementary functions are required, you have to select the Multiple-object-selection FU or the Filter FU along with the kernel FU. The functional unit Multiple reply makes it possible for more than one reply to be returned in response to the same operation. This is a useful feature because, with scoping, subtrees in the object hierarchy can be addressed as candidates for a management operation.

Figure 5.9 gives an overview of the CMIS primitives and their parameters. It is beyond the scope of this book to explain each parameter individually; most of them are self-explanatory or have been described before. So, we restrict ourselves to some of them: Invoke ID (ID assigned to this operation), Linked ID (used if multiple replies are to be sent for one operation), `Mode` (confirmed or unconfirmed), `Access control` (input to access control function; see Figure 5.5), `Get invoke ID` (ID assigned to the previously requested and currently outstanding M-GET-operation), and `Reference-object instance` (specifies an existing instance of an object of the same class as the managed object to be created).

In Figure 5.10 a time-sequence diagram for M-GET service (taken from [STA93]) is given as an example. It shows three out of several possibilities. You are invited to think about further situations not shown in the figure. CMIS also provides an extensive list of error values. The CMIS standard allows the errors to be reported, as shown in Figure 5.11.

5.4.2 Layer Management

Layer management deals with functions, services, and protocols that are specific to a layer and do not require the services of higher OSI layers. Examples of layer-specific management functions are loop tests (for level 1), the exchange of routing information (for level 3), and loading protocols for boot software (e.g., at level 2).

Layer management

Although the OSI management architecture explicitly designates layer management as a category, the ISO has hardly dealt with this area—except for defining protocols for exchanging routing information and specifiying catalogs for layer 3 and layer 4 managed objects. So this will not be discussed in depth. However, a number of specifications for layer management were developed by the IEEE in the IEEE 802.X standards in conjunction with the introduction of LAN and MAN technologies.

The communication entity of layer management is called *(N)-layer management entity* (LME) and the corresponding protocol *(N)-layer management protocol*. The LME controls the layer entities; it monitors layer-specific management information, is able to load protocol parameters, and can activate or reconfigure a layer's resources. An LME can also act on behalf of systems management.

5.4.3 Protocol Management

Of course, management information and functions are also an element of normal layer protocols, as described in earlier chapters. Examples include window sizes and timers, the test frame in HDLC and RESET-PDU in X.25, as well as protocol parameters for the connection

Protocol management

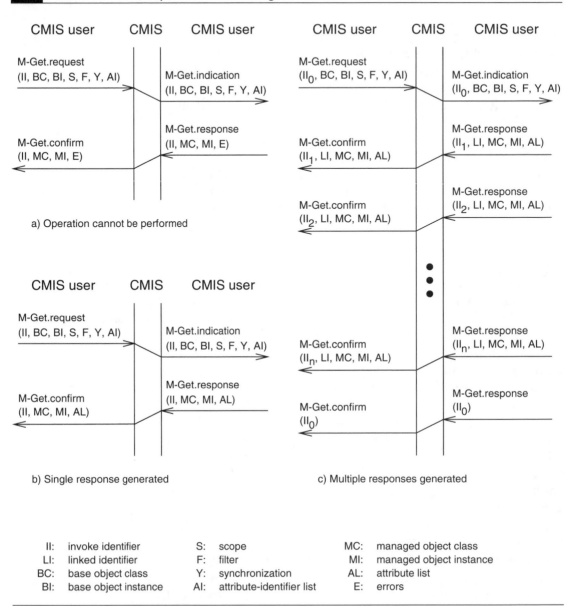

Figure 5.10
Time-sequence diagram for M-GET

ERROR	EVENT REPORT	GET	SET	ACTION	CREATE	DELETE	CANCEL GET
Access denied		X	X	X	X	X	
Class instance conflict		X	X	X	X	X	
Complexity limitation		X	X	X		X	
Duplicate invocation	X	X	X	X	X	X	X
Duplicate MO instance					X		
Get list error		X					
Invalid argument value	X			X			
Invalid attribute value					X		
Invalid filter		X	X	X		X	
Invalid object instance					X		
Missing attribute value					X		
Invalid scope		X	X	X		X	
Mistyped argument		X	X	X	X		X
No such action				X			
No such argument	X			X			
No such attribute					X		
No such event type	X						
No such invoke identifier							X
No such object class	X	X	X	X	X	X	
No such object instance	X	X	X	X	X	X	
No such reference object					X		
Processing failure	X	X	X	X	X	X	X
Resource limitation	X	X	X	X	X	X	X
Set list error			X				
Sync not supported		X	X	X		X	
Unrecognized operation	X	X	X	X	X	X	

MO:　Managed object

Figure 5.11
CMIS errors

establishment phase, error information, and elements of resources supporting quality of service guarantees, as can be found in protocols that support isochronous traffic or sophisticated data streams.

It would naturally be desirable if management-relevant protocol elements could be recognized as such. The need for this has recently been recognized and was taken into consideration during the development of the newer protocols (e.g., ISDN, ATM, FDDI, DQDB) and in the revision of some of the application protocols (e.g., X.400, X.500). But there is still a great deal to do in this area.

5.5　OSI Functional Model

OSI management has five functional areas (see also section 3.2), namely, fault, configuration, accounting, performance, and security management. With OSI, these areas are called *systems management functional areas* (SMFAs). As a result of the specification of functional models (see section 4.5) for different management functions, a number of general management functions (*systems management functions*, SMFs) were

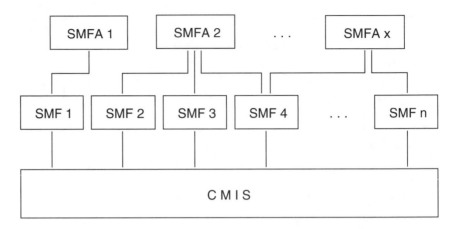

CMIS: Common management information service (e.g., GET, SET, CREATE, DELETE)

SMF: Systems management function (e.g., Object Mgt, State Mgt, Alarm Mgt)

SMFA: Systems management functional area (e.g., Fault, Config, Perf)

Figure 5.12
Functional structure of systems management

developed for use by the functional areas (Figure 5.12). The definition of an SMF comprises the specification of the related MOCs. A given SMF may support requirements for one or more of the five SMFAs; a good example is the event report management function. Each SMF provides a mapping onto CMIS. A management application can make use of the SMFs as generic predefined functions.

Some of the SMFs are very complex functions that, for flexibility and reuse, are usually defined generically. Function-specific models are used to define the functions and the associated management information as so-called support managed object classes. The functions specified by OSI systems management (ISO 10164-n) encompass the following list, in which the given number corresponds to n in the ISO document number:

Brief description of OSI-SMFs

1. *Object management function*: This function provides a uniform scheme comprising a number of predefined notifications for reporting creation and deletion of MOs and changes to MO attributes.

2. *State management function*: This function provides general operations for the state management of MOs. It involves setting up a general state model and defining a set of operations for controlling

and monitoring the state transitions. The model for this function was outlined in section 4.5.

3. *Attributes for representing relationships*: These support the establishment and manipulation of relationships between MOs, using, for example, "operated by," "replacement for," "primary/secondary." A separate relationship template was introduced to describe the roles and properties of related MOs. (The relationship MOC has already been mentioned in section 5.2.)

4. *Alarm reporting function*: This is a generic classification of alarms (i.e., special events), according to cause type ("`communications alarm`," "`quality of service alarm`") and is refined through a definition of the probable cause and specific problem (`communication protocol error, I/O device error`).

5. *Event report management function*: This is described at the end of this section.

6. *Log control function*: This function provides operations for collecting and filing notifications about or emitted by MOs into logs. A generic model is defined for logs and their manipulation.

7. *Security alarm reporting function*: This is an analog of the alarm reporting function that relates specifically to matters of security management. The generic classification of alarms differentiates, for example, between "violation of integrity" and "physical use of force"; alteration of information and attachment of eavesdropping devices are some of the probable causes.

8. *Security audit trail function*: This is a refinement of the log control function in which requirements relating to the filing and collection of security-relevant notifications and operations are met through the generation of audits, in other words, special logs.

9. *Objects and attributes for access control*: A definition of the operations for introducing and manipulating access control rules ensures that MOs are protected from unauthorized external management operations. Event reports are available that monitor if management information is requested by nonauthorized receivers. The same applies to the establishment of nonauthorized management communications connections. The *access control decision function* (ADF) allows the formulation of different security policies. On this basis, the *access control enforcement function* (AEF), which can be set up between the initiator and the target of a management function, ensures that security policies are being enforced.

10. *Usage metering function for accounting purposes*: The definition of a uniform description scheme for accounting data and the specification of the functionality required for compiling this data ensure that an efficient and effective exchange of accounting information is supported.

11. *Metric objects and attributes* (previously the workload monitoring function): A generic model for threshold monitoring provides the functionality for the ongoing monitoring of dynamic attributes and the triggering of alarms when selected thresholds are exceeded.

12. *Test management function*: A general taxonomy for tests is used to provide operations for starting and ending tests and interchange formats to convey the results of these tests. Managed object classes such as `Test Performer`, `Test Conductor`, `Test Objects`, and `Uncontrolled Tests` are introduced as part of this SMF. The most widely used definitions are those for OSI conformity tests.

13. *Summarization function*: This function allows data within the agent system to be preprocessed and reduced even before it is transmitted to the management system. Statistical algorithms such as averaging and the calculation of standard deviations are provided for this purpose.

14. *Confidence and diagnostic test categories*: The taxonomy introduced for the test management function is refined through the definition of concrete test categories that support tests on the availability and functional performance of resources. Examples of test categories include internal resource tests, connectivity tests, data integrity tests, loop tests, echo tests, and protocol tests.

15. *Scheduling function*: This function supports the time control of management operations on the basis of selectable periods. In particular, it enables any operations to be started or ended at daily, weekly, or monthly recurring intervals.

16. *Management knowledge management function*: This function allows a system to query another system about which management-relevant capabilities are supported. This relates to supported MOCs, MIT, MO relationships, naming schemes, domains, policies, and users.

17. *Changeover function*: This function models support functions in order to communicate relationships and roles between MOs that enable redundancy and automated fail-over, such as `active/standby`, `backup/backed up`, and `primary/secondary role`.

18. *Software management function*: This function is used to model software activation and deactivation as well as the interactive aspects of software downloading.

19. *Management domains and management policy management function*: This function supports the establishment and administration of domains and the assignment of policies—in other words, behavior rules or policies that should be enforced.

20. *Time management function*: It defines a generic time service using time-synchronization protocols and various time-synchronization mechanisms for the purpose of management.

21. *Command sequencer*: This control mechanism uses a script language for the execution of management functions. It can improve the way in which management functionality is "tailored" to an agent by allowing dynamic delegation through scripts rather than static implementation. This SMF is the OSI approach to management by delegation.

22. *Response time monitoring function*: This function measures delays and round-trip delays of PDUs for a predetermined point-to-point or multicast connection on the basis of different evaluation procedures.

In connection with the definition of SMFs, a whole range of generic specifications for useful managed object classes (support and control MOC) was standardized for describing log objects, test objects, control objects, statistics, performance measurement procedures, and accounting procedures. It would be impossible to describe these objects and other SMFs in detail. We refer you to ISO 10164 and ISO 10165-2 for further information.

The functional model is continually being expanded. This is allowing more and more formalized management functionality to be defined generically, thereby enabling its reuse as an application module for management solutions. What is also interesting is that the development of languages for management by delegation is under work. Depending on suitability and need, these could be used in the dynamic allocation of management functionality to the individual components of distributed systems.

The *event report management function* is used as an example of SMF in the following illustration. According to ISO 10164-5, the purpose of this function is "the ability to specify conditions to be satisfied by a potential event report. . . in order to be sent to specified destinations." Figure 5.13 presents the concept behind this function.

Description of event reporting

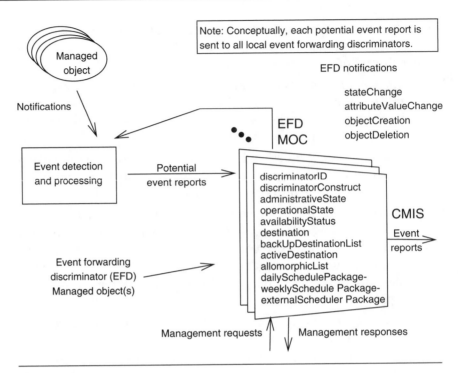

Figure 5.13
Event report management model

The notifications generated by managed objects are initially received by a nonstandardized local detection and processing mechanism (*event preprocessing*) and assembled into a potential event report. This potential report is submitted to a filter mechanism that is controllable by management, the *event forwarding discriminator* (EFD), and this then decides if and where the report is to be forwarded. The EFD is an example of a managed object that controls the operations and notifications of other managed objects. The EFD represents a refinement of the "discriminator" superclass. The general attributes of a discriminator include:

- *Discriminator name:* Identifies the EFD in the MIT.

- *Discriminator construct:* This specifies the tests that should be carried out on potential reports and therefore constitutes the filter mechanism. Similar to the CMIS filter, it has the ability to formulate logical statements about attributes such as "(objectClass equal to protocolEntity) and (entityId starts with 123) and (perceivedSeverity not equal to minor)."

- *Discriminator status:* For filter control. The components are management status (i.e., administrative state) and operating status (i.e., operational state; compare state management function).

- *Schedule packages* (optional): These are used for time-dependent course planning and define the start time, stop time, and activity intervals for the discriminator to be operational.

With EFDs the application processes (i.e., SMAEs or application entities) to which the event notifications that pass the filter are to be sent also have to be specified. The services of the event report management function include creation, deletion, suspension, and resumption of EFDs as well as change of discriminator attributes to control which events are forwarded to where. The same discriminator superclass is refined into a log object that stores events as log records for subsequent retrieval by the manager.

5.6 Telecommunications Management Network (TMN)

The situation faced by public network providers (public carriers, PTTs) has hardly been different from that of the private networks: The management systems from different manufacturers and with different user interfaces manage only individual service networks such as SDH, ATM, FR, X.25, the telephone network, and mobile radio or components within these networks. The ITU-T reference model for the *telecommunications management network* (TMN, [ITU-TM.3xxx, SID98]) represents a management architecture that is tailored to the specific needs of operators of public networks and is aimed at supporting an integrated management of these networks. From the standpoint of the service networks being managed, TMN represents an "overlay network" for management purposes. The aspect of management integration is dealt with in many different ways (see Figure 5.14).

- It should take only one management network with distributed management functionality to manage different basic networks. This includes the different service networks, network technologies including their components, intelligent networks, virtual private networks, user terminals, and PBX systems.

  TMN objectives

- All OAM aspects should be taken into account; this includes the control and supervision of carrier networks, services, and user man-

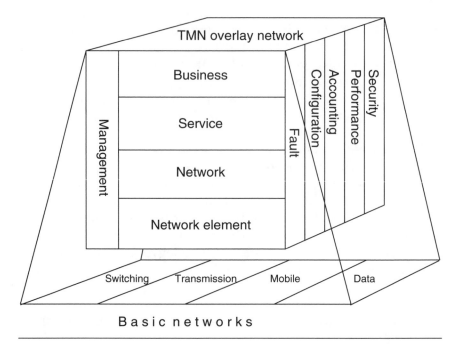

Figure 5.14
TMN management dimensions

agement including maintenance. With carrier systems, we traditionally talk about operations, administration, maintenance (OAM) or
OAM&P (& provisioning) instead of management. However, these
map to the five functional areas (FCAPS) of OSI.

■ All functional areas should be taken into account, as should the entire management pyramid. This is reflected by the different management layers shown in Figure 5.14. The business layer is concerned
with planning and engineering, domains allocation, administrative
policies, interjurisdictional policies, provisioning policies, service
availability, pricing strategies, tariffs filing, legal review, and security policies. The service layer applications are responsible for
service creation, service deployment, service testing, service provisioning and operation, service billing, security administration, and
interjurisdictional service connections. The network layer deals
with normal network management tasks like network monitoring and control, circuit provisioning, access infrastructure, routing,
end-to-end visibility, and usage. The network element layer is related to component management (i.e., it comprises monitoring and
control of network elements, installation and configuration supervi-

sion, element inventory, fault correction, alarm surveillance, usage generation, etc.).

- Manufacturer-specific OAM concepts should be supported (heterogeneity aspect).

- Interfaces should be defined between domains of the carrier, between provider and customer, as well as between the different systems for the purposes of management information flow.

TC networks are normally a great deal more complex than ordinary LAN environments. The first factor is size; large SDH and ATM networks consist of thousands of network components each in turn containing large numbers of managed objects. If a considerable amount of preprocessing were not carried out in the agents, network operators would be confronted with thousands of events per second. The scalability of management functions, the openness of system interfaces, access security, and heterogeneity also place major demands on the TC environment. Compared to LAN environments, TC networks also historically incorporate a strong service and business orientation that is still in the beginning for commercial data networks. The OSI management architecture has a special approach to addressing these requirements.

- The object orientation of OSI promotes a top-down approach and reuse of specifications and therefore implementation.

- OSI also offers ample options for modeling complex resources and structuring MIBs to reflect relationships and decomposition of complex systems into user–provider layers and subcomponents.

- The SMFs of OSI offer a wealth of standardized generic management functions that can be used to solve many problems with reusable software modules.

- The SMFs, configurable discriminators (e.g., EFD), scoping, and filtering offered by OSI allow a considerable share of the processing load to be transferred to the agents.

- OSI supports the domain concept that models telco jurisdictions.

TMN is the result of the planning that went into developing a management architecture for TC networks. TMN is based to a large degree on the concepts of OSI management, which is why it is covered in this chapter. The TMN reference model incorporates a logically separate management network (the TMN overlay network) for the interaction between different management-relevant components. The

TMN architecture

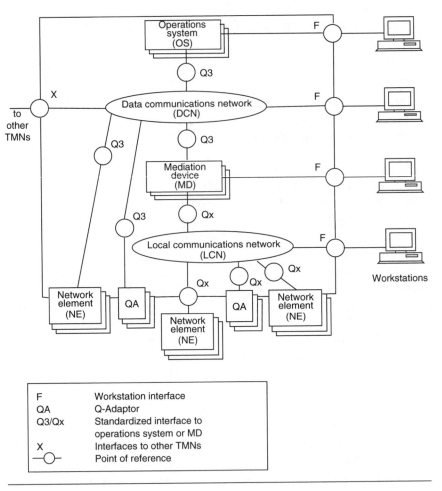

Figure 5.15
TMN reference model

TMN organizational model (actors, roles, function modules) is designed to take into account the special operator situation that exists with public networks.

The TMN architecture and all the management activities are based on so-called *function blocks*. Function blocks can be implemented on a single platform or distributed over several platforms. Interfaces are defined between the function blocks. Figure 5.15 shows TMN blocks in a sample physical arrangement.

Functional blocks of TMN reference model

- *Telecommunications networks* (TNs): Individual subnetworks offered by a carrier, such as telephone networks, ISDN, X.25 networks, mobile radio networks, videotext networks, and videoconferencing networks. According to Figure 5.15, a TN would be located outside TMN, containing NEs.

- *Network elements* (NEs): These are components that provide TN users with the network functionality (services) needed and with interfaces to TMN. Examples include switching nodes, multiplexers, and cross-connects.

- *Operations systems* (OSs): These TMN components process management information for the purposes of controlling and monitoring TNs. Data analysis and global control take place in the OS, the actual management system.

- *Mediation devices* (MDs), *Q-Adaptors:* These TMN components support the forwarding of management information between NEs and the OS and are therefore management gateways between Q3 and Qx interfaces (i.e., they provide a bridge between TMN components and non-TMN components or legacy systems). These mediators between the OS and NEs can incorporate the following management functions: data collection and provision, data preprocessing and concentration, data selection ("forwarding discriminator"), and network component identification. The necessary protocol conversion is also carried out (e.g., connection oriented to connectionless, access protocols) and mediation of information models.

- *Workstations* (WSs): These TMN components enable *human* users to access the TMN. Part of this function block operates outside the TMN.

- *Data communications networks* (DCNs), *local communications networks* (LCNs): These TMN components allow communication to take place between other TMN entities. These are therefore the transport networks for management information.

Figure 5.15 also contains some TMN reference points that are interfaces between TMN entities and must be specified by services or protocols. Final specifications are not yet available for all reference points:

TMN reference points

-F: Interface to WS.

-X: Interface to other TMNs (i.e., between jurisdictions or domains).

-Qx: Originally, Q1 and Q2 are interfaces for the connection of simple transmission and switching equipment via nonstandard protocols.

-Q3: Standard TMN interface for the connection of complex equipment or entire switching nodes and OSs.

To reiterate, TMN is based on OSI management concepts and standards. This applies in particular to the information model. All OSI object classes and template specifications can therefore also be reused in a TMN environment. However, as already mentioned in section 5.2, on a generic level TMN has also defined TMN-MOCs, which as superior classes for specific MOs, can be used across all TC technologies, services, and architectures. These classes are defined in the *TMN generic network information model* (M.3100): for example, network fragment (models a network or subnetwork), termination point fragment (models a network access point), managed element fragment (models a network component), transmission fragment (models transmission routes and communication mechanisms between elements), cross-connection fragment (models relationships between the ports of a switching node including the switching fabric).

Even the OSI functional model is incorporated. The *functional area fragment* describes OSI systems management functions and the corresponding MOCs (per section 5.5). Specific TMN management functions and services are then defined on this basis. These include switching management, routing management, customer administration, restoration and recovery, traffic management, tariff and charging administration, staff work scheduling, and trouble administration.

The Q3 interface is based on the OSI communication model, in particular the CMIS/CMIP. Several different versions are available of profiles of the management protocol and management functions and of their reliance on the underlying protocol stacks. Recommendations Q.811, Q.812, Q.821, and G.773 are examples of Q3 specifications.

Significance of TMN

The TMN has a major role due to the importance of the underlying networks. First, it represents a management applications architecture primarily aimed at providers of public networks. The fact that it is based on OSI management concepts adds to its importance because of the key role these providers play in the market. [FHN96] describes the commercially successful development environment for OSI agents and managers in the TMN area. Issue 3 of *IEEE Communication Magazine* (Vol. 34, March 1996) deals exclusively with MOC specifications and model development for telecommunications networks. We also refer you to the book [AIP98], which is dedicated totally to the management of TC networks (including mobile, satellite, and CATV networks).

Other consortia involved in the further development of TMN concepts and TMN-MOC definitions aside from the ITU and ETSI are ANSI T1M1, EURESCOM, ATM Forum, and NM Forum (recently changed name to TeleManagement Forum) [SID98]. Because they are based on TMN specifications, TMN solutions are, of course, interoperable.

OSI stacks (Q3) are highly portable due to standardized application interfaces. Agent development kits are also relatively portable; many use industry standard interfaces like XMP or TMN/C++ API (see Chapter 15). Management platforms do tend to be proprietary and offer less portable environments, but this depends on the platform and programming language used. Here again, TMN/C++ API is finding its way into many products today. Originally, OSI management has not defined an application API because it has focused instead on the communication aspects. The situation with the CORBA architecture (Chapter 7) is more favorable because of the CORBA services. CORBA does provide an excellent interface definition and infrastructure for object-to-object communication. But still there are portability issues and interoperability issues. Consortia that favor managing TC networks using OMG concepts therefore also exist in the TC environment, for example, the OMG Telecommunications Working Group and TINA-C (Telecommunications Information Network Architecture Consortium) [PAT98].

5.7   Chapter Summary

The OSI management architecture has defined the four submodels of a management architecture. It has particularly played a significant role in the telecommunications environment; TMN is based on the OSI architecture.

The OSI information model is strictly object oriented. Strict multiple inheritance is used for the specification of MOCs; allomorphism is also allowed. The MOC specifications are written in a template language using ASN.1 macros. The naming makes use of relative distinguished names. This produces a containment relationship that allows the modeling of composite objects. Three tree structures are typical of OSI: inheritance trees, containment trees, and registration trees.

The OSI organization model differentiates OSI systems according to manager role (managing system) and agent role (managed system); this means that an asymmetrical cooperation schema exists. Systems can be combined to produce functional or administrative domains to which policies can be allocated.

The OSI communication model has three categories for the exchange of management information: layer operation (exchange within a protocol), layer management (layer-specific exchange of management information), and systems management (exchange of management information through management applications). A general service, CMIS, with its own management protocol CMIP has been standardized for the latter. CMIS is a connection-oriented service that can be used to access OSI MOs. Access to subtrees and layers within an MIT is possible through only one operation with scoping, and filtering can be used for making further object selections.

The OSI function model provides an extensive range of generic systems management functions (SMFs). These can be used as building blocks in the development of management solutions.

The TMN architecture uses OSI management but offers even more features. In addition to component and network management, it also offers business and service management in separate management layers. The organization model has also been extended, thereby enabling all management activities to be distributed over so-called function blocks.

Reference points or interfaces are defined for the interaction of the different function blocks. CMIP is used for Q3. The OSI information model is used as the TMN information model. The OSI-SMFs have been expanded to include functions that are typical for the telecommunications environment. The TMN/C++ API has succeeded as the API for the development of management applications.

Internet Management

Internet management architecture is defined by a large number of standards that also refer to several different versions, thereby making it difficult to provide a structured description. Our presentation of the material is structured as follows. Section 6.1 provides a general overview. Section 6.2 presents the Internet information model (SMI), broken down into version 1 and version 2. Section 6.3 then presents the communication model (SNMP), also broken down into version 1 and version 2. Section 6.4 deals with RMON, and section 6.5 outlines some of the newer developments that have not yet been completely standardized.

6.1 Overview

The Internet management architecture—frequently also called SNMP management because of its management protocol—clearly forms the basis for the majority of multivendor management solutions in the data communications environment. This dominance is due, on the one hand, to the widespread use of IP-based protocols as a result of the Internet but also to the fact that, compared to OSI and OMG, Internet management concepts are simpler and lend themselves to implementation by relatively small components and inclusion within inexpensive products at a reasonable cost. Another reason is that the standardization process in the Internet area is less complicated and more open to informal participation. Even ordinary users are able to familiarize themselves quickly with the development of a standard using the request-for-comments (RFC) procedure. This procedure is controlled by the Internet Architecture Board (IAB) through the Internet Research Task Force (IRTF) and the Internet Engineering Task Force (IETF). Workgroups on different subject areas produce recommendations for standardization that, after appropriate review processes, become either a proposed or a full standard category draft. The documents are assigned a corresponding RFC number. IETF is largely vendor driven, whereas ISO and ITU are largely carrier driven.

Management protocols first came on the scene in the late 1980s with the development of the host monitoring protocol (HMP), the high-load entity management system (HEMS), the simple gateway monitoring protocol (SGMP), and CMOT (i.e., CMIP over TCP/IP). The one that enjoyed the greatest success, however, was the simple network management protocol (SNMP), a further development of SGMP.

This basic SNMP, now also called SNMPv1 as a result of further development, is used widely today. Because of various weaknesses in the original design (relating to the transmission of high-volume management data and to security requirements such as authentication and encryption), the first follow-up version SNMPv2 was introduced. Although appropriate products were available from the outset, version 2 had difficulty gaining full acceptance due in part to its controversial security concept. It may also be mentioned that SNMPv2 suffered from the success of SNMPv1. Vendors saw little market motivation to incur cost of migration because the market was largely still happy with SNMPv1. In the meantime, yet another version, SNMPv3, is at an advanced stage in the standardization process.

The Internet management architecture does not incorporate a very distinctive organizational or functional model. Compared to OSI management, even the information model (section 6.2) is simpler and not truly object oriented. The development goal was to produce uncomplicated concepts and therefore products. Flexibility and functionality are therefore not incorporated into the information model but are achieved through the management applications. Despite or because of their simplicity, Internet MIBs and SNMP offer considerable advantages. Although the lack of special inheritance techniques restricts the reuse of specifications and makes it less convenient to carry out systematic object manipulation in the MIB (e.g., efficient MIB browsing or scoping), it makes it easier for developers and users to understand and implement the concept, often assisted by freeware and publicly available tools. This explains why the Internet approach has caught on quickly, especially in the LAN area.

In section 6.2.1, we describe the information model in terms of the way it was defined for version 1 of SNMP. Section 6.2.2 looks at the extensions to the model that were introduced with SNMP version 2.

What also makes the Internet communication model (section 6.3) less complicated is the fact that the management protocol task pro-

Historical development of Internet management

Chapter overview

vides access to the MIB according to the information model. SNMP can run over any transport network but is usually deployed over the connectionless UDP protocol. Version 1 of the management protocol is introduced in section 6.3.1.

In section 6.3.2, we describe the further development of the Internet management protocol as it exists with SNMPv2, which was published in 1993. Several SNMPv2 dialects have been developed further since then, essentially differing in the security concept used. We cover the variants SNMPv2p and SNMPv2c.

Section 6.4 is dedicated to remote monitoring MIB I and II (RMON-MIB). This is an approach in which the managed component already carries out and controls the standardized collection and preprocessing of management information, thereby reducing the workload of the manager and the network. This illustrates a function model defined for use with SNMP.

We conclude in section 6.5 by briefly describing the latest state of development, namely, SNMPv3 and DISMAN. An attempt is made in SNMPv3 to achieve a convergence of the different SNMPv2 variants and to design a modular, expandable architecture for SNMP entities. DISMAN relates to an Internet approach for management by delegation.

An enormous number of documents (RFCs) are available for Internet management, but only a small number of them have the status of a full standard. This is partly because the IETF will obsolete or downgrade full standards if replaced by later standards or found to be lacking in deployment. The main standards for SNMPv1 are RFC 1155 (describing the information model), RFC 1213 (describing the original Internet MIB), and RFC 1157 (describing the management protocol SNMP). The text makes reference to other RFCs. All RFCs and current designs for further development are accessible to the public through electronic means (*http://www.ietf.org*).

It should be mentioned that there is the need for coexistence of Internet management and OSI management. This makes necessary some mediation architecture that performs the translation of, for example, the different information models. This topic will be discussed in Chapter 10.

6.2   Internet Information Model (SMI and MIB)

The Internet information model (structure of management information, SMI) is available in two versions. SNMPv1-SMI is the original

Internet management structure

version and continues to be the most widely used one. In the course of the development of a successor version of the SNMP management protocol, the information model has also been extended to SNMPv2-SMI. The basic concepts of version 1 have been retained, however.

6.2.1 SNMPv1-SMI

Internet management is based on the client–server principle in which the client is usually designated as the management station (in short, manager) and the server as the management agent (in short, agent). In this asymmetric cooperation model (Figure 6.1), the manager is the carrier system for all management applications; it provides an interface to human operators and maintains a (logical) database for all relevant data of the network it monitors. Using the SNMP management protocol, a manager communicates with the monitored resources (managed nodes), more specifically, with the "management representative" of the resource, the agent. Through the agent, the manager has read or write access to the agent MIB (management information base). This *agent MIB* is a collection of variables that are characteristic of the behavior of the managed node. With Internet management, these MIB variables are also called *managed objects*, although they do not incorporate any kind of object orientation in the sense of encapsulation, inheritance, or the like. The variables represented by Internet MOs are similar to the MOC attributes of OSI.

Internet MIBs and agent MIB

The *Internet MIBs* define the structure of the agent MIB. These specify which managed objects are even allowed to appear in an agent MIB, how they are structured, which meaning they incorporate, and how they can be identified. Internet MOs are related hierarchically and named according to the same registration tree used by ISO and ITU. The agent MIB contains the MOs provided by the managed nodes. Each variable is a leaf on the registration tree with a dependency on a typically concrete (can be logical, too) resource. The MO variables of the agent MIB can be queried about current values; if need be, a value can be changed, which then has an effect on the represented resource. An agent MIB therefore represents the instantiation of (sometimes more than one) Internet MIBs (Figure 6.2): The latter defines the "object types" that are allowed in principle; the former contains the "object entities" that are supported by the respective concrete agent.

Internet registration tree

An important objective associated with the specification of multivendor management information is the development of a unique form of identification and description of information worldwide. To do jus-

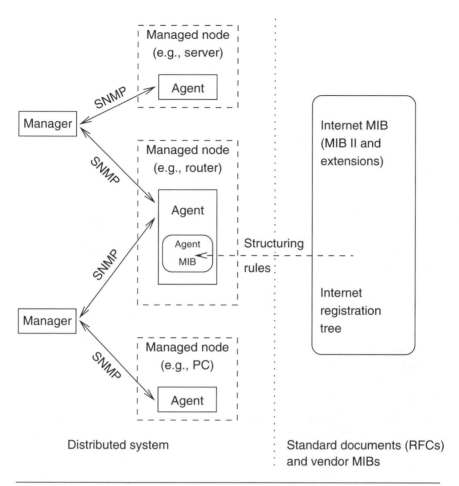

Figure 6.1
Internet architecture model and MIBs

tice to this requirement, the ISO and the ITU-T have introduced a global *object identifier tree*, which permits any objects, not just those in the management domain, to be assigned to a unique worldwide identifier. The assignment of the object identifiers is extremely simple: The name space is organized like a tree in which each tree node is assigned a name and a number, with the numbers beginning with 1 enumerating all the nodes belonging to a parent node. This allows delegation of naming authority (e.g., the IETF is responsible for numbering all nodes registered under "1.3.6.1"). Figure 6.3 shows the organization of the Internet name tree (i.e., the part of the registration tree below the node with object identifier "1.3.6.1" and the name "iso.org.dod.internet").

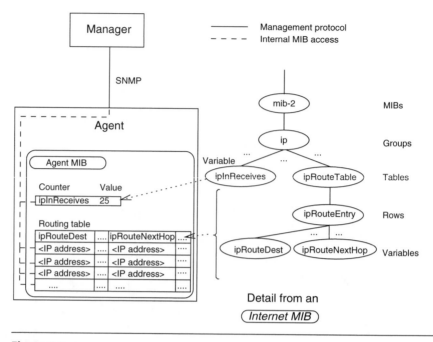

Figure 6.2
Example of an agent and Internet MIB

Management information is scattered over several subtrees of the registration tree

- Below the "mgmt" node with object identifier "1.3.6.1.2," currently only one node, "mib-2," is defined, below which is the standard MIB (currently MIB-II defined by RFC 1213). Each management agent is required to have the capability of interpreting MIB II. We will look at its content later.

- The *experimental MIBs* are incorporated below the "experimental" subtree. This generally relates to technology-specific management information for FDDI, frame relay, the DS3 interface, ISO CLNS objects, X.25, ATM, UNI, and SONET—a total of more than 70 MIBs [MIL97]. The management information contained in these MIBs is a candidate for extending future standard MIBs. In practice, many MIBs become mature without moving to the "management" branch.

- The "enterprise" subtree is reserved for enterprises that want to de-fine manufacturer-specific management information in accordance with the Internet information model. More than 3000 enterprise-specific subtrees already exist [MIL97]. The explosion of proprietary *manufacturer MIBs* is having an effect on the interoperability of management systems because MOs are addressed through their position in the registration tree and this has to be reflected in the management applications. Moreover, many MIBs contain hun-

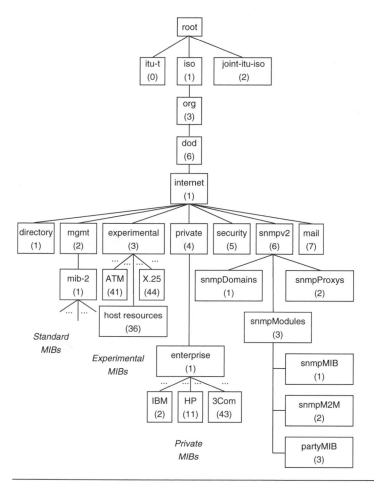

Figure 6.3
Organization of Internet registration tree

dreds of MIB variables, and it is often difficult to understand the true relevance of these variables to management. The type and number of MIBs implemented are gradually becoming product-differentiating characteristics in the immense set of management product offerings.

Initially, only the first four subtrees appeared below the "internet" node; the others were added later as a result of further developments. The internal nodes of the registration tree are pure structuring nodes and do not contain supplementary information. They are used exclusively for registration and object identification; the actual management information is located only in the leaves. In a certain way, the structuring nodes fill the role of class definition, the attributes of which are the leaves. However, their position in the tree induces neither a containment (at least not in every case) nor an inheritance hierarchy.

The IETF defined an ASN.1 OBJECT-TYPE macro for the nodes that contain the "real" management information; this macro allows the specification of the following information:

Description of object types, generic object type macro

- Name and object identifier of the node

- Syntax of the management information referenced by or available through accessing the node in the form of an ASN.1 data type

- Informal description of the semantics of this management information

- Specification status information that determines whether the management information is mandatory, optional, or obsolete because it has been made superfluous as a result of a new specification for the MIB

Nodes that contain this information are designated as *object types*. The instantiation of object types, the *object instances*, produces the actual *managed objects* (MOs) in the agent MIB. All the managed objects of the different Internet subtrees per Figure 6.3 are specified in accordance with the preceding scheme.

Let us use an IP packet counter as an example. The concrete syntax in the form it was used for the object ipInReceives in the original standard MIB (RFC 1213) reads:

```
ipInReceives OBJECT TYPE
SYNTAX Counter
ACCESS read-only
STATUS mandatory
DESCRIPTION
>>The total number of input datagrams received from
interfaces, including those received in error.<<
::= { ip 3 }
```

The specification clarifies that the object is a "counter" that can be accessed only through reading and must be supplied by an SNMP agent. An informal description of what is to be counted by the object is also supplied. The description concludes with details on how the object can be identified. It also identifies the branch the object is located on relative to the parent node; in the example, it is branch 3 below the node "ip."

Counter is one of the following six ASN.1 data types predefined in the Internet information model (RFC 1155, structure of management information, SMI) to describe the syntax of Internet objects:

Allowable ASN.1 data types, generic object types

- *Network address* enables the selection of a protocol family. Initially, this selection was limited to Internet protocols.

- *IpAddress* is used in the representation of the 32-bit-long Internet address.

- *Time ticks* allow the specification of periods of time with each time tick comprising 1/100 second, relative to the last boot time at the agent.

- *Gauge* defines a counting object that can assume a value between 0 and $2^{32} - 1$, can be increased and decreased, and does not loop.

- *Counter* defines a counting object that can assume a value between 0 and $2^{32} - 1$ and can only be increased. The counter is cyclical (modulo numbering).

- A variable of the type *opaque* contains the value of any ASN.1 type desired (i.e., this allows late binding of types).

In addition to these specifically defined ASN.1 types in the Internet information model, the simple types `INTEGER`, `OCTET STRING`, `OBJECT IDENTIFIER`, and `NULL` are also supported. `SEQUENCE` and `SEQUENCE OF` are permitted as ASN.1 types for combined objects also referred to as "constructor types"; these two data types are used to construct Internet tables. Tables are the only combined objects that occur in an Internet MIB. They are constructed on the basis of the following principle: The object type that describes an entire table consists of a "`SEQUENCE OF` ⟨table row⟩" with each row of a table in turn consisting of a "`SEQUENCE` ⟨table column⟩." The two different ASN.1 types `SEQUENCE OF` and `SEQUENCE` take into account the fact that the entries in a table can be added or removed dynamically as table rows, whereas the columns that describe the MIB variables stored in the table must be established when the table is defined. (Note: This restriction no longer applies to the expanded information model SNMPv2-SMI [RFC 1902], sometimes also referred to as SMIv2, and therefore table columns can also be expanded through subsequent refinement, but still not added to at runtime.)

Tables as object types

We demonstrate the Internet approach to table descriptions on the basis of the specification for the routing table (i.e., the description of the managed object `ipRouteTable`). We have chosen this example for didactic reasons because the description is still based on the

Example of a table structure

conventions of SNMPv1-SMI. In a now obsolete version of MIB II (RFC 1213), different object types were used to describe the table. Because space is limited, we are listing only 2 of the 13 total table columns:

Structure of the whole table

```
ipRouteTable OBJECT-TYPE
SYNTAX SEQUENCE OF IpRouteEntry
ACCESS not-accessible
STATUS mandatory
DESCRIPTION
>>This entity's IP Routing table.<<
::= { ip 21 }


IpRouteEntry OBJECT-TYPE
SYNTAX IpRouteEntry
ACCESS not-accessible
STATUS mandatory
DESCRIPTION
>>A route to a particular destination<<
INDEX { ipRouteDest }
::= { ipRouteTable 1 }
```

Structure of a row

```
ipRouteEntry ::=
SEQUENCE {
ipRouteDest IpAddress,
...
ipRouteNextHop IpAddress,
...
}
```

A column element

```
ipRouteDest OBJECT-TYPE
SYNTAX IpAddress
ACCESS read-write
STATUS mandatory
DESCRIPTION
>>The destination IP address of this route. An entry with ...<<
::= { ipRouteEntry 1 }
```

Another column element

```
ipRouteNextHop OBJECT-TYPE
SYNTAX IpAddress
ACCESS read-write
STATUS mandatory
DESCRIPTION
"The IP address of the next hop of this route...."
::= { ipRouteEntry 7 }
```

According to the description, access is not possible to the table object `ipRouteTable` or the table row object `ipRouteEntry` itself. In other words, a manager cannot retrieve the entire table or table row—it must retrieve individual columnar variables. In terms of how they are described, the object types `ipRouteDest` and `ipRouteNextHop`, which are columns of a table row, seem no different from the so-called simple MIB variables, such as the counter `ipInReceives`. The differences are first evident when the respective instantiations are referenced. This also applies to the INDEX entry that appears in the table row object `ipRouteEntry`. At least one appropriate OBJECT-TYPE, which has to appear as one of the columns in the table, is specified as an index for each table. This is called an *index object type* (`ipRouteDest` in the example). If access to a specific table row is desired, then the current value of the index object type in this line is appended to the identifier for the object itself to form a "name." The operation "getnext" mentioned later is utilized to "walk through" table rows by following this name structuring.

It should be pointed out that the example given was used only to provide a general description of a table. As we have already mentioned, the example selected `ipRouteTable` is now obsolete as a managed object. `ipRouteTable` from RFC 1213 was replaced by *ipForwardTable* in RFC 1354, which in turn has now been replaced by RFC 2096 to allow different options for specification. The Internet information model in the extended SNMPv2-SMI version (which we cover in section 6.2.2) is already being used for description purposes. The new routing table structure is provided by the combined object type `ipCidrRouteTable` (an excerpt will be given in section 10.3.1), which is registered in the IP group under `ipForward` (4) in MIB II. This table, which even has an index consisting of four object types, can be used to support policy-controlled interdomain routing.

MIB II is the currently valid basic specification of management information. Eleven other structural nodes called *groups of MIB II* (Figure 6.4) are attached to structuring node 1.3.6.1.2.1 assigned to mib-2 itself. The rule is that if one device (agent) supports an MIB group, then all objects (leaves of the tree) must support this group.

- *Group system*: The objects in this group supply general information about the managed node (`sysDescr`, `sysObjectID`, `sysLocation`, `sysUpTime`), information about contact partners and system names (`sysContact`, `sysName`), and information coded in an integer number identifying which services of which protocol layer are supported by the managed node (`sysServices`).

Groups in MIB II

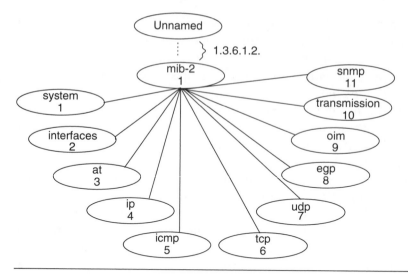

Figure 6.4
MIB II groups

- *Interfaces group*: This group consists of the number of network interfaces (ifNumber) provided by the managed node plus a table (ifTable) containing the following information for each interface: type (ifType) and description of the interface (ifDescr), information on the configuration of the interface (ifSpeed, ifMtu, ifPhysAddress), status information (ifAdminStatus, ifOperStatus), and finally statistics counters (ifInOctets, ifInUnknownProtos, ifOutUcastPkts, ifOutErrors, etc.). The latest extension to this information can be found in RFC 2233.

- The *address translation* (at) *group* was a part of MIB I but was assigned the status "deprecated" in MIB II, meaning that it is being continued only for compatibility with MIB I. It was a table for mapping IP addresses to hardware addresses. In the future, each protocol group is being defined with its own address mapping tables.

- *Protocol groups ip, icmp, tcp, udp, egp, snmp*: Statistics counters appear in each group and are used to count different types of incoming and outgoing protocol data units as well as different kinds of error situations. Other tables that contain specific information about routing, connections, and neighboring nodes for each protocol are also available. We have already referred to the current valid structure of the routing table (RFC 2096).

- *Transmission group:* This group contains management information for a number of different transmission protocols and network interfaces such as X.25, Ethernet, Token Ring, FDDI, LAPB, DS1, E1, PPP, DS3, SDMS, frame relay, RS232, ATM, and SONET. The DS1 interface alone contains almost 100 MIB variables known as DS1-MOs. Each transmission protocol is represented by an MIB beneath this group.

- *OIM group:* OIM, which stands for OSI Internet Management MIB, is already considered a "historic" group and contains managed objects for CMOT, thus CMIP over TCP.

Details about object types and their precise specification will not be included in the context of this discussion. In-depth knowledge of all protocols and network technologies is required in order to develop a full understanding of the information defined in these groups.

But to reiterate, the original Internet SMI information model is not object oriented, which means that it does not contain object classes or inheritance. The large number of MIB catalogs that exist in the Internet area would suggest that the simple registration tree (which does not provide a complete or flexible representation of containment) does not allow an adequate structuring of management information. The lack of a mechanism for refining and reusing object definitions particularly results in logically related management information being maintained in totally separate subtrees within the registration tree. This is obvious, for example, when you need all the available information for a particular interface card; the information is dispersed over all sorts of different tables of MIB II, of the vendor MIB, and of the RMON-MIB. In this sense, too, the many private MIBs are largely redundant. This is where the hidden heterogeneity surfaces again: The management applications must be able to recognize these many MIBs since MOs of different subtrees have to be addressed separately. Related MOs are often specified in different MIBs or registered in different branches of the registration tree; besides, object identifiers (OIDs) in the tree are used as names and the SNMP protocol is structured only to traverse OIDs, but not relationships.

The MIBs mentioned so far have all been network oriented (i.e., they have all concerned the network management of the Internet, its protocols, components, underlying networks, and access networks). In recent years, Internet management has also recognized the importance of not limiting integrated management to specifics of the networks but also applying the concept to aspects of systems management and application management. Definitions of management information based on the principles of the SMI information model have therefore

MIBs for systems and application management

also been available in these areas. Examples of MIBs that can be used beyond pure Internet network management include:

- Host resources MIB (RFC 1514)
- Mail monitoring MIB (RFC 2249)
- X.500 directory monitoring MIB (RFC 1567)
- DNS server/resolver MIB extensions (RFC 1611/1612)
- Network services monitoring MIB (RFC 2248)
- Printer MIB (RFC 1759)
- Uninterruptible power supply MIB (RFC 1628)
- Relational database management system MIB (RFC 1697)
- System-level MOs for applications (RFC 2287)
- Application MIB [STB98, IET98]

The host resources MIB enables hosts to specify management information that characterizes the system; this includes information indicating characteristic sizes of the different memories, describing attached peripherals, documenting installed software, and relating to running processes. From the standpoint of a systems administrator, this MIB information is, of course, still too limited [GUN95, HKN96]. But the RFCs mentioned also signal an opening to other areas of application for Internet management. We will talk about the RMON-MIB again in section 6.5.

6.2.2 SNMPv2-SMI

This section will discuss the development of the Internet information model and the resulting enhancements to SNMPv1-SMI. The first set of SNMPv2-RFCs (RFC 1441 to 1452) was published in 1992; it was relieved by the current specifications RFC 1901 to 1908.

Extension of information model, new subtrees in the registration tree

The original Internet registration tree contained only subtrees (1) to (4) under 1.3.6.1 (compare Figure 6.3); the subtrees security (5) and SNMPv2 (6) were added during the development of SNMPv2. The nodes snmpDomains (1), snmpProxys (2), and snmpModules (3) appear under SNMPv2. The structural node snmpModules contains the subtrees snmpMIB (1), snmpM2M (2), and partyMIB (3). SnmpMIB (1) largely replaces the subtree snmp (1) in MIB II and refers to SNMPv2, which is not directly interoperable with SNMPv1. The system group and other MIB II groups have been extended by several MOs. The snmpDomains group refers to the different versions of SNMPv2 on underlying protocol stacks. Details about the MIB extensions can be found in RFCs 1906 and 1907 and in [MIL97, PEM97].

The ASN.1 data types allowed in the *object type macro* (compare section 6.2.1) have also been extended. New ones that have been added since version 1 include nonnegative integers ("Unsigned32"), larger counters ("Counter64"), OSI addresses ("Nsap address"), and BITS, a construct that represents an enumeration of named bits.

New object types in SNMPv2

Even the macro itself defined by SNMPv1 has been altered in SNMPv2 (RFC 1902) and now contains the parts SYNTAX, UnitsParts, MAX-ACCESS, STATUS, DESCRIPTION, ReferPart, IndexPart, and Def-ValPart. The extended object types appear in SYNTAX; UnitsParts contains as optional text "dimensions" such as "seconds" and "notifi-cations" associated with the MIB variable. In a (semantically) orderly form, MAX-ACCESS has the values not-accessible, accessible-for-notify, read-only, read-write, and read-create. The new STATUS values are current, deprecated, and obsolete. ReferPart can con-tain reference text to other modules. IndexPart permits flexible table descriptions, and DefValPart the definition of default values. It is im-portant to mention the problem caused by having different versions of the Internet information model. The addition of new MIB groups or variables means adding new branches to the registration tree; however, if variables are no longer necessary because of new versions, they still have to remain in the MIB (once registered, the number is forever assigned to the original object).

Changed structure of object-type macro

In SNMPv1, events were simply defined by the protocol and not by individual MIBs. SNMPv2-SMI (SMIv2) introduced new macros, such as the NOTIFICATION-TYPE macro (RFC 1905), which permits a flexible specification of traps. Macros incorporating text conventions (RFC 1903) for specifying frequently used reference types are also available. The AGENT-CAPABILITY macro describes the capabilities of SNMPv2 agents in the form of supported modules, MOs, and values. It roughly corresponds to OSI management knowledge. And, lastly, the MODULE-COMPLIANCE macro can be used to describe the minimum requirements for an MIB implementation. This replaces the use of "mandatory" and "optional" in the OBJECT-TYPE macro itself.

New SNMPv2 macros

To sum up, SMIv2 advances management information modeling. The object type macro allows finer granularity when defining MOs. The text conventions allow more formal specification of behavior and reusability of specification. Also table handling has become more flexible. Formalizing "row status" allows manager create and delete table rows; also a certain refinement of table rows is allowed in version

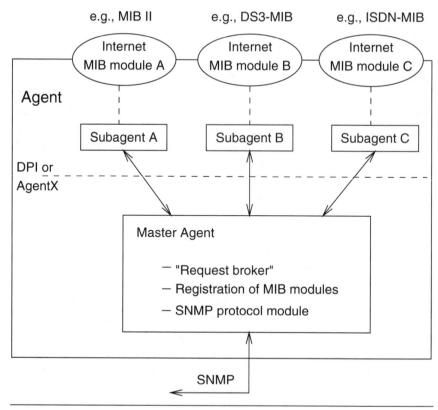

Figure 6.5
AgentX and DPI

2. For more details with respect to SMIv2-tables, see RFC 1902 or [STA96].

Although the SNMP version 2 management protocol has not caught on, the same does not apply to the expanded information model SNMPv2-SMI (abbreviated to SMIv2). According to IETF specification rules, object type macros based on SMIv2 are being used to describe all newer Internet MIBs. Since SMIv2 is largely a superset of SMIv1, publicly available translators can be used to convert a v2-based MIB for use in a v1-product or agent or manager. Some loss of functionality does occur.

The existence of so many MIBs from different sources has inevitably resulted in a move to support the coexistence of several MIB models on one agent. This possibility is described in RFC 1592. Subagents that communicate with the (main) agents of a managed node over the *distributed protocol interface* (DPI 2.0) are allocated to the individual MIB modules (see Figure 6.5). The master agent distributes the requested

Coexistence of independent MIBs on an agent through DPI

operations of the manager transmitted by the management protocol SNMP (see section 6.3) among the subagents. The subagents collect the management information relating to their MIB modules and pass on the results to the master agent. DPI allows subagents and MIBs to be added and removed dynamically without the need for a recompilation of the master agent. The local MIB modules are addressable by names since the DPI contains a registration mechanism. The agent systems are therefore more flexible and easier to scale because not all subagents have to run at the same time.

The *agent extensibility (agentX) protocol* is a further development of DPI (RFC 2257). This protocol makes an even more distinct separation between master agent and subagent. According to the RFC, "The master agent is MIB ignorant and SNMP omniscient, while the subagent is SNMP ignorant and MIB omniscient for the MIB variables it instantiates." The master agents interpret the SNMP protocol operations and transform them into agentX protocol operations; the subagents themselves are responsible for any management-relevant instrumentation, such as connections to concrete resources. Subagents can be developed with agentX with no need to consider other subagents that might already exist on the component.

AgentX as a further development of DPI

6.3   Internet Communication Model (SNMP)

The core of the Internet communication model is the simple network management protocol (SNMP). So far, two versions of SNMP exist—version 1 and several variants of version 2. We describe these two versions in the following subsections. In section 6.5, we will sketch a third version, SNMPv3, which is still in the design process.

6.3.1   SNMP Version 1

In Internet management, resources are also managed, in other words, supervised and controlled, through access to the characteristic values of the MIBs representing the resources. As demonstrated in section 6.2, managed objects are the leaves in the agent MIBs. Communication between manager and agent is over the simple network management protocol (SNMP), which was initially specified in RFC 1157.

The manager is able to access the remote agent MIB using SNMP operations. An SNMP agent receives the manager's requests, carries out the actions required, and generates an appropriate response. During

Description of SNMP operations

this process, the protocol works asynchronously, meaning that the manager can initiate a request without having to wait for the agent to supply a response (implementations of SNMP may or may not "block" while a request is outstanding). In addition to various manager-initiated operations, SNMP also provides a trap message that can be used by agents to transmit information to the manager without having received a prior request from the manager. SNMP provides a total of four protocol interactions, which are shown in Figure 6.6.

Get-request-operation

■ Read access (get-request-operation): The manager generates a *GetRequest* PDU in which it enters the object instance values from the agent MIB that should be transmitted in a *GetResponse* PDU from the agent. This operation is atomic with SNMPv1: Either all the values are retrieved or none is. The identifier given in the PDU structure (Figure 6.7) identifies an MO entity. With simple MIB variables, the identifier is formed by a "0" being attached to the object identifier in the Internet MIB. As explained earlier, access to table values is controlled by a yet-to-be-specified index column of the table; this specifies the index object type. Access to the *n*th entity (therefore the *n*th table row) of object type X in a table is through an access identifier ⟨object ID of X⟩, ⟨value of the index object type in the *n*th table row⟩. The question arises concerning the calculation of the actual value of the index object type in connection with this access method: Looking at the example in section 6.3, how is it possible to access entries in the table `ipRouteTable` if the IP destination address contained in the `ipRoute Dest` is not known? The answer to this question is closely linked to the SNMP operation `get-next`, which allows table columns to be retrieved row by row even if the precise access identifier is not known.

Get-next-operation

■ Browsing the agent MIB (`get-next`-operation): The get-next PDU is almost identical to the get-request PDU; it has the same PDU exchange pattern and the same format. In the get-request PDU, each variable in the variable-bindings list refers to an object instance whose value is to be returned. With get-next there is a difference. The manager generates a *GetNextRequest* PDU, in which it enters the object identifier of an object type or an object instance. In a *GetResponse* PDU from the agent, it receives the access identifier and the value, in lexicographic order, of the "next" object instance for the object identifier indicated in the request. More than one object identifier can be entered in a `get-next-request` PDU, and the next object instance for each object identifier is determined by the agent. Typically, the get-next operation is used to access the

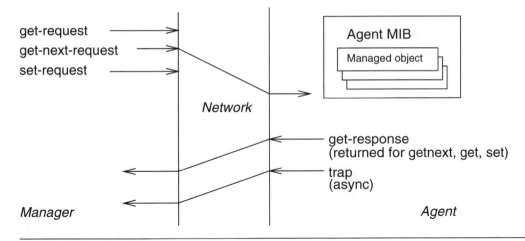

get-request
get-next-request
set-request

Agent MIB

Managed object

Network

get-response
(returned for getnext, get, set)

trap
(async)

Manager

Agent

Figure 6.6
SNMP operations

next instance of an object in the MIB. It could access the next object in the database, or it could access the next row entry in a table. The get-next PDU invokes the accompanying get response. The keys to the search in the database for the get-next are the MO names of the previous get. There are several possible outcomes of a get-next operation depending on what is requested (e.g., object ID of a simple object in MIB, object-instance ID of a simple object in MIB, OID of table, OID of table entry, columnar-object ID, columnar-object-instance ID, OID that does not match). Get-next provides an elegant way for retrieving unknown objects and accessing table values. For example, to get the first row of a table, perform a get-next with every object in the table, identified by ⟨object ID of X⟩.0. To get the next row, resend the response returned to the first get-next, and so on.

- Write access (set-operation): The manager generates a *SetRequest* PDU for the agent in which it enters the object instances together with the new values to be set. The agent indicates the success or failure of the write action in a *GetResponse* PDU. (Note: There are no *SetResponse* PDUs.)

- Notification by agents (trap-operation): The agent generates a trap PDU in which it notifies the manager of certain events without having received a prior request from the manager to do so. In SNMPv1, these were limited to a set of seven trap types.

The different interactions are described in more detail in the description of the PDUs used in SNMP. The exact syntactic PDU structure is defined in the form of an ASN.1 specification in RFC 1157. `GetRequest`, `GetNextRequest`, `GetResponse`, and `SetRequest` have the same structure and consist of the following parts (Figure 6.7):

- *request-id* is used for the unique identification of a request (i.e., for correlation of get response with request).

- *error-status* enables the agent to notify the manager of possible errors that occur during the execution of a request. The following error states have been standardized: `noError`, `tooBig`, `noSuchName`, `badValue`, `readOnly`, `genErr`.

- *error-index* can be used by the agent in the case of an error to identify the first variable responsible for the error.

- *variable-binding* consists of a sequence of pairs of variable names and variable values. It is here that the manager enters the variable (object) names appearing in the request; with write access the value of the variable is the value to be set; otherwise, the variable value for a request is set to 0. In its response, the agent transmits the variable names provided by the manager with the corresponding values (i.e., it fills in values by modifying the request buffer for simplified implementation).

With the SNMP PDUs described so far, the manager can carry out polling only. Polling is based on a request–response scheme like the one that occurs in the PDU structure described. The trap PDU is the only protocol data unit in SNMP that allows the transmission of information that has been initiated by an agent and therefore is not based on the polling principle. Many SNMP implementations use the so-called trap-directed polling: A trap tells the manager to get object values (i.e., poll them), for example, in case of an event having occurred. This is in contrast to OSI events; here notifications issued asynchronously by an agent carry all affected attribute values with them. This trap PDU is structured as follows:

- *PDU-type* for trap PDU is characterized by type = 4.

- *enterprise* contains the object identifier of the object that has produced the trap.

- *agent-addr* describes the network address of the SNMP agent that sent the trap.

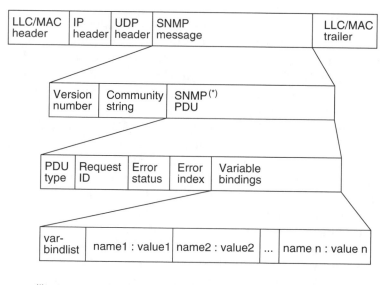

$^{(*)}$ Instead of an SNMP PDU, a trap PDU also may be contained in an SNMP message

Figure 6.7
SNMP message format

- *generic trap* provides a rough identification of the trap based on the following standardized trap types: coldStart (e.g., if agent's configuration or SNMP entity was altered—typically, an unexpected restart), warmStart (e.g., after reinitializing—typically routine restart), linkDown (e.g., failure in one of the agent's links—variable-bindings field refers to related interface), linkUp, authenticationFailure, egpNeighborLoss (signals that an EGP neighbor is now down), and enterpriseSpecific (signals that an enterprise-specific event occurred).

- *specific trap* allows a further enterprise-specific classification of "enterpriseSpecific" type traps beyond the seven generic types.

- *time stamp* contains the time ticks that had passed since the last initialization of the network, at the time this event occurred at the agent.

- *variable-bindings* offers additional information relating to the trap. The significance of this field is implementation specific.

Traps are therefore similar to "predefined weak interrupt conditions." The manager can but does not have to react. On the agent side, some threshold monitoring can be carried out before a trap is sent. A manager will normally respond to a trap using selective polling.

Figure 6.8 sums up the SNMP definitions as specified in RFC 1157. An SNMP entity constructs the appropriate PDU using the ASN.1 structure given in the definitions. Then the PDU is passed to an authentication service (if present) together with the source and destination transport addresses and a community name. The authentication service may perform encryption or any other transformation. Then the SNMP message is constructed according to Figure 6.7. This new ASN.1 object is then encoded, using the basic encoding rules, and passed to the transport service (e.g., UDP). At the destination, an SNMP entity does a syntax check of the SNMP message. Then it verifies the version number. If there is an authentication service, the message is delivered to it. If authentication succeeds, the SNMP PDU is returned as an ASN.1 object. After some syntax check, the SNMP PDU is processed. Figure 6.9 illustrates the receipt of the SNMP PDUs on the agent side.

Community string as an SNMP security mechanism

The security mechanism used in SNMP is an extremely simple concept: In SNMP, each protocol data unit to be transmitted is packed into an SNMP message (Figure 6.7), which in addition to the PDU itself, contains a version number and a community string relevant to the security aspect. The community string serves as a type of password for MIB access since the agent processes only those SNMP messages that match the string configured in the agent, received from authorized managers.

Because of the simple concept, this form of authentication is also called a *trivial authentication algorithm*. A major disadvantage of the procedure is that by listening in on the network traffic a nonauthorized user (or a router on the path between manager and agent) can easily determine the community strings (the permitted passwords) configured in the SNMP agents and therefore carry out any number of operations on an agent MIB. The procedure also lacks the mechanism to cope with other threats, such as the falsification of SNMP messages (alterations of bridge filter settings), the repetition of SNMP messages (e.g., reboot requests to components), and the unauthorized disclosure of the contents of SNMP messages that have been listened in on (e.g., passwords for terminal servers).

In the IAB's view, extending SNMP to include appropriate security procedures such as the cryptographic checksum algorithm MD5 (RFC 1321) and the data encryption standard (DES) in cipher block chaining mode [FIPS-PUB46-2 and 81] was an urgent priority in its efforts to improve new SNMP versions (e.g., SNMPv2p). However, IP itself has since been extended to provide both confidentiality and packet authentication for application protocols, not just for SNMP. This simplifies the

```
RFC1157-SNMP DEFINITIONS ::= BEGIN

IMPORTS
        ObjectName, ObjectSyntax, NetworkAddress, IpAddress, TimeTicks
            FROM RFC1155-SMI;

-- top-level message

Message ::= SEQUENCE {version INTEGER {version-1(0) },        -- version-1 for this RFC
            community OCTET STRING,                           -- community name
            data ANY            -- e.g., PDUs if trivial authentication is being used

-- protocol data units

PDUs ::= CHOICE { get-request        GetRequest-PDU,
                  get-next-request   GetNextRequest-PDU,
                  get-response       GetResponse-PDU,
                  set-request        SetRequest-PDU,
                  trap               Trap-PDU}


-- PDUs

GetRequest-PDU ::=          [0] IMPLICIT PDU
GetNextRequest-PDU ::=      [1] IMPLICIT PDU
GetResponse-PDU ::=         [2] IMPLICIT PDU
SetRequest-PDU ::=          [3] IMPLICIT PDU


PDU ::= SEQUENCE { request-id INTEGER,
                   error-status INTEGER {            -- sometimes ignored
                                  noError(0),
                                  tooBig(1),
                                  noSuchName(2),
                                  badValue(3),
                                  readOnly(4),
                                  genErr(5)},

                   error-index INTEGER,             -- sometimes ignored
                   variable-bindings VarBindList}    -- values are sometimes ignored


Trap-PDU ::= [4] IMPLICIT SEQUENCE {
                   enterprise OBJECT IDENTIFIER,     -- type of object generating
                                                     -- trap, see sysObjectID in RFC 1155
                   agent-addr NetworkAddress,        -- address of object generating trap
                   generic-trap INTEGER {            -- generic trap type
                                  coldStart(0),
                                  warmStart(1),
                                  linkDown(2),
                                  linkUp(3),
                                  authenticationFailure(4),
                                  egpNeighborLoss(5),
                                  enterpriseSpecific(6)},

                   specific-trap INTEGER,            -- specific code, present even
                                                     -- if generic-trap is not enterpriseSpecific
                                                     -- enterpriseSpecific
                   time-stamp TimeTicks,             -- time elapsed between the last
                                                     -- (re)initialization of the network
                                                     -- entity and the generation of the trap
                   variable-bindings VarBindList}    -- "interesting" information

-- variable bindings

VarBind ::= SEQUENCE {name ObjectName,
                      value ObjectSyntax }

VarBindList ::= SEQUENCE OF VarBind

END
```

Figure 6.8
SNMP definition (RFC 1157)

```
procedure  receive-getrequest;
begin
    if  object not available for get   then
        issue getresponse (noSuchName, index)
    else if   generated PDU too big   then
        issue getresponse (tooBig)
    else if   value not retrievable for some other reason   then
        issue getresponse (genErr, index)
    else   issue getresponse (variablebindings)
end;


procedure  receive-getnextrequest;
begin
    if  no next object available for get   then
        issue getresponse (noSuchName, index)
    else if   generated PDU too big   then
        issue getresponse (tooBig)
    else if   value not retrievable for some other reason   then
        issue getresponse (genErr, index)
    else   issue getresponse (variablebindings)
end;


procedure  receive-setrequest;
begin
    if  object not available for set   then
        issue getresponse (noSuchName, index)
    else if   inconsistent object value   then
        issue getresponse (badValue, index)
    else if   generated PDU too big   then
        issue getresponse (tooBig)
    else if   value not settable for some other reason   then
        issue getresponse (genErr, index)
    else   issue getresponse (variablebindings)
end;
```

Figure 6.9
Receipt of SNMP PDUs

special security requirements that must still be addressed by extending SNMP.

Figure 6.7 also illustrates the normal embedding of SNMP in the Internet protocol world. SNMP is typically based on the connectionless transport protocol UDP. SNMP PDUs are therefore coded in accordance with a simplified subset of the ASN.1 basic encoding rules (ISO 8825-1). SNMP traps are normally received at UDP port 162, the other SNMP messages at UDP port 161.

In addition to the most frequently used mapping of SNMP to UDP, SNMP can now also support OSI protocol stacks, Ethernet, Novell-IPX, and AppleTalk. SNMP proxies, or management gateways, are then used to manage the resources that do not support SNMP. In order to ease the use of SNMP functionality when writing SNMP-based management applications, SNMP APIs were developed, such as SNMP++ (see Chapter 15).

6.3.2   SNMP Version 2

As mentioned earlier, SNMPv1 is the dominant management protocol in the data communications environment. It can even be implemented in relatively simple resources. Almost all devices support SNMP, at least to the extent that interoperability is guaranteed within the scope of MIB II. Many management applications are available, and SNMP has proved itself in many areas of application.

Nevertheless, a number of disadvantages and limitations have already surfaced:

Weaknesses in
SNMP version 1

- SNMPv1 incorporates a very weak security concept. Community strings are "clear text" transmitted passwords.

- SNMPv1 does not support the efficient transmission of large volumes of management data.

- SNMPv1 supports only a polling scheme that is always initiated only by the manager. However, an agent can initiate polling through the use of traps (trap-directed polling). All management information must be requested explicitly by the manager.

- SNMPv1 allows only primitive support of asynchronous events. There are very few permanent and globally defined traps. The trap mechanism functions only for previously specified events. Supplementary management information is not specified for traps, and traps are not related to MIB definitions of objects that generate them.

- The reliance on connectionless UDP results in the danger of data loss.

Work on proposals aimed at improving SNMPv1 therefore commenced in 1992, and a preliminary version of SNMPv2, including initial prototype implementations (RFC 1441 to 1452), was proposed as a set of draft standards in April 1993. This SNMPv2 version, described later, is also called SNMPv2 Classic or sometimes, because of its party-based security model, SNMPv2p. However, because of the extensive and complicated security mechanisms, the new proposals were not well received in the market. Attempts at simplifying the proposal were undertaken by the SNMPv2 working group in 1994–95 and recorded in draft standards RFC 1902 to 1908 in 1996. Other developments were produced under the names SNMPv2*, SNMPv2u, and SNMPv2c. The last is a version that uses community strings (compare with SNMPv1). SNMPv2u is based on a user-oriented security model, and SNMPv2* attempts to present an approach that is a mixture of v2p and v2u. Needless to say, this proliferation resulted in market confusion.

New PDU types and protocol operations

The new SNMPv2-PDU structure is the same for all SNMPv2 variants. It has the same structure for all protocol operations. The new PDU types *GetBulkRequest, InformRequest,* and *SNMPv2-trap* are particularly singled out for mention. Added to the already existing SNMPv1-PDU types GetRequest, GetNextRequest, GetResponse, and SetRequest, this makes seven PDU types that are available. Another one, the report PDU, is under consideration. *GetBulk* requires only one call for

Get-bulk-operation

a readout of a whole table (or parts of a table). The purpose of this PDU is to minimize the number of protocol exchanges required to retrieve a very large amount of management information. This means it takes only one PDU to be executed instead of the previously necessary sequence of lexicographically ordered GetNextRequest PDUs. One GetBulk identifies the max-repetitions and is handled by the agent as though that number of GetNext's had been received in sequence. This means that the GetBulkRequest operation uses the same selection principle as the GetNextRequest operation. That is, selection is always of the next object in lexicographic order. The difference now is that multiple lexicographic successors can be selected. In essence, GetBulk works as follows. It includes a list of (N+R) variable names in the variable-binding list. For each of the first N names, retrieval is done in the same fashion as for GetNext; for each of the last R names, multiple lexicographic successors are returned. The GetBulk is controlled by two fields: nonrepeaters (the number of variables for which a single lexicographic successor is to be returned) and max-repetitions (the number of successors to be returned for the remaining variables in the variable-binding list that has the length L). The following holds: $N = \max(\min(\text{nonrepeaters}, L), 0)$; $M = \max(\text{max repetitions}, 0)$; and $R = L - N$. The total number of variable-binding pairs that can be produced is $N + (M \times R)$.

The InformRequest PDU is used for manager-to-manager communication (not agent-to-manager). All PDU types, including the trap

PDU, now have a uniform syntactical basic structure. Compared to SNMPv1, the new PDUs offer much more diversity in the error codes.

The controversy surrounding the entire version 2 development centers on the security concept. There was an interest in countering the security deficiencies mentioned in section 6.3—masquerades, information modification, message stream modification, disclosure. Although the security concepts of SNMPv2 were not successful, they will be described here because the same problems exist as before. Even if an accepted standard fails to incorporate an adequate security specification, this has to be considered relevant as far as actual implementations are concerned because of the impact on the security of management. Although SNMPv2p has now been classified as historic, it is the SNMPv2 variant that offers the most comprehensive security concept. It uses the following security mechanisms:

Extensive security concept with authentication and encryption for SNMPv2p variant

- The data encryption standard (DES) is applied as the encryption cipher algorithm.

- Packet source and content authentication is implicit through the use of a shared secret key based on the MD5 (message digest no. 5) algorithm.

- A time stamp procedure using weakly synchronized clocks is offered. This enables the monitoring of sequences that are out of order (i.e., prevents replay attacks) and also offers clock synchronization.

These three mechanisms allow the implementation of three different security levels that are activated in accordance with the relevant management transaction per the coding in the SNMPv2 message:

- No authentication; no encryption (`nonsecure`)

- Authentication using MD5; no encryption (`not private` or `confidential`)

- MD5 authentication; DES encryption (`authenticated, private`)

The security-relevant context, called party, of an SNMPv2p entity must always be entered in the header of an SNMP message for the sender and the receiver (compare Figure 6.10). Different parties can be used between the same manager and agent to define authorized views of particular MIBs or objects. An SNMPv2p message contains the format fields privDst, authinfo, dstParty, srcParty, and context in front of the actual SNMPv2 PDU. *dstParty* and *srcParty* contain the security-relevant role (context, party) of the receiver or the sender. *Context* indicates the MIB view (section of the MIB). *Authinfo* provides

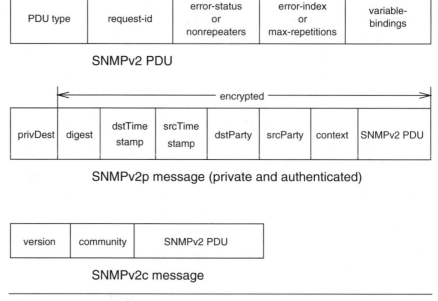

Figure 6.10
Structure of an SNMPv2 PDU and SNMPv2 message

information (e.g., digest, time stamp) that is relevant to the authentication protocol. *PrivDst* repeats the object identifier of dstParty. If encryption (privacy) is selected, then all fields of the SNMPv2p message except privDst are coded using DES. Refer to RFCs 1445 to 1447 or to [STA96] for information on how security procedures are actually carried out.

The controversy over security (e.g., complexity of implementation and administration, limitation to single authentication and encryption algorithm was considered too weak but required for export) is avoided in SNMPv2c although it also uses SNMPv2 PDUs (compare Figure 6.10) to take advantage of the new protocol operations. The security provisions in the SNMPv2 message of this variant are limited to the community string familiar from SNMPv1.

The SNMPv2c variant uses the community string for security

The last modification to version 2 that deserves mention is the one to the organizational model. As illustrated in Figure 6.1, SNMPv1 incorporates only manager-to-agent communication. It has long been recognized that substructures are required for the management of large networks in order to keep certain activities as local as possible. Version 2 supports hierarchical management structures (compare Figure 4.4). Managed nodes can have a dual role (dual-mode nodes)—as managers for nodes at a lower level in the hierarchy and simultaneously as agents

Introduction of intermediate managers and manager-to-manager communication to a superior manager. The manager-to-manager MIB (M2M-MIB) and inform-PDU were developed to enable this communication between managers. However, as a result of subsequent developments, M2M-MIB has achieved the status of historic and therefore is not currently valid.

It should be obvious from the discussion that SNMPv1 and SNMPv2 are not interoperable. This fact and the complicated security mechanisms that impact the implementation and time budget of agents are the reasons why SNMPv2—despite existing products—has not yet been successful in the market; only very few firms have supported SNMPv2p or the later SNMPv2c. The market is waiting for the standardization of SNMPv3 to be completed (see section 6.5). Yet the expanded SMIv2 information model is being widely used already. Coexistence with SNMPv1 is essential for a migration strategy to SNMPv2; this is dealt with by RFC 1908. The latter recommends two solutions for protecting SNMP investments: a proxy agent or managers that can cope with both versions (bilingual managers). Recommendations are also available for bilingual agents (RFC 2089).

6.4   Remote Monitoring MIBs

The remote monitoring (RMON) standard was developed on the basis of experience gained with proprietary network probes. Probes are measurement logging components used to monitor LAN traffic in different LAN segments; the logged values are then fed to an evaluator component, usually a LAN analyzer. A certain amount of data preprocessing can take place in the probes.

The RMON-MIB (RFC 1757) describes the managed objects of a standardized remote network monitoring device and to a certain extent represents an abstraction of a probe. The demands placed by its objects on the supporting agents are higher than those of a standard MIB II because RMON also defines the results of statistical calculations as managed objects. In this sense, RMON can be interpreted as the first extension of Internet management in the direction of OSI systems management functions. The network traffic resulting from polling is reduced somewhat because of the additional preprocessing that takes place in the agents. Furthermore, the quantity of SNMP-standardized manageable resources increases due to the RMON-MIB because RMON is particularly oriented toward LAN supervision, thus also below the IP layer. So long as sufficient agent resources are available, supervisory data can continue to be collected even if the SNMP connection to the

The RMON-MIB represents a standardized probe

manager is broken off. Moreover, in principle, RMON agents can be managed by more than one manager.

We are describing the RMON-MIBs in detail because of their important function in actual network management compared to the other MIBs mentioned at the end of section 6.2.1. RMON is the first standard to provide more flexible monitoring. It also illustrates a kind of functional model defined for use with SNMP.

The RMON-MIB is subtree mib-2.16 in the Internet registration tree

The RMON-MIB (RFC 1757) occupies subtree 16 below structural node MIB II (i.e., node 1.3.6.1.2.16) in the Internet registration tree and consists of ten MIB groups (see Figure 6.11). The RMON2-MIB (RFC 2021), which was developed later, currently consists of additional groups that are attached as additional subtrees below mib-2.16; the first ten groups are also referred to as RMON1. Overall, RMON comprises more than 200 managed objects. All RMON groups are optional, which means that "RMON-conformant" products do not have to support all groups. This is taken into account when interoperability is being considered for heterogeneous environments. However, certain dependencies exist: the `event group` is a prerequisite of the `alarm group`; the `filter group` is necessary for the `packetCapture group`; and the `hostTopN group` needs the `host group`.

The RMON-MIB consists of ten MIB groups

The `statistics group` supplies the following management information (per segment): number of packets, bytes, broadcasts, multicasts and their distribution, information about lost packets, and five other error types (e.g., collisions, CRC errors, packets that are too small or too large). Some of the same parameters also exist in the interface group of MIB II, but there they relate to individual devices, whereas the focus here is on traffic load and the error rates of LAN segments. The granularity of the collected data depends, of course, on the quality of the underlying LAN attachment units.

The `history group` provides the basis for a trend analysis that allows the recording of monitoring information from the statistics group. Monitoring frequency and measurement intervals for individual interfaces are specified in the `controlTable`. The results are then filed in other tables (`historyTable`). Table management (conventions, arithmetic, changes and deletions to the table rows) in the SNMP area is very complicated and cannot be covered in detail in this book. We direct you to the original documents (RFCs 1757 and 2021) or to the literature (e.g., [STA96]). There is some analogy to the OSI summarization function.

The `alarm group` uses threshold analyses to define alarms. A hysteresis mechanism referring to absolute and relative changes in measurement values is specified using the upper and lower threshold values

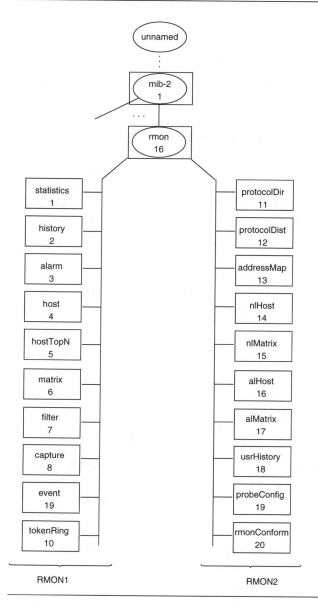

Figure 6.11
RMON-MIB

assigned to individual measurement values (load values, error rates). The alarms are then transmitted in trap notifications from SNMP to the manager.

For each host initiating network traffic in the segment, the `host group` contains statistical information derived from the monitoring of

MAC addresses in the packets. The host group (see Figures 6.12 and 6.13; the latter taken from [STA96]) for its part consists of tables. A control table (`hostControlTable`) defines which hosts are to be monitored and the measurement period. The `hostTable` contains the measurement data (e.g., packets sent or received, broadcasts, defective packets) organized according to MAC addresses, whereas the `hostTimeTable` essentially contains the same information but organized by the time when it originated.

The `hostTopN` group enables statistics to be obtained from those hosts that maintain statistics lists on projected measurement values. Yet this evaluation is carried out by the agent and not by the manager for the projected measurement interval, thereby producing a reduction in SNMP traffic.

The `matrix group` allows direction-related traffic matrices to be established for the source–sink pairs of MAC addresses (i.e., the hosts).

The `filter group` provides for the definition and application of filters (i.e., the conditions for recording packets). Data filters specify packet selection on the basis of bit patterns in the packets; status filters define the selection using status information such as CRC errors and packet length violations. Complex filter conditions can be formulated using condition expressions (AND/OR expressions). A packet stream that successfully passes a filter test is called a *channel*. It is possible for counters and events to be associated with a channel. There is some functional analogy to an ISO discriminator.

The `packetCapture group` permits the definition per channel of buffer hierarchies for the packet streams received from the filters.

Lastly, the `event group` supports the definition of events that, if necessary, trigger actions that are defined elsewhere in the MIB. The conditions for the events could also be defined in other RMON-MIB groups.

As mentioned earlier, the RMON-MIB was originally developed for Ethernet LANs. RFC 1513 contains extensions for Token Ring LANs (IEEE 802.5) that include the addition of specific table objects in the statistics and history groups and in the supplementary tokenRing group.

RMON2 extends the original RMON-MIB to include ten more groups

Whereas RMON1 primarily carries out a protocol analysis of OSI levels 1 and 2, RMON2 (RFC 2021) extends this analysis to include levels 3–7. This extended analysis improves the monitoring of the internetworking as well as of the application level (email, file transfer, WWW) because important information for the manager is already processed on the RMON agent, in other words, on remote systems. Further, the agent can process data that represents more closely a

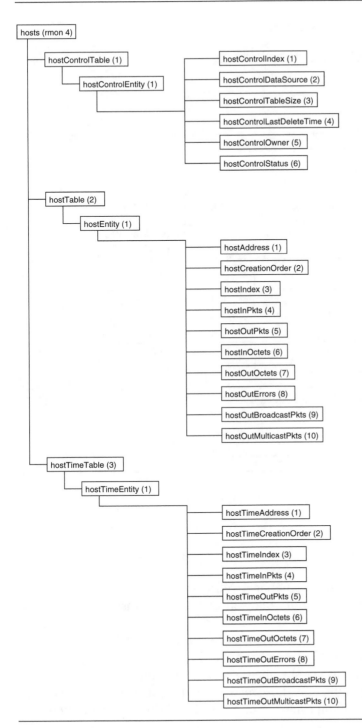

Figure 6.12
Host group of RMON

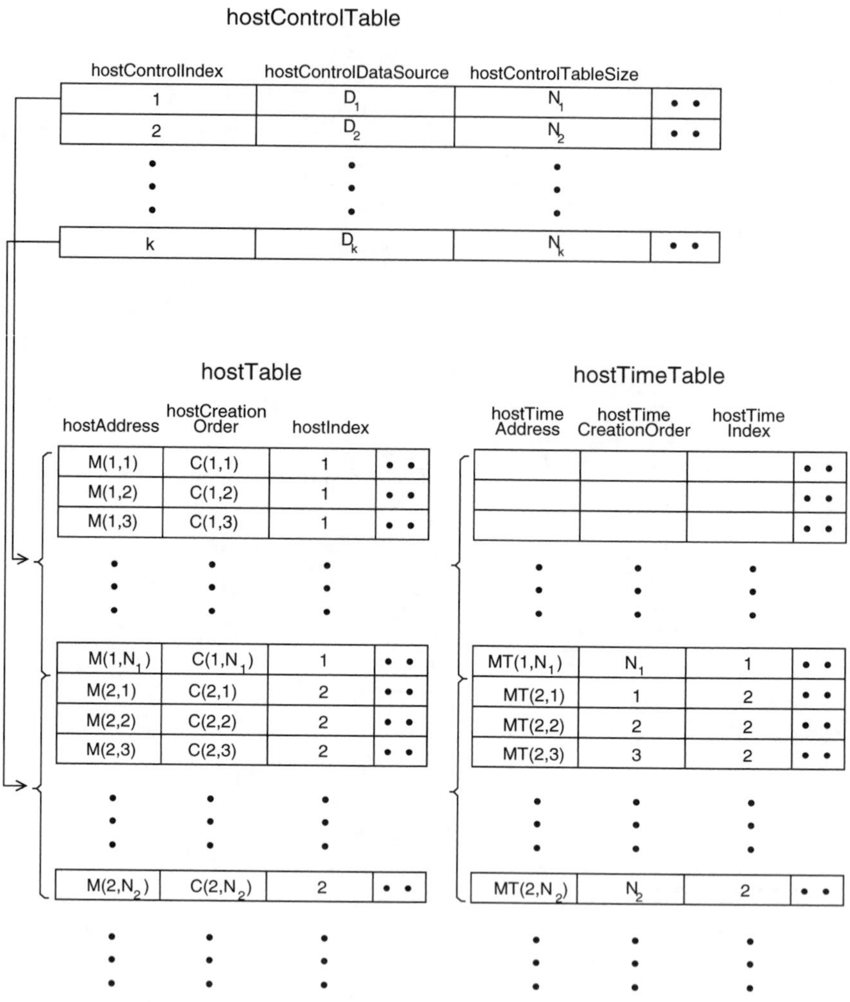

hostControlTable

hostControlIndex	hostControlDataSource	hostControlTableSize	
1	D_1	N_1	• •
2	D_2	N_2	• •
•	•	•	
•	•	•	
•	•	•	
k	D_k	N_k	• •

hostTable

hostAddress	hostCreation Order	hostIndex	
$M(1,1)$	$C(1,1)$	1	• •
$M(1,2)$	$C(1,2)$	1	• •
$M(1,3)$	$C(1,3)$	1	• •
•	•	•	
•	•	•	
•	•	•	
$M(1,N_1)$	$C(1,N_1)$	1	• •
$M(2,1)$	$C(2,1)$	2	• •
$M(2,2)$	$C(2,2)$	2	• •
$M(2,3)$	$C(2,3)$	2	• •
•	•	•	
•	•	•	
•	•	•	
$M(2,N_2)$	$C(2,N_2)$	2	• •

hostTimeTable

hostTime Address	hostTime CreationOrder	hostTime Index	
			• •
			• •
			• •
•	•	•	
•	•	•	
•	•	•	
$MT(1,N_1)$	N_1	1	• •
$MT(2,1)$	1	2	• •
$MT(2,2)$	2	2	• •
$MT(2,3)$	3	2	• •
•	•	•	
•	•	•	
•	•	•	
$MT(2,N_2)$	N_2	2	• •

Figure 6.13
Example of hostTables

temporal "snapshot." A manager retrieving data, even with GetBulk, has only data that is not collected at the same instant and can be difficult to relate.

Compared to RMON1, RMON2 offers more flexibility in the use of tables. First, external objects can also be used as index types when object type macros are specified; second, time filters are available for indexing. As a result, only those measurement values that have changed since the last polling cycle are addressed and then transmitted to the manager.

RMON2 extends RMON by ten further MIB groups (11–20) below the Internet structural node mib-2.rmon (see Figure 6.11).

The `protocolDir group` lists in a table all the protocols that can be monitored by the agent. The group also supplies information about monitored protocol parameters, PDU structures, and so forth.

One of the tasks of the `protocolDistribution group` is to collect protocol-related statistical data about packets. This enables bandwidths to be established according to the respective layer.

The `addressMap` contains mappings between MAC and network addresses and supports the generation of topology maps and autodiscovery.

The `nlHost group` keeps track of the network traffic (especially IP traffic) related to a specific network address (IP address), allowing the requested data to be made available over an appropriate control table. The `nlMatrix group` incorporates the traffic matrix at the network level. The `alHost` and `alMatrix groups` are the groups for the application layer that can be queried for specific management information relating to certain hosts and in accordance with application protocols supported by the `protocolDir group`.

The `usrHistory group` permits application-specific data to be collected and stored with the assistance of the alarm and history groups.

The `probeConfig` and `rmonConformance groups` describe information that is needed in order to evaluate and manage the interoperability of RMON implementations. This includes knowledge about the MIB groups supported by agents and the values of the configuration parameters for the probes as RMON agents.

Compared to the MIBs outlined in earlier sections of the book, the RMON-MIB is all and all considerably more advanced when it comes to the important task of remote network monitoring. But it has to be borne in mind that RMON is standardized only for Ethernet and Token Ring but not, for example, for Fast Ethernet or FDDI. The RMON-MIB offers a number of advantages such as a reduction in network traffic, data preprocessing, proactive management, offline data entry, and the availability of several managers for the RMON agents. The prerequisite is that the probes are well placed in the network. The advantages are offset by complicated table management and the need for complex agents. As a consequence, dedicated devices may be needed to cope with this aspect. However, a number of network components (such as hubs and switches, or even interface cards for PCs) already integrate RMON agents, but often only the first four groups (statistics, history, hostTable, alarm) are supported. Any evaluation of RMON products

Evaluation of RMON

must take into account the number of supported RMON groups, the maximum number of nodes that can be monitored, necessary CPU and storage capacity for filtering, the recording and storage of traffic information, packet throughput (maximum clearance time), and which RMON applications are available on a specific management platform. The latter applies to follow-up procedures for RMON data; these particularly include procedures for demand assessment, QoS management, capacity planning, and reporting systems. Although RMON probes are capable of collecting all types of data, the managers are responsible for all management-relevant responses through the use of appropriate applications.

6.5   SNMP Version 3 and Other Developments

SNMPv3 as convergence of SNMP proposals

There have been various efforts in recent years to integrate a new security concept and other improvements into Internet management. Owing to a considerable difference of opinion within the SNMPv2 working group, no final proposals have yet been drawn up. Since 1997, the SNMPv3 working group has been working toward a convergence of previous proposals. Since the work is still ongoing, we can present only some of the known objectives.

The goal of the working group is to produce a uniform security and management framework for SNMP that will enable the implementation of a secure "set," in other words, a secure controlling management, using the simplest means possible and incorporating modularity for adaptability to different areas of application. Modularity and coexistence are required to enable agents to operate several different security models, encryption mechanisms, and SNMP message formats simultaneously and to allow the replacement or expansion of agent modules. It has now been recognized that a static allocation of management functionality is not useful against the background of the functional diversity and dynamics of management requirements, and that this kind of approach is also not scalable. These considerations also dictate that it should be possible to apply a modular structure to an MIB so that the modules can more readily be used to deal with processing needs, specifically that they can be allocated to management-relevant functional areas. This is another case where an object-oriented approach would be more effective in satisfying the respective requirements!

The current results of the working group have been compiled in the overview document "An Architecture for Describing SNMP Management Frameworks" (RFC 2271). The architecture presented is modular

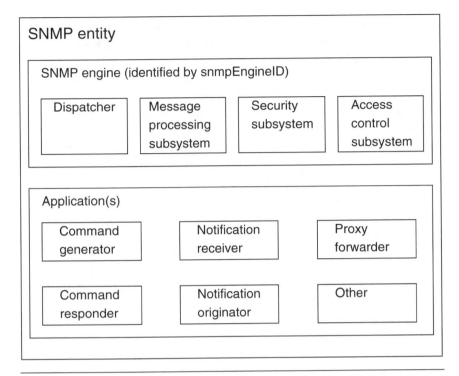

Figure 6.14
Structure of an SNMPv3 entity

and flexible in structure, enabling it to incorporate other standard developments. At the core and consisting of several subsystems is an *SNMPEngine* on which all different kinds of SNMP applications can be run (Figure 6.14). The subsystems in turn each consist of different modules capable of coexisting with one another.

The SNMP management system developed within this new SNMPv3 framework overall consists of:

- Several nodes each with an SNMP entity containing a *notification originator* and a *command responder* application. These correspond to the previous agents.

- At least one SNMP entity that contains a *command generator* or a *notification receiver* application. This corresponds to the traditional manager.

- A management protocol for exchanging information between SNMP entities.

It is obvious that the fundamental structure is the same for all SNMP entities, irrespective of whether their traditional role has been that of a manager, a midlevel manager, a proxy, or an agent.

The engine consists of a dispatcher and the message processing, security, and access control subsystems. The *dispatcher* coordinates internal communication between the subsystems and is able to differentiate between the different modules coexisting within a subsystem. It directs incoming PDUs to the correct applications and maps outgoing PDUs to the appropriate underlying transport systems. The dispatcher provides applications with a service interface for which a whole range of service primitives has been specified.

The SNMP engine is the basic system for all SNMP entities

The *message processing subsystem* handles incoming and outgoing SNMP messages. In so doing, it supports a number of coexisting modules each corresponding to a different message format or protocol version (e.g., SNMPv3, SNMPv1, SNMPv2c). The fact that modules can be replaced or added lays the migration groundwork for future protocol developments (RFC 2272).

The *access control subsystem* deals with issues controlling access to MIB objects and the corresponding access rights. This is another area where there is fundamentally support for more than one module; the standard module is based on the view-based access control model, for which modularized MIBs are a prerequisite (RFC 2275). This is a functional replacement for SNMPv2 parties.

The *security subsystem* also is designed to allow for the coexistence of different security modules that are controlled by the message processing subsystem. For example, one module could be based on SNMPv1 communities; another could implement the user-based security model (USM, RFC 2274) approach preferred by SNMPv3. The USM attempts to answer the following questions: Is the SNMP message genuine as well as on time, and who is requesting the SNMP operation? The USM therefore concerns itself with the threats "modification of information," "message stream modification," "masquerade," and "disclosure," but not with "denial of service" or "traffic analysis." The user for whom a security-relevant service is provided is called the "principal"; this user is identified by a *userName* that is mapped to a *securityName*. Hash functions first transform user passwords into nonlocal codes; from this code each SNMP engine is able to extrapolate its own local code (public and private keys) for the user. The USM also specifies algorithms for key update and authentication. Two protocols are defined for the latter: MD5 and secure hash algorithm (SHA, FIPS-PUP 180-1). Perhaps this will be replaced by the use of IPSEC. As with SNMPv2, loosely synchronized clocks are used to monitor the timeliness of SNMP messages. DES is used for data encryption.

The *applications* in Figure 6.14 are management-relevant applications. In particular, these also contain the basic applications for an SNMP entity that are linked to the SNMP operations. For example, the SNMP operations SET and GET then are forwarded to the command responder application. This then has local access to different contexts supported by different MIB modules (RFC 2273).

Overall, SNMPv3 promises to be a flexible framework that will allow previous as well as new Internet management versions to coexist within one management architecture. Owing to the importance of compatibility, the SNMPv3 working group has also addressed this issue in a separate Internet draft document, "Coexistence Between Version 1, Version 2, and Version 3 of the Internet Standard Network Management Framework" (August 1998).

Another new approach that promotes flexible and dynamic agent structures is *agentX*, which was covered at the end of section 6.2.

AgentX development

New developments are also evident in another area. In section 4.4, we mentioned that a static allocation of management functionality is not appropriate for very large and dynamically distributed systems because of the lack of scalability. We referred to the development of management by delegation. The DISMAN working group is also looking at this concept for use in the Internet world. An Internet draft *Distributed Management Framework* has been drawn up by the group. To the DISMAN group, distributed management does not mean management functionality distributed in a statically set way according to one of the different possible forms of arrangement, but something that is "movable." This approach will allow the "distributed management" application to keep pace (scalability) with the changing needs of large distributed systems. This kind of dynamic adaptability is also optimal for dealing with changes in conditions (such as organizational changes and changed processes).

DISMAN—a concept for management by delegation

The idea behind the DISMAN framework is that the manager as the "DISMAN user" turns over jobs backed up with "credentials" to a "distributed manager" that executes the applications in a distributed form in entities called "management targets." A number of relevant services are recommended for, among other things, domain formation, describing management targets, and the safe delegation of credentials and their control. Domains are groups of systems that are subject to a management policy according to certain criteria. A description of the target systems of a delegation is required to enable criteria to be applied in determining whether a target system is even in a position to carry out a particular task. The function of "credentials" is precisely as the name implies, and these are indispensable for security. Lastly, the delegated task itself must be described in a script language and its actual delegation controlled as a management action.

DISMAN-MIBs   Proposals for several related MIBs already exist. Among these are DISMAN-SERVICES-MIB, TARGET-MIB (to express targets for traps and script transfer), EVENT-MIB (based on the RMON alarm and event groups and intended as a replacement of those groups; it is also the successor and update of the SNMPv2's manager-to-manager MIB), Notification LOG-MIB, Expression MIB (to provide custom objects for the EVENT MIB), Schedule MIB (definitions of MOs for scheduling management operations), Remote Operations MIB, and SCRIPT-MIB (defines a standard interface for the delegation of management functions based on the Internet management framework; this comprises capabilities to transfer management scripts; for initiating, suspending, resuming, and terminating scripts; to transfer arguments and results; and to monitor and control running scripts). The respective documents have the status "Internet draft" (i.e., working papers of the IETF and its working groups, published in the last quarter of 1998). They are not yet standardized, but these efforts signal the first step the Internet has taken toward implementing management as a dynamically distributed application.

It is still not clear whether the high implementation cost will have an effect on the acceptance of the powerful DISMAN concept. It is also not definite whether DISMAN will require an SNMPv3 implementation or can also be used in SNMPv1 environments.

Internet management is undisputedly the dominant management architecture in the data communications world, particularly in the LAN and intranet areas. But the original simple concepts also have their limitations in terms of scalability, modeling complex managed objects, and the complexity of intelligent agents. In this respect object-oriented approaches offer definite advantages. But the Internet world is very dynamic, which is also evident from the Internet management concepts currently being developed in many different areas.

Anyone who wants to be kept up-to-date on the developments outlined in this chapter can do so over WWW. The general URL is *http://www.ietf.org/html.charters*. Information on the individual working groups can be obtained by adding */disman-charter.html, agentx-charter.html*, or *snmpv3-charter.html*.

6.6   Chapter Summary

Internet management is dominant in the field of classic data communication networks. The Internet management architecture is conceptually simpler compared to the OSI one.

The information model (SMI) is not truly object oriented; this means that the inheritance principle cannot be used for things like class definitions and allomorphism in the specification of managed objects. The Internet information model is oriented toward data type. The data types (referred to as object types) permitted for management information are simple ASN.1 data types or tables. The Internet MOs are specified as object types (grouped in MIBs) in the leaves of the Internet registration tree. The object entities (managed objects) are accessed through the identifier in the registration tree. The registration tree expresses only partial containment relationships. Agent MIBs implement entities of sections from the Internet MIBs. The object types are described on the basis of simple ASN.1 macros. MIB II is currently the standard MIB. A range of technology-specific MIBs as well as a large number of manufacturer-specific MIBs are also available. Although most MIBs have been oriented toward network management, MIBs are now increasingly available for systems and applications management.

RMON was introduced in order to take advantage of the increasing processing capability of agents, to handle the preprocessing of management information in agents, and to relieve the workload on the network and the management system. RMON allows management data to be collected and evaluated in agents on a table-controlled basis. To a degree, RMON thereby carries out the tasks handled by some of the systems management functions (SMFs) in OSI.

There are two versions of the Internet SMI. Version 2 adds several new subtrees to the registration tree. The macro that is used to define an object type has been changed slightly. Overall SMIv2 offers advancements in the modeling of management information. The formalization of row status allows table lines to be added or deleted (a rough and limited analogy to CMIS M-Create/M-Delete). The refinement of table lines that is possible has a slight analogy to ISO inheritance. The inclusion of text conventions allows a more formal specification of behavior and permits the reusability of specifications. SMIv2 is therefore the only version being used in new documents.

The Internet communication model defines the management protocol SNMP that provides access to agent MIBs. The use of simple operations enables read (get) or write (set) access to values of object instances. GetNext can be used to browse through MIBs or tables. In version 1, data access by the manager consists of atomic operations with the response providing either all the data requested or none of it. There are few predefined traps that the agents are able to send asynchronously. These traps have been defined for SNMP, and in contrast to OSI notifications, they cannot be defined as object specific. SNMP version 1 is not a truly secure protocol; the community strings it uses are "clear text" passwords. SNMP version 2 offers many different variants of SNMP messages that differ from one another in the security features offered. The now standardized PDU structure, which also includes a trap PDU, is common to all the variants. GetBulk is a new PDU type and allows large quantities of management information to be requested and transmitted in a single operation. (However, the new PDU is not able to offer the flexibility of CMIS scoping and filtering.) Because of the success of SNMPv1 and because of the discrepancies existing in its security concept, SNMPv2 has not been able to make an impact on the market.

New developments in the Internet management environment are focusing on a general and flexible protocol platform for the coexistence of SNMP variants (SNMP engine of SNMPv3) and the aspect of management by delegation (DISMAN). However, none of these developments has been standardized as of yet.

CORBA as a Management Architecture

In contrast to the other architectures that have been mentioned, the OMG (see section 2.3.2) approach is not specifically oriented toward the management of DP infrastructures. In principle, it is designed for all distributed applications. Recently, however, it has become an important architecture in the integrated management area, particularly because products used in the management of end systems and applications are or will be based on OMG technology. The aim is to have *one single* architecture for the development, use, and management of distributed systems. This means that there is no longer a fundamental difference between management applications and other applications in development; the same methods can be applied to modeling both user and management data. To some extent, even some of the same tools can be used, thus canceling out the need for as many special management development tools and improving the efficiency and cost-effectiveness of the development process overall. Furthermore, the user and management data of an application is transmitted via the same mechanism; you only have to acquire one communications system and then install and maintain it.

CORBA is becoming an important architecture for management applications

This chapter presents an overview of *object management architecture* (OMA). Section 7.1 outlines the different components of the architecture and their interrelationships. The other sections then discuss the most important components in more detail. Section 7.2 deals with the information model of OMA, specifically, the object model and the interface definition language (IDL), and then leads into the communication model that specifies the communication system for objects (the object request broker) and protocols between ORBs in section 7.3. The OMA organizational model is described in section 7.4. Sections 7.5 (CORBA Services), 7.6 (CORBA Facilities and Systems Management Facilities), and 7.7 (Domain Interfaces) explain the OMA functional model. Section 7.8 contains an assessment of OMA as an architecture for network and system management.

The standards and documents referenced in these chapters are all available over *http://www.omg.org*. [ORH98], [VOD97], [MOR97], [SIE96], [OPR96], and [OHE96] provide further information on OMA and CORBA.

7.1   Object Management Architecture

The object management architecture (OMA) for distributed object-oriented programming (see Figure 2.9), first published in 1992, provides a framework that primarily allows a location-transparent cooperation of objects in a heterogeneous environment.

CORBA: the
core of OMA

Several different subarchitectures and specifications have been defined within this framework. The *common object request broker architecture* (CORBA) described in the following section forms the core of the framework. It specifies all the submodels of a management architecture as described in Chapter 4, except for the functional model.

In addition to the ORB, OMA specifies four categories of object interfaces that enable access to different categories of services. Section 7.1.2 outlines the basic characteristics and relationships of these object interfaces.

The OMA is constantly being expanded and improved by the OMG. The OMG is an industrial consortium with more than 800 members that was founded by eight companies in 1989. It is organized into task forces for specific areas. If a task force feels that a particular subject area could be important enough to be examined and standardized by the OMG, it publishes a so-called *request-for-information* to which it also accepts responses from nonmembers. If, after having evaluated the responses, the task force concludes that there is a concrete requirement for a detailed specification, it formulates a *request for proposal* on the basis of the responses and sends it to the members. The proposal contains detailed requirements of the technology being developed. A member company responds with a *letter of intent* if it plans to submit a proposal for a solution. This is followed by concrete proposals on technology that are then evaluated by the task force. Finally, the members take a vote on the proposals. The process is completed once a particular proposal reaches the required quorum and is then published as an OMG specification. In practice, there is much work done between request-for-proposal responses and published specification, as submissions are merged and modified to meet the requirements.

7.1.1   CORBA

An object request broker (ORB) is an infrastructure component that mediates interactions between client applications that require services and the server applications that provide these services. It establishes the client–server relationships between objects. If an ORB is used, the client object can invoke a method on a server object with total transparency, irrespective of whether this object is located on the same computer or on another computer in the network. The ORB receives the request and is then responsible for locating the server object, transferring the parameters, invoking the method, and delivering the results. It is therefore often also referred to as an "object bus."

ORB: infrastructure component for client–server communication

CORBA introduces components that not only support the interaction of objects with the ORB but are also needed for the communication between different ORBs in a hetergeneous environment over so-called inter-ORB protocols. This standard therefore defines the OMA *communication model*.

CORBA defines the OMA communication model

A common open object concept is required for the interaction between objects in a heterogeneous environment. CORBA therefore specifies a fundamental object model and with the interface definition language, the syntax for describing the object interfaces. CORBA therefore also defines the OMA *information model*. The same model is used to define IDL interfaces for higher-level objects used in the OMA functional model (i.e., CORBAservices and CORBAfacilities).

CORBA object model and IDL: the OMA information model

The interoperability architecture, a subarchitecture of CORBA, introduces a domain concept as well as concepts for bridging domain boundaries. In other words, it also refines the OMA *organizational model*, the core of which is fundamentally based on a symmetric cooperation of equal objects.

CORBA interoperability architecture: central component of the OMA organizational model

The specifications and components defined by the communication, organizational, information, and functional OMA submodels are summarized as an overview in Figure 7.1.

7.1.2   Categories of Object Interfaces

In addition to the ORB, the OMA includes the following four categories of object interfaces:

- The *common object services specification*, the standard for *CORBAservices*, forms the heart of the OMA functional model. CORBAservices supply the basic functionality needed to enable a system and the objects to be used effectively in a distributed environment.

CORBAservices: the lower layer of the OMA functional model

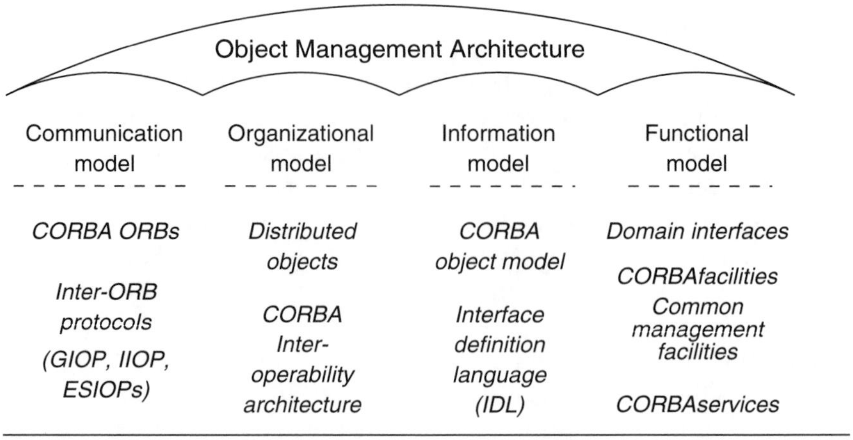

Figure 7.1
OMA submodels

Different types of services are available, including those for instantiating objects, naming, and providing permanent storage for objects as well as for receiving and sending event messages. CORBAservices are standardized by the OMG. It is mandatory for CORBA-compliant systems to adhere to these standards. Until now, 15 object services have been specified; others are currently in the process of being standardized.

CORBAfacilities for systems management: management services in OMA

■ The second layer of the OMA functional model is formed by *CORBAfacilities*. In principle, these provide universally applicable services for all applications. The *common facilities architecture* identifies the following areas as those from which these services originate or will be originating for the first phase of the definition process: user interface, information management, systems management, and task management. On the one hand, CORBAfacilities, like CORBAservices, are subject to standardization by the OMG, but, on the other hand, they are optional and not mandatory for implementations. CORBAfacilities for the systems management area therefore enable the integration of management services into the OMA. Until now, these services have been primarily specified by the X/Open Systems Management Working Group (XoTGsysMan).

Domain interfaces: services for special applications areas

■ *Domain interfaces* are services of the highest layer below the actual applications themselves. They are usually designed for use in special areas of application (domains) such as health care and the financial world. Frequently also referred to as business objects, some of them are to be standardized by the OMG but, of course, will not be mandatory for implementations.

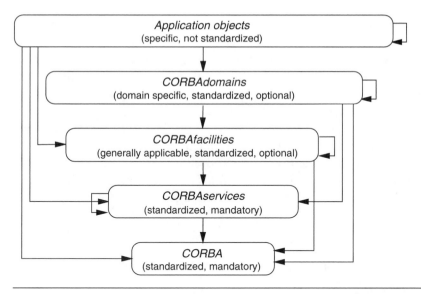

Figure 7.2
Support relationships between services and application objects

- Although *application objects*—the objects that execute the actual applications (e.g., a CASE tool) or even management applications—are considered in the OMA, they have not been standardized by the OMG. Therefore, they do not constitute an independent subarchitecture of the OMA.

The first three categories listed define the functionality that is available in principle to all applications, particularly even to management applications. These categories offer the flexibility required for the delegation of functions and represent the OMA *functional model*.

OMA: layered functional model

Support relationships that exist between the services of the different categories and the application objects can be modeled appropriately through the use of object-oriented techniques. These are presented in Figure 7.2.

CORBAservices supply the *basis* for the support relationships by providing the *elementary* functions that even enable objects to be used in a CORBA environment. CORBAfacilities are based on these services and increase the scope of their functions. They can, for example, either use the CORBAservices or inherit and adapt the properties and operations of the interfaces of the CORBAservices. Similarly, domain interfaces can be based on the interfaces of CORBAservices and CORBAfacilities, or they can be derived from them. This is the way, for example, the notification service (see section 7.7.1) is based on the event service (see section 7.5.1) and extends and refines it. Support relationships can also exist between objects belonging to the same service layer. The interfaces of the application objects then consist of interfaces from CORBAservices and CORBAfacilities, of domain interfaces, and other interfaces.

Boundaries between the categories of the service hierarchy are not fixed

The *boundaries* between application objects, CORBAdomains, CORBAfacilities, and object services are partially *fluid*. Software modules that are frequently used in applications but have not yet been specified as CORBAfacilities are candidates for new CORBAfacilities; likewise, the functionality of CORBAfacilities could be transferred to CORBAservices (i.e., moved to new infrastructure standards and objects).

7.2   Object Model and Interface Definition Language

OMA: object-oriented information model

As the name indicates, the OMG information model is based on an *object-oriented approach*. Because the architecture is not specifically oriented toward network and system management but in principle should support all distributed applications, the information model is also less specific. Unlike OSI or Internet management, it does not define managed objects but instead the fundamental properties of very general objects. For example, operations (such as reading and setting attributes) already offered by other architectures are not specified for objects, and instead only a model is provided that allows the invocation interfaces of the objects to be defined for the cooperation among themselves or for interaction with an object request broker.

OMA information model: core object model and extensions

The *OMA core object model*, which mainly provides design portability for distributed applications, serves as the basis for the information or object model. It defines the object concept, the interfaces, and inheritance and originally supplied the conceptional basis for extensions and refinements in the form of components. The core model combined with one or more components is called a profile. Although in principle several different profiles were conceivable, the only one that exists today is the CORBA-specified use of the core model. No alternative profiles are currently being developed, nor are any expected. We will therefore not differentiate between the core model and the CORBA refinements.

The programming language-independent notation *interface definition language* (IDL) is introduced to describe the invocation interfaces.

It ensures that there is a uniform approach to invoking the operations of objects in a CORBA system. For a cooperation, it is irrelevant which programming language these objects are implemented in, provided a mapping of the IDL exists to the actual implementation language.

IDL: programming language-independent notation for object interfaces

The following sections describe the object model, IDL, and mapping to programming languages in detail.

7.2.1   Object Model

Objects within the OMA are very general models for things and concepts. A differentiation is made between:

OMA differentiates between object reference and object implementation

- The *object implementation* representing the program code that implements the operations that can be carried out on the object
- The *object reference* that represents the identity of an object. This reference is used by clients to address an object when an operation is being invoked

An *operation* is an interaction provided by an object. The *signature* of an operation consists of:

Operations: interaction with objects

- An identifier (the name) of the operation
- The result type
- A (possibly empty) list of parameters

The name, type, and direction are given for each parameter. The directions that are possible are `in`, `out`, or `inout`. Other optional elements of a signature include:

- A list of exceptions
- The keyword `oneway`, which indicates a "best-effort" semantic
- A clause specifying context information that is to be transmitted with the invocation of an operation

The syntax of all these signature elements is IDL. The possible execution *semantics* for operations are "at-most-once" and "best-effort." Both are available at the static and at the dynamic invocation interface (see section 7.3.1). The latter additionally offers a type of invocation referred to as "deferred synchronous," which allows nonblocking invocation.

Execution semantics: at-most-once and best-effort

In contrast to other models where they are provided as a separate concept, the *attributes* of an object are equivalent to a pair of opera-

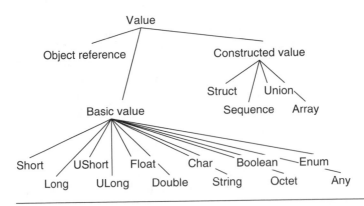

Figure 7.3
Data types in the core object model

tions: a read operation that allows the value of a defined type to be read and a set operation that allows a modification of the value. Attributes can also be declared as `readonly`, in which case only the read operation is available. That is, each attribute defines its own read or read–write interfaces.

Unlike the object models in Smalltalk and Eiffel, the OMA object model incorporates types that are not objects. These are usually referred to as *data types*. Normal basic types for numerical values, characters, and Boolean values are available, along with an abundance of constructed types such as structures, unions, and variable-length sequences (see Figure 7.3).

Interfaces are nonempty sets of signatures for operations, notated with IDL. The interface to an object typically consists of the set of operations possible on an object. Currently, each object has exactly one interface. This limitation will probably be addressed by future versions of CORBA.

Multiple inheritance is possible between interfaces

Interfaces can be in an *inheritance relationship* to one another. If interface A inherits from interface B, then A contains all the operations from B and possibly even others. The object model refers to this as the "substitutability" of interface B by interface A. B can be substituted by A without triggering any "interaction errors." Multiple inheritance between interfaces is possible. It should be emphasized here that the inheritance understandably relates only to the interface definition and not to object implementations, since IDL is only a specification and not a programming language. If a concrete implementation language incorporates inheritance, it is possible that the inheritance of interface definitions can also result in an inheritance of implementations.

The object model itself does not incorporate asynchronous object notifications

The transmission of asynchronous *event messages* by objects is not part of the OMG object model. This is realized through the *object event service* (see section 7.5.1).

7.2.2   Interface Definition Language

IDL is a declarative language. It defines the syntax used to notate the object interfaces described earlier. Major grammatical similarities exist with declarations in C++; however, some of the keywords in IDL are different, and IDL also has supplementary ones. Since this is interface description language, the language naturally does not contain any procedural elements.

IDL: interface definition language, based on C++

IDL contains the following important elements:

- *Constants and data type declarations*: The basic types available include signed or unsigned integers either 16 or 32 bits in length, IEEE single-precision or double-precision floating-point numbers, characters, variable-length strings, Boolean values, octets, and enumeration types. One special basic type is any that is able to express the value of any IDL type. The constructed types comprise unions, sequences, and arrays of basic types.

- *Operations*: Operations are declared in a similar way to C++. The declaration contains the name of the operation, a result type (void in case no result is expected), and a possibly empty list of parameters. The optional raises clause states the exceptions supplied by the operation.

- *Attributes:* Declarations of attributes help to simplify the interface definition. They always represent one pair of operations for reading and setting a certain type of value. The readonly attributes represent only read operations. Modifying operations are not available in this case.

Attribute: short form for a pair of access operations

- *Interface declarations*: These declarations group constant, data type, attribute, and operation declarations into one single interface per object.

- *Module declarations*: These declarations can contain any correct IDL declarations as well as other module declarations. They define scopes for names and are therefore used to structure large declarations and should help in preventing name collisions in the case of reuse of identifiers.

The following example shows a segment from the IDL declaration of the object event service (see section 7.5.1):

```
module CosEventComm {
  exception Disconnected {};
  interface PushConsumer {
    void push(in any data) raises(Disconnected);
    void disconnect_push_consumer();
  };
  interface PushSupplier {
    void disconnect_push_supplier();
  };
  interface PullSupplier {
    any pull() raises(Disconnected);
    any try_pull(out boolean has_event)
      raises(Disconnected);
    void disconnect_pull_supplier();
  };
  interface PullConsumer {
    void disconnect_pull_consumer();
  };
};
```

The module CosEventComm defines an exception and four interfaces (i.e., a supplier and a consumer interface each for the push–pull model). The push consumer interface contains an operation without a result type that allows the transmission of any kind of event message and in some cases supplies the exception defined earlier.

7.2.3   Mapping IDL to Implementation Languages

Today IDL can be mapped to diverse implementation languages

If objects are to cooperate in a heterogeneous environment but their interfaces, although all notated in IDL, are to be implemented in different programming languages, then the *mapping* of IDL to these *languages* must be defined (language binding). Mappings are currently available for the languages C, C++, Smalltalk, Ada, COBOL, and Java.

IDL compilers create stubs specific to particular programming languages from IDL declarations

If, say, an object that produces messages uses the push variant (see section 7.5.1) of the event service, it invokes the operations of the PushConsumer interface of the receiver. An IDL compiler is used for the IDL interface outlined earlier to generate client stubs (see section 7.3.1) in the language in which the object is to be implemented. Based on the stubs, the operations of the receiver can be invoked from the code of the object implementation.

If the pull model is used, the generating object must implement the IDL interface `PullSupplier` itself, thus functioning as a server. This definition is inherited at the interface of the object for this purpose. An IDL compiler generates a server *skeleton* (see section 7.3.2) in the implementation language of the object for the interface operations; the programmer then fills these skeletons with code that implements the operations. The skeletons ensure that operations are invokable by the clients (in this case, by the receiver) that want to fetch an event message.

Using the language Java as an example, the following list presents the mapping of some IDL constructs. Since Java (see [CAW98] or [FLA97]) is an object-oriented language and its object model shares many similarities with the OMA object model, this mapping can often be very direct.

- IDL modules are mapped to Java packages; IDL interfaces to Java interfaces and helper classes.

- Direct equivalents exist in Java for most of the basic types of IDL.

- Enumeration types and unions become Java classes; sequences and fields become Java arrays.

- IDL operations are mapped using Java methods.

- A `readonly` attribute becomes a method for read access to the value of the attribute; `readwrite` attributes become methods for read and modification access.

- IDL exceptions generate special Java exceptions.

The following example shows an excerpt from the IDL interface description for the event service from the Java code generated in section 7.2.2:

```
package CosEventComm;

final public class Disconnected
  extends org.omg.CORBA.UserException {

  public Disconnected() {
  }
}

public interface PushConsumer
  extends org.omg.CORBA.Object {
```

```
public void push(org.omg.CORBA.Any data)
  throws CosEventComm.Disconnected;

public void disconnect_push_consumer();
}
// Interface definitions for additional three IDL
// interfaces follow here
```

7.3   Object Request Brokers and Inter-ORB Protocols

ORB: communications entity for objects

An ORB mediates interactions between client applications that require services and server applications that provide these services. Objects can invoke operations to other objects at the (system) interface to the ORB and obtain results. The ORB accepts the request, forwards it to a suitable object, and then delivers the result to the client once the operation has been completed. It is transparent to the invoking object regardless of whether the invoked object is located on the same or on a different computer in the network.

Supporting components and specifications are required in three areas in order to implement this form of communication (also see Figure 7.4):

■ Clarification is needed on the client side on how operations of remote objects with a known IDL description can be used locally. This requires mechanisms permitting this kind of invocation to be executed from the code in the programming language that is to be used for the implementation of the client (section 7.3.1). This interface is called ORB API.

■ On the server side, the operations of an interface defined using IDL are implemented in a programming language. Mechanisms are required that allow the ORB to invoke these operations on the local server implementations and, in some cases, to receive results that it then forwards to the remote clients (section 7.3.2). The respective component is called an object adapter.

■ If the client and the server are not in the same system or supplied by the same vendor, a protocol for the cooperation of independent ORBs is necessary in heterogeneous environments. These kinds of *inter-ORB protocols* were defined within the framework of version 2 of CORBA; the currently most significant one, the *Internet inter-ORB protocol*, is based on the TCP/IP protocol stack. It is specified

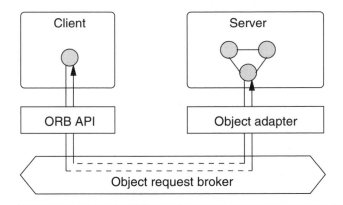

Figure 7.4
Client–server communication with an ORB

as being mandatory for CORBA 2.0–conformant ORBs. This makes this communication model usable in heterogeneous distributed environments (section 7.3.3).

The CORBA standard specifies the mechanisms mentioned as well as protocols for ORBs. Version 1 did not incorporate any provisions for the interoperability between ORBs of different vendors. Version 2 is a superset that provides interoperability, which is essential in integrated management. We will concentrate only on the current version.

CORBA 2.0: interoperable ORBs

On the basis of the three areas outlined, CORBA defines a complete communication channel between client and server, therefore defining the OMA communication model.

CORBA de-fines the OMA communication model

7.3.1   The Client Side of CORBA

CORBA specifies the following infrastructure components for the interaction between the client objects and the ORB, therefore the ORB API (Figure 7.5):

- *Client IDL stubs* provide the static invocation interface to objects and the services they offer. The methods and parameters are specified already at the time of *translation* through the use of IDL. The stubs are generated by IDL compilers from the IDL descriptions. They also contain code for so-called data marshaling, which is a transformation of methods and their parameters into a syntax that is suitable for transmission to a server. This kind of stub is required for each interface of a server object that is used. In the view of

Client IDL stubs: static invocation interfaces

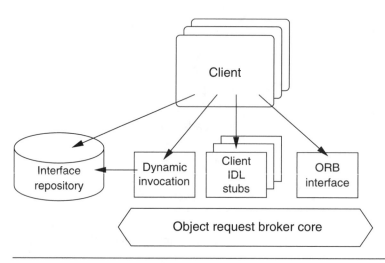

Figure 7.5
Components of the client side of CORBA

the client, invocations of IDL operations are local invocations; the interface acts as the local proxy for a remote object. The name service (see section 7.5.2) allows names to be resolved to object references that are used in invocations.

DII: dynamic invocation interface

- With the *dynamic invocation interface*, methods and their parameters that are to be invoked do not have to be determined until the *runtime*. CORBA defines appropriate programming interfaces that allow method specifications for the server object to be extracted from the interface repository, method invocations to be generated with their parameter lists, invocations to be executed, and results obtained. Management applications using the dynamic invocation interface do not necessarily have to be changed when the interfaces of the server objects change. The price to be paid for this flexibility is a complicated implementation mechanism for client invocations since one or more requests to the interface repository are needed before each invocation.

Interface repository: metadata

- The *interface repository* contains interface signatures for the registered objects in IDL notation, called *metadata*. A programming interface enables this metadata to be stored and accessed.

ORB interface: helpful for using the ORB

- The *ORB interface* supplies certain functions that are generally useful for applications, such as conversion of object references into strings and the reverse, access to metadata from the interface repository, and provision of implementation information on objects based on their object references.

In the narrower sense, an ORB, usually referred to as an *object request broker core*, accepts and analyzes the requests and their parameters received by way of the invocation interface. It identifies the code that implements the referenced object and transfers the parameters and assigns control to the object implementation (see following section).

The CORBA framework allows implementers of management applications to choose between the static invocation interface, which is easier and faster to use, and the dynamic one, which is more flexible but also more complex. This flexibility is one of the major advantages of using CORBA for management tools. For example, consider the case that a generic management application like an MIB browser has to use MIBs that were not yet known when the application was compiled. The dynamic invocation interface allows the implementation of this application in a way that it does not have to be recompiled to be able to use these new MIBs.

If an acceptable level of performance is desired, method invocations by management applications must often be executed asynchronously. Since asynchronous, thus nonblocking, invocations are currently not considered in the CORBA specifications, the use of so-called deferred synchronous requests is provided; synchronous requests are also possible. The first type of request is appropriate for management purposes. A management system making a request receives a so-called *handle* (temporary identifier) for the target object, allowing it to query the status of the operation or to request the result at a later time. The client is able to invoke other requests while the request is being processed by the server without having to generate a separate thread for each request.

7.3.2   The Server Side of CORBA

If an ORB core receives an operation request from a client, it must select the appropriate server object and invoke the operation using the parameters supplied by the client. To do so, it selects an object adapter to the server object, forwards the parameters, and transfers control to the object implementation. The individual components involved are as follows (Figure 7.6):

- *Static skeletons*, also referred to as server IDL stubs, provide the static interface to the services offered by an object. They are generated by IDL compilers in the same way as client IDL stubs.

Static skeletons: static method invocations

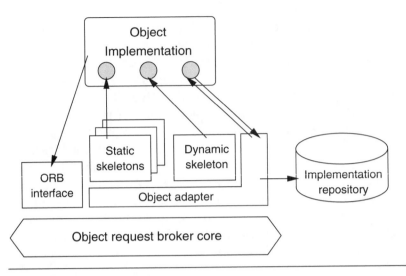

Figure 7.6
Components on the server side of CORBA

Dynamic skele-
tons: dynamic
method invocations

- The *dynamic skeleton interface* enables method invocations for which no static request description is provided to be processed during runtime. It interprets incoming messages while establishing the respective target object and the method invoked at the same time. It is comparable to the dynamic invocation interface on the client side and was introduced within the scope of ORB interoperability for the implementation of bridges (section 7.4). Dynamic skeletons are also useful in the implementation of management gateways on the CORBA side. They allow gateways to be adapted to new managed object classes and methods without having to be compiled again.

Object adapter:
invocation of
server objects

- The *object adapter* forwards method invocations from clients to the server object, thereby providing a link between the ORB and the skeletons connected to the server objects. It provides a runtime environment for the initialization of server objects and transfer of requests, thereby allowing the ORB to start server objects and to transfer control to them.

Implementation
repository: objects
and references

- The *implementation repository* stores information about the object classes implemented by the server, the instantiated objects, and the object reference. It can also contain other information such as management data affecting the ORB itself.

The components for the clients and the servers described provide the mechanism needed for object interaction with the ORB. What still has to be determined is how ORBs, when there is more than one,

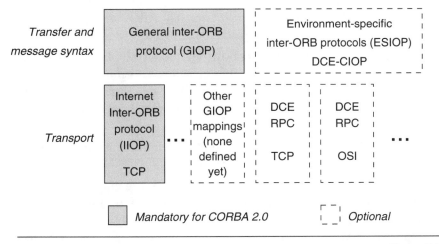

Figure 7.7
Inter-ORB protocols

communicate with one another in a heterogeneous environment. The relevant protocols are dealt with later.

7.3.3 Inter-ORB Protocols

If communication is to take place between ORBs of different vendors, then specifications are required for the protocol between the ORBs themselves and for mapping this protocol to the transport protocol. The protocols described next are compiled in Figure 7.7.

- The *general inter-ORB protocol* (GIOP) specifies the syntax and semantics of the messages exchanged between ORBs. For this purpose, it defines seven PDU types for the following:

  GIOP: communication between ORBs

  - Invocation of a method, return of results, and termination of a request
  - Queries to test the validity of the object references and to determine the location of the objects and the corresponding responses
  - Termination of connections and error notifications

  The GIOP is designed to be used with any connection-oriented transport protocol. It also specifies the transfer syntax for method invocations and their parameters, called *common data representation* (CDR). It contains specifications on byte order and for representing simple IDL data types such as strings, Boolean values, integers, and floating-point numbers. The GIOP also defines the linearization of more complex IDL data structures.

The third important specification defined by GIOP relates to *interoperable object references*. This provides a format in which the associated ORB domain and the protocol enabling access to the object (protocol profile) can be communicated for a given object reference.

The specifications of the GIOP therefore relate to layers 5, 6, and 7 in the OSI model.

IIOP: GIOP over TCP
- The *Internet inter-ORB protocol* (IIOP) defines the mapping of GIOP to TCP. It defines how GIOP PDUs should be framed into TCP PDUs. The TCP connection is used asymmetrically, meaning client and server are allowed to use only a subset of each of the PDUs available. The initiative for establishing a connection is exclusively taken by the client. IIOP allows a number of different method invocations to be transferred over the same connection. The status of the connection itself can be manipulated by IIOP messages (e.g., `cancel`, `shutdown`).

  Because TCP is currently the most widely used connection-oriented transport protocol, ORBs must support IIOP to conform with CORBA 2.0. This creates the basis for the unlimited interoperability of all ORBs, assuming CORBAservices also exist for naming and so forth. In principle, the entire Internet can be used as a "backbone" for communication between ORBs.

The first ESIOP: inter-ORB communication over DCE-RPC
- *Environment-specific inter-ORB protocols* (ESIOPs) are designed for communication over other protocols or protocol stacks. CORBA 2.0 contains DCE-CIOP as the first of many possible ESIOPs. It specifies communication between ORBs over the DCE-RPC. One of the objectives was to enable the use of services, such as the security service, offered by DCE. Since DCE-RPC uses *network data representation* (NDR) as the transfer syntax, IDL must be mapped to it. First, the CDR representation of IDL is used, which is then directly mapped to NDR. DCE-IDL, not to be confused with CORBA IDL, is not used by DCE-CIOP.

7.3.4   Example Products and Solutions

In the following, we will briefly sketch two important products from the management area that use CORBA as the underlying communications platform for management applications.

Tivoli Management Architecture

The *Tivoli Management Architecture* is the basis for Tivoli Enterprise, a suite of products for systems management. The architecture is basically structured using a three-tier approach:

- The *management server* acts as the management supervisor for the entire management environment.

- *Management gateways* provide communications between a group of management agents and the rest of the environment.

- *Managed endpoints*, the management agents, run on hosts, Unix workstations, desktops, or network devices.

The management framework that forms the basis for the solution is built on top of a CORBA communications platform. It runs on the management server and the management gateways. The framework consists of some basic services that enable the use of ORBs, management services, user interface services, and advanced application services. These combined services form the application programming interface to which systems management applications are written.

Based on CORBA platform

The framework is used to tie the various different applications together. These applications include, for example, inventory management, software distribution, monitoring of a distributed environment, security management, user administration, and event management.

For more information, we refer you to *http://www.tivoli.com* or *http://www.ibm.com*.

HP OpenView Distributed Management

The HP OpenView distributed management platform is a software platform for telecommunications management. In the past, it was primarily a TMN platform based on OSI management standards. Recently, a CORBA-based application development environment has been added to the platform. Besides a CORBA 2.0–compliant ORB, it includes a set of object services supporting the implementation of management applications (e.g., naming, event, and lifecycle services; transaction services; and trading services—see section 7.5). Two additional services of the development environment relate to domain interfaces that are developed by the *Telecom Domain Task Force* of the OMG (see also section 7.7):

CORBA support added to platform

- The *notification service*, which provides enhanced event management, can be seen as a predecessor of the notificaton service described in section 7.7.1.

- The *topology service* has been submitted to the OMG in response to the request for proposals of the OMG for a service with the same name. As of the beginning of 1999, however, the OMG Telecom Domain Task Force has suspended the work on the topology service (see section 7.7.2).

The primary goal of the development environment is to support the implementation of CORBA-based applications for the service management layer and the network management layer of TMN. It aims at a tight integration of all applications in these areas. CORBA-based applications access managed objects in the OSI domain using Q3 adapters that follow the mapping specified by the JIDM group (see section 10.4). With these adapters, applications also can communicate with other TMN platforms. For further details, see *http://www.hp.com/ovtelecom/*.

7.4   Organizational Model

OMA: symmetric organizational model

The OMA *organizational model* follows a symmetrical approach. Unlike the hierarchical model for Internet management, this model is based on a cooperation between fundamentally equal objects (*peer-to-peer approach*). It enables manager–agent and manager–manager relationships as in OSI and SNMP-based management as well as agent–agent relationships. This not only allows management functionality to be distributed to hierarchically equal management systems and management services to be delegated to hierarchically lower systems but in principle also permits an autonomous cooperation between agent systems.

The *actors* in this model are exclusively objects. Depending on requirements or the implementation, these objects can assume the role of a client, a server, or both simultaneously.

The OMA organizational model takes into account domains and bridges

This originally very simple organizational model was extended considerably for *version 2* of CORBA to include an interoperability structure. The new version principally aims at addressing the previous lack of interoperability of independently developed ORBs. The technical interoperability of ORBs (see section 7.3.3) serves as the basis for forming *federations* of ORBs, which are loose unions of independent ORBs. These federations are meant to overcome organizational and technological boundaries. The existence of these boundaries should be

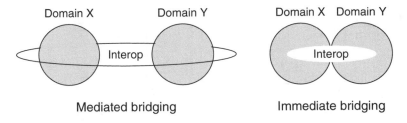

Figure 7.8
Bridges between domains

totally transparent for method invocation, which means that it should not be visible whether the invoked server object is within or outside the boundaries. The prerequisite for these types of unions are a domain concept and concepts for bridges between different domains since not all ORBs within a federation are obligated to use the same protocol.

A *domain* is a set of objects, the members of the domain, that share certain properties. Domains themselves can be modeled as objects, in turn becoming members of domains. Domains can be administrative as well as technical and are not necessarily linked to the domain of an ORB installation. Examples of domains include scopes for object references, domains with the same transfer syntax or the same communication protocol, and scopes for network addresses or a certain security policy.

Since different exchange formats and protocols can be used within different domains, a format or protocol conversion is sometimes needed for communication across domain boundaries. This *bridging of domain boundaries* can basically be implemented in the following two ways, which are also illustrated in Figure 7.8:

- With *mediated bridging*, interactions of the format internal to the domain are translated into an agreed common interchange format. This common format can be either GIOP (see section 7.3.3) or even a proprietary format agreed upon by both domains.

- With *immediate bridging*, an intermediate format is not required. The internal formats of the interactions are merged together. The elements of the interactions are directly transformed between the internal format of one domain and the internal format of the other.

These bridges provide the technical basis for concealing the existence of domain boundaries from clients and servers; in other words, they make them transparent.

However, there are many cases when it is undesirable to have complete transparency of communication beyond domain boundaries,

Domains: sets of objects with shared properties

Bridging domain boundaries: mediated or immediate

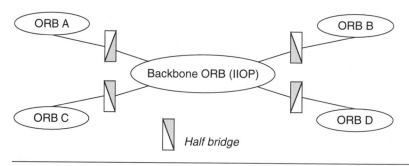

Figure 7.9
Federation of ORBs

such as for reasons of security or secrecy. On the contrary, there could be a reason for restricting, controlling, and monitoring the communication that is taking place. To deal with these limitations from an architectural standpoint, the OMA organizational model introduced the concept of *policy-mediated bridging*. If the policy is a security-oriented one, then the bridge could be designated as a CORBA firewall.

ORB backbones: structuring major ORB federations

Totally analogous to other communication infrastructures, it may often be convenient to structure complex configurations of domains and bridges as backbones with connected "subnetworks." IIOP is the protocol that is most often used within the backbones (see section 7.3.3). The protocol used in the bridges to the attached ORBs is always translated to IIOP. In this case, these bridges are referred to as "half bridges," first, because one side of the bridge is always an IIOP and, second, because the boundaries between two domains connected to a backbone are bridged by two of these half bridges (Figure 7.9).

7.5 CORBAservices

CORBAservices: fundamental supplementary functions for ORB-based communication

Object services in CORBA (CORBAservices) are a collection of system services assembled in the form of IDL interfaces. On the one hand, they extend and supplement the range of ORB functions through the addition of important and useful functions that are available to all applications. On the other hand, they prescribe standards for interfaces that need to be implemented by applications when they want to participate in certain interactions. An example IDL definition for the event service is given in section 7.2.2.

Similar to the approach taken for the definition of the systems management functions of OSI management, the OMG identified the functions that many if not all applications require. These functions are gradually being standardized within the framework of the *common object services specification* (COSS).

Although they are by no means management specific, the functions are almost without exception also essential for management applications, or at least beneficial to them. The name service and the event service are essential; consequently, the latter is described in more detail in the next section. Only a brief description can be given of all the other services within the scope of this discussion.

CORBAservices are not management specific

7.5.1   The Event Service

The event service supports the communication of objects using asynchronous messages (i.e., messages that have not been directly requested). This requires defining two roles for objects: *suppliers* that generate and transmit event messages and *consumers* that receive and further process the messages.

Two different concepts are provided for the interchange of messages (see also IDL declaration in section 7.2.2):

The event service supports push as well as pull communication

- With the *push model*, the `PushSupplier` itself notifies the `PushConsumer` of the occurrence of an event using the operation `push` of the `PushConsumer` object.

- With the *pull model*, the initiative is taken by the consumer. The `PullConsumer` requests event messages by invoking the operation `pull` of the `PullSupplier`.

Event channels allow communication between supplier and consumer to be decoupled. Suppliers send the messages to the channel that, if necessary, buffers them and forwards them to the consumer. The channel itself thereby incorporates the role of supplier as well as consumer. Any number of suppliers and consumers can communicate with one another without direct interaction over the channel. This allows consumers flexibility in registering for the receipt of messages that are relevant to them. Either the push or the pull model can be used for communication between suppliers or consumers and the channel. Figure 7.10 illustrates possible interactions for a push model between channel and supplier and a pull model between channel and consumer.

Channels decouple supplier and consumer

In addition to the differentiation between push and pull model, a distinction is also made in the event service between generic and typed communication:

Communication can be typed or generic

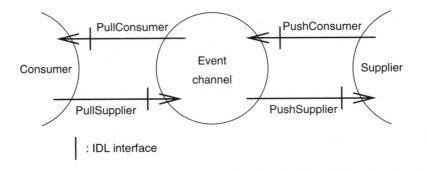

Figure 7.10
Communication over channels

- With *generic communication,* push and pull operations only have one type `any parameter` in which all data is encapsulated into the message.

- With *typed communication,* events are transmitted through the invocation of operations that have an "application-specific" IDL definition.

The IDL example in section 7.2.2 showed an excerpt from the interfaces provided for generic communication. This section also explained how interface definitions are used in the implementation of suppliers and consumers of messages.

This service allows all objects to communicate over event messages, which, in contrast to other architectures like the OSI management or version 2 of the Internet management, are not contained in the CORBA information model.

7.5.2   Other Services

- The *naming service* allows names relative to a name context to be bound to objects and names to be resolved into object references, therefore locating objects in an environment. A link to existing directory services such as X.500 and network information service (NIS) is possible.

- The *persistent object service* supplies standard interfaces for the persistent storage of objects independently of the concrete storage or database technology (ODBMS, RDBMS, files).

- Conventions and standard interfaces are defined within the scope of the *lifecycle service* to allow the creation, deletion, copying, and migration of objects. This enables a uniform manipulation of distributed objects at different locations.

- The *concurrency control service* controls simultaneous access to resources. It introduces a component that manages locks to resources that have been requested for use by transactions.

- The *externalization service* defines conventions and protocols that allow the status of an object to be externalized in the form of a data stream. This data can then be used in the same process or in another process to internalize an object with the identical status.

- The *relationship service* enables dynamic relationships to be established and managed between components, with no need for these components to be informed of this relationship or even the existence of the other components.

- The *transaction service* coordinates interactions between components using a two-phase commit protocol to guarantee transactional properties. It supports flat as well as nested transactions.

- The *query service* is used to carry out query operations to sets of objects. The query language is a superset of SQL based on SQL3 specifications and the object query language.

- The *licensing service* supplies flexible fundamental mechanisms for the licensing control of finely granulated objects that SW suppliers can use to implement their own respective licensing policies.

- The *property service* allows properties (i.e., named and typed values) that do not exist in the static IDL description of the object interface to be dynamically assigned to objects.

- The *time service* provides the current time with an estimate of inaccuracy, generates time-triggered messages, and calculates the interval between two event messages.

- The services of the *security service* include the identification and authentication of subjects, authorization and access control, and the guaranteeing of message integrity and confidentiality.

- The *trading object service* allows services to be offered, whereby they are registered with a broker object, and services to be located, whereby the broker object is queried about services with certain properties.

- The *object collection service* offers uniform mechanisms incorporating the use of objects such as sets, lists, and trees for the manipulation of the most frequent structures.

CORBAservices: basis for service hierarchy

The OMG assumption is that practically every application program that is based on distributed objects will use a subset of these services. The services are usually implemented by the vendor of the ORB and supplied packaged with the ORB. The ones listed previously can be used directly by application objects as well as by the CORBAfacilities and domain interfaces described next.

7.6   CORBAfacilities and Systems Management Facilities

CORBAfacilities: horizontal functions for many application domains

The next layer of the functional model is represented by CORBAfacilities (also called *common facilities*). These facilities provide services that, although no longer incorporating the fundamental character of CORBA-services, can still be used jointly by a variety of different application areas. It is not necessarily assumed that these services will be implemented by the same vendor as the ORB. Owing to their horizontal function, these services were previously referred to as *horizontal facilities.*

Up to now four areas have been defined for these services:

- The *user interface* area contains services for document processing, such as the printing and displaying of objects, the presentation of objects in compound documents, and the management of help systems.

- Services from the *information management* area support information modeling, storage, processing, and exchange.

- *Task management* supplies functions for automating and coordinating workflows.

- *System management* is concerned with the administration of complex DP systems. These services supply basic functions for the monitoring, control, and protection of systems.

Common management facilities: OMA management functions

The latter service area forms the basis for the integration of management services into the OMA. However, the concrete specification of these services is still in the early stages. The driving force behind the design of common facilities for systems management is the Systems Management Working Group of the Open Group, which originated as a result of an association between X/Open and OSF. This group introduced the systems management services into the OMA.

7.6.1   The Managed Set Service

The managed set service allows *sets of related objects* to be assembled and administered for management purposes. Its activities include adding and deleting members and acquiring information about members of a particular set.

The service is defined by the following interfaces:

- The interface `set` contains the normal operations for manipulating sets; it defines objects that implement the sets. The implementations of these objects use the interface `member` of their elements.

- The interface `member` allows set objects to notify their elements of membership to a set or even to withdraw it. Upon request implementations must supply references for those sets in which they are contained.

In this model, therefore, the elements of sets are familiar with all the sets of which they are members. Objects can be elements only if they implement the interface `member`. This is the principal difference compared to the relationship and object collection concept in the corresponding CORBAservices, in which objects themselves are not aware of the relationships in which they are found. As a result, no additional requirements are then made of the object implementations.

7.6.2   The Instance Management Service

The instance management service supports lifecycle management, hence the creation or deletion of managed objects. At the same time, it also defines the fundamental characteristics of managed objects within the OMA.

Managed instances: managed objects in the OMA

The module `ManagedInstances` defines three basic roles:

- An administered resource (in Figure 7.11, instance 1), thus a managed object, is designated as a *managed instance* here. It implements a refinement of the interface `member` from section 7.6.1, which can be used by the instance manager to execute operations on it.

- Constructor objects (factories) for managed objects or managed instances, so-called *instance managers*, encapsulate important aspects of the functionality of general factory objects and factory finder objects.

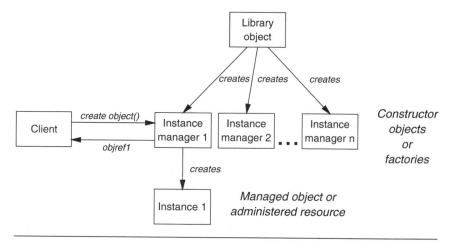

Figure 7.11
Creation of managed objects

- A *library object* represents a constructor object for instance managers.

Figure 7.11 illustrates the relationships between the individual roles.

7.6.3   The Policy Management Service

Policy management: management-specific refinement of the organizational model

The purpose of the policy management service is to assist administrators in adapting the behavior of a management system according to the management policies of their own specific environment. It supports the definition of policies to object groups (domains) as well as the monitoring of them. In addition to management functionality, this specification also introduces a management-specific refinement of the OMA organizational model.

Policy regions: domains with associated policies

Management domains, which are sets of managed objects for which the same policies apply, are called *policy regions* here. These are refinements of the managed sets from section 7.6.1 and therefore administer the references to the contained managed objects, or managed instances, from section 7.6.2. Of course, there are different types of managed instances. A reference to one or more constructor types appears in the domain object for each possible object type.

Initialization and validation policies: adherence to policies

Domain objects also contain references to *initialization policy objects* that are used to set required attribute values for new managed objects. On the other hand, they do not define any operations that monitor that these policies are being adhered to on an ongoing basis. This is

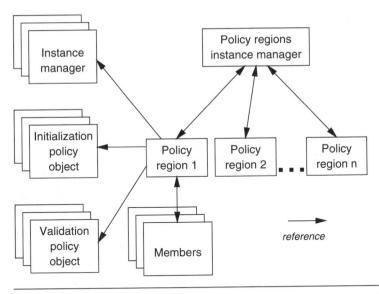

Figure 7.12
Reference structure in management domains

the task of the *validation policy object*. Figure 7.12 provides an overview of the existing reference structure for the described components.

The specification contains no operations for enforcing a compliance to policies. This is left to the management application itself, which can, of course, rely on the initialization and validation policies to do so.

7.7   Domain Interfaces

Domain interfaces define services at the highest hierarchy level. (The notion domain here relates to business domains, which should not be confused with management domains.) These interfaces no longer incorporate the horizontal function of common facilities but instead support only applications of a particular domain. They were, therefore, previously referred to as *vertical market facilities*. Today, they are often also called *business objects*. Just as CORBAfacilities, these interfaces are at an early stage of development since the OMG has primarily been concentrating on ORBs and CORBAservices.

Following are some of the *areas* or *domains* in which specifications are currently being drawn up by special working groups (see *http://www.omg.org/about/report.htm*):

■ Health care (CORBAmed)

Domain interfaces define services for specialized application domains

- Factory automation
- Office automation
- Financial world
- Traffic
- Electronic commerce
- Telecommunications

The last domain, which the *OMG Telecom Domain Task Force* is promoting, is the most important one for applications in network and systems management. Example services specified by the task force will be briefly described in the following sections.

If CORBA is to be positioned as a cooperation and management architecture in the telecommunications field, then clear migration policies will have to be specified. Other activities in the group are therefore geared toward CORBA cooperation with existing systems. The first steps planned in this direction include:

- A definition of the mappings required to enable a cooperation of CORBA with TMN (also see section 10.4).

- The development of concepts for a cooperation of CORBA with existing *IN systems* (e.g., by mapping GIOP to signaling system no. 7 or using gateways to this protocol).

No detailed specifications are yet available for the activities described in section 10.4 for these domains.

7.7.1   The Notification Service

The notification service extends and enhances the event service for management purposes

The *notification service* was introduced as a result of the realization that the general event service (see section 7.5.1) was not meeting all the requirements of network and systems management. The notification service introduces the following extensions and improvements to the event service:

- *User-definable event filters* and priority definitions enable the suppression of irrelevant messages. This helps prevent an overloading of applications due to the processing of large numbers of unimportant messages.

- *Time stamps* for messages support performance measurements and error diagnosis.

- Message *buffering* allows receivers to interrupt their connections to event channels without losing their messages.

- Defined *quality of service criteria* allow applications to specify their requirements regarding the reliability of deliveries, the issuance of acknowledgments of receipt, and the maximum age of messages being delivered.

For further details, refer to *http://www.omg.org*. As of the beginning of 1999, the current OMG document number is telecom/98-11-01.

7.7.2 The Topology Service

One of the central functions of a management system is to administer and represent the *logical topology* of distributed systems. Almost all applications rely on topology data or manipulate it. However, the interfaces that exist to the services of topology management in current platforms are proprietary. Consequently, the effort involved in porting management applications to other platforms is very high.

The topology service administers topology data and associated metadata

The object of the *topology service* is therefore to simplify access to and manipulation of topology data. The following interfaces are defined for this purpose (Figure 7.13):

- The rules applying to topology relationships between objects can be defined and read at the interface for *metadata manipulation* (*metadata manager API*). These rules can relate to the specification of the object types in the relationship or to cardinality.

- Concrete topological relationships can be entered or changed, thus the topology set up and administered, at the interface to the *administration of topology data* (*data manager API*). Before each change is implemented, a check is carried out to ensure that the rules contained in the metadata are being followed.

- The *query interface* (*query manager API*) is used by management applications for read access to the topology.

There are different alternatives for the implementation of the topology service. One way is to implement it "from scratch," which was the original plan; another way is to base it on other services such as the relationship service. Recent developments by the OMG, such as metaobject services and objects by value, would support the latter option. This led to a suspension of the work on the topology service

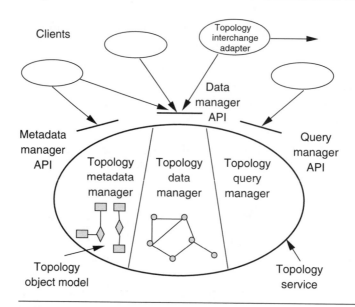

Figure 7.13
Interfaces for access to topology data

and will undoubtedly result in a new edition of the request for proposal (RFP).

7.7.3   The Log Service

As mentioned in section 7.3.4, the network, service, and business management layers of TMN are candidates for the development of CORBA-based management applications. To support the integration of these new applications with existing TMN products, CORBA counterparts for the OSI systems management functions (see section 5.5) are needed.

The *log service* as specified by the OMG Telecom Domain Task Force conforms to the functionality of the log control function of the OSI management as defined in ISO 10164-6 or ITU-T X.735. It stores events that are supplied to the log as `log records` and also forwards them to other logs or to any application that wishes to receive them.

The log service is implemented as an event channel. It can therefore support both push and pull communications and multiple suppliers and consumers of events. Logs can form log networks of various topologies by simply connecting the logs as event channels. Support of TMN systems can be achieved via a gateway because the GDMO definition of `log` is fully preserved.

Log service: implemented as event channel

For further details, refer to *http://www.omg.org*. As of the beginning of 1999, the current OMG document number is telecom/98-12-04.

7.8   Extensions in CORBA 3.0

As of the beginning of 1999, the specifications of the new features in version 3.0 of CORBA are not completed. In the following, we will briefly sketch the extensions that have been announced by the OMG:

- *Distributed component support*
  - The *CORBA component model* specifies a framework for the development of plug-and-play CORBA objects. It encapsulates the creation, lifecycle, and events for a single object and allows clients to dynamically explore an object's capabilities, methods, and events. It also facilitates tighter integration with Java and other component technologies.
  - The *CORBA scripting language* specification makes composition of CORBA components easier using scripts.
  - Support for *objects by value* provides an additional method of passing information across a network. This will foster a more seamless integration of CORBA with modern programming languages like Java.
  - *Multiple interfaces* allow a single object to present multiple views of itself through an interface selection mechanism.
- *Java and Internet integration and legacy support*
  - A *Java language to IDL* mapping specification allows developers to implement applications completely in Java and to generate the IDL from Java classes. This enables other applications to access Java applications using RMI over IIOP.
  - The *firewall* specification defines interfaces for passing IIOP through a firewall, including options for filtering and proxying.
  - *DCE/CORBA interworking* specifications provide a road map for integrating DCE applications into CORBA environments.
- *Quality of service specifications*
  - *Minimum CORBA* addresses the need for CORBA-compliant systems that can operate in embedded environments.
  - *Realtime CORBA* introduces so-called realtime ORBs in the CORBA specification that give developers a more direct control over resource allocation.

– The *asynchronous messaging* specification includes levels of quality of service (QoS) agreements and IDL changes that are necessary to support asynchronous method invocations. QoS policies tell the ORB how to handle various scenarios such as unreachable objects.

7.9   Chapter Summary

CORBA's importance as an architecture for integrated network and systems management will no doubt continue to grow in the future. This is due not only to the existence of well-known CORBA-based tools and platforms such as Tivoli TME10 and HP OV Telecom but also to a number of technical reasons:

- Vendors find it attractive to be able to use the same architecture for both "normal" and management communication mainly because of cost reasons. This means that the same object model and the same tools can be used in both cases. It enables a seamless integration of the management interface into applications.

- If development continues to proceed at a rapid pace, the systems management common facilities and domain interfaces for the telecommunications area could provide an open platform for management applications. This would enable many interfaces that today are available only in proprietary variants of platform manufacturers to be simplified into vendor-independent interfaces. It would also make it easier to port management tools to different platforms, which is a very complicated process today. Despite all their efforts (such as the TMN/C++ API; see section 15.3.1), neither OSI management nor Internet management has anything comparable to offer. The SW development process enables an easy integration of the mechanism for the inheritance of interfaces.

- The different existing standardized mappings of IDL to implementation languages find no parallel in the other management architectures. The effects of the attachment of IDL to Java and of CORBA support in version 1.2 of the Java platform (see *http://java.sun.com/products/jdk/1.2/index.html*) will be particularly evident in the short or medium term.

- A solution for the coordination of different subagents on one machine has already been found in the basic CORBA architecture. In Internet management, for example, addressing this problem later had produced a diversity of competing and mutually replace-able standards such as DPI (RFC 1592), agentX (RFC 2257), and EMANATE (see *http://www.snmp.com/emanate/emanate.html*).

- Users are able to make multiple use of the CORBA infrastructure. This means that there is one infrastructure less to acquire, install, and maintain. Expensive services such as the event service, which has to be acquired anyway, can also be used for management (i.e., total cost of ownership can be reduced through reuse).

- There is a popular and widely used Web browser that is already equipped with an IIOP-compatible ORB. This browser is therefore a potential CORBA client. If an ORB is not installed from the outset, it can be loaded to a Java-enabled browser without any difficulty. The support of CORBA in version 1.2 of Java, mentioned earlier, will probably have an impact on browsers as well.

The main disadvantage of CORBA is that no management informa-tion that can even remotely compete with most OSI and SNMP MIBs has been defined for this architecture. A fundamental component for truly open management on a CORBA basis is currently still lacking. The development of standardized translation procedures that would allow the MIBs mentioned to be used in a CORBA environment (see Chapter 10) could constitute a short- or medium-term solution to this problem.

Another disadvantage is that, compared to Internet management, the architecture is relatively complex and expensive to implement. This could prove to be an obstacle in the introduction of low-cost components.

An area in which these disadvantages do not carry a lot of weight is telecommunications network management. Especially the service management and business management layers of TMN look promising for CORBA-based management. This trend is fostered by the work of the JIDM group (see section 10.4) on CORBA/CMIP gateways, which eases usage of the wealth of OSI management information by CORBA-based applications.

All in all, CORBA provides a cost-effective platform for distributed applications, but to meet management needs, it must be supported by management-specific device interfaces (agents) and information (MIBs), neither of which has been assisted sufficiently by CORBA.

8

DMTF Desktop Management Interface

Workstation computers (*desktops* such as PCs and Unix workstations) far and away represent the lion's share of the typical components used in distributed processing infrastructures today. For a long time the perception was (and in some ways still is) that they were difficult to administer in an automated or centralized manner. The main problem was attributed to the difficulty in access from standardized management architectures.

The *Desktop Management Task Force* (DMTF) consequently undertook the task of integrating heterogeneous workstation computers with all of their components into an integrated management. This involved the development of a new management architecture, the *desktop management interface* (DMI), with its emphasis on:

- Definition of an information model, the so-called *management information format* (MIF)
- Specification of concrete management information for workstation computers and their components using this model
- Coordination and integration of several management agents (subagents) within a workstation
- Creation of communications infrastructure for remote and local access to management information

The DMI is designed to create a *bridge* between operating system-specific proprietary *device interfaces* and configuration or registration files on the one hand and standardized *management architectures* on the other. Although the DMI is a complete and separate management architecture, special additional provisions were made to ensure that integration with Internet management would be as seamless as possible.

DMTF-DMI: management of heterogeneous workstation computers

DMI is supposed to bridge the gap between proprietary device interfaces and standardized management architecture

Without exception, all the documents and standards referenced in this chapter can be accessed over *http://www.dmtf.org*. Other information on DMI can be found in [HEW97].

The DMTF was founded in 1992 as an association of HW and SW manufacturers. In 1994, version 1 of DMI was published. The initial economic driver was mainly not integrated *distributed* management, but rather integrated *local* management (i.e., the ability for third-party components to be manageable). DMI 2.0 became available in early 1996. The main difference between DMI 1.0 and DMI 2.0 is that the latter one was extended to include remote access to the management entity as well as integration with Internet management architecture (i.e., the main emphasis shifted from local to remote management). We will concentrate on version 2.0 in the following.

8.1   Architectural and Organizational Model

DMI service provider: management entity on workstation computers

The central element of the architecture (see Figure 8.1) is the *service provider* (SP), which mediates between the managed resources of a workstation computer and the managing units. It represents an entity with functions roughly comparable to those of an SNMP master agent or even of a rudimentary ORB (see section 7.3) in a computer that mediates between components (object implementations) and management applications (client objects).

DMI management interface: interface to management applications

The SP receives queries and requests from local or remote management applications over an RPC mechanism at an interface called the *management interface* (MI). At this interface, event messages are forwarded from resources to their receivers. A separate information model, the *management information format* (MIF), is defined to describe the resources at this interface. The SP either processes the requests itself or passes them on to the resources, the *managed components.*

DMI component interface: interface to resources

The *component interface* (CI), the interface to the resources, executes the last-mentioned request. It goes without saying that the implementation of the CI is specific to the operating system. The architecture also allows the SP to implement the functionality of the CI using other system-specific resources instead of standardized operations. So, for example, Microsoft can supply an SP for Windows that provides the standardized MI but replaces the functions of the CI through operations of the proprietary device driver interface.

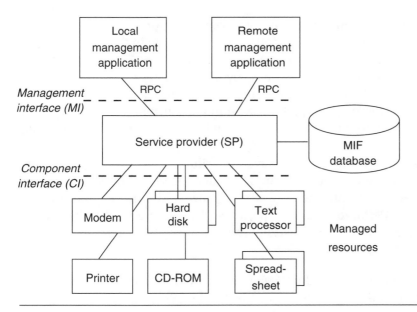

Figure 8.1
Desktop management interface architecture

8.2 Information Model

The information model used to describe the workstation computer resources and their manipulation at the MI and (at least conceptually) also at the CI strongly resembles the information model of Internet management. It too uses a *data type approach*.

The information model resembles Internet SMI

8.2.1 Management Information Format

The orientation of the information model, called *management information format* (MIF), to two different interfaces accounts for the major conceptual difference between this model and the Internet SMI: In addition to normal definitions for component properties, the MIF contains specifications for the technical implementation of the cooperation between components and the SP. An example of this are references to functions (object code) that can be used to read or modify values with changeable attributes during the runtime of the SP on a particular operating system. In other words, the MIF defines an object interface (like IDL), not just properties.

MIF: The object-based DMI information model

A component is described in an *MIF file* that is transferred to the SP during registration. This file contains all the static properties of

MIF file: description of a resource

the component that the SP is able to supply upon request. The access operations for dynamic properties are also stored in the MIF file.

The *component description* (an example follows) is structured as a list of attribute groups, followed by a list of tables. Attribute groups, on the other hand, are lists of attribute definitions. Attribute types are the usual basic types, including enumeration types. The same as in the Internet SMI tables, combined data types are available in variable lengths.

The DMTF standardized several attribute groups with concrete attribute definitions in the form of so-called *standard group definitions* (see section 8.2.3). The aim is to achieve widespread uniformity in attribute definitions for components of the same class across manufacturer boundaries. Basically, two classes of *standard groups* are differentiated:

Management information standardized through predefined attribute groups

- Definitions within the DMI architecture specification for the generation of *uniform basic attributes* for the following purposes:
  - Configuration of the SP itself
  - Guarantee that a minimum amount of information is available for each component (type of component, time of installation)
  - Definition of asynchronous event messages or the subscription and filtering of messages

- Definitions of working groups for specific *component classes* to ensure that uniformity exists in the basic groups of these multivendor components (see example in section 8.2.3)

MIF files for resources contain values for static attributes and access functions for dynamic attributes

The standard groups for the component classes are frames. They provide quasi "generic managed object classes" that can then be refined by manufacturers for their specific components. This means presetting values for attributes and specifying access functions, differentiated according to operating system. For each attribute, the MIF file for a component contains either a value if the attribute is static or an access function used by the SP to read or set the value at the time of the query if the attribute is changeable.

Another feature of the MIF is the syntactic constructs that facilitate or allow (pragma statement) mapping to the Internet management information model or assist management applications in the efficient storage of attributes (storage statement).

The way in which access possibilities to an attribute (`read-only`, `read-write`, and `write-only`) or the binding nature of the implementation (`required`, `optional`, or `obsolete`) is expressed closely resembles the Internet SMI version 1.

The MIF provides *asynchronous event messages.* The generation of events is linked to groups in an MIF file. If the group displays a table, the event is allocated to a particular table row (such as a specific processor in a multiprocessor machine).

MIF provides asynchronous event messages through resources

The events are defined with the help of the *event generation group,* which provides a *structure* for the *event data.* This data can refer to the type of message, the functional unit in the component triggering the event, or the importance of the event.

There are two different groups of event messages:

- *SP* messages (such as `DmiComponentAdded`, `DmiComponentDeleted`; see section 8.3.2)
- Messages (i.e., asynchronous event notifications from *components*)

Producers of event messages, in other words, the subagents in the resources, can be stateful or stateless. Stateful computers store a history of transmitted messages on abnormal status and produce a message if the abnormal status is removed. Stateless computers do not store any histories and therefore are unable to submit any "OK" messages related to earlier messsages.

8.2.2 Example of an MIF Definition

The following example is an excerpt from the *software standard group definition* (see section 8.2.3). The excerpt contains parts of the definition for table rows that define the paths on which different parts of SW products are installed.

```
Start Group
Name = "Location"
        Description = "This group identifies the
various locations where parts of a software product
have been installed."
        Key = 1
Start Attribute
        Name = "Index"
        ID = 1
        ...
End Attribute
Start Attribute
        Name = "Location Type"
        ID = 2
        Description = "The type of this location entry"
```

Definition of a group of standard attributes

Only read access
to attribute

```
Access = Read-Only
...
Type = Start ENUM
1 = "Unknown"
2 = "Other"
3 = "Product base directory"
4 = "Product executables directory"
5 = "Product library directory"
...
12 = "Shared library directory"
...
15 = "System executables directory"
...
End ENUM
```

Default value

```
Value = 1
End Attribute
Start Attribute
      Name = "Path"
      ID = 3
      Description = "The path to this location."
      Access = Read-Write
```

Suggestion for
efficient storage

```
      Storage = Common
      Type = DisplayString
      Value = ""
End Attribute
End Group
```

8.2.3   Standardized Attribute Groups

Working groups
standardize at-
tribute groups for
resource classes

Using MIF, the DMTF working groups standardized the following concrete attribute groups for important components of workstation computers and attached devices. These groups are meant to be used by the manufacturers of components in their definition of MIF files. This includes assigning concrete values to attributes.

- The *systems standard group definition* (previously called *server MIF*) covers the main components of servers with emphasis on the hardware. It deals with processors, main memory, cache, BIOS, video adapters, I/O interfaces, (uninterruptible) power supply, cooling, and chassis.

- The *mass storage standard group MIF definition* contains a large number of technical and some very detailed attributes and statistics on the mass storage of all relevant types (hard disks, tape drives, CD-

ROMs, DVDs, magneto-optical drive assemblies). The associated controllers and system bus interfaces are included. A remarkable number of event messages are available to report initialization, warnings, errors, and so on.

- The *monitor MIF* groups supply information for monitors, such as tables containing the different possible horizontal and vertical resolutions and the accompanying refresh frequencies.

- The attributes from the *software standard group definition* are supposed to serve as the basis for the management of applications. They relate to installation paths; dependencies between individual SW packages; old versions that have been replaced by new ones; files from which packets are obtained, including checksums; and so forth.

- In contrast to the other ones, the *cost of ownership MIF* supplies technical definitions for commercially relevant data such as prices, warranty periods, maintenance information, and leasing contracts.

Other current attribute definitions are found in the *printer MIF*, the *LAN adapter standard group definition*, and the *finisher MIF*. The finisher MIF deals with the management of large-scale printing jobs that can involve several different devices. The *mobile supplement to standard groups* supplements existing definitions with typical attributes of mobile end systems, such as infrared adapters, energy supply, and PCMCIA modules.

8.3 Communication Model

The DMI communication model provides mechanisms that allow the SP to exchange management information with the components and management applications. In the first case, the communication is exclusively local, whereas in the second case, communication can be with local or with remote entities.

DMI communication model: information exchange between SP and components or applications

8.3.1 Component Interface

The *component interface* (CI) is defined in version 2 of DMI. For reasons of backward compatibility, a data block interface like the one in version 1 is still being provided; however, it is no longer being recommended because of its inefficiency.

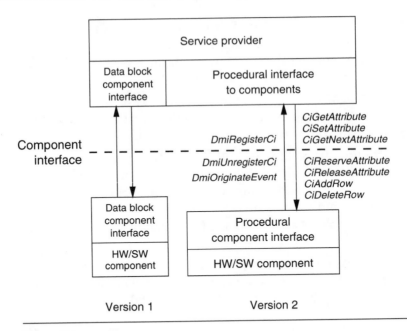

Figure 8.2
DMI component interface

The components offer the SP the following different operations at the CI interface (also see Figure 8.2):

- `CiGetAttribute`, `CiSetAttribute`, and `CiNextAttribute` for the manipulation of attributes in the component. The function of these operations is comparable to the operations of SNMP.

- `CiReserveAttribute` allows the SP to test the executability of a `CiSetAttribute` operation and to lock the attribute. The attribute can be released again by `CiReleaseAttribute`. These operations support atomic write operations on several attributes.

- `CiAddRow` and `CiDeleteRow` are used for manipulating tables (i.e., instantiating and deleting rows).

The SP executes the following CI operations:

- `DmiRegisterCi` and `DmiUnregisterCi` allow components to register or unregister with an SP to reflect (e.g., installation or removal).

- `DmiOriginateEvent` allows components to send asynchronous messages to the SP.

Unlike the functions of the MI, which are mandatory for DMI-conformant systems, the functions of the CI in their standardized form are only optional. As was outlined in the introduction to this chapter, there is another option for implementing communication between components and SP, provided the functionality of the interface to management applications is not affected. For instance, a common driver interface can be used so that there is no need for equipment manufacturers to implement any other interfaces.

Implementation of CI optional

8.3.2 Interface to Management Applications

Communication with local and remote management applications is effected over the *management interface* of the SP. In both cases, it is supported by common RPC variants (such as DCE-RPC and Sun RPC). Similar to CI, a data block interface is offered for compatibility reasons (exclusively for local use) but is no longer being recommended.

MI based on RPCs

The following functions are provided to management applications by the SP over the *MI server* (see Figure 8.3):

SP implements MI access functions for management applications

- *Attribute access operations*, which also allow the execution of a single operation to several attributes
- *Administration operations* such as the registration and unregistration of applications for receiving event messages
- *Inventory operations* used by an application to obtain information about existing components, to add new ones, and to delete existing ones
- Functions for the *manipulation of metadata*, such as the addition of new attribute groups

Management applications must implement an interface at which an SP is able to deliver event messages. These messages can include notifications by components (`DmiDeliverEvent`) or notification of components that have been added or deleted (`DmiComponentAdded`, `DmiComponentDeleted`).

Management applications implement an interface to enable SP to supply events

If the management application is not located in the same system as the SP and the functions of the MI should therefore be accessible remotely through RPC, then these functions must be available in an appropriate interface description language. In the case of a DCE-RPC, the DMI standard defines a specification for MI operations using DCE-IDL from which the appropriate stubs for management applications or for the implementation of the SP can be generated. This is comparable

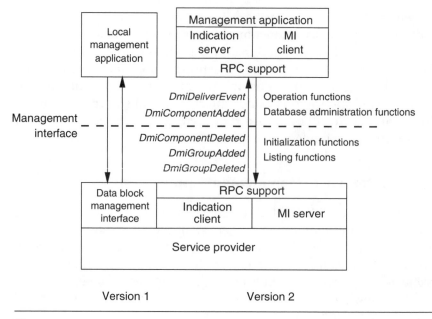

Figure 8.3
DMI management interface

to the generation of client interfaces for a CORBA ORB from the interface descriptions in OMG-IDL.

Mapping to SNMP is standardized

If SNMP is to be used for access to the management information provided by the SP, most fundamental SNMP attribute access operations (get, set, getnext) can be mapped directly. Event messages at the MI are converted into SNMPv1 traps or SNMPv2 notifications. A standard adopted by the DMTF for the conversion of the MIF to an Internet SMI specifies the necessary mappings.

8.4 Functional Model

Functional model: subscription and filtering of messages

The DMI functional model is not a fully developed model. It incorporates only event management, but this function is comparatively highly advanced due to its filter and message subscription options.

The procedure for subscribing and filtering messages is implemented in two stages:

- During the first stage, the management application requests all the messages of the service provider.

- If the first stage is successful, the management application uses filter definitions to request selected messages from components during the second stage. The criteria used in filtering are the component that triggers the event, the event type, and an attribute that indicates how critical an event is.

In addition to a large number of defined messages, event management supports the transition from polling-based management to event-based management.

8.5   Chapter Summary

DMI is an architecture specifically designed for the management of end systems such as workstation computers and servers. Its information model, the MIF, with its data type approach is heavily based on the Internet SMI. In addition, it contains statements that support intrasystem communication between the management entity and the agents in the resources. The architecture contains mechanisms allowing the integration and coordination of several subagents to the resources of a system through the execution registration operations. Similar approaches are being worked on by the *agent extensibility working group* of the IETF (see section 6.2.2 or RFC 2255). Extensive and in-depth information definitions are now available on an MIF basis for end systems. Nothing closely comparable is being offered by other architectures.

The communication model is actually based on RPCs. The recently added standardized mapping to SNMP offers additional flexibility and allows for seamless integration into Internet management for remote, distributed use.

Although the functional model is not yet particularly well developed, it does provide essential mechanisms for the management of event messages. By so doing, it alleviates one of the major weaknesses that still exists in Internet management—the need for extensive polling.

The recent excellent integration options with Internet management do much to improve the future prospects for the architecture. It is totally conceivable that Internet management and DMTF-DMI will be sharing the management of LAN components in the medium term:

Integration with SNMP improves future prospects

- Management of the network components with Internet MIBs and SNMP
- Management of the end systems with DMTF MIFs, SNMP, and RPCs

What kind of an effect the minimal success of SNMPv2 and the development of SNMPv3 will have on DMI remains to be seen. It is also difficult to project what kind of manufacturer support will be available for the, in part, extremely extensive MIF standard groups (i.e., whether there will be enough market penetration in this area for the architecture to establish itself in the long term). Based on the current state of development, it could also be that subsets roughly comparable to the profiles in OSI management (see section 5.3) are formed for selected scenarios. Approaches such as the specification *wired for management baseline* introduced by Intel are pointing in this direction. A great deal depends on factors such as Microsoft's strategy, which has not always been very clear on how it views DMTF and DMI. What is certain right now is that Microsoft will not be implementing CI in a standardized form but instead will be relying on its device driver interface; however, this does not necessarily have to spell ruin for the future prospects of DMI. It is not yet definitively clear how DMI will slot into the overall Microsoft management strategy, the "Zero Administration Initiative."

Web-Based Management Architectures

9.1 Motivation and Objectives

The installation of corporate intranets during the last few years has experienced an enormous dynamic. Entire communication structures are being based on Internet protocols, and Web browsers are being used as universal, easy-to-use graphical "user terminals" over which all applications and corporate data are accessible. For example, 3270 terminal emulations are being replaced by Web browsers, and Web servers are being attached to the "legacy" applications in order to gain HTTP access. If this works with all applications, no further consideration will have to be given to different HW architectures and operating systems on the user terminal side; Web browsers are available across all platforms. The application is practically accessible from any end system. However, care has to be taken when activeX controls, Java applets, or very specific features of HTML are used. Differences in browser platforms might lead to undesirable results.

Web browsers: universal user terminals in intranets

This strategy could also be pursued for management systems. The prerequisite for efficient integrated management is that management applications can be accessed anywhere and that management agents are available on all resources. As a result of SNMP market penetration, the latter requirement is mostly being met in many resource areas. On the other hand, for administrative tasks users are often still tied to local management consoles or may need an X-server for the ability to access the functionality of remote management platforms. If Web browsers were used as management consoles, management applications would be available practically anywhere. Two basic options are available:

Goal: Web browsers as management consoles

- The resources themselves are instrumented using HTTP servers and accessed directly over a Web browser, thus HTTP is directly used as

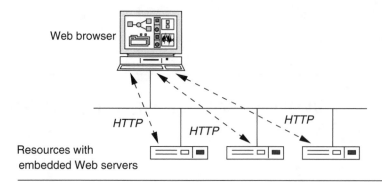

Figure 9.1
Web-based management with embedded Web servers

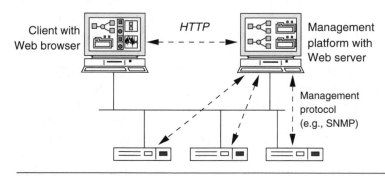

Figure 9.2
Web-based management with proxies

the management protocol (see Figure 9.1). This is referred to as an embedded approach for Web-based management.

- An existing management platform is equipped with an HTTP server that allows each Web browser to have access to the platform functionality (see Figure 9.2). Communication with the resources continues to take place over SNMP or CMIP, and HTTP is used only as a "GUI protocol." This is referred to as a proxy solution.

Many manufacturers today are not only equipping management platforms but also stand-alone management tools with Web servers so that the respective functionality can be accessed via a Web browser. The tools usually communicate with the resources over a proprietary protocol or over SNMP or CMIP. This can be viewed as a special case of a proxy solution, which, however, allows only an integration of the user interface. Even if several of these tools can be operated over the same user interface, their functionality is still always isolated from other tools.

The main objective in using an *embedded approach* is the expectation of lower entry costs for management solutions because for simple tasks and smaller environments there is the chance that complex and expensive management platforms can be avoided altogether. In fact, the embedded approach is rapidly replacing telnet or serial port–based command line interfaces as the most primitive configuration interface offered by network equipment.

The main motivation behind using a *proxy solution* is the protection of investment in other architectures and products because of the support of existing standards. This approach is particularly attractive for environments in which the existence of central facilities for the collection, correlation, and processing of large volumes of data is essential.

Of course, the two approaches are not mutually exclusive and can easily be combined. A migration path based on existing solutions exists since the transition from the available specialized consoles to Web browsers usually does not pose a problem for the operators. In principle, Web-based solutions can easily be scaled for different-sized infrastructures. A management platform is neither required for small environments nor completely ruled out for large ones. The simple and intuitive usability of browser user interfaces simplifies the task of administrative personnel.

Web-based solutions: scalability for different-sized organizations

Aside from ease of use and cross-platform availability, Web browsers are attractive for management purposes for another reason: They offer a platform-independent execution environment for programs (Java applets) that, if necessary, can be loaded by servers. The main advantages of this are as follows:

Web browsers: platform-independent execution environment for management applications

- It is easier to achieve short *innovation cycles* and a favorable price–performance ratio for management software because no software has to be installed on the management consoles, and the different HW and SW architectures used with the clients do not have to be taken into account. However, differences in browser platforms and Java versions may decrease this advantage.

- If the functions are implemented as Java applets, the often heavily burdened platforms can *delegate* the execution of these functions to the consoles. Another reason why this is advantageous is SNMP-based management today rarely allows functions to be delegated to agents and, consequently, the workload created by polling is frequently very high.

Some browsers already have ORBs integrated into them. The ORBs allow Java applets direct access to CORBA server objects.

Further information about Web-based management can be found in [BDF97], [MAS97], [RPR97], [HEW97], and [JAN96]. Today, most manufacturers of management systems are working on Web-based solutions. In addition to the many purely proprietary solutions available, two approaches aim for an open architecture for Web-based management:

- *Java Management API Architecture*, which is being developed by the Sun subsidiary JavaSoft but is also supported by other manufacturers

- *Web-Based Enterprise Management Initiative*, which is being promoted by a consortium of different manufacturers dominated by Microsoft

Because of rapid technological advances in this area, it is not easy to project the future prospects for either architecture. However, both will be dealt with in detail because they represent the first attempts to offer a manufacturer-neutral basis for Web-based management solutions.

9.2   Java Management API

The Java Management API (JMAPI) was introduced by JavaSoft to support the use of the language Java in the implementation of management applications. The specification first defines a new management architecture that contains several central elements of the proxy solution for Web-based management described in the preceding section. But, on the other hand, it is in many ways much more than a purely architectural definition in that it also specifies a detailed implementation reference model for this architecture and implements fundamental components in the form of extensive class libraries.

JMAPI: architecture for Java-based management applications

The JMAPI architecture was first published in 1996. Version 1.0 of the tool kit for JMAPI was announced for 1998 but never has been released. During December 1998, Sun announced a new effort to develop the JMAPI architecture. The new initiative should produce version 2.0 of JMAPI. The specifications were announced for public review by March 1999. See *http://java.sun.com/products/JavaManagement* for current information about the status of the project. Information about Java can be found, for example, in [FLA97] and [CAW98].

The announcements of Sun state that JMAPI 2.0 shall use technologies from the previous prerelease of JMAPI as well as from Java Dynamic Management Kit 3.0 (see section 15.2.5). At the time of writing, no details about the new architecture were available. Therefore, we will give an overview of the existing architecture.

9.2.1 Architecture

Conceptionally, the JMAPI separates the management system into two components (management console and platform), an approach that is familiar to other architectures (e.g., TMN with its separation into OSF and WSF; see Chapter 5). The manager system is therefore structured according to the client–server principle; the management console (*Java-enabled Web browser*) assumes the role of client, the platform (*managed object server*) that of server. In addition, the JMAPI has two fundamentally different types of agents. The JMAPI architecture therefore consists of four fundamental elements (see Figure 9.3):

Separating managers into two components

- The *managed object server*, also called *admin runtime module* based on the name of the associated class library, represents the *basic infrastructure* of a *management platform*. Its core consists of a constructor component (managed object factory) that allows applications to coordinate in the creation, manipulation, and deletion of managed objects. It incorporates the following interfaces for this purpose:

  Managed object server: core of a management platform

  - Database access to persistent storage of managed objects (managed data interfaces and JDBC interfaces)
  - Communication with agents implemented in Java over RMI
  - Communication with agents over SNMP to access Internet MIBs (SNMP interfaces)

  It also stores Java code for implementing management applications or agents that, if required, can be loaded on the Java machines of the management consoles or the agents. The code for management applications is usually Java applets that are available from an HTTP server; the code for agents is Java applications.

- The *management console* decoupled from the platform appears as a *Web browser with an integrated Java machine*. It implements the graphical user interface and provides an operational environment for applications that are Java applets. This environment allows applications to communicate with the platform and, together with the class library *admin view module* (AVM), offers fundamental

  Java-compatible Web browsers: GUI and operational environment for management applications

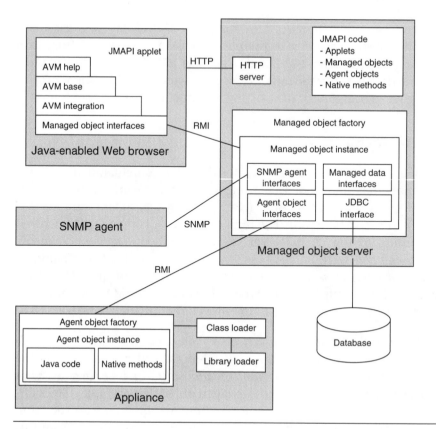

Figure 9.3
JMAPI architecture

integration and coordination mechanisms for different applications running on a console at the same time.

- *Managed object interfaces* allow access to the objects of the managed object server through RMI. These are stubs that can be used to invoke the methods of the managed object factory.
- *AVM integration* is for the coordination of different applications. For example, client stubs provide methods on servers that are used to register new applets, management-related HTML pages (*PageRegistryMO*), or extensions of interfaces for managed objects.
- *AVM help* is a general help system into which applications-specific help functions can be integrated.
- *AVM base* extends the Abstract Window Toolkit by various GUI classes ranging from simple windows to complex versions of tables and hierarchies.

AVM help and AVM base are in no way management specific and can be used completely independently of the libraries outlined here. These modules are therefore adopted into the general Java development environment.

■ *Management agents* that are implemented in Java are called *appliances*. They contain a constructor function for managed objects that are implemented by Java code, in some circumstances with program parts in architecture-specific object code (*native methods*). The code for the objects can be either integrated into the agent or loaded from the management server, if required.

Appliances: Java management agents

■ The architecture also facilitates access to *SNMP agents*. This access is usually through a managed object in the managed object server and using an *SNMP agent interface*. Communication with agents directly from applications on a console using SNMP is also possible. However, the security restrictions of applets could prove to be a hindrance.

Access to SNMP agents possible

9.2.2   Object Model

The JMAPI *management information model* is a *refinement* of the *Java object model* and incorporates well-known object-oriented principles. It separates interface definitions (an example is given in section 7.2.3) on which multiple inheritance is provided from implementations of the interfaces in the form of object classes that incorporate only single inheritance.

JMAPI information model: refinement of Java object model

The *model* for *managed objects* is provided by the definition of the *ManagedObject* interface, which can be inherited and refined from the concrete interface definitions for managed object classes. The interface is implemented by the abstract class *ManagedObjectImpl*, which similarly can be inherited and specialized from implementations of the refined interfaces. In the process, the abstract methods are overwritten with a concrete implementation.

The ManagedObject interface defines access to managed objects

Managed objects in this model are embedded in a managed object server, hence in a management platform. These are database objects that are either proxy objects for real resources in the agents, the *agent objects*, or pure database objects for which no counterparts exist in the agents. The *ManagedObject* interface provides fundamental methods for use in the following areas:

Managed objects are database objects

■ Read and write *access* to *attributes*

- *Administration* of *relationships* involving a managed object, such as the addition or deletion of relationships or the querying of existing relationships

- Methods for the *management* of *event messages,* such as the registration of objects that seek to subscribe to specific event messages of an object

- Basic mechanisms that support the *execution* of *transactions* on several objects, such as locking or resetting an object or committing a prepared modification

ManagedObject is the root of a hierarchy of refined definitions for diverse resources

This interface was used as the basis for defining a fundamental object class hierarchy (see Figure 9.4) for management purposes. These classes too are for the most part still abstract; in other words, they cannot be instantiated. They serve as a structuring framework for manufacturers who should be refining them into instantiable concrete classes for resources. For example, the class `LogicalElem`, which is derived directly from `ManagedObject`, is refined further into a logical component, and this class in turn is refined into logical storage. External elements are objects that, although they must be described within the framework of the JMAPI, are not administered with this architecture; an example is people.

Figure 9.4 shows the currently valid JMAPI object class hierarchy. Some of it is based on an earlier version of CIM (see section 9.3.2). At the time of writing, it is not clear whether JMAPI 2.0 will be information model independent or whether CIM will be adopted.

9.2.3 Communication Model

Communication in JMAPI is based on RMI, SNMP, and HTTP

The JMAPI communication model includes three different communication protocols:

- *HTTP* is used to load Java applets, which represent parts of management applications, from a managed object server to the management console, thus to a Web browser with a Java virtual machine.

- On the one hand, management applications use *remote method invocation* (RMI) to communicate with managed objects on the managed object server. On the other hand, these managed objects use RMI to access agents in which Java code implementing the agent objects is run.

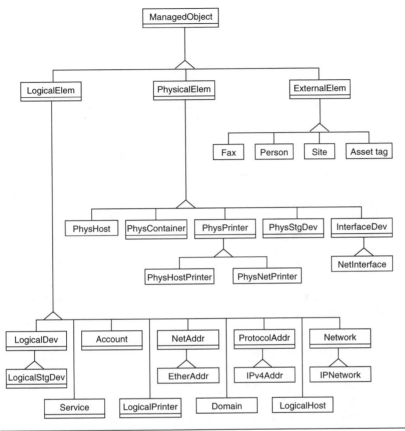

Figure 9.4
JMAPI object model

- To enable direct access to the large number of SNMP agents, the architecture allows managed objects to access agents in the resources through RMI as well as over *SNMP*.

9.2.4   Functional Model

The aim in using Java applets to implement management applications is to use the processing capacity available on management consoles. Function execution is not only delegated from the platform to the agents but also to the consoles; this provides enormous flexibility as far as the arrangement of the functional modules is concerned.

Since the JMAPI is a very new architecture compared to those discussed in Chapters 5–8, few concrete definitions of management functionality can be transferred and also shared by many applications

Java allows a flexible delegation of functionality

JMAPI provides classes for event management

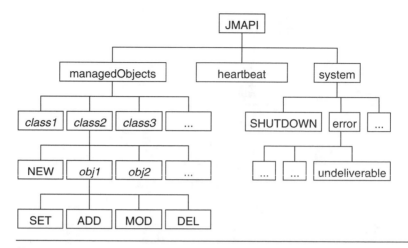

Figure 9.5
The standard event tree for JMAPI

aside from the fundamental specification given. The only function that has been defined so far is the one on event management that is implemented in the form of diverse classes.

Event dispatchers on Java agents transmit event notifications

The JMAPI *event management service* model specifies that *event dispatchers* are run in agents, the appliances. Resources direct their event notifications to these dispatchers. The notifications can then be subscribed to from the dispatchers by interested applications.

Option for subscribing to and filtering notifications

The different types of notifications are arranged in the form of a tree in which generic notifications can be refined into more and more specific notifications. (Figure 9.5 presents the standard JMAPI event tree.) An application subscribes to the notifications of the branch of a tree by indicating the root of the subtree, a filter class, and an action class. If an event occurs from the subtree, the dispatcher instantiates the filter class and applies the filter method defined there to the event notification. If the method evaluates the Boolean value `true`, the action class that contains the specification on how the message can be delivered to the receiver is then instantiated.

Notification model: management-specific extension of generic event management

The JMAPI uses this general event management model as the basis for defining a management-specific refinement in the form of a *notification model*. This includes defining the following standard event notifications:

- Addition, modification, or deletion of managed objects in the database
- Creation of new managed objects (`NEW`)

■ Termination of a managed object server (SHUTDOWN)

ObserverProxy, another class that has been introduced, contributes considerably toward simplifying the subscription of notifications for management applications compared to the basic event service.

9.3 Web-Based Enterprise Management

A consortium of manufacturers, called the *Web-Based Enterprise Management Initiative* (WBEM) and consisting of Microsoft, Intel, CISCO, Compaq, and others, was formed at about the same time that development started on the JMAPI. The goal of this consortium was to develop an open, vendor-neutral architecture for the Web-based management of the entire enterprise DP infrastructure of an organization. The new architecture, called *hypermedia management* (HMM), was supposed to bring the different existing management approaches under one umbrella. The central elements of the architecture were to include Web technologies, specifically Web browsers and a management protocol based on HTTP.

During the course of development, a management protocol, the so-called *hypermedia management protocol* (HMMP) was specified, which contrary to original intentions, was not based on HTTP but directly on transport protocols and overall had very little in common with HTTP. HMMP also failed to deliver any major new approaches for the integration of Web browsers into management architectures.

The difficulties of succeeding in the market today with a totally new management architecture and, particularly, a new management protocol were not recognized until later. Consequently, what was considered to be the most promising component of the architecture, the information model called *common information model* (CIM), was removed early from the development process of the architecture and turned over to the *Desktop Management Task Force* (see *http://www.dmtf.org*). CIM is already being used or supported by some manufacturers.

Common information model (CIM) is currently a key component of WBEM

In the meantime, the rest of the architecture has also been transferred to the Desktop Management Task Force (DMTF) for development, with the result that some major changes have been instigated. Work on HMMP was suspended, and a new initiative has been started to define a mapping of CIM to the *extensible markup language* (XML) (see *http://www.w3.org/XML/*). In other words, the original intention to create a management architecture based on Web technologies and HTTP has been reestablished.

As of the beginning of 1999, it is difficult to assess the future prospects and positioning for the WBEM architecture. The influence of the DMTF and its member firms has to be weighed against the problems created by establishing new management standards in the market. For example, Microsoft considers WBEM to be a key component of its management strategy (*Zero Administration Initiative for Windows*) and has announced the integration of WBEM technologies into future versions of Windows, starting with Windows 2000 Server (formerly Windows NT Server 5.0).

Up-to-date information on WBEM is available at *http://www.dmtf. org/* or *http://www.microsoft.com/management*.

9.3.1 Architecture

Key components: CIM, MOF, and a mapping from CIM to XML

As of the beginning of 1999, the WBEM architecture addresses mainly management information aspects. The most important parts of the architecture are:

- The *common information model* (CIM), an object-oriented model for the description of management information

- The *managed object format* (MOF), a syntax specification for managed objects that have been modeled using CIM

- A specification for the representation of CIM in the *extensible markup language* (XML) (see *http://www.w3.org/XML/*), an XML grammar, written in document type definition (DTD) that can be used to represent CIM classes and instances

HTTP is used to transfer management information

Mapping CIM to XML means that any Web browser that ships with an implementation of an XML parser can be used to display and render management information. No specialized management protocol is needed in this context; HTTP (see *http://www.w3.org/Protocols*) is used to transfer management information.

In the following, we will be looking briefly at CIM, MOF, and representing CIM in XML.

9.3.2 Common Information Model

CIM is to form the "umbrella" over existing information models

The main component of the WBEM is the *common information model* (CIM), previously called *hypermedia management schema* (HMMS) and currently undergoing further development by the DMTF. The definition of a completely new management information model was motivated by the central requirement of integrated management for as unrestricted and loss-free information exchange as possible. Most of the different information models available today cannot easily be mapped directly to each other, and the transitions between them almost inevitably result in considerable information loss.

The aim is to create a common "umbrella" for existing models on which management applications can be run. The integration of existing models is to be resolved in a way that minimizes losses from mapping. Furthermore, a possibility should be created for gradually replacing the data type–oriented information models of Internet management and DMTF-DMI with an object-oriented model.

CIM is consequently based on an object-oriented, programming language–independent approach. It defines:

CIM: object oriented and programming language independent

- A basic information model referred to as a *metaschema*

- A syntax for the description of managed objects (*managed object format*, MOF)

- Two layers of generic managed object classes, called the core model and the common model

As of the beginning of 1999, the current version of CIM is 2.1. The metaschema is defined with the help of unified modeling language (UML) (e.g., see [RJB98], [BRJ98], [MUL97], or [ERP97] and *http://www. rational.com/uml/documentation.html*). It contains the following key elements (named elements; see Figure 9.6):

- *Classes* characterize sets of objects with shared properties. Only single inheritance is possible between classes. Inheritance relationships are not strict; therefore, inherited properties or methods can be overwritten.

- *Methods* define the signatures of operations that can be executed on the objects of a class.

- *Qualifiers* are used to specify the additional characteristics of classes or the properties and methods of the classes. Examples include the different access options to properties (READ, WRITE), information on mapping attributes to an existing MIB (MappingStrings), the classification of attributes as keys (i.e., names) for entities (Key), and the identification of classes that cannot be instantiated (ABSTRACT).

- *Associations* are classes (or the instantiations of them) that represent relationships between two or more objects. They therefore contain at least two references.

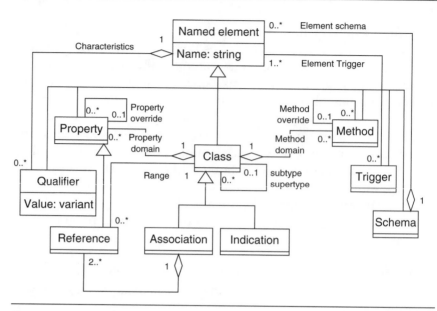

Figure 9.6
Structure of the CIM metaschema

- *References* are special properties. They make reference to other objects.

- *Event classes* (*indications*) are used to define different types of event notifications. The instantiations of these classes are the corresponding type of concrete event notification generated by the *trigger* mechanism.

- *Schemas* are groups of elements combined for administrative purposes (e.g., naming).

The concrete managed object classes defined on the basis of the metaschema and MOF are arranged into a three-layer inheritance and specialization hierarchy:

Core model: basis
for the inheritance
hierarchy

- The *core model* provides a small number of classes, associations, and properties usable in all management domains and disciplines and serving as the starting point for all refinements. Examples include classes such as ManagedSystemElement, the classes PhysicalElement and LogicalElement derived from it, and then in turn the classes System and Service derived from the latter.

- The *common model* refines the core model into classes that, on the one hand, are still not dependent on specific technologies or implementations, but, on the other hand, are already concrete enough so that they can serve as the basis for many management applications. Areas to be covered by the classes are applications, networks and network components, end systems with attached devices, and databases.

■ *Extension schemas* refine the common model for special technologies. For example, Microsoft specified an extension schema (*Win32 Schema*) that specializes the classes for the common model for Windows 95/98 and Windows NT.

9.3.3 Managed Object Format

The *managed object format* (MOF) specifies the syntax for managed object definitions that are based on the CIM metaschema. The MOF notation is a customary template language, comparable to GDMO or to Internet SMI.

The following example incorporates an excerpt from the definitions for the classes mentioned in MOF syntax. Defined are the abstract class CIM_ManagedSystemElement with the attributes Description and InstallTime, the class CIM_LogicalElement as a subclass of CIM_ManagedSystemElement, and the class CIM_OperatingSystem in turn as a subclass of CIM_LogicalElement with the attributes NumberOfLicensedUsers, LastBootUpTime, NumberOfUsers, NumberOfProcesses, and so forth. In each case, a description of the semantics of the attribute appears in English. Other language elements are used to indicate the key attributes for identification of the objects (key) and the mapping to management information that is defined in other architectures or information models such as DMTF MIF or in an Internet MIB (MappingStrings).

```
    [Abstract,
    Description(...)]
class CIM_ManagedSystemElement
{
    ...
        [Description ("The Description
        property provides a textual description
        of the object."), ...]
    string Description;
        [Description ("A datetime value
        indicating when the object was installed.
        A lack of a value does not indicate that the
        object is not installed."),
```

Suggested mapping to DMTF MIF

```
        MappingStrings {"MIF.DMTF|ComponentID|001.5"}, ...]
    datetime InstallDate;
    ...
};
class CIM_LogicalElement:CIM_ManagedSystemElement
{
};
```

System: subclass of LogicalElement

```
class CIM_System:CIM_LogicalElement
{
        [Key, ...]
    string CreationClassName;
        [Override ("CIM_ManagedSystemElement:Name"),
        Description ("The inherited Name serves as key of
        a System instance in an enterprise environment"),
        Key, ...]
```

Key to instances consists of two elements

```
    string Name;
    ...
        [Description ("An array (bag) of strings that
        specify the roles this System plays in the
        IT-Environment."), ...]
    string Roles[];
};
class CIM_OperatingSystem:CIM_LogicalElement
{
    ...
        [Description ("Number of user licenses for the
        OperatingSystem. If unlimited, enter 0. If
        unknown, enter -1.")]
    sint32 NumberOfLicensedUsers;
        [Description ("Time when the
        OperatingSystem was last booted")]
    datetime LastBootUpTime;
    ...
        [Description ("Number of user sessions for which
        the OperatingSystem is currently storing state
        information"),
```

Suggested mapping to an Internet MIB

```
        MappingStrings {"RFC1514|hrSystemNumUsers"}]
    uint32 NumberOfUsers;
        [Description ("Number of process contexts
        currently loaded or running on the
        OperatingSystem"),
        MappingStrings {"RFC1514|hrSystemProcesses"}]
```

```
uint32 NumberOfProcesses;
    [Description ("Total swap space in bytes"),
    Units("Bytes")]
uint64 TotalSwapSpaceSize;
    [Description ("Number of Kbytes of virtual
      memory supported"),
    Units("KBytes")]
uint64 TotalVirtualMemorySize;
    [Description ("Number of Kbytes of virtual
    memory currently unused and available"),
    Units("KBytes")]
uint64 FreeVirtualMemory;
    [Description ("Number of Kbytes of physical
    memory currently unused and available"),
    Units("KBytes")]
uint64 FreePhysicalMemory;
...
};
```

Supplementary information on the attribute

9.3.4   Representing CIM in XML

The MOF provides a textual representation of management information modeled using CIM. However, this representation alone is not sufficient to transfer management information in heterogeneous environments. For the latter, a mapping of the representation to a communication protocol is needed. As mentioned before, in the earlier stages of the WBEM initiative, it was planned to introduce a completely new management protocol for this purpose. When DMTF took over the responsibility for the development of the WBEM architecture, the original goal of using HTTP as the management protocol had been reestablished. This led to the specification of a mapping of CIM to XML.

Mapping CIM to XML

XML is a subset of the standardized generalized markup language (SGML). It is used to represent structured data (such as management information) in textual form. In XML, a document can optionally have a description of its grammar attached. The grammar for an XML document is described using a mechanism known as document type definition (DTD). The DTD describes the allowable elements in the XML document. A document that is structured according to the rules defined in the XML specification is termed "well formed." In addition to being well formed, an XML document can be "valid." A valid XML document must contain a DTD, and the grammar of the document must conform to that specified in the DTD.

XML: subset of SGML

Metaschema mapping

In order to make use of XML to represent management information, an XML vocabulary (i.e., a DTD for CIM classes and instances) must be defined. Several alternatives exist for such a definition. The DMTF used a so-called *metaschema mapping* (i.e., one in which the XML schema is used to describe the CIM metaschema), and both CIM classes and instances are valid XML documents for that schema. The DTD is used to describe in a generic fashion the notion of a CIM class or instance.

HTTP as management protocol

XML documents do not necessarily contain information about the rendering of the data contained. This can be achieved by the use of extensible style language (XSL) style sheets. They can be used both to render XML information graphically and to transform it into other formats. Any number of XSL style sheets can be associated with an XML document. For example, XSL style sheets can be written that graphically present managed objects or provide a transformation to MOF.

All in all, the definition of a DTD for CIM, together with the capabilities of XSL, provides a way to communicate CIM-based management information in heterogeneous environments via HTTP, provided that XML parsers (i.e., XML-capable browsers) are available. XSL can be used as a standardized way to render management information.

9.4 Agent Technology

Variety of agent technologies

Agent technology is one of the fastest growing areas of information technology. The wide deployment of Web browsers, Web applications, and Java provided the means and the infrastructure for development, implementation, deployment, and usage of new agent technologies. These are known under a variety of terms, including intelligent, flexible, learning, rational, or autonomous agents. Recently, application of these technologies in network and systems management yielded very promising results.

It would lead far beyond the scope of this book to review all these approaches and technologies. We therefore refer you to [JEW98] for a first overview. In the following, we will only briefly sketch the components of a typical framework for the application of intelligent or flexible agents in network and systems management.

Applying agent technology to management

In the context of management, applying intelligent agent technology today mostly means that only a lightweight basic agent is initially present on systems that have to be managed. Management functionality then is configured on this agent when required (i.e., additional components are downloaded or existing functionality is modified to meet the new management requirements on a case-by-case basis). Such a management agent in principle consists of the following components:

- The *agent core*, also called management framework or agent backplane bus, that provides the runtime environment for the other components. It controls the latter, enables communication between them, delivers incoming requests to the appropriate component, and allows managers to install new components or to delete existing ones. The agent core may be implemented, for example, on the basis of a Java virtual machine and the components as JavaBeans.

- *Basic management services*, such as notification services, filtering, or persistent storage of objects that can be commonly used by the other management components.

- *Protocol adapters* (i.e., implementations of management protocol entities) that enable communications via SNMP, CMIP, IIOP, RMI, HTTP, and so on.

- *Management components* that execute a specific management task. They are typically loaded to the agent core when required and use the basic management services and the protocol adapters.

Many vendors have implemented agents or agent frameworks of this type. Examples are Sun's JDMK (see section 15.2.5) or Odyssey from General Magic (see *http://www.genmagic.com*). Tivoli and Computer Associates also use a comparable technology for their agents.

9.5 Chapter Summary

In this chapter, we tried to point out the basic concepts that lie behind the buzzphrase *Web-based management*. First of all, we sketched the two basic schemes that can be followed when Web-based management is implemented: the *embedded approach* and the *proxy solution*.

Then, we gave an overview of two important approaches to Web-based management: Sun's Java Management API (JMAPI) and the Web-Based Enterprise Management (WBEM) of the DMTF. Although the two have been started both with the same vision (i.e., implementing an open approach to Web-based management), the outcome is completely different.

JMAPI focuses on APIs for the support of agent and application developers. Its main goal is the rapid and efficient implementation of portable and reusable management agents. The component-based approach was used to foster adaptation to or integration of new management requirements. WBEM, on the other hand, concentrated on the development of a completely new management information model. This was motivated by the central requirement of integrated management for as unrestricted and loss-free information exchange as possible. The aim is to create a common umbrella for existing models. In conjunction with the approaches described in the following chapter, this could lay the foundations for a *deep integration* of management architectures.

Gateways between Management Architectures

As outlined in previous discussions, different types of management architectures are available today, and they are all designed for different application areas. Each architecture incorporates advantages as well as disadvantages. Today, OSI management is being used primarily for telecommunications networks within the framework of TMN, and Internet management is finding its application with LAN components. DMI is becoming an important architecture in the area of workstation computers and their components. CORBA will undoubtedly establish itself in the management of end systems and applications. But what happens is that "management islands" are created, and initially there is no link between them. The problem will possibly even be accentuated if the new architectures that were covered in the last chapter gain acceptance. The integration needed in the management of all the information processing systems of an individual organization is therefore still not available.

Different management architectures lead to management islands

The problem does not arise only when different classes of resources, such as network components, and applications require administration. Several management architectures and models are often available for a single class of resources. Today, DMTF MIFs (see section 8.2.1) and Internet MIBs are both specifying the management-relevant properties of end systems. Furthermore, systems often contain an ORB that offers management from a CORBA-based platform.

Several management models often exist for just one class of resources

Another example can be seen in the framework that was defined by the ATM Forum (see *http://www.atmforum.com/*) for the management of ATM networks (see, e.g., [BLA95b]). It also uses several management architectures. A change in (management) technology is required at the LAN–WAN transitions, although the systems being managed implement the same fundamental communications mechanisms. The framework defines five different *M-interfaces* for management (also see Figure 10.1):

Example: ATM management from the ATM Forum

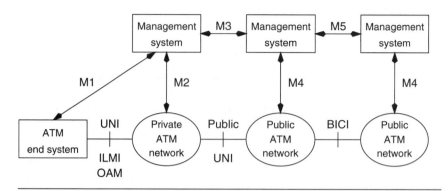

Figure 10.1
ATM management of the ATM Forum

- *M1* for the management of ATM end systems. This is based on the integrated local management interface (ILMI) [ATM96], the user-network interface specification (UNI) [ATM94c], and the managed objects for ATM management (RFC 1695). The ILMI uses SNMP for message exchange; RFC 1695 specifies an Internet MIB. M1 is therefore completely oriented toward Internet management.

- *M2* for the management of private ATM networks and ATM switches. Like M1, M2 relies on SNMP and RFC 1695 and can be extended to include additional MIBs; thus, it too uses the Internet management architecture.

- *M3* for the management of relationships and connections between private and public TM networks. This interface is also referred to as a CNM interface [ATM94a] and, like M1 and M2, is based on SNMP.

- *M4* for the management of public ATM networks. M4 provides functionality that is similar to M2 but is directed toward large public networks. It is primarily based on CMIP, which is the dominant protocol used in the telecommunications area. However, SNMP is also accepted. Different MIBs for M4 are specified for the two different protocols.

- *M5* for the management of relationships and connections between two public ATM networks. It mirrors the broadband ISDN intercarrier interface (BICI) [ATM95] on the management side and, like M4, is primarily based on CMIP.

It is therefore evident that a technology and even a single interface can involve the use of several management architectures! The examples show that a great deal of attention must be given to the gateways

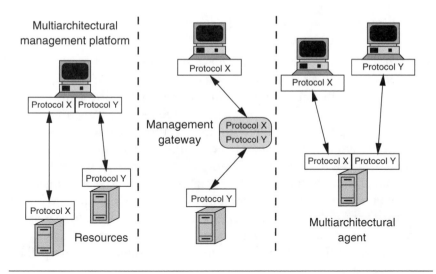

Figure 10.2
Different types of architectural transitions

between management architectures today if the objective is to achieve integrated management.

10.1 Different Types of Architectural Gateways

With the growing number of management architectures in the market, increasing importance is being attached to architectural gateways that allow a comprehensive view of information processing infrastructures even in environments that incorporate different architectures. These architectural gateways also take into account relationships between resources that have to be accessed by different management protocols. Basically, there are *three variants* of architectural gateways (also see Figure 10.2):

The importance of the transitions between management architectures is growing

- *Multiarchitectural platforms:* The transition is implemented within the management platform, thus within the managing system that "speaks several management languages." There is therefore no need for a direct translation of the protocols, and instead, mapping is carried out to the corresponding communications API of the platform. The translation of the management information often does not take place within the infrastructure of the platform but is instead carried out in the management applications. The differences between the architectures are thus even reflected in the applications; the

Transition in the management platform: multiarchitectural platform architectures frequently simply coexist alongside each other on a common user interface.

Transition in an intermediate system: management gateway

- *Management gateways:* In this case, the transition is implemented by an intermediate system that not only translates the management information but also converts the management protocols. To the manager that was developed for management architecture X, the *gateway* appears as an agent for architecture X. On the other hand, from the standpoint of agents or resources that are implemented on the basis of a different management architecture, Y, it represents a manager for architecture Y. The gateway functions as a "translator" between the two management languages. When it operates without causing any data loss, its existence is totally transparent to managers as well as to agents; managers or agents just see the agents or managers of their own architecture. Management gateways will be dealt with in detail later.

Transition in the agent: multi-architectural agent

- *Multiarchitectural agents:* Here the necessary mappings are carried out in the agent, which means in the system being administered; in this case, it is the agent that "speaks several languages." As with a multiarchitectural platform, no protocol conversion is required. In contrast to the management gateways, no general additional translation is required between standard information models. Local information is merely mapped onto different management information from different architectures. If several management protocols are required for write access to the same resource, then access must be properly coordinated by the agent that can use locking mechanisms for this purpose. Multilingualism is not particularly suitable for use with simple components. Yet in practice multilingual agents frequently exist because SNMP agents are preconfigured for most systems today and because management agents of other architectures are often installed as extras on workstation systems and servers. In fact, all agents map from one language (local data) to another language, a standard management language like GDMO or Internet SMI.

Objective of the transitions: concealing the existence of different architectures

The aim with all variants is to conceal the existence of different management architectures as much as possible from users, thus the operators of DP infrastructures, and from the management applications. The goal is to offer users a uniform view of all the systems being administered and to design an efficient implementation of the applications.

In the following sections, we will take a closer look at management gateways, that is, architectural gateways. The problems involved in implementing gateways are a superset of the problems that have to be addressed with the other two types. As we already mentioned, no protocol conversion is required with multiarchitectural platforms that expose architectural differences to applications directly, and no translation of information models is needed with multiarchitectural agents that map directly into more than one architecture.

Further information about architectural gateways can be found in [KAS94], [KAS93], [KEL98], [KEN97b], [ACH93], and [MBL93].

10.2   Management Gateways

At the heart of every management architecture are the definitions of concrete managed objects in the respective information model. Transitions are introduced between architectures with the aim of allowing unrestricted access to these managed objects across all architectural boundaries. Management information available in one architecture has to be translated into the information model of the other architecture to enable it to be used in the other architecture (see section 10.2.1). This process is carried out only once for each of the concrete managed object classes of the different architectures. This mapping of information models or managed object classes is therefore also referred to as a "static aspect" of gateways.

Translation of management information

Clarification is also needed on how the communication mechanisms of one architecture are converted to the processes of another architecture during the runtime of gateways, in other words, how the different management protocols and services are mapped to each other (see section 10.2.2). This is referred to as the dynamic aspect of the gateways.

Protocol conversion

10.2.1   Translation of Management Information

Information definitions can basically be translated in two different ways: at a syntactical level or at a semantic level.

- *Translation at syntactical level:* With this translation, an attempt is made to map the information models along with their description syntaxes to one another. An algorithm is developed that translates the elements of one specification language into the equivalent elements of the other specification language. The implementations

Translation of syntax: mapping the specification languages

of this algorithm are often referred to as specification compilers. The translators operate at a purely syntactical level; an interpretation of the semantics of the information being translated is not required. This variant is often referred to as *specification translation.* An example is the translation of Internet SMI to GDMO, which is explained in more detail in section 10.3.1.

Translation of semantics: mapping of concrete managed objects

- *Translation at a semantic level:* With this type of translation, the semantics of the information definitions of one architecture are analyzed and an attempt is made to map these semantics as closely as possible to the management information that exists in the other architecture. The aim in so doing is to achieve a maximum integration of the information of both architectures. The abstract, generic classes of the target architecture can be used as the basis. For example, if you were translating MIB II of Internet management into the managed object classes of OSI management, you would try to map the information contained in the group `tcp` to classes derived from the OSI managed object classes `communicationsEntity`, `coProtocolMachine`, and `singlePeerConnection` (see ISO 10165-5) or, even preferably, to `transportEntity`, `comodePM`, and `transportConnection` (see ISO 10737). This would produce an optimal integration of the management information of the two architectures.

Translation of specification languages can be automated

The advantage of translation at the syntactical level is that it can be automated and even standardized. Separately executed translations therefore deliver identical results. However, the resulting information is only integrated syntactically into the target architecture, meaning that although it is based on the information model of this architecture, it does not take into account management information with the same or similar semantics that may already exist. Two inheritance hierarchies already separated at the root emerge. The classes outlined in section 10.3.1, which are produced from the translation of Internet SMI to GDMO and without exception are derived from `top`, are an example of this.

Translation of concrete managed objects provides deeper integration of architectures

Translation at the semantic level avoids this disadvantage. With this approach, the only inheritance hierarchy produced is one that integrates the management information from both architectures. But there is a price to pay for this advantage, which is that translations cannot be executed automatically because an in-depth analysis of the semantics of the information of both architectures is required. Furthermore, separately executed translations can sometimes provide different results since different translators could be selecting different mappings. So when the information contained in group `tcp` is mapped to classes

in the preceding example, for the managed object class you can select communicationsEntity, coProtocolMachine, and singlePeer-
Connection from ISO 10165-5, or you can select transportEntity,
comodePM, and transportConnection from ISO 10737.

The most appropriate method differs according to business needs. If
no parallel MIB exists (see, for example, section 10.4.1) or development
time is short, syntactic translation may be desired. If parallel MIBs exist,
semantic translation may be the only method to achieve the desired
goal.

10.2.2   Protocol and Service Conversion

During the runtime of a gateway, the different protocols and services
must be mapped to each other in such a way that the existence of the
gateway is transparent to the management system and to the agents.
The following interactions occur:

- *Information queries* and *control messages* from the manager are
  received by the gateway, converted into the appropriate queries
  and control messages of the target protocol, and forwarded to the
  agent.
- Analogously, the resulting *responses* from the agent are accepted by
  the gateway, converted, and delivered to the management system.
- *Asynchronous event notifications* from the agents are received by
  the gateway, converted, and forwarded to the manager system.

> Protocol conver-
> sion deals with
> control messages,
> queries, responses,
> and asynchronous
> event notifications

The protocol conversion can be divided into two largely independent task areas:

- *Name mapping:* Identifier properties in the original request must
  be mapped to corresponding properties of the target.
- *Service mapping:* Services or the functionality requested through the
  use of the protocol of the original architecture must be mapped to
  the corresponding services or functionality of the target architecture
  and appropriate protocol elements.

> Mapping of object
> identifiers
>
> Mapping of
> functions

A gateway can either convert each query from a management
system directly into a query to an agent or otherwise attempt to deal
with the query itself using earlier responses from the agent.

The first gateway is a *stateless gateway*. It does not store any management information from the agents, which is superfluous to what it
requires itself in order to access the agents. A *stateful gateway*, on the

Two types of gateways: stateless and stateful

other hand, entirely or partially replicates the MIB of the agents in a local database and is therefore in a position to process certain queries from the management system itself without having to forward them to the agents. Mechanisms need to be implemented in this case to ensure that the replicated information and the original information in the agents are consistent with one another, at least to the extent that any deviations are within an acceptable limit.

An important difference between the two types of gateways is the handling of management information that cannot be appropriately mapped directly to the other side. A stateful gateway can use data from other sources (e.g., other tools) to add information to its responses (i.e., enhance incomplete mappings between the two domains). This in general is not possible when using a pure stateless gateway.

Stateful gateways require complex mechanisms for ensuring consistency

Ensuring that this consistency exists is usually very complex mainly because:

- The existing information models do not contain any constructs to indicate whether certain information is static or dynamic. It is therefore not possible to automate the derivation of this property from the definitions for concrete management information.

- Many variables often show a very low dynamic over long periods, but this dynamic starts to increase rapidly when faults occur. These are the types of changes that are particularly important for management. If the mechanisms for ensuring consistency that are used derive update cycles from the dynamic of the variables in the past, there is a danger that important changes, in particular, will not be mirrored in the replications, and the management system will therefore not be aware of fault situations.

- Changes are often not only carried out by one but by several management systems, some of which do not use a gateway but access the agents directly. This even presents a problem for the replication of information that does not show any of its own dynamic but can be changed only through the use of explicit write management operations.

- Variables are often also changed as a side effect of management operations, but there is no mechanism that allows the reason for the change to be recognized unequivocally in the information definitions. An example is counters that are reset as a side effect of a general change to state.

Despite all these problems, intensive efforts are currently under way to produce suitable mechanisms for guaranteeing consistency. The anticipated gain in performance is not the only reason behind these efforts. Stateless gateways are no longer an efficient option if the extended functions of management protocols such as scoping and filtering of CMIP are also mapped in the gateways.

10.3   ISO/CCITT and Internet Management Coexistence (IIMC)

It was already foreseeable in 1992 that in the medium term neither OSI management nor Internet management would be able to succeed on its own and that both of them would have to establish themselves in different areas of application. It also became obvious that a seamless gateway between these two architectures would be necessary for the purposes of integrated management. The specifications required for a *gateway* between the *two architectures* was therefore developed within the framework of the *ISO/CCITT and Internet Management Coexistence* (IIMC) initiative, which was primarily spurred on by the Network Management Forum (now Telemanagement Forum). The most important of these specifications relate to translation algorithms for management information in both directions and to a protocol conversion from CMIP to SNMP. The documents and specifications produced by the IIMC initiative can be accessed at *http://www.nmf.org* or *http://www.tmforum.org*. The specifications are currently being supported by a number of products, such as *Sun Solstice TMN/SNMP Q-Adaptor* (see *http://www.sun.com/solstice*) and *Multi-Protocol CMIP Mediation Solution* from Netmansys (*http://www.netmansys.com/*). An overview of the products of the different vendors is available from NMF (TM Forum) at *http://www.nmf.org* or *http://www.tmforum.org*.

IIMC: gateway between OSI management and Internet management

10.3.1   Translation of Management Information

Translation algorithms from ISO GDMO to Internet SMI (see [NMF30]) and conversely from Internet SMI to ISO GDMO (see [NMF26]) were developed by IIMC. Both procedures operate at a purely syntactical level. Therefore, no attempt is made, for example, to classify existing information in the inheritance hierarchy under *generic managed object classes* of OSI management in the translation of MIB II to GDMO.

Translation of management information is on a syntactical level

Although translations in both directions are specified, in practice, it is only the translation of Internet SMI to GDMO that has been commercially deployed on a wider scale. Even the protocol conversion deals only with the scenarios involving a CMIP-based management system and SNMP-based agents. Consequently, we will focus only on this direction of translation and conversion.

Registration and *naming* are important operations in the unique identification of management information. During the translation of Internet MIBs to GDMO, new object classes and name bindings occur that must be registered. Yet there is the advantage that each managed object of Internet management is contained with an object identifier in the subtree of the ISO registration tree (see section 5.2). The information that is produced is registered with the retention of the OID in another subtree.

For the naming, an attribute with the name of the class and the suffix "Id" is added to each class that is created. In object classes that are allowed only one instance per Internet MIB, the value of the attribute is set to `ASN.1 NULL`. For classes that are allowed more than one instance (corresponding to table rows), the respective index in the SNMP table is allocated to the name attribute.

The actual translation algorithm consists of the following main rules:

Groups and rows of tables become object classes; other Internet objects become attributes

- *Groups* of the Internet MIB being translated, such as the groups `system`, `ip`, `tcp`, from MIB II, become object classes.

- Table definitions, such as `tcpConnTable` and `ipRouteTable` from MIB II, are not translated. The *table rows* (e.g., `tcpConnEntry` and `ipRouteEntry`) become object classes. Instances of these classes are contained in instances of those classes that represent the corresponding group.

- All *other objects* of the Internet MIB become attributes of the appropriate class.

- *SNMP traps* are frequently not allocatable to any particular class or particular object. A generic notification is therefore defined to which all traps are mapped. This notification is sent out by the class that represents the group `system` of MIB II.

Example: OSI object class for an MIB II table

The following example shows the translation of `ipCidrRouteEntry` from `ipCidrRouteTable`, a new version (RFC 2096) of `ipRouteTable` from MIB II (RFC 1213). An excerpt of the definition in Internet SMI reads as follows:

```
ipCidrRouteTable OBJECT-TYPE
    SYNTAX SEQUENCE OF IpCidrRouteEntry
    ...
    ::= {ipForward 4 }
ipCidrRouteEntry OBJECT-TYPE
    SYNTAX IpCidrRouteEntry
    ...
    INDEX {
        ipCidrRouteDest,
        ipCidrRouteMask,
        ipCidrRouteTos,
        ipCidrRouteNextHop
        }
    ::= {ipCidrRouteTable 1 }
IpCidrRouteEntry ::=
SEQUENCE {
ipCidrRouteDest IpAddress,
...
ipCidrRouteNextHop IpAddress,
...
}
ipCidrRouteNextHop OBJECT-TYPE
    SYNTAX    IpAddress
    MAX-ACCESS    read-only
    STATUS    current
    DESCRIPTION
        "On remote routes, the address of the next system
        en route; Otherwise, 0.0.0.0."
    ::= { ipCidrRouteEntry 4 }
```

Definition in
Internet SMI

The GDMO object class `ipCidrRouteEntry` is derived from this definition with the use of the translation algorithm. Instances of this class represent the rows of the `ipCidrRouteTable`. The attributes `ipCidrRouteDest` and `ipCidrRouteNextHop` of the class correspond to the table columns of the same name. The definition of the attributes refers to the MIB objects (REFERENCE). The description of the attributes (DESCRIPTION) is taken unchanged from the translated MIB. Instances of the GDMO object class `ipCidrRouteEntry` are contained in instances of the class `ip`, which represents the group `ip` of MIB II.

```
ipCidrRouteEntry MANAGED OBJECT CLASS
    DERIVED FROM "Rec. X.721 | ISO/IEC 10165-2:1992":top;
    CHARACTERIZED BY ipCidrRouteEntryPkg PACKAGE
    BEHAVIOUR ipCidrRouteEntryPkgBehaviour BEHAVIOUR
        DEFINED AS
```

...and associated
GDMO definitions

```
!BEGINPARSE
REFERENCE
    !!This managed object class maps to the
    ipCidrRouteEntry with object id
    {ipCidrRouteTable 1} in RFC 2096.!!;
DESCRIPTION
    !!A particular route to a particular
    destination, under a particular policy.!!;
INDEX   RFC2096-MIB.ipCidrRouteDest,
    RFC2096-MIB.ipCidrRouteMask,
    RFC2096-MIB.ipCidrRouteTos,
    RFC2096-MIB.ipCidrRouteNextHop;
ENDPARSE!;;
ATTRIBUTES
    ipCidrRouteEntryId  GET,
    ipCidrRouteDest     GET,

    ...

    ipCidrRouteNextHop  GET,

    ...

REGISTERED AS { iimcAutoObjAndAttr
        1 3 6 1 2 1 4 24 4 1};
ipCidrRouteNextHop ATTRIBUTE
    DERIVED FROM {iimcIIMCIMIBTRANS}: ipAddress;
    BEHAVIOUR
        ipCidrRouteNextHopBehaviour BEHAVIOUR
        DEFINED AS
        !BEGINPARSE
        REFERENCE
        !!This attribute maps to ipCidrRouteNextHop with
         object id {ipCidrRouteEntry 4} in RFC2096.!!;
        DESCRIPTION
        !!On remote routes, the address of the next
        system en route; Otherwise, 0.0.0.0.!!;
        ENDPARSE!;;
    REGISTERED AS {iimcAutoObjAndAttr
            1 3 6 1 2 1 4 24 4 1 4};
```

It is clear from the example that a structured convention is used to apply the free-form text in the BEHAVIOUR clause defined by GDMO; it differentiates between the reference to the translated Internet management information (REFERENCE), the description of which corresponds to the MIB definition (DESCRIPTION), and the index of the SNMP table (INDEX).

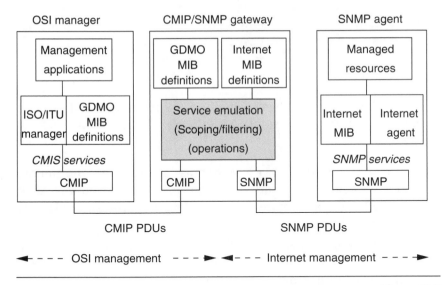

Figure 10.3
Structure of CMIP/SNMP gateway

10.3.2   Protocol and Service Conversion

As briefly mentioned, the only protocol conversion offered as part of the IIMC initiative is one that allows CMIP-based managers access to SNMP-based agents. It does not deal with the management of CMIP agents by SNMP managers.

Protocol conversion allows OSI managers access to SNMP agents

The IIMC approach describes a stateless gateway for the conversion of CMIS services executed over CMIP to SNMP PDUs. Figure 10.3 presents the architecture of the gateway. The main components of this conversion are briefly outlined here.

Object Selection

With CMIS requests, the set of instances to which an operation is applied is determined by the specification of a scope and a filter. Since the IIMC approach defines a stateless gateway, it has no knowledge about which objects are currently available in the agents. Therefore, SNMP-Get and SNMP-GetNext PDUs are used to establish which instances currently exist in the scope and the values of the attributes used in the filter. This is followed by the application of the filter statement to the values received of those instances that are in the scope. If this delivers the value `true`, the operation is executed on the object, otherwise not. However, the IIMC specification does not prevent the

Before each operation, a stateless gateway must first determine which instances exist implementation of stateful gateways that store management information tree data to optimize requests.

Service Emulation

Emulation of CMIS services with SNMP PDUs

Once the object selection has taken place, the requested CMIS service is emulated through the use of SNMP PDUs. The following rules are applied:

- If a read operation (M-GET-Request) is involved, the appropriate SNMP-GetRequest PDUs are sent to the agent. The results are then compiled into one or more M-GET-Response and transmitted to the manager.

- If a write operation is involved (M-SET-Request), the appropriate SNMP-SetRequest PDUs are generated. Similar to the read operation, these results are also compiled into one or more M-SET-Response.

Only table entries can be created and deleted

- SNMP has no operations for generating and deleting managed objects. The table entries that can be created or destroyed are an exception. An M-CREATE-Request can therefore be executed only if it relates to objects that represent table rows. In this case, it is mapped to SNMP-SetRequest PDUs, which manipulate certain columns of the table, particularly SNMPv2 row status.

- The same statements that apply to M-CREATE-Requests also apply to M-DELETE-Requests. The corresponding table row is deleted if the value of the column entry is set appropriately.

Because with CMIS one operation request in some cases can be used to access several MOs, an indication must be given of what the semantics of the request should look like if the operation cannot be executed to all MOs. As part of the service feature *synchronization*, CMIS offers the variants atomic and best effort (see section 5.4). If the CMIS services are mapped to SNMP, a CMIS request may result in several SNMP requests to carry out scope and filter. In this case, as a general rule, only best effort can be supported. Atomic synchronization is possible only if the CMIS request can be mapped to a single SNMP request PDU.

All traps are mapped to a generic notification

As we mentioned in the previous section, all SNMP traps are mapped to a generic notification internetAlarm. If the gateway receives an SNMP trap PDU, it generates an M-EVENT-REPORT that appears to originate from the object of the transmitting agent, which represents the group `system` of MIB II. The trap type is coded in the probable cause field of the `M-EVENT-REPORT`.

10.4   Joint Inter-Domain Management (JIDM)

The subject of management gateways has gained new relevance as a result of CORBA's use as an architecture for the management of networked systems. The Network Management Forum (Telemanagement Forum) and the Open Group consequently founded the *Joint Inter-Domain Management (JIDM) Group* in 1993 as a joint initiative. There was a recognition of the fact that a universal architecture for distributed applications like CORBA could also offer some advantages for management compared to the familiar specialized management architectures. This would allow conventional SW development methods to be applied in the management area as well, thereby enabling the use of reasonably priced standard development tools. The disadvantage is that only very few management-specific definitions and services are yet available in CORBA. What is almost completely lacking are definitions for concrete management information in the form of numerous MIBs that exist in other architectures. There is an obvious interest in exploiting the advantages of CORBA and of the specialized management architectures.

CORBA as a management architecture raises the issue of gateways again

There is a particular interest in mapping the languages of OSI management and Internet management to the OMG approach because extensive object specifications exist specifically for management purposes in both of the first cases and could be adopted for CORBA-based management.

Gateways between CORBA and OSI or Internet management should allow the use of the existing MI

The aim of JIDM is therefore to implement gateways between CORBA on the one hand and OSI management or Internet management on the other. CORBA-based management applications should be able to transfer information using an ORB that has been specified with IDL but originated from a translation of GDMO MIBs and Internet MIBs. Because of an interest in protecting investment, no changes are to be made to OSI agents and SNMP agents. These supply information from the corresponding MIBs over CMIP or SNMP to the gateway that makes it accessible to the manager via ORB and IIOP. It should also be possible to access CORBA agents using existing OSI-based management tools (see Figure 10.4).

The translation procedures required for implementing the gateways shown either were recently passed by the JIDM Group or are in the final stages of development. A brief overview of the specifications follows.

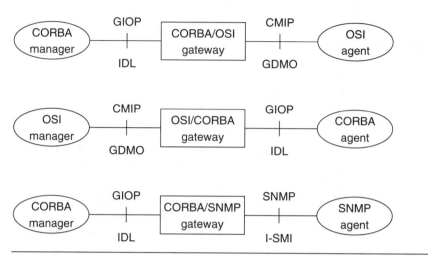

Figure 10.4
The key JIDM interoperability scenarios

The referenced documents and specifications are accessible at *http://www.opengroup.org* or *http://www.omg.org*. Additional information can be found in [SOH97]. The specifications (or parts of them) are already being supported by products such as MASK by ISR Global Telecom (see *http://www.isrglobal.com/*), the Q3ADE product suite from UH Communications (*http://www.uhc.dk/*), the HP OpenView Distributed Management Platform (see section 7.3.4 and *http://www.hp.com/ovtelecom/*), and products from Smile (*http://www.smile.fr/*). An overview of the products of different vendors is available from NMF (now Telemanagement Forum) at *http://www.tmforum.org*.

10.4.1   Translation of Management Information

Translation of GDMO and Internet SMI to CORBA IDL and of IDL interface definitions to GDMO

The scenarios given require that management information definitions in Internet SMI (I-SMI) and GDMO are translated into IDL interfaces and data type definitions. This process represents the main element of the work. Conversely, IDL interface definitions also have to be transformed into GDMO. Since CORBA does not yet incorporate object or interface definitions for management into which the translation results could have been inserted, a translation at the syntactical level has been selected. The appropriate translation algorithms specified in [OG509] are outlined next.

Mapping from ASN.1 Data Types to IDL Data Types

OSI and Internet management both use subsets of ASN.1 to define data types. The mapping of ASN.1 data types to IDL data types can therefore be used for CORBA/OSI gateways as well as for CORBA/SNMP gateways and consequently is specified separately in advance.

The translation of ASN.1 to IDL is required for GDMO to IDL and Internet SMI to IDL

In the mapping, each ASN.1 module is transferred to an IDL module. The mapping of the individual type definitions is carried out on the basis of a predetermined allocation table of ASN.1 types to IDL types. Parts of it cannot be executed directly or loss-free because ASN.1 has a more extensive type system than IDL. For example, ASN.1 contains a larger number of primitive types and, compared to IDL, hardly has any restrictions on the recursive definition of data types. In order to retain information identifying the original ASN.1 type, IDL types with identifiers that contain this information are introduced as an interim step. For example, the ASN.1 type `INTEGER` is mapped to the IDL type `long` for which the additional identifier `ASN1_Integer` is defined. All in all, the ASN.1 definition `"T0 ::= INTEGER"` is mapped to `"typedef long ASN1_Integer; typedef ASN1_Integer T0."`

Mapping of GDMO Definitions to IDL Interfaces

The previous data type mapping can now serve as the basis for the translation of the definitions of the GDMO template language into IDL interfaces. The IDL interface ManagedObject is introduced as the root of the inheritance hierarchy from which all translated interfaces inherit. The translation of GDMO definitions obeys the following rules:

Each managed object class creates an IDL interface with the appropriate attributes and operations

- Each *managed object class* is mapped to an IDL interface with the same name. The interface inherits from all interfaces that belong to the superior classes mentioned in the `"DERIVED FROM"` clause.

- Each *attribute*, depending on the types of access allowed (e.g., `GET`, `GET-REPLACE`), is mapped to a set of access operations the names of which always contain the name of the attribute as a prefix and the operation (e.g., `Get`, `Set`) as a suffix.

- *Operations* (`ACTION`) are mapped directly to IDL operations with the same name.

- *Notifications* are mapped to a number of separate interfaces. The interfaces support the typed or untyped event notifications of the CORBA event service and both types of delivery (`push` or `pull`).

The following example shows an excerpt from the GDMO definition for the managed object class `top`:

```
top MANAGED OBJECT CLASS
CHARACTERIZED BY
topPackage PACKAGE
BEHAVIOUR topBehaviour;
ATTRIBUTES
objectClass GET,
nameBinding GET;;;
CONDITIONAL PACKAGES
packagesPackage PACKAGE
ATTRIBUTES
packages GET;
...
```

The corresponding IDL definitions are:

```
interface top : ManagedObject {
X721Att::ObjectClassType
objectClassGet()
raises (CMIS_ATTRIBUTE_ERRORS);
X721Att::NameBindingType
nameBindingGet()
raises (CMIS_ATTRIBUTE_ERRORS);
X721Att:: PackagesType
packagesGet()
raises (CMIS_ATTRIBUTE_ERRORS);
```

The main complication with this procedure is caused by the different inheritance and specialization mechanisms for multiple inheritance incorporated in GDMO and IDL. Certain inheritance relationships that are possible in GDMO cannot be mapped to IDL. The solution consists of mapping a slightly altered inheritance hierarchy in these cases. This mapping can be carried out automatically, as is the case with any of the mappings mentioned earlier.

Mapping from IDL to GDMO and ASN.1

Translation of IDL
to GDMO is simpler
because GDMO and
ASN.1 are more
expressive than IDL

Mapping in this direction is simpler than the one just described because ASN.1 has a more extensive type system than IDL and also because more language constructs are available in GDMO than in IDL interface specifications. The key parts of the translation algorithm are as follows:

■ A managed object class is created for each IDL interface.

- A GDMO attribute is created for each attribute of the IDL interface.
- An ACTION is produced for each operation of the interface.
- Each IDL data type is mapped to an ASN.1 data type.

No templates are created for attribute groups, behavior definitions, or notifications.

Mapping of Internet SMI to IDL Interfaces

The translation of the template language of Internet SMI into IDL interfaces obviously has certain similarities to the mapping of Internet SMI to GDMO as specified within the framework of IIMC. The main translation rules are as follows:

Translation of Internet SMI to IDL is similar to the IIMC procedure

- Each MIB module results in an IDL module.
- A separate IDL interface is created for each group of the module being translated.
- Scalar variables of the group are mapped to IDL attributes within the interface.
- Separate IDL interfaces are created from the definition of the table rows. The elements of the rows provide the attributes of the interface.
- SNMPv2 notifications are mapped altogether to two interfaces, one each for the event transmissions according to the push and pull procedures. Each notification produces an operation by the same name in the push interface and one `pull` and one `try` operation in the `pull` interface. SNMPv1 traps are handled in the same way.

The following example presents an excerpt from the translation of the table `ipCidrRouteTable` from MIB II based on RFC 1213 and RFC 2096, which has already been used in previous sections. The parts of the IDL definition that relate to the excerpt from the definition in Internet SMI shown in section 10.3.1 are:

```
typedef sequence<octet, 4> IpAddressType;
...
interface ipCidrRouteEntry : SNMPMgmt::SmiEntry {
...
attribute IpAddressType ipCidrRouteDest;
...
attribute IpAddressType ipCidrRouteNextHop;
...
};
```

Example:
IDL interface for
`ipCidrRouteTable`
of MIB II

A specification is not provided for mapping IDL to Internet SMI because there is no knowledge of any practical applications or scenarios.

10.4.2 Protocol and Service Conversion

Interaction translation

The efforts of the JIDM Group in protocol and service conversion (which they call *interaction translation*) led to specifications of CORBA/CMIP and CORBA/SNMP gateways. In both cases, the conversions are based on the *specification translation* that provides the principal mapping between CORBA requests and simple GET or SET services. This is where OSI attributes and SNMP variables are mapped, depending on the access possible, to either IDL Get or even IDL Set operations that can be invoked upon the receipt of a CMIS request or an SNMP operation, respectively.

The work in interaction translation then has to deal with aspects such as differences in object models, object identification and naming, creating and deleting of objects, handling of notifications, and so forth. Obviously, parts of these aspects have to be considered separately for the CORBA-to-CMIS/CMIP and the CORBA-to-SNMP mapping. In the following, we will briefly sketch the common parts of the mappings, then the CMIP part, and finally the aspects that are specific for SNMP. For further details, refer to the original JIDM specification, which is available at *http://www.omg.org*. As of January 1999, the current OMG document number is telecom/98-08-14.

Common Aspects

For both mappings, one design goal was a high flexibility regarding the possible usage scenarios. Therefore, two approaches have been followed at the same time with respect to the mapping of objects as seen from the manager and from the agent side:

Two approaches for object mapping

Coarse-grained: one CORBA object per managed domain

- In the *coarse-grained approach*, one CORBA object exists per managed domain that is accessed by a CORBA manager. All requests are directed to a single proxy agent that provides an appropriate interface and handles the interactions with the (generally many) objects in the managed domain. With this approach, only a small number of object references have to be maintained and manipulated at the expense of two different object models: one object in the CORBA domain versus multiple objects in the CMIS or the SNMP domain. Type safety of communications is achieved at runtime, not at compile time.

- In the *fine-grained approach*, one CORBA object exists per managed object being accessed in the CMIS or the SNMP domain. With this approach, we have therefore a one-to-one correspondence between objects as seen from the manager and from the agent side. The disadvantage lies in the larger number of object references that have to be maintained.

Fine-grained: one CORBA object per managed object

The fine-grained approach is further subdivided into two different schemes to cope with access to the various different MOCs in the OSI domain or the many Internet MIBs in the SNMP domain.

- The first scheme uses so-called *generic operations* to access the managed objects (i.e., one common interface definition is used for operations on all classes of managed objects in the OSI domain, and one common interface definition provides access to different Internet MIBs). This allows both single-object as well as multiobject (scoped) operations. Type safety of communications is achieved at runtime, not at compile time.

Generic operations: one common interface for all MOCs or MIBs

- The second scheme uses *specific operations* to access the managed resources (i.e., a separate interface is provided for each relevant MOC in the OSI domain, and separate interface definitions are used for each object group in the SNMP domain). These interfaces are the output of the specification translation as described in section 10.4.1. This scheme is highly type safe (safety achieved at compile time), but allows only single-object operations.

Specific operations: separate interfaces for each MOC or MIB

Besides these general considerations, some specific aspects apply both to the mapping to the OSI domain and to the mapping to the SNMP domain. They have led to the specification of a number of interfaces that are combined in the *JIDM facilities specification*:

- The interfaces `ProxyAgent`, `ProxyAgentController`, `ProxyAgent-Finder`, `DomainPort`, and `DomainPortFactory` enable CORBA managers to get access to a given managed object domain (e.g., to find factories that allow creation of new objects or to obtain references to existing managed objects).

- The interfaces `EventPort`, `EventPortFactory`, and `EventPort-Finder` provide CORBA managers with means to receive event notifications from agents and CORBA agents to obtain object references to the event ports of managers.

OSI Management Facilities

Specific aspects of mapping to OSI management

OSI management facilities comprise interfaces that support functionality specific for the mapping to OSI management. This functionality includes:

- Invoke operations using scope and filtering
- Name objects according to OSI principles
- Create and delete OSI managed objects

The most interesting interfaces in this specification are as follows:

- The interface `ProxyAgent`, which provides coarse-grained interactions with OSI managed objects; besides other functions, this interface allows CORBA managers to perform `GET`, `SET`, and `ACTION` operations on OSI managed objects.
- The interface `ManagedObject` provides fine-grained, generic access to managed objects and forms the basis for fine-grained, specific operations because all interfaces for managed object classes, including class `top`, inherit from this interface; it provides `GET`, `SET`, and `ACTION` operations on OSI managed objects, and so on.
- The interfaces `LinkedReplyHandler`, `EndOfRepliesHandler`, and `MultipleRepliesHandler` allow managed objects or proxy agents to send multiple replies to a single scoped operation. `BufferedRepliesHandler` enables the use of a deferred synchronous model to retrieve responses for multiple replies.
- With the operations of `LName`, OSI names can be translated into names according to `CosNaming::Names` and vice versa.

SNMP Management Facilities

Specific aspects of mapping to Internet management

The interfaces included in the SNMP management facilities specification provide specific operations for the mapping to SNMP. These operations include:

- Name MIB entries according to SNMP management principles
- Create and delete MIB entries (table rows)
- Communicate traps and notifications

The interfaces in this specification are as follows:

- The interface `ProxyAgent` provides an analogy with its OSI counterpart coarse-grained interactions with SNMP managed objects; it allows CORBA managers to perform `GET` and `SET` operations, and so on.

- The interface `SmiEntry` is the counterpart of the interface `ManagedObject` in the OSI domain; that is, it provides fine-grained, generic access to MIB entries and forms the basis for fine-grained, specific operations because all specific interfaces for MIB groups as produced by the specification translation inherit from this interface; it provides `GET` and `SET` operations on MIB variables. With `SmiTableIterator` and `GetNextEntryIterator`, the information within a table can be traversed and retrieved.

- `GenericFactoryInterface` enables creation of managed objects in the SNMP domain (i.e., table rows).

- `NamingContext` and `NcEntryIterator` provide the capability to navigate in the SNMP name space in the lexicographic order.

10.5   Chapter Summary

The work of IIMC and JIDM has laid the foundations for integrated management across the boundaries of established management architectures. It has shown that gateways are possible despite the enormous problems that exist due to the profound differences between architectures. This is particularly important because of CORBA's growing role as the future communications infrastructure for TMN.

The issues concerning gateways that remain unresolved are those relating to a deeper integration of managed objects. Both approaches are based on a translation of information models at a syntactical level that, on the one hand, can be automated but, on the other hand, does not deliver the in-depth integration required. Although management information can easily be accessed from the "other architectures," it remains "information from the other architecture" and does not become "information of the particular architecture."

This is the starting point for CIM (described in Chapter 9), which the DMTF wants to establish as the future information model. If it succeeds as such and allows the many existing Internet MIBs or even OSI MIBs to be mapped to CIM, which is based on a semantic level, then a deep integration could be possible.

On the other hand, the introduction of new management architectures with new protocols also means that new architectural gateways need to be specified and implemented.

Part III

Management Tools and Techniques

W ith the increasing importance of management in networked systems, there has been a steady increase in the number of management tools available in the market. It is almost impossible today to keep track of the abundance of tools and their functions. Part III therefore provides a classification scheme that can be followed for the different *management tools* and describes the *structure*, *functionality*, and *use* of representative classes of tools. The descriptions are first presented without reference to any concrete products, followed by information about typical products currently available in each class.

Chapter 11 begins with a short overview listing examples of *management tools* and derives from it criteria for a classification of tools that can be used for a general classification scheme.

Although the general aim today is to integrate the management of preferably large subareas of networked systems, this is not possible without the additional use of *stand-alone tools*, in other words, *test* and *monitoring tools* that operate autonomously without the cooperation of other tools. Chapter 12 therefore describes tools such as test equipment and interface testers, protocol analyzers, and stand-alone tools from the Internet area, even though the main focus of this book is integrated management.

A central element of Part III is the description of *management platforms* with their software architectures, functions, and some typical management applications, outlined in Chapter 13. These software systems are the carrier systems (i.e., platforms) for a large number of integrated management solutions today. They implement the management architectures that were discussed in detail in Part II.

In most cases, it still is not possible today to administer and oversee the entire IT infrastructure of a company using only one management platform. The use of more than one platform can create management islands that contradict the overall objective of integrated management. Consequently, tools are used that integrate certain aspects of management beyond specific management architectures, platforms, and tools. Chapter 14 thus deals with so-called enterprise management systems, trouble ticket systems, and documentation systems—in other words, with *integrating tools* that unify separate management systems.

The development of management systems is a complex task, especially against the backdrop of complex management architectures and the manufacturer-independent interoperability of tools, and often requires the support of special tools to make the process an easier one. Chapter 15 therefore presents the important *development tools* such as MIB compilers, tools for management agents and management applications, and tools for generating user interface elements.

Lastly, the first part of Chapter 16 structures and, using examples, describes *concrete management tasks* that arise during the installation and the operation of *network components*. The second part of this chapter then highlights concrete management tasks and functions for *end systems* and *applications*, as well as the typical mechanisms used in the implementation of tools.

Classification of Management Tools

A great variety of management tools have appeared on the market during recent years. There are a number of reasons for this development:

- Diverse *classes* of resources requiring administration are available within the management disciplines of network, systems, and applications management. The spectrum ranges from simple hubs to complex, distributed telco services.

- Tools have to deal with the various *characteristics* of resources, such as electrical properties of a line or configuration parameters of complex software packages.

- Management tools are needed for *IT infrastructures of varying size and complexity*, ranging from small PC networks with ten workstation systems to corporate networks with tens of thousands and even hundreds of thousands of systems.

- Tools have to meet all sorts of different *requirements*. These range, for example, from modifying simple parameters to distributing and installing software packages in heterogeneous environments.

- Some new *technologies* are so complex that they can be utilized only in conjunction with specially designed tools. The technologies (such as VLANs) are therefore often supplied bundled with a management system.

As a result of these factors, all sorts of different versions of management tools were developed. Some typical examples include the following:

- *Test equipment* is used for testing the characteristics of lines and attachment components. Although this was the first type of management tool to be developed, it has remained an important instrument against the background of interface diversity in current transmission technology.

- *Protocol analyzers* support the diagnosis of problems in different protocol layers. Previously only available as stand-alone hardware–software units, the functionality of protocol analyzers is found today within the scope of RMON (see Chapter 6), often as firmware or a software supplement to network components (such as routers).

- *Tools* from the Internet area (e.g., `ping`, `traceroute`, `dig`) are part of the standard repertoire of every administrator of a TCP/IP-based computer network. The advantage of these tools is that they are based on standard protocol mechanisms, which means that no management-specific requirements are placed on the agents (i.e., the responding systems).

- Even if the tools differ in their functions and complexity, they are partially based on the same basic components (e.g., databases and protocol entities). *Management platforms* therefore provide applications with a management-specific common runtime environment.

- Many management tasks involve compiling the results from different tools, reprocessing these results, or forwarding them to a common user interface. So-called *enterprise management systems* therefore implement interfaces for several different management architectures or other tools and integrate this data.

- One of the core functions of resource management is to support and monitor the handling of problem situations and faults. This is the task of *trouble ticket systems* (TTSs). Since problem or fault reports are frequently generated by other tools, the TTSs implement the respective interfaces to those tools.

- In complex networks, it is not only the logical topology or functions that require computer-supported administration but also physical infrastructure, the geographical arrangement of components, organizational responsibilities, and operationally relevant data. This is the task of *documentation systems* that supply management information.

These classes of obviously very different tools will be described in more detail later. First, we want to present the criteria for structuring the sets of tools.

11.1   Criteria for the Classification of Management Tools

Different, sometimes also orthogonal, criteria exist for classifying management tools into a scheme. The characteristics of the user interface constitute a general criterion and one that is obvious to the user. The spectrum here ranges from simple, command line–based interfaces all the way to high-resolution graphical displays of the network topology. In addition to this criterion that does not specifically relate to management tools but can be applied to most tools, there are other more specific criteria such as the following:

> Several criteria can be used for classifying tools

- *Structure and components of a tool*: Management tools can be implemented as either a pure software solution that can be run on the usual platforms of hardware and operational software or a combination of special hardware and the software run on it. (Pure hardware solutions have almost no relevance today.)

  > Pure software solutions or a hardware–software combination

- *Autonomy of a tool*: Management tools are either *totally autonomous* or *executable only in interaction* with other tools, components, or a management platform. Furthermore, some tools are in principle executable on their own but do not provide the user with sufficient or useful functionality when used in isolation. This applies, for example, to management platforms on which applications are run to provide users with the functionality they require.

  > Completely autonomous or only useful in combination

  The second case can be broken down further:

  - The other parts that are required are components whose *functionality*, including *access* to this functionality, is based on a *standard*. These components can therefore originate from any number of manufacturers. Examples include tools that are based on CORBA services or require agents that provide MIB II or RMON-MIB over SNMP.
  - Special *proprietary interfaces* are used for cooperation with the other components. These components must be precisely defined and originate from a particular manufacturer. Examples of these are applications that are integrated into a specific management platform, therefore using its specific interfaces, or event management tools that reprocess vendor proprietary alarms of other tools.

- *Local or distributed implementation:* Management software can be run either *locally* on a system or *distributed* among different systems.

  > Local or distributed implementation

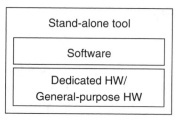

Figure 11.1
Stand-alone tools

A distributed implementation inevitably requires the use of a communication protocol. Standardized management protocols or even proprietary protocols can be employed for this purpose.

Task areas covered

- *Area of functionality:* Each tool is used to perform one or more management tasks, each of which can usually be categorized according to a particular functional area. The different areas mentioned in section 3.2 offer a possible classification criterion. But there are other ways of differentiating between tools and, particularly, software solutions according to the tasks they perform. Chapter 18 covers this topic in more detail.

The criterion of task area to be covered in Part IV

The criterion that is important for operators of DP infrastructures or users of management tools is, of course, the area of functionality being covered. The relationship between the activities carried out by the operator and the tool functionality is therefore handled in depth in Part IV. Consequently, in our categorization, we will focus on the other two criteria we deem most interesting: *structure and components* and, more important, *autonomy* (see the following section).

11.2   A General Classification Scheme

Based on the *autonomy* criterion, management tools are categorized into the following classes (Figure 11.1):

- *Stand-alone tools* (see Chapter 12 and Figure 11.1), which contain the following important classes of tools:
    - Testing devices (see section 12.1)
    - Protocol analyzers (see section 12.2)
    - Tools from the Internet area (see section 12.3)
- *Platforms,* which in principle can be executed autonomously but on their own still do not offer users sufficient or useful functionality.

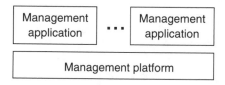

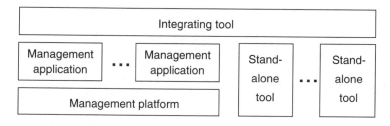

Figure 11.2
Platforms and platform-based tools

Figure 11.3
Integrating tools

They provide an infrastructure and an operating environment for applications. The *platform-based tools* that make use of this infrastructure and provide user-oriented functionality are dealt with together with the platforms in Chapter 13 (also see Figure 11.2).

- *Integrating tools*, the main task of which is to integrate other tools, for example, to compile or reprocess the results of those tools or present them in a compiled form to the user (see Chapter 14 and Figure 11.3). In section 11.3, we will briefly discuss the possible forms that can be used for this integration.

In addition to the management tools outlined, another class of tools, called *development tools*, is available *in the narrower sense* for applications in the management area. *In a broader sense*, we also see these programs as management tools (see Figure 11.4) because of the fluid transitions that exist. It is not always possible to define the dividing line between tools that are used by an operator to customize applications and the actual development tools used to implement applications. Figure 11.4 provides an overview of the tools from the classes shown in Figures 11.1 to 11.3, which we will describe in the following sections. The four types of development tools that will be discussed in Chapter 15 also appear in the same figure.

Management tools in the broader sense are also development tools

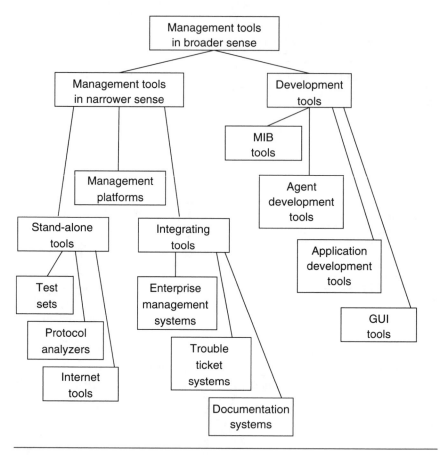

Figure 11.4
Classification of management tools

11.3　Forms of Integration

Figure 11.3 highlighted the fact that a variety of tools are available to support operators with their management tasks. Managing the entire IT infrastructure of an organization mostly results in the need to use a number of different tools. The cooperation and communication between these tools has to be as seamless as possible to support efficient management.

Before we describe the various classes of tools and tools whose main task is to integrate other tools, we first give a rough classification of the different possible forms of integration. In principle, we can distinguish four forms of integration: user interface integration, proxy- or gateway-based integration, data integration, and total integration. We will briefly sketch each of these forms.

11.3.1 User Interface Integration

In this simplest form, the tools that have to be integrated can be used from a common GUI and thus at least some common look and feel can be achieved. A typical example is an API that can be found in most management platforms, which allows linking some sort of start script of other tools to the menu bar of the platform (i.e., starting of different tools can be done in a uniform manner by the operator). Another example would be the integration of help files for a number of tools under a common help system.

The main characteristic of user interface integration is that the respective information bases in these tools are unaffected by the integration; on the one hand, this is advantageous since it results in considerable cost savings for the integration itself. On the other hand, the disadvantages are also clear: management procedures in the tools are running uncoordinated, probably resulting in inconsistent data, and relations between the data of different tools have to be found and interpreted by the operator, which in general, is impossible due to the large amount of management data found in typical organizations.

Information bases not affected

11.3.2 Proxy- or Gateway-Based Integration

Reducing or even eliminating the inconsistencies in management data is the primary focus of proxy-based or gateway-based integration. The task of the proxy or gateway is to make the management data of one side visible at the other side and to reflect changes on data at one side to data of the other side.

The main advantage of this form is that neither side has to be modified—both tools or both domains operate on their original data or on their original information model; the existence of the gateway should be more or less invisible to both sides. This protects investments in the management infrastructure on both sides. The disadvantage is that in most cases no one-to-one mapping can be found for the management information on the two sides of the proxy or gateway (see sections 10.3 and 10.5 for a discussion of this issue). Additionally, many technical details of proxies (e.g., simultaneous writing access from both domains to the same information) have not been finally solved.

Neither manager nor agent has to be modified

Examples for this form of integration are the management gateways described in sections 10.3 and 10.4 that form the basis for integrating tools from the Internet, OSI, and CORBA management domains. Other examples are the various so-called Q-Adaptors that can be found in TMN systems. They are essentially gateways between TMN-compliant (i.e., CMIS/CMIP-based) tools and other management systems. Especially important today are Q-Adaptors for management systems based on Transaction Language 1 (TL1) (see, e.g., [BELL1], [BELL2], or *http://www.tl1.com\/*). TL1, first defined by Bellcore in the early 1980s, is a management protocol that is widely used in telecommunications. Example products are Vertel's TMN QxDE (see *http://www.vertel.com*), TL1 EMS components from Lumos (see *http://www.lumos.com*), or the TL1 package from DSET (see *http://www.dset.com*).

11.3.3   Data Integration

As mentioned before, eliminating any data inconsistencies between the different sides is in general not possible with the proxy or gateway approach. This is where data integration starts; in this case, all affected tools operate on the same, mostly distributed, information base. Obviously, this requires that on either side the same information model or data model is used (i.e., seamless integration is achieved at the expense of a redesign or reimplementation of tools).

Here, the common information model of DMTF comes into play. It was specified with the goal in mind to become the integrating model in the future. Other examples for approaches to data integration are the data models provided by management platforms that can be used by the tools that are programmed to the API of this platform.

11.3.4   Total Integration

In addition to data integration, total integration means that tools share the same user interface and use the same management infrastructure. This encompasses, for example, the use of the same event management system, the same APIs for registering and unregistering or logging, or the same APIs to access all elements of the user interface like maps.

Tightest form of integration   Obviously, this tightest form of integration is very difficult to achieve. However, many recent efforts point toward this direction. Examples are the nonproprietary, open specifications of the OMG Telecom Domain Task Force for notification, logging, and topology services that have been sketched in section 7.7.

In commercially available integrating tools, typically not only one of these forms has been implemented; mostly, a combination can be found. For example, tools for the management of corporate applications (see section 14.1.1) aim at a data integration for the management models of the applications themselves and often use proxies or user interface integration for monitoring tools. High-end enterprise management platforms (see section 14.1.2) often include management gateways and approach some aspects of total integration. Event management systems (section 14.1.3) integrate tools that are sources of event notifications via proxies and aim at data integration for event messages and logging. Roughly the same applies to trouble ticket systems (section 14.2). Documentation systems point toward data integration since they provide a source and repository for information such as inventory, organizational, geographical, and process information. We will refer to our classification in the following chapters where appropriate.

Stand-Alone Test and Monitoring Tools

Stand-alone tools are aids that can be used in isolation, therefore without being integrated into a management system or a management platform (see Chapter 13) for special management-relevant tasks. Stand-alone tools originated in the network management environment, specifically for testing and monitoring the lower layers of the transport system.

A number of network failures are caused by faults in cable systems, attachment components, and connection elements that are due to installation and configuration faults. Chapter 2 showed us that an abundance of transmission media and access interfaces as well as interface protocols are available. It is in this environment that test sets and interface testers (section 12.1) for fault indication in layer 1 and protocol analyzers (section 12.2) for layers 2 and 3 of the transport system find their application. In section 12.3, we will then identify some of the stand-alone tools generally available in the Unix and Internet environments.

We will sketch these tools although these are mainly troubleshooting tools, not management tools in the narrower sense. But they are part of the tool kit of a network manager; they are used to verify or diagnose issues that the management systems (see Chapter 13) discover.

The following criteria are relevant for the categorization of stand-alone tools:

Criteria for evaluating tools

- What can be tested? Specific test and monitoring equipment is available for the different transmission media, interfaces, and components. Is the functionality of a monitoring device fixed or extensible?

- Which transmission level can be tested? Does the tool generate a signal as the applied voltage over an electrical medium, or does it generate the signal as a modulation pattern (the bit pattern coded by a signal) or the syntactic structure of a PDU?

- Interaction options for test equipment. Is the analysis purely passive, or can active test patterns be generated for the network segment being monitored?

- Can a test be carried out during running network operations without adverse impact, or do normal operations have to be interrupted for the test?

- Does the test equipment have to be permanently installed in the subnetwork or transmission path being monitored, or is it portable?

- How does a tool fit into a larger scheme of integrated network and system management? (See also section 11.3.)

12.1 Test Devices and Interface Testers

Test devices and interface testers are used to test transmission media and the physical signals transmitted on the media in accordance with current interface conventions. These are considered elementary tools and therefore deserve brief mention. *Analog test devices* check signal behavior during analog transmission, whereas *digital test devices* check digital transmission paths and device interfaces; see the overview in Figure 12.1. The scope of testers is usually restricted to a transmission section or a LAN segment.

Analog test equipment

Analog test devices measure values, such as voltage level, resistance, jitter, modulation, attenuation, signal-to-noise ratio, and bandwidth, that are characteristic of signal behavior. Test devices are available for practically all types of media and all transmission rates, including E1/T1 and satellite links.

Frequency generators

The simplest test that can be executed by a *frequency generator* involves establishing the energy loss of the test signal using a *decibel meter*. This test is mainly applied to check twisted-copper cable.

Multimeters

Multimeters, also known as multitesters, volt meters, or ohm meters, are used to measure the voltage, current, and resistance of electrical conductors. If the measured values deviate from the permitted values, the test could possibly show a fault in the electrical conductor. The types of faults that can occur include broken cables, short circuits, cables without resistive termination, and damaged cables.

Time domain reflectometers (TDRs)

Time domain reflectometers (TDRs) send pulses to a medium (electrical media in the case of a TDR, optical media in the case of an OTDR) and measure the time until the possible return of (partial) reflections. This kind of reflection can occur in situations involving broken cables, passive branching, nonadapted components, or miss-

Test devices	
Analog	*Digital*
Frequency generator	Breakout box
Circuit quality monitor modem	Bit error rate tester
	Block error rate tester
Multimeter	
	Modem tester
Time domain reflectometer	DTE/DCE emulator
	Data recorder
Oscilloscope	

Figure 12.1
Examples of test equipment

ing terminating resistors. The reflection point can then be calculated from the known signal speed. This allows cable faults as well as unknown components (e.g., the not yet documented branching of an AUI cable) to be localized or the length of a cable to be established. Modern TDRs are capable of visualizing test results and even storing them. This enables differential analyses to be produced when further tests are undertaken. It is recommended that each cable installation be calibrated using a TDR.

The large number of high-speed modems available today allow line quality to be monitored during normal network operations. This *circuit quality monitor* (CQM) capability of modems allows almost all the quality parameters of an analog line to be monitored. The monitoring is controlled either from a console attached to the modem or via a management system in which the CQM parameters are then analyzed further.

Circuit quality monitor modems (CQMs)

A classic form of signal monitoring that is still often used today involves the use of oscilloscopes. These can be used to determine so-called eye patterns, which are the characteristic patterns of a modulated signal. Different types of interference, such as noise and phase jitter,

Oscilloscopes

have a definite effect on these eye patterns that can be visually detected through the use of oscilloscopes.

Digital test devices

Digital test equipment can encompass a broad spread of equipment, ranging from simple breakout boxes to bit error rate testers and programmable devices, the most convenient of which is the protocol analyzer (section 12.2).

Breakout boxes

Breakout boxes are the simplest form of digital test equipment and are used to monitor and test plug connections and interfaces (e.g., electrical interfaces such as V.24, V.35, RS-449, and RS-332 and optical interfaces such as G.703). The box contains the signal lines that are accessible through test sockets (passive boxes) or are arbitrarily linkable together (active boxes). Thus a null modem can be constructed by swapping the appropriate signal lines in an active box. *DTE/DCE emulators*, which not only operate at the signal level but also at the character level, are a more advanced version of active breakout boxes and can therefore be used as modem testers.

Bit error rate testers (BERTs)

Bit error rate testers (BERT) create test patterns that can be transmitted to the circuit or the device being tested (such as a modem) and mirrored there (loopback mode). The test pattern comparison takes place in the BERT where the bit error rate is also calculated. Similarly, the *block error rate tester* (BLERT) tests entire blocks. Individual applications have different requirements for maximum tolerable error rates. Modem testers usually also contain a B(L)ERT module.

Data recorders

Data recorders, which simply record traffic for offline analyzers, are not test devices in the narrower sense but are considered stand-alone tools.

A lot of digital or analog access, test, and performance monitoring equipment in the market falls under the category of stand-alone devices. These units (e.g., products from companies such as HEKIMIAN) are testing solutions for E1, T1, E3, T3, DS1, DS3, and DDS testing. They incorporate functions from the devices described before, but also functions from protocol analyzers described in the following section. The test units provide nonintrusive and intrusive test access, long-term test capability, and remote control. They also provide automatic alarm-reporting capabilities, including loss of signal, alarm indication signal, severely errored seconds, remote frame alignment signal alarm, error-free seconds below threshold, and so forth. Some test units provide a performance monitoring feature that reports on demand, for example, consistent with ITU-T G:821 framing bit error (FBE) count, FBE ratio, discarded FBE seconds, bipolar violation (BPV) count, BPV ratio, degraded minutes, and so on. The test units can be multiuser and multifunction units.

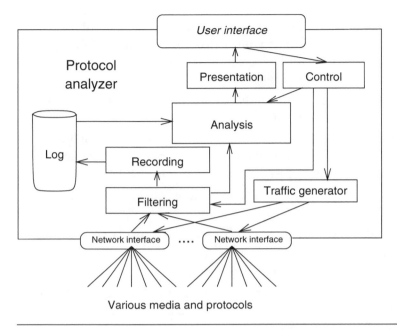

Figure 12.2
Functional model for a protocol analyzer

12.2 Protocol Analyzers

Protocol analyzers are an indispensable tool for the network administrator. These tools (Figure 12.2 shows how they are structured) are capable of eavesdropping on, storing, and analyzing network traffic. A knowledge of the PDU structure of the monitored layers (e.g., signal coding, frame structure, packet structure) is required for the analysis, thereby making these analyzers protocol specific. Modern analyzers support entire protocol hierarchies. Many protocol analyzers also integrate functions like the ones mentioned in conjunction with test equipment. Following is a list of requirements for analyzers:

- Complete recording and storage of the network traffic being observed. Time stamp accuracy is required (with Ethernet and X.25 in the range of microseconds, with fast transmission systems such as Fast Ethernet, Gigabit Ethernet, and ATM in the range of nanoseconds).

- Extensive filter facilities. These include the definition of filters using Boolean expressions, agreement on triggers for starting the protocol recording, and support of alarm filters in the creation of sound or video signals.

Requirements of
protocol analyzers

- User-friendly interfaces for the network administrator on which information is represented in the form of text, graphics, or histograms. Online monitoring on the screen is also desirable, even in the case of higher transmission rates.

- Support for monitoring traffic over different types of media and multichannel measurements.

- Provision of facilities for testing the physical state of lines, for example, using an (integrated) time domain reflectometer (i.e., integrated test devices as described in section 12.1).

- Collection and clear presentation of statistical information describing network load and error rates.

- Automatic detection of changes describing network configuration.

- Functions for generating network loads to enable load tests to be carried out under controlled conditions.

- Facilities for remote operation, for example, over a dialup port (outband) or remote login (inband) used to initiate and control tests performed by the analyzer.

- Online and offline analysis of test results.

- Convenient facilities for storing and reactivating analyzer configurations.

Protocol analyzers are implemented in dedicated devices (particularly for high-speed protocols) or as software packages that run on PCs and workstations. Analysis of performance and data entry throughput for network cards constitute important criteria; the ultimate aim is to monitor all the traffic on a transmission link or segment.

Extensive possibilities for carrying out analyses

A recording filter usually at least describes the following variants: all packets, all defective packets, all packets with predefined types of errors, senders, destinations or traffic volume, or packets of a certain type (e.g., broadcast) or of a source–sink pair. The analysis encompasses all different types of errors (e.g., CRC errors, misaddressing, packet length errors, unauthorized packet types, and collisions), counters (sent, received, delayed packets), and statistics (throughput, network load, and workload as peak values, mean values, or statistical distribution). Protocol analyzers are therefore indispensable tools for fault and performance management.

New protocol analyzer developments

Protocol analyzers can, of course, analyze only certain predetermined protocols. Some analyzers support protocol description languages allowing them to be open to new developments in the protocol sector; this enables the analysis capabilities of the tool to be extended to accommodate new protocols. Another development involves a more intelligent analysis that is rule based and therefore provides more than an evaluation based on the syntax of the PDU.

Since a protocol analyzer, like a test device, usually addresses only one transmission link or one segment, the basic principle of protocol analyzers has also been extended into a *distributed monitoring system.* This involves separating the recording part from the analyzer and using a corresponding module as a measurement *probe* in each network segment being monitored. The data that is transmitted inband or outband to an analyzer, where it is then evaluated. The direct next step is to integrate the probes into the network components. If this process is taken yet a step further and the information recorded by the probes, including a preprocessing of the data, is standardized, the result is remote monitoring MIBs (compare with RMON in section 6.5).

A rich product range of protocol analyzers is available to administrators. In the LAN area, there is support of Ethernet, Fast Ethernet, Token Ring, and FDDI. At WAN interfaces, the following are among those supported: V.24, X.21, V.35, V.36, RS449, RS530, E1/T1, $ISDNS_0$, $ISDNS_{2m}$, ATM (E1, E3, DS1, DS3, OC-3C). Of course, analyzers also exist for X.25, FR, SDMS, IP, and other standards. Support even exists for wireless transmission. However, the more complex the protocol or the higher the transmission rate, the higher the reliance is on dedicated devices since purely software-based analyzers are not able to cope with the throughput required (high recording speeds without data loss).

12.3 Tools from the Internet Environment

The Internet environment has fostered the development of a number of useful individual tools, most of which are available as standard operating system features or as public domain software solutions. More than 100 tools, some of which are in competition with commercially available packages, are listed in "Tools for Monitoring and Debugging TCP/IP Internets and Interconnected Devices" (RFC 1470).

The catalog is organized by certain functional groups (e.g., map, status, traffic, security, debugger, analyzer, alarm), network components, underlying operating system environments (OS/2, NT, Windows, Unix, etc.), and the basic protocols used (e.g., ICMP, SNMP). The examples mentioned for the support of configuration management are `ping` (network layer reachability analysis using ICMP Echo Packet), `(x)netmon` (querying of configuration data using polling and traps), `snmpset` (setting of parameters for each Internet resource), and

Tools for network management

traceroute (reachability analysis with path detail results). Examples for the support of performance management include spray (load generator) and snmpxperform (simple traffic monitor).

Other examples are netstat and tcpdump. Netstat displays management information (i.e., traffic counters) that is useful for evaluating the status of the network. This also pertains to the status of sockets and interfaces, including the addresses of the hosts using the system, the routes available, and the members of the multicast groups. Tcpdump is likewise a very useful tool; it implements analyzers for protocols such as Ethernet, FDDI, ARP, RARP, TCP, and IP. An appropriate Boolean expression can be expressed with parameters such as protocol, direction, host, port, or (group) addresses to specify the filter. This analyzer can be run on practically any Unix system.

Another example is tcptrace from Ohio University. It is not a packet capture program. It reads output dump files in the formats of several popular packet capturing programs (e.g., tcpdump, snoop, etherpeek, netm). For each connection, it keeps track of elapsed time, bytes per segment sent and received, retransmissions, round-trip times, window advertisements, throughput, and so forth and can produce different types of graphs. Flstats is a tool for extracting flow statistics from tcpdump files, and tracelook aids in looking at tcpdump files and determining what is actually in the trace. The MGEN-Toolset from Naval Research Laboratory provides programs for sourcing or sinking realtime multicast–unicast UDP/IP traffic flows with optional support for operation with ISI's rsvpd.

TCP-Wrapper is an example of a security management tool. The aim of this tool is to restrict access to TCP servers by using IP address checking (RFC 1413) and recording each use that takes place. SATAN is a tool that is capable of pinpointing various network-relevant security problems in connection with NFS, NIS, remote shell, and FTP use. Tripwire is able to detect whether an attempt has been made to break into a system by using a mechanism that records system status for later analysis.

Tools for system management

This is only a partial list of the available tools. New tools that combine different tools or provide comparable functionality are being developed all the time. But it should be pointed out again that all these tools are stand-alone tools and therefore do not satisfy our requirements for integrated management. What is particularly apparent is that the tools mentioned are mostly applicable for use in the network management area. The same variety of tools is not available for the system management area; the only tools that exist here are some Unix commands, some of them vendor specific, for rudimentary system management. Examples of these tools include `rup` (calculates fault-free runtime of remote computers), `rusers` (identifies users of a machine), `rpcinfo` (lists services of a server), `fuser` (lists users of a file system), and `COSprint` (a print manager). Of course, manufacturer-specific tools are available for the different variants of operating systems and for the individual functional areas, but these tools are not the subject of our discussion.

It is useful to point out here that some network management system platforms incorporate the aforementioned tools (e.g., launch ping from icon or map, examine disk utilization from some icon), but they do so using rlogin and other command line tools. Importantly, the results returned are often visual and do not feed an upstream OSS or integrated management system (in general, exceptions exist, particularly for ping). These tools work without any underlying management architecture, and they do not require special-purpose agents. This is so because they can rely on a common set of operating system services or protocols in a homogeneous environment. In section 11.3, we discussed methods for integrating stand-alone tools and devices.

The tools can be applied without management platforms and special agents

Management Platforms

In the earlier chapters, we discussed that integrated management of distributed heterogeneous systems is practicable only on the basis of standardized management architectures. Part II of this book concentrated on the key open management architectures that currently exist. We described (open) *management platforms* as those runtime and development environments for distributed management applications that operate according to the concepts for (standardized) management architectures and therefore provide the basis for an integrated approach (refer to Figure 4.2).

Whereas conventional and stand-alone tools often support one particular applications area (e.g., LAN or WAN, individual functional areas, manufacturer-specific products) in an often proprietary way, platforms incorporate the following features:

- They are run in open systems environments.
- They offer a runtime environment based on standards (architectures) for distributed management applications and an appropriate development environment.
- They offer open programming interfaces for applications. This means that they can also be expanded through software of third-party suppliers.
- They provide different options for management integration: Thanks to the common underlying information model, a unified modeling and description framework exists between the different managed objects (objects of network, system, and applications management). There is also functional integration because of the uniform platform database and shared basic applications.

The first platforms were developed in 1989 (OSF, DEC, HP, Cabletron, Tivoli, Sun, IBM). The architectural aspects of OSF in particular have had a considerable influence on the fundamental platform architecture [GHE97].

The next sections describe platform architectures as they appear in general, basic applications that are common for most platforms, management applications that are available for specific management areas, and selection criteria for management platforms. Though platform products are quite diverse and requirements may vary, we try to help you to visualize what platforms can do by describing a decomposition of functions and components. In doing so, it is unavoidable that our opinions concerning platform approaches become apparent.

13.1   Platform Architectures

Figure 13.1 illustrates the functional structure of a management platform. The infrastructure (section 13.1.1) provides the runtime environment for management applications over a programming interface (API). A platform is normally supplied with a number of basic applications (see section 13.2) that can be accessed by the management applications and the development tools. The user interface module again is separated by an open API.

Tools support the development of new applications using CASE tools and the integration of new management objects through MIB editors, MIB compilers, and MIB browsers; in some cases, application generators and modules for interface layout are available. These development tools are covered in Chapter 15.

The platforms can often be coupled with other management tools or support systems, such as trouble ticket systems, cabling management systems, or documentation systems. There can also be a coupling with the management systems of other architectures. This possibility is dealt with in Chapter 14.

13.1.1   Infrastructure

Modules of platform infrastructure
The infrastructure is the platform in the narrower sense. It coordinates the processes of the runtime system and provides applications with the basic services they require. These services include access to managed objects and to other management systems (communication module) along with services for the administration and storage of management information (information module).

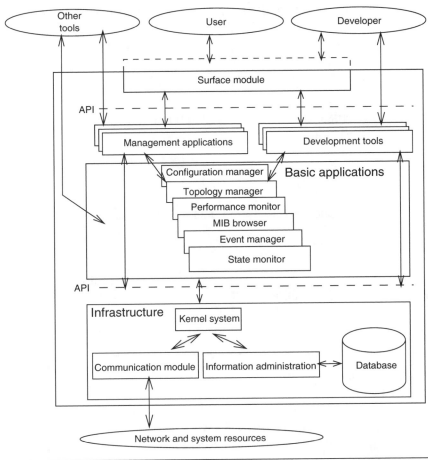

Figure 13.1
Structure of a management platform

The *communication module* provides services that enable access to managed objects in remote systems; it also supports the different cooperation models. The communication partners of a platform are other managers, agents, and proxy systems. In the case of distributed (so-called scalable) platforms, the communication module also enables communication within a platform. The cooperation forms can either be symmetrical (peer to peer) as in CORBA or asymmetrical (client–server) as with OSI and Internet. Depending on the respective management architecture, the different management protocols to which the communication module can map the cooperation mechanism are SNMPv1, SNMPv2, and dialects; CMIP, RPC, CORBA, GIOP, ESIOP, and SIOP; or proprietary management protocols. These protocols must then be mapped to the appropriate underlying transport

Tasks of communication module

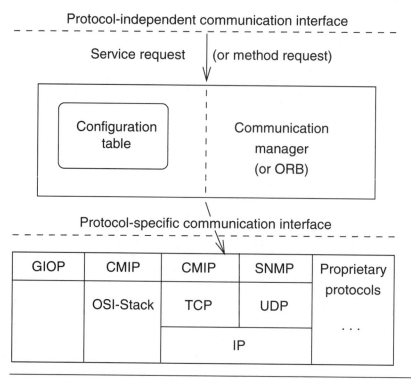

Figure 13.2
Communication module

protocols (SNMP over UDP/IP, SNMP over TCP/IP, CMIP over OSI, CMIP over TCP/IP, CMIP over LLC, RPC over TCP, GIOP over Internet). Figure 13.2 shows the modules contained in a communication module. Access to a communication module is over an appropriate service interface (usually a protocol-independent communication interface). This can be an API similar to CMIS (X/Open-XMP), the NMForum API (TMN/C++), the SNMP API SNMP++, or an ORB service interface. Some of these APIs are discussed in section 15.3.1. If an application utilizes these services, then, depending on the destination object, the corresponding addressing information is obtained either from directory services (similar to CORBA) or from mapping tables configured by the system administrator. Furthermore, the supported management protocols are selected on the basis of the communication destination, and the management PDUs are structured according to the purpose of the communication. The module must also include mechanisms for the security of the communication (encryption, authentication).

Each platform offers an extensive database for management purposes. The *information module* is responsible for administration of

Information module

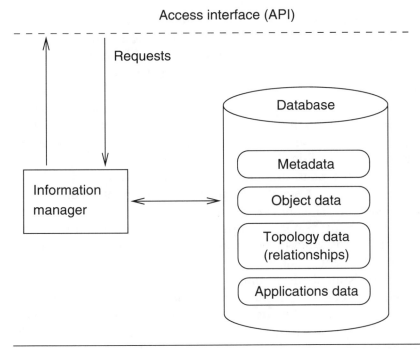

Access interface (API)

Requests

Information manager

Database

Metadata

Object data

Topology data (relationships)

Applications data

Figure 13.3
Information module of a platform

and access to this database. A (flat) file system or relational or object-oriented database can serve as the underlying basis for these functions. The information can consist (refer to Figure 13.3) of metadata (e.g., template definitions, managed object class definitions, IDL declarations, object type macro definitions, concise MIB format), object data (MO variable values, MO attribute values, MO status information), MO relationships, topology information, event notifications, maps, archival information, or data from the management applications. The data can be filed in the different storage facilities of a platform (RAM, disk, tape).

Administrators, applications, programmers, and remote systems potentially access this information. Standardized access languages such as SQL or interfaces such as ODBC and RDA often are used to access the information so that an easy export-import can be supported between platforms and other integrating tools (e.g., trouble ticket systems and documentation systems). Another approach is that a management interface can be applied to access the data (e.g., CORBA IDL). The trend is moving away from raw data access (through SQL, etc.) toward objectified access for greater application module independence.

Data models for a platform

Each management platform administers an image of the network being monitored in accordance with the underlying information model. Most platforms primarily support a *system-oriented* data model; that is, they model each system monitored within the platform. The advantage of *network-oriented* data models, on the other hand, is that associations can directly be made between related information of different systems or components within the platform infrastructure (as opposed to within a single application) since the underlying data model of the platform can express relationships between managed objects.

In the case of system-oriented data models, each application always has to carry out the respective correlation between information from different systems. The individual applications themselves in turn store information about the relationships between objects. This produces an undesirable redundancy in the storage of network-relevant information within the different applications.

Another distinction is the one that exists between *passive* and *active* information models. With passive information models, information about individual components is stored within the management platform. Applications have access to this information and can process it. Active information models do the same thing, but in addition, they support active elements, such as procedures and functions, that allow information to be interpreted automatically whenever any changes take place and can trigger follow-up actions. This then allows networked information structures to be established within the platform, thereby permitting an automatic response to faults or providing significant information about the performance capabilities of the network as a whole. (Cabletron's Spectrum platform utilizes this capability using the inductive modeling technique.)

Setup of the data of a platform

There are different ways of storing information. Some systems distinguish between a long-term external database and an internal runtime database (e.g., active memory), which can be used by the system while programs are being executed. All changes are initially implemented in the internal database and are written back into the external database if so requested by the user. These external databases are usually runtime versions of well-known SQL-RDBMSs such as Sybase, Informix, Ingres, and Oracle. The database structure is fed by different tools:

- MIB tools (see Chapter 15)
- Interactive setup by the user using a graphics editor; this is supported by most products

- A population of object instance data from existing databases (NIS, name servers, a user's own data)

- Discovery mechanism; special applications existing within the platform generate data (e.g., topology data) based on an observation of the network (see section 13.2)

- Management applications (see section 13.3)

The *core system* is also part of the infrastructure of a platform. This system is responsible for the coordination and monitoring of all processes or modules in a platform (process start, process status monitoring, interprocess communication). With distributed platforms, the core system functions also include the distribution of services, databases, and applications. The core system supports the installation and configuration of services, databases, and logfiles, as well as the registration and integration of applications. In some cases, it also offers security and backup functions (the latter is often also available through external tools over the appropriate interfaces). The core system, of course, uses the platform of the operating system services of the underlying host system. Unix and NT workstations are the most common management platform operating systems with Unix-based systems still dominating, especially in wide-scale enterprise management arenas (also because of their robustness).

The core system offers help and coordinating functions for the platforms

13.1.2   User Interface Modules

Graphical user interfaces (GUIs) allow users interactive access to the functions and applications of a management platform and display the network or distributed system being observed. The display on the screen is based on the terms *symbol, map,* and *submap,* which are explained later. Some GUIs are often based on window-based systems using the standards OSF/Motif and X/Windows; other GUIs (compare Chapter 9) are Web based and make use of Java. So, the GUI model described in this subsection is just one of the many interfaces that are available. Not all tools are based on this mapping model, but the most common are.

A typical viewing area of a window breaks down into the usual main divisions: menu list, system menu, windows for maps, dialog box for applications control, push buttons for monitoring and control, help, scroll bars, and a selection field for tools. The symbols generally fall into three different information planes: background plane, application plane, and user plane. The background plane is normally an inactive

GUI components

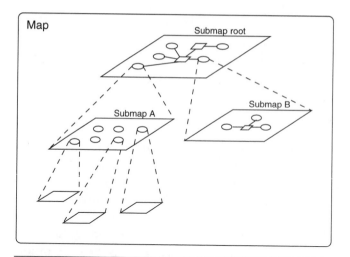

Figure 13.4
Graphic display of a network topology

graphic plane for the deposition of the other planes; it uses geographical cards and building floor plans that can be incorporated into the platform through use of the customary graphic exchange formats, such as GIF. The application plane is the dialog plane for applications, and the user plane is for user-specific extensions. Java applets are also being used more and more as front ends.

Chapter 15 includes additional information about tools for user interface design. Before we look at the display issues, we first want to define some of the terms used.

Basic concepts

An *object* represents a resource within the management platform based on the supported information model. The properties of the resource are modeled by the appropriate object attributes. A *symbol* is a graphical representation of a managed object within the user interface. Some symbols are not based on physical objects, such as those used to visualize relationships between objects (e.g., logical connections between systems). Accordingly, objects also exist that are not represented by any symbols within the user interface. A *submap* is a set of symbols that represents part of a network topology or parts of a system within a window. A *map* (see Figure 13.4) is a set of hierarchically related submaps that present the user with a view of the entire network being observed or of parts of a system's containment hierarchy. The particular submap that constitutes the top of the hierarchy is usually called a *root map*. The individual submaps contain symbols that are linked to other submaps and enable access to these submaps.

Symbols, submaps, and maps are themselves objects within the management platform and contain attributes describing their properties. Examples of attributes for symbols include:

- The symbol name, which can be different from the object name, especially when several symbols exist for one object in different submaps.
- The symbol type, which is usually represented by a corresponding graphical icon. The symbol type is usually determined by the properties of the underlying object.
- The symbol's affiliation to a submap with the corresponding graphical coordinates that determine the position of the symbol.
- Access rights that specify which users or which management applications are allowed to change a symbol.
- Behavior of a symbol when being accessed (clicked on) by a user (opening an associated submap or activating an associated application).

Examples of attributes of submaps include:

- The embedding of the submap into the hierarchy tree of the map; this embedding involves assigning the submap to symbols in the other submaps over which the submap can be opened.
- An algorithm that determines the layout of the symbols within a submap. If a layout algorithm is specified, submaps can be generated automatically by programs. This is particularly important when maps are automatically being set up and maintained by a discovery function.
- Access rights.
- Representation of a submap within a window (e.g., zooming or scaling with a settable scaling factor).

An important prerequisite for the use of a platform as a management station within a concrete network environment is the facility to construct submap hierarchies with arbitrary depth. A facility should also exist to allow an object to be represented in different submaps by different symbols. This is the only way of realizing different *views* (e.g., topological, organizational, geographical, or device views) of the network that can be adapted to the particular tasks of different user groups. These views are so important because of the need to split up the responsibility for planning and operation, particularly of complex

Margin notes:

Symbols, submaps, and maps are themselves MOs

Views support management domains

networks, among several groups or persons or roles within the provider organization (formation of domains). A view can therefore be described as consisting of:

- A set of symbols hierarchically arranged into submaps
- A set of functions that can be used on the symbols of the underlying objects
- A set of users with access rights to the submap hierarchy, functions, and objects

It should be mentioned that not all products realize domain and access controls based on GUI representation. Although this description makes it easy to visualize, it unfairly implies more uniformity across management platforms than really exists today.

The implementation of views within a management platform depends on the attributes that are supported for the different elements of the user interface:

- Are access rights to the map, submap, object, or symbol plane settable?
- Can management functions be assigned for the map, submap, object, or symbol plane?

Realistic display of connections and systems is helpful

Another important property required of the graphical interface is that it should allow as realistic a presentation of managed objects as possible from the standpoint of appearance and physical arrangement. This can be supported by various techniques. Submaps can be overlaid with graphical information such as geographical maps, building plans, or room layouts. The symbols in the submaps are then arranged to correspond with the background picture so that it is possible to see exactly where a component is located in a building or a room or where the wiring is run. This kind of information is useful for the quick localization of components when faults occur so that it can be dealt with by direct physical intervention (e.g., by pushing a reset button). Consequently, most platforms support the facility of overlaying digitalized images, thereby supporting different picture formats.

Even components themselves can be represented realistically. The user is presented with a view of the system that corresponds to the actual layout of the system. This display includes things like boards, existing interfaces, switches, and light indicators. The advantage of this kind of display is that users at a management console are able to form a true visual picture of the components. Diagnostic instructions referring to the display of the components can also be provided ("If the second diode from the left lights up, the switch below it should be turned on"). The pictures and operating instructions provided make it easier for users with less training to locate a system and carry out the necessary tests and diagnostic measures. In addition to being able to see the display with the associated information, most users would welcome a facility that enables them to print it out. The display itself can be either a simple picture or an ordered set of picture objects. In the latter case, individual picture objects, such as interfaces, can then be selected and specifically interrogated for further information (How is the interface configured? Is a cable attached? Where does the cable go?).

The user interface module provides users and administrators with a set of functions that can be organized into the following groups.

Map management functions are used for managing maps and their associated objects. These functions provide services such as map creation and deletion, access right administration, and map saving through the creation of *snapshots* that can be used in the restoration of maps.

Editing functions for submaps provide users with access to the elements of a map. The functions offered include creation and deletion of submaps and symbols, insertion of submaps into the submap hierarchy, attribute changes and access rights, symbol copying between maps, and symbol linking using appropriate representation elements.

Search functions help users locate information. A major aim of these functions is to provide users with sufficient support in formulating search queries. This can be done through the use of so-called wildcards or regular expressions. The attribute sets of the objects supply some of the possible search criteria. A search function would ideally incorporate the power of the SQL database query language; however, this is not always supported by the products currently available. The results of a search query are displayed to the user in a list form and through a marking of the related elements in the map.

Navigation functions support the movement of users through the submap hierarchy or through the different views that exist. Two different techniques are applied for navigating users through a map hierarchy:

Functions of the graphical user interface

- A submap is always displayed in one single window. If a new submap is opened, the old one is overwritten.

- A separate window is used to display each submap. The disadvantage of this technique is that the screen often becomes overloaded with many windows, but the advantage is that different submaps can be displayed at the same time.

In both cases, users require assistance to help them find their way around the hierarchy:

- An indication is given for each submap on how it is incorporated into the hierachy.

- The subnetwork hierarchy is displayed also indicating which sub-network is currently open. The display can also be used to open other submaps for processing.

- Based on a symbol within a submap, other submaps containing symbols that represent the same object as the original symbol can also be opened. This function is used to change different views between submap hierarchies.

Invocation of management functions

Management functions are made accessible to users through menus. Functions are usually called up after the selection of a set of symbols and the choice of a function from the menu offered. Functions are sometimes activated indirectly through the editing of object properties in a template when the closing of a template triggers the functions associated with that template. It is not usually sensible to allow every function to be available for all symbols, and instead there should be a possibility of restricting which functions can be chosen when symbols have been selected. This restriction can depend on:

- Authorized operations for the user: Configuration operations can be prohibited in a map used by network operators to monitor a network.

- The map or submap in which the selection was made: A user can be prohibited from editing a submap in maps in which management applications have the responsibility for the construction and maintenance of submaps.

- The properties of the symbols or objects selected: Access to certain management information makes sense only for those resources that actually can also provide this information.

- The number of symbols selected: Certain functions are meaningful only if a certain number of symbols have been selected. An example of these functions would be the specification of a route or a cable path between two network components or end systems.

This ends the discussion of user interface modules. Again, as mentioned earlier, though the general functions of the user interface have been discussed with a certain GUI in mind, this is not universally implemented by all management platforms. GUIs, in particular, can be quite diverse; this diversity mirrors the variety of user interface style guides, GUI builders, windowing tool kits, Web browser forms, and so on. We describe some GUI development tools in section 15.4.

13.2   Basic Applications

This section describes some of the basic applications that are part of almost all management platforms. It should be noted, however, that from the administrator's point of view, these are relatively primitive applications often limited to a visualization of the information retrieved by network components and end systems. *MIB browsers*, which enable direct access to a system's management information, are one example of these applications. The operation of an MIB browser is adapted to a specific information model. MIB browsers with SNMP capabilities therefore allow users to move through the treelike structured MIB and access the current values of MIB variables. MIB browsers are also seen as teaching aids that enable users to understand the structure of an MIB and also as testing aids that are used to analyze the management functionality of a system.

MIB browsers

The functionality of the basic applications listed next has not been standardized; as a rule, they are platform dependent but similar as far as the basic functions are concerned. But the trend toward standardization is growing in this area as well. An example of this is the specification for CORBA services that defines quasi-basic applications. Refer specifically to the *topology* and *notification services* of CORBA telecom DTF mentioned in Chapter 7.

13.2.1   Monitoring the State of Resources

The objective of monitoring the state of resources is to ensure that the information on the state of the resources is as up-to-date as possible at the management station. The monitoring involves accessing attributes of the resources. Unlike event management, which is described later, the initiative in this case is mostly taken by the management station. We mentioned earlier that agent-initiated polling at manager-defined intervals or on the basis of agent-internal events is also in use (e.g.,

Monitoring the state of resources is a basic task

trap-directed polling). The manager polls the resources and evaluates the results of the poll queries. The monitoring function is therefore heavily dependent on the protocols used to address the individual resources. The following mechanisms are used:

- Simple echo and test protocols: The management station sends a PDU to a system that is acknowledged by the system. If a response reaches the management station within a certain period, it is then assumed that the system is operational. The best-known examples of these protocols are ICMP requests, which are the basis of the ping command described earlier (also known as "heart beat").

- Connectionless management protocols: A specific kind of management protocol is used to send queries to the systems being monitored. In response, these systems send the current values of those MO attributes that were specified within the query. If a response reaches the management station within a certain period, then the values contained in the response are interpreted. SNMP over UDP is an example of this kind of protocol.

- Connection-oriented management protocols such as CMIP: The management station establishes connections to the systems being monitored and regularly accesses certain MO attributes of the components over these connections. If one of these connections is terminated on the system side, this is interpreted as a fault in the system. Compared to connectionless protocols, this method offers the advantage that a more reliable assessment of the state of the systems can be made. The downside is that it requires connections to be established and maintained for all the systems being monitored.

The disadvantage of monitoring by polling, such as in the case of SNMP, is that direct information is not available about the state of a resource if no response has been received. The following reasons can be the cause of a response failing to appear:

- The query or the response has been lost because ICMP and SNMP are both based on unreliable datagram services.

- The query reaches the resource, but the resource either cannot respond at all or cannot respond in the allotted time because it is overloaded.

- The query or the response is delayed because of a high network load.

The monitoring process can be individually configured in order to increase the reliability of the monitoring. This can be done by:

- Setting time-out intervals for the systems. The time-out interval specifies how long the management station is to wait for a response from a system.
- Setting retry counters that specify how often a query can be sent to a system before a conclusion is reached on the availability of the system.

In other words, apply the same techniques used by reliable transport protocols. Both values should be individually settable for different systems to enable the monitoring to be adapted to the topology of the respective network or the domains. For example, if certain resources can be accessed only over narrowband or unreliable communication paths from the management station, then the time-out interval and the retry counter have to be set correspondingly high. The exact setting of both values depends to a large degree on the previous experience of the network operator. However, the setting of high values can result in the delayed detection of a resource failure.

13.2.2   Threshold Monitoring

In addition to monitoring general availability, a management protocol can also check the current quality of service. This enables a provider to define threshold values that are then compared to the actual attribute values of the components. With SNMP, these threshold values usually have to be defined, administered, and monitored within the management station. With CMIP or in the Internet environment with RMON, threshold values can be created as objects within the system being monitored or within a proxy agent and monitored there.

Threshold value monitoring is important for QoS analysis

The following parameters are important for defining threshold monitoring: measurement points within a system, polling intervals, threshold values, and the conditions that dictate when an event should be generated. If it is determined that a threshold value has been exceeded or a value has dropped back under a previously exceeded threshold, an appropriate event is sent to event management. The setting of threshold values is heavily influenced by a provider's own previous experience. The user must therefore follow an iterative approach:

- Define a monitoring process, including critera for creating an event.

- Activate the monitoring process and observe whether it is providing useful results vis-à-vis operational objectives (Are errors being detected early enough? Are performance bottlenecks being identified? Are a large number of useless events being created?)

- Change the procedure, usually by modifying the measurement point or the threshold values.

Current monitoring procedures are mainly system oriented, meaning that all measurement points for a monitoring process are located within one system. Cross-system monitoring requires either a network model within the platform or special applications.

13.2.3   Event Management

Event management is a triggering mechanism for management actions

The function of *event management* is to accept and to process events. These events can be *external events* that are generated by resources (network components, end systems, applications) and are sent to the management station or *internal events* that are generated by other modules of the platform, such as resource monitoring. External events are determined through periodic polling or through asynchronous operations, such as traps and notifications. The causes that lead to event messages include exceeded threshold values, time expirations, state and configuration changes, test results, certain errors, and user reactions. Events are assigned different priorities. An event notification generally contains the attributes of event type, event cause, priority (severity), and additional information such as MO identifier, network address, event description, and time stamp. The subfunctions of event management are listed as follows (see Figure 13.5):

Subfunctions of event management

- Collection of data (e.g., polling RMON probes), acceptance of external events, generation of internal events.

- Storage of events in various internal or external logfiles, in some cases already sorted by origin, type, priority, and time.

- Provision of a filter mechanism for the search of events by a user or for the further processing of incoming events.

- Filter-controlled notification of events to the user or forwarding of events to other management applications or systems.

- Filter-controlled execution or triggering of actions, based on received events.

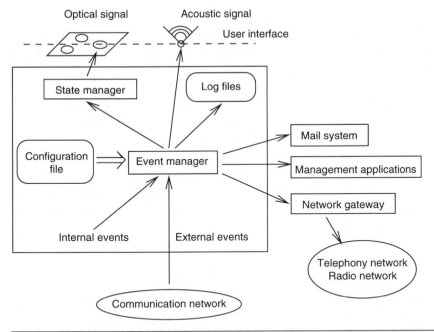

Figure 13.5
Embedment of event management

■ Support of alarm or event correlation in order to reduce possible "event storms" (which are symptomatic notifications of follow-on events caused by one original event) to the most important events. This is important for ensuring that management actions respond only to actual "root" causes. An event correlation usually requires the support of a network-oriented configuration model. We will discuss this later.

The different possible reactions to events should be defined in corresponding configuration data. Examples include sending an email, starting specific diagnostic functions, creating a trouble ticket, invoking system commands, and notifying maintenance personnel.

An important subfunction is the visualization of events for users. The visualization is based on a state model for resources, which describes states and the events that lead to state transitions. Different levels of priority, sometimes indicated by color coding, are assigned to the individual states. If the display of a symbol changes, users should be able to understand which event caused this change so that the appropriate action can be taken. Some platforms allow users freedom in defining state graphs for certain components or classes of components. When a graphic representation of state information exists, it must be taken into account that a user possibly has not opened the submap containing the corresponding symbol. State information can be shown within the graphic network display in two ways:

- A separate state window exists that displays how many systems are in states with a particular urgency. This window can be used to dump lists of systems found in a particular state.

- State changes are displayed in the map. Therefore, if the state of a symbol changes, the state, and consequently the representation of the symbol for the submap in which the symbol is contained, also changes. That is, the color change "bubbles up" to superior maps and symbols.

13.2.4   Configuration Management

Different capabilities of configuration applications

In contrast to most of the applications described earlier, which in general, allow just read-only access to the MIB, configuration applications also allow users additional write access to resources. There are different ways of implementing configuration applications:

- Information about the current configuration of resources: SNMP can be used to interrogate tables such as the routing table, the interface table, the address table, or the ARP table. Another important facility is one that allows access to information of the systems group of the Internet MIB, which contains information about current hardware–software versions, contacts, and installation sites.

- Use of management protocol to make configuration changes: A SET-PDU can be used to change the configuration information in a component. The problem is that many manufacturers do not implement write access to resources because of security concerns (this applies to all management protocols). In most platforms, therefore, the use of SET is limited to only a few selected MIB variables. Additional security mechanisms are often incorporated and can allow users to log into a system directly and supply a password before a state is changed.

- Configuring by logging into a system: Some component manufacturers also offer an option that allows users to log into a system to make configuration changes directly in the system. Platforms support this capability, allowing users to log directly into systems over the GUI using telnet as a standard application. This is referred to as cut-through access to the managed device.

- Configuration using manufacturer-specific modules: Owing to the difficulties of using SNMP for the configuration of resources, many manufacturers offer software modules that are specifically designed for their own product when managed through different management platforms. These modules offer a GUI, usually with a display of the resource, its replaceable components (e.g., plug-in modules), and management interfaces for generating, changing, and calling up the configuration data. Loadable configuration files are generated from the configuration data within the management station, and in a second step, are loaded over the communications network into the resource. A requirement of configuration applications is that they not only support loading but also incorporate a facility for dumping or storing existing configuration files from systems to the management station; this data then has to be usable as the basis for other changes. (In telecommunications management, this process is sometimes referred to as memory administration or provisioning.)

13.2.5   Topology Management

The *autodiscovery* function is an important function of management platforms. In conjunction with the use of different protocols, this function allows an extensive range of configuration information to be gathered over the network and the contained resources and filed in the database of the management platform. The term *autotopology function* is used when the information collected is used at the same time to build a map of the network topology obtained. Examples of discovery include:

Autodiscovery and autotopology

- The learning mechanism that has already been mentioned in connection with LAN bridges is used at level 2a.

- Host and router availability can be determined at level 3 from the combination of IP broadcasts and ICMP (e.g., echo). Traceroute (establishing the route to a destination) is also a helpful discovery program. The different routing protocols, of course, offer supplemental information.

- If systems run TCP/IP (this can be CORBA over TCP/IP, etc.), the identity of the communicating partners can be established through

MIB access to the routing table and to the ARP table and entered into the platform database.

- In some cases, it is possible to determine which management protocol is used for systems that have been discovered. Access to the interface table can identify the interfaces used by a particular system. Organizational data on systems (software–hardware versions, contact partners, installation site, manufacturer) can be acquired through access to system parameters, for example, to the system group of MIB II. If systems provide management data, this data is used as the point of departure for the next discovery cycle. Name servers are also useful for a discovery.

- Attempts are often made to access popular vendor MIBs (e.g., Windows NT WS MIB, HP Printer MIB) to determine more about a discovered system.

It is interesting to note that administrators are able to control the scope of the discovery function. This includes restricting use to certain subnetworks or restricting the routes used by specifying "boundary systems" (e.g., gateway routers to a public network). Failure to bound a discovery process can overload a network and the higher-level network in which it participates.

Integration of discovery function into platform
There are different ways to integrate a discovery function into a management platform. It can permanently be run as a background process in which discovery intervals are set as object specific or map specific. An elegant implementation involves setting the discovery interval automatically according to the quantity of current configuration changes taking place. But the discovery function can also be an autonomous application that is triggered by general or privileged users. In the first case, an automatic comparison is immediately made with the existing database, and newly discovered systems are inserted into an existing map. This insertion process can be carried out only if a view that has been established and maintained by the discovery function exists. No changes are allowed to be made to the view by the user. Changes should, however, be displayed to the user so that the new information can be copied to other views. Another option is to allow the discovery function to set up its own network database and the user to be given tools that allow the content of this database to be transferred to the actual database of the respective platform (comparison of different discovery maps or between discovery map and platform map, generation of submaps from the discovery map information).

Besides, another basis for the topology management should be mentioned, namely, self-discovery or announcement paradigms like CMIP object creation–deletion notifications. These complete the measures described in this section.

13.2.6   Performance Monitoring

A performance monitor enables measurements to be defined and executed for performance management. Similar to threshold value monitoring, measurements are defined by the following parameters:

> Performance monitoring is the basis of performance management

- Selection of a measurement point by entering the identity of a system and the attributes to be monitored, such as response time, throughput, resource use, and threshold values.

- Selection of measurement intervals, in other words, determining when the measurement point is to be read.

- Specification of the duration of the measurement (sample period) through the definition of a start and end time. The end time can also be provided implicitly by the input of the number of samplings to be executed.

- A facility for controlling the measurements (sample period) using functions such as start, hold, continue, and interrupt.

- A definition of rules to be followed if a measurement cannot be executed in accordance with its definition because of component failure. In most cases, the measurement is simply terminated, although it would be better if the measurement were temporarily interrupted and resumed again once the fault has been corrected. In any case, these kinds of unexpected events should be indicated to the user to ensure that a sensible interpretation of the measurement results can be made.

- Measurement results are usually stored within the platforms for analysis at a later time. Simple help tools such as displayed graphic curves or diagrams and calculations of minimal, mean, and maximum values are available for carrying out analyses. Separate application programs exist for more complex analysis (such as capacity planning).

A certain amount of preprocessing can take place in the agents. In the Internet, this entails accessing RMON-MIBs and with OSI a number of SMFs like workload monitoring function or summarization function (refer to section 5.5), which are then used by the performance monitor.

(Having a device sample and report performance management is more efficient and allows for temporal synchronization of measurements needed for proper analysis.)

Here's a hint: When CORBA is used for the infrastructure of the platform, CORBAservices and -facilities (see sections 7.5 and 7.6) can, of course, be used to support the basic applications.

13.3 Management Applications

Management applications represent solutions for specific management domains

The basic applications described here are also management applications, and some of them can even be used on a reciprocal basis. But these basic applications are not adequate for managing large or complex distributed systems. First, some of them use too much network capacity, and second, depending on the platform product, the basic applications are available only in an "economical version," meaning that they offer minimal functionality. The use of other management applications with the platform is therefore unavoidable. An extensive selection of these management applications is offered by platform manufacturers, component and system suppliers, and software houses. Examples include:

- *Trouble ticket administration* and *help desk support* (these systems will be dealt with in Chapter 14).

- *Event correlation systems*. These systems help reduce event and alarm storms. Examples are Seagate NerveCenter/Pro (state transition diagram), Tivoli TME/Enterprise Console (rule-based correlation), and SNI Event Center (rule-based correlation). A correlation system that is based on service-dependent graphs is being developed at our own institute at the University of Munich.

- *Inventory management, asset management*. This entails the collection, storage, and display of technical and operational data on components, systems, and software. In some cases, these applications resort to autodiscovery mechanisms (section 13.2). Examples of inventory applications are SMS from Microsoft, AssetView from HP, and TME/Inventory from IBM.

- *Facility management*. This relates to planning, documentation, and management systems for cabling and other building infrastructure. Examples include Physical Network Management (PNM) MT923 from Accugraph, COMMAND from Cambio Networks, and CCM from ComConsult (see also section 14.3). Facility management is also the term used by telco carriers for their inventory management. The TIRKS System from Bellcore is an example in this context. It is a fully integrated database that provides a total network provisioning process for special service circuits, message trunks, carrier systems, and span facilities as well as complete inventory management of telecommunications facilities and equipment.

- *Accounting and billing.* The modules and data structures for accounting management were already discussed in section 4.6. The tools that are relevant are the metering of accounting-related resources based on consumption and facilities for processing log entries. Management applications control the usage metering and the specification of necessary log data structures. Subsequent processing (e.g., billing) is usually carried out outside the platform. Especially in telco environments collecting and storing billing-related information in a fault-tolerant manner is extremely important. In this context, the use of adjunct processors is quite common. A good many customer management and billing applications in the market integrate the functionality for each stage of customer interaction (account creation, authentication and authorization, activity tracking, rating, billing, journaling, and business analysis). Examples of such solutions are Infranet of Portal or Arbor/BP of Kenan. Examples for accounting applications for more specific network environments are CISCO Enterprise Accounting for NetFlow or CISCO Enterprise Accounting for ISDN.

- *Software distribution.* This application is especially important because of the high staffing required for individual system software distribution. The management applications that are available for this application vary considerably in terms of the functionality supported. They range from simple distribution functions (file transfer) all the way to automatic software installation and licensing control. Subfunctions of this kind of management application can include [TER95]:

  - Checking the target machine for free storage capacity and other compatible software versions (preinstallation check)
  - Taking over the control of the target machine during installation, including backup of running software
  - Editing and configuring distributed software on the target machine
  - Postinstallation checking (i.e., verifying new software is functioning, rolling back to backup copy if not)

– Linking to inventory management to update software version levels, and so on.

The different phases of this management application comprise provision of the distribution packages, planning the distribution, distribution based on the push or pull model, installation, licensing control, and monitoring different versions. Examples of SW distribution products include TME10 Software Distribution, CA Unicenter Software Delivery, and Microsoft SMS (refer to section 16.2).

■ *Security management.* Encryption procedures, key management, and use of certificates are included in this category. A single sign-on is important for integrated user authentication. Examples of security management products include certificate authorities (VerSign, Entrust) authentication tools (Kerberos, RADIUS servers), physical tokens, and so forth. There are security products that provide high-level APIs that hide the complexities of key, signature, and certificate management from developers and allow developers to quickly and easily incorporate best-in-class security into their applications with confidence that the security implementation has been done correctly. Product examples include Entrust/Toolkit from Entrust Technologies and OnSite from VeriSign, which provides an application integration tool kit for an enterprise public key infrastructure.

■ *Systems management.* Applications are available for file management, print management, user administration, host management, email and directory management, and PC management (see section 16.2).

■ *Network management.* A number of technology-related applications packages are available for network management in the LAN, MAN, and WAN areas. TMN-conformant platform applications are also offered. (Examples include IBM NetView TMN Portable Agent Facility, HP OpenView Telecom TMN platform and related telecom products, Siemens ONMS portfolio, Diamond Lane, and Stratus/Nortel.) CNM applications that support service-oriented instead of component-oriented management [LLN98] also merit mention.

Management applications are integrated into platforms in different ways

When management applications are being selected, some consideration should be given to *integration depth*, which is an important factor with integrated management, and even with enterprise management. The first step should be to identify which agents will be supported by the application. Some application products support only the management of the resources of specific vendors. This especially occurs in Internet management where the heterogeneity of the real world is often reflected in incompatible vendor-specific MIBs due to the lack of an object orientation of the underlying information model.

A second issue concerns vertical integration depth. Which interfaces, services, and data of the platform itself are actually being used? Is there a synergy, or does the application not support the sharing of data and functionality in the platform? The third issue relates to horizontal integration. How does the application interact with other applications? Can application chains be formed so that one application automatically becomes a preceding application for another one over a shared database so that an integrated solution can be created? All that is usually offered in the real product world is an integration of menu groups or of user surfaces. In the former, an application is merely adopted into the menu group of the main menu over an application registration service of the platform; otherwise, it runs autonomously alongside other applications. With surface integration, the GUI of the application is structured on the same principles as other application surfaces, which means that the same symbols and maps are used.

13.4   Selection Criteria

This chapter concludes with a list of criteria that should be considered in the selection and the use of management platforms. The following factors add to the difficulty of selecting a concrete system:

- Products are often the result of a rapid deployment of new technology. Functions that are not yet available in a supplier's product are often announced in new versions that quickly appear on the market without integrated management.

- Products can often really be evaluated only in concrete operating environments; in other words, the strength and weaknesses of a product are not usually evident until different groups of users actually start using the product to monitor and control a specific set of networks and systems. However, it takes a great deal of time and effort to familiarize users with new products and to adapt and configure products to test environments in order to reach the stage where real evaluation can occur.

- The selection of a particular product has long-term implications for an enterprise, particularly because of the high investment costs associated with the introduction of the product (procurement, staff training, development of special modules) and the frequently required adaptations to operational procedures.

Some of the factors that could play a role in the selection process are listed next. The first set of criteria is of a more general nature, whereas the second set aims at differentiating between products. A comparative analysis of platform products can be found in [GHE97].

- *Flexibility.* The platform should be adaptable to the existing operational environment. It should be possible to adapt the platform to the organization of the enterprise, to the technology that is being used, and to the existing components. Flexibility is guaranteed through open interfaces, the configurability of individual modules, the adaptability of the user interface to different user groups through the use of views, and the availability of modules that enable an attachment (i.e., integration) to other management systems. (Note: This is the kind of flexibility being sought with CORBA services.)

- *Integrability.* The platform should be integrable into a management environment or itself act as an integrating module. Above all, there must be an assurance that using the management platform will not result in an entirely new database being created alongside the existing one. It is desirable that it is possible to easily link the database of the platform to the existing database of an organization (e.g., to the user data, inventory data, cost data, building data, and accounting data).

- *Security.* In view of the growing importance of communications networks and distributed systems and, consequently, management, a platform must be capable of offering sufficient operating security. Appropriate mechanisms are required to ensure that unauthorized and improper operation due to the wantonness or misbehavior of a user with the resultant negative effects on network operations is avoided or at least kept to a minimum.

- *Ease of use.* A management platform should offer interfaces that conform to the state of knowledge of the different user groups involved. For example, operators should be able to use the various functions without having detailed knowledge about the underlying management information model and object-oriented paradigms. Both the maps and symbols interface style, and an interface offering menus of functions, can satisfy this requirement.

■ *Viability.* The costs related to using the platform should be balanced with the potential benefits. The overall cost comprises the procurement of necessary hardware and software, individual adaptations to the environment of use, training of future users, maintenance, and personnel required in the use and servicing of the system.

■ *Future prospects.* Another consideration in the acquisition of a system is whether it will continue to be successful in the market. The main purpose of a platform is to provide an operational environment for management applications, so it is important that a sufficiently high number of these kinds of applications will be readily available in the long term. Suppliers of platforms have consequently established special programs that are aimed at persuading a maximum number of manufacturers of management applications and network components to base their development on their particular platform. The more popular a platform is in the market, the more likely third-party software manufacturers are to develop software for the platform, and this in turn increases the attractiveness of the platform itself.

■ *Supported platform services and basic applications.* There are many facets to this criterion. Platform services are heavily oriented toward supporting management architectures; that is why SNMP, TMN, and CORBA platforms exist. This fact, of course, has an effect on the underlying mechanisms and structures of basic applications (MIB structures, MIB browsers, MIB compilers, metadata, event mechanisms, communication modules, and information modules). Basic applications vary considerably in their functionality (compare with section 13.2). On the other hand, platform manufacturers offer different combinations of basic modules for their platforms. This "packaging" is frequently designed for a specific application. Platforms therefore specifically exist for network management (e.g., HP OpenView Network Node Manager, DEC TeMIP, Cabletron Spectrum, IBM NetView/6000) and for systems management (e.g., HP OpenView IT/Operations and IT/Administration, Tivoli TME10, CA Unicenter TNG, Sun Solstice System Management). PC management is another key application area (e.g., Microsoft SMS, Novell ManageWise, Intel LANDesk Management Suite).

■ *Supporting applications.* An important aspect of the selection process is the list of applications that can be run with a platform. It is not only important to consider the type of application per se but also to identify which agent products (e.g., which component types of which manufacturer) can be managed with an application.

The integration depth of an application is also an issue (compare with section 13.3). A list of SW cooperation partners is helpful in determining the future prospects of the platform. The portability of applications, namely, the support of open APIs, is also a platform criterion.

- *Scalability.* Scalability is especially important for networks and system numbers that are expanding at a fast rate. The issues that are of interest in this case are the number of manageable systems, components, and managed objects; the number of simultaneously executable applications; the number of simultaneously supported operator consoles; transaction rates; image setup rates with new information, and so forth.

- *Other evaluation criteria.* This includes the following: modularity of the platform structure, HW/SW requirements for the carrier system, number of platforms already installed, availability of platform user groups, product availability, release plans and product announcements, reports on the experience of other users and references, the quality of the documentation, and customer support (customizing, help desk, maintenance). The criteria relating to development tools are covered in Chapter 15.

13.5   Chapter Summary

Although the extent of dependence on the underlying management architecture and application environment (e.g., network management or system management and management area) varies greatly from platform product to platform product, it is possible to provide a general description of these products according to a breakdown of functions and modules. A sample platform is presented in Figure 13.1.

The platform infrastructure that is run on normal (usually Unix) workstations comprises a communication module and the information administration along with a kernel system. The communication module converts service requests for the infrastructure API that affect the agents or other systems into management protocols. The information administration module administers directories and information of managed objects and the data from management applications. The platform infrastructure is therefore heavily dependent on the management architecture that is supported. It is accessed through an API; SNMP-API (SNMP++), TMN-API (TMN/C++), and XOM/XMP as well as the ORB service interface are examples of APIs.

User interface modules can differ greatly and are usually based on Windows-based systems or on Web-based GUIs. It should be possible to display symbols, submaps, and maps; to initiate functions through the clicking on of icons; and to open other representation layers. The user interface should be capable of being adapted to concrete applications environments.

Most platforms are offered with a set of basic applications. In addition to an MIB browser, these include applications for state monitoring, threshold monitoring, event management, configuration management, topology management, and performance monitoring. OSI SMFs, RMON, or CORBA services and facilities, for example, are used for the implementation of these applications. The actual management applications themselves rely heavily on the applications environment of the relevant platform and are procured and installed according to the needs of the respective requirement. Solutions are offered for practically every area of management and business. A number of examples were given in the chapter. In practice, most management applications are not really deeply integrated and are run alongside each other on a common user interface.

Integrating Tools

The previous chapters in Part III highlighted the fact that a variety of tools and diverse platforms are available to support operators with their management tasks. If a company or an organization wants to integrate the management of its entire data processing infrastructure on this basis, then the cooperation between different tools must be as seamless as possible. A reciprocal exchange of information should be ensured. Tools whose main function is to integrate other tools were developed for this purpose, thereby reducing the gap that exists between tool functionality and the overall requirements operators have for fully integrated IT management; this topic will be discussed further in Part IV.

Integrated management requires the integration of existing tools

We will be describing the three most important classes of integrating tools. Section 14.1 analyzes the meaning of functionality inherent in the catchphrase *enterprise management system*. We found that three categories can be distinguished among the tools and platforms that are called enterprise management systems. The first category approaches the goal of integration from the perspective of managing corporate applications. The systems outlined in section 14.1.1 aim at the integration of the variety of tools that are needed to manage a distributed corporate application. A second category of enterprise management systems (section 14.1.2) starts at the infrastructure that is needed to foster an efficient integration of different tools. The systems in this category are mainly comprised of extensible high-end management platforms. The third category (section 14.1.3) focuses on the integration of event notifications and alarms from different sources, which is important for timely reactions to critical circumstances and increases the efficiency of management personnel.

The latter aspect (integration of event notifications and alarms) is also one of the goals of another class of integrating tools, namely, trouble ticket systems (section 14.2). However, here the focus lies mainly on the support and tracking of the processing of trouble reports and related workflows by management staff instead of on the more technical aspects of event integration.

The major problem of integrated management and related workflows today is that inventory and configuration information is scattered all over different management tools. This creates serious problems with consistency and produces inefficient updating processes for the information. The goal of the last class of integrating tools we want to describe, namely, documentation systems (section 14.3), is the integration of other tools through a virtually single source of inventory and configuration information.

14.1   Enterprise Management Systems

There are different ways of interpreting enterprise management

Anyone looking at the current publications of software providers and consulting firms and paying attention to current market analyses could not fail to notice that enterprise management is currently a hot topic. We introduced it in Chapter 1 as the level above network, systems, application, and information management. According to our definition, enterprise management encompasses the activities of finance, personnel, technology, and production management from a corporate point of view (fields of business, business processes) and derives from them policies for IT infrastructure, operating processes, associated services, and databases. Enterprise management therefore roughly corresponds to the concept *business management* from TMN (see section 5.6 and Figure 5.10).

Integration of management levels is the core of enterprise management

Although this definition supplies the motivation or vision behind the products of enterprise management, comprehensive and in-depth solutions for the whole problem area do not yet exist. Manufacturers all have different interpretations of enterprise management; consequently, the products offered focus on different things. But they all have the same goal, which is to achieve an integrated management of the entire DP infrastructure. In particular, this means ensuring that accessibility to all management information is seamless irrespective of the sources or degree of processing. This information relates not only to the raw data of agents but also to preprocessed data from intelligent agents and data from applications. The different points of focus are:

■ *Management of applications:* Here the focus is on the operation of corporate applications that represent the actual business purpose for the IT infrastructure. This is often referred to as *end-to-end management* because the emphasis is on the accessibility of the application to all clients. In this case, the first step of enterprise management is therefore to concentrate on the *integration of the layers* network, systems, and applications management (see Figure 1.2). An obvious analogy exists with the *service management* of TMN and its relationship to the *network management layer* and the *network element layer*.

The end-to-end management of applications must also include networks and end systems

- *Scalable platforms, integration of management architectures:* The tendency here is to start with a redesign of the technical basis and not to layer one or more additional tools above existing ones. This means that additional functionality is implemented in the management infrastructure that supports integration. The "classical" approach is followed in which the management platform is an integrating component but extendable through the addition of components, such as for the transition between management architectures. An assurance is needed that the platform itself can be distributed to guarantee that a system is also scalable for large environments. The approaches described in Chapter 10 provide the foundations for implementing an infrastructure on which the solutions for enterprise management can be based.

Scalable platforms, integration of management architectures: technical basis for enterprise management

- *Event management:* Again the goal is the *integration* of network, systems, and applications management, but with the emphasis on the management of event notifications and alarms from different sources. An attempt is made to increase the availability of applications and to improve the efficiency of management through a filtering, correlation, prioritization, and integrated reprocessing of all notifications.

Event management: integrated processing of all messages and alarms

- *Direct support and implementation of operating processes:* This element comes the closest to the definition of enterprise management as we presented it in Chapter 1 and will also be covered extensively in Part IV.

The following sections look closely at the characteristics of the preceding aspects. It would be wrong, however, to conclude from the classifications given that the enterprise management systems available in the market can all be allocated precisely to one of these categories. Combinations of the different variants also exist.

14.1.1 Management of Corporate Applications

Enterprise management: management of company-critical applications

Some products interpret enterprise management as the management of company-critical applications. These applications often incorporate all the popular operating system platforms. In a typical "three-tier model" application, for example:

- The clients are based on a Windows variant, OS/2, or Novell.
- The server is based on a Unix variant.
- The databases run on OS/390 or another mainframe processor.

Cover the entire lifecycle of an application

In this case, the goal of enterprise management is to cover the *entire lifecycle* of an application in heterogeneous environments; this is also referred to as *deployment management*. It entails:

- *Preparation* of the entire *application*, especially of the clients, for distribution and installation
- *Checking* the equipment and *configuration* of the *target systems* to guarantee the installability and operation of the application
- *Distribution* of software packages that contain the individual components of the application to the appropriate target systems
- *Installation* and configuation of the components of the application on the target systems
- *Monitoring* of the *application* during operation (i.e., checking status and measuring performance on an ongoing basis)
- *Deinstallation* of an application

These activities should be covered by a set of highly integrable tools. There should be minimal restriction in using the data of a tool in the other tools. Important requirements of the management system include:

- Automatic or at least easy creation of the packages for the distribution.
- Autodiscovery functions that enable automatic detection of as many properties of the target system as are needed for the installation. These include technical characteristics, such as the version of the operating system or processor, disk space availability, and DLLs installed, as well as those of an organizational nature, such as identification of department and cost center.

- A hierarchical structuring of software distribution to make efficient use of expensive or limited bandwidth on WAN routes through the deployment of software depots at several levels and to control the workload of the software server.

- Transaction support for software distribution and installation in order to execute a simultaneous version change on all the participating systems and eliminate problems due to the interaction of incompatible versions.

- Integration of inventory management and software distribution so that a distributed and installed version is compatible with the equipment and characteristics of the target system. This relates to data integration in our classification in section 11.3.

- Interfaces to network and system status monitors to monitor the availability of all clients.

- Interfaces to architecture-specific software distribution tools.

- Interfaces to performance monitors for network components and end systems, such as Windows NT and OS/390.

Regarding our classification in section 11.3, the last three items in the list mostly implement either user interface integration or proxy-based integration. Since the interfaces mentioned are usually proprietary, integration with the enterprise management system is mostly carried out in the form of separate modules.

Today, some of the requirements mentioned can be met only through the integration of various tools. A management model for applications common to all tools is required to ensure that an integration is implemented efficiently. The core of a management system for corporate applications provides a generic management model for all applications and is usable in heterogeneous environments. This model provides the basis that enables the applications of different suppliers to be uniformly "manageable." AMS from Tivoli/IBM is an example of this kind of model. It will be described more extensively in section 16.2.

Core area: management models for applications

Products for use in this environment include Tivoli TME10 Global Enterprise Manager and Tivoli Manager for Applications (*http://www.tivoli.com/*) and HP OpenView IT/Administration (*http://www.hp.com/openview/*).

Different subareas such as inventory management and software distribution are covered in section 16.2.

14.1.2　Scalability, Integration of Architectures

Enterprise management systems are often also defined as *high-end management platforms*, platforms that owing to their scalability and range of functions are suitable as the basis for the management of an entire IT infrastructure.

Scalability through distribution

Scalability inevitably requires that a platform is itself *distributed*. At the same time, the distribution of the platform should largely be transparent to users and applications. Distribution in this context, therefore, does not mean the use of a distributed database but a distribution of the entire core structure of the platform. Mechanisms are required for transferring messages between the distributed entities of the core infrastructure. Furthermore, a distributed transaction monitor is needed to implement the transaction properties in operations to several objects.

If the *range of functions* of the platform should be suitable for the management of the entire IT infrastructure, then a large number of the functions described in Chapter 13 should be available in a particularly well-developed form. Following are some of the characteristics that distinguish these systems from simpler management platforms:

Implementation of more than one management protocol

- The communication system supports *several management protocols*. In addition to an implementation of CMIP and SNMP and an integration of ORBs, the system often incorporates different RPCs or other protocols such as TL1 (see [BELL1], [BELL2]).

Integration of gateways

- *Management gateways* are frequently bundled with the products; these could be CMIP-TL1 gateways or CMIP-SNMP gateways based on the specifications of the IIMC Group (see section 10.3). Support of gateways between CORBA and OSI management based on JIDM specifications (see section 10.4) has already been announced by several manufacturers.

Platform's own user administration

- The platforms contain their own *user management* with several user classes (e.g., operator, administrator) and extensive functions for access control and view creation.

Domains and policies

- Well-developed mechanisms exist for forming *domains* or groups of objects to which *policies* can be assigned.

Several DBMSs

- The platform supports several DBMSs, thereby allowing or facilitating the integration of existing corporate databases with management tools.

With respect to our classification in section 11.3, this class of platforms aims at data integration and partly total integration. As mentioned, management gateways are also provided. Products found in this environment include Sun Solstice Enterprise Manager (*http://www.sun.com/solstice/*) and HP OV Telecom (*http://www.hp.com/openview/*).

14.1.3   Event Management

A mechanism that enables a speedy response to faults (events) is an important prerequisite for ensuring a high availability of applications. This applies all the more since "proactive" management today is often sooner a vision for the future than a reality. There are various reasons why it is often difficult to respond appropriately and efficiently to faults:

- The large number of different possible event notifications and the fact that in type and content the majority of them are proprietary, meaning that they are not based on any standards and thus require custom interpretation.

- The different types of sources, such as diverse management protocols and management tools, which technically complicate the collective processing of notifications and control over distribution.

- The necessity of requiring different tools to process event notifications from different sources adds to the user's orientation time and provides an opportunity for error, confusion, and oversight.

- The lack of a general classification of notifications, which makes it difficult if not impossible for notifications to be forwarded automatically to the respective expert.

- The difficulty in determining and recognizing priorities so that service-affecting faults are given expedited handling.

- The incredible increase in the number of notifications when certain errors occur, that is, the "ripple effect" a fault has on the operation of an enterprise network.

As a result of these problems, critical notifications are often detected too late or not at all because of the flood of notifications, notifications are not processed in the correct sequence, or errors are processed in multiple because they have triggered notifications that are to be handled with different tools.

Notification flood hinders efficient management

In view of these problems, many software manufacturers (and operators as well) consider the efficient management of all the event notifications of an IT infrastructure as a core area of enterprise management. Systems therefore contain components supporting the following:

- Integration of event notifications from *different sources* so that they can be processed collectively. This requires that the different formats of notifications are mapped to one common format (i.e., data integration for events or proxy-based integration; see classification in section 11.3).

- Flexible *filtering* of notifications in order to eliminate duplicates and unimportant ones. The latter currently still usually requires a considerable configuration and programming effort on the part of the organization.

- Assignment of *priorities* to notifications on the basis of diverse criteria such as type of notification, source, or time of day, that is, according to business impact.

- Intelligent mechanisms for the *grouping*, *correlation*, and *automatic forwarding* of notifications.

Special language for rules or graphical tools

Tools usually establish the basis for these functions and allow organizations to formulate rules defining the stated functionality for their environments. These rules are either formulated with a specialized programming language or compiled using a graphical tool.

These rules can usually determine how a message should be forwarded automatically or escalated. These functions are explained in section 14.2.

Products for event management include Boole & Babbage COMMAND/POST and MAX/Enterprise (*http://www.boole.com/*), Avesta Trinity (*http://www.avesta.com/*), Micromuse Netcool/OMNIbus (*http://www.micromuse.com/*), Objective Systems Integrators NetExpert (*http://www.osi.com/*), and Tivoli TME10 Enterprise Console (*http://www.tivoli.com/*).

14.2   Trouble Ticket Systems

Motivation for the introduction of TTS

In section 3.1, we used scenario 5 to describe how a trouble ticket system (TTS) can be used as a support tool for help desks (also see section 17.5). We now want to take a more detailed look at TTSs, and what soon becomes obvious is why a TTS is perceived as being an "integrating" tool. This point is also clarified in Figure 14.3 (see page 354).

Because of networked systems, applications-oriented services are becoming more complex and being implemented as distributed applications. (This has been mentioned several times elsewhere in our discussions.) Within an organization, this means that a number of people are jointly involved in solving problems or processing requests; so there is an information aspect as well as a workflow aspect involved. When you consider the cooperative processing of problem messages within the customer-provider chain (see scenario 1 in section 3.1), these aspects even begin to cross over into other organizations. This creates the need for a common data structure that allows all participants to query and document the status of the cooperative processing. Each problem (e.g., user complaint, failure, alarm) documented according to this data structure, in the context of TTS called *trouble ticket* (TT), describes one case. If the data structure is selected cleverly, a collection of TTs can be expanded into a case database containing expert knowledge, for example, on error diagnosis and error recovery [DRV95]. TTs have different states depending on the status of the entries and the processing. A change in state can be used as a trigger to instigate actions or to allocate responsibility for processing to other experts or to another system. To this extent, TTs also play a role in workflow management. In some cases, they can also be used to formalize workflow, to allocate work steps to those responsible for certain tasks, and to coordinate activities and information flow (e.g., during a repair process).

14.2.1   Structure and Functions of TTSs

The keystone of every TTS is a database in which the trouble tickets, thus the documented errors and other problem descriptions produced by a person or a management application, are collected. A TT represents an ongoing activity or workflow. The related information includes errors, problem description, status, owner, and so forth. We will break down the TTS into individual modules and describe the functions implemented by each module. Problem messages are recorded as TTs by an *input module* and entered into the database. The services of the *output module* provide a readout of the TT data records. Of course, it is vital that these input and output modules can be used by multiple users and also offer technical interfaces to couple other systems online (such as email, WWW, and documentation systems). As shown in Figure 14.1, the TT database, the input module, and the output module constitute

Basic modules

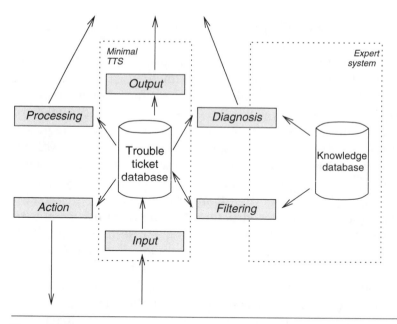

Figure 14.1
Structure of a TTS

a "small-scale" TTS. The illustration also shows that a TTS usually can also provide a variety of other functions. These extended functions are briefly described next.

Action module   Frequently, some of the work to be carried out after the arrival of a TT is known about beforehand. An example of this is the notification to a user that his or her error message has been recorded as a TT. These sorts of simple tasks can be dealt with by an *action module*. The "programming" of this module is effected in the form of rules stating that action Y is to be carried out upon arrival of a trouble ticket with the property X. The action module would also establish the link to the workflow management component in the TTS if one exists; otherwise, it does so to a separate workflow management system possibly using a workflow API (e.g., OMG specified one).

Processing module   The information contained in the TT database must be processed in a way that ensures that a maximum benefit is derived from it. Various types of statistics can particularly be helpful in the overall evaluation of faults that have occurred. These statistics can include:

- Display of TTs according to their state of processing.

- Identification of the most frequently reported types of faults, including the steps taken to resolve them, and of the resources or services that generally were the cause of the faults.

- List of the amount of time elapsed to correct the different classes of faults (meantime to repair, MTTR, or meantime between failure, MTBF) and comparisons with the allowed values due to respective SLAs.

It is not only these simple statistical values that are of interest but also the benchmarks derived from them relating to service quality, workload in terms of personnel (such as hotline, second-level support), and weaknesses in workflow. Trends can also be identified from these values. Frequently asked questions (FAQs) will give an indication of the kind of corrective action required but also will give an indication for which problem area an additional training of staff will be advisable.

It is not the quantity but the quality of the trouble tickets contained in the TT database that will determine how effective a TTS is for a network provider. It may therefore not be feasible for every TT initiated by applications or users to be entered into the database. A TT is usually generated only if a particular problem cannot be resolved immediately at the help desk and requires several experts to deal with it. Even if a problem can be resolved quickly, there are times when it could be feasible to generate a "quick ticket" for statistical purposes (e.g., to evaluate customer behavior, to ascertain the most frequent hotline questions); the quick ticket contains a minimum amount of requested information but is not forwarded to any other experts. Generally speaking, however, multiple TTs relating to the same symptoms can be generated if tickets are automatically produced as a result of events or alarms or if more than one help desk exists in the hotline. In this situation, a *filter module* or a *correlation module* should decide what is acceptable for creation of a TT and inclusion in the database. The filter module would then be able to determine that two trouble tickets from different users are describing the same fault or that the causes of faults for a trouble ticket that has been received have already been diagnosed, and delete these TTs accordingly (possibly after the respective user has automatically been informed of the processing state of a "similar" ticket). It must be mentioned that there are regulatory and business metric consequences of creating TTs since both public and private organizations are measured on the number of TTs and the time to resolve them. However, these examples highlight the problem of deploying filter modules: appropriate specialized knowledge is required

Filter module

for use of this kind of module. The same applies to the diagnostics module described.

Diagnosis module

As Figure 14.1 illustrates, the *diagnostics module* provides a smooth transition from the extended TTS to an expert system. The ultimate objective of a TTS is to determine the cause of faults and to restore service. Trouble tickets provide the symptoms of the faults for this diagnostic process. A certain type of knowledge is required to correlate the trouble tickets and fault causes. [LEW93] presents and analyzes two AI approaches (rule-based and case-based reasoning) based on a TTS diagnostics module. An intelligent investigation into the ticket database of a TTS can be important for many reasons: for automating and reducing the amount of time required for the diagnostic process, for producing trend analyses, for optimizing workflow, and so forth.

14.2.2 The Information Structure of a Trouble Ticket

TT format

To a large extent, the efficiency of a TTS hinges on the accuracy and completeness of the information available with a TT. Figure 14.2 illustrates the information structure for a TT. The basic data of a TT is provided during the fault reporting or detection phase. This data comprises the following [VAD93]. (Some of the data may be multiple in the cases where inputs are correlated into a single TT.)

- Ticket identification and ticket state (the conceivable states are open, accepted, rejected, diagnosed, assigned, in progress, resolved, verified, closed).
- Data about the user or system that is reporting the fault.
- Data about the components or the service in which the fault has occurred.
- Time stamp indicating when the fault occurred or was reported.
- Data describing the fault.
- Organizational data on how the fault was repaired (e.g., person who accepted the fault, experts assigned to resolving the fault, current state of resolution, priority). These fields represent the link to the workflow management component, which in many products, is integrated into the TTS system and also implements escalation mechanisms.

During fault diagnosis, this basic data is expanded on the basis of the descriptions of the diagnostic actions undertaken (action list) and the changing responsibilities (responsibility list). Actions are documented

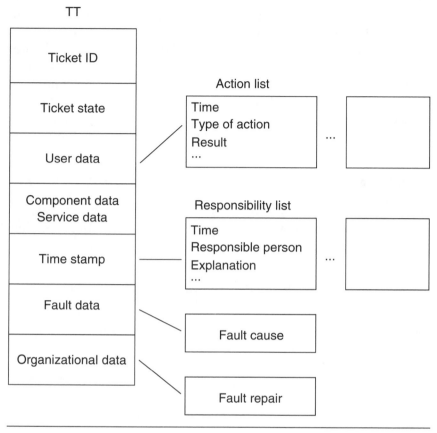

Figure 14.2
Information structure of a trouble ticket

according to the time of the diagnosis, the person responsible for the diagnosis, the type of action taken (e.g., restart of a component), and the results achieved. If the fault is located, then the cause of the fault and the measures taken to repair it are added to the TT. The time stamp is recorded with each phase to enable information to be produced later about how long the fault lasted and how much time was required to repair it.

A fundamental question that arises is whether a fault should be described using free format text (e.g., "File cannot be fetched") or through the selection of fault classes from given lists (e.g., type of fault = file transfer problem). The advantage of using descriptions from predefined lists is that it is much easier to correlate faults and to produce evaluations and statistics later. The more formalized the TT information is, the more suitable it is for use in automatic evaluations (use of

Free format text versus predefined lists

correlators, linking to information databases). Problem identification and classification is also important for assigning the fault diagnosis to the appropriate expert. On the other hand, free format text comes closer to the way users work and think. If lists are used, it is necessary that appropriate analyses are carried out in the provider organization and fault classes are defined before a TTS is used. A multilevel classification is useful for this purpose to enable the proper modeling of a user or a provider view. (Note: Both classifications can be used together!)

14.2.3   Integration of TTS into an Operating Environment

Figure 14.3 shows a TTS as an integrating tool in an operating environment. In particular, a TTS is a central support tool for the hotline

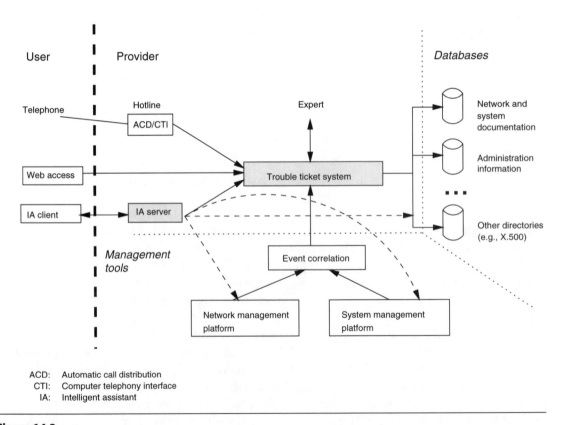

ACD: Automatic call distribution
CTI: Computer telephony interface
IA: Intelligent assistant

Figure 14.3
Integration of TTS

and the help desk. The following functionality should be provided by a help desk: call management, problem documentation and tracking, document backup, maintenance history, case databases, access to documentation systems, trend analyses, management reports, and escalation procedures. Not all these functions are implemented in the TTS; some are provided in conjunction with other management tools. The TTS's role as a central function adds to the importance of its integration into operating environments. An integration using management tools (e.g., network and system management platforms) with the aim of automatically generating tickets can be effective only if an event correlation tool is used. When causally linked event storms occur, this tool reduces the event quantity to a small number of causative fault symptoms (i.e., root cause events) to which tickets are then allocated for diagnostic workflow purposes.

Significance of event correlation

But not only fault diagnosis can be integrated with a TTS as indicated. Performance management tools are extremely important in enterprise and applications management. They can also easily be integrated with a TTS. The easiest way of doing so is to consider any appropriate results of some threshold analysis performed in the performance management tool as an event triggering for generating a corresponding TT. The TT then will trigger the necessary workflow and at the same time log the ongoing activities. In this way, a TTS works as an integrating tool.

The illustration also shows database integration. The databases that can be linked effectively are the network and system documentation systems (see also section 14.3), user databases (e.g., an X.500 directory), and administrative information. There is an inclusion of lists for checking whether experts are available (can be busy or absent) to process the tickets. This is particularly important when a customer is being promised access to certain processing times.

Integration of databases

TTSs can also be integrated into telephone systems through *automatic call distribution* (ACD) or *computer telephony integration* (CTI). This kind of integration would enable the access to customer call-related databases to be automated.

Integration of CTI and ACD

Special note should be taken of the user interface of a TTS. Traditionally, users talk with a hotline or a help desk, in other words, with staff of the provider who make an effort to obtain the TT information. Because of the personnel costs involved, direct TTS interfaces are becoming more and more important. The goal is to progress from less helpful statements such as "nothing functions" to accurate descriptions of symptoms ("host 129.187.10.32 not available"). There are two types of direct interfaces:

User interface of TTS

- *A form completed by the user* (email or Web): This technical interface helps the provider by cutting out the recording process and is also relatively easy for the user. The data entry process can then be done by the user or by a third party (e.g., help desk operator). However, only simple information can usually be queried (e.g., Until when did it function? What changes did the user notice? Is the fault reproducible?). Furthermore, the TT usually cannot be generated automatically because the user is not familiar with the service classification of problems used within the TTS and therefore would not be in a position to categorize the problem. Therefore, a dispatcher who analyzes forms and creates TTs is required by the provider.

Intelligent assistant as an interface

- *User-implemented fault localization and automatic compilation* of relevant information: A corresponding procedure has been developed by the authors and is being used under the name of *intelligent assistant (IA)*. It involves using Java applets to load decision trees for certain classes of problems (such as accessibility problems, throughput problems, and acquisition requests) into the user's workstation system; these decision trees roughly correspond to the interrogation by experts at the first-level support stage. In principle, each tree node can be linked to management tools (such as monitors, platforms, and databases). Actions (such as accessibility tests) are triggered automatically as the tree is scanned. The results are displayed online to the user and logged for the subsequent generation of TTs. Hence, faults are localized and precise information is recorded according to predefined goals and within a specified time without the involvement of hotline staff. In other words, form entry makes the user do the data entry job, but this makes the user (without being an expert) do part of the diagnosis and correction job.

Because the service classification is determined by the decision trees, the TTs can be generated automatically with information that is more accurate than when they are recorded over a help desk later. Our experience shows that there is a higher level of customer satisfaction because of the improved transparency in the service provided. The experts are also impressed by the improvement to the TT quality. The downside of this approach is that it is the experts who have to set up and maintain the decision trees, but this activity can free them from some of the ordinary frustrating routine work that exists in some of the problem areas [DRK98]. To summarize, this kind of automation helps the organization reduce total cost of staff to support the services being offered.

14.2.4   Standardization of Trouble Ticket Systems

Various standardization bodies and consortia have recognized the need to standardize tasks and the associated objects in the context of TTS. This also makes sense if you view the TTS illustrated in Figure 14.3 as an integrating tool. The ITU-T defined a *Trouble Management Function for ITU-T Applications* (ITU recommendation X.790, 11/1995) for telecommunications applications. The document puts forth proposals for the standardization of the functionality and information structure of TTSs in accordance with the OSI management approach. Individual actions are described for the generation and processing of trouble tickets, and the roles of manager and agent are assigned. These actions roughly correspond to the TTS modules described earlier. An inheritance hierarchy is defined for the managed object classes (MOCs) deemed necessary for trouble management. Examples of these MOCs include trouble reports (provider trouble report, telecommunications trouble report), trouble report format definition, log records (event log record, trouble history record), repair activity objects, and contact objects. The attributes approximately correspond to the information provided earlier in this section. The complete ITU model is presented in Figure 14.4.

TTS approach of ITU

The diagram should be largely self-explanatory from the standpoint of the descriptive details. However, we have to mention that, in the context of X.790, emphasis is on exchange of TTs between jurisdictions or organizations (carrier to carrier), allowing automation outside the span of control within a single provider (e.g.,TTs between service provider and user). In contrast, the TT structure in NMF601 is used for customer to carrier; there are therefore some differences in the requirements. This makes a difference on at least two counts (NMF 501). First, the range of services and the business relationships are usually different; relationships between service providers are often subject to industry or even government regulation, whereas relationships and service offerings to end customers are proprietary and constantly evolving. Second, the technology of implementation is impacted since the end user customer typically seeks a trouble administration solution available off-the-shelf and capable of supporting connections with a few service providers. The service provider, however, is prepared to invest heavily in OSS systems to protect his or her core business,

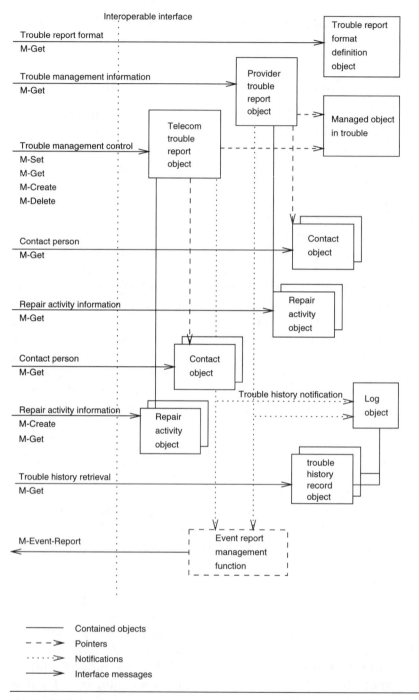

Figure 14.4
ITU model for trouble ticket management

and furthermore needs a system supporting high transaction volumes and a large, often distributed, organization. (note: The TT in X.790 is protocol dependent, i.e., CMIP; with NMF the TT structure is defined as protocol independent.)

The IETF is also concerning itself with TTSs in RFC 1297 (NOC Internal Integrated TTS). This document describes the desired functionality and information structure of a TTS from the view of the network operator. The following is being proposed on the basis of the Internet information model:

TTS approach of IETF

- User complaint tickets to describe fault reports from end users
- Trouble tickets to describe faults detected by the network operator
- Engineering tickets to describe familiar or possible problems (e.g., maintenance times for network components, overloading of certain network segments)
- Metatickets in which requests for changes or proposals for improvements to the TTS itself are documented (e.g., expansion of the data stored in the TTS, improved statistics)

The information stored in these tickets can then be queried by other systems through the SNMP management protocol.

The NM Forum has also produced some new and promising work in the TTS area. The consortium has dealt with service management at the customer–supplier interface in two documents (NMF501 "Customer to Service Provider Trouble Administration Business Agreement 8/96" and NMF601 "Customer to Service Provider Trouble Administration Information Agreement 3/97"). The NMF work is based on X.790, and the documents complement each other. In the first document, typical workflows are defined at this interface on the basis of different business scenarios and functional as well as technical requirements derived from them. NMF501 specifies the functional requirements for the customer-to-service-provider trouble administration interface. These requirements refer among other aspects (e.g., business, technical) to the specific trouble administration one. Requirements referring to this aspect are discussed in several sets such as *trouble report creation, trouble report tracking, trouble report management and trouble report clearing and closure.* For example, the first set covers the initial creation of trouble reports by either a customer or a service provider, whereas the second set is concerned with the tracking of the problem resolution process by the customer.

TTS approach of NMF

NMF601 defines the functionality and information for the exchange of management information to meet the requirement sets as specified in NMF501. Results of the analysis are defined in the form of an object, dynamic, and functional model. The functional model provides specifications of the operations at the following interfaces:

- The customer_TTR interface type for the purpose of entering a telecommunication trouble report and tracking the status of trouble resolution
- The TTR_Notification interface type to inform customers of events related to telecommunication trouble reports (e.g., status change)
- The TTR_Notification interface type to inform customers of events related to provider trouble reports (e.g., scheduled maintenance on a service)

Operations at the customer_TTR interface type allow the customer, for example, to:

- Cancel trouble resolution on (TTRCancel)
- Request the creation of (TTRCreate)
- Modify (TTRModify)
- Track status of (TTRStatusTrack)

Operations at the TTR_Notification interface type are invoked by the service provider to convey notifications of a TTR, as for example:

- Cancellation of trouble resolution (TTRCancellationNotify)
- Creation (TTRCreationNotify) in case a service provider has detected a service failure
- Status change (TTRStatusUpdate)

The same operations are used at the PTR_notification interface type. They are invoked as well by the service provider to convey notification of a provider trouble report (e.g., scheduled maintenance on a service).

The second document provides the associated object model that is specified with OMT and UML. There are tools to map UML to CORBA IDL or Java interface objects. Commercial trouble ticket systems implement the specified operations mostly via an API. For example, the Remedy ARS API calls for creating and deleting a trouble report as well as for modifying an attribute are ARCreateEntry, ARDeleteEntry, and

`ARSetField`. Some of the operations like `TTRCreate` can be directly mapped to `ARCreateEntry`, whereas the implementation of, for example, `TTRModify` would request to use `ARDeleteField`, `ARCreateField`, or `ARSetField`.

In general, the quality of a trouble ticket system product can be measured also by the flexibility of the provided API.

The IT Infrastructure Library (ITIL) of the UK Central Computer and Telecommunications Agency (CCTA), which is becoming more and more of an industrial standard, also contains specifications for functions from the TTS environment.

A TTS is an important cross-section tool that is effectively integrated with a number of other tools. It plays an important role in service-oriented management at the interface between operator and user of an IT infrastructure. This tool is used for collecting data (of which tickets are only one example) as well as for monitoring activities. TTS input systems (see intelligent assistant (IA), described earlier in this chapter) can also be interpreted as workflow management front ends. Up-to-date product overviews for TTS and for help desk systems can be found in the current documents of the Datapro Information Service Group, a subsidiary of Gartner Group (McGraw-Hill).

14.3   Documentation Systems

In the discussion on MIB catalogs in Part II, it was frequently pointed out that management information does not only consist of technical and dynamically changing parameters such as current resource use, operating states, and acute alarm reports. There is other information relating to procurement, installation site, type of maintenance contract, accessibility, and names of contacts that is also vital for management. The function of documentation tools is to support the recording, display, and administration of management-relevant information that describes the infrastructure of a distributed system and is usually considered to have long-term value. This includes the following (enumeration is not exhaustive):

Documentation systems are sinks and sources of management information for all kinds of tools

- Information about systems and components. This includes type of device, structure of device with number and type of boards and interfaces, and version numbers of hardware and software used.

- Information about cabling systems and connections (physical inventory).

- Ordering and inventory information (business management information). This includes asset-relevant information (costs, payment schedule, taxes, cost sharing, procurement data, depreciation, value, useful life) and service conditions (type of maintenance contract, warranties, supplier contact, hotline, maximum time before start of repairs), inventory numbers, serial numbers, and licenses. This category of information is particularly important for *asset management.*

- Information on procedures. Description of management procedures, data flows, operational procedures, and organizational practices.

- Organizational information. This comprises information about the structure and the personnel of the network provider and of user organizations. Information about certain staff of the network and system operator is important in terms of responsibilities and accessibility (telephone number, email, or postal address). The allocation of data terminating equipment (terminals, PCs, workstations) to users, cost centers, and organizations must be documented.

- Geographical information (different locations, topology). The description of the locations at which cables, cabling components, and terminating devices are situated constitutes an important part of network documentation. The information can be managed in a hierarchically structured form (country-city-site-building-floor-room). Pictures and plans that realistically represent a location have a high informative content. Information about rooms that is important includes number of telephones in a room, access to the room (who is in charge of or has the keys?), dimensions of the room, cabling infrastructure (cable ducts and conduits, wall sockets), infrastructure for equipment (air-conditioning, monitoring of access, electrical connections, furniture, wiring cabinets, load-bearing capacity of the floor, failsafe power supply).

- Directory information (names, addresses, accounts) for both humans and systems.

- Information necessary for the purpose of service management (subscriber details, contracts, service level agreements, usage details, account information, tariffs, etc.).

A common data model is essential for information integration

The sources of this information can vary greatly, as can the tools used to manage it. How this information is used can also vary according to the procedure and the tool employed. The goal is the availability at any given time of a complete and up-to-date documentation of the physical

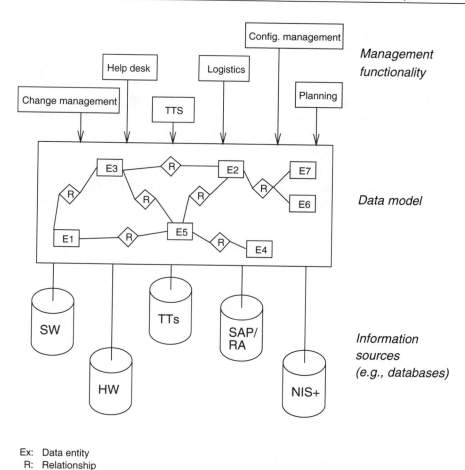

Management
functionality

Data model

Information
sources
(e.g., databases)

Ex: Data entity
R: Relationship

Figure 14.5
Integration of documentation components through a common data model

and logical infrastructure of networks, systems, and applications. The
information provided is relevant for technical management and for a
managerial evaluation of inventory (asset management). It offers the
only means for achieving transparency from the standpoint of cost,
contractual obligations and a commitment of funds, and technology
and business processes. It is therefore important to specify a *tool-
independent data model* of the required management information.
Figure 14.5 clarifies the role of this type of data model, which could
be represented in the form of an entity-relationship model. The actual
provision and storage of data can be implemented on a distributed
basis and in different forms (database systems, file systems, tools,
platforms, TTS). The significance of the integrating aspects of the data

model will be immediately evident because of its tool-independent specification. This also supports flexibility in the context of change management.

Figure 14.6 presents a section of a concrete schema of network documentation. It shows just how interwoven the different information can be, and yet only a small section of data is shown. With distributed and redundant information storage, it is important that a safe mechanism exists for ensuring data consistency. In our work, we have used the options provided by trouble ticket systems (specifically, ARS from Remedy) as described in section 14.2, which allows additional management integration. Instead of trouble tickets for problem management, different *documentation tickets* (common docu tickets, device tickets, single component tickets) were designed for compatibility with the data structures of the TTS. This design reflects the fact that a device consists of several components, and accordingly certain information is device specific (e.g., IP address) or component specific (e.g., serial number). Process-oriented actions were also defined (e.g., allocation of inventory numbers, generation of new equipment, affixing of inventory numbers, shutdown, exchange of parts, installation into existing equipment) that trigger documentation changes or are initiated by such changes. The workflow management aspects of a TTS can thereby also be used advantageously to integrate the documentation.

Because of the data exchange required, the different documentation systems should be easy to couple to other tools (such as platforms, TTS). It is therefore important that they use standardized database access interfaces (SQL, RDA) or object interfaces (CORBA), which also provide the flexibility needed to design a management solution based on the principles of the corporate operations framework concept (see section 17.4). Automatic update mechanisms for the maintenance of consistency can also be easily employed only if open interfaces exist. Another important option is the availability of *view forming* to data because certain users or procedures are interested only in some of the information or have restricted access only to information (perhaps for reasons of security).

14.3.1   Cable Management Systems

Cable management systems represent a class of documentation systems worthy of mention. They initially originated as isolated tools and were either database based or CAD system based.

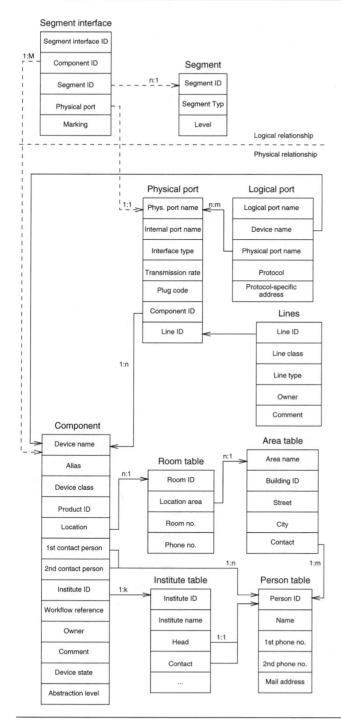

Figure 14.6
Network documentation layout

Database-based
approaches

In a database-based solution, a database system is used to store and manage all the information. Access to the information is effected over standard tools that are part of the respective database system and to which only the database structure defined for the network documentation is adapted, such as form-oriented interfaces, report generators, and SQL procedures. An important advantage of this approach is the usability of standard database software for access to the information. An easy mechanism is also available for the exchange of information with other databases that already exist within an organization.

The main disadvantage of a pure database solution is the lack of appropriate graphical representation of topology information. Tables and lists do not provide as clear a picture of a complex topology (e.g., a local network) or cable running through a building as does an illustration of the configuration that displays the individual systems and modules and how they are cabled together. Documentation systems are therefore enhanced with special applications that generate configuration and topology maps from existing data. These maps can then also be used to make subsequent changes to data. However, the representation displayed is usually only schematic and cannot take into account the true spatial conditions. So although this kind of a display can show that two terminals are connected together, it cannot show exactly where the associated connecting cable is laid within a room.

CAD-based systems

CAD-based systems mainly use CAD standard software from the building technology or facility management area for the documentation of the physical cabling of terminals. Room and building plans in which terminals and cabling components as well as the cable itself are shown realistically and to scale are used as the basis for the documentation. The supplementary information available for the separate elements is stored as part of the CAD plans. Some CAD systems support different display planes, thus a room plan can be superimposed by various separate display planes (e.g., displaying power and water supply, air-conditioning, telephone network, and the data communications network).

The advantage of these systems is the realistic graphical representation of information. Users are able to use the CAD plans to form an exact picture of their networks that conforms to the actual on-site configuration. However, the disadvantage of this type of documentation is the general lack of powerful functions like those provided by database-based solutions that enable access and allow a linking of the different information that relates to the displayed elements.

Because the advantages and disadvantages of database and CAD solutions complement each other, over the last few years products have been developed that attempt to combine both approaches. These systems are based on a CAD system, a database system, and a special integration component that is responsible for the exchange or comparison of information between both systems. These integrated systems incorporate various features:

Integrated database/CAD systems

- Information is stored not only in CAD plans but also in the database tables, with an integration component responsible for ensuring the consistency of the data.

- Changes are implemented at the CAD interface, and the corresponding database tables are automatically updated at the same time. For example, the symbol for a terminal being installed is created over the interface of the CAD system and positioned within a building plan. Entries for this system are then automatically made in the appropriate database tables in which the properties of the terminating device, such as name and telephone number of the system manager responsible, are stored. Conversely, changes on the database side should automatically trigger updates in the CAD displays.

- Depending on the task, information can be accessed either over the CAD user interface or over nongraphical database interfaces.

- The information accessed can be displayed on the user interface of the CAD system. Let us take the display of a communication path between two terminating devices as an example. The user selects two devices over the CAD user interface and chooses the function "communication path" from the menu system. Access to the database provides the information about the communication path with all the elements (cables, cabling components) highlighted through the use of different colors. If necessary, the relevant CAD plans containing the elements to be displayed are loaded.

Cable management systems vary according to the number of object types supported and whether the object descriptions are fixed or changeable. Objects of cabling management include:

Objects of cable management

- *Cable:* Products vary according to the type of cable supported, such as data cable, telephone cable, or distribution cable. Modern products follow an object-oriented modeling approach and provide class definitions for the different types of media (compare Chapter 2). The transmission characteristics on their own are not sufficient, and attributes usually also have to be specified, including structure of the cable (number of wires, tensile strength, type of sheathing, length), the course of the cable, supplier and date of installation, and service interface.

- *Cable administration:* This includes a description of cable routes, shafts, conduits, ducts, pipes, and so forth.

- *Cabling components* such as boxes, junction boxes, splice boxes, connection elements, tee couplers, and boosters.

- *Connection elements* and their internal switching: jumpering panels, matrix switches, wiring cabinets, coupling fields, LAN coupling elements, and ports.

It goes without saying that some of the attributes of the objects mentioned are identical to those of other devices and systems; these include name of owner, contact persons, accessibility, telephone numbers, purchase date, location, commissioning, and last change made.

Good documentation systems offer extensive plausibility tests to prevent the incorrect entry of object descriptions. These include tests to check conformance to standardization regulations (e.g., IEEE 802), occupancy levels of cabling routes, and plug compatibility. The systems also usually support bulk recording to provide efficient and cost-effective data recording. New products not only support the building cabling standard (EIA/TIA 568 Intrabuilding Wiring Specification) but also the associated administration standard (EIA/TIA 606 Administration Standard for the Telecommunications Infrastructure of Commercial Buildings), which defines the data structures for cabling documentation.

Many of the modular cabling documentation systems can be expanded into general integrated documentation and administration systems, as clarified by Figure 14.7, which illustrates an example product: *ComConsult Communication Managers* (CCM). With the availability of a modular, freely configurable, and object-oriented data model, the same documentation tool that produces the cabling documentation can be used to set up equipment and configuration management, topology and connection management, telephone administration, and so forth. Each documentation, of course, contains an analysis component, history administration, and a report generator. For the purposes of achieving an overall integrated management solution, it is important that a documentation system can be used in conjunction with the applications of other suppliers (e.g., platform applications and facility management). Applications are frequently integrated directly into the documentation tool; these can include planning and change management, contract and inventory management, space management, and

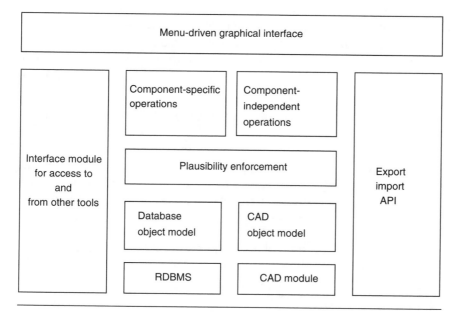

Figure 14.7
Structure of a modular cabling documentation system

reporting. The actions of change management will be dealt with in Part IV.

14.3.2   Introduction of Documentation Systems

Selecting and using a documentation system is a strategic decision for a provider and requires some thorough preparation. The introduction of a documentation system is foremost an organizational undertaking because these systems operate efficiently and profitably only if a systematic approach is followed in how they are used and maintained. This requires:

Organizational conditions

- Specification of responsibilities and procedures for incorporating and changing information. Depending on the desired organizational form, this can be carried out as a central function by a person with a high level of responsibility or as a decentralized function by equal-ranking users.

- Introduction of mandatory documentation, which means that changes to real configurations can be implemented only if they were documented beforehand.

- Introduction of mandatory reporting, which means that anyone who undertakes changes to a real configuration or detects that changes have been made to a configuration is obligated to document these changes or to report them to those in charge, and this is enforced by the system.

- Incorporation of documentation into general workflow management.

Integration with other databases The database that is built up within a documentation system in many cases overlaps with other databases that already exist within the provider organization. The following points therefore require clarification before a documentation system is used:

- Whether an existing database can or should be used; if necessary, the underlying database scheme for the documentation system must be altered accordingly.

- How the consistency of the overlapping databases should be controlled; an example would be to specify reference data that is regularly entered into the documentation system (management of replicated data).

- Whether products come with solutions that can automatically be used for data exchange with other systems. Some manufacturers of documentation systems may be able to offer solutions that support linking documentation systems to a management platform (e.g., through the use of standard documentation interchange formats or standard access functions).

- How a comprehensive data model should look (see Figure 14.5).

Setup of a database There should be no underestimation of the effort involved in building up the necessary database when a documentation system is introduced. Ideally, the database could be generated from existing data. The difficulty, however, is in building up a CAD database if no corresponding computer-supported plans are available. This then requires the undertaking of one of the following time-consuming measures:

- Recapturing of all buildings using a CAD system.

- Scanning and adaptation of the resulting pixel files to the possible functions of the CAD system through, for example, vectorization or defining objects, groups, layers, and so on.

- Scanning of plans and input into a CAD system without previous vectoring; some of the functions of the CAD user interface of the documentation tool will then not be available because of the prerequisite for vectorized information.

It should also be noted that during initial data entry, changes have to be recorded to data that has already been entered to ensure that the initial data entry and the updating process are always running in parallel.

14.4 Chapter Summary

Fully integrated management from the viewpoint of the service or the network provider means that a single tool or a seamless integration of different tools must exist that meets all the provider's management requirements. Truly integrated management that addresses all these needs of providers does not yet exist today. However, products are available that address some of the problems identified in the previous section of this book. Substantial progress has been made toward a fuller integration of management during recent years. Means for integration include enterprise management systems, trouble ticket systems, and documentation systems.

The management of corporate applications in heterogeneous environments has suffered in the past from the lack of standardized or published management models that cover the whole lifecycle of an application and are equally suitable for all functional areas of management. This situation has been recently improved through the introduction of open management models for applications, for example, the application management specification (AMS; see section 16.2.2) from Tivoli/IBM and the accompanying development tools. Another problem—the lack of management instrumentation for applications with standardized interfaces—has been alleviated through the development of application response measurement (ARM; see section 16.2.6) and standardized interfaces for recent software component models such as Enterprise JavaBeans.

High-end enterprise management platforms have to cope with a variety of management information models and protocols. This makes the development of an infrastructure that supports the efficient integration of different management tools a complex and time-consuming task. However, recent advances in development gateways between architectures (e.g., the work of the JIDM Group; see section 10.4) and efforts toward an integrated information model, namely, CIM (see section 9.3), should promote the implementation of integrating platforms.

Event integration and management in heterogeneous environments is hindered by the vast number of different formats for event notifications and alarms. This situation should be alleviated through ongoing efforts to define common templates and classification schemas for event notifications and alarms.

The integration of alarms and events as well as user complaints is the goal of trouble ticket systems. Trouble tickets trigger actions and workflows; the states of related IT processes are documented in the TTs too. The structure and functions of TTSs as well as the standardization work concerning TTSs have been discussed in this chapter. From this it became clear that a TTS plays an integrating role. Documentation systems also play an integrating role if there exists an integration of documentation components through a common data model.

Development Tools

As with any software solution, an analysis of needs and requirements tha serves as the basis for the specification of functionality and procedures is a prerequisite for the development of management tools. The interfaces between the individual components of a distributed application are then specified subsequently.

With management applications, this usually also includes the interface between manager and agent. Depending on the information model used, the definition of the management information exchanged between these components can be complex; the availability of a tool is often desirable. *Modeling tools* therefore support the description of the management information on the basis of the respective information model.

Modeling tools support the specification of management information

If these kinds of tools are used, the information being exchanged is in a format that serves as the starting point for *support* in the *implementation* of *managers* and *agents*. This information is used to generate interface stubs for the applications, thus structures enabling communication with agents, and implementation structures for agents that are then expanded through the use of code for access to the actual resource. A fluid transition therefore exists between the modeling of the management information and agent or applications development. Furthermore, depending on the information model used, pieces of code that support an application in the display of this information at the user interface can be derived from the definition of the management information. Another form of support consists of making nonmanagement-specific components such as databases, transport systems, and Web servers usable for management applications or management agents.

Support in the implementation of managers and agents

Another important aspect in the development of management applications is the integration with other applications under a shared user interface, preferably with a shared look and feel. Development

Development tools for user interfaces

373

tools such as *GUI builders* are typically used for this purpose, for the *generation* of management-specific as well as general *user interface elements.*

Chapter
organization

The different sections of this chapter provide an *overview* of the *development tools* available for the areas mentioned. Section 15.1 is concerned with modeling tools for management information, which are also referred to as MIB tools. Section 15.2 then outlines how software can support the development of agents. Section 15.3 provides a general description of tools used for the implementation of management applications. Section 15.4 is devoted specifically to development tools for user interfaces to management applications because of the importance of the support of applications development in this area and the wide availability of relevant products.

15.1   MIB Tools

MIB tools support a specific information model

MIBs define key parts of the semantics of the interface between managers and agents. The definition of these semantics is inevitably strongly guided by the information model of the underlying management architecture. Because these information models can be very different, the tools are usually tailored to a specific model. A broad spectrum of functions is available:

- The relatively simple types of information models, such as Internet SMI or DMTF-MIF, usually require less support; consequently, the *tools* are *simpler*. The dominant tools are those that can be used to check definitions in the Internet SMI or the DMTF-MIF for *syntactical accuracy.*

- The expectation with powerful object-oriented models such as GDMO and UML/CIM, on the other hand, is that the tools will provide *more extensive functionality*, which also includes support of allomorphic concepts or relationships between classes of objects. These typically tend to be *complex modeling tools*, with less emphasis on syntax, more on semantics.

Our discussion will be limited to a description of the more complex tools. These include management-specific products, typically GDMO tools and general tools, as well as modeling tools for UML or OMT.

15.1.1 GDMO Tools

As section 5.2 already emphasized, the information model for OSI management may be very powerful, but it is also very complex for the modeler to use. General object-oriented principles such as specialization along with the comparatively complex inheritance mechanisms, the concept of allomorphism, the number of and relationships between different template types, and the conditional packages all contribute to this complexity, which makes modeling a very complicated operation and prone to error if adequate tools are not available. Typical functions of GDMO tools include:

The complexity of GDMO requires powerful modeling tools

- *Syntax tests* for imported and generated ASN.1 and GDMO definitions
- *Input* of existing *ASN.1* and *GDMO definitions* and conversion into the internal format of a tool
- *Output* of the internal format into an *ASN.1* and *GDMO format*
- *Mask-controlled editing* of the information specified in different template types
- (Graphical) display of the *inheritance hierarchy*
- Clear *display* in an overview format of the *relationships* between the templates that together completely describe a class
- Control of the display using *filters* or *domain definitions*, particularly, for example, to mask out the irrelevant parts of the model for a specific application
- Assurance of the *consistency* of the definitions; this includes, for example, checking whether referenced classes or attributes have been defined, whether circular references exist, and so forth.
- *Navigation* in the relationships, such as from the definition of a class to the exact definition of an attribute
- *Search functions* that, for example, respond to questions like "Which classes use a given attribute definition?"—in other words, navigate in relationships and references in the reverse direction
- *"Pretty printing"* of the models

Implementation skeletons for the CMIP agents and *interface stubs* for the applications may then be generated from the internal or an external format. This function therefore represents the transition between the modeling and the implementation of agents and applications (see sections 15.2 and 15.3). The code parts can normally be produced for

Generation of code skeletons and stubs

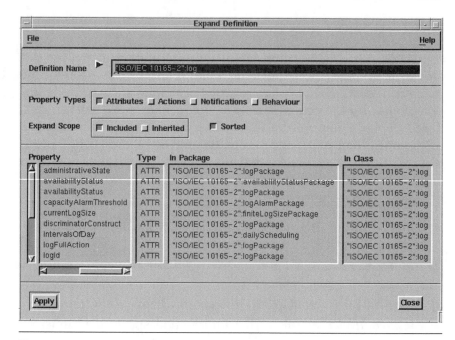

Figure 15.1
Class browser for the tool Damocles

C or C++ in the OSI environment and may reflect standard APIs like TMN/C++.

Examples of tools that at least partially contain the functions mentioned are presented in [FHN95] or under *http://www.dset.com*. Figure 15.1 shows the class browser of the tool Damocles (see *http://www.ikv.de/products/damocles.html*). It provides an overview of the definitions in the different ASN.1 or GDMO templates and their relationships, and allows the display to be controlled through filters and domain definitions and a navigation through the relationships. The example in Figure 15.1 shows the log managed object class and its attributes. Radio buttons allow the user to also view attributes inherited from superclasses or other properties such as actions and notifications.

15.1.2   Modeling Tools for UML and OMT

Use of SE modeling tools in management

With the increasing use of CORBA as an architecture for network and systems management, more and more importance is also being given to general (i.e., nonmanagement-specific) software development tools in the management area (see first paragraph of Chapter 7 and section 7.8). Use of OMT [RBP91] and more recently of UML [RJB98], [BRJ98] for modeling management information merits particular mention. UML is used more frequently in management during the introduction of CIM (see section 9.3.2). We will therefore briefly outline some of the relevant parts and functions of typical tools for OMT and UML.

The tools are usually based on a common *database* (*repository*) of all components and functions, which managed by a standard DBMS. The database contains all information from the models and the tables. To ensure that the information contained in the tables and the models is consistent, an object is entered into the repository only once, even if it is used more often. The products can, of course, be used concurrently by many users.

Common database for tools

All diagram editors, table editors, and other functions can be called up from one common *desktop*. This includes project and user administration as well as database administration.

Common user interface

Various *editors* are available on the desktop for the creation of *diagrams*. For the OMT, these include the editors for the object model, the dynamic model, and the functional model; for UML, these editors are for the diverse types of diagrams such as object diagrams, use-case diagrams, and sequence diagrams. Consistency checks between the diagrams would be useful but do not yet exist in most products. The most important editors today for the modeling of management information are those for object models or class or object diagrams. Figure 15.2 presents a view of an object model editor.

Diagram editors

Information about the objects that are not displayed graphically is recorded with *table editors*. A class table can, for example, contain the type definitions for attributes and method parameters for the classes of the object model. Supplementary information that is necessary for the generation of interfaces (such as in IDL; see section 7.2.2) can also be contained in these tables.

Editors for different types of tables

A number of other tools are available that provide the user with a diversity of *useful functions*, such as printouts of diagrams and tables, administration of the repository or of the users, and conversions of internal formats to third-party formats.

Functions for the *generation of interface descriptions* and *implementation skeletons* provide the transition between pure modeling tools and software development tools that are then used to implement agents or management applications. A typical feature of tools for UML and OMT is that they generate IDL interface descriptions as well as stubs and implementation skeletons for C++ and Java. Sections 15.2 and 15.3 cover this in more detail.

From pure modeling tools to software development tools

Examples of tools in the category just described are Rational Rose (see *http://www.rational.com/*) and Software through Pictures (StP) (see

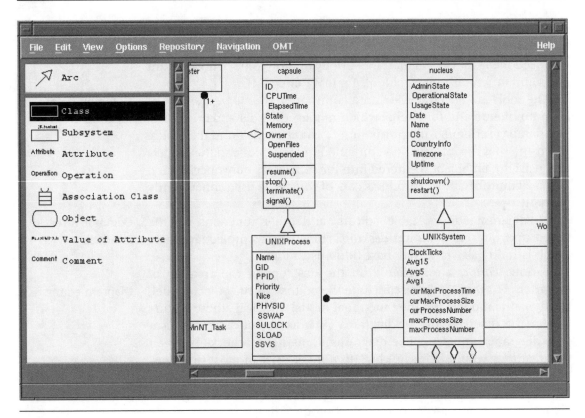

Figure 15.2
StP object model editor

http://www.aonix.com/) from Aonix. Figure 15.2 shows the object model editor from StP, which enables an editing and graphical structuring of the OMT static model, thus of the classes with their attributes and inheritance and containment relationships.

15.2   Tools for Developing Agents

Interaction
between
protocol entity
and resources

The management information modeled with the tools described earlier must be provided by the agents. Code pieces are implemented that enable interaction between the *management protocol entity* and the *resources* it manages and therefore acquire information from the resources for control by management.

The various management architectures follow different approaches in their *definition* of the interface between the management protocol entity in the agent and these code pieces. Three different approaches are common today:

Different approaches to interface specification

- The architecture omits defining this interface and leaves it completely *unspecified*. It is viewed, as by OSI management, as a "local matter."

- The *principal range of functions* of the interface is defined but not the mapping of the functions to the implementation languages. DMTF-DMI is an example of this (see section 8.3.1 and Figure 8.2). The definitions for *SNMP Agent Extensibility* (RFC 2257) in Internet management are also in this category (also see section 6.2.2).

- In addition to the range of functions for the interface, mechanisms for the *mapping to implementation languages* are also defined. This applies to CORBA (see sections 7.2.2, 7.2.3, and 7.3.1).

The more comprehensively the interfaces are defined, the more fluid the transitions between architecture specifications and development environments become. The development environment is then defined within the framework of the implementation of the architecture; it is part and parcel of it. The following sections look more closely at the examples mentioned and describe how agents for these architectures and interfaces can be supported through the use of tools.

Some transitions between architecture specifications and development environments are fluid

15.2.1   Tools for OSI Management Agents

The *GDMO* and *ASN.1 specifications* mentioned in section 15.1.1 serve as the starting point for the coding of the agents. Like the functions that implement access to the real resources, these specifications are specific for a particular *agent*. All other parts (e.g., the protocol machine or scoping and filtering) are functionally equivalent for all OSI agents.

Only few agent parts are specific

In addition to the modeling tools from section 15.1.1, development tools for OSI agents provide important components in the form of *program libraries* that *implement the parts* that are *common* for all OSI agents and support integration with the specific parts.

The following description is based on the tool TMN Workbench for AIX from IBM (see, e.g., [FHN95]). To a large extent, it also applies to the tools of other manufacturers, such as the DSET Agent Toolkit (see *http://www.dset.com/*). The key parts of the tool include the following (also see Figure 15.3):

Common parts are contained in development environments

- The *infrastructure* provides the basic functionality of the agents. It contains implementations of protocol entities for CMIP (CMISE)

Infrastructure: basic agent functionality

and ACSE (see section 2.2.2) and a directory service to locate agents and managers. In other products, a standard API may be used to bind other protocol stacks to the agent.

Part common to all agents
- The *agent services part* provides services that are common to all agents.

  - The component *naming and replication* manages the containment hierarchy of the objects. It determines, for example, which objects fall within the scope of an incoming CMIP query and forwards copies of the query to the core agent for further processing.
  - The *core agent* accepts these queries and forwards them to the resources.
  - The *event* and *log handlers* are implementations of the event report management functions and log control functions outlined in section 5.5. Other agent development kits support additional SMFs as well.
  - The *Callback CMIS/CMIP Interface* (CCI) enables CMIS requests to be initiated from the specific agent parts through the use of callback functions. In the view of the CMIS entity, the specific part therefore assumes the role of manager. This is how the implementation of the dual role of manager-agent in an entity promoted in the OSI architecture is supported.

Specific part of a certain agent
- The *agent-specific part* is the part the developer produces using an MIB composer. As was mentioned in section 15.1, C++ code parts such as stubs and program skeletons can be generated from the ASN.1 and GDMO specifications. The developer then has to expand these parts with C++ code, which implements access to the actual resource ("user-defined behavior"). In most products, this process is supported by a number of example code pieces implementing access to resources. From this, the MIB composer produces the agent-specific part, which can be combined with the common part and the infrastructure to form a complete executable agent.

When this tool is used to generate an OSI agent, the developer only has to code those program parts that are directly associated with access to the resources being managed. All the other parts are either delivered as part of the development environment or generated from the ASN.1 and GDMO specifications. In our example, infrastructure, agent services, and MIB composer are included in the development kit. Additionally, large portions of the agent-specific part are generated by

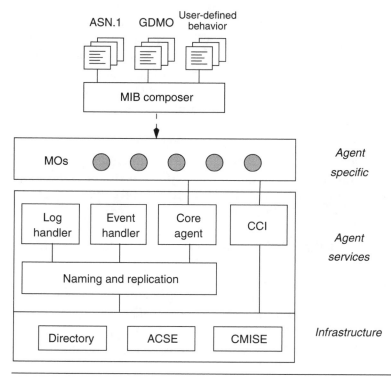

Figure 15.3
Tool-supported implementation of OSI agents

the MIB composer. The main thing is that the developer does not have to be concerned with complex mechanisms such as scoping.

15.2.2   Tools for SNMP Management Agents

With the development of SNMP agents, as with OSI agents, large parts of the agent code are the same for many agents. Consequently, the basic starting point of the development tools for SNMP agents is very similar to that for OSI agents.

In this case, the tool provides the *master agent* (see section 6.2.2), which roughly corresponds to the infrastructure and the common agent part of the previous section. This master agent is, however, less complex because SNMP is a simpler concept than CMIP, incorporates no mechanisms like scoping, and usually does not incorporate any functions for event or log management. However, it includes GetNext, GetBulk, and often RMON features.

Many parts are also identical for different SNMP agents

Master agent provided by development environment

Several standardized protocols (see section 6.2.2) and proprietary technologies, such as EMANATE from SNMP research (see *http://www.snmp.com/*), are available for *communication* with the *subagents*. EMANATE has an important place in the market because of its use by well-known firms, such as HP in its HP OpenView Extensible SNMP Agent. Subagent skeletons that implement these protocols are usually part of the tool.

MIB compilers generate subagent stubs

Some products in this environment have some similarity with the MIB composers described earlier; these are usually called *MIB compilers* and are used to generate Internet MIB *stubs* for the *subagents*. The stubs are supplemented with code by the developer for actual access to the resources. No further code is required to produce an executable subagent.

Integration of new subagents during runtime

It is possible for the individual subagents to be developed separately from one another. The development of a new subagent does not require a new translation of the master agent or even new binding. The new subagents register with the master agent during runtime and indicate which managed objects they are providing over the protocol. As of the beginning of 1999, the dominant implementation languages supported are C and C++, although Java will also be making a mark in the future.

15.2.3 Tools for DMTF-DMI

Similarity between Internet management and DMTF-DMI also exists in development environments

Because of the many similarities between the Internet management architecture and DMTF-DMI, particularly between the information models, the development tools for the two architectures also show major similarities. Within the DMTF architecture (see Chapter 8), the service provider (SP) roughly corresponds to a master agent, the component interface (CI) to the interfaces between master agent and subagent, and the component instrumentation to the subagent.

Tools contain master agents and sample subagents

The tools contain the *service provider*, thus the master agent, and often sample code for *component instrumentation*, which can be modified as necessary for the respective MIF. Because a distinction is made between static and dynamic information in this architecture, or information model, very little code has to be produced by the developer. The static information is conveyed to the SP through the help of the MIF file for the component (see section 8.2.1); the only operation requiring programming is access to the dynamic attributes.

The similarities that exist with the tools for SNMP agents also continue to the implementation languages that are supported; the dominant language is currently C. Products for the category described include DMI 2.0 Software Developer's Kit from Hewlett-Packard and LANDesk Client Manager Software Development Kit from Intel (*http: //developer.intel.com/*).

15.2.4 Tools for CORBA Agents

If management agents are developed for the CORBA architecture, they will not differ substantially from the development of general CORBA-based server objects; use of the *general* CORBA development tools will be possible. This was actually one of the motivations for using CORBA for the management of networked systems. The books listed at the beginning of Chapter 7 provide a good overview on this subject, so our treatment here will be limited to a brief outline of the tools and their uses.

CORBA: use of general tools for management agents

The starting point is usually the IDL interface specifications that have been produced manually by the developer or generated by modeling tools (see section 15.1.2). These serve as the input for IDL compilers (see section 7.2.3) that use the specifications to produce the implementation structure for the desired programming language. These structures then still have to be extended by the code that enables access to the resource. In principle, the latter is not different from the extensions undertaken to complete the structures described in the previous sections for the agents to other architectures.

15.2.5 Other Tools for Management Agents

In addition to the tools designed for a specific management architecture, other tools are now becoming available for use with different management architectures and management protocols. The products particularly worth mentioning in this context are those using the programming language Java to access agents that at least to a partial degree are not dependent on tl.e computer architecture and operating system on which the agents should be run.

Architecture-independent agents

The Java Dynamic Management Kit (JDMK) from Sun (see *http: //www.sun.com/*) is typical of some of the products available in the market. The objective of this development tool is to use Java to support the implementation of flexible agents. The aim is to ensure that key parts of the agent code are *architecture independent*, and that the *functionality* of the agents can be *modified* during runtime.

Agents developed with JDMK run on a Java virtual machine and consist of the following components:

JDMK: develop-
ment of flexible
Java agents

- *Managed objects* created as JavaBeans, which have to be implemented by the developer of the agent
- *Adapters* for a number of protocols (RMI, HTTP, SNMP)
- Availability of *basic services* in the form of JavaBeans, such as simple
  notification mechanisms, filtering, object databases, and loading of
  classes
- A *core structure* that supplies the runtime environment for the other
  components and controls the cooperation between them

The tool is supplied to the components for the agents, except the
managed objects. Either the push or the pull model can be used in
the modification of the agent functionality during runtime; services in
the forms of beans can be loaded on the agents, modified there, or
deleted again.

15.3   Development Environments for Management Applications

Limitation to
management-
specific aspects

Management applications themselves are primarily applications; the
customary software development environments therefore also apply
here. It would be impossible to provide an overview of all the relevant
tools, so we will limit our discussion to the *management-specific* aspects
of applications development.

Fluid boundaries
between realiza-
tion of architecture
and development
environment

It should be pointed out at the outset that fluid *boundaries* exist
today between the implementations of architectures and platforms, applications development, and applications customizing . For example,
the implementation of a CORBA service can be seen as an implementation of the architecture, but on the other hand, it also supports the
development of applications.

Many "applica-
tions" are really
development tools

Owing to the expansion of integrated management from network
management toward systems and applications management, more
requirements are being placed on management applications, and needs
are differing from user to user. Many applications are therefore *less of
a tool* for management than *development environments* for those tools
that allow users to produce their own management solutions or to
produce them with the help of third parties. Our emphasis will be on
development tools in the narrower sense.

We will be describing the following aspects:

- *Interfaces to management protocols*, such as XMP/XOM and TMN/C++ APIs
- Management-specific *interfaces to databases*
- Refined *event services*
- *MIB compilers* that produce internal data structures from MIB specifications that can be used by applications

To the extent possible, no distinction will be made between platform-based and other tools; the transition here too is fluid, as shown by the example of XMP/XOM, which can be found within platforms as well as on its own.

15.3.1 Interfaces to Management Protocols

If support is not available, a comparatively complicated procedure is involved in programming access to management protocols, thus *converting the information* (marshaling) between an internal format (e.g., C-data structures) and an interchange syntax (e.g., ASN.1, BER) and assembling the PDUs. The following list includes tools that can support an applications programmer with these tasks:

Access to a protocol requires conversion of format

- *XMP/XOM:* The programming interfaces X/Open management protocol (XMP) and X/Open OSI abstract data manipulation (XOM) are meant to standardize access to the CMIP or SNMP implementations of different manufacturers and, to the extent possible, to hide the differences between the two management protocols. XMP [OG306] is the interface for access to CMIP and SNMP protocol functionality. Because of the existing functional differences, the goal of standardizing access to the two protocols can be only partially achieved. Applications therefore continue to require adjustment to the different protocols; however, the process is simplified due to the common syntactically standardized interface to data elements carried by protocols. XOM [OG607] allows a local manipulation of ASN.1 data types, such as for the conversion of parameters between ASN.1 and C structures during access to XMP.

XMP/XOM: access to CMIP and SNMP

- *TMN/C++ API:* This programming interface (see, e.g., [CCS97]) consists of three layered APIs (also see Figure 15.4). *ASN.1/C++ API* provides mapping between ASN.1 constructs such as types and values and C++ classes or objects, logically addressing the same problem space as XOM. *CMIS/C++ API* enables access to CMISE and ACSE. It comprises C++ classes and objects that represent this

TMN/C++ API: access to CMIP and manipulation of GDMO objects

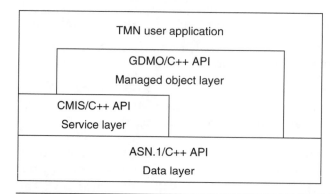

Figure 15.4
Architecture of TMN/C++ API

applications service, logically addressing the CMIP part of XMP. The *GDMO/C++ API*, which is based on the two other interfaces, allows applications to manipulate managed objects directly without having to understand CMISE. Operation is therefore no longer at the protocol level but directly on the management information.

SNMP++: set of C++ classes for access to SNMP services

- *SNMP++ API*: This API consists of a set of C++ classes that provide access to SNMP services for applications. SNMP++ is not an additional layer or wrapper over existing SNMP engines, but utilizes existing SNMP libraries. It is not meant to replace other SNMP APIs such as WinSNMP, but will ease the object-oriented development of applications with access to SNMP.

SNMP access from Java programs

- With the growing use of Java as a language, the demand for tools that simplify *SNMP access* from *Java programs* is increasing. Several Java class libraries are now available that provide SNMP operations and allow manipulation of the data types of Internet SMI in Java programs. Examples of these libraries include the SNMP class library from AdventNet (see *http://www.adventnet.com*) and the class library available with JMAPI (see section 9.2) for SNMP access.

In addition to the aforementioned examples, many other interfaces to protocols are available for applications development; an overview of these interfaces can be found in [GHE97]. The benefit they have in common is that they support application portability and allow reuse of a common protocol infrastructure.

15.3.2   Interfaces to Databases

From the standpoint of management applications, the properties or required operations of MOs that are of interest are not always limited to those attributes or actions that are provided by the agents. What is also important for an application is whether and how the object is represented at the user interface, that it can be stored persistently, and that operations on the object and on other objects can be executed with transaction protection. Hardly any management protocols today allow the latter. Applications therefore file information about many objects in a *database*. A standard database interface is therefore incorporated into every platform.

Filing MOs in databases

For applications this means having to deal with two or more models for MOs (database scheme and information model/s of the management architecture/s). As a result, interfaces are now being offered that, although they are ultimately based on standard DBMSs, actually augment the general interfaces to these systems (SQL interfaces, ODBC, etc.) through the addition of *management-specific functions*. An example of this is the provision of a common data model for applications, for example, to represent objects in a platform.

Augmenting DB interface with management specifics

New approaches are trying to provide applications with a *standardized MO model* that, in a sense, combines the "agent view" and the "database view" on the MOs. It should be transparent to an application whether a particular property of the MO that it is accessing is implemented in the agent or in a local database. The advantages of databases, such as persistent storage and the execution of operations with transaction protection, should be retained as far as possible.

Uniform access to DB objects and agent objects

The *managed objects* from JMAPI (see section 9.2) exemplify this kind of approach. These are primarily database objects, and applications operate exclusively on them. Database access and access to agents are then hidden by the managed objects. The development environment supplies the implementation of a basic class `ManagedObject`, the properties of which can be inherited to specialized object classes. Basic mechanisms enabling database access and locks to realize transactions are therefore supplied with the development environment.

15.3.3   Refined Event Services

Functions that occur with frequency in management applications are those involving the receipt of selected *event notifications* from certain objects and filtering or correlation based on defined criteria.

Receiving, filtering, and sending notifications

Mechanisms that support these functions are available in all management architectures (see sections 5.5, 6.4, 7.5.1, 7.7.1, 8.4, 9.2.4, and 9.3.1).

Subscribing to notifications

The development environments usually provide applications with services that allow the *subscription* for certain events. The criteria applied are the type of event notification, the source, and the value of specific parameters of the notification.

The abstract definition of these services is partially a subject of the management architecture. The function of a development environment is to allow the use of these services by programs.

CORBA notification service: support for event management

With CORBA, the mapping of the "abstract" definition (of the IDL interface specification) to programming languages is part of the architecture. A development environment that should simplify the management of event notifications for applications could therefore provide an implementation of the *notification service* (see section 7.7.1) and the associated IDL interface. Developers of applications can use IDL compilers (see section 7.2.3) to generate stubs for the functions in the programming language they use.

JMAPI: classes for event management

The translation step mentioned can be eliminated if the programming language has definitely been decided. This means that the classes provided by the development environment can be used directly. An example of this are the different *classes for event management* supplied with JMAPI (see section 9.2.4). The use of `EventDispatcher`, `EvdController`, `ObserverProxy`, and so forth provide the applications programmer with extensive functionality for sending, filtering, and receiving event notifications.

For other examples, refer to the comprehensive compilation of services for event management in [GHE97]. Functionality for event processing that goes a lot further than the functions mentioned in this section is part of TTSs (see section 14.2). It includes, for example, rule engines for correlation of events.

15.3.4   MIB Compilers

MIB compilers generate stubs for applications

There is an effort to make maximum use of MIB specifications in the development of management applications, just as there was with management agents. Numerous references have already been made to the possibility of using these specifications to generate *stubs* for access to the *management information* from the applications (see section 15.1). Some overlapping occurs with section 15.3.1 because access to the protocol is, of course, also contained in these stubs.

This facility is provided as part of the architecture for CORBA anyway; comparable functions are furnished for GDMO, for example, from the top layer of TMN/C++ API (GDMO/C++ API).

In addition to generating stubs, an MIB compiler can also produce an *internal format* from the specifications, thus, for example, a representation of ASN.1 types in the form of data structures in programming language. These representations (metadata) can be shared by all applications. The metadata can also serve as the basis for the generation of the associated user interface elements, such as the frames for entering values with range checks. These elements are the subject of the following section.

Internal format of MIBs

15.4   Tools for Designing User Interfaces

The previous sections of this chapter discussed the current extensive availability of management tools with different functionality that providers of DP infrastructures have to combine to address their own particular requirements. The key in ensuring that this kind of "building-block" approach will be an efficient and accepted solution is uniform operation achieved through an *integration of the tools* under a *common user interface* (see section 4.1).

Integration of tools using a common user interface

A uniform operating interface (look and feel) is achieved through the establishing of *guidelines* that dictate what this interface should look like (*user interface style guide*). These guidelines will be effective only if an appropriate *tool* (*GUI builder*) exists for allowing an easy and rapid implementation of *conformant user interfaces*. We will provide a brief overview of elements that are typically supplied by these tools.

Uniform look and feel

Previously, tools were supplied together with the management platform and conformed to the associated user interfaces such as HP OpenView Windows and a standard for graphical user interfaces. X Windows and the user interface from Windows NT still dominate the field. With the growing popularity of Web browsers as management consoles, we are seeing the development of tools that attempt to establish a cross-platform standard; these tools are based on the Abstract Windowing Toolkit (AWT) from Java or on SWING/JFC (Java Foundation Classes).

Tools for different user interfaces

Because user interfaces for management (see also section 13.1.2) inevitably also contain *general elements*, tools are incorporating functions—for example, for creating the components of a window (e.g., title, menu, scroll bars) or pop-up and pull-down menus, for controlling user dialogs, and for using the mouse. Our intention is to stress the

General user interface elements ...

Host Name	Type	Arch	IP Address
archimedes	Standalone	SPARC	123.456.789.010
barney	AutoClient	SPARC	456.789.010.123
bigbang	Standalone	x86	789.010.123.456
cypress	Standalone	PowerPC	010.123.456.789
elvira	Server	SPARC	101.123.456.789

Figure 15.5
System table (from JMAPI)

management-specific aspects, so we will not look at these functions or tool sets like SWING/JFC in detail.

...And management-specific elements

Through function and class libraries, tools for designing management interfaces typically offer the following *management-specific interface elements*, which then in part still need to be parameterized, combined, or refined by the applications:

- *Icons* for certain types of *resources*, such as network components, desktops, and servers. All applications are thereby able to use the same symbols for resources, a feature that contributes toward making the interface easier for the user to understand.

- Elements for structuring *hierarchies* of objects or *maps*. Object hierarchies are displayed in a way familiar from Windows Explorer. Maps were covered extensively in section 13.1.2.

- Elements to display an *overview* of the management-relevant *attributes* of an object (*property books*). A registry or filing box metaphor is often used.

- Elements for the *tabular display* of a set of same type objects. These basic elements can be used to build overviews of systems or event notifications. Figure 15.5 shows a system table that was created with the user interface element table from the Admin View Module (AVM) from JMAPI (see section 9.2 and *http://www.javasoft.com/*). With this element, all tables are presented with the same look and feel, regardless of content or source of information contained.

- Elements for *displaying dynamic values*, among other things as a function of time. Typically, this would be displayed as a meter (see Figure 15.6) or a graph (Figure 15.7).

- Elements used to *configure* the displays mentioned in the previous point in accordance with their own requirements. Figure 15.8 illus-

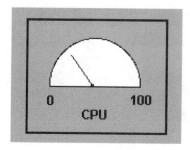

Figure 15.6
Variable display as a meter instrument

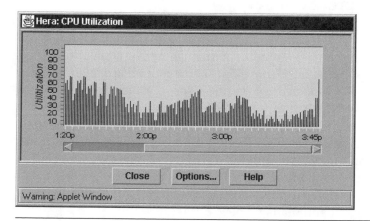

Figure 15.7
Graph display

trates a display of the disk utilization of file systems produced with elements of JMAPI. Again, all such displays would have the same style. Furthermore, application developers do not have to write much custom code for these graphic displays.

Figure 15.9 presents the related interface element that controls this display. In this case, developers do not code the GUI controls (radio buttons, high–low value boxes); they simply map the resulting values into their effect on managed objects and management application operation.

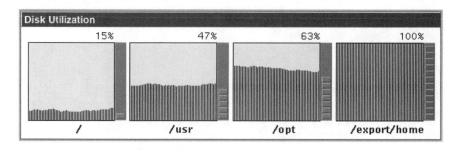

Figure 15.8
User interface element (from JMAPI)

15.5   Chapter Summary

In this chapter, we have shown how development tools support the specification and implementation of management systems. We started with MIB tools that assist the developer in the modeling of management information. The modeled information specifies key parts of syntax and semantics of the interface between managers and agents. Because the underlying information models can be very different, the tools are usually tailored to a specific model. In our brief description, we focused on tools for GDMO and for UML or OMT. Besides information modeling, these tools often include functions for the generation of interface descriptions and implementation skeletons. This links pure modeling to agent and manager development.

The information that has been modeled as described here must be provided by the management agents. That is, code pieces have to be written that implement the interaction between the managed resource itself and the management protocol entity of the agent. Supporting this process and providing the protocol entity and an agent skeleton is the main part of the functionality of tools for agent development. We have briefly described tools for OSI agents, SNMP agents, DMTF agents, and CORBA agents. Additionally, we gave a short overview of a typical tool set for agents implemented in Java.

Many of the typical functions of agent development tools apply to development environments for management applications as well. Analogous to the implementation skeletons that are generated from the modeled information in the case of agents, interface stubs can be generated by MIB compilers. These stubs are used as a basis for realization of management applications. Implementations of management protocols, including interfaces for access to the protocol functionality, common interfaces to different DBMSs, and tools for efficient event

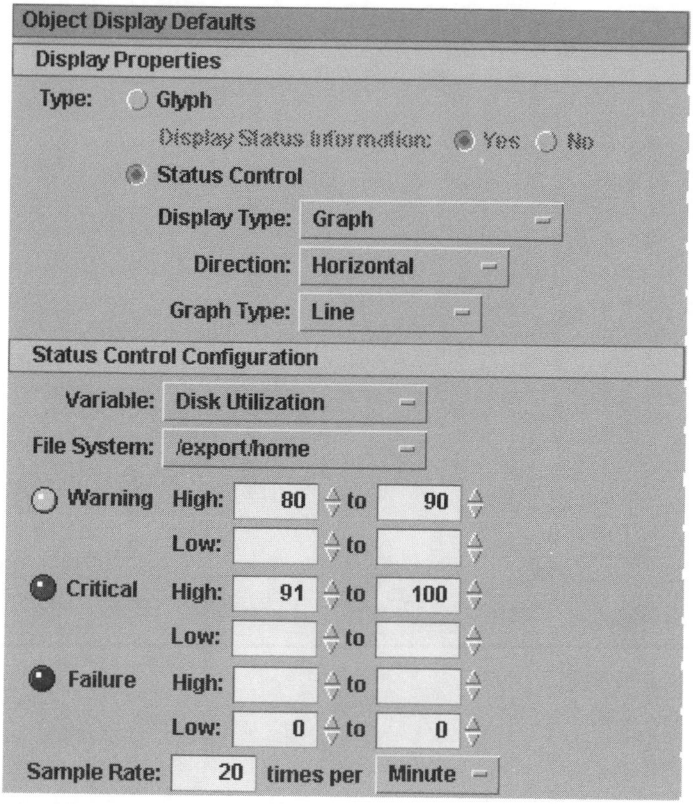

Figure 15.9
...and the associated configuration window

processing, are other examples for typical functionality of application development tools in a management context.

To round off our overview of management development tools, we have shown some examples of tools that support design and implementation of user interfaces for management applications. We focused on tools for the aspects of user interfaces that are specific for the management context.

Selected Solutions and Tools for Network and Systems Management

The preceding chapters have no doubt succeeded in conveying the sheer magnitude of the problems and issues that exist for management. It would be impossible even to attempt to outline all the approaches that are relevant to solving the problems of management. We are therefore focusing on two management layers, namely, network and component management (section 16.1) and systems management (section 16.2).

Section 16.1 focuses on issues concerning the management of network components. It emerges that a large number of management tasks are basically the same for each type of component (e.g., physical installation, basic configuration). These are summarized in section 16.1.2 under device-independent component management. Section 16.1.3 deals with device-dependent component management, covering the characteristic functions of certain types of devices. Owing to the large number of component types available (compare with Chapter 2), it is not possible for us to look at all the different types or functions. We have therefore decided to concentrate our discussion on bridges, LAN switches, ATM switches, and routers. Nevertheless, we have had to be selective about which devices to highlight and how much detail to provide.

The same applies to the area of system and applications management (section 16.2). We again had to be selective in our choice of material because of the many issues that exist. We have limited ourselves to the areas of inventory management tools for software management, software distribution and installation, server monitoring, desktop management, application monitoring, user administration, and briefly, other areas such as license management and printer and spooling management. We offer problem descriptions as well as approaches to solutions.

16.1   Network and Component Management

Network management is mainly component management and topology management (i.e., management of the interconnection network between network components and end systems). In the following subsections, we concentrate on component management. First, we summarize the tasks that come up in general, then we deal with aspects of component management that are relevant for every type of component. Finally, we discuss device-dependent component management by considering several specific network devices in more detail.

16.1.1   Tasks

For a communication network to function properly, controlling and monitoring measures have to be applied regularly to central resources, the network components (see section 2.4). Collectively these measures are described by the term *component management*. In section 2.4, we covered the functionality of resources but with no reference to the management aspects. Component management is complicated by different factors:

Challenges
presented by
component
management

- Complexity of activities: The network manager responsible for the orderly operation of communications components is confronted by different tasks comprising complex activities and requiring extensive resource-specific expertise. What particularly adds to this complexity is that it often takes more than just looking at a component in isolation; information about the general network environment also has to be taken into account when problems arise.

- Heterogeneity of components: Because components are supplied by different manufacturers, the management tasks required for functionally comparable components vary by manufacturer and product.

- Multiplicity of components: In a large communication network, a single component type can exist in large numbers; this can contribute quantitatively to the effort required even to execute simple management tasks.

As a rule, network administrators are faced with a multiplicity of LAN and WAN components. And, in many cases, manufacturer-specific solutions are a typical aspect of component management. This manufacturer dependence can be manifested in two places: in the agent and in the management application.

Agents are management-relevant representatives of concrete resources; the respective information model largely determines the extent to which generic agents are possible. If the underlying management architecture is a proprietary one, the agents as well as the tools will be manufacturer specific as it is. With Internet management, the device characteristics of the components are usually reflected in the manufacturer-specific MIBs because standard MIBs generally do not allow the mapping of many vendor-specific characteristics of the concrete devices.

The manufacturer orientation of component management can even be evident on the manager side in manufacturer-specific management systems that offer solutions for the manufacturer's product families but are not able to satisfy the requirements of a platform architecture with open programming interfaces (as described in Chapter 13). However, more and more solutions for integration into platforms are now being offered for component management (e.g., by treating these stations as element management systems that offer standard "northbound" interfaces for integration).

Some of the functions of component management are generic in the sense that they apply to almost all devices. These functions will be covered in section 16.1.2. Other functions, on the other hand, specifically relate to a particular component type; a selection of components is covered in section 16.1.3.

Typically for component management, the areas of configuration, fault, and performance management (of the different functional areas presented in Chapter 3) dominate when it comes to the core functionality of components such as hubs, switches, and routers. When it comes to IT processes (see Part IV), the emphasis is on the operation, monitoring, and change management of components.

It has already been covered in section 3.2 that many enterprise Internet MIBs include settable objects for not only configuration but also security and accounting management. Configuration information allows display of topology (see section 3.2.1) and maps (see section 13.2) to represent relationships.

One major monitoring task that falls under the area of fault management involves the early detection and diagnosis of faults in components (e.g., due to defects). The function of performance management, on the other hand, is to detect the bottlenecks that occur in components or in the connected lines and to establish the causes of the problem. Security management's role consists of monitoring components so that

Component management often incorporates manufacturer-specific aspects

Configuration and monitoring tasks form the focus of component management

any threats to the security of the communication network are detected early or can be prevented altogether. In terms of accounting management, components can supply important information about the usage of resources.

The management of security is a less typical aspect of component management in the narrower sense, whereas the security of management (e.g., access protection for configuration or other management operations) is typical. Any extension to the core functionality of a component, such as the addition of firewall functions to a router, will of course add to the scope of component management. Accounting management is not a typical activity in the LAN environment, but is, of course, very important in the carrier and provider area.

RMON is an important aid

RMON and trap mechanisms have a key monitoring function in the private data network area. Management applications for the processing of monitoring results and component queries exist both for manufacturer-specific and platform-based component management; these applications are described in sections 13.2 and 13.3. Event management, including event correlation as well as state and threshold value monitoring, is also a particularly important activity of component management.

Many manufacturers typically combine the component management for all of their components (hubs, switches, routers) under the name of a particular management product. Well-known examples of this practice include Optivity from Bay Networks, Transcend from 3Com, CiscoWorks from CISCO, ForeView from Fore Systems, and Spectrum Element Manager from Cabletron Systems.

There has recently been a tendency toward Web-based management (see Chapter 9). With this type of management, each system with a WWW browser can be used as an operating console for component management. Components can also be configured with Java applets and applications. Management by delegation is also emerging as an application that allows agents to be loaded into components for management purposes.

16.1.2 Device-Independent Component Management

Most network components (hubs, switches, bridges, routers) roughly have the same basic structure as the one illustrated in Figure 16.1(left side). The MIB contents are also structured on the same basis (right side). Therefore, along with other information, each agent MIB at least contains information about a device in general and its internal

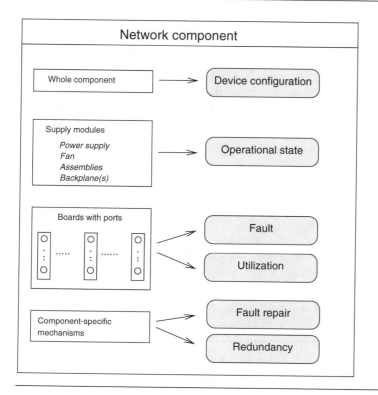

Figure 16.1
Basic structure of a component

structure, the different interface cards (boards), and the ports available on the boards. The ports are characterized by information provided about their media interface (e.g., signal characteristics, code, transmission rate, supported protocols). The "component-specific mechanisms" module is representative of the component type; it therefore applies to device-dependent management.

The *overall configuration* of a network component includes:

- Physical installation.

- Basic configuration. Basic initialization by a device-specific setup procedure (e.g., using boot disks or configuration files stored in NVRAM). Provisions for future start and reset operations.

The overall configuration is the same for all component types

- Allocation of names, addresses, domains, and so forth for subsequent identification within a networked system.

- Basic configuration of device-specific functions.

- Configuration of separate physical assemblies (frames, racks, slots, cards).

- Configuration of ports.

- Configuration of security parameters that protect access to components or to their management module (passwords, encryption, authentication, access control lists, community strings).

- Setting of basic parameters related to monitoring tasks (polling cycles, timers, enabled traps).

Support through configuration protocols

To support a configuration, some components even offer simple protocols for transmitting configuration information. These include the boot protocol (BOOTP), the dynamic host configuration protocol (DHCP), and a very simple file transfer protocol (e.g., trivial file transfer protocol, TFTP). TFTP can be used to load configuration data as a file from a boot server located anywhere. The more rudimentary bootstrap protocol BOOTP is used for loading configuration parameters (such as IP addresses or subnet masks) and a bootfile from a BOOTP server on the same LAN. DHCP, a further development of the bootstrap protocol (RFC 1541), additionally allows a dynamic allocation of temporary IP addresses and name servers. Many components also allow telnet access for remote interactive configuration of the components. Almost all modern components are configurable through the use of a standardized management protocol, usually over SNMP. This enables access to all the MIBs supported by the agent in the component. Newer developments also provide a facility (built-in HTTP server) for configuration over a Web browser. A Web server function is implemented in the component for this purpose.

The majority of component management products allow a direct interrogation of the whole configuration and its individual parameters. A *physical view of the components* (including boards, switches, and LED displays) is typically offered. The physical display is also often used to control and to monitor operations; a click of the mouse on a switch icon displayed in this way creates the same effect as the actual physical operation of the switch. States of components are represented on the same indicators in the display as they are on the actual components.

Operating state monitoring reproduces the states of the different modules of the components. This includes:

- Monitoring power supply, with an option to handle internal, external, and main sources of power separately, if required. This also includes the activation of a UPS. A separate upsMIB (MIB for uninterruptible power supply, RFC 1628) that contains parameters for amperage, voltage, output, frequency, and battery status is available for SNMP management. Control mechanisms that enable modules to be prioritized differently depending on the source of power supply also exist. Power Net SNMP from APC is one of these products.

Operating state monitoring is a management task common to every type of equipment

- Monitoring temperature. This includes measuring internal and external temperatures and operating the controls for the fans based on current temperature.

- Monitoring devices to detect unauthorized physical access (e.g., opening the chassis, removing or adding modules).

- Execution of self-tests to check whether certain subassemblies of the components are defective. Some components support "hot swapping," which enables defective modules to be exchanged during running operations.

- Many components (e.g., routers) also offer a mechanism to control overloading, which includes a check on CPU utilization. This will enable the detection of any bottleneck behavior in the components, particularly from the standpoint of the component-specific mechanisms.

Port monitoring, of course, depends on the individual interfaces and protocols that are supported. The functions normally supported include:

Port monitoring is another task common to all components

- Monitoring the state of boards and ports. Modern components incorporate a facility for the detailed analysis of the operational state of their boards and ports. Examples of port states are `Ok`, `Receive Link Down`, `Transmit Link Down`, `Local Jabber`, `Remote Jabber`, and `Illegal Synchronization`.

- Monitoring the counters used to register the defective blocks received by the components. Errors that can occur in this connection include packets that are too short or too long, alignment errors, collisions, and fragmentation errors.

- Setting threshold values for the automatic monitoring of error counters. Some of these threshold values are automatically set by a component on the basis of the monitoring of statistical benchmarks.

- Querying and setting port parameters. Activation and deactivation of port administrative state.

Today, it is taken for granted that status indicators will be expressed in real time and that devices will be represented realistically. All recording rates (e.g., polling cycles) and monitoring time frames are configurable.

All measurement data can be compiled to produce different kinds of statistics or be arranged for different kinds of presentations. In this way, performance management, including the monitoring of QoS and component utilization, is supported by all component management.

In addition to access over the normal communication network effected by the component, a second access (e.g., serial port access via a telephone network) is often available for the management of important components to enable management operations to be initiated when serious network failures take place (inband versus outband management).

16.1.3   Device-Dependent Component Management

The module "component-specific mechanisms" in Figure 16.1 conceals the different types of devices available. This module incorporates the typical mechanisms for bridges, switches, routers, and other components. For component management, this means the addition of type-specific tasks to those tasks that were mentioned in the last section. These supplementary tasks for the management of certain types of components are outlined next to illustrate the variety of device-dependent component management offered.

Star Couplers

Star-coupler management
Star couplers (see section 2.4.1) incorporate numerous mechanisms, including fragment extension and jabber control, that are activated when corresponding faults are detected. A network manager cannot manipulate these mechanisms (e.g., switch them on or off) since the standard precisely specifies when and in which form they should be implemented. Some products do offer interrogational counters that provide information about the frequency of the occurrence of these faults.

The same situation applies to another fault handling mechanism, "autopartitioning," in which a segment is automatically switched off when a fault persists (64 data collisions in a row or a data collision lasting more than 1 ms). The counterpart of this mechanism is "reconnection," which involves the automatic reconnection of a segment to the rest of the network as soon as it is operating properly again.

Bridges

Two aspects central to bridge management determine the functionality of a bridge: the configuration and the monitoring of the traffic separation mechanism and the configuration and the monitoring of the loop suppression mechanism. We presented the fundamentals of these mechanisms in section 2.4.1; they are mentioned again in terms of possible management action. As an example, we are looking at transparent bridges conformant with the IEEE 802.1d standard.

Bridge management

The traffic separation mechanism is based on the concept that a bridge is capable of "learning" on its own which end systems exist in the attached subnetworks. For this purpose, during backward learning (see section 2.4.1), the address of the sender is read for each frame received at a port and then noted with a time stamp in the address table. In addition to the memorized address table, there is a filter table in which the network manager can specify which MAC addresses (or specifically the frames that carry these as the destination address) are allowed to be transported by the bridge and under which circumstances. There are different ways in which the network manager or a management application can have an effect on the mechanism, such as by switching off the learning mechanism or making or specifying extensions to the filter table or address table to indicate how the information for the transport decision is to be used. The management actions include:

Controlling traffic separation

- Activation and deactivation of the learning mechanism; deactivation results in shorter packet processing times. However, this is not a key issue with the efficient bridges today, and therefore, the mechanism usually remains activated.

- Activation and deactivation of the address table that has been learned; deactivation means that only those MAC addresses that have been entered statically will be taken into account.

- Alteration and updating of the filter table.

- Configuration of aging timers that are used to specify how long a MAC address is held in the address table and still considered valid although no transmission has taken place from that address during this period.

Controlling the
loop suppression
mechanism

The spanning tree algorithm [PER92] shown here serves as the basis for the loop suppression mechanism with transparent bridges. (Some of the management tasks for source routing, which is a "competitor" to this algorithm, are different from those listed here.) The spanning tree algorithm produces the definition of a "spanning tree" from the bridges accessible from each other over the subnetworks; this spanning tree is specified according to the following characteristics:

- A bridge, specifically the one with the highest priority according to certain criteria, is defined as the root of the tree and is called the root bridge.

- For each bridge, the spanning tree algorithm specifies as the root port the port from which the root bridge is accessible over the cheapest path (as defined by the network manager).

- For each subnetwork, the spanning tree algorithm identifies the bridge and in this bridge the port that is the most optimal for reaching the subnetwork from the root bridge; these are referred to as designated bridge and designated port.

Alternative routes between any two end systems and any loops possibly resulting from them are avoided through the activation only of the root port and the designated ports for each bridge, meaning that they are in "forwarding state"; all the other ports are deactivated ("blocking state"). These can be activated again if any changes occur in the existing configuration, such as a fault in a line or a bridge or the addition of new subnetworks or bridges to extend the network. The bridges inform each other of these sorts of changes by transmitting bridge protocol data units and appropriate adjustments are made to the spanning tree.

The intervention options open to the network manager include activation and deactivation of the entire procedure, specification of input parameters for the stipulation of the spanning tree, and the setting of timer values for the reconfiguration.

- Activation and deactivation of the spanning tree procedure. Because of the additional network load, the procedure should be activated only if cycles can actually occur.

- Specification of bridge priorities used to determine the root bridge. Bridges that have a "central" position in the network are those that should be awarded a high priority.

- Determination of the path costs for the communication links between bridges and their allocation to the ports. An appropriate formula is the following: path cost = 1000/line capacity, with 1 Mbit/s used as the basis for one unit of line capacity.

- Setting timer values that determine the dynamic of the procedure when reconfigurations are necessary.

A number of managed objects are available to the administrator for an execution of the necessary management operations. Approximately 20 variables and 5 tables are provided in 4 groups for bridge management in the Internet Bridge MIB (RFC 1493). For our example, we have taken the MIB group dot1dStp, which defines the management variables for the loop suppression mechanism outlined earlier. The group encompasses the object types ProtocolSpecification, Priority, TimeSinceTopologyChange, TopChanges, DesignatedRoot, Root-Cost, RootPort, MaxAge, HelloTime, HoldTime, ForwardDelay, Bridge-MaxAge, BridgeHelloTime, and BridgeForwardDelay. This group also defines the table PortTable, which consists of the columns Port, Priority, State, Enable, PathCost, DesignatedRoot, DesignatedCost, DesignatedBridge, DesignatedPort, and ForwardTransitions. To familiarize you with the notation, we are providing definitions of some of the object types; their allocation to the algorithms and actions described is easy to recognize. RFC 1493 uses version 1 of the Internet information model (SMIv1) for the specifications.

Managed objects of a bridge

```
dot1dStpPriority OBJECT-TYPE
    SYNTAX      INTEGER (0...65535)
    ACCESS      read-write
    STATUS      mandatory
    DESCRIPTION >>The value of the writeable portion of the
                Bridge ID, i.e., the first two octets of
                the (8 octet long) Bridge ID are given by
                the value of dot1dBaseBridgeAddress.<<
    REFERENCE   >>IEEE 802.1D-1990:Section 4.5.3.7<<
    ::= {dot1dStp 2}

dot1dStpTimeSinceTopologyChange OBJECT-TYPE
    SYNTAX      TimeTicks
    ACCESS      read-only
    STATUS      mandatory
    DESCRIPTION >>The time (in hundredths of a second)
                since the last time a topology change
                was detected by the bridge entity.<<
```

Excerpt from the bridge MIB definition

```
            REFERENCE    >>IEEE 802.1D-1990; Section 6.8.1.1.3<<
            ::= {dot1dStp 3}


dot1dStpTopChanges OBJECT-TYPE
            SYNTAX       Counter
            ACCESS       read-only
            STATUS       mandatory
            DESCRIPTION >>The total number of topology changes
                         detected by this bridge since the
                         management entity was last reset or
                         initialized<<
            REFERENCE    >>IEEE 802.1D-1990; Section 6.8.1.1.3<<
            ::= {dot1dStp 4}


dot1dStpRootCost OBJECT-TYPE
            SYNTAX       INTEGER
            ACCESS       read-only
            STATUS       mandatory
            DESCRIPTION >>The cost of the path to the root as seen
                         from the bridge<<
            REFERENCE    >>IEEE 802.1D-1990 Section 4.5.3.2<<
            ::= {dot1dStp 6}


dot1dStpRootPort OBJECT-TYPE
            SYNTAX       INTEGER
            ACCESS       read-only
            STATUS       mandatory
            DESCRIPTION >>The port number of the port, which offers
                         the lowest cost path from this bridge to
                         the root bridge.<<
            REFERENCE    >>IEEE 802.1D-1990; Section 4.5.3.3<<
            ::= {dot1dStp 7}


dot1dStpMaxAge OBJECT-TYPE
            SYNTAX       Timeout
            ACCESS       read-only
            STATUS       mandatory
            DESCRIPTION >>The maximum age of Spanning Tree Protocol
                         information learned from the network on
                         any port before it is discarded, in units
                         of hundredths of a second. This is the
                         actual value that this bridge is currently
                         using.<<
            REFERENCE        >>IEEE 802.1D-1990; Section 4.5.3.4<<
            ::= {dot1dStp 8}
```

```
dot1dStpPortEnable OBJECT-TYPE
    SYNTAX       INTEGER
                     {enabled (1)
                      disabled (2)}
    ACCESS       read-write
    STATUS       mandatory
    DESCRIPTION >>The enabled/disabled status of the port<<
    REFERENCE   >>IEEE 802.1D-1990; Section 4.5.9.2<<
    ::= {dot1dStpPortEntry 4}
```

Sample columns
from a port table

```
dot1dStpPortPathCost OBJECT-TYPE
    SYNTAX       INTEGER (1. 65535)
    ACCESS       read-write
    STATUS       mandatory
    DESCRIPTION >>The contribution of this port to the path
                 cost of paths toward the spanning tree root
                 that include this port. 802.1D-1990
                 recommends that the default value of this
                 parameter be in inverse proportion to the
                 speed of the attached LAN.<<
    REFERENCE   >>IEEE 802.1D-1990; Section 4.5.5.3<<
    ::= {dot1dStpPortEntry 5}
```

LAN Switches

The function of LAN switches (a further development of multiport bridges; compare with section 2.4.1) is to provide fast port-to-port connections, specifically so that a number of these connections can be operated at the same time. The switching times are so short that there is no impact on the full transmission rate to ports, even due to the latency of the transmitter. Management operations relating to switches include:

Switch
management

- Setting options for function mode. In section 2.4.1, we discussed a variety of different internal switching techniques (e.g., Cut Through, Store-and-Forward) and operating procedures (e.g., Error Free). Some switches allow operating procedures to be configured; in other words, they select the procedure on the basis of the current network state (e.g., dependent on counter values and alterations). The operation mode Cut Through, of course, makes sense only if the same port characteristics exist (e.g., transmission rate).

- The actual switching is based on the addresses in the PDUs. Aging mechanisms can be specified for the port mapping tables. Hub management also includes the mapping of port numbers to the MAC addresses of the equipment.

- Traffic flow analyses can be produced on the basis of internal connections. The results can, for example, be made available to the TopN Group of the RMON-MIB.

VLANs

- Many switches allow the configuration of *virtual LANs* (VLANs). A VLAN is the formation of logical LANs on a physical LAN. A VLAN is provided by a group of users (= ports). A distinction is made between *single-device VLANs, multiple-device homogeneous VLANs*, and *multiple-device heterogeneous VLANs*, in which the VLANs are always defined by groups of ports. With the latter two VLANs, a group comprises the ports of several switches. VLAN management encompasses the definition of groups and the altering of groups. The groups control the allowed port connections in the switches; communication is always restricted to group members, which means it is restricted to a VLAN (port based, MAC based, or policy based). VLAN configurations can be displayed and are usually represented in different colors on top of the physical LAN segments. Some switches even allow automatic VLAN configuration on the basis of setup policies.

ATM Switches

ATM management

First of all, management functions similar to those with LAN switches also exist with ATM switches. Even ATM-based VLANs (on the basis of LAN emulation, LANE) can be managed.

The features offered by ATM switches over and above those available with LAN switches are established in the ATM concept (see section 2.4.1).

- PVC management: Establishing and managing permanent virtual circuits for certain transmission rates

- Bandwidth management: Configuration of service-related bandwidth per port and PVC

- Service management: Controlling the permitted QoS per port (e.g., ABR only, ABR and CBR together)

- Autodiscovery of ATM devices and ATM topology (VC, VP, and switch)

- Monitoring and display of UNI and NNI (see Figure 2.21)

The ATM-specific managed objects also have to be defined in accordance with these tasks. A corresponding MIB definition (RFC 1695) is available for Internet management. The management information covers ATM interfaces, ATM virtual connections (PVCs and SVCs), ATM cross-connects, AAL5 entities (these are the entities of the adaptation layer that map connectionless traffic with variable bit rates and without a time relationship, thus IP or frame relay, to the ATM cells), AAL5 connections, ATM switches, and ATM networks.

Managed objects for ATM

Our example is extracted from the description of ATM interfaces. The management information in the example is organized as a table; the definition of it suffices for the Internet information model version 2 (SMIv2). The table contains only ATM-specific information, which exceeds the information contained in the interface group of the standard MIB II (see "List of Abbreviations" for identification of abbreviations).

Excerpt from the ATM interface MIB

```
atmInterfaceConfTable   OBJECT-TYPE
    SYNTAX            SEQUENCE OF AtmInterfaceConfEntry
    MAX-ACCESS        not-accessible
    STATUS            current
    DESCRIPTION       >>This table contains ATM local
                      interface configuration parameters,
                      one entry per ATM interface port.<<
    ::= {atmMIBObjects 20}


atmInterfaceConfEntry   OBJECT-TYPE
    SYNTAX            AtmInterfaceConfEntry
    MAX-ACCESS        not-accessible
    STATUS            current
    DESCRIPTION       >>This list contains ATM interface
                      configuration parameters and state
                      variables.<<
    INDEX             {ifIndex}
    ::= {atmInterfaceConfTable 1}


AtmInterfaceConfEntry    ::= SEQUENCE {
    atmInterfaceMaxVpcs               INTEGER
    atmInterfaceMaxVccs               INTEGER
    atmInterfaceConfVpcs              INTEGER
    atmInterfaceConfVccs              INTEGER
    atmInterfaceMaxActiveVpiBits      INTEGER
    atmInterfaceMaxActiveVciBits      INTEGER
    atmInterfaceIlmiVpi               INTEGER
    atmInterfaceIlmiVci               INTEGER
    atmInterfaceAddressType           INTEGER
```

```
        atmInterfaceAdminAddress            OCTET STRING
        atmInterfaceMyNeighborIpAddress     IpAddress
        atmInterfaceMyNeighborIfName        Display String}


atmInterfaceMaxVpcs                     OBJECT-TYPE
    SYNTAX                              INTEGER (0..4096)
    MAX-ACCESS                          read-write
    STATUS                              current
    DESCRIPTION             >>The maximum number of VPCs (PVCs and
                            SVCs) supported at this ATM interfaces.
                            At the ATM UNI the maximum number of
                            VPCs (PVCs and SVCs) ranges from 0 to
                            256 only.<<
    ::= {atmInterfaceConfEntry 1}


atmInterfaceMaxVccs                     OBJECT-TYPE
    SYNTAX                              INTEGER (0..65536)
    MAX-ACCESS                          read-write
    STATUS                              current
    DESCRIPTION             >>The maximum number of VCCS (PVCs and
                            SVCs) supported at this ATM interface.<<
    ::= {atmInterfaceConfEntry 2}


atm InterfaceConfVpcs                   OBJECT-TYPE
    SYNTAX                              INTEGER (0..4096)
    MAX-ACCESS                          read-only
    STATUS                              current
    DESCRIPTION             >>The number of VPCs (PVCs and SVCs)
                            configured for use at this ATM
                            interface. At the ATM UNI, the configured
                            number of VPCs (PVCs and SVCs) can range
                            from 0 to 256 only.<<
    ::= {atmInterfaceConfEntry 3}


atmInterfaceConfVccs                    OBJECT-TYPE
    SYNTAX                              INTEGER (0..65536)
    MAX-ACCESS                          read-only
    STATUS                              current
    DESCRIPTION             >>The number of VCCs (PVCs and SVCs)
                            configured for use at the ATM interface.<<
    ::= {atmInterfaceConfEntry 4}


atmInterfaceMaxActiveVpiBits            OBJECT-TYPE
    SYNTAX                              INTEGER (0..12)
    MAX-ACCESS                          read-write
```

```
    STATUS                      current
    DESCRIPTION         >>The maximum number of active VPI bits
                        configured for use at the ATM interface.At
                        the ATM UNI, the maximum number of active
                        VPI bits configured for use ranges from 0
                        to 8 only.<<
    ::= {atmInterfaceConfEntry 5}


atmInterfaceMaxActiveVciBits   OBJECT-TYPE
    SYNTAX                      INTEGER (0..16)
    MAX-ACCESS                  read-write
    STATUS                      current
    DESCRIPTION         >>The maximum of active VCI bits configured
                        for use at this ATM interface.<<
    ::= {atmInterfaceConfEntry 6}


atmInterfaceIlmiVpi            OBJECT-TYPE
    SYNTAX                      INTEGER (0..255)
    MAX-ACCESS                  read-write
    STATUS                      current
    DESCRIPTION         >>The VPI value of the VCC supporting the
                        ILMI at this ATM interface. If the values
                        of atmInterfaceIlmiVpi and
                        atmInterfaceIlmiVci are both equal to zero
                        then the ILMI is not supported at this ATM
                        interface.<<
    DEFVAL                      {0}
    ::= {atmInterfaceConfEntry 7}


atmInterfaceIlmiVci            OBJECT-TYPE
    SYNTAX                      INTEGER (0..65535)
    MAX-ACCESS                  read-write
    STATUS                      current
    DESCRIPTION         >>The VCI value of the VCC supporting the
                        ILMI at this ATM interface. If the value
                        of atmInterfaceIlmiVpi and
                        atmInterfaceIlmiVci are both equal to zero
                        then the ILMI is not supported at this ATM
                        interface.<<
    DEFVAL                      {16}
    ::= {atmInterfaceConfEntry 8}
```

In terms of Figure 16.1, the preceding MIB excerpt describes only the segment of management information that in the management view characterizes a board in an ATM switch or cross-connect. The actual switching function of the component is defined in a different ATM-MIB group, such as the `Virtual Path Cross Connect Group`. For VPs, this group contains the configuration and status information for all point-to-point, point-to-multipoint, and multipoint-to-multipoint connections within an ATM switching component.

A comprehensive survey of ATM switches also includes the ATM access interfaces and components and the interaction between public and private ATM networks. One area that causes particular problems for ATM management is the guarantee of connection-related service quality in the performance management area. The requirements of this guarantee are usually in conflict with the maximization of statistical multiplex gain and the associated favorable utilization of network resources. Traffic models are a prerequisite for an optimal component configuration. We discussed the ATM management architecture of the ATM Forum in Chapter 10 and will not delve further into this subject.

Routers

Router management

The main task of this component is global network routing at layer 3. This routing usually takes place in connection with store-and-forward switching, which explains why routers contain extensive analysis mechanisms and other measures (such as firewall tasks).

Identification

To use the services of a router, the attached end systems must identify themselves to the router (unlike the bridges). The same applies in reverse in the sense that the network address of the router (often also ambiguously called a "gateway," such as in Unix, Windows, or DHCP) must also be made known to the end systems since routers have to be explicitly addressed by the end systems. The management tasks comprise:

- Entry of the addresses or subnetworks of the attached end systems in the routing table of the router. This "static route entry" is one option. Usually the router is configured with interface addresses and receives packets from any system connected to that interface. It can use routing protocols to learn network topology (RIP, OSPF, etc.) and ARP to learn MAC addresses of stations on the LAN.

- Configuration of the network address of the router in the respective end systems, provided this is not carried out automatically within the framework of the routing protocol.

The upside of this additional configuration effort is greater management flexibility:

- Control of access to the router through appropriate entries in the routing table
- Logical division of the network into subnetworks, which improves the structuring of the network overall

The management functions provided in connection with routing are to a large degree dependent on the respective routing procedure used. Generally, *adaptive routing* is employed. Instead of forcing the network administrator to react to changes in network configuration, such as line outages, the routers themselves make the necessary adjustments to their routing tables. What is important is that the routers are able to exchange the appropriate routing information with one another. A separate routing protocol (e.g., RIP, OSPF, EGP) is used to carry out this communication; sometimes the router address is made known over a BOOTP or a DHCP. Even if an adaptive routing procedure is used by the network administrator, the routing function is controlled on the basis of a definition of the corresponding configuration values:

Routing in the router

- Stipulation of costs incurred as a result of transmission over a line. The decision criteria, also referred to as "metrics," can be based on the number of hops, the financial costs incurred through the use of the line, or other characteristics of the line such as capacity and error rate.
- Monitoring current entries in the routing table in order to determine which faults are being caused by the automatic updating of the routing tables.
- Carrying out long-term statistics in order to optimize the results of a procedure by implementing corresponding changes to the cost parameters (or even to the entire network configuration).

It should be noted that all management functions pertaining to the routing procedure always relate to a particular layer 3 protocol; a multiprotocol router maintains a separate routing table, independent of the other tables, for each layer 3 protocol it supports.

The routing procedure is embedded in a chain of protocol processing tasks that are always performed by a router when a data packet is ready for processing at one of the interfaces. We will use the example of the IP router widely used today to review this processing procedure and show the different options open to a network administrator in connection with each processing step. Yet we are aware that increasing transmission rates in the Gigabit/s area, for example, will result in the development of other router architectures. First the packet that is at

Protocol processing in the router

the interface and is ready for processing is copied in the main memory of the router (usually through the use of efficient pointer operations).

- All routers allow network administrators or management applications to become informed about the occupancy level of the internal buffer and the utilization levels of the processor so that they can determine early enough whether the network is becoming overloaded. Short-term overloading can generally be dealt with by congestion control measures. Preventive measures are applied (compare with [TAN96]): retransmission policies, out-of-order-caching policies, acknowledgment policies, flow control policies, time-out determination, packet discard policies, routing algorithms, packet lifetime management, and so forth. Defining these parameters again becomes a management task. Long-term overloading can result in the need to exchange components or to make changes to the topology.

Different checks are carried out in the router, and the results are made accessible to the network administrator over different fault counters.

- Identification of packets discarded by a router because of a non-supported protocol type.
- Identification of the other errors, differentiated by protocol type (e.g., FCS errors, length errors, PDU-type errors), which may have caused the router to discard the incoming packets.

After all checks of the packet have been carried out and no errors are determined by the router, an access filter for the respective layer 3 protocol may be applied to the packet. These access filters enable the network administrator to decide whether to allow the explicit relay or forwarding of packets with certain layer 3 addresses and other parameters (protocol type, port, etc.); alternatively, the network administrator can prohibit this forwarding.

Using routers as firewalls

- Setting and monitoring access filters serves as the basis for the use of routers for firewall purposes (packet filtering). Packet filters constitute an easy way to compartmentalize service access or a communication relationship. The filtering process is based on a check of the source and destination addresses and of the port numbers of UDP or TCP packets, as well as on an analysis of individual flags or fields of the packets. The definition of the filter rules depends on management policy. Packet filters at layer 3 guarantee only limited security. Dynamically allocated IP addresses and address spoofing (faking addresses) create the problems here. Another problem is that user authentication is generally not possible at layer 3. One way of increasing security is through the instigation of firewalls on the application layer and so-called application gateways or proxies (also called SOCKS proxies). Activities that run over the packet filter should also be documented so that this information is available when security violations are analyzed at a later date.

When a packet has also passed through an access filter, it is delivered to the routing function described earlier. When this function is executed, it may become evident that no route exists to the desired destination network.

- A check should be made to determine whether certain destination networks are accessible, and if necessary, the routing tables or the default route should be reconfigured accordingly.

The result of the routing function is the selection of the port leading to the next router (possibly in another subnetwork) on the way to the destination system or leading directly to the addressed terminal equipment. The router must produce the appropriate layer 3 and layer 2 headers (includes mapping layer 3 addresses in packet to appropriate layer 2 address on next hop) and copy the packet in the output queue of the ports selected; this concludes the protocol processing process for the packet.

More about Components

Previous routers have dealt with device-specific execution through the use of software. For certain layer 3 protocols (e.g., IP, IPX), the first routers implementing routing at "full wire speed" using ASIC hardware are now on the market. This development is gradually blurring the difference between switches and routers: hardware-based routers are turning into layer 3 switches.

Layer 4 switches are also available. These offer the possibility of using an applications-specific port, thus layer 4 service access points, for controlling and monitoring purposes (i.e., redirection based on application protocol, e.g., load balance across Web servers or redirect to Web cache).

The calculation of connection times and transfer volumes is an important aspect of WAN switches and WAN access components, particularly since WAN services are usually provided by a separate network provider. WAN components therefore frequently allow the activation of an accounting mechanism (thus a user-related measurement of accounting units) and an accumulation of measurement values, with this information accessible to a management system or a billing system on the basis of configurable triggers (e.g., IP "flow" accounting that relates all packets between a given source and destination IP address is provided by NETFLOW from CISCO).

16.2   Systems and Software Management

Systems management is a concept that is interpreted and used in different ways. Within the meaning of Figure 1.2 in Chapter 1, it relates to the *management* of *end systems* and their *resources*. This is also an area in which a variety of different tools are available, including stand-alone as well as platform-based and enterprise tools (see section 14.1). Every operating system contains functions and tools for system administration. The orientation of this book dictates that we not deal with stand-alone or purely local administrative tools but only with tools that are geared to heterogeneous environments and incorporate a certain minimum of integration with other tools. This delineation inevitably has to remain vague.

Management of end systems and their resources

16.2.1   Functional Areas and Resources

Two approaches can be followed to describe the tasks that arise in the context of systems and software management and that are supported by tools:

Different classifications of systems management tasks

- On the basis of *functional areas*
- On the basis of the *resources being administered*

Both approaches are commonly used and are also reflected in the way in which tools available in the market are described. They are, however, not orthogonal to each other and do not always provide a breakdown of tasks into truly disjoint subsets.

Classification According to Functional Area

With end systems, there is less of a tendency to follow the familiar network management approach of dividing tasks into fault, configuration, accounting, performance, and security management (FCAPS); instead, tasks are usually broken down into different areas:

FCAPS classification in systems management is less common

- *Monitoring*, which mainly combines aspects from fault and performance management but partially also touches upon the other functional areas.

- *Software distribution* and *deployment*, which falls into the classic classification of configuration management.

- *Inventory management*, also often called documentation, which is also allocated to configuration management.

- *User administration*, which is classified into security and accounting management.

Compared to the FCAPS classification, this organization by area has the advantage that it comes closer to the actual allocation of tasks to roles and people within the provider's organization. It also achieves a better mirroring of the distinction often made between operating and administration. Operating is interpreted as relating to the short-term routine activities that mainly focus on availability, whereas administration mainly encompasses change and configuration management. From the preceding list, operating therefore contains monitoring, whereas administration contains the three other areas.

Classification According to Administered Resource

Because of the large variety of resources administered in the end system and applications area, there are also a large number of terms relating to management tasks, ranging from more universal aspects such as:

- *Server management*
- *Desktop mangement*
- *Applications management*

to specific aspects such as:

- *Management of storage media* (management of archiving, backup media, etc.)
- *Printing management*

Overview of the Tools Described

In this chapter, we particularly want to focus on solutions and tools. As already mentioned *both* classifications are reflected in the descriptions of tools available in the market. On the one hand, we want to cover all the typical classes of tools but without causing any major repetition of the topics in the following subsections; on the other hand, it is not possible to base the following discussion on only one of the two classifications, nor is it possible to select both of them for the description.

Description on the basis of deployment management

We will therefore structure our description of the solutions and tools for the task areas mentioned by again referring to the *cycle of deployment management* already discussed in section 14.1.1, and we will describe tools roughly along the lines of the *lifecycle of an application.*

Inventory management

The tools required at the beginning of the cycle are tools that support *inventory management* (see also section 14.3) and can be used to clarify which components (hardware, software packages) are deployed in the end systems. What this serves to resolve is whether a particular application can be installed on a system, whether the requirements have been fulfilled, or which ones should be created at the outset. This is called inventory management.

Software distribution

The information supplied by inventory management provides the basis for *software distribution and installation*, which then transfers the software packages to the target machines, installs them there, and handles the configuration.

Monitoring ...

If an application has been successfully installed, the user must *monitor* its *function*, its *performance*, and its *availability* during the runtime. In addition to the application itself, the server and, to a certain degree, the clients have to be monitored and continuously administered.

... servers

A breakdown or the overloading of the associated server is frequently the cause of the availability and performance problems of an application. The task of monitoring these systems generally falls under *server management*, which represents a central component of the management of corporate applications.

Management of desktops and ...

Not only the servers but also the workstation systems, or desktops, have to be administered. In addition to the functions for inventory management and software distribution already mentioned, tools for *desktop management* often also contain a remote control function for the user interface that enables the administrator to display the screen contents of the desktop on a central console; this allows entries to be simulated, commands to be executed, and the users' entries to be monitored.

But monitoring the server and the clients is not enough to ensure that all the possible availability and performance problems are being detected. In many cases, direct monitoring of the application itself is necessary (e.g., for a direct measurement of response times). Furthermore, regular tests are required to ensure that the conditions tested during installation continue to be met. This is the task of *application monitoring* in the narrower sense.

...monitoring the application itself

The main task of management when an application is being run is not only to monitor the participating systems but also to administer user authorizations. From their desktops, users today usually are able to access a number of applications and servers, which in many cases, are based on different operating systems or communication architectures. Consequently, tools that can also be used in heterogeneous environments are required for *user administration.*

User administration

In addition to tools for these major areas of application, many *other tools* are especially designed for use with important components, with the peripheral devices of systems, and with specific applications. Examples of these include printing management, management of storage media (archiving and backup systems), management of certain middleware systems (message transport, transaction monitors), and management of workflow or database applications.

Other areas

Individual aspects of tools for the areas mentioned are described in detail in the following sections.

16.2.2 Inventory Management Tools for Software Management

As explained in section 14.3, there are technical, organizational, and legal reasons for having a full familiarity with the hardware and software components installed in a company as well as for logging them and keeping track of them. Section 14.3 discussed the architecture of a documentation system. An *inventory database*, which contains precise and up-to-date information on the type, the properties, and the equipment of the end systems, serves as the basis for many tools. In addition to their importance for fault detection and for commercial matters, such as establishing depreciation requirements, they are also particularly important for *software distribution and installation* and licensing control.

Inventory database is the basis for systems and software management

In addition to organizational data (user, department, responsible administrator, installation location of a system) and economic data (cost center, purchase price and date, depreciation time frame, warranty period, supplier, information about maintenance and leasing contracts), the following data is typically maintained by a system:

- Data on hardware, such as type of processor and BIOS; size of cache, main memory, and disk storage; network interface; video adapter; and type and characteristics of attached monitors and other peripherals.

- Data on software, such as name, manufacturer, version of operating system and the installed software packages, installation paths and parameters, license information, and so on.

Difficulty in keeping data up-to-date

An important aspect of software distribution and installation is ensuring that this data is *maintained consistently* and *kept up-to-date*, and in many cases, this is a time-consuming process. One reason is the very large number of systems often involved; another reason is that users and administrators sometimes do not forward locally implemented changes to inventory management. This can include extensions to the hardware, deinstallation of some of the hardware, or the installation of additional components or other software packages. The problems therefore also apply to the data that is specifically required for software distribution planning.

Autodiscovery functions

Tools for inventory management that are geared to software distribution therefore contain as central components functions for the *automatic collection* of data and for ensuring that it is kept up-to-date (*autodiscovery*), which can also be executed in heterogeneous environments. For this purpose, data is obtained directly from the end systems. This then produces a distributed database situation with the central database always containing only copies and the primary inventory data stored in the systems or generated when required.

MIFs: important sources for inventory information

Inventory tools for software management should contain as many mechanisms for *autodiscovery* as possible and have the capability of automatically locating a maximum amount of the information mentioned. Along with diverse proprietary and system-specific options (e.g., evaluation of *windows registry*) for reading data from the systems, the *MIF standard groups* (see section 8.2) specified by the DMTF have recently been established as the standard supported by a large number of hardware manufacturers. More and more data from the systems standard group, the monitor MIF, the software standard group, and the LAN adapter standard group is being provided over an SP and evaluated by inventory management tools.

Some of the definitions from the software standard group were included in section 8.2.2. The following example is also an excerpt from the systems standard group and is used to identify the processor installed in a system:

```
Name = "Processor Family"
        ID = 1
        Description = "The family of processors to which
                       this processor belongs."
        Access = Read-Only
        Storage = Common
        Type = "Processor Family"
        Value = 0

Start Enum
Name = "Processor Family"
        0x01 = "Other"
        0x02 = "Unknown"
        . . .
        0x0A = "80487"
        0x0B = "Pentium Family"
                // Use this if specific Pentium version is
                // not enumerated; 0x0C through 0x11 are
                // reserved for specific Pentium versions.
        0x0C = "Pentium Pro"
        0x0D = "Pentium II"
        0x0E = "Pentium MMX"
        . . .
        0x21 = "Power PC 601"
        0x22 = "Power PC 603"
        0x23 = "Power PC 603+"
        . . .
        0x62 = "68000"
        0x63 = "68010"
        0x64 = "68020"
        0x65 = "68030"
        . . .
End Enum
```

Other standardized information sources exist in the diverse Internet MIBs mentioned in Chapter 6.

Examples of tools that contain functions for inventory management and are specifically designed for software distribution are Tivoli

Product examples

Inventory, MS Systems Management Server, HP OpenView IT/Administration, and CA Unicenter AimIT.

MIFs not yet sufficient

Although the information provided in the different MIFs and MIBs serves as a basis, it is far from being adequate for efficient and problem-free software distribution. What the MIFs lack is important information about the components of software packages and, above all, about the relationships that exist between the components.

A popular model currently being used to provide the required information in heterogeneous environments is *application management specification* (AMS). The objective of this tool is to *standardize the contents* of a distributed *inventory database* for software management, which can be used as the basis for managing the entire lifecycle of an application. Because of its importance, a brief description of this tool follows.

Application Management Specification (AMS)

AMS: management model for applications

The AMS ([TIV97a], available at *http://www.tivoli.com*) represents a pragmatic approach to producing a quick initial uniform description of applications through the use of generic management information. It was developed by Tivoli, but today is also being supported by other manufacturers. The following design criteria were selected in order to force a quick acceptance of the model:

- *Use of an existing information model:* In the first version, AMS uses the management information format (MIF) of DMTF (see section 8.2); in version 2.0, it uses CIM (see section 9.3.2).

- *Use of standardized management information:* AMS is based on the *software standard group definition* of the DMTF (see section 8.2.3), and in the future, will be using the *common model* (see section 9.3.2) for applications from CIM.

- *No instrumentation required of an application:* AMS has been specified so that a software manufacturer can implement it without any instrumentation of the applications, meaning that the application requires no modification. On the other hand, instrumentation is not excluded.

- *Separation of static and dynamic information:* In connection with the criteria already listed, an AMS-conformant description of an application contains only static information. This means that the information is provided in the form of one or more files, and a special agent is not required. The files thereby provide the inventory database for software management.

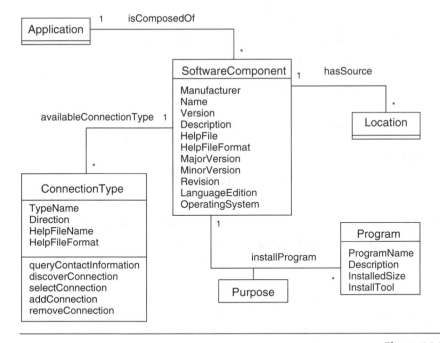

Figure 16.2
Excerpt from AMS

Purely static information is usually sufficient for inventory purposes but not for the tasks of application management overall. An AMS-conformant description therefore contains references to commands or programs that dynamically supply information or execute actions. The references themselves, however, are static.

References to commands and programs

Figure 16.2 presents an excerpt from an AMS. It shows how an AMS specifies the structure of an application (isComposedOf) on the basis of an arbitrary number of software components. Several self-explanatory static management attributes are assigned to the components. Each component is linked over relationships of the hasSource type to Location objects that indicate where, for example, executable code, configuration files, log files, or the required program libraries are located for a component. Relationships of the installProgram type link the components to programs that implement the installation or deinstallation of the components. The attribute Purpose of the relationship installProgram can adopt the values Before install, After install, or Before remove. In the first case, for example, Program indicates the tool that can be used to test the installability of the component. availableConnectionType provides information on the types of dynamic dependencies that can exist for a component in

Examples from AMS

relationship to other components, including references to programs in which information about these dependencies can be obtained and manipulated during running time (`discoverConnection`, `addConnection`, `removeConnection`).

Overall, the AMS supplies information about:

- The *topology* of an application, thus its arrangement of components and subcomponents, including important characteristics of the components
- Programs for *installation* and *deinstallation*
- *Monitoring programs*
- Possible *management intervention* allowed by a component
- *Security requirements* and *access control information*
- Types of *dynamic dependencies* and the associated *manipulation programs*

Foundation for software inventory database

The *software inventory database*, which is compiled using the AMS-conformant descriptions of the applications, therefore supports tools for the entire lifecycle of an application. It is obvious that it can be used as the database for software distribution and availability and performance monitoring. But some applications are less evident. For example, during the runtime of an application, a constant check is made to establish whether the conditions specified and tested before or during the installation still apply or whether another package that is required has been deinstalled or replaced by a nonsuitable version or a hardware change has been carried out. These checks can be supported by tools based on inventory management.

Basis for application management tools

The AMS is therefore the first basis for tools such as *Tivoli Manager for Applications* (*http://www.tivoli.com/*) for application management in heterogeneous environments that is not overly demanding of software suppliers. Tivoli supplies Module Designer, which supports the generation of AMS specifications for applications.

16.2.3 Software Distribution and Installation

Tools for efficient software distribution are an absolute necessity

In DP infrastructures, which today typically consist of enormous numbers of decentralized systems, automated software distribution and installation is one of the areas that requires a high participation of personnel. Support by a wide range of tools is a necessity.

The tools described in the previous subsection are used to clarify how systems are equipped with hardware and software. Once these details have been established, the planning and execution of software distribution can begin in the narrower sense.

The *distribution process* can be organized into the following *stages:*

Phases of the distribution process

- *Assembly* of the software and data parts, including guidelines on installation.

- *Planning* of the distribution (e.g., defining the target machines, selection of distribution time frames against the background of operating times and available transmission capacities).

- Actual *distribution*, which is implemented using a push or pull model, sometimes over distribution stations called depots.

- *Installation* and *configuration* of the delivered packages and checking that the installation has been carried out correctly.

These different stages are described next. Differences can exist with the individual steps depending on the class of the distributed software application or operating system. These issues will be dealt with briefly in section 16.2.4.

Assembly of Software Packages

Before software can be distributed, the distribution units—usually called *packages*—have to be assembled. There are very few cases where a package can be used just the way it was delivered by the supplier. First of all, configuration parameters such as installation paths have to be adapted to the company's own guidelines; second, often only a small fraction of the data contained on the data medium supplied by the vendor is actually required for a specific installation. A distribution of the entire package is basically out of the question for reasons of cost or line capacity.

Packaging for distribution

It is helpful if a tool can offer extensive assistance in the assembly of the packages. Tools are now available in the market that create snapshots of the disk on a reference system before and after installation of the software and then use the difference between the two snapshots for an automatic generation of the actual package that is to be distributed.

Distribution Planning

When planning software distribution, it is helpful if the tool used integrates well with inventory management, in other words, receives all the relevant properties of the possible target systems and also evaluates these properties. The efficiency of software distribution depends

Planning on the basis of inventory

largely on the relative proportion of unsuccessful installations, the frequency of which can be reduced through an in-depth analysis of the configurations of the target systems. Other conditions relating to the distribution (e.g., time of day, network load) should be specified so that they are flexible, simple, and as complete as possible in order that the actual distribution itself can be carried out without supervision outside normal operating hours.

Distribution

Two distribution models

Two different models exist for the distribution itself:

- With the *push model*, the server, or the distributor, initiates the transmission. The advantage of this model is that it offers a more reliable way of timing the distribution process, but it requires that the target machine is active and accessible or that it can be activated remotely (also see section 16.2.5). This model is not fully suitable for mobile systems.

- With the *pull model*, it is the target system that takes the initiative by "checking" with the distributor to establish whether new software is to be installed.

Software distribution is a multilevel process

If software is to be distributed to a large number of target systems in a large company spread over several locations, a single-step procedure involving one server will not suffice. The load on the server and on the communication links makes this an unsuitable option. Tools used in these environments have to support multilevel distribution concepts with intermediate distribution depots at different levels (see Figure 16.3).

In some cases, because of the size of program packages today and the load already existing on data lines, it may not be possible or desirable to send software packages over a line to the depot. Some tools therefore allow large packages to be stored on transportable data media (e.g., written on CD-ROM) and first to be distributed, for example, by post, to the depots (see Figure 16.3). This means that only the initiation of the distribution and the event reports are run over the communication network.

Installation and Configuration

Steps for installation and configuration

If the software packages have been successfully transferred to the target

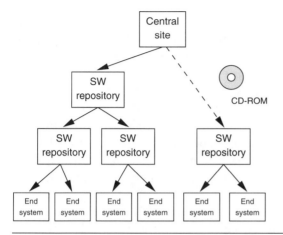

Figure 16.3
Software distribution is a multilevel process

machines, then the software is installed and configured. The following steps are carried out:

- *Unpacking of the software:* The package compressed for transmission is decompressed and unpacked and the different files are usually filed in a temporary directory.

- *Execution of preinstallation routines:* Test routines in the package are executed before the final installation. These test routines check that the conditions required for a successful installation that could not be tested from the inventory information in advance have been met. A typical example of this is the existence and version of necessary function libraries. A mechanism is sought that involves carrying out as few and uncritical routines on the target system as possible in order to improve the security and the stability of the procedure.

- *Installation and configuration:* The files of software are copied or transferred to the appropriate target directories, and the system configuration is modified.

- *Execution of postinstallation routines:* These routines test as far as possible whether the installation was successful and whether an executable installation of the application is available. Depending on the success of the tests, success or fault reports are distributed, temporary directories are deleted, or applications that are not executable are deinstalled again.

Software distribution agents are necessary

The execution of the steps mentioned requires that *agents* that are compatible with the distribution tool are installed on the target systems and that these agents take over control of the target machine during the installation process.

Criteria for tools

Tools are evaluated according to the hardware and operating system platforms for which they provide these agents. Other criteria relate to whether and to what extent the tools support all the steps listed and the described different distribution concepts and to the class of software (only application software or even operating systems) for which they are suitable. Added to this are general aspects such as integration with other tools and user friendliness.

Product examples

Products that contain software distribution functions include HP OpenView IT/Administration, HP OpenView Software Distribution, Novadigm EDM, MS Systems Management Server, CA Unicenter Software Delivery and ShipIT, Tivoli Software Distribution, and BB Data ASDIS.

16.2.4 Server Monitoring

In the lifecycle of an application, successful distribution and installation of software is followed by the operational phase. This phase should provide a constant guarantee of the function and performance of the application.

Monitors for important resources

A variety of different tools are generally required to enable an application to be monitored in terms of availability and performance in the broader sense because both the network infrastructure and the configuration and availability of the end system resources are relevant to guaranteeing the availability of an application to the user. Tools for application monitoring therefore consist of an integration of all sorts of different monitors for the individual classes of resources. They should at least be combined under one common user interface and transmit messages about critical states to a common event management system in the respective format.

Product examples

Examples of this include Distributed Monitoring from Tivoli, which cooperates with the Tivoli Enterprise Console, and diverse monitors such as HP OpenView PerfView and MeasureWare, which are compatible with the platform HP OpenView IT/Operations with its event management.

Server monitoring

The main starting point for the monitoring of applications is, of course, the server. Tools are required that allow a uniform mechanism for monitoring the different server types, such as the different Unix servers, Windows NT servers, Netware servers, or Banyan Vines servers. The typical values monitored include:

- *Operational status* of the server overall

- *Use of resources* and *performance-related values,* such as utilization of the processors, main memory and disk storage use, number of processes and active sessions, and open files, as well as more specific data such as hit rates in the cache, page errors, and available I/O buffer.

- Operational status of important *components* such as uninterruptible power supply and fans

This basic data is used, for example, to trigger alarms when critical values have been reached or to produce statistics and trends as the basis for capacity planning, for the transfer of applications, and for the upgrading of servers.

The information sources are the specific monitors of the operating systems as well as certain Internet MIBs. The host resources MIB (RFC 1514) in particular is sometimes implemented by the operating system manufacturer and evaluated by certain tools.

Internet MIBs as information sources

The following example is an excerpt from this particular MIB and supplies information on the utilization of processors and storage devices:

```
HrStorageEntry ::= SEQUENCE {
        hrStorageIndex           INTEGER,
        hrStorageType            OBJECT IDENTIFIER,
        hrStorageDescr           DisplayString,
        hrStorageAllocationUnits INTEGER,
        hrStorageSize            INTEGER,
        hrStorageUsed            INTEGER,
        hrStorageAllocationFailures Counter}
...
hrStorageAllocationUnits OBJECT-TYPE
        SYNTAX  INTEGER (1..2147483647)
        ACCESS  read-only
        STATUS  mandatory
        DESCRIPTION
                >>The size, in bytes, of the data objects
                allocated from this pool. If this entry is
                monitoring sectors, blocks, buffers, or
                packets, for example, this number will
                commonly be greater than one. Otherwise
```

```
                              this number will typically be one.<<
                ::= { hrStorageEntry 4 }


      hrStorageSize OBJECT-TYPE
                SYNTAX   INTEGER (0..2147483647)
                ACCESS   read-write
                STATUS   mandatory
                DESCRIPTION
                         >>The size of the storage represented by
                         this entry, in units of
                         hrStorageAllocationUnits.<<
                ::= { hrStorageEntry 5 }
```

Utilization
of storage
```
      hrStorageUsed OBJECT-TYPE
                SYNTAX            INTEGER (0..2147483647)
                ACCESS            read-only
                STATUS            mandatory
                DESCRIPTION
                         >>The amount of the storage represented by
                         this entry that is allocated, in units of
                         hrStorageAllocationUnits.<<
                ::= { hrStorageEntry 6 }
      ...
      HrProcessorEntry ::= SEQUENCE {
                hrProcessorFrwID        ProductID,
                hrProcessorLoad         INTEGER}
      ...
```
Processor utilization
```
      hrProcessorLoad OBJECT-TYPE
                SYNTAX   INTEGER (0..100)
                ACCESS   read-only
                STATUS   mandatory
                DESCRIPTION
                         >>The average, over the last minute, of
                         the percentage of time that this processor
                         was not idle.<<
                ::= { hrProcessorEntry 2 }

      ...
```

Product examples   One of the products that belongs to the category described is HP OpenView Expose, which can be used to monitor servers under Windows NT, Netware, and Vines. Other products include Seagate Manage Exec and Intel LANDesk Server Manager.

16.2.5 Desktop Management

Management of workstation systems and specifically of PCs is an area in which tool support is particularly important because of the problems arising in connection with the use of large numbers of systems. This area of management often places a heavy demand on staffing requirements in the IT departments. It concentrates on:

Main emphasis of desktop management

- *Inventory management*
- *Software distribution* and *installation*, along with licensing management
- *Remote control*
- *Virus protection*

Inventory management has already been dealt with extensively in section 16.2.1. Some of the MIFs that were mentioned are specifically designed for desktop management. This particularly applies to the monitor MIF because the features of a graphics card or a monitor play a minor role for servers.

We have also already dealt with software distribution and installation and licensing management. The two key *features* of PCs in this connection are:

Features of PCs in software distribution

- They can be *activated* and *deactivated* by the user. What this means for software distribution is that either the pull model must be used or a facility should be available that permits a remote activation of the PCs, for example, to move from energy-saving mode to operating mode (remote wakeup).
- Owing to the quantity problem and decentral installation of the systems, a mechanism is required that also allows an automated complete *reinstallation* of the *operating system* from a central location. PCs must be able to load a minimal system from a server (remote new system setup), even if a local OS is not available or there is a problem in loading the OS (e.g., because of a failed OS update). In this case, PCs behave like NCs (network computers).

The specification *Wired for Management Baseline* from Intel [INT97] proposes solutions for the two areas mentioned: Tools for *remote control* are systems that allow an administrator to control the user interface of a PC from a remote location; the administrator sees the screen contents of the PC on his or her management console and is able to transmit keyboard entries and mouse movements to the PC (see

Remote control of PCs

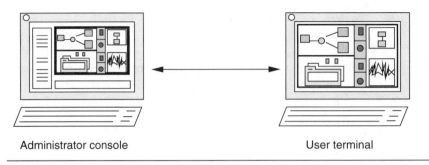

Administrator console   User terminal

Figure 16.4
Remote control for PCs

Figure 16.4). This greatly simplifies the process of providing advice or solutions to problems over the telephone. The following factors have to be considered:

- *Transmission bandwidth:* If the communication connection between the administrator's console and the user PC has only a low bandwidth, it is not practical to use a large amount of graphical information. A possible way to resolve this problem is to reduce the number of colors used or to use grayscale displays.

- *Graphics standards:* If the administrator and user consoles use different display formats, a conversion is required.

- *Legal issues:* Remote control mechanisms allow users to be monitored. The legislative frameworks of some countries, such as data protection laws and rights to privacy, sometimes dictate that users must be made aware of this fact.

Virus protection

Virus protection (see [KSC97]) is not a topic we will cover in any depth. Many products are available for this area, but most of them are not integrated with other management tools. It should be pointed out, however, that virus descriptions should be updated frequently to ensure that adequate protection is provided. If products themselves do not provide special mechanisms for updates, then this problem can be addressed through efficient software distribution.

Product examples

Numerous products are available in the market for the management of PCs. The Systems Management Server from Microsoft supports all the areas mentioned except for virus protection. HP OpenView Desktop Administrator supplies solutions for inventory management and software distribution. Other products include Novell ManageWise, the Intel LANDesk Management Suite, and the Intel LANDesk Configuration Manager, which is geared to the installation of operating systems.

16.2.6 Monitoring Tools for Applications

A constant check is required during operating time to ensure that applications are available to users and that their performance-related characteristics (such as response times) meet the various needs. A monitoring of network infrastructure (see section 16.1), server utilization, and the state of processes (see section 16.2.3) will provide only an indirect and usually unreliable assessment of the function and performance of an application.

The only way this issue can be addressed is if *data supplied directly by the application* is made available to tools for reprocessing. This requires the definition of an interface to applications that allows an application to communicate with a management entity. Several approaches exist, including some Internet MIBs that unfortunately have not yet received the support required from software suppliers. One of the reasons for this could be that there are no APIs for these definitions, or maybe the problem is that there are several competing MIBs. The latter applies to Internet management with the competing definitions for the master agent–subagent interface (see section 6.2). Furthermore, some APIs are tied to specific implementation languages.

Direct monitoring of an application

The ARM-API currently appears to be a potential solution to this problem, but it has not yet been integrated into any of the existing management architectures. It is briefly outlined in the following section.

Application Response Management (ARM)

The AMS approach in which static files are used to describe applications for management purposes and an attempt is made to avoid making modifications to the applications themselves is not sufficient on its own to offer extensive *performance monitoring* of the applications. An *instrumentation* of the applications themselves is what is required. The Application Response Measurement API (ARM-API, see *http://www.hp.com/go/arm* or *http://www.tivoli.com*) defines an interface that allows the response times of individual transactions to be monitored. This API was developed jointly by Tivoli/IBM and Hewlett-Packard, and the concept has purposely been kept simple in order to improve its chances for broad support by application manufacturers. It is to support the popular programming languages. Although ARM can be used independently of an AMS, the two approaches tend to complement each other. The AMS contains information on whether and how an application uses ARM and threshold values for the response times to the different transaction types.

Measuring response times for transactions

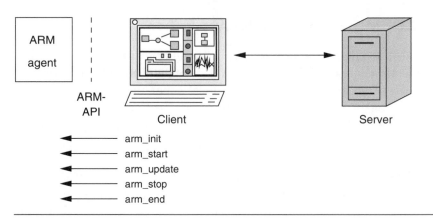

Figure 16.5
Functions of ARM-API

ARM-API: communication between application and ARM agent

The ARM-API allows applications (also see Figure 16.5):

- To *register* or *deregister* with an ARM agent (`arm_init`, `arm_end`), which usually takes places at the start or at termination of the application.

- To report the *beginning* and the *end* of a *transaction* (`arm_start`, `arm_stop`) or to indicate that a transaction that is running a long time is still active (`arm_update`).

ARM agents

Management tools that communicate with *ARM agents* are therefore able to derive data on the performance and availability of an application. The interpretation of response times ("good," "OK," "too high") is supported, whereby the AMS specification supplies the respective application with the threshold values for the response times for different transaction types. Of course, these values provide only a guide and have to be adapted during running operations to the concrete configuration.

Data supplied by the ARM agent is reprocessed into statistics, trend calculations, and similar output. Event reports can be generated in the event that threshold values are exceeded. The data can be used for accounting purposes as well as for availability and response time monitoring.

Products based on ARM include HP OpenView PerfView (management application) or HP OpenView MeasureWare (ARM agent, see *http://www.hp.com/openview/*) and Tivoli Distributed Monitoring (*http://www.tivoli.com/*).

16.2.7   User Administration

A problem in heterogeneous information processing environments is that users always have to be registered separately for each system they use. Users today require identification for Netware, for databases under Windows NT, in some cases for several Unix variants, for the mainframe, for access to internal Web pages and Web servers, for the email system, and so forth.

Multiple user administration

The administrator is therefore faced with a needlessly inefficient situation because of tasks like the following that have to be executed separately for each system used:

Tasks

- *Administration of user-specific objects* (identification, group affiliation, authorization)
- *Establishing of quotas* for resources that are in short supply (e.g., disk space)
- *Accounting* of resources used (see also section 3.2.4)

For the users, this means that they require *more than one identification*, each with a different password, and that they or their cost centers receive several invoices with no real way of checking how they relate to one another.

Tools for user administration in heterogeneous environments should therefore:

Requirements

- Allow the setting up, modification, or cancellation of *user identification* with authorization for *as many systems as needed in one step*. This is referred to as single sign-on. It will not only help to improve the efficiency of user administration but also the security of the systems because of a reduction in the danger of "abandoned" identifications.
- Provide a safe mechanism for *delegating the administration* of identification to several administrators, particularly in large firms with large numbers of users.

The objective of these measures is a *single sign-on* that allows users to register and become authorized for the use of different applications in one step. This option is not yet available for all the identification requirements mentioned, but a first step in this direction is being offered by products such as Single-Sign-On Option from CA Unicenter TNG.

The following section provides several examples of areas that require user administration or a link to systems for user administration. Further details of user administration and accounting can be found in [VAR94].

Product examples

Tools that contain functions for user administration include HP OpenView IT/Administration and Tivoli User Administration. Further examples for accounting and billing tools were given in section 13.3.

16.2.8   Other Areas

Tools for specific resources

In addition to the management areas described in the previous section, a variety of products and solutions are available that are geared to specific resources. Selected examples are summarized in this section to give you an impression of the variety of tools that exists. The list presented is not meant to be complete, nor do we touch upon the extremely complex security issues that have arisen in this context. Instead, we refer you to [GAS96].

Licensing Management

Measuring software usage

With the growing number of distributed systems, the task of software distribution along with the tracking of software use is becoming an ever-more important task, especially from an economic standpoint. On the one hand, licensing agreements for software should be administered from a central location; on the other hand, there should also be some flexibility in the administration of these agreements. Licensing management should cover the following schemes or combinations thereof:

- *Fixed number of licenses*, purchased in advance
- *Variable number of licenses*, billed afterwards on the basis of usage depending on *average* usage during a particular period or a time of the day or based on *maximum* simultaneous usage

Licensing management in the MS-Windows area has been simplified through the introduction of the Licensing Service API. The CORBA Licensing Service of the OMG represents another attempt at establishing a standard in this area.

Products for licensing management are usually supplied by the manufacturers that offer solutions for software distribution, but they can also exist within the framework of inventory management or as individual solutions.

Printing Management and Spooling

The first thing that comes to mind when you think about asynchronous output to different *media* are the different types of printers available; however, the media could also be plotters, slide or video production equipment, CD writers, or magnetic tape. In addition to different types of equipment, a variety of *document formats* exist, such as PDF, PostScript, PCL, ASCII, diverse bitmap formats, and ISO 9660.

Diverse output devices and formats

A problem that still has not been resolved satisfactorily is how to use this equipment from heterogenous systems and select equipment according to the format of the data. The process involved is still usually prone to error and requires an unnecessary amount of expertise on the part of a user; this is particularly the case if a user wants to use a printer in someone else's group or in a different department. For example, functions for querying the status of or deleting a request operate differently from system to system. The administration involved, particularly in granting authorization, routing requests, and monitoring printing quotas, is extremely time consuming. The situation will not improve until there is an acceptance of standardized specifications at least for printers, such as the printer MIF of DMTF (see section 8.2.3) or the printer MIB (RFC 1759). The Internet printing protocol of IETF (see *http://www.ietf.org*) could also prove helpful in this area.

Management of output devices

A product that is designed to resolve or at least alleviate the problems mentioned is HP OpenView OpenSpool.

Product examples

Administration of Archiving and Data Backup Systems

Data archiving and backup has taken on an important dimension with the growing quantity of applications being transferred from mainframes to distributed Unix or NT servers. In many cases, it is also being run as a central facility for distributed systems to enable the efficient use of expensive special systems such as tape archives and robot systems.

As with many other systems, the administration of these systems includes dealing with users and their authorizations, setting quotas, and billing for used resources. Furthermore, because these are important components of the information processing infrastructure, messages about critical events or states in the systems have to be forwarded to the operator consoles of the different systems.

Consequently, the tools needed for the administration of these systems should ideally be integrated into a general management

Integration into platforms

platform. There should at least be an integration of the user interface and operation of the event management of the platform.

Product examples

Some of the products that follow this course include HP OpenView OmniStorage and HP OpenView OmniBack, which are integrated with HP OpenView IT/Operations; Tivoli ADSM, for which an integration exists with TME; and Solstice Backup from Sun.

Management of Important Middleware Systems

Middleware, such as transaction monitors and message transfer systems, often provides the basis for a number of company-critical applications. Constant monitoring and consistent configuration are extremely important for systems such as CICS and MQSeries. Tools were therefore developed that are specifically designed for the fault, performance, and configuration management of these systems.

Integration with event management

Along with the general integration aspects of these tools, integration with the event management of a management platform is particularly important for guaranteeing a speedy reaction to faults by notifying the responsible experts.

Examples of relevant products are the options from CA Unicenter for CICS and the MQSeries, Tivoli Manager for MQSeries, and BMC Patrol Knowledge Modules for the MQSeries and Tuxedo (see *http://www.bmc.com*).

Management of Directory Services

During recent years, many companies have experienced a proliferation of directory services based on different standards. Examples of these are X.500 Directory, LDAP-conformant systems, DNS, NIS and NIS+, NDS, Windows DNA, and Active Directory. Other directories are contained in Lotus Notes and MS Exchange for email.

Consistent management of several directory services

Systems therefore are needed that support the simultaneous and consistent modification of data in different directories. User administration is inefficient and error-prone if different directories have to be modified individually. If an employee leaves a company or a department or changes jobs within the company, errors in the administration of the directories could result in abandoned IDs or authorizations, which in turn represent a security problem.

Products that are geared to the joint management of different directory services include Directory Management Option and DirectIT from CA Unicenter TNG.

Management of Information Services

With the trend toward intranet solutions, Web servers are becoming important programs for companies. For example, if important database applications are accessed over a Web interface, the same demands for availability and performance behavior are placed on the Web server as on the DB server.

Products are now available that specifically monitor the status and performance of the different types of Web servers, take over the management of the server logs, and produce statistics from the log files. Owing to the high requirement for availability in some circumstances, integration with the event management of a management platform is also important for ensuring that there is a speedy reaction to critical events or states.

Status and performance monitoring of Web servers

Examples of relevant products include Tivoli Manager for MCIS for the Internet server from Microsoft or Tivoli Manager for SuiteSpot for the server products from Netscape, TME10 NetCommander, the CA Unicenter Web Server Management Option, and BMC Patrol Knowledge Module for Internet servers.

Management of Database Systems

There is no need to emphasize the importance, scope, and complexity of databases and DBMSs today. The availability and performance of these systems is of central importance in most companies. In many companies, it was and still is not possible to manage with only one of the leading DBMS products such as DB2, Oracle, Sybase, Informix, Ingres, or MS SQL Server.

Administrators are therefore confronted with the problem of having to evaluate the different specific values of different systems when monitoring availability and performance. Furthermore, the products are often supplied with their own user administration facilities. What is needed are tools that at least standardize the administration of the different DBMSs. What would be preferable are solutions that allow a complete integration with existing systems for user administration. As has been mentioned in the context of several other areas, integration with the event management of a management platform is essential here too because of the high requirement for availability.

Uniform management of more than one DBMS

Examples of products for database system management include Tivoli Database Management (for DB2, Oracle, Sybase, Informix, MS SQL Server), the CA Unicenter options for DB2, Ingres, Informix, Sybase,

Oracle, MS SQL Server, and the BMC Patrol Knowledge Modules for DB2, Ingres, Informix, Sybase, Oracle, MS SQL Server.

Management of Important Applications

Actual corporate applications such as SAP R/3 and the applications from Baan and PeopleSoft are based on the databases just discussed. The availability and performance of these applications is ultimately the goal of all areas of management, from the management of simple network components all the way to the management of complex DBMSs.

In many cases, the applications are systems that are customized to a particular company and have evolved over many years. The management of these systems is therefore usually proprietary.

Management modules are offered for some systems, such as SAP R/3, that are used by many companies. The requirements placed on these modules are roughly comparable to those placed on the management of database systems.

Applications such as Lotus Notes and MS Exchange have attained company-critical status today. Specially customized management modules are therefore also available for these applications.

Products in this area include the CA Unicenter management options for SAP R/3, MS Exchange, and Lotus Notes; the Tivoli Manager for Exchange, R/3, and Domino; and the BMC Patrol Knowledge Modules for Baan applications, PeopleSoft applications, Lotus Domino/Notes, and MS Exchange.

Management modules available for certain applications

16.3   Chapter Summary

This chapter presented a wide variety of management examples, including both problem descriptions and the tools necessary to deal with them. The examples have been taken from the area of network and component management as well as from the management of end systems and applications.

Starting with some practical scenarios, we analyzed the specific requirements that stem from these scenarios and described the functionality needed to meet these requirements. We also presented examples of standardized MIBs that support the implementation of functionality in heterogeneous environments as well as a breakdown of the products commercially available in the respective management area.

We have been more specific in our attempt to tackle the management of components such as hubs, bridges, LAN switches, ATM switches, and routers and to describe the key areas of systems and applications management, namely, inventory management, SW distribution and installation, server monitoring, desktop management, monitoring applications, user administration, and briefly, other areas such as license management and printer and spooling management.

The development of new products in the systems and applications management area has experienced a high momentum during recent years. A vast variety of tools are currently available on the market. It is not a lack of tools for solving a problem but the ability to find the right tool for a specific problem that creates the main problem for providers. Selecting a tool does not necessarily mean that the provider has resolved a problem since problems are often shifted elsewhere or new ones are created. Installing and configuring a tool and integrating it with existing ones is often a complex and time-consuming task.

Additional problems are created through the overlapping functionality of tools and different combinations of functionalities in tools. In this chapter, we described two different approaches that can be followed in combining the functionality of tools for systems and applications management:

- On the basis of functional areas, resulting in tools for inventory management, SW distribution and installation, user administration, and the monitoring of distributed environments.

- On the basis of the resource being administered, thereby producing the need for tools for server management, desktop management, applications management, or more specifically, the management of storage media and printer management.

Tools can be found on the market for both approaches, with the result of obvious overlaps in functionality.

The current situation calls for further efforts in the area of integrated or integrating management tools as described in Chapter 14. Integrated management should pursue a highly modular approach in order to meet the needs of network and service providers. This approach should resemble a Lego-like construction kit that enables a flexible combination and seamless integration of almost any selection of modules.

The key prerequisite for this approach is the existence of standardized or commonly agreed-upon management models or management schemas for all the resources being managed, thereby forming a global management database as a common basis for all tools.

Operational Implementation

The first three parts of this book examined the architectural principles and tool technologies required for the design and creation of integrated management solutions. The aim of Part IV is to show how these management solutions can be used systematically within the operation of networked systems. To deal with this subject from the standpoint of the provider,we need to analyze the operational processes in which management tools are used in the provider organization.

Chapter 17 develops an in-depth understanding of the *operation of networked systems* and the provider organizations responsible for their operation. IT services that represent the objective and the result of the operation of a networked system are the starting point for the discussion. The object of the corresponding service level agreement is to identify which services will be supplied by a provider, the quality of these services, and the cost of these services to the customer. The service offering directly establishes which task areas will fall within the responsibility of a provider organization. In this part of the book, we deal exclusively with those tasks that are directly linked to the networked system. After a review of existing preliminary studies, we conclude the chapter by introducing a *process model* in which the activities of the task area of IT operation are described in the form of operational processes. These three procesess are called routine management, problem management, and change management.

Chapter 18 then looks at the *requirements of management tools* from the *perspective of the provider*. The analysis is conducted on the basis of the three operational processes introduced in Chapter 17. We then investigate the kind of support available to a provider in the form of so-called *process-oriented management means* in the individual actions of an operational process. We first look at the types of management means accessed by operating personnel during the execution of an action. In this connection, the purpose of management tools is to provide (a computer-based) implementation of the process-oriented management means derived from the operational processes. There is a direct correlation between the demands on management tools and the requirements of operating personnel in terms of management means. We use the example of the operational process change management to show how the requirements for a provider-accepted tool can be converted into a tool implementation.

Chapter 19 deals with the important aspect of the *quality monitoring and assurance of an operation* and expands the process model through the addition of a quality layer. First there is a motivation of an additional quality layer (besides the operational level), and the contents are introduced in the form of the quality processes being established. The discussion that follows then focuses on the quality process that incorporates the goal of operational quality monitoring and assurance. Similar to the procedure followed in the description of operational processes, the process-oriented management means needed to implement the quality process are identified and the requirements for (quality) management tools established accordingly. The management resources needed for operational quality monitoring and assurance and their computer-supported conversion into provider-accepted tools are clarified in an appropriate case study.

Chapter 20 concludes Part IV with a brief presentation of the products *Tivoli Management Environment* and *Mansys Expert Desk*, which meet certain requirements from the operational standpoint and represent management concepts that are oriented to the provider. However, the examples presented also indicate that considerable work is still needed in this area of integrated management.

Introduction to the Operation of Networked Systems

Complex networked systems that provide communication and information processing services to large numbers of users do not run on their own; in addition to the management tools described extensively in Part III of this book, these systems require the involvement of trained staff to execute operational tasks with the right level of quality to ensure the orderly running of IT operations. For the user, orderly and secure operations mean that the provider is maintaining the service quality promised [WLA98, WIL94], as already discussed in the different scenarios described in the introduction to Part I.

Relationship between management tools and the operation of a networked system

Management tools therefore cannot only be considered from the view of the developer of these tools; more important, the needs of the provider as a tool user must also be incorporated into the planning that goes into the development of integrated management solutions. As shown in Figure 17.1, the developer and the provider are both concerned with completely different aspects and issues relating to management tools. The most important aspects based on the views of both the developer and the provider are as follows:

The provider is a user of the management tools

- The *management architecture* represents the development basis for the management tool prescribed by the standardization (see Part II of this book). The architecture specifies the underlying information model for the specification of the management information and identifies which management protocols are supported for the exchange of management information.

- The *software technology* selected by the developer completes the development basis for a management tool (Chapters 7 to 9 and Part III). It is used to convert the content of the communication, information, functional, and organizational model prescribed by the management architecture into an executable implementation.

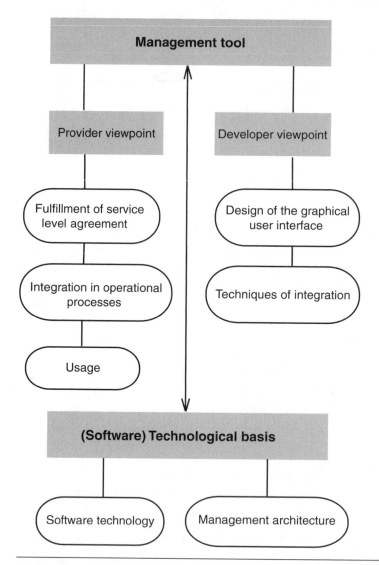

Figure 17.1
The two views of management tools

- Over and beyond the technical development of the management tool, the developer is also concerned with a variety of other different aspects, some of which directly touch upon the provider's needs. One aspect is the *technologies* the developer can use to integrate a tool into the existing environment of the provider. Transitions often have to be created between the different management architectures (see Chapter 10) for this purpose. *User interface design* is a particularly provider-oriented development aspect of management tools since the user interface represents the technical component of the tool that the operator directly experiences.

- An aspect directly related to tools and of importance to the operator is the *operation* of these tools, which is primarily determined by the design of the user interface. Good operability means that the operator is able to use the functions offered by the tool efficiently, in other words, easily, quickly, and securely. From this standpoint the Web-based user interfaces described in Chapter 9 are becoming more and more important.

- A relevant issue for the provider is the extent to which a *tool can be integrated into its operational processes*. This aspect is closely tied into the main question the provider has to ask, and that is whether the functions offered by a particular tool will even be useful in the operation of the networked system and whether use of this tool will make a substantial contribution toward meeting the requirements placed on the operation.

- Lastly, providers are assessed by *their ability to comply with the service level agreements negotiated with their customers*. In this context, management tools represent a technical resource (along with other technical as well as, particularly, personnel resources) used by the operator to achieve a particular goal.

This chapter deals with the fundamentals required for developing an understanding of the provider-oriented view of management tools. We first take a black-box view of the provider organization providing a description of the interfaces to other organizations. Different approaches are available for the internal structure of provider organizations, but we will concentrate on what we consider to be a future-oriented, process-oriented structuring. The chapter is therefore structured as follows.

Content and organization of the chapter

The starting pɔint is the main objective that is pursued by a provider organization in its operation of a networked system, and this is to provide services with a guarantee of the quality agreed on with the customer (section 17.1).

Different approaches exist for setting up and structuring provider organizations so that services agreed on with a customer can be provided efficiently. Section 17.2 discusses these approaches and highlights the advantages of a process-oriented approach.

A process-oriented approach is used in section 17.3 as the basis for structuring the tasks and interfaces of a provider organization. The results of current research projects and contributions from the literature provide the relevant foundation for this approach (section 17.4).

Section 17.5 rounds off the chapter by presenting a consolidated general process model that is appropriate for modeling the operation of a networked system from the standpoint of the derivation of provider-accepted management tools. This process model is then used in Chapter 18 as the basis for specifying the operational requirements of (integrated) management tools and their systematic implementation into solutions for providers.

17.1 Services Offered by Providers of Networked Systems

Service level agreements (SLAs)

In recent years, providers of networked systems have been under increasing pressure by their customers (thus the users of networked systems) to describe their services in the form of precisely defined service level agreements (SLAs). Obviously not every service that has been described by an SLA is provided by the resources of the networked system, as the following classification of IT services indicates.

17.1.1 Structure and Content of Service Catalogs

The provider is an IT service provider

Providers of networked systems use service catalogs as the vehicle for describing the services they offer to their customers. The provision of a service catalog (see, e.g., [WAL93]) therefore forces the provider to see itself no longer solely as an expert of the IT technology offered but as an *information processing service provider*. From the customers' standpoint, it is important that they are receiving the "right" IT services for coping with their tasks. The question of how the service is to be provided is largely left up to the supplier of the service, in this case, the provider of the networked system.

Two types of IT services

The service offering of a provider of networked systems contains two fundamentally different types of services (also see Figure 17.2):

- *Core services*, which are characterized by the fact that they are directly implemented through the use of the (network, system, application) resources of the networked system being operated.

- *Supplementary services*, which provide users with the necessary foundation for using the core services.

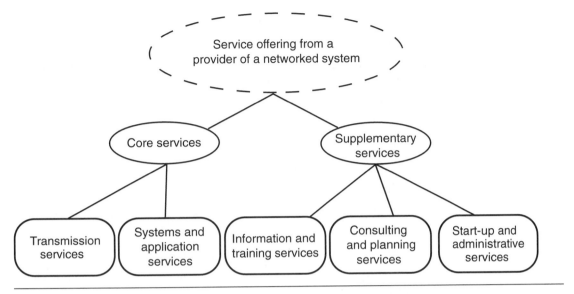

Figure 17.2
Structure of the service offering by a provider of a networked system

The most important services that exist in these two categories are described next, starting with the supplementary services.

Information and Training Services

The information and training services offered by the provider give customers an opportunity to learn how to work with networked systems and to find the best way of using them to execute their own tasks. Examples include:

Supplementary services of a service catalog

- Introduction to the service offering of the operator
- Provision of certain specialist literature (e.g., manufacturer's documentation)
- Introductory courses (e.g., on operating systems, programming languages)
- Training on the use of concrete software systems (e.g., word processing, CAD systems)
- Further training courses (e.g., to become a network or system administrator)

Consulting and Planning Services

What characterizes the services in this group is that they are geared directly to the specific needs and concerns of the customers. These services should ideally produce solutions that are customized as closely as possible to a customer's own environment. Examples of services offered include:

- Advising on use of network or computer technologies
- Advising on use of software systems
- Evaluating and selecting hardware–software components
- Testing the compatibility of hardware–software components
- Planning transmission networks
- Planning the introduction of computer systems
- Providing expert opinions (e.g., technological trends, specific management tools)

Start-Up and Administrative Services

The services in this group provide support to customers who are responsible for maintaining their own hardware and software components. Examples include:

- Testing of hardware functions
- Installation and configuration of network components
- Installation and adaptation of operating systems software (e.g., Windows, Unix)
- Installation and adaptation of application software

Transmission Services

Core services of a service catalog

This class of core services allows customers to transmit data according to a specified range of functions and agreed-on quality.

Systems and Application Services

The services in this class provide customers with access to systems and application components with a specified range of functions and agreed-on quality.

For the core services, it is assumed that all the network, system, and application resources needed to provide these services will be made available and administered by the provider of the networked system. This premise does not apply to the group of start-up and administrative services where the provider supports the customer in the operation of the customer's own components.

17.1.2 Service Level Agreements Between Provider and Customers

In principle, SLAs should exist for all the services listed in a provider's service offering and used by customers. The SLA contains an exact description of what is offered in a service and defines which costs are applied when a customer uses the service. Since providers of networked systems are just now slowly being accepted as IT service providers, a large number of services in the IT area are still being used without explicit SLAs.

Advantages of an SLA for the customer

SLAs are particularly important with core services, that is, transmission and systems or application services, since they contribute toward ensuring that a networked system is structured and run strictly in accordance with the goals that have been established. Furthermore, customers require these specifications for planning the use of the IT services in their own business processes [COR97, DHM93].

SLAs for core services between an operator and a customer contain agreements on the following aspects.

Functional Specifications for the Services

The function provided by a service should be described informally or (partially) formally but in a way that is easily understood not only by an expert but also by the customer. The specification should also identify the target group of customers for the service and the conditions that are appropriate for the use of the service.

Technical Requirements on the Customer Side

In some cases, the use of a service requires that a certain technical infrastructure exists on the customer side; a description of the infrastructure can be included optionally in the SLA. Examples are as follows:

■ Customer-supplied hardware and software required for the configuration and use of a transmission service

■ Type of terminal needed for access to an application

Operating and Maintenance Times

Information in SLAs about operating times is especially important for application services. A provider can be obligated to a user to maintain 24-hour operations 7 days a week or to define separate time windows broken down by weekday, holiday, and weekend. In addition to agreeing on maintenance window times with the customer, the provider is also committed to providing the services on the basis of the following service levels.

Service Levels

Service levels represent the elementary agreements for a core service

Service levels define the level of quality required and promised to the customer for a specific service. These particularly include information about the following two aspects:

- *Availability.* The availability aspect specifies the maximum amount of time a service can be unavailable to the customer due to faults that occur during the agreed-on operating time. The information is indicated in percentages and provides a ratio between availability and nonavailability from the standpoint of the customer. It should be emphasized that the concept of availability can be defined in different ways depending on the service being offered and the goals that have been set. The contract must therefore contain a stipulation clarifying the conditions under which a service is no longer available to a user.

- *Performance parameters* (e.g., response times). Customers are also interested in knowing which performance features (QoS parameters) are part of the service being offered by the provider. A central performance criterion with application services is response times that can be defined on a scale (maximum n seconds in x percent of availability time frame, maximum m seconds in y percent of availability time frame, etc.) in the service level agreement. The introductory description of performance management in section 3.2.3 lists the steps for measuring performance.

A service level can also contain details on data safety and data security as well as other service-specific information.

System Faults and Penalties

Noncompliance with an SLA

An SLA should include a provision outlining the provider's obligations to the customer in the event that a major fault in the operation of the networked system prevents the operator from meeting the terms of the agreement. In special cases, the customer can influence the decision on which contingency plans should be adopted. Each SLA should stipulate which penalties are borne by the provider in the event that the terms of the service level cannot be met during normal operating times. The penalties usually comprise adjustments to billing of the service in favor of the customer (so-called money-back guarantees).

Costs

If an SLA is produced, the provider agrees to provide the service with the quality specified and the customer agrees to pay a certain price for the service. The cost billed to the customer for the use of the service rises commensurately according to the functions and quality requested by the customer.

The particular service determines how the costs are defined in the SLA. Examples of the basis on which costs are calculated in the area of core services include:

Cost units for a core service

- Network connection: one-off connection charge, basic charge per station and month, usage charges
- Computer use: number of instructions
- Disk space: gigabytes per day
- Data archiving: storage or removal, storage per month
- Printers: number of printed pages

The accounting forms given represent only simple examples. In practice, there is a great deal of complexity in the accounting of IT services used. For example, numerous tariff structures usually exist to specify how costs should be calculated based on a variety of parameters (such as customer type, time, and distance). The quality stipulated for the service also has a major bearing on the costs that are charged to a customer using the service.

Accounting and billing, of course, play a major role in the service-related approach described here. Similar to the activity of quality monitoring and assurance presented in Chapter 19, appropriate management information from the networked system and the operational processes is required to ensure that services are billed according to the actual service used and to the correct user.

The following sections of this chapter outline what a provider organization should be considering in its efforts to provide the aforementioned IT services on an effective and efficient basis.

17.2 Current Approaches to Structuring the Operation of Networked Systems

Alternative options for structuring an IT operation

Different alternatives to structuring the operation of networked systems will be presented and discussed. The structuring approach selected is mainly determined by the role of the networked system in the respective company or institution. Although the continuing technological development of systems is constantly producing new possibilities, it is also placing new demands on the operation of these systems, and these demands in turn are affecting the structure of operations.

17.2.1 Goals and Tasks

Alternative orientations

The importance of a networked system to a company greatly depends on the development state of the system and on the users' requirements for this system. The role of the system has a bearing on the orientation within the company on the operation of the networked system.

- If the networked system supports only one single activity that is not particularly critical for the success of the company, the operation of the system is usually implemented on a decentralized basis and distributed among the appropriate company divisions. The goal is to operate the systems for only these selected activities. The operational tasks are then heavily influenced by the *specialist knowledge* that exists about the respective system within each division.

- If the networked system plays a central role in the processing of company-critical information, then the goal of the provider is to coordinate the use of the networked system in its entirety. The resulting tasks are then mostly allocated to certain *functional aspects*, such as security, performance, and fault susceptibility, that concern the overall operation of the networked system. As a consequence, the tasks involving specialist knowledge about certain systems are extended to include tasks relating to the functional aspects that encompass the entire networked system.

- If the provider takes on the role of a service provider, the networked system then represents the central basis for operations. Then the goal of the provider is to supply the services required by the user at the level of quality requested. To achieve this goal, the provider extends the tasks relating to specialist knowledge and functional aspects to include those necessary to provide the required service quality. All procedures are geared to satisfying the terms of the service level agreement. This produces a *process-oriented* structure based on the operation of the networked system.

17.2.2 Mapping to the Operational Structure of the Provider

The goals mentioned here are geared either toward delimiting or expanding the tasks of the provider of a networked system. Certain activities have to be carried out by corresponding roles to perform these tasks. These roles represent a relationship between the operational structure and the organizational structure of the provider.

Organizational structure of an IT operation

The organizational structure is set up to meet the goals of the operational structure. Another criterion that is important in the selection of an organizational structure is the complexity in the *coordination and communication* between the individual organizational units involved in the operation of the networked system.

Experts for Certain Systems

The structuring of the provider organization according to the specialist knowledge required for certain systems is strongly oriented toward the technology applied. This leads to the existence of organizational units, each of which is responsible for certain parts of the networked system. In line with its *linear responsibility*, the task of a higher-ranking organizational unit is to coordinate the different subareas in accordance with the requirements of the networked system. A correspondingly high effort is involved in the communication between the various organizational units.

Figure 17.3 shows an organization structured into specialized organizational units. In this example, the operation of the networked system is a provider organization organized into specialist departments for:

Example of a provider organization

- The SNA or 5080 systems used
- The communications components in the LAN–MAN area (Ethernet, Token Ring, FDDI)

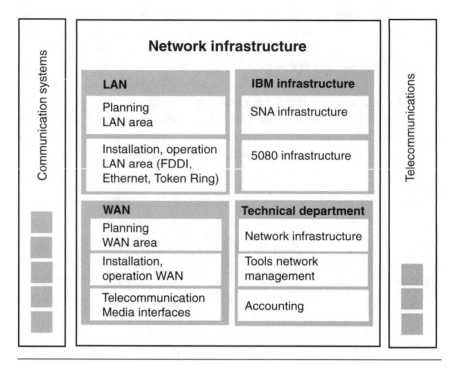

Figure 17.3
Example of an organization according to specialist knowledge

- The components in the WAN area (telecommunications, media interfaces)

These areas are supplemented by the technical departments responsible for network infrastructure, tools, network management, and cost accounting that with their own staffing are part of the provider organization.

A disadvantage of an organizational structure based on specialist knowledge about the individual systems is that the heterogeneity of the networked system is transferred to the organization of the provider. This produces a complex form of coordination and communication between the different specialized organizational units. Furthermore, technological change implies organizational change.

Structuring According to Functional Aspects

Functional organizational structures

A grouping of related tasks according to functional aspects will produce the first performance gain for the operation of a networked system. Mapped to the organizational structure, this creates organizational units whose tasks are always based on a specific function. This function is executed by the respective organizational unit for the entire operation of the networked system. The performance gain is achieved as a result of the less complicated coordination and communication of the respective function. Furthermore, the expansion of each staff members' area of responsibility increases the motivation factor. Organizational forms that take into account specialist knowledge as well as the functional aspects are *staff line organizations* and *matrix organizations.*

A central security department responsible for all security-related functions of an entire company is an example of an organizational unit that is grouped according to a specific function. These tasks comprise technical aspects as well as the monitoring of the systems, along with operational aspects such as the compliance with contractual agreements with customers. Specialists are available to deal with detailed queries about specific security systems.

The security department as an example of a functional organizational unit

Orienting All Processes to the User

As a result of service level agreements with users, providers of networked systems orient all operating processes so that the requirements of their users are satisfied. The orientation to these processes produces additional tasks for the provider. Among other things, the processes must be run within a specific time (time management) to ensure the compliance with the times and schedules stipulated in the SLAs. Properly qualified and authorized personnel (personnel management) is required to fill the roles involved in carrying out the operations of a process.

Customer orientation of an IT operation

For the organizational structure of the provider, this means:

- A single employee is involved in the entire process of the service. This gives the employee added responsibility, thereby acting as a motivating factor.
- There is flexibility in grouping employees according to current requirements and, to a large extent, to integrating them into the procedural process.

An organizational form that adopts these approaches is the *modular factory.* This concept involves forming individual groups to deal with the entire process, thereby having direct responsibility for the process. The outsourcing of a subsidiary is a special case. With outsourcing, processes and the services provided by these processes are delineated from other processes to the extent that they are separated from the company and are able to exist on their own. This requires a rigid structuring of the organizational structure according to these processes to enable the identification of personnel required for the outsourced processes. Two organizations then exist that remain related through the provider–user relationship and define a service catalog as the interface. The advantage is that both organizations are now able to concentrate on their core competences and improve their processes through the use of appropriate tools.

17.3 Interfaces and Tasks of a Provider Organization

A provider organization walks the delicate tightrope between customers as service users on the one side and manufacturers as suppliers on the other:

The provider on a tightrope between user and manufacturer

- *Help desks* offer users a defined access to the provider organization for conveying queries, faults, complaints, and other service requests. In addition to the telephone, which remains the most frequently used medium, other options that are becoming important for communication with users are Web-based interfaces (also see Chapter 9) and email. There is clear evidence that these different media and tools are now being combined to create integrated environments.

- The interface to *developer support* is used by the provider when special questions arise about products of the manufacturer (e.g., in connection with a fault occurring during operation) that can be dealt with only by the manufacturer. Manufacturers also use this interface to inform providers about new versions and releases of their products. In complex networked systems, a considerable coordination effort is required to deal with the resultant changes to a provider's network, system, and applications components, as we will describe later.

A provider organization can consist of autonomous (sub)organizations

- A third interface results from the further and further switching of individual networked systems in producing a global networked system [CAL97]. Services in this kind of system are not provided by a sole provider but through the interaction of several different provider organizations. As a result, each provider organization must maintain an interface to the other providers involved. In the telecommunications area, the management aspects of this interface are examined in the context of *customer network management* (CNM, [PLH97]).

In this case, the central management tools are a component part of the manufacturer's interface. The objective of the tools is to support the provider in using the hardware and software systems that build the networked system so that services with the appropriate quality are available at the user interface. In this respect, the management tools act as a link between the interfaces to the manufacturer and to the user.

Significance of management tools

Figure 17.4 illustrates the interaction between the roles of the developer of the management tools, the provider of the networked system, and the users of the services of the provider.

The suitability of a management tool ultimately depends on its usability in the operation of networked systems. The mistake that was made in the development of management tools in the past was that too little importance was attached to operational requirements. The result was a low acceptance of the tools, which became evident because a significant part of the tool functionality either was not being used at all or was not being used properly in the provider organization [EMA94].

Management tools only partially meet the operational requirements placed on them

The observations presented thus far serve as the motivation for the underlying approach of this part of the book. The management techniques accepted by provider organizations, that is, the management solutions designed for *providers*, can be implemented only if there is a clear link between management techniques and the operational processes in which these techniques are to be used. This requires a clear understanding of how a networked system operates. The operation of the system—which encompasses using the network, system, and applications components of the system for the purposes of providing IT services—is the core function of a provider organization. Before we completely devote ourselves to the tasks involved in the operation of a networked system, we first want to look at the different task areas that have to be dealt with by a provider organization.

17.3.1   Company Management

The provider organization's company management defines the goals of the organization. Its responsibility is to ensure that the operative tasks can be carried out efficiently and that the goals that have been set can indeed be achieved. Some of the goals that have been specified for the management level of a provider organization include:

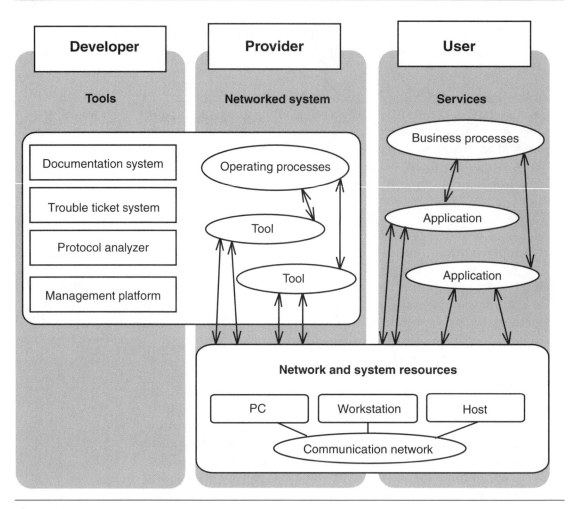

Figure 17.4
Interaction between developer, provider, and user

- Maintaining a good and successful relationship with customers and suppliers
- Assuring the agreed-on quality of the network, system, and application components of the networked system and the associated support services
- Hiring personnel and promoting the further training of this personnel
- Checking and guaranteeing that the services are provided at an economical cost

A department closely linked to company management is *(IT) controlling*, which conducts performance evaluations of all the departments in the provider organization and is responsible for general control functions. We will not cover the separate task area of controlling as such since it focuses too much on the managerial aspects.

Cost–benefit analysis of the provider organization

A central performance goal that ultimately determines the success of an entire provider organization is the one seeking to ensure the satisfaction of the customers with whom service level agreements have been established. Customer satisfaction depends to a strong degree on the quality of the staff and technical resources used in providing the service. The role of management is to create the basic conditions assuring that this quality will also be provided.

17.3.2   Planning

Planning describes the way the provider organization can reach the goals defined by the company management. The following activity areas make up planning.

Planning: from market observation to requirement and procurement plans

Market Observation

An observation of what is happening in the market is important for developing an awareness of the innovative IT technologies and associated products that are available. The sources of this information are technical trade magazines and relevant events such as seminars and product presentations organized by manufacturers. The information that is collected is organized and evaluated in terms of its applicability to the networked system of the provider organization.

Individual Tests of Possible Products

The knowledge gleaned about a product through information available in the market often does not suffice for a final decision on the usability of a network component or a system component for the networked system. When this is the case, special individual tests are carried out that reflect the provider organization's own specific requirements for a component. The result is a test report containing recommendations on the suitability of the respective product. If a particularly important decision is linked to the results of the test, a detailed presentation is prepared for management.

Establishing Future Capacity Needs

Knowledge about the current utilization of IT components and a projection of future capacity requirements form an elementary foundation in the planning of a networked system. Current utilization values are made available in the form of reliable statistics and evaluations. (This aspect will be covered extensively in connection with the operation of networked systems in the sections that follow.) Future requirements depend to a large degree on the strategic goals of a provider organization and on the market situation. A close link between the planning area and the company management of a provider organization is necessary for tackling these issues.

Producing a Requirement and Procurement Plan

The result of the planning process

All the input from the planning activities mentioned is merged into one planning instrument that lists requirements and contains a procurement plan for the continued upgrading of the networked system for a specific period (e.g., between three months and one year). This plan incorporates aspects such as:

- Upgrading certain parts of the communication network with network components from a particular manufacturer
- Expanding and extending existing computer systems
- Introducing a new processing technology
- Configuring one or more existing applications so that they can be run on the new processing technology

The interaction between the planning activities described here is graphically illustrated in Figure 17.5. The conversion or implementation of the requirement and procurement plan is an operational task handled concretely by so-called change management, which will be discussed later.

17.3.3   Development

The goal of the provider is to minimize its own development work

Provider organizations try to "purchase" most of the development for the network, system, and applications components for their systems from the manufacturers. Planning controls the selection process and is responsible for ensuring that the products for the most part satisfy the needs of the provider organization. Despite widespread efforts in the software development area [OHE96], there is still a strong

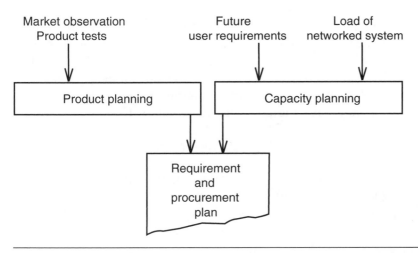

Figure 17.5
Planning tasks in a provider organization

sole reliance on commercially available products, particularly with network and system hardware and with system-oriented software. The more applications oriented the software is, the more difficult it is to find the right commercial off-the-shelf product to suit the provider's requirements. As a consequence, the provider organization is forced to become active in software development itself, whereby it either develops certain applications-oriented software totally on its own or customizes existing products to suit its requirements, usually in conjunction with a software company or systems integrator.

A compromise: customizing commercial products

Previously, the only option available to provider organizations was to develop their own software because of the poor selection of products available; today, the interest is focused more on finding "open," or adaptable, product solutions in order to minimize the considerable maintenance and updating cost of software to provider organizations and to unload this responsibility onto the software suppliers. This option can be realized only if an improved and open design of applications software is available for networked systems.

17.3.4   Training

In addition to guaranteeing a high level of quality in the technical resources, specifically the IT components of networked systems, provider organizations also have to make sure that they employ properly trained personnel. This manifests itself in the acquisition and the hiring of new personnel. The personnel policies laid down by the

The overall quality depends substantially on the quality of staff

company management of provider organizations provide the appropriate guidelines. Suitable training of personnel is required so that the provider organization is able to keep pace with the high level of complexity and rapid developments in the networked system area; this training ensures that staff are constantly receiving further training so that they have the competence to adapt to new operational circumstances.

Typical situations requiring training include:

- New employee joining the provider organization or an employee changing jobs within the organization
- Introduction of new network components, processing systems, and applications in networked systems
- Introduction of new working procedures and processes

Training can be offered either in-house or externally through workshops or seminars. Intensive efforts are currently under way to provide computerized training over the existing wide area networks (telelearning). The hope is that this technology will provide more efficient use of available training facilities in the long run.

17.3.5   Operation

Management tools constitute the primary support for operating personnel

From the viewpoint of IT management, the operation of the networked system is the most important task in a provider organization. Therefore, the following sections deal solely with this task area. The staff responsible for this area are part of the provider organization in which employees are responsible for certain tasks and use different types of supporting tools to ensure that these tasks are carried out efficiently. The management tools that were described earlier in this book constitute a major portion of the tools required for the operation of a networked system. For example, it would be impossible to monitor a transmission line without the appropriate monitoring tools. Another example is the support of problem repair using a trouble ticket system. Provider organizations are therefore dependent on appropriate management techniques supplied by the developers of management tools.

17.4   Existing Work on Structuring Operations

Very few contributions can be found in the literature on the structuring and optimization of the operations of networked systems. The explanation for this is as follows:

Very little preliminary work available

- The hardware and software components of a networked system

  are subject to so much change that it has not been possible to produce any consolidated results.

- The operation of a complex networked system is so complicated and affects so many levels that it is difficult to produce a systematic description of the content.

- In the past, the emphasis in computer science research was more on the development of information systems and less on the operation of these systems.

- There are very few academics active in computer science research who have the practical knowledge required for authoritatively dealing with this subject.

- Different organizations have widely varying structures and thus structuring needs.

It is particularly for these reasons that the following contributions from the standardization and scientific areas originate to a large degree from industry-related projects and tend to have the character of progress reports. However, the experience from these projects is highly valuable in consolidating the content of the operation of networked systems.

The foundations are provided by practical experience gained

17.4.1   OSI Functional Areas and IT Infrastructure Library

The *functional areas of OSI management* [ISO 10040] described in Chapter 5 of this book represent a widely established and accepted attempt to structure the functions required for the management, that is, the monitoring and control, of a networked system. The five well-known functional areas (configuration, fault, performance, accounting, and security) largely provide the management functions needed in an integrated management approach broken down into sufficiently separate areas. The functional areas of OSI management produce a *functional* separation of the task content for the operation of networked systems. However, they should not be used for structuring operations into organizational units, as has already been clarified in section 17.2.

OSI functional areas provide a starting point ...

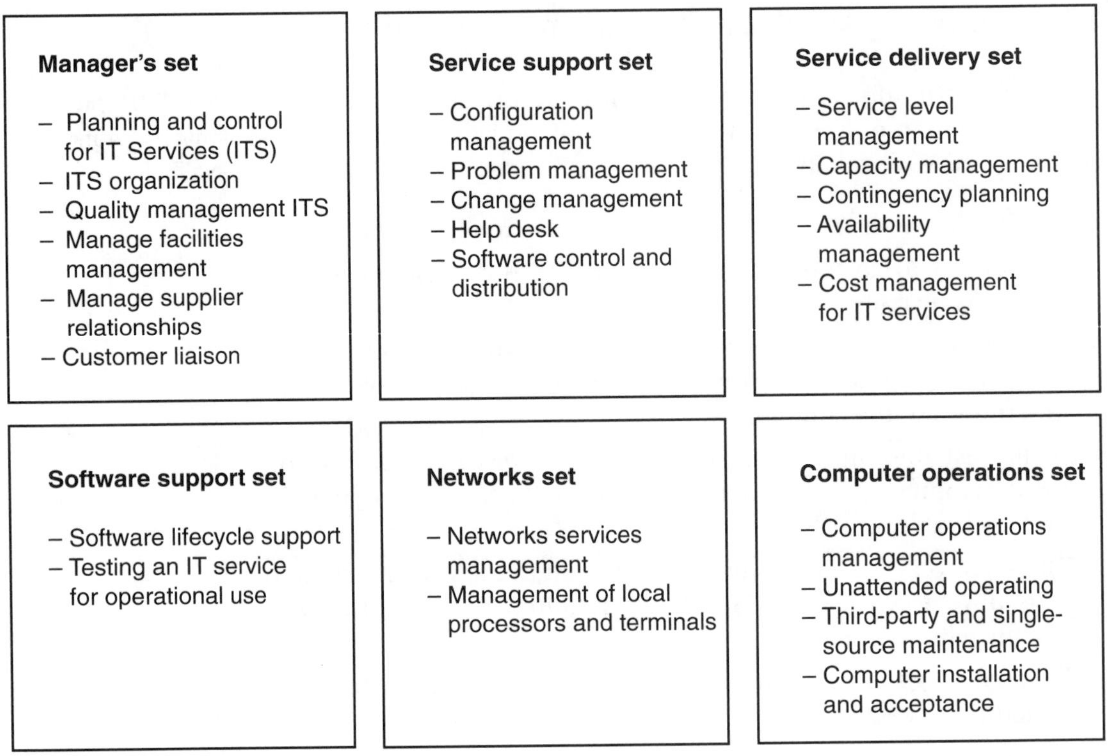

Manager's set	Service support set	Service delivery set
– Planning and control for IT Services (ITS) – ITS organization – Quality management ITS – Manage facilities management – Manage supplier relationships – Customer liaison	– Configuration management – Problem management – Change management – Help desk – Software control and distribution	– Service level management – Capacity management – Contingency planning – Availability management – Cost management for IT services
Software support set	**Networks set**	**Computer operations set**
– Software lifecycle support – Testing an IT service for operational use	– Networks services management – Management of local processors and terminals	– Computer operations management – Unattended operating – Third-party and single-source maintenance – Computer installation and acceptance

Figure 17.6
ITIL sets for the operation of networked systems

...which has been adopted by the ITIL

The IT Infrastructure Library (ITIL, [CCT94]) produced by the Central Computer and Telecommunications Agency (CCTA, [CCT97]) represents important groundwork for the *process-oriented structuring* of provider organizations. The ITIL takes the functional areas of OSI management and compiles them into a collection of organizational and technical parameters for the operation of complex IT infrastructures. As Figure 17.6 shows, the part of the ITIL that deals with issues relating to service provisioning and the management of infrastructure consists of six so-called sets, which in turn, contain two or more modules. The content of each of the sets is briefly outlined next.

Manager's Set

See section 17.3

This set concentrates on the organization of operating personnel and cooperation with suppliers that are involved in providing a service. The set applies to all (senior) IT service managers.

Service Delivery Set

This set deals with providing quality and cost-assured IT services. The starting point is the service level agreements (SLAs) and associated issues relating to which functions need to be established in a provider organization in order to provide services with the agreed-on quality.

See section 17.1

Service Support Set

The functions contained in this set are designed to ensure flexible and reliable service provisioning. Configuration management as the basis for change management and help desks as the interfaces to customers are important functions for achieving necessary flexibility and reliability.

Computer Operations Set

This set combines all the functions directly associated with the operation of large computer installations, particularly mainframes and centralized machines.

Software Support Set

This one handles all aspects of IT service management that are related to software development. In particular, this includes communication with software developers to convey requirements for operation.

Networks Set

The networks set is devoted to the special requirements of distributed infrastructures and concentrates on communication and the local processing systems. This set is particularly geared to those providers who are planning to downsize in the direction of client–server architectures.

The ITIL consists of a further three sets that are concerned with environmental infrastructure, such as buildings, cable routes, and other supply infrastructures for IT resources. These will not be covered in our discussion.

Other ITIL sets

The ITIL can be viewed as the first systematic approach that consciously addresses the problems of IT systems from the side of the provider. It produces an extensive collection of sets containing modules that focus on the organizational aspects of operation. However, the tools that could be used to meet the operational requirements

Appreciation ...

efficiently are only alluded to and not described sufficiently to allow a derivation of the provider's tool requirements.

...and criticism of the CCTA approach

Although the CCTA has tried to bring a uniform structure into the operational aspects of IT management, its approach is lacking an integrated and comprehensible overall model. As a result, there is a lack of clarity for the reader in the important relationships between the operational processes specified in the ITIL and a difficulty with the orientation in the numerous modules. This shortcoming also explains why an inconsistency exists between the horizontal relationships between modules stipulated by the CCTA and the operational processes described.

In section 17.5, we will introduce a process model that is relatively simple in comparison to the CCTA approach but nevertheless substantially incorporates the IT infrastructure library. Owing to the emphasis on the technical aspects, and specifically on tool support, this model incorporates other, yet overall considerably fewer, aspects.

17.4.2 Service Management in TMN

The work of the ITU on the subject of service management is worthy of mention in the area of integrated management. As the fourth layer of the "pyramid" (see Figure 17.7) of the Telecommunications Management Network (TMN), service management encompasses the processes for monitoring and controlling the services provided by network and system resources [MAS97].

The content of service management can be described by the following two phases: (1) service offering and service contract and (2) service provisioning.

Within the context of TMN, the service offering comprises the telecommunications services that a provider offers potential customers. Customers who want to use a telecommunications service are first checked out by the provider and then enter into a service level agreement with the provider.

A service must be established and tested in accordance with the service level agreement. This involves carrying out the appropriate measures at the underlying network management, element management, and network element layers.

By incorporating service management and business management into the management framework, the TMN approach does not restrict itself only to the technical resources of the networked layers (the lower layers "network element management layer" and "network manage-

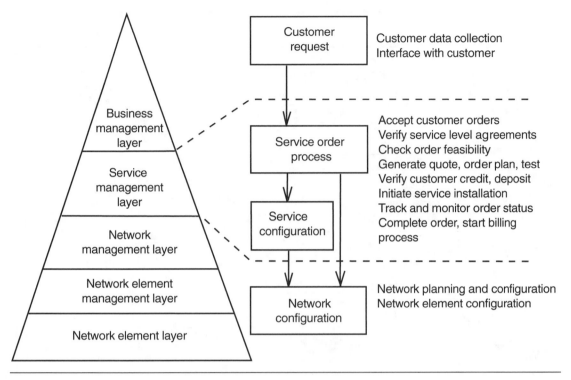

Figure 17.7
The service management level in TMN (partially adopted from [CHK97])

ment") but also takes into account the needs of the provider and its customers.

The process model described in section 17.5 slots into the service management layer of the TMN framework since it describes the operational processes required for providing services in a provider organization. In contrast to the TMN itself, the process model is not restricted only to the telecommunications network area.

Relevance of the TMN reference model

17.4.3   Framework Operating Concept

The framework operating concept (FOC; [HAW96]) is the result of extensive project experience we gained in connection with the structuring of provider organizations from different areas (public network and IT service providers, information departments in the automobile and chemical industries). As should be clear by the name itself, FOC is a framework that has been designed for the creation and implementation of operating concepts in the IT area. An operating concept

One of the preliminary projects we conducted: creation of a framework for operational concepts

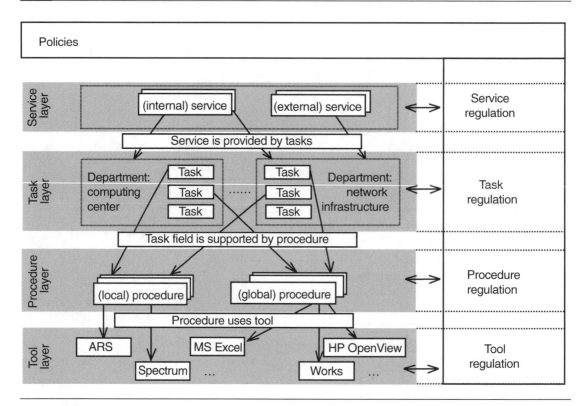

Figure 17.8
Framework operating concept

contains the organizational and technical specifications for the operation of networked systems that ensure that the corporate objectives associated with the system will be achieved. The specifications deal with organizational and operational structure, procedures for service- or process-related tasks, and the supporting tools.

The information that is important in conjunction with the FOC shown in Figure 17.8 can be summarized as follows:

Promoting the FOC: clear separation in terms of content between service, task, procedure, and tool in one operating concept

- An operating concept should specify what a provider organization is providing (*service*), who is involved in providing the service (*task*), how the task should be carried out (*procedure*), and what is used in the procedure (*tool*). These four aspects can be separated into individual entities in terms of content and described in a layered structure.

- All *services* are characterized by their content and by service level agreements that have been concluded. Services can be offered to internal as well as to external users. The difference is that internal services are offered only between the organizational units of the respective area of operation (e.g., between a computer center and a network control center), whereas external services are offered to customers who operate outside the respective area of operation.

- *Tasks* are controllable units within an organizational unit. They also include the assignment of personnel to certain tasks (role distribution). A distinction can be made between service-related tasks, which are directly associated with the provisioning of a service, and basic tasks, which are required for the implementation of a variety of services. An example of a basic task would be tuning measures to the networks and the computer systems used for the service-related tasks.

- When it comes to *procedures*, a distinction is made between local and global procedures. Local procedures would exist in only one organizational unit, whereas global procedures provide a horizontal function and are implemented in different organizational units. Examples of local procedures include network access procedures that specify the authorization and setting up of network access points and maintenance procedures for specific network, systems, and applications components. Problem reporting and accounting procedures are typical global procedures because they function only on a cross-departmental basis.

- A *tool* is interpreted as a technical system that supports certain steps described in a procedure.

- Regulating entities that can also be effective on a cross-layer basis exist at each layer of the FOC. The regulating part of the overall framework consists of *policies* that in turn define the required behavior of the objects and the subjects existing at the individual layers of the FOC. Examples of policies include directives dictating the conditions under which a task is to be carried out within a provider organization or how certain tools are to be used.

The framework operating concept is a pragmatic approach to structuring the diverse content of an operating concept and existing internal relationships and providing the appropriate descriptive framework. The process model introduced later and the specification of the processes with respect to tool functions concern the lower two layers of the framework operating concept.

Relationship between FOC and process model that follows

17.5 Introduction of a Process Model for Describing the Operation of Networked Systems

Motivation behind the process model: provider-accepted tools

Against the background of the preliminary work already described, this section introduces a process model that serves as the starting point of our discussion on management tool functions for the provider. The concept for the process model is kept as general as possible so that the model can be used in the process-oriented structuring of any provider organization.

The process-oriented approach that has been followed always keeps sight of the goal of the operation of the networked system: a guarantee of the quality of the IT services provided in accordance with the requirements of the IT user. Yet the process-oriented approach does not restrict itself only to individual areas or disciplines of networked systems (network, systems, applications, service, or enterprise management) or functional areas (configuration, performance, fault, security, and accounting; see Figure 1.3), but instead looks at the operation of networked systems across different areas and functions. The management functions and tools needed (described in earlier parts of this book) are integrated into the appropriate processes. Networked systems can operate effectively and efficiently only if proper interaction exists between the different (sub)processes.

17.5.1 The Three Central Operating Processes

IT operations are bound by two elementary conditions "toward the bottom (networked system) and toward the top (user)":

- The *networked system* with its network, systems, and application resources serves as the foundation and basis for IT operations.
- The goal of networked systems is to provide IT services with the service quality stipulated in the comprehensive service level agreement (SLA) with the customer.

Starting point: daily (routine) operational tasks

The overview of a networked system shown in Figure 17.9 follows the assumption that the operation is based on an existing networked system that was planned and installed beforehand. Certain routine tasks are carried out in order to provide services. Examples of these tasks include monitoring the functioning of the components, resetting individual components when a fault occurs, or implementing

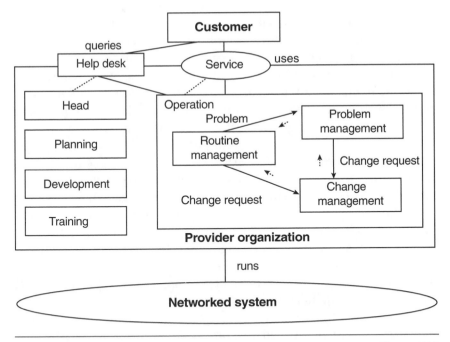

Figure 17.9
Central processes for the operation of a networked system

data backup to avoid any data loss. These tasks are consolidated into so-called *routine management*. To fulfil these tasks, routine management requires direct access to the network, systems, and application resources.

One of the main tasks of routine management is to detect any deviations from the target state of running operations. These deviations can include a partial or total breakdown of a component or an overloading of the network. If a problem that shows up cannot be resolved through measures that are part of routine management, a problem notification is sent to *problem management*. The fault is analyzed there, and a diagnosis of the possible cause is produced. This process is organized in the form of so-called support levels: If the problem cannot be diagnosed at one of the support levels, the process is escalated to the next highest level. A precise diagnosis will enable an efficient resolution of the fault. The task of repairing problems falls to problem management but can also be carried out by routine management or change management on the basis of an (internal) instruction.

Networked systems usually have the characteristic that they evolve themselves—for example, through the process of network and system

Transition from routine management to problem management

Networked systems are always undergoing change

components being exchanged and new versions of system and applications software being introduced on one or more systems. These major interventions into a networked system can be due to a number of different reasons (explained in detail later) and can be outside the scope of routine management. Instead, they are part of *change management*, in other words, a task area that is responsible for the careful planning of changes and ensuring that their implementation into a networked system is monitored and protected, particularly with a view toward minimizing the risk of violating existing service level agreements. New or changing customer requirements that are reflected in new or changing service level agreements can serve as the trigger for changes to networked systems. This always occurs when service level agreements cannot be fulfilled by routine management on an existing networked system. Another reason for a change could be the repair of a fault. If the intervention into a networked system by problem management exceeds a certain scope of responsibility, an appropriate change request is sent to change management.

Routine, problem, and change management are the three operational processes

Each of the three *operational* task areas of routine, problem, and change management is based on a *process* (to be introduced in the next chapter), which also explains why the term *operational process* is used in this context.

Within a provider organization, the three operational processes address all aspects relating to the technical operations of networked systems. However, these operational processes have no bearing on aspects such as contract design, training, or development, which likewise constitute task areas within provider organizations.

A close link exists between the process in the help desk and the operational processes

In addition to the interface supplied through the operational process of routine management, a second important interface exists to the customers that is realized through so-called *help desks*. Customers can use this interface to direct any of their queries to the provider organization. Queries that refer to operations but cannot be fully processed by the help desk are forwarded to the appropriate operational process. Customer queries that result in a change request are then forwarded to change management, and problem reports that the help desk is unable to resolve completely on its own are turned over as problem reports for processing by problem management.

17.5.2 Interfaces to the Help Desk and between Operational Processes

Help desks offer customers a uniform interface to operations and all other task areas within the provider organization. As already explained,

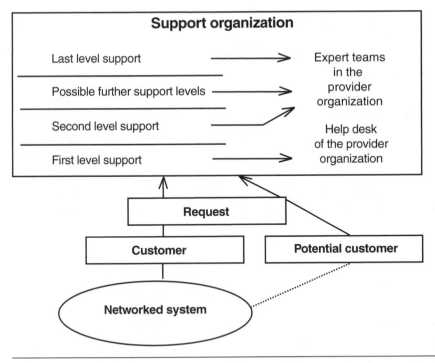

Figure 17.10
Structure of a support organization

the interface to operations is provided through the interaction between change management and problem management.

Help Desk—Change Management

A change request to a networked system received by the help desk from a customer is forwarded to change management. Change management also conveys information to the customer that is relevant in connection with the changes.

Help Desk—Problem Management

From the standpoint of problem management, the help desk is the first point of contact for the acceptance of problems reported by customers. This first point of contact is a component part of the support structure of the provider organization and is regarded as first-level support.

Help desk and problem processing constitute the support organization

As shown in Figure 17.10, in the view of the support structure, the interface from the help desk to problem management represents a transition from first-level support to second-level support. Beginning with second-level support, all other support levels are implemented within the problem management.

The close interplay that exists between the three operational processes is reflected in the form of the following interfaces.

Routine Management–Problem Management

Problem notifications are not only submitted by users but can also be sent directly from routine management to problem management. Similar to the procedure with the help desk, routine management first tries to resolve the situation that has occurred. Conversely, problem management instructs routine management to use a routine action in order to repair a problem or to help repair part of the problem.

Problem Management–Change Management

If a problem cannot be resolved totally or even partially through intervention by routine management and a change to the networked system is required, a transition is made from problem management to change management. The provider organization must therefore define precisely what the difference is between a routine action and a change because both actions are processed differently. The delineation between the two can vary according to provider organization, as we will see later.

Change Management–Routine Management

Changes are usually executed as a result of corresponding requests to routine management. The important effect of change management on this process is that it coordinates and therefore safeguards the intervention to networked systems carried out by routine management.

17.5.3   Allocation of Operational Occurrences to Operational Processes

The guidelines for establishing which operational occurrences are allocated to which operational processes or determining when the processing of an occurrence requires the transition to another operational process cannot be generalized or regulated for all provider organizations. The aim of Table 17.1, therefore, is merely to provide a guide to the type of allocation possible and should be adapted to suit the needs of the respective provider organization.

Table 17.1 Examples showing the delineation between routine actions, problems, and changes

Part of Networked System	Routine Actions	Problems	Changes
Network	Resetting a network component	Network component indicates a fault that cannot be repaired through a routine action	Introduction of a new network component
	Switching a backup connection	Interruption to a connection	Expansion of network through addition of additional backup lines
	Regular replacement of fans	Replacement of a faulty network component	Introduction of a new network technology (e.g., ATM)
			Planned interruptions to network connection
System	New user entry	User not able to access his or her system resources	Changes to access rights with high security risk
	Resetting a system	Partial or total breakdown of a computer system	Exchange of a defective computing system
	Execution of constant data backup	Fault in data backup that cannot be repaired through a routine action	Switch to another data backup system
Application	Entry of a user		Introduction of a new application or a new version of an application
	Assignment of rights for access to an application	User cannot access application	
	Reconfiguration of input–output channels		Mass configuration with far-reaching effects

The delineation of actions has far-reaching consequences

In actual provider organizations, the delineation between routine actions, problems, and changes depends to a great extent on the responsibility and competence awarded to the individual operational processes. Precise specifications are therefore necessary to clarify which (routine) actions are allowed to be carried out during routine management so as to allow any operational exceptions to be eliminated. This specification defines the dividing line between routine actions and faults. This is analogous to the definition of changes in the provider organization: When is intervention in the networked system allowed within the scope of routine management, and when should there first be a switch to change management? The key criterion for this decision has to do with the range of responsibility and interference risk associated with this intervention, and this can depend on two factors:

- Location in the networked system of the components in which intervention is taking place. Intervention to a central production server is more serious than the same intervention to a test server.

- Experience gained from the same intervention in the past. Interventions that initially take place over change management can turn into routine actions.

Specifications should be adapted to current state of knowledge

The last point emphasizes the importance of reviewing and revising the specifications drawn up by a provider organization in order to keep pace with constantly changing operational conditions and to guarantee that networked systems operate efficiently as well as safely.

Use of Management Tools in Operation

The process model developed for the operation of networked systems presented in the last chapter laid the foundation for the specification of management tools from the standpoint of the provider's requirements. An understanding of the operational sequence in the form of the three operational processes that were introduced is important because it provides the essential starting point from which providers can determine their requirements for management tools.

As shown in Figure 18.1, management tools represent a certain kind of computer-supported aid that providers can use in the design and efficient execution of their operational processes. This chapter introduces the term *process-oriented management means* (PoM) and clearly differentiates it from a management tool: A specific PoM is introduced as a result of an activity that is to be carried out within the scope of the operational process; a management tool is introduced as a result of the decision by the provider to provide this PoM on a computerized basis.

To a certain extent, the layer with the process-oriented management means represents a link between operational processes and management tools. This intermediary layer is helpful in ensuring that an analysis of the operational process is in the foreground when a provider's requirements are established. There is a special effort to avoid limiting the view of a tool function that already exists and usually originated solely from the view of the developer. The aim is therefore to avoid linking provider requirements too closely to what management tools offer today: First the provider requirements are clarified on the basis of the requested PoMs; then a determination is made whether and to what extent the management means can be supplied by one or several tool functions.

This clarification of the relationship between processes or operational sequences and the personnel and technical resources required

Operational processes and management tools

PoM stands for process-oriented management means

The aims of PoMs

Workflow management

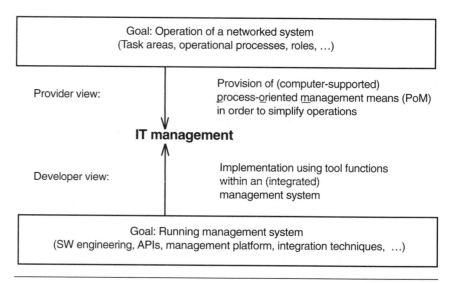

Figure 18.1
Relationship between a tool and a PoM

for their efficient execution is a central task of *workflow management*. Workflow management is based on the modeled (business) processes [VOB96], aiming to create from them "executable mappers" [JAB95]. A pragmatic and widely accepted definition of the word *workflow*, which originates from the *Workflow Management Coalition* (WfMC, [TAT97]), can be found in [WOR96]:

> Workflow is the automation of a business process, in whole or part, during which documents, information, or tasks are passed from one participant to another for action according to a set of procedural rules.

Despite intensive debates on the subject of process modeling and the workflow management associated with it, a consolidation of the different strains of thought [VOB96] has not yet been achieved. It is therefore not possible to orient the following observations about operational processes and the management tools used in them to any hard-and-fast specifications (e.g., in the form of a description technique for the processes). The description and structuring forms selected are purposely so general that WMF can easily be embedded, for instance, in a workflow reference model [HOL94].

Chapter structure and content
The requirements for the use of management tools are specified from the provider's view and the process-oriented management means needed. Section 18.1 begins by introducing the key types of PoMs that

appear in operational processes. Section 18.2 then goes on to describe a procedure for the systematic analysis of an operational process from the standpoint of the management functions required by the provider and supplied by the developer; process-oriented management means play a central role in this procedure. In the sections that follow, this procedure is then applied to the process model for the operation of networked systems that was presented in section 17.5; the different possible uses of the management tools and the related requirements from the provider's view are examined in detail for the three operational processes (routine management, problem management, change management). Particular attention is paid to the last operational process, change management.

18.1 Types of Process-Oriented Management Means for the Operation of Networked Systems

The different architectures and tools described in Parts II and III of this book gave an indication of the diverse and extensive possibilities available today to assist providers of networked systems in dealing efficiently with their processes (routine, problem, and change management). A systematic analysis of the actions carried out in the processes and of the process-oriented management means required is necessary in order to make these concepts and techniques suitable for use by providers.

Relationship to other parts of the book

Because of the extreme complexity and multifaceted aspect of the tasks involved, a large number of different types and versions of PoMs are needed for the operation of networked systems. Despite this fact, past experience in the operation of networked systems enables a differentiation between certain characteristic types of management means that appear in the different operational processes.

The descriptions of the types and versions of process-oriented management means introduced later are specifically not initially oriented toward the established architectural and tool definition world in the integrated management area (see the previous parts of the book for this information); the reason is that this would not have established a sufficient reference to the operational use of the PoMs and therefore to the provider's requirements. At first glance, the PoM types and versions may appear "traditional" and not very advanced technically. This is due to the aim of the approach, which largely seeks to derive the management means from the operational processes and not from the

Designations selected for PoM types and versions are consciously "traditional"

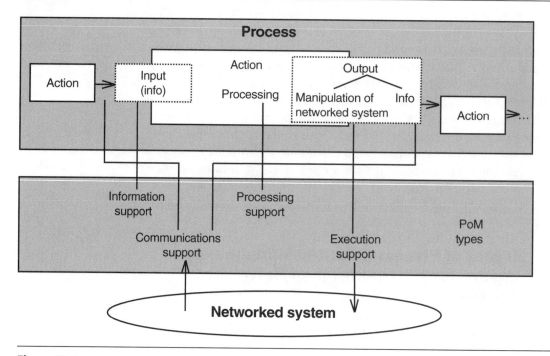

Figure 18.2
PoM types

rapidly changing tool technologies. The implementation into the very advanced tool technologies that promote integration, such as CORBA, Desktop Management, and WBEM, does not take place until the second step (see Chapters 7 to 9). Important advances have been made at the tool level because the PoMs identified are largely available on a computerized basis and with a minimum of media breaks, thereby resulting in the desired efficiency gain in the operational processes.

Classification of PoMs   As Figure 18.2 shows, the three different types of process-oriented management means that appear in the operation of networked systems can be derived appropriately from the observation of any one action occurring in the operational process. These three PoM types—*information support, communication support,* and *processing support*—clearly show that the information aspect plays an important role in the specification of management means for the operation of networked systems. This type of process-oriented management means supplies providers with the information needed to carry out work on a networked system at the right time and at the right place. The fourth PoM type, called *execution support,* comprises all the management means that offer providers with direct support for executing a specific activity on their networked systems.

The aspect relating to the support aids needed to execute activities is not particularly detailed in the process descriptions and workflow approaches that currently exist. For example, the workflow reference model [HOL94] introduces nondifferentiated applications concealing all sorts of computer-supported functions. In addition to applications, [JAB95] also explicitly incorporates noncomputerized functions for supporting manually executed activities in the workflow.

Specifications generated by workflow management

The four types of PoMs that are suitable for our purposes are defined more closely in the following sections on the basis of a description of the characteristic attributes of process-oriented management means for the operation of networked systems.

18.1.1 Information Support

Suitable carriers for the acceptance of the information required for the operation of a networked system are a prerequisite for the efficient processing and distribution of this information within the provider organization. Some of the information carriers required to execute activities in the operational processes are:

Carriers of management information in a process

- *Configuration bases:* Contain relevant configuration information—such as type, location, and addressing information—for components of networked systems.

- *Monitors:* Contain current status information (e.g., load state, faults) for components in networked systems.

- *Logbooks:* Contain descriptions of historical situations to document events or circumstances in the IT operation. The form of the entries can be specified by predefined information fields.

The preceding list of examples of process-oriented management means is not meant to be complete and will be expanded upon and defined in conjunction with the description of the three operational processes (sections 18.3 to 18.5).

The first two examples of information support listed contain important information about components in networked systems. The *management information bases* (MIBs) described in Chapters 5 and 6 of this book provide an important foundation for this kind of standardized information. The information is provided by the management means that support information transport and is described later.

Information support is closely associated with the class of management tools referred to as *data storage tools*. These types of PoMs supply the information required for the operation of networked systems, such as the configuration base that should be filed in a data storage tool. The documentation systems discussed in section 14.3 can be clearly allocated to the class of data storage tools.

A data storage tool is used by all the other management tools to store the information needed or produced by these tools. A *monitoring tool* therefore provides the current status of the component provided as information support by a PoM "monitor" at appropriate locations in the operational processes. Status monitoring of resources and threshold value monitoring (see section 13.2), which are implemented as basic applications in management platforms, are typical functions of monitoring tools.

18.1.2 Communication Support

Two concrete management means are used to clarify the function of communication support:

Exchange of management information between actions in a process

- *Request/job forms:* Forms have a defined layout that specifies the information fields and their position in the form. An information field consists of a description field and an input field. The provider sometimes specifies which information fields must be filled in by the party making the request and which field entries are optional. The precise framework stipulated through the form structure simplifies the systematic processing of queried information.

- *Work progress slips:* This is a special type of form that is passed on after various actions of a process have taken place. The work progress slip has one or more information fields that are used to describe each of the processing points that have been passed. When a work progress slip is received, the information contained on the slip is usually first checked to determine which of the processing points on the slip have already run through.

Special role of management agents and protocols

A totally different type of communication support is used to extract relevant information about operations from the networked system itself. The *management agents* and *protocols* described in connection with management architectures in Part II are used in this case. Since a provider only indirectly comes in contact with these technical components (through the use of the appropriate processing support described later), they do not appear explicitly at the level of the operational processes and therefore are not classified as *process-oriented management means*.

The exact nature of communication support heavily depends on the information being transported. If the information carrier is in a paper form, the communication support used in a provider organization can be the interoffice mail for internal communication and facsimile or the public postal system for external communication. The variety of possible management means increases if the information is stored electronically. In this case, all forms of computer communication can be used as communication support; examples include email, file transfer, and especially, the WWW. Web technology offers providers numerous options, specifically (also see Chapter 9) because of its capability to provide and communicate forms (through appropriate dynamic Web pages) through electronic means. The goal is to use computer-supported solutions to achieve a greater uniformity in communication channels, and this is possible only if there is an integration of solutions at the technical level.

The management means used for communication within operational processes, such as forms and work progress slips, can easily be implemented and processed electronically. Systems that support computerized processing originate from the workflow management area where they are referred to as *workflow support tools.*

18.1.3   Processing Support

As shown in Figure 18.2, certain information and communication support entities provide the input and output information for processing support.

Processing of management information within a process action

Examples of different types of PoMs for processing support include:

- *Checklists:* A certain type of form for the structured querying of conditions that must be met before one or more actions can be executed. A checklist contains information fields, each of which queries an aspect that requires checking. Each information field is processed so that the appropriate aspect is checked and the corresponding results based on the performance level are achieved and other related comments are documented.

- *Checking support:* A management means that monitors specific stipulations for IT operations and produces a reaction if any irregularities occur. The information required is the observed current information and the requested target information. An example of checking support is a network status monitor, which is used to check whether the current status of components used in a networked system corresponds to the desired target status. The previous checklists also have the character of checking support because they systematically provide information on whether a certain aspect of IT operations has actually been fulfilled.

- *Analysis support:* Analysis support helps operating personnel to reach an immediate decision through an analysis of a situation that has occurred during an action. As input, this management means requires peripheral and background information that can be used as the basis for the analysis and decision making. In addition to the input information, a certain type of knowledge is required to provide analysis and decision support. The peripheral and background information required can be entered interactively, controlled by the process-oriented management means. The process is completed as soon as the person using the PoM is able to reach a decision.

The management means that offer the provider processing support conceal management functions that process the given input information in different forms.

If the processing involves an analysis of information (such as PoM problem diagnosis support), the relevant management means can be provided on a computerized basis by a *diagnostic tool.* If the processing involves a preparation of information (e.g., in the form of statistics; PoM statistics generator), the management means are provided on a computerized basis by a *reporting tool.* Note that the statistics resulting from this process represent a separate PoM offering the provider information support. These types of tools were covered extensively in connection with the stand-alone test and monitoring tools (Chapter 12) and management applications run on integrated platforms (section 13.3).

18.1.4　Execution Support

The fourth and last differentiated type of PoM supports providers directly with the work carried out to the components of networked systems. The processing within an action determines exactly which activities are involved.

Support of intervention into networked system

Management means allocatable to the PoM type execution support can be divided into two categories:

- *Configuration and control:* Using the management means for configuration and control, a provider is able to change the current configuration parameters set in a component and intervene in the networked system for control purposes. The management means can provide further support by alerting the provider to inconsistencies in the configuration changes or suggesting or directly carrying out useful configurations. This provides a fluid transition to automated configuration.

- *Automation:* This involves management that allow one or more actions to be carried out totally or partially without any intervention or support by operating personnel. Automation support normally requires availability of the appropriate control information (e.g., in the form of operating scripts or redundant resources with fail-over rules). Once the automation support mechanism has been set, there is normally no further interaction between operating personnel and this management means. However, operating personnel must monitor operations closely to ensure that the automation support is functioning correctly, which is why this management means contains process-oriented aspects and therefore is regarded as a PoM.

There is a direct correlation between this type of management means and management tools that require the appropriate execution support requested by the provider. It should be emphasized that management means of the execution support type inevitably have to be provided on a computer-supported basis; this requirement does not apply to the three other types of PoMs.

18.1.5   Relationship between PoMs and Management Tools

The different types of PoMs offer a new view of the management tools that are used in the operation of networked systems. This view emanates from the provider and the work processes it provides. The work processes describing the operation of a networked system were introduced as three operational processes in the last chapter. As the preceding discussion and Figure 18.3 show, there is an evident connection between the PoM types presented and the management tools that were extensively dealt with in Part III of this book. Certain classes of management tools are suitable for providing certain types of PoMs on a computerized basis. PoMs (types) and management tools (classes) are loosely connected, which means that a clear differentiation is not always possible.

A new view of management tools

Goal and purpose of PoM types

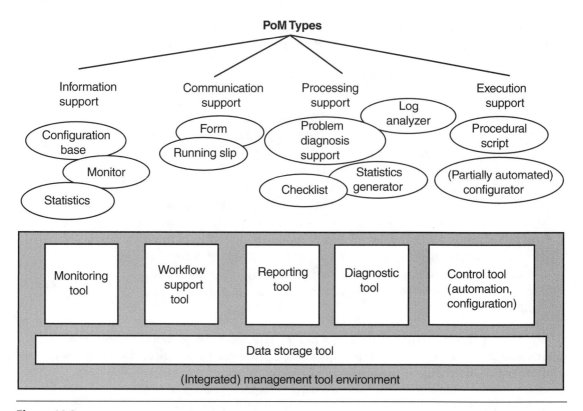

Figure 18.3
Allocation of management tools to PoMs

The list of PoM types described is not meant to be exhaustive or universally valid. It instead constitutes a first attempt at exploring and categorizing the tools of the trade for the operation of networked systems. Furthermore, the list is used in the procedure introduced in section 18.2 to provide a systematic allocation of the PoMs required for the execution of each operational process.

18.2   Pragmatic Procedure for the Determination of Provider-Oriented Tool Functions

Starting point: the process model introduced in the last chapter

The process model presented in the last chapter provides an organization of logical task areas, and the processes to carry out these tasks, that could be applicable to almost any provider organization. It goes without saying that the model can provide only general specifications with a certain level of detail because starting from a certain level the features that appear are specific to a provider organization and cannot be generalized.

A knowledge of the processes involved in the operation of networked systems is essential for the developer of management tools. Basically, each segment of an operational process should be examined from the standpoint of which management tool functionality should be offered to the staff involved in this part of the process. This lays the groundwork for a provider-based analysis of the management tools required or the functionality provided by these tools. Particular attention is initially paid to those tool functions that support the general parts of the process description; these functionalities can be seen as *generic* in the sense that they can be used directly in any networked system environment. Tool functions that cover process segments tending to deal with specific aspects are provided either through the appropriate expansion or customizing of generic tool functions or through specialized tool functions.

Goal: an analysis of requirements for management tools from the view of the provider

Generic and specific tool functionality

A simple initial example is provided by the following description: The network and system components are monitored within the framework of routine management. An activity that falls under the general part of the process description is the facility of being able to specify the status of each component. The appropriate generic tool functionality for status queries is requested at one or sometimes different points in the process of routine management; this kind of status query and status change function was described within the framework of the specification for the systems management function in OSI management. In this example, the specific part of the process description contains all those aspects of status monitoring that mirror the special requirements of the provider and cannot be supplied directly by generic functions. These aspects can relate to:

Introductory example

- How the status information is represented by a tool
- An appropriate mechanism for changing the status information provided by the generic function
- How special actions are used to react to certain status changes

The introduction of process-oriented management means and their organization into four types was a deliberate attempt to address the issue of tool support from the standpoint of the provider. Used within a systematic approach, the PoMs close the gap between the *requirements* of the provider from the standpoint of its work ("requires") and the *offering* of a developer from the standpoint of the management tools provided ("enables").

Role of PoMs

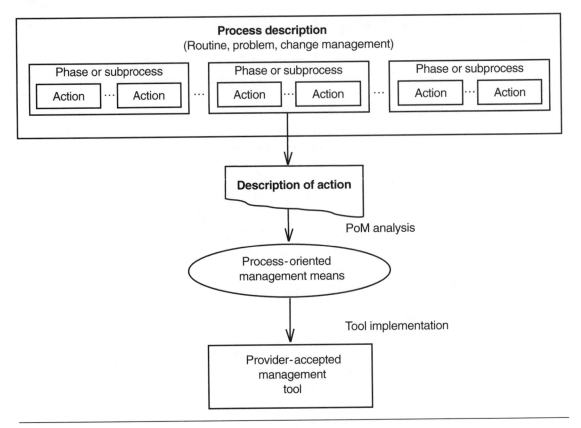

Figure 18.4
An overview of the procedure

The individual steps involved in the procedure presented in the overview in Figure 18.4 are explained in the sections that follow.

18.2.1   Process Description

The approach to process description pursued here

There are many areas within and outside the sphere of informatics where a need exists to describe the content of processes [VOB96]. Yet it should be emphasized that there is no generally accepted single definition of the process concept and that, because of the very different objectives that exist in connection with processes, it would be impossible to supply one. It is a similar case with the techniques used for describing these processes [HUP97]. A simple and easily comprehended description and structuring approach that examines the content of each operational process suffices for the objective here that forms the basis for the description of operational processes.

The first thing that needs to be determined within the framework of the procedure followed here for process description is whether the respective operational process can be divided into large time-delineated blocks. These blocks are referred to as *phases* of the operational process. The definition of the phases allows a rough structuring of the overall process along the time axis. There are processes to which this kind of structuring is not appropriate (e.g., in the case of the parallel operation of the time-delineated blocks of a process). These processes are not divided into phases but instead into *subprocesses*.

Phases versus subprocesses

The actual content of each phase or each subprocess is described according to the specification of the actions that are executed therein.

Actions as the smallest units in a process description

18.2.2   Action Description

The actions identified in the process description are the main subject of investigation in the further operation of the procedure. The following aspects can be relevant to an understanding of an action:

Content of an action description

- Goal and purpose of the action
- Input and output behavior of the action
- (Process) state before and after execution of the action
- Participants in the execution of the action (personnel resources)
- Components of the networked system used in the execution of the action (technical resources)
- Information used and processed during the action

The process description approach followed here is referred to as *activity-oriented process description*. Refer to the literature [COR97, DAD97, VOB96] for information that distinguishes between the process description approaches (e.g., object oriented).

Selected form of process description

18.2.3   Analysis of Requested PoMs and Their Implementation into Tools

The process-oriented management means identified for each action in the following step of the procedure constitute a particularly interesting aspect of the process description. In this connection, an orientation exists to the list of PoM types given in the last section in which the type needed for each support aspect occurring in the action is determined and an indication of the process-oriented management

PoMs selected for each action

means is introduced. Each management means appearing in the table is described informally and positioned in the overall relationship of the process.

From PoM to management tool

The transition from the provider view to the developer view occurs at this point in the procedure. Each of the management means appearing and being used in an operational process can be implemented through the use of computerized tool functions provided by a management system.

Identifying provider requirements

The provider's demands on the system are essentially mirrored by what the operator has to do and in certain functional or performance-related quality features. These operational requirements provide the developer with important guidance on how to design the tool functions in the event that the process-oriented management means are to be computerized within a management system. Attention thereby must be paid to a provider-accepted implementation of the operating requirements to a user interface design and the algorithmic conversion of the functional requirements of the provider.

Content of following sections

The procedure described is applied to the three operational processes outlined in the following sections. Change management (section 18.5) is given particular attention because of the interest in using this operational process to show how the provider's requirements for management tools can be converted into a provider-accepted tool implementation (section 18.6).

18.3 Routine Management

Kernel process of operation

Routine management can be viewed as the core process of the operation of a networked system. The use of routine measures allows services to be provided for the customer with the agreed-on quality. However, there must first be an assurance that the networked system is installed in a suitable configuration guaranteed by change management, and is installed in a largely fault-free state guaranteed by problem management.

A graphic overview and informal introduction of the three operational processes appeared in section 17.5. These operational processes will now be looked at in depth on the basis of the pragmatic procedures described in the last section, with routine management playing a key role in establishing the provider requirements for tool functions with routine management.

Activity cycle

Routine management is characterized by a cycle in which certain types of activities run in parallel with one another and constantly re-

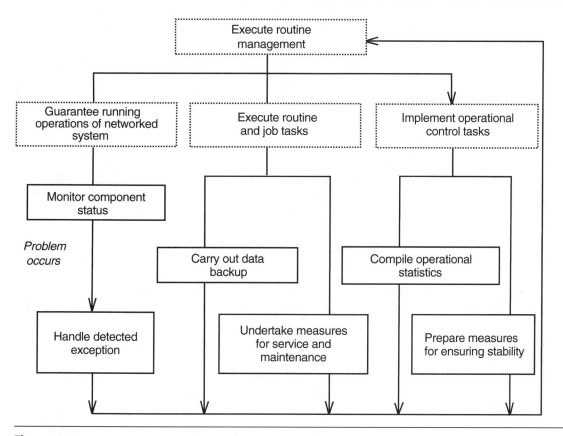

Figure 18.5
The routine management process

peat themselves. Because of this characteristic the operational process cannot be divided into phases and instead operates in parallel with the subprocesses provided.

As Figure 18.5 shows, a distinction is made between three subprocesses to which the key actions of the entire process can be allocated. The process structure is kept general so that the actions in principle occur in the routine management of every organization that operates a networked system. It is taken for granted that the process content cannot be complete. The approaches described in [CCT97, MOL94] have been incorporated into the proposal presented here for the structure of routine management.

Three subprocesses of routine management

Subprocess ⟨Guarantee Running Operations of Networked System⟩

Monitoring components in a networked system

All the actions that directly affect the running operations of the components of a networked system are combined in this subprocess of routine management. This includes the action ⟨*monitor component status*⟩ through which the operating status of all the network, system, and applications components involved in affecting the service level agreements (SLAs) are monitored. If any deviations from the desired operating status are established, then the action ⟨*handle detected exception*⟩ is executed. If the exception cannot be resolved completely within this action, a changeover takes place to the process of problem management or of change management.

Subprocess ⟨Execute Routine and Job Tasks⟩

Intervention into a networked system

The routine and job tasks that are part of routine management are each executed in the appropriate action. Two examples are shown here.

The action ⟨*carry out data backup*⟩ describes one of the particularly important routine tasks. This action ensures that access to consistent data is still possible after the breakdown of one or more computer systems.

The activities involved in the action ⟨*undertake measures for service and maintenance*⟩ differ considerably depending on the IT components that appear in the networked system being operated. Typical examples of these activities are the initiation of self-tests or a check of the functionality of expendable parts (e.g., on printers).

Subprocess ⟨Implement Operational Control Tasks⟩

Short-term planning

This subprocess of routine management comprises actions that concern the short-term planning of the operation of a networked system. The request usually takes place in the form of regular status dialogs that occur at frequent intervals (e.g., daily).

The action ⟨*compile operational statistics*⟩ provides the basis for short-term planning within routine management. An operating statistic provides information about the running operations of the networked system.

Speedy action may be necessary in routine management to counteract situations that could also threaten the provider's ability to comply with the SLA guarantee to the customer. This can particularly be the case when serious faults occur or a short-term overloading of the networked system could not be foreseen. This objective is pursued through the action ⟨*prepare measures for ensuring stability*⟩. The de-

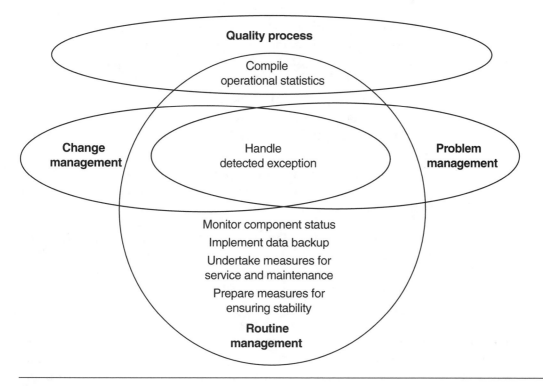

Figure 18.6
Central position of routine management

cision of which measure should be undertaken in this case is usually based on the specifications generated by the problem management process.

The actions introduced here emphasize that routine management is at the center of the process model because it is where all areas that come into play in the operation of a networked system are linked together. As Figure 18.6 clarifies, the action ⟨handle detected exception⟩ serves to describe the transition from routine management to the two other operational processes.

Transitions to the other two operational processes

The action ⟨compile operational statistics⟩ produces a transition to another type of process that can be viewed as having a direct relationship to the operational processes. The aim of these processes, called *quality processes*, is to monitor and guarantee the quality of the operational processes. The operating statistics supplied by routine management represent an important source of quality information for this purpose. Quality processes are covered in depth in Chapter 19.

Reference to quality processes

Certain management tools can be used to provide the computer-supported PoMs required by routine management personnel in the three "interface" actions of routine management mentioned.

Management tool requirements in the actions

- The action ⟨monitor component status⟩ represents a key element in the analysis of management tools in routine management. In other actions of routine management, tools for network and systems management play only a subordinate role.

- The action ⟨carry out data backup⟩ is mostly executed by the respective data backup systems. These special automation tools for the operation of networked systems will not be dealt with further here.

- Different kinds of automation tools that have little relationship to management tools are also used in the action ⟨undertake measures for service and maintenance⟩.

To a limited extent, certain derivations from the measures for supported management tools can be used by a provider in the action ⟨prepare measures to ensure stability⟩. A quality process called ⟨operational quality monitoring and assurance⟩, which is introduced in Chapter 19, covers this in depth.

Specification of three actions in routine management   Three actions of routine management—⟨monitor component status⟩ and the two "interface" actions ⟨handle detected exception⟩ and ⟨compile operational statistics⟩—are therefore analyzed in a PoM context. The provider's requirements are then given for each of the management tools used for converting this PoM on a computer-supported basis.

18.3.1   Monitor Component Status

An indication about the status of the running networked system can be supplied only if the appropriate information is delivered directly or indirectly from the individual components. If this status information is available, it is evaluated within the action with the aim of establishing any deviations from the target state. This kind of deviation of the actual status from the target status is referred to as an exception and will be explained in more detail as an action of routine management (see Table 18.1).

Relevant management tools   The management agents and protocols shown in italics in Figure 18.7 are not process-oriented management means. They provide the basis for enabling the management means ⟨monitor⟩ to receive the management information needed by the components of the networked system.

As Figure 18.7 shows, the management protocol and the management agent are used by a monitoring tool that implements the PoM

Table 18.1 Support needed in the action ⟨monitor component status⟩

Support Requirements	Type	PoM
Information about which components in the networked systems are to be monitored	Information	Configuration base
Availability of status information	Information	Monitor
	Communication	(Management agents, management protocols)
Display of status information	Information	Monitor
Evaluation of status information	Processing	Operational monitoring sheet

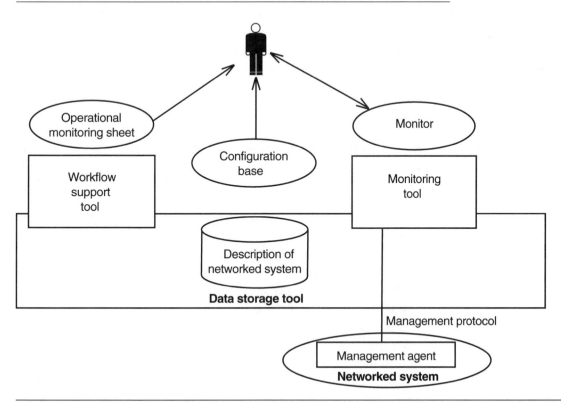

Figure 18.7
Action ⟨monitor component status⟩

⟨monitor⟩. Another tool that is essential in addition to the monitoring tool is a data storage tool, which provides the PoMs ⟨configuration base⟩ on a computer-supported basis. Furthermore, a workflow support tool can be used for forwarding and storing the PoM ⟨operational monitoring sheet⟩.

The following section clarifies which process-oriented management means are required by the provider within this action and the requirements for providing them on a computer-supported basis.

Configuration Base

The configuration base is a fundamental management resource for the operation of networked systems and contains important information about the components used in the system. The configuration base can be viewed as a "basic management resource" since it is used as information support in numerous actions occurring in routine, problem, and change management. The PoM ⟨configuration base⟩ can be accessed whenever specific basic information is required about the component of a networked system. At this juncture, the specifications for *managed objects* (see Chapters 5 and 6) defined within the information models of the different management architectures supply the essential information source.

Fundamental ⟨basic management means⟩

Content　　From the view of the provider, the following different types of basic information should be provided:

- Information about the various participants. The names of the manufacturer, the supplier, and the responsible staff member within the provider organization are relevant to each network, system, or applications component used. Other details, such as a customer service contact or the provider to be used in an emergency (hotline), can also be entered into the configuration base.

- Commercial and legal information. This includes all information concerning the financial or legal aspects relating to a component, such as procurement price, inventory number, details on licensing, maintenance, and depreciation.

- Equipment information. The type designation assigned by the manufacturer and a possible general type designation provide detailed information about the technical characteristics of network, system, and applications components. This also includes the development level (e.g., storage development stage, network connections) in which the component is used.

- Configuration information. This type of basic information represents the nucleus of the configuration base. This information (depending on the type of component) establishes the settings of the components made by the manufacturer or selected by the provider itself. Examples of this comprehensive type of information are network addresses allocated by the manufacturer and the provider, the current software version being run, buffer lengths, routing tables, and other control information on algorithms that are run in the respective network, systems, or applications component.

The provider's requirements for data storage tools that provide a computer-supported configuration database for networked systems include:

Provider requirements

- Support in setting up a configuration base that meets the provider's requirements. Many of the configuration bases available today for the operation of networked systems have evolved historically and are limited in their ability to meet requirements resulting from the operational processes. As a result, a reorganization of the existing configuration base is often needed, thereby necessitating the appropriate tool functions for data modeling. There has to be an assurance that the data model actually reflects the provider's requirements.

- Support in ensuring that data is consistent. In complex networked system environments, the configuration base consists of a variety of different data sources. The content of the data sources is usually not disjunctive, meaning that the same information can appear in different places. Appropriate tool functions can ensure that the information in the configuration base is consistent; they can also verify the validation of the information. These functions are achieved either by merging the data sources or by using reliable update mechanisms.

- Faster and easier access. If it has been ascertained that the configuration base contains the information necessary for operation, there has to be a guarantee that this information will also be available at the right time and in the right place. The issue of access organization is closely linked to the issue of distributed and redundant data storage.

Operational Monitoring Sheet

Measurable requirements for components in networked systems

For routine management, operational monitoring sheets describe concrete, that is, measurable, requirements for the operation of the network, systems, and applications components that make up the networked system. They are therefore component-oriented SLAs (in contrast to service-oriented SLAs). Because of the complex interaction between components and other factors (such as fault and load situations) [DRK97, FLY94], there is no complete or satisfactory answer to the question determining which operational requirements should be placed on interacting network, systems, and applications components in order to achieve a certain service quality.

Content

The content of an operational monitoring sheet can be structured in accordance with the five management functional areas:

1. *Configuration*
   - Information about location.
   - Unique address or names (e.g., IP address, computer name).
   - Version state.
   - Equipment type and number.
2. *Faults*
   - Online availability. With applications, this information can be obtained directly from the service level agreement. For network and system components, the aim is to achieve the highest availability level possible.
   - Monitoring online availability. The tools (also see PoM ⟨monitor⟩) used to monitor online availability are indicated in this location on the operational monitoring sheet.
   - Maintenance and security windows. A window in which certain routine and job requests are undertaken must be provided for each component of a networked system. These windows should be incorporated into the operational monitoring sheet and strictly adhered to by routine management personnel.
   - Information about problem repair. This category includes the assignment of contact names. Other information could relate to existing backup options for minimizing the impact of problems.
3. *Performance*
   - Specification of capacity needs. At this location in the operational monitoring sheet, an estimate is made of the processing performance required for the applications along with the requirements for main and backup in order to specify a minimum capacity for the computer hardware.

- Response times. The response times to be complied with are contained in the SLA and should be communicated to the network, systems, and applications components used. We have already discussed the difficulties that arise in connection with complex networked systems.
- Monitoring response times. At this location, there is a reference to the tools used to monitor response times (also see PoM ⟨monitor⟩).

4. *Accounting*

- Accounting number. Information about accounting procedures relevant to (routine) management (e.g., charge back data).

5. *Security*

- Security provisions existing for a particular component.
- Information about security procedures relevant to (routine) management (e.g., authentication and access controls).

A provider's main requirements for workflow support tools for providing computer-supported operational monitoring sheets can be summarized as follows:

Provider requirements

- Support functions for the generation of the sheets. When new service level agreements are drawn up or existing ones modified, the requirements for the quality of the operation of the components in the networked system also change. Thus, for example, network and system components sometimes have to be expanded or upgraded in order to achieve suitable response times.

- Easy and constant access to operating personnel. The content of the operational monitoring sheets for this condition are stored and maintained electronically. Integration should be promoted with other documentation bases, such as those provided by the PoM ⟨configuration base⟩, to avoid a duplication in the storage of the same information and to avoid the possibility of inconsistencies.

- Support in setting the PoM ⟨monitor⟩. The central information contained in the operational monitoring sheets can be used to advantage in the specification of the monitors used in operations. The support of this mapping of content from the operational monitoring sheets to the monitors is an important requirement of providers.

Monitor

Monitors represent a central process-oriented management means for the provider to record and evaluate the current status of resources in a networked system [HOJ97]. In Chapter 13, the management functions needed for this kind of PoM were introduced and described in detail as the basic applications provided by an integrated management platform. In terms of content, the monitoring aspects that have to be dealt with by a provider in routine management are:

Status monitoring of operated components

- Monitoring basic functioning. An identification is required of the components that are not even capable of entering into a functioning state due to defects. This kind of monitoring is especially difficult with defects that do not show up as normal allocatable symptoms.

- Monitoring of operational requirements. Operational requirements are specified for each component in the operational monitoring sheet (e.g., information about availability and performance). The information included in an operational monitoring sheet is similar to the information that appears in the service level agreement described in Chapter 17. The key difference is that a monitor usually supplies component-related information rather than service-related information. The allocation of component-related information to the respective services is not an easy task.

Specification of monitoring function based on component type

The individual component types of a networked system provide a further basis for the specification of monitoring tasks undertaken by a provider. The expanded management information bases (MIBs) standardized and supplied by vendors in the *network* component area offer an important monitoring basis. Records of traffic streams can provide information about the (fault and load) state of communication networks.

In the *systems* area, along with the respective MIBs, the operating systems also offer monitoring functions that characteristically reproduce the state of the computer system. The system MIBs for workstations and PCs are based on those MIBs. In the mainframe area, for example, MVS, operating systems and enhanced vendor-specific tools provide extensive and wide-ranging monitoring functions.

Applications are essentially monitored for the provider at the system level. Extensive monitoring functions can also be incorporated within individual applications. However, these functions are frequently not visible to the provider but help an application to cope independently with critical situations (e.g., resource bottlenecks or errors) without the need for operator intervention (e.g., SAP R/3, [BUG95]). From the standpoint of the operator, it would be desirable to have a monitor that could be used for a large number if not all applications, and this issue is the subject of important research taking place in the area of integrated management [BRU96, CHW97].

The following are important requirements of providers for monitoring tools that offer computer-supported management means for monitors:

Provider requirements

- Integration of monitors. It would be impossible to have one monitor system that integrates all monitoring aspects. Instead, different systems incorporating relevant monitoring concepts are required to deal with the different monitoring tasks that arise in the network, systems, and application areas. This multitude of different systems makes it difficult to follow systematic procedures based on the operational monitoring sheets. It is therefore essential that monitors are integrated from the standpoint of the provider.

- Clear display of critical situations. Monitors are used in routine management for the fast and reliable detection of critical operating situations. In this case, it is necessary that a monitor not only recognizes a critical situation (also see requirements on operating monitoring sheet) but that it also makes it obvious to operating personnel. A problem that arises in this connection is the handling and display of sequence errors that occur as a result of a critical situation [DEV92].

18.3.2 Handle Detected Exception

Clarification is required if an exception, in other words, a deviation of the current state from the target state, is detected. If the exception cannot be dealt with completely within the action of the routine management process, then a fault message is generated and forwarded to problem management, or a change request is supplied and made accessible to change management.

Handling an identified (routine management) exception

Only a limited amount of processing of an exception can and should be carried out by routine management (also see section 17.5). The analysis conducted by routine management establishes whether the exception can be dealt with through an appropriate routine action in the networked system. If routine management is able to deal completely with the exception, it directly carries out or initiates the necessary measures (see Table 18.2).

Table 18.2 Support requirements in the action ⟨handle detected exception⟩

Support Requirements	Type	PoM
Recording of exception and the supplementary information important for the analysis	Information	Operational logbook
Support in determining the cause	Processing	Exception evaluation support
Support in the execution of the short-term measures to be taken	Execution	Routine action support
Generation and forwarding of a problem notification	Communication	Problem notification form
Generation of a report for change management	Communication	Change request form

Relevant management tools

Operational logbooks, problem notification forms, and change request forms are the information and job objects provided as process-oriented management means and needed by operating personnel to carry out an action (see Figure 18.8). At least these forms (and the necessary distribution lists) should be prepared (and forwarded) electronically by a workflow support tool for the computer-supported distribution of the problem notification forms and change request forms to the appropriate locations.

Providers also want suitable computer-supported management means for coping with the "creative" part of an action, namely, the analysis of a problem and the potential repair. The PoM ⟨exception assessment support⟩ is part of the diagnostic tool. A routine action support tool must always be a computer-supported control tool because the execution of the corresponding routine action in the networked system has a direct controlling effect on the respective IT component(s).

Documentation of operational exceptions

Operational Logbook

Operational exceptions that arise in routine management should be appropriately documented. Operational logbooks are used by providers

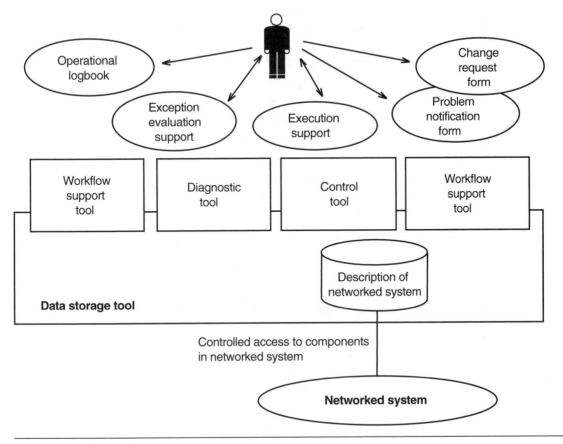

Figure 18.8
Action ⟨handle detected exception⟩

for this purpose. The entries that are made overlap to a degree with the content of the problem notification forms or change request forms that are described here.

The typical information fields that should be included in entries to operational logbooks are: Content

- Identification of the person making the entry (e.g., name or clear job title)
- Time when the entry was made
- Particulars about the exception
    - Selection of a class to which the exception can be allocated
    - Time when the exception was discovered in routine management
    - The components in the networked system that caused the exception or are affected by it

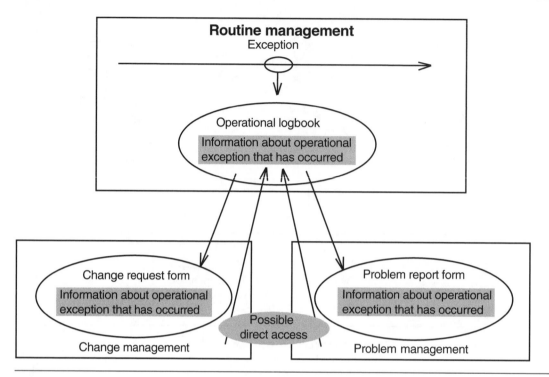

Figure 18.9
Classification of PoM ⟨operational logbook⟩

  – Other symptoms established in connection with the exception

- Analysis of the exception (including indications to related exceptions)

  – Assessment of the consequences
  – Assignment of a priority to determine the urgency for correcting the exception (e.g., high, medium, low), often based on perceived consequences

- Description of measures undertaken (including an indication of whether the exception could be corrected or a problem notification has been generated)

Relationship to other PoMs

If routine management is not able to process the exception completely, the content of this list should be totally or partially adopted into the problem notification form or the change request form (see Figure 18.9).

Problems relating to the delineation of responsibility and competence

The quality and the detail of the information noted in an operational logbook depends on a number of different factors. A major factor is the time allowed to personnel for documenting the executed activities.

The more important the documentation aspect is to a provider organization, the more precise and reliable the information entered into the logbook will be. Another factor is the competence of the operating personnel in routine management and, directly linked to that, the accountability and competence interfaces between routine management and the other two operational processes defined in the respective provider organization. The more competent the staff engaged in routine management is, the clearer the lines of authority and consequently the higher the intensity and quality of the processing of exceptions. The basic principle is that the more extensively an exception is processed in routine management, the fewer the number of problem notifications and change requests that have to be generated. Furthermore, the analysis by routine management will enable problem and change management to process problem notifications more quickly.

In many provider organizations operational logbooks are still being filled in manually. Workflow support tools must meet the following requirements to provide computer-supported process-oriented management means:

Provider requirements

- Appropriate access possibilities. In principle, it should be possible for all personnel in routine management to make entries to the operational logbook at any time. If possible, access should be available from each workplace.

- Easy operation. The operation essentially consists of filling out a form; consequently, the form should be structured so there is enough free space for describing the operational problem. The functions of a standard text editor familiar to operational personnel should be used to input the text. It should not be necessary to make manual entries for fields in which content can be extracted from a given operational situation (e.g., unique identification of the person making the entry or of the component concerned). Part of the time problem mentioned will be eliminated if this information can be generated automatically.

- Forwarding possibilities to the other operational processes. A major advantage of computer-supported operational logbooks is that documented operational exceptions can be electronically processed within the actions that follow. Flexible options should therefore exist for inserting the information from an operational logbook into the corresponding forms for forwarding to problem or change management. As shown in Figure 18.9, the availability of access to operational logbooks from other operational processes can contribute substantially toward increasing the efficiency of communication within an organization.

Exception Assessment Support

Target–actual comparison

If an exception occurs—i.e., a predetermined operational target value (PoM ⟨operational monitoring sheet⟩) does not agree with the actual value established—routine management must decide how to deal with the exception. The exceptions that can occur in a system are so diverse that it takes competent and appropriately trained personnel to execute them. A variety of different sources of information (e.g., extensive system documentation on the network, systems, and application components used) is available to personnel for this purpose.

Computer-supported documentation of expert knowledge is desirable …

The provider introduces the PoM ⟨exception assessment support⟩ in order to document and make available the expert knowledge of routine management personnel. The major advantages of this procedure are:

- A mastering of the more and more extensive and complex operational knowledge, thereby making it impossible for even the best expert to know everything about complex networked systems.

- Secure routine management of the networked system with fewer trained personnel (e.g., during night or weekend shifts).

- Cost savings through the automation potential or the use of fewer trained personnel.

…but not yet satisfactorily resolved

It is very difficult to use a management tool to achieve suitable computer support for exception assessment. The main problem is the acquisition, maintenance, and availability of a knowledge base that contains the necessary supplemental information for processing an exception. Since providers face a similar problem with problem diagnostics, users are referred to the PoM ⟨problem diagnostic support⟩ developed in problem management.

Routine Action Support

Intervention with minimal impact

A routine action is a manipulation of a networked system that routine management is allowed to carry out without explicit agreement with change management because of the limited effect of the action. Since the process-oriented management means for the routine action support has a direct impact on one or more network, systems, or application components of the networked system, this management means is frequently available as a computer-supported resource. Table 18.3

Table 18.3 Routine actions and management tools that can be used

Type of Routine Action	Tool That Provides Computer-Supported PoM
Resetting network component	Element management system Management application (manual activation of reset button)
Resetting system	System administration tool
Registration of new user	User administration tool
Change to configuration of a network component (e.g., routing table)	Element management system Operating terminal (attached locally to component)
Change to configuration of a system component (e.g., priorities)	System administration tool
Installation of software	Installation script

provides examples of different routine actions with the corresponding management tools that were covered in detail in Part III.

Delineation between routine actions and changes

The routine actions listed in the table clarify the distinction between these actions and changes to networked systems. The provider organization must make clear which actions can be undertaken to the networked system within the scope of routine management. For example, certain system and applications software can be installed as a routine action if the effects of this installation on the overall system are made known to routine management personnel and a widespread coordination through change management is no longer required.

No static line of separation

The example shows that the dividing line between routine actions and changes can shift over time. As a result of the experience of change management with the installation of certain software, routine management is also able to install the software with a reasonable risk. This helps to reduce the higher planning and administrative effort associated with change management.

Problem Notification Form

This process-oriented management means is used for the systematic compilation of all information that is required for the further processing of an exception (within the framework of the process of problem processing). The following information fields are included in the form:

Also refer to ⟨operational logbook⟩ described earlier

- Details about the user reporting the problem. A determination is made whether the person is an external user or whether the problem notification has been submitted by operating personnel responsible from the routine management area.
- Type of problem
- Hardware–software components of the networked system that have been affected
- Additional details about the problem symptoms that have been established

Provider requirements

The provider's requirements for workflow support tools that provide (routine) management personnel with the PoM ⟨problem notification forms⟩:

- Support in filling in the form through automatic completion of input fields on the basis of previously entered information
- Checking of entries for accuracy and consistency (syntactically and semantically)
- Availability of special information fields to accommodate the exception being recorded
- Flexible options for forwarding the form to the location where the problem notification will be processed (see PoM ⟨operational log⟩)

Change Request Form

Described more extensively under change management

In structure and content, this form is similar to the problem notification form described earlier. This request form is used by routine management to provide change management with additional information (e.g., for planning an appropriate implementation of a change). It is dealt with in detail in connection with the description of the change management process (section 18.5).

18.3.3   Compile Operational Statistics

Significance of operational statistics

Operational statistics that provide information about the stability of a networked system form the basis for routine management. The content of these statistics can cover the utilization level of the processing system (CPU, disks) and networks or provide information about problems

Table 18.4 Support requirements for the action ⟨generate operational statistics⟩

Support Requirements	Type	PoM
Information on which components in the networked system require collection of operational data	Information	Configuration base
Collection of operational data and provision thereof at the location where it is to be processed	Information Communication	Monitor
Consolidation of collected operational data to produce reliable statistics	Processing	Operational statistics

with IT resources (applications, processing systems, storage systems, network components, transmission lines).

Informative operational statistics can be used to determine whether service level agreements concluded with customers are possibly being violated and which short-term measures ensuring stability should be undertaken (see Table 18.4).

Derivation of measures

Configuration bases and monitors were introduced and described extensively in the earlier action ⟨monitor component status⟩ as process-oriented management means. These PoMs provide static (configuration base: which components) and dynamic (monitor: current status information for components) operational data for the compilation of operational statistics in connection with this action.

Relevant management tools

At the center of the action is the process-oriented management means for the operational statistics that process the operational data in a usable form. Operational data even in simpler networked system environments represents mass data, which is why the PoM ⟨operational statistics⟩ must be provided by a computer-supported statistical tool.

The operational statistics compiled by routine management are of interest to a number of departments within the provider organization. Distribution lists are used for the orderly distribution of these statistics. A workflow support tool can be used for computer-supported distribution.

Operational Statistics

Informative operational statistics represent an important and valuable management means to help providers assess the operational state of networked systems and take the necessary measures to improve operational quality.

The following questions have to be clarified before a provider can make a suitable assessment of the operational statistics provided:

Provider's view of operational statistics

- To which part of the networked system do the operational statistics apply?
- Which properties are dealt with in the statistics?
- What period of time do the statistics cover?

Provider requirements

Suitable tool functions are required in order to generate extensive operational statistics. The following requirements have to be met by these types of tool functions to enable the provider of a networked system to derive maximum benefit from this PoM:

- High-quality raw data. The quality of the operational statistics generated depends directly on the quality of the raw data used as the basis for the statistics. Most of the raw data is supplied by the monitors that are used. Appropriate checks for consistency and completeness can indicate to the provider whether the quality of the raw data delivered by the monitors is satisfactory.
- Flexible format. Operational statistics are used by different employees in a provider organization for totally different purposes. The statistics should therefore be compiled in a format that is flexible enough to make them useful to a wide spectrum of users. This flexibility can be achieved, for instance, by ensuring that the process is controlled individually in order to accommodate special requirements.

18.4   Problem Management

Step-by-step processing at support levels

Problem management is responsible for dealing with problems that occur in networked systems. Reports of problems from external users are first channeled to a help desk and, if they cannot be handled there, are forwarded to problem management. The process involved in attempting to repair the problem involves different support levels that also determine the phases of the operational process for problem management.

Problem management is characterized by numerous interactions and an accompanying exchange of information within the provider organization for the repair of problems. The PoMs that are used in this process largely support these interactions and flow of information in problem management. As in routine management, a workflow support tool that incorporates concepts for workflow management [FLO94, VOB96] is used to provide the necessary support of the management means.

Numerous inter-actions and information flows

Another important management tool can be used in the diagnosis of problems. So far the developers of management tools have done an inadequate job of meeting providers' requirements for diagnostic tools, and therefore this aspect of problem management is still for the most part being carried out by human experts who are not receiving adequate support from computer-supported PoMs.

Diagnostic tools

The content of the operational process for problem processing is dealt with by the support organization, which determines how reports from users or to users within the provider organization should be handled. The previous chapter provided an introduction to the structure of support organization. Through the support organization, a close relationship develops from problem management to the help desk because the latter is the first point of contact for all questions relating to support that are directed to a provider organization. The function of the help desk is referred to as "first-level support" by the support organization and represents a special process for problem management. We will briefly look at the process executed in the help desk that not only affects operations but all other task areas within the provider organization, and therefore is not introduced as an operational process in the process model (see section 17.5).

Support organi-zation (also see section 17.5)

As is shown in Figure 18.10, the process is triggered by a query raised by an external user or by an in-house employee of the provider organization. Once important basic information such as the identity of the user and the content of the query is registered, a decision is made about whether the query can even be processed by the help desk. One reason for rejecting a query could be that the person making the query does not even have the right to make use of the help desk service. If the query is accepted, processing begins as soon as further information has been requested. The goal of many provider organizations is to have as many queries as possible processed completely in the help desk in order to minimize the effort involved in forwarding partially processed

Description of the process

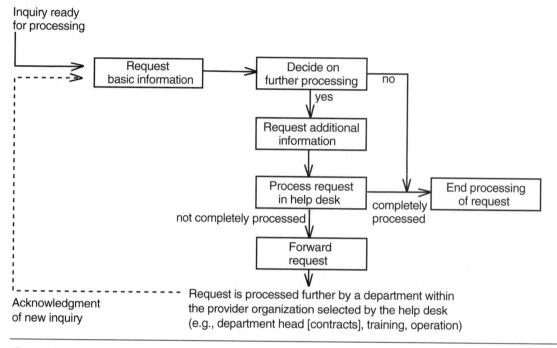

Figure 18.10
Help desk process

queries. The destination address for a query can be one of various locations within an organization:

The help desk does not only forward inquiries to operations

- If the person making the query wants to make use of the provider's service offering and is not yet a customer, he or she will be transferred to the department that handles contracts with customers.

- If the person is interested in certain additional training, he or she will be transferred to the training area.

- If the query concerns the use of networked systems, the person is transferred to operations if the query could not be dealt with by the help desk.

Only the last case is interesting from the standpoint of the problem management process. As is shown in Figure 18.11, problems can be reported by a help desk as well as directly by routine management. When the problem processing commences, it is assumed that the necessary basic information for categorizing the problem will originate either from the help desk or from routine management.

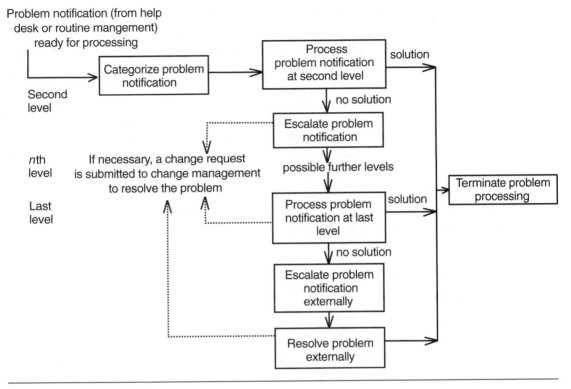

Figure 18.11
The problem management process

Since, according to the concept of the support organization, the help desk provides first-level support, the first phase of problem management constitutes the second level. Other support levels can follow that form the subsequent phases of this operational process. The process concludes with the last level of support.

The actions that take place in the different phases of the process are described next.

- *Second-level phase.* Three actions are carried out by operational personnel during this phase. In the first action, ⟨*categorize problem notification*⟩, an initial analysis is conducted to determine how to categorize the problem from the standpoint of content. The problem notification is then analyzed in detail through the action ⟨*process problem notification at second level*⟩, and if possible, the problem is processed and resolved. If this is not possible, the process switches to the next level of action, ⟨*escalate problem notification*⟩.

Categorize, process, and if necessary, escalate

- *nth-level phases.* During each subsequent phase in the problem management process, each action instigates a further step in the problem notification processing, and when necessary, escalating to the next higher support level if a solution cannot be found. It is up to the provider organization to determine how many of these levels should be provided in a concrete support organization (often there are three levels: first level, second level, and third level as the last level). A level is mostly characterized by the capabilities for problem solving embedded in it and, therefore, as a direct consequence, by which problems can be resolved in the level or have to be escalated to a different level.

Last level of support organization reached

- *Last-level phase.* A problem is processed analogously with the preceding support levels. At this last support level, the problem notification is turned over for processing by the experts with the most competence in dealing with the problems of the provider organization. If the problem cannot even be resolved at this level, external support (manufacturer or consultant or other provider) will be sought, which is instigated by the action ⟨*escalate problem notification externally*⟩.

The action ⟨*terminate problem processing*⟩ ends the problem-solving process. This stage of action is not reached until all measures for handling and resolving the problem have been undertaken in the view of problem management.

Focusing on two actions

In our continuing study of process-oriented management means and management tools, we focus on the actions in which the diagnostic tool is of particular interest in connection with problem management. This tool is used in conjunction with the first two actions: ⟨categorize problem notification⟩ and ⟨process problem notification⟩.

18.4.1   Categorize Problem Notification

Acceptance of the ⟨problem notification form⟩ (from routine management or the help desk)

The first action in problem management involves the acceptance of the problem notification form generated by the help desk or in routine management (action ⟨handle exception detected⟩ in section 18.3.2). The categorization of the problem notification at the very beginning of the problem-solving process facilitates the detailed planning of the subsequent processing involved. This includes identifying which department at the support level will be responsible for processing the problem notification. The categorization process can also produce other information that can be useful in resolving a particular problem.

Table 18.5 Support requirements for the action ⟨categorize problem notification⟩

Support Requirements	Type	PoM
Indication of problem notification being categorized	Communication	Problem notification form
Support in establishing to which category the problem notification is to be allocated	Processing	Problem categorization support
Identification of the measures to be undertaken to repair a problem as a result of the categorization	Processing	Problem-solving plan

The objectives in categorizing problem notifications are as follows:

- Personnel who accept problem notifications should have the appropriate competence to evaluate how to proceed.

- The approach taken to initiating the problem-solving process should reflect the difficulty of the problem.

- Problem notifications should include additional information that could be valuable in resolving the respective problem.

- A decision should be planned on where to forward a problem notification for further processing.

If the problem that has been reported to problem management can be resolved promptly, in other words, without the need for time-consuming analysis and diagnosis, there is no reason to expend the effort involved in providing an explicit categorization of the problem (see Table 18.5).

As is shown in Figure 18.12, the problem notification form and the problem processing plan are closely linked PoMs in this action and should be provided on a computer-supported basis by a workflow support tool. The process-oriented management means for problem categorization support is part of a diagnostic tool with access to a knowledge base that must contain the different categories with their characteristic properties.

Relevant management tools

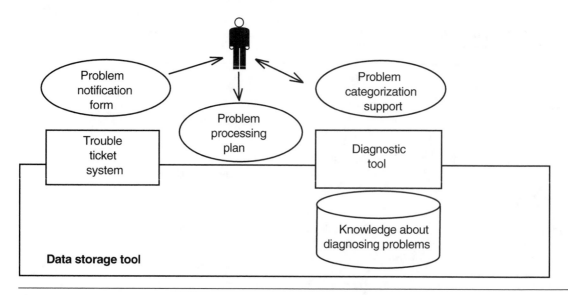

Figure 18.12
Action ⟨categorize problem notification⟩

Problem Notification Form and Problem Processing Plan

Problem notification forms were described in the action ⟨handle detected exception⟩ in conjunction with routine management. Problem processing plans supplement these forms with the following information:

Additional content of a ⟨problem solving plan⟩

- Location that accepted the problem notification
- Location(s) that will be involved in processing the problem notification
- Category to which the problem notification is assigned
- Priority to be given to the processing of the problem notification
- Any other information relevant to the processing

Problem notification forms are implemented as trouble tickets

As the central process-oriented management means of this action, these two documents (the problem notification form and the problem processing plan) can be converted appropriately into a workflow support tool. In concrete tool products, a problem notification form is called a *ticket* or a *trouble ticket*. This kind of trouble ticket also contains information on which work has already been done or is being planned to resolve a particular problem ("trouble"). This corresponds to the information contained in the PoM ⟨problem processing plan⟩.

Table 18.6 Examples of problem categories

Information in ⟨problem notification form⟩	Primary Problem Categories
Networked system component in which problem has occurred	Network problem System problem Application problem
Person reporting the problem	End user problem (user is one reporting problem) Operational problem (Operational personnel) Component problem (agent in the component)
Type of problem	Total breakdown Malfunction Overloading ...

To meet the provider's needs, the workflow support tool referred to as a *trouble ticket system* in the context of problem processing should provide the following functions:

Provider requirements

- Clear presentation of information for problem processing

- Support in establishing the plan in which certain information (e.g., current location processing the problem notification) is automatically amended

- Support in forwarding the completed problem processing plan

- A facility for checking the completed problem processing plan for completeness and consistency

Problem Categorization Support

The categorization of a reported problem is an important first step in the analysis process in problem management. The starting point for the categorization is the information contained in the problem notification form. Many details in the form provide the basis for different fundamental problem categories.

First step in analysis procedure

Table 18.6 shows some of the fundamental categories that can be derived from the information in a problem notification form.

Information in Problem Notification Form

Combination of basic problem categories ...

The primary problem categories can be combined to provide more detailed and informative categories. The transition to the diagnosis of the problem that is handled in the next action is then fluid.

...and allocation of solutions for problem repair

There are different ways of using the identified problem category for the subsequent processing of a problem. For example, the category to which a problem notification has been assigned can be used to determine which location will process the problem or might even indicate a possible solution to eliminating the problem.

Provider requirements

Computer-supported problem categorization support as part of a diagnostic tool can assist the provider with the following aspects:

- Compilation of a catalog of problem categories and a flexible means for expanding the catalog. The catalog is an important element of the knowledge base to be developed in a diagnostic tool.

- Identification of typical properties that can characterize the problems in a certain category.

- Support in the navigation and search of a catalog. This involves the selection of the most appropriate category to which the current problem notification is to be allocated.

18.4.2 Process Problem Notification (at the *n*th Support Level)

The aim of the previous action, ⟨categorize problem notification⟩, is to ensure that a problem (through the problem processing plan) is forwarded to the department within the provider organization that is responsible for processing the particular problem and has the related expertise to do so. It is here that the actual diagnosis is carried out by the *n*th support level, and if possible, the necessary measures to resolve the problem are executed or triggered (see Table 18.7).

Relevant management tools

The problem processing plan contains all the information required to process the fault at the *n*th support level. If this process-oriented management means is computer supported, the information is provided by a workflow support tool, referred to here as a trouble ticket system (see Figure 18.13). This system can also be used to monitor the entire problem repair process on a computer-supported basis.

The central part of the action is the search for the cause of a problem; the appropriate PoM ⟨problem diagnostic support⟩ can be provided as a computer-supported diagnostic tool. The PoM problem

Table 18.7 Support requirements for the action ⟨process problem notification⟩

Support Requirements	Type	PoM
Acceptance of information relevant to processing a problem notification	Communication Information	Problem resolving plan
Support in the cause of the problem	Processing	Problem diagnosis support
Implementation of measures for problem repair	Execution	Problem repair support
Guarantee of problem repair measures	Information	Status monitoring

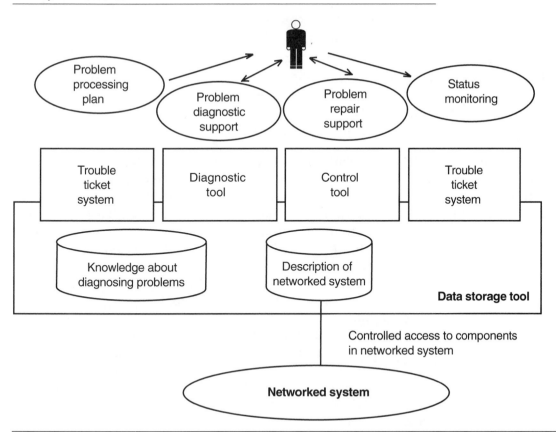

Figure 18.13
Action ⟨process problem notification⟩

repair support, which is based on functions supplied by configuration and control tools, implements the necessary processing measures.

Problem Diagnostic Support

Allocation of problem notification to cause of problem

The efficiency of problem management and the closely affiliated help desk critically depends on how quickly and how accurately a problem notification can be diagnosed, or a particular cause of error can be correctly categorized. An exact diagnosis of a problem is required in order to correct a problem in the networked system.

Complexity of problem diagnosis

Although it is desirable, it is also very difficult to provide support in the form of computer-supported process-oriented management means to operational personnel involved in problem management. The key reasons for the complexity associated with problem diagnosis are:

- Each individual component in a networked system (such as the extensive software components) is in itself very complex.

- The variety and heterogeneity of the components increases this individual complexity.

- Owing to the flexible and dynamic configurability of the components in networked systems, it is very difficult, if not impossible, to use the diagnostic models developed successfully for other technical systems (which tend to be static).

Computer-supported diagnosis in the area of the operation of networked systems...

It is particularly for the last reason that experts are for the most part still able only to conceptualize but not implement the intellectually difficult part of the diagnosis, namely, concluding the cause of a fault from the symptoms—despite extensive efforts that have been made in this area and the promising approaches available [DMN97, DRE95, HOJ97, LEW93]. Initial research results [GRA97, MOU97] show that the agent technology [JEN94], which originates in the distributed artificial intelligence area [OHJ96], promises to offer providers with the support they need in coping with these complex problems.

...has not yet been satisfactorily resolved from the view of the provider

As a result, very few providers have been using computer-supported PoMs to support problem diagnosis in problem management. Yet there is a considerable demand from providers for this kind of technology because it represents the only option for substantially improving the problem management process. Furthermore, because of the increasing complexity of the networked systems, diagnosis is becoming a more and more extensive process.

The following requirements for management means for fault diagnosis must be met to enable their use by providers in problem management:

Provider requirements

- Justifiable effort in the initial acquisition of diagnostic knowledge
- Simple yet largely automated updating of diagnostic knowledge
- Simple operation with reasonable response times
- Support in the problem resolution

Problem Processing Plan

There is a seamless transition between successful diagnosis and the repair of the cause responsible for a problem. If repairing a problem requires more extensive measures and possibly the involvement of a number of experts, the management means of the problem processing plan is used in the systematic repair of the problem; the progress that is made in this repair can also be monitored on the basis of this process-oriented management means.

Coordination of problem processing

The content of the problem processing plan consists of the measures to be taken and, in some cases, a time stipulation. It is also used to coordinate the joint efforts of different locations within and outside the provider organization that are responsible for repairing the problem (manufacturers, third-party firms).

Content

The management means problem processing plan should meet the following requirements to enable it to be used by providers in structuring their problem management operations:

Provider requirements

- Automatic generation of the problem processing plan
- Distribution among companies and departments involved in the problem handling process
- Update of the current processing state
- Detection of conflicts in schedules

Status Monitoring (of Problem Processing)

A provider must always ensure that it is aware of the processing status of each problem notification being dealt with in problem management and, if required, can provide this information to the user who reported the problem. The appropriate PoMs allow the provider to determine and monitor the progress of the problem processing at any given time.

Monitoring progress in problem processing

Content

The documentation of the processing process is an important prerequisite for status monitoring. The following information is needed to describe the processing:

- Clear identification of the problem notification. The information that unambiguously identifies the notification is included with the initial problem notification. All other details about the report are found in the PoM ⟨problem notification form⟩.

- Current processing status. Possible status indicators are ⟨being processed⟩, ⟨processing delayed⟩, ⟨processing completed⟩. Different information is provided depending on which state in the process has been reached (e.g., reason for delay, name of location currently processing the problem notification).

- Processing history. In addition to the current processing status, this PoM should provide the provider with a rundown of the different processing states reached in the past (status history).

Provider requirements

The provider's requirements for PoMs essential to status monitoring in problem management can be summarized as follows:

- Support in the documentation of problem processing. This is particularly important for the querying of current processing status.

- Evaluation of processing status. Particularly important problem messages and long delays in the processing of problem messages should especially be emphasized so that operational personnel are alerted accordingly. This particularly applies to those faults that are in danger of violating the terms of customer service level agreements.

18.5   Change Management

The operational process ⟨change management⟩

Change management is the last of the three operational processes differentiated in the process model. The change management process will be used to illustrate how provider requirements derived for the computer support of support tools can systematically be taken into account in a tool implementation (section 18.6). Change management and the tools used in the different actions will therefore be dealt with comprehensively.

Function of change management

The function of change management [CCT97, MOL94] is to plan and coordinate the implementation of changes to networked systems. In the process, the networked system is transferred to a new technological state. Examples of changes that would fall under the process of change management are the installation of new (application) software and the introduction of new hardware systems. Changes to in-house technology that are directly related to the networked system also fall within the scope of change management.

The goal of change management is to implement changes to networked systems so that new services affected through the service level agreements are provided but existing SLAs with other users are not affected by intervention to the system. Because of the complex interrelationships that exist between networked systems today, change management plays a major role and requires well-defined procedures [ABM97].

Not all activities that relate to networked systems fall within the scope of change management. Changes that are part of the change management process include:

Object of change management

- Changes that transform a networked system from one state to a new technological state in order to satisfy the requirements of the customer. The reasons for the transformation could be the danger of noncompliance with existing service level agreements or the existence of new requirements that are being placed on the system.

- Changes that because of their consequences require thorough planning, taking into account all eventualities and conditions. These kinds of changes are usually triggered by other operational processes since a higher degree of coordination is required than is available in routine and problem management.

There are three reasons why change management is instructed to make a change:

Reasons for a change

- The provider is committed to have the latest state of technology in order to remain competitive. Because of technological advances in software and hardware development, the networked system is updated at regular intervals. The changes are initiated by the developer (e.g., through the release of new software versions by developer support).

- Because of the high degree of coordination needed during the operation of a networked system, a change may be required in other processes (such as routine management or problem management) in the networked system. This can be the case if a serious problem cannot be repaired only by problem management. Change manage-

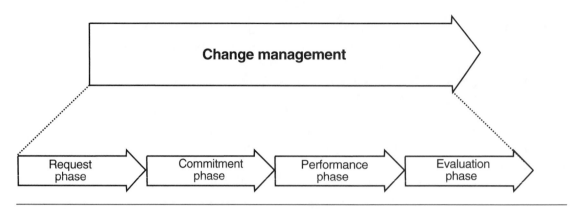

Figure 18.14
Phases of the process ⟨change management⟩

ment is then instructed to make a change to the networked system in order to repair the problem.

- New requirements of the user cannot be met in routine management with the current state of the networked system. This could be a request for new application software or the need for higher availability of an existing application. A request is made to change management to adjust the system to a new technological state so that the user's requirements can be accommodated and the terms of the SLA guaranteed.

Phases of change management

In accordance with the concept of user and provider [SCH96], the process of change management can be divided into four subprocesses that are also referred to as *phases* because of their chronological sequence (see Figure 18.14).

Request Phase

The request for a change to a networked system is made during this subprocess. All the requirements for the system are compiled. The origination of a change request and its transformation into a concrete form constitute the forerunner to the other subprocesses. The request phase is mostly rooted with the service user of change management. This can be a normal user or other operational processes. The concrete change request is submitted to change management and formulated into the action ⟨*formulate change*⟩. This action is usually a part of other processes such as routine or problem management. The action becomes part of change management itself if a change escalates into further changes.

Commitment Phase

The change request then progresses to the second phase. The action ⟨*agree technical performance characteristics*⟩ entails compiling the technical performance characteristics of the networked system into a set of functional specifications. The action ⟨*classify change*⟩ is used to analyze and classify the respective request. Criteria that play a role in the classification process include urgency of the request, estimated effort involved, and foreseeable risks. The conditions for making the change are examined so that a rough estimate can be made of the effort involved. Operational conditions as well as the current state of the networked system and the state of the technology are taken into account. If certain conditions do not exist, this means that nonexisting prerequisites have to be created. This allows a rough estimation of the cost required for a particular change. Depending on the rough assessment and the urgency of the change request, the request is assessed as urgent, executable, or not executable. With the action ⟨*assign priority*⟩, each request is assigned a certain priority that establishes its sequence in the global timetable for the processing of changes. As a result of this subprocess, all the change requests that have been received are classified by priority and provided with the appropriate technical service agreements.

Performance Phase

The changes that have been requested are processed in accordance with their respective technical requirements during the performance phase. Each change is first checked out in a test environment through the action ⟨*execute change in test operations*⟩. The test operations are set up so that no interventions into the networked system pose any threat to existing service agreements. The closer the test operations emulate the later actual operations, the more comprehensive the test can be executed. However, it is never possible for a test to incorporate all the aspects of actual operations. After having successfully passed the testing stage, the change is then introduced into actual operations through the action ⟨*accept change in actual operations*⟩. This step particularly requires careful planning since intervention into the networked system during actual operations could have an impact on existing TSAs.

Evaluation Phase

This phase concludes the actual operative work to the networked system. The action ⟨*release change*⟩ indicates that the networked system that has been changed is ready to be turned over to the responsibility of the service user—in other words, other operational processes or users. Routine management continues to receive and evaluate feedback from the user concerning the change after the release in order to improve the quality of the change process.

Operational management establishes roles that are necessary for carrying out the individual activities that enable the change process to be executed. These roles are filled by appropriate personnel from the organizational side of the provider. In some cases, one role can be covered by several different people, and in other cases, one person can also carry out several roles at the same time. The following roles can be identified within the context of change management: the change manager as the one responsible for the process, the initiator of the change request, the technicians involved in the system, and the developers and the users of the networked system. Certain roles, such as that of the initiator, can also be rooted in other processes.

Actions in the phases
The different actions and the PoMs of change management required for executing the actions are described next. The list can be expanded depending on different needs or scenarios.

18.5.1   Formulate Change

The action ⟨formulate change⟩ is used to formulate a request for a change to the system. The change request (CR) aims at extending the functionality or increasing the quality of a networked system. The change transposes the system to a state that allows it to provide new services or services with improved quality.

A change request is implemented when it is submitted to a defined interface in change management and formulated accordingly. The description of the change request contains mandatory as well as optional information. The mandatory information includes a finely detailed description of the change request along with the name, address, and telephone, fax, and email (if applicable) numbers of the initiator in case further information is required (see Table 18.8).

Table 18.8 Support requirements for the action ⟨formulate change⟩

Support Requirements	Type	PoM
Formulation of change request	Processing	Change request form
Submission to change management	Communication	Telephone, facsimile, email, WWW

Change Request Form

The change request form (see Figure 18.15) is used to structure the information required so that an adequate description of the change exists. The information in the form can also be organized so that it can be used during the subsequent processing stages. The change request form also constitutes part of the documentation for the change. It also documents the relationship between service user and service provider.

The change request form is expected to provide information about the initiator and the time the request was initiated (date and time stamp). The change request must also be described with sufficient detail (objects affected, deadline). The reason for the change and the consequences of not implementing the change must be made known so that the urgency of the change can be assessed. The change request must provide for the entry of necessary information. Furthermore, it should be possible for the information to be expanded at any time during the processing process.

Requirements of change request

The initiator of a change request is the one who describes the change request with as much detail as possible. Yet it must be taken into account that the initiator in some situations has only a limited view of the networked system. An overview is required of all requests submitted (compare with help desk) so that similar requests can be consolidated and processed efficiently in the same processing sequence.

Telephone, Facsimile, Email, WWW

PoMs such as the telephone, facsimile, electronic mail, and the WWW are used as the communication resources between the service user and the service provider to convey a change request to change management. The use of an automated tool at the beginning of change management will help to ensure the effectiveness and efficiency of the change management process.

Supporting communication

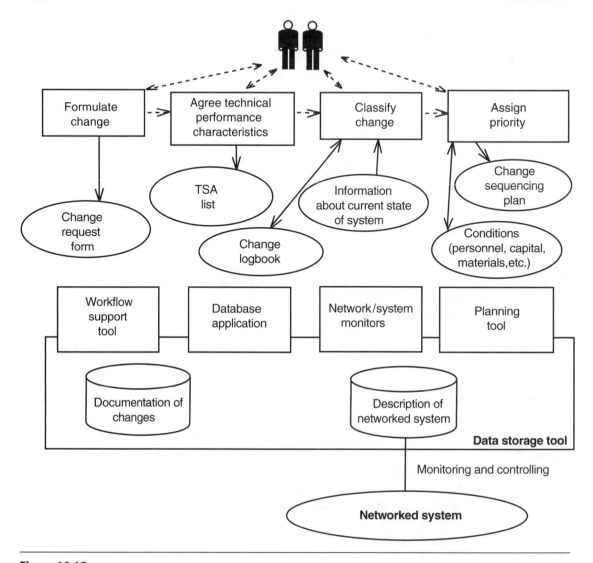

Figure 18.15
Actions, PoMs, tools (part 1)

Provider requirements

Following are the provider requirements for change management tools:

- The tool must initiate the input of the information mentioned previously. It is essential that the mandatory information is provided. An adequate possibility must be provided for entering optional information. The change request must be completed carefully so that there is no chance of a misinterpretation of the information

Table 18.9 Support requirements for the action ⟨agree technical performance features⟩

Support Requirements	Type	PoM
Demands on networked system	Processing	Technical service agreement (TSA)

provided. The contact address of the initiator is required in case further information has to be requested.

- The information must be structured so that it can be used for further processing. A template should be devised that serves as a guideline for the information being entered.

- The information relating to the change request should be available in electronic form as quickly as possible to enable an effective and efficient processing of the request by automated tools. The use of communication tools, such as email or the WWW, would facilitate the process. The other advantage of the WWW is that the user-friendly interface allows for an easy input of the information required.

- Another requirement is that the administration and storage of the requests submitted can be automated. The use of a provider-accepted database in which the different requests can be filed and the processing of these requests documented is desirable.

Tools that are implemented to support the initiation of change requests [CCT97] will be described later. The functional specifications of these tools have a major impact on the design of the user interface. The entry process can be simplified through automatic extension and default settings.

Prototype of a tool for supporting a change request

18.5.2 Agree Technical Performance Characteristics

The requirements for the networked system are formulated in the action ⟨agree technical performance characteristics⟩. Some of the technical requirements can be derived from a request or from a service level agreement. Basically, a possibility should be provided for negotiating the technical performance agreement with the customer. As with the previous actions, appropriate PoMs are required for the support of communication (see Table 18.9).

Specification of the performance features of a technical system

Technical Service Agreement (TSA)

Technical per-
formance agree-
ments as a set
of functional
specifications

The TSA (see Figure 18.15) corresponds to the operational monitoring sheet in routine management. It lists the technical requirements for the networked system that result from the change request and therefore corresponds to the functional specifications for the hardware and software systems to be used.

The service provided by change management is measured on the basis of the TSA. There can usually be financial consequences if requirements are not met.

Provider
requirements

Following are the provider requirements for TSA tools:

■ Tools should allow the extension of a change request to include the technical performance agreements.

■ An extension to an agreement contains detailed information about which features the networked system should have once the change has been made.

■ An indication of the technical performance limits of the current state is helpful as a negotiating basis.

■ TSAs can be adequately structured in a tabular format, with the individual rows listing information about each performance feature requested. Information about each performance feature is added to the columns: performance feature exists (yes/no, percentage), performance feature provided (yes/no, when, percentage, etc.).

18.5.3   Classify Change

The action ⟨classify change⟩ takes the change request that has been entered and analyzes it. The aim of analyzing the request is to classify the change. Important criteria for this classification include:

■ Urgency of the change

■ The implications of not executing the change

■ Risks associated with the implementation of the change

■ The costs (rough estimate based on experience) that will be incurred if the change is made to the networked system and that often represent a criterion for the change request

Classification of
change requests

The change classification action establishes whether the change request falls into one of the following classes:

- *Urgent change:* These changes usually originate in problem management and are important from the standpoint of ensuring that the services agreed on can be provided. The decision determining whether a change is urgent is made by weighing the effort and risks associated with the change against the consequences of not executing the change with consideration of deadlines. There is usually not sufficient time to plan urgent changes, and they therefore have a high risk potential associated with them. A compromise has to be sought between a time delay and the acceptance of risk.

- *Executable change:* These changes are assessed on the basis of empirical values and an estimation of their feasibility. Conditions such as available resources and time pressures are important for the classification.

- *Nonexecutable change:* The decision against making a change is based on past experience and a rough assessment. The policy on meeting user requirements plays a big role in this decision. On the other hand, the current state of a networked system or the state of current technology can represent a criterion for a change request.

Information from different sources is required for a classification of changes. First, there must be an assurance that the conditions required for implementing the change indeed exist. Information is collected on the current state of the system and on the resources to be used (personnel, data, capital). If the right conditions do not exist, a decision must be made whether the change should be implemented nevertheless. This decision can lead to other changes that must be reflected in the planning process. If it is not possible to create the right conditions for making the change (too expensive, too time consuming, or technically not possible), this situation will be considered a reason to stop the change. Technical conditions would be based on the availability of sufficient hardware resources to introduce new software.

Criteria for change classification

A detailed overview of the networked system is helpful for the action ⟨classify change⟩. In addition, an estimate is made of the cost and work required in order to create the right conditions. The result of this action is information that details the feasibility of the change, the cost involved, and the time required. The more experience there is in executing changes, the more accurate and reliable this information will be. The action ⟨classify change⟩ provides an evaluation of the change requests submitted (see Table 18.10).

Table 18.10 Support requirements for the action ⟨classify change⟩

Support Requirements	Type	PoM
Checking of conditions	Processing	TSA list
Current state of networked system	Information	Configuration base, monitoring support
Experience from previously executed changes	Information	Change logbook

TSA lists

TSA lists (see Figure 18.15) serve as checklists for this action and are used to check the current state of the networked system. The completed TSA list provides information about the conditions that exist for a particular change and where action is still required. Conditions that are lacking give an indication of which work steps have to be taken into account during further planning.

Listing technical conditions

The TSA list contains an almost complete list of all the technical conditions required for the respective change. The checklist can be used to determine whether a requirement is being met. A provision is also made for comments on the degree to which a requirement is met (in percentage terms).

Configuration State, Monitoring Assistance

Information about the networked system

Information from the networked system is required so that a reliable comparison can be made between the requirements of the networked system and the current state of the system. This information falls into different types:

- *Static information:* This is information about the state of the configuration that does not change in the medium to the long term. Examples of this information include maximum hardware performance, maximum storage capacities, name of vendor, and addresses.

- *Dynamic information:* This information has a short life and changes at short notice; consequently, appropriate monitoring support may be required when this information is provided. This category of information could cover the current usage of disk space or CPU capacity utilization. Snapshots usually have little informative value. Dynamic information, which is usually provided in the form of statistics, is therefore useful only for consideration over a specific time frame.

Provider requirements for a tool-supported configuration state and monitoring support are as follows:

- Static as well as dynamic information about a networked system is required for decision making in change management. The requirements for the configuration state are similar to those for routine management.
- Monitoring support must provide adequate information about the status of the software and hardware in the networked system. The information should be edited as far as possible to increase its informative value.
- Static and dynamic information should be stored and updated efficiently. A suggestion about a tool that mirrors the configuration state has already been described in the section on routine management. Management platforms today implement monitor functions for different types of information about networks and systems. These platforms are also capable of collecting individual information over a specific period and collating it into statistics. A cooperation between documentation tools (see routine management) and management platforms would be desirable.

Change Logbooks

Experience gained from changes implemented in the past are recorded in a change logbook to help in making an assessment of new changes that are being implemented and to provide information about the possible risks involved. The change logbook (see Figure 18.15) can also assist in diagnosis of those problems that result from unforeseen consequences of a change. The more experience available, the more accurate the assessments can become.

The change logbook supplies information about changes in the past that could have some correlation with current changes being submitted. Details are provided about the length of time required, the quality achieved (references to problems and risks), and the cost of implementing the changes. Each individual execution in change management is accompanied by the change logbook that documents all relevant information regarding a change. Because of the large quantity of information available, there must be a facility for a search mechanism. If required, the collection of experience in the logbook is used to compare current changes with previous similar ones. This helps to provide an estimate of the effort and risks involved.

Provider requirements for a tool-supported change logbook include the following:

- There must be a guarantee that the documentation on changes is carefully being maintained. This means that information about throughput times, costs, quality achieved, and problems that occurred must be entered accurately and completely. The use of the change logbook should be designed so that it makes it easy to document the activities and most of the information is entered automatically. Processed PoMs such as checklists and change plans can be entered into the logbook.

- The change logbook contains the results of previous experience. Fast access and the possibility of an effective and efficient means of querying this history of information is necessary if the logbook is to provide helpful support for new changes being planned. The logbook should therefore be structured to suit the provider's needs. A possibility would be to divide the change logbook roughly according to change tests, change acceptances, risks, evaluations, resources, duration, costs, and so forth. It is important that plans that were drawn up for changes are stored since they serve as a starting point for plans for new changes.

- Similar to problem management, functionality is needed that provides automated support for current changes from the existing change documentation. An appropriate structure is required in order to automate processing.

18.5.4 Assign Priority

This action, which follows next, assigns a priority to each request on the basis of its classification and appropriately files the request into a global change plan. Because of the priority assigned to a request, it is sometimes necessary to delay a change that is in progress in favor of one with a higher priority. Once the urgent change has been implemented, the one that was on hold can be resumed (see Table 18.11).

Change Sequencing Plan

A change sequencing plan (see Figure 18.15) supports the action ⟨assign priority⟩ by organizing the entered changes into the right sequence

Table 18.11 Support requirements for the action ⟨assign priority⟩

Support Requirements	Type	PoM
Establishing processing sequence based on priority	Processing	Change sequencing plan

according to priority and timetable. A rough schedule is drawn up for all the changes that are to be executed. The planning involved in this particular action is based on an assessment of the effort and time required, with the information from previous experience (see change logbook) enabling this information to be more precise.

Sequence of changes being executed

Provider requirements for change sequencing plans are as follows:

Provider requirements

- The change sequencing plan should provide an overview of the changes to be executed over an extended period (usually one year). All the changes should be listed in sequence according to the priorities assigned to them.

- The preparation of the change sequencing plan must also take into account general conditions such as personnel and capital requirements. These conditions should be incorporated into the individual change plans.

- It should be possible to make changes to the plans. Changes could be required, for example, if an urgent request has to take precedence.

- The change sequencing plan should allow a comparison of the target and actual state of a change. This functionality should be automated as much as possible.

18.5.5   Execute Changes in Test Operations

This action tests certain important aspects of a change in an environment that as closely as possible emulates the actual operational environment. These testing environments can be structured in different ways. Depending on the risk involved, it may be sufficient to carry out tests of individual aspects separately. With a high risk, it is recommended that a reference system be created that closely resembles the actual system used later in normal operations. The action substantially pursues the following aims:

Execution of a change in a test environment

- Detailed implementation of the planning

- Operational implementation of changes in test operations

An important criterion for test operations is that changes do not pose a threat to existing service level agreements since there is no intervention into the actual networked system. The disadvantage is that it is sometimes not possible to test all aspects of a change sufficiently because the testing conditions only emulate the real environment.

Knowledge from the test environment

First, all the conditions required for a change have to be created in the test operation. This mainly relates to the provision and reservation of (software and hardware) resources. As soon as the conditions are available, the change is introduced operatively into the test environment of the networked system. The vendor's hardware and software documentation and some of the historical experience provide some important guidance in this process. The steps that are to be taken and the risks that occur are documented in the change test logbook. The detailed information about duration, effort, and risks that is provided is important for the success of the change in actual operations. An example is the installation of new software. Each version of software differs from other versions from the standpoint of the time it takes to install the software, the work steps involved, and in some cases, the options used. The action ⟨execute change in test operations⟩ exposes the problems of changes planned in the context of an individual networked system. These could be compatibility problems or performance bottlenecks that would not have been recognized before the testing.

If required, the change that is introduced is adapted to the existing networked system and the requirements of the user configured accordingly. The function of this action is to integrate a change into an existing system technically and in compliance with the service requirements. After this action has taken place, the testing more or less mirrors the same state as the later actual operative state of the TSA networked system.

When a change is accepted into test operations, a comparison is made between the technical requirements outlined in the TSA list and the performance attributes of the changed networked system. If the attributes agree with the requirements, the change is released for actual operations (see Table 18.12).

Change Procurement List

Creating necessary conditions

The change procurement list (see Figure 18.16) is based on the processed TSA list. It lists all the resources that a check of requirements disclosed were not adequately available and therefore have to be pro-

Table 18.12 Support requirements for the action ⟨execute change in test operations⟩

Support Requirements	Type	PoM
Listing of resources needed	Processing	Change procurement list
Ordering of resources not available	Communication	Change order form
Documentation of test change	Information	Change test logbook
Comparison of test service provided with requirements	Processing	TSA list
Release of change for acceptance in actual operations	Communication	Acceptance release form

vided and reserved for the current change. A frequent problem is a lack of available storage space in main memory as well as in secondary storage (hard disk). The change procurement list provides information on other resources needed in addition to what is already available. An example would be the additional acquisition of main memory or hard disk storage.

The change procurement list can also contain requirements for resources such as entire hardware or software systems. Items of this sort in the list can escalate the current change to the need for other changes.

Escalation of a change

Following are the provider requirements for tool-supported change procurement lists:

- A provider-accepted tool for the creation of a change procurement list is based on the TSA list that has been processed and completed. This list identifies which resources are lacking. The change procurement list itemizes all the resources that still must be acquired.

- Detailed specifications are listed in the change procurement list for each resource required. The TSA list provides appropriate support.

- The completed change procurement list functions as a checklist for monitoring the acquisitions required. Details about the amount of

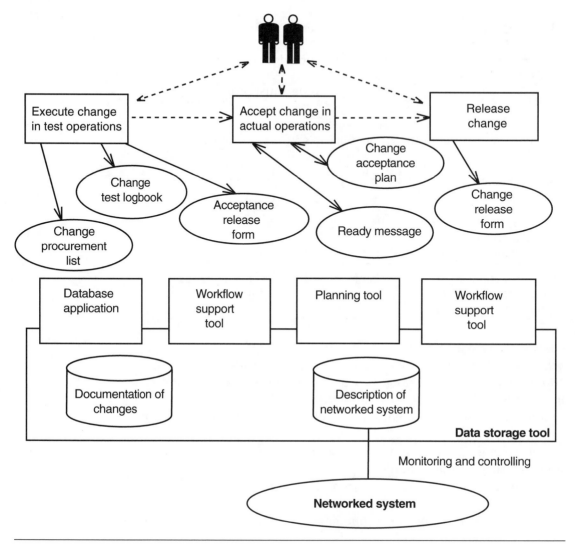

Figure 18.16
Actions, PoMs, tools (part 2)

time required to make the acquisition, cost, and so forth are added to the list.

Change Order Form

Ordering technical resources

The change order form is a PoM that informs the (software and hardware) developer of which resources are required. Similar to the change request, it formulates the requirement for a resource needed for the networked system and usually refers to software and hardware systems. The form contains a detailed description of the performance requirements for the systems.

Provider requirements for order tools include the following:

- Similar to change request tools, order tools must provide users with support in providing sufficient information for ordering resources. To be helpful, the information should be structured in a way so that these needs are clearly described. A template is useful for implementing this kind of structure.

- The customer must be in a position to provide additional (unstructured) information about the order. An information field is provided in the template for this purpose.

- The order form should be processed efficiently. Ideally, the order tool would electronically forward and store the order form.

- Similar to a change request, the change order form would have a provision for including important information such as how the sender could be contacted for feedback.

Change Test Logbook

The change test logbook (see Figure 18.16) is generated while a change is being tested. If problems surface during the testing of the change, the logbook can be helpful in resolving the problems. The notes in the logbook make it possible to retrace individual steps and return to an earlier state. If the change fails completely during test operations, the logbook is used to analyze the problem and avoid the same problem happening again.

The change test logbook represents a concrete implementation of the planning of changes. It documents in detailed form the individual operative steps involved for a particular change in a concrete networked system. What it does not include are activities that cannot be reflected in test operations. The logbook provides extensive guidance on planning the acceptance of a change into actual operation.

Provider requirements for tool-supported change test logbooks are as follows:

- A tool should be able to document in detail the execution of a change in test operations. The information should include a description of the individual operative activities, the duration of the execution, and an indication of the possible risks involved.

- The tool should provide the user with guidance on how to present the information required. A graphical user interface is helpful for this purpose.

- A tool-supported change logbook provides important detailed information for the acceptance of a change into actual operations. It is therefore important that the documentation can be stored and processed.

Acceptance Release Form

Release report for change to actual operations

Once a change has been successful in test operations, it is ready to be accepted for actual operations. An acceptance release form (see Figure 18.16) is used to formulate the release of the change. This form serves at the same time as a request to transfer the action from test operations to actual operations and signals that the testing has been completed. The form is sent to all parties who are affected by the change. It signals the provider's readiness to implement the change and the need for all affected parts of the networked system to be prepared for the change.

Provider requirements

Provider requirements for tool-supported acceptance release forms include the following:

- The acceptance release form contains important information for the execution of a change in actual operations. The form includes concrete details about the change as well as milestones that are to be observed.

- The acceptance release form contains references to other information sources regarding the change. One of these sources is the change test logbook.

- Since the acceptance release form is usually sent to more than one party, an effective and efficient distribution and administration of the acceptance release forms must be guaranteed.

18.5.6   Accept Change in Actual Operations

A separate action ensures that a change is accepted into the actual operations of the networked system. The action requires sensitive operations to the system and therefore must be planned carefully. If adequate planning is not undertaken, there is an increased risk that existing services will be endangered through the intervention to the system. Depending on the type of test operations carried out and the existing empirical values, it should more or less be possible to plan accurately for changes to actual operations.

There are different ways in which a change can be accepted, yet the type of change involved may mean that there is no freedom in selecting how the acceptance will be implemented:

- *Floating acceptance:* With floating acceptance, a change is gradually accepted into the entire networked system. There is very little risk to existing service agreements since these changes are mainly small ones that usually do not affect the efficiency of the networked system.

- *Acceptance in one step:* The *all-or-nothing* rule applies with this kind of acceptance and means that a change can be either accepted globally at the same time in the networked system or not at all. These sorts of changes are associated with high risk potential since almost all services are endangered if unforeseen problems occur. This kind of acceptance in one step is usually necessary when changes are undertaken to client–server systems, specifically when the server and the client both require having the same version for compatibility. If the server is changed, then all clients also have to be changed. The same applies to the change of communication protocols in networked systems.

Alternative options for the acceptance of a change in actual operations

The following sections describe the different basic steps involved in the acceptance of changes to the actual operations of networked systems. The list can be expanded or concretely defined according to the respective scenario.

The action ⟨accept change in actual operations⟩ includes drawing up a detailed plan for implementing changes to a system. All parts of the system that are directly or indirectly affected by the change are included in the planning. The plan therefore comprises all the operative steps required for a coordinated change. Some of the operative activities undertaken for the actual change to the networked system can be derived from the change test logbook.

Different types of information are needed to produce a plan. An important factor is the current state of the networked system, as well as knowledge about the available resources (personnel, resources, capital). It is essential that a timetable is set up for all the parts of the system that will be affected. User profiles also provide important information. This information is helpful in establishing suitable times for the changes to be made (consideration of time zones in which

Acceptance of a change in actual operations

Table 18.13 Support requirements for the action ⟨accept change in actual operations⟩

Support Requirements	Type	PoM
Generation of plan for coordinated change acceptance	Processing	Change acceptance plan
Coordination with affected parts of networked system	Communication	Acceptance ready message
Acceptance of service supplied	Processing	TSA list

certain components of a networked system are not allowed to be changed, so-called *frozen zones*).

The parts of the networked system affected by the change rely on the change acceptance plan and introduce the change to actual operations accordingly. Individual operations are carried out in tandem with the change in test operations. As each step is completed, attention should be paid to the synchronization points with other parts of the system. All difficulties relating to delays or technical problems should be reported immediately.

If required, other adaptations are made that can be implemented only within the overall context of the system. These adaptations usually relate to the configuration of the changes for actual operations in accordance with the TSA. In addition, optional settings are carried out when necessary to suit the needs of the user.

After the operative work has been completed, the TSA is used again to check performance in the context of the entire networked system in actual operations in order to determine any deficiencies. The results of the actions involved in acceptance of changes are translated into empirical values for use in the planning of future changes (see Table 18.13).

Change Acceptance Plan

Detailed planning of all activities for the acceptance of the change in actual operations

A change acceptance plan (see Figure 18.16) comprises a detailed listing of all the (operative) activities required for incorporating a change into actual operations. It always identifies one change in the change sequencing plan and contains information from the change (test) logbook. The planning involved extends to all the affected parts of the networked system. Overall conditions such as available personnel, blocked time zones (the *frozen zones*), and important milestones for the synchronization of individual subareas of the system are reflected in this planning. The change acceptance plan initiates the execution of the change in actual operations. The plan supports the monitoring of the synchronized acceptance of the change.

Following are the provider requirements for tool-supported change acceptance plans:

Provider requirements

- A tool for the change acceptance plan requires the context information of the change from the change sequencing plan. This usually includes information about timetables, personnel, and so forth.
- With these conditions taken into account, the individual (operative) activities required for the acceptance of the change are listed. This includes incorporating the documentation on the different steps involved and supplementing it with additional activities that are required for the change.
- The change acceptance plan should be allocated to the individual subareas of the networked system.
- An automated monitoring and controlling of the change acceptance in accordance with the change acceptance plan is desirable. This requires a comparison of the actual implementation with the target implementation of the change and a reporting of any time delay.

Ready Message

A ready message (see Figure 18.16) is a PoM that acknowledges the acceptance request for each affected subarea of the networked system. It confirms the readiness of the individual subareas to accept the change. This enables a synchronized acceptance of the change across the entire networked system, which is initiated by the change acceptance plan.

Ready message for the acceptance of a change in actual operations

Provider requirements for tool-supported ready messages are as follows:

Provider requirements

- The tool for the ready message enables a confirmation of a particular acceptance release. The acknowledgment must therefore be referenced to the corresponding release form.
- There should be a technical implementation to equal the tool for acceptance release to facilitate the operation.

Table 18.14 Action ⟨release change⟩

Support Requirements	Type	PoM
Formulation of change release	Processing	Change release form
Submission to routine management	Communication	Telephone, facsimile, email, WWW

- Information is required about the readiness to accept a change and a description of potential problems. An appropriate template should be used to structure the acknowledgment.

18.5.7 Release Change

Release of changed networked system

The last phase of change management involves the release of the change (ROC) through the action ⟨release change⟩. This action turns over the changed state of the networked system to the responsibility of routine management. The assumption is made that the changed system was sufficiently tested during the phases in change management and at the time of handover is largely error-free. Since errors that were not detected early enough can still occur, it should be possible to refer to the respective change (see Table 18.14).

Change Release Form

Instructing routine management to operate the changed networked system

Similar to the change request form, the change release form (see Figure 18.16) supports the completion of the change management process. This form is used to indicate that the change has correctly been implemented and that responsibility for the networked system is now being turned over to the routine management area. The form contains information about the process involved in making the change and the level of performance achieved in terms of the requirements.

Provider requirements

Provider requirements for tool-supported change release forms include the following:

- The change release form confirms that the change request has been executed. For efficiency purposes, this tool should have the same technology as the tool for the change request.
- The tool turns over the change to the responsibility area of the customer. Consequently, there should be a reference to the evaluated performance features in the TSA list.

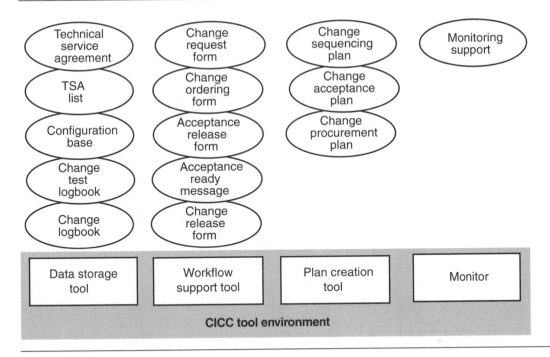

Figure 18.17
Allocation of PoMs to tools

- Contact names should be provided for any queries.

The following sections describe a tool that takes into account the provider requirements described and implements these requirements modularly and flexibly into an appropriate software module.

18.6 Provider-Accepted Tool for Change Management

This section outlines how a provider-accepted tool for change management can be developed from the description of the processes and process-oriented management means. The specifications for the PoMs are based on the needs of the provider (see section 18.5) and converted into suitable applications. The name of the tool environment that evolves is cooperative IT change control (CICC, [ABM97]) and supports the process of change management in networked systems.

Provider-accepted CICC tool environment for change management

Figure 18.17 shows an allocation of PoMs to the corresponding tools. The list of PoMs and tools in the figure is not meant to be exhaustive and can be expanded as needed.

Mapping PoMs to tools

The description of change management and the PoMs required to support the process produce some basic requirements for a CICC tool environment.

Flexibility

- *Flexibility through modularity.* The details of the way in which change management is implemented can vary and change in the long run for each scenario depending on the different organizational structure and overall conditions that exist. For the PoMs used in the process, this means that additional PoMs are added with the introduction of new actions but can also become unnecessary as entire actions are eliminated. Likewise, only selected PoMs are used when required. CICC should be kept as flexible as possible to enable a CICC tool environment to be adapted to the respective provider requirements. For the architecture of the CICC tool environment, this means each PoM initially is implemented as an autonomous module. Each module can be used independently on its own in the support of individual actions. The necessary information for the tool environment is provided through the interaction with the user.

Effectiveness

- *Effectiveness through communication and cooperation.* The individual, largely autonomous tool modules each support selected actions. The aim is to make effective use of the tool modules in each action. This means that information processed by one module is required for processing by another module. In order to provide effective support to change management, the autonomous modules must communicate and cooperate with each other. This is reflected in intensive data exchange and mutual interrogation. The CICC architecture specifies the appropriate relationships and functions for communication and cooperation.

Efficiency

- *Efficiency through coordination.* The CICC tool modules are independent and communicate and cooperate with each other. A coordinated communication and cooperation between the tool modules as well as between the tool modules and the user is necessary to assure the efficiency of CICC in change management. The coordination consists of the initiation of the use of the tool modules in accordance with the process description for change management. The right tool module is thereby offered at the appropriate time in the process, and if required, the user then starts to interact with the tool environment. The CICC tool environment should initiate change mangement on a largely automated basis.

Cooperative tools are characterized by the aspects modularity, communication, cooperation, and coordination. These aspects are essen-

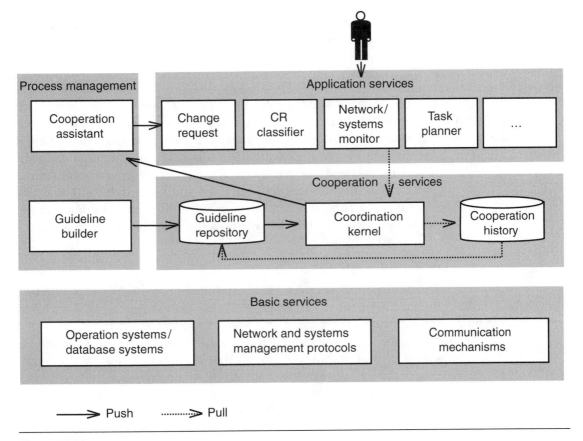

Figure 18.18
CICC architecture

tial to guaranteeing the effective and efficient operation of networked systems.

18.6.1   CICC Architecture

The architecture of the CICC tool environment can be derived as follows by the general requirements as well as by specific provider needs for tool-supported PoMs (see Figure 18.18).

Basic Services

The basic services for data storage and communication form the foundation of the CICC architecture. These services are provided today

Communication and data storage

through the functionality of operating systems and database systems in conjunction with high-performing communication networks.

Cooperation Services

Cooperation services

The cooperation services for the CICC tool environment are based on the basic services. The cooperation services mainly support the technical cooperation of the individual tool modules in distributed environments by concealing the heterogeneity and therefore the complexity of the basic services from the users. This is important for the exchange of information between roles and tool modules. The cooperation services particularly assist in providing the conditions for the operational cooperations between roles within change management.

Application Services

Conversion of PoMs into tool modules

The application services of CICC implement the process-oriented management means (PoMs), which can be automated and useful in the support of the actions in change management. These applications are derived from the specifications of the PoMs. Yet each application is a largely autonomous tool module that guarantees a flexible configuration of the tool environment according to the provider's requirements. The communication and cooperation between the application modules provide the necessary overall functionality for change management.

Process Management Services

Monitoring and control of tool environment

The process management services in the CICC tool environment support the efficient communication and cooperation of the roles using automated PoMs in change management. These services enable a monitoring and initiation of change management without forfeiting the possibility of dealing with exceptions at any time.

The individual layers are examined more closely in the next section. Examples are used to illustrate the different implementation approaches. The implementation heavily depends on a provider's requirements and can vary accordingly. It is possible that advances in technology will create an improvement to these implementations in the near future.

18.6.2 Basic Services

Data storage is a basic functionality of the CICC tool. It serves as a comprehensive mechanism for holding information that is used by the cooperating modules in the persistent storage of their information.

The prototype for the CICC tool contains all the information needed for the execution of a specific change in a database. This includes *user data*, which is processed and forwarded by the tool modules, and *control information*, which is needed to control the process sequence and track status. The status of request processing is an example of control information. The plans in the planning module are collected as data in the database so that background information on steps to be taken and the risks involved is available for similar changes.

Prototype of CICC tool environment

The database is implemented through a relational database (Oracle, Access). JDBC/ODBC is used for the bridging between the WWW and the database. Access to the database is by SQL commands embedded in Java that are transmitted to the database. The result of a query is transmitted in the reverse direction.

The communication services have a special importance since the CICC is a cooperative tool environment for the operation of networked systems. They can be divided into two classes.

Communication services for CICC tool environment

The first class supports the *vertical* exchange of information between the change management process and the networked system being managed. These are services that enable systems and networks to be monitored and controlled. The services are mainly provided by tools, mechanisms, and protocols, as described in the earlier parts of this book. Examples of these protocols include simple network management protocol (SNMP) and common management interface protocol (CMIP). Provider-oriented PoMs enable these mechanisms to be used at the appropriate locations within the change management process.

The second class of communication services supports *horizontal* information exchange during the process sequence between roles that interact with the tool modules through the use of PoMs. These services use only the networked system as a transport medium. Examples of these *communication mechanisms* are remote procedure call (RPC) and, in particular, email, the World Wide Web, and file transfer protocol (FTP). These services are also used through the appropriate tool modules implementing PoMs in change management.

18.6.3   Cooperation Services

Cooperation services create the conditions for the cooperation between roles through the use of the tool modules of CICC. The following components are required for this purpose.

Communication, cooperation, and coordination

The *coordination kernel* is the central component. Its task is to support the communication and cooperation between the individual tool modules and also to provide technical support between the participating roles. The CORBA standard developed by the OMG shows promise as an effective approach to the implementation of this service.

Guideline co-operation concept (GCC)

Operational guidelines (e.g., for security) have to be followed so that the communication and the cooperation can be coordinated to ensure efficient processing performance. Two fundamental techniques are used for this coordination effort: the *push* technique and the *pull* technique. The push technique uses the guidelines filed in the *guideline repository* to coordinate the CICC tool environment by offering a supporting PoM to a role in an actual situation. The workflow management approach [HOL94] is familiar as a similar approach. The flexibility required in order to process each exception that has not been predefined for filing in the repository is supported by the pull technique. The different roles are allowed to deviate from the guidelines, and if required, use the tool modules. In this case, the coordination kernel initially takes on the task of documenting the situation that has occurred in the *cooperation history* in order to synchronize itself with the process operation at some time. This can be done through a comparison of the situation that has occurred with the knowledge from the guideline repository or through the input of additional information from the user. Both techniques for the use of tool modules together produce the *guided cooperation concept* (GCC), which as far and as helpful as possible, initiates the roles for the execution of the change process but leaves open the possibility of deviating from these guidelines in valid situations.

18.6.4   Application Services

Section 18.5 described PoMs for change management from the viewpoint of the providers of networked systems. These descriptions were taken over by developers and examined from the standpoint of which functionalities could meaningfully be automated. The PoMs that can be automated become modules for the CICC tool environment. How the functionalities are to be implemented is derived from detailed provider requirements for PoMs. By following this systematic procedure, a provider creates a tool environment called CICC that suits its requirements.

Examples are used to show how PoMs are implemented in the CICC tool environment.

Examples of application modules

Change Request Tools

The goal of this application is to provide automated support for the instruction of change management by the submission of a *change request* (CR). The corresponding PoM is the change request form. It is characterized by a high degree of interaction with the initiator of the change.

Change request (CR)

One of the requirements is that the initiator, when formulating the request for a change, is instructed on which information is needed by the provider. This can be provided through the submission of a template that identifies and clarifies which information fields are to be completed. The information fields are differentiated according to those requesting mandatory information and those requesting optional information (e.g., the field *Comments*) for the change request. The template also allows the details provided by the initiator to be structured for automated processing. To meet these requirements, a request form in hard copy would be sufficient. Figure 18.19 shows a sample template for instruction to change management.

The completed template is submitted to the provider, which means that a means of communication must exist between customer and service provider. A facsimile machine could be used for transmitting the hard-copy request to the provider.

As a result, the application service supplies the necessary information for motivating a certain change and to a certain extent implements the request into a concrete form. A change request tool should be used to digitize the information so that automated processing is possible.

Since a CR application is a module that is heavily influenced by the interaction with the user and by the communication between initiator and service provider, WWW technologies are appropriate for the implementation of this application. A prototype of the CR module has been implemented as a Java applet. The now familiar Web browser can be used to call up the CR application. Through the integration of multimedia functions (audio, video), WWW technology supports the completion of the request. After it has been entered for processing, the information is transmitted to a database (Oracle, Access). The linking of the database to the WWW is implemented in the prototype using the object-oriented language Java (RMI, JDBC, ODBC).

CR implemented through Java applet

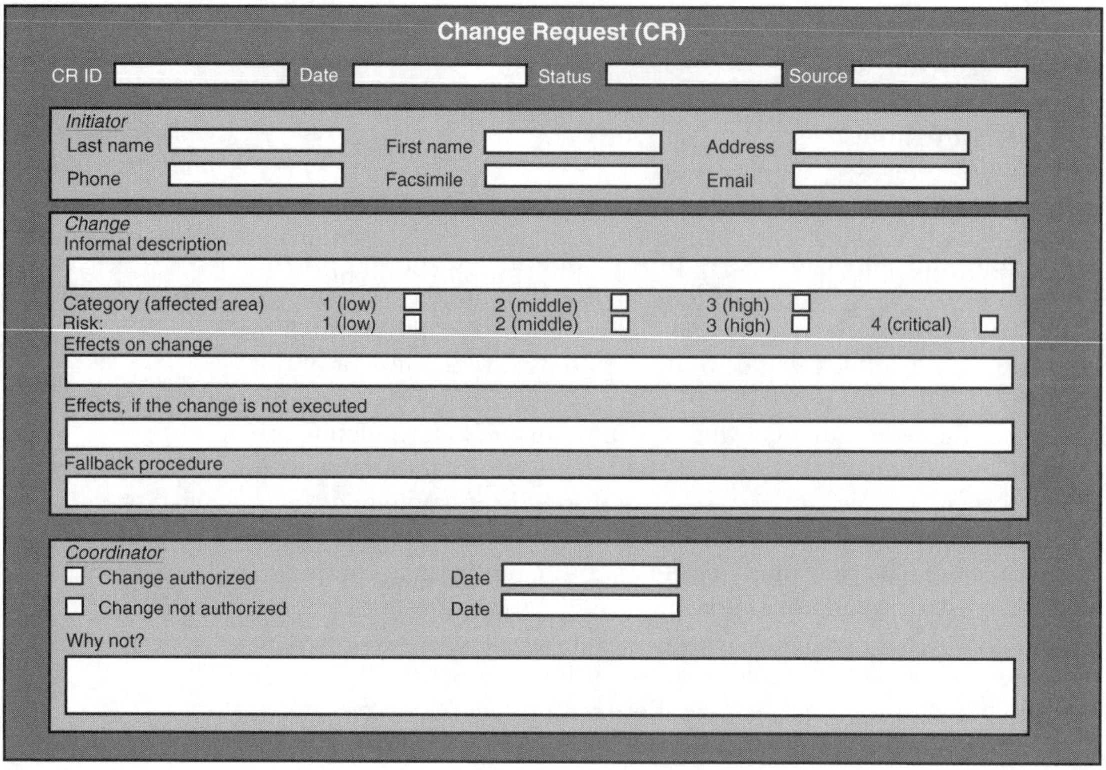

Change Request (CR)

CR ID [   ]   Date [   ]   Status [   ]   Source [   ]

Initiator
Last name [   ]   First name [   ]   Address [   ]
Phone [   ]   Facsimile [   ]   Email [   ]

Change
Informal description
[   ]

Category (affected area)   1 (low) ☐   2 (middle) ☐   3 (high) ☐
Risk: 1 (low) ☐   2 (middle) ☐   3 (high) ☐   4 (critical) ☐
Effects on change
[   ]

Effects, if the change is not executed
[   ]

Fallback procedure
[   ]

Coordinator
☐ Change authorized   Date [   ]
☐ Change not authorized   Date [   ]
Why not?
[   ]

Figure 18.19
Template for change request

TSA Tools

These tools are used to support the documentation and processing of the PoM TSA list. Since these functionalities are required in a number of different actions, we find it useful to summarize the provider requirements for TSA tools from various PoM descriptions and to integrate them into an application service.

A table is appropriate for listing the different performance features. The first column of the table lists the technical features that are particularly important to the customer. The second column provides quantitative and qualitative details about the services to be provided. It is important that the requirements are kept within the technical limits of the performance features listed. These limits can be based on empirical values and inserted automatically into the tables. A further column implements the checklist function and allows the insertion of details about the existence of certain conditions (yes/no, percentage). The next column documents the compliance level for performance factors in test operations, and the following one documents the compliance level after a change has been accepted into actual operations. Sufficient options will exist for inserting additional information about the technical performance features.

An Excel spreadsheet that is passed from one action to the next could be used for the technical implementation. A database application that provides the required table functionality is being planned for the prototype of the CICC tool environment. Integration conditions will be taken into account when the different fields are filled in. This will also require an adherence to the technical performance limits that can be displayed as default values. An automatic reference to the change request entry in the database will appear.

Database application for description of technical performance agreements

Network and System Monitors

A network and system monitor provides tool-supported monitoring assistance and supplies information about the actual state of a networked system. The monitor should be integrated into a CICC tool environment so that it can be employed, for example, in the processing of TSA tables.

Since the monitor mainly supplies dynamic information from the network and the systems, the information must be reliable so that it can be used for other applications. The monitor therefore incorporates functions for the generation of statistics that can present dynamic information based on certain criteria, such as times or percentages. For instance, these could be statistics on the capacity utilization of a CPU over a certain period, indicating peak usage and average usage.

Network and system monitors today incorporate this functionality, which is an important component of integrated management platforms such as OpenView (Hewlett-Packard), Spectrum (Cabletron), Solstice Enterprise Manager (Sun), Netview (IBM/Tivoli), and ISM/Openmaster (Bull).

Management platforms

Planners

Planners implement the PoMs ⟨change sequencing plan⟩ and ⟨change acceptance plan⟩. The change sequencing plan contains a timetable for all pending changes over a long period (e.g., one year). It also includes planning for the use of resources (such as personnel). It initiates the sequence of the changes, serves as the target sequence, and can be compared to the current sequence for intervention into a system for control purposes. The change acceptance plan contains detailed

Planning tool

information for each change on all the operative activities required for acceptance to actual operations. Comparable to the change sequencing plan, it contains information on the use of resources and a timetable for a specific change.

The planning module provides a mechanism for listing the operative activities involved. In some circumstances, a (partial) parallelization of activities is useful. Milestones are established for the synchronization of the individual activities, and possible risks are explicitly indicated. Roles (people) are assigned to the individual activities.

Integration of existing tools

The project planning application MS Project is used to implement the planner in the CICC tool environment. MS Project offers a clear overview of conditions (e.g., load charts, network plans) and a facility for processing change plans. MS Project with Java is linked to a database to enable the further processing of information.

ROC Applet

Release of change (ROC)

The ROC (release of change) applet implements the tool-supported change release form. Similar to the change request tool, Internet technologies (WWW) are used for this purpose. The functionalities of this tool module are similar to those of the change request tool, but the information it contains relates to the results of the change. This information can be taken from the TSA tool.

18.6.5 Process Management Services

Coordination of tool environment through specification of guidelines

Two other components allow an efficient use of PoMs in conformance with the specifications in change management: guideline builders and cooperation assistants. The *guideline builder*, for example, allows the change manager responsible for the process to specify guidelines for the cooperative operation of change management. These guidelines can relate to a basic sequence of actions as well as a distribution of responsibility or assignment of rights. The specification serves as a guideline for using the coordination kernel to initiate the roles and use of PoMs. The function of the guideline is to make recommendations, and can be deviated from in valid situation (e.g., when dealing with nonspecified exception situations). The guideline builder is directly linked to the cooperation kernel through the guideline repository.

Monitoring and initiation by the cooperation assistant

Another component of process management services is the *cooperation assistant*. On the basis of the current situation in change management, the cooperation assistant recommends to a role that it should use an appropriate PoM to handle an upcoming need for action. The actual status is conveyed to the cooperation assistant by the cooperation kernel. But the user is not forced to follow the recommendation. In valid special cases, it can be necessary to use other PoMs or tool modules without causing any inconsistencies in the CICC tool environment. To do so, the cooperation assistant uses the next opportunity to synchronize with the process again. There is an advantage to using a cooperation assistant compared to the worklist handler in the workflow management approach [HOL94]: It offers a straightforward option for not only using the push technique to assign roles to the pending steps and PoMs being used but also for using the pull technique recommended by the cooperation assistant to ensure access to the PoMs. The cooperation assistant even supports an operational cooperation between roles if a suitable application module is not available by making a request to the role responsible and requesting a short confirmation once the task has been completed.

18.6.6   Other Aspects

Internet technology is being used to implement the communication aspect in the prototype for the CICC tool. A WWW browser enables multimedia interaction with the user and also provides other data exchange services (e.g., FTP, email).

Applications must be coordinated to ensure that change management is supported efficiently. A sufficiently detailed process description of change management [ABM97] provides an appropriate guide. The aim is to use this guide to control the use of tools in interaction with the tool users. This is the aim pursued by developers of workflow management systems [DAD97, HOL94]. These systems enable a detailed modeling of a process and initiate the use of integrated tools during runtime. Yet current workflow systems are still not flexible enough to meet provider requirements in the services area.

Workflow management systems are not flexible enough

The goal in the development of the CICC tool environment is to assemble an offering of modular application services that can be configured to produce a provider-accepted tool environment that meets the respective provider's needs. The roles are supported during the processing of their tasks to ensure that these application services can also be used efficiently in change management.

Because of the modular architecture and the underlying cooperation services of the application services, the CICC can be expanded at any time through new or existing applications. For example, if there

Scalability of CICC tool environment

is a change in procedures at the process level, the CICC tool can be expanded by the corresponding modules.

Gaining experience in the execution of changes

The changes that are executed are documented in a logbook. There is an analysis of the extent to which these empirical values can be processed and used in actual change situations. The maintenance of this logbook through the storage of information gained from experience is similar to a learning process that always allows for more precise evaluation and planning within change management. This results in an acceleration in the process sequence and an improvement in the quality of change management.

Quality Monitoring and Assurance of Operations

The operations of a networked system must be structured to comply with the quality parameters stipulated in service level agreements with the customers. An effective and efficient implementation of the processes of routine, problem, and change management extensively described in the last chapter provides the foundation needed. The procedure of checking that the operations of a networked system are actually being carried out effectively and efficiently is the subject of a process we refer to as operational quality monitoring and assurance.

Significance of quality aspect

The quality issue has already been raised in a number of places in connection with the description of the operational processes. Quality parameters are agreed on with a customer in a service level agreement and must be complied with at the operational level as follows:

Existing points of contact

- In routine management some of the quality parameters flow directly into the process-oriented management means of the operational monitoring sheet that is used within the action ⟨monitor component status⟩.

- Problem management must be organized in such a way that the quality parameters agreed on with the customer can also be complied with in the event that a problem occurs in the networked system.

- The aim of change management is to ensure that new and extended service level agreements incorporate the quality parameters required. Changes are implemented so that there is no impact on the quality agreed on in the other service level agreements.

Through the appropriate actions undertaken and the management means used in these actions, each operational process therefore already plays its role in "producing" quality. This begs the totally justified question of why these procedures in the operational processes do not

Motivation for independent quality level

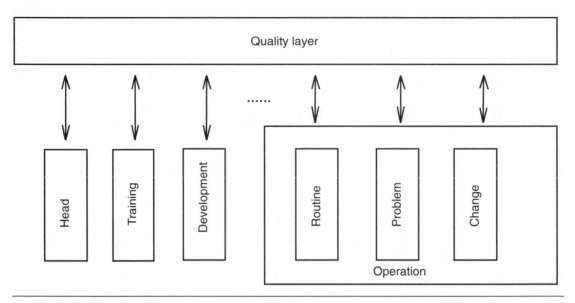

Figure 19.1
Breakdown of quality level

suffice and a *separate quality* layer is needed in the process model in addition to the operational layer. The introduction of a separate quality layer is motivated by the following two reasons:

- Each operational process tackles impending quality issues from a *local* and limited view. In the quality layer that spans the operational processes, these local views are merged into a *quality policy* that is applicable to the entire provider organization and incorporates the agreed-on overall goals for quality.

- The operational processes tackle only the *operative aspect* linked to quality. If quality is to be produced, there are *planning and strategic aspects* that, additionally, must be dealt with by the processes of the quality layer.

As shown in Figure 19.1, the quality layer can do justice only to the global orientation addressed in the first point mentioned if it forms a relationship not only with operations but also with all the other operating areas of the provider organization (e.g., planning, development, training, and controlling).

Chapter structure and content   Section 19.1 clarifies these interfaces to the different operating areas in descriptions on the individual quality processes. Sections 19.2 and 19.3 then focus totally on the quality process responsible for quality monitoring and assurance in the operations of networked systems.

19.1   Content and Processes of the Quality Layer

This section begins with a brief introduction to the issue of quality as addressed in the ISO 9000 standards series and the application of these standards to the information processing area, followed by a description of the key quality processes carried out by the provider organization of a networked system.

19.1.1   Quality in Accordance with ISO 9000

The concept of *quality* is used to describe the nature of the result of every form of economic creation. Since the nature of a result that represents a product or a service is particularly of interest to the person using this product or service, the discussion about quality is strongly linked to the issue of customer orientation.

Clarification of terms

The International Standards Organization offers a binding and generally accepted definition of the term *quality* in the standard ISO 8402, which describes it as *the aggregate of the characteristics of a product or a service in respect to its suitability to meet defined or given requirements*. Numerous publications, particularly those from the management and commercial informatics areas, devote a great deal of attention to the aspect of quality.

Definition per ISO

The standardization work of ISO in the area of quality in the past was not only restricted to a specification of terms but also involved the development of a standardized procedure for the introduction of so-called *quality management* (QM) systems in companies. This procedure is documented by the ISO 9000 standards, which in essence, are made up of five standards (ISO 9000 to ISO 9004). In ISO 9000, the quality management system is introduced as *the organizational structure and the responsibilities, processes, procedures, and resources required for the implementation of quality management*, with quality management described as *that aspect of the overall management task that defines and implements quality policy*. Quality policy is defined as *an organization's comprehensive intentions and goals concerning quality as formally stipulated by top management*. The definition from the standard [ISO 9000] just mentioned unequivocally states that any introduction of quality management in conformance with the ISO 9000 specification must be approved and promoted by company management.

Quality management per ISO 9000

In addition to providing a comprehensive clarification of definitions, the ISO 9000 series also includes concrete specifications for the introduction of a quality management system that can be officially certified by authorized bodies. The standard ISO 9004 therefore serves as an industry-endorsed guide that specifies all possible aspects of the quality of a QM system in the form of *quality management elements*. Some of the total of 20 QM elements are as follows:

Selection of
QM elements

- *Contract checking:* Each contract that has been agreed on with a customer must first be checked to ensure that the conditions can be met.

- *Control of documents and data:* A suitable procedure has to be established and used for monitoring documentation with a facility for the removal or identification of invalid or outdated documents.

- *Control of faulty products:* Faulty products should be identified so that unintentional use can be avoided.

- *Internal quality audits:* Regular audits should be carried out to determine whether the different elements of the quality management system are effective for meeting the stipulated quality objectives.

- *Training:* Training should be provided to ensure that employees develop an awareness of what quality means. Furthermore, training related to tasks and workplace functions should ensure that employees are able to meet the requirements placed on them.

Different ISO 9000
applications models

The standards ISO 9001 to ISO 9003 introduce three different validation levels for specific company areas. The ISO 9001 standard is the most extensive one of the three validation levels and encompasses the areas of development, design, production, installation, and customer service. ISO 9002 covers only the areas of production and installation, and ISO 9003 is limited to product final inspection.

19.1.2 Quality Management Systems in Information Processing

The IT sector can
also be certified
per ISO 9000

The ISO 9000 standards series has recently become of particular interest for the issues of quality in the information processing area because more and more IT companies are introducing quality management systems in compliance with ISO 9000 and are also having IT products and services certified. An IT service provider such as a computer center or a network of computer centers can therefore use the ISO 9002 standard as the foundation for the introduction of a QM system. In this context, the term *production* is interpreted as the production of the service offered to the customer, which is something the ISO 9000 series also allows. Developers of IT systems, on the other hand, will

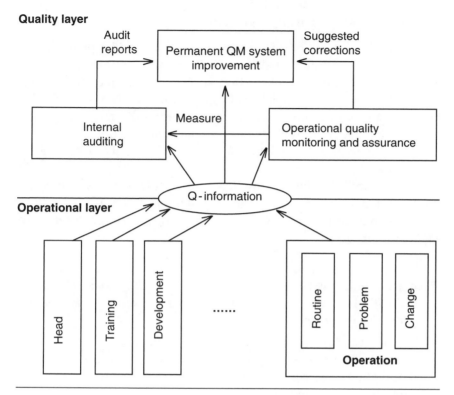

Figure 19.2
Three key quality processes

strive for certification in compliance with ISO 9001 since the aspects of (software) development and design have to be incorporated into the QM systems they introduce.

19.1.3   Quality Processes

From the view of the standard, the QM elements described present a standardized approach to structuring the content of the quality layer. Process-oriented quality management has already been successfully tested [WLA97] in connection with the introduction of QM systems for the IT area. Figure 19.2 presents three important quality processes that are of particular interest to us in this context and should be introduced by any quality-oriented provider organization that places an emphasis on quality in its operations. Each of these quality processes will be described briefly.

Continuous QM System Improvement

Within the framework of this quality process, a provider organization introduces a procedure that allows existing shortcomings (e.g., in work processes or in the tools used) that surface in a variety of different ways to be eliminated systematically and permanently. The corrective measures introduced involve a strict monitoring of scheduling and a critical evaluation of the effectiveness of the measures undertaken. The measures are to be corrected appropriately in the event that there is no improvement.

The quality information supplied by the individual areas provides the basis for the validation carried out. Other quality processes can also contribute as follows toward making continuous improvements to a QM system:

Relationship to other quality processes

- The aim of the audit report produced in the process ⟨execute internal audit⟩ is to reveal shortcomings in the processes and to deal with these shortcomings through the process ⟨*permanent QM system improvement*⟩.

- The process ⟨*operational quality monitoring and assurance*⟩ can produce proposals for improvement that extend beyond the area of operation (e.g., improvement to the skills of operating personnel through appropriate training).

From the view of the standard, the quality process ⟨permanent QM system improvement⟩ is of major importance if a provider organization wants to be certified in accordance with the ISO 9000 standard. The only way to close gaps in quality successfully in a provider organization and therefore meet the ongoing demands for increasing quality is through a systematic pursuit and evaluation of corrective measures.

Execution of Internal Audits

Direct reference to a QM element

The quality process ⟨*internal auditing*⟩ specifies a measure for revealing gaps in quality that is promoted by the standard in a separate quality management element.

The process roughly comprises the following steps:

- *Development of an audit plan* defines which location will be audited by an auditor and when. The audit plan should be agreed on with all participating parties.

- The *audit* should evaluate the effectiveness of the quality assurance measures executed by the location being audited. These measures are a component part of the quality management system and should be documented therein in accordance with certain specifications dictated by the standard.

- The process is completed with the *generation of an audit report*, which documents the results of the audit. This report identifies shortcomings that have been found and the appropriate corrective measures required.

The execution of the corrective measures defined in the internal audit is the task of the process ⟨continous QM system improvement⟩.

Operational Quality Monitoring and Assurance

The fundamentals of the quality processes presented can be applied to any IT organization. The quality aspect that relates to the area that is of interest here, the operation of networked systems, will be looked at more closely. The following sections therefore concentrate solely on the quality process that is responsible for the monitoring and assurance of operational quality. As Figure 19.2 highlights, the process ⟨operational quality monitoring and assurance⟩, abbreviated here to *operational QMA process*, is closely linked to other quality processes. For example, transitions always occur between the operational QMA process and other quality processes when the measures for quality assurance require the involvement of more than just the provider organization.

19.2   Operational Quality Monitoring and Assurance (QMA)

In this section, the procedure used earlier in conjunction with the three operational processes is applied in a slightly modified form to the quality process from the view of the operation of a networked system. The allocation of the process-oriented management means (PoM) required is based on the process content, which is executed more precisely in the form of actions. The features required by the provider are then described for each PoM. The section concludes with a list of the key requirements for suitable ⟨quality management⟩ tools that can provide the computer-supported management means required.

Use of the PoM concept with quality process

19.2.1   Content and Structure of the Quality Process

The core of the quality process ⟨operational quality monitoring and assurance⟩ consists of the execution of a target performance comparison. The target quality is determined by two important sources:

Target quality value and ...

1. A customer is given certain guarantees of quality in the *service level agreement*, and the provider organization's primary aim is to comply with these guarantees [STI95]. The content of the guarantees can roughly be broken down into the following areas:

   - Stability: availability, guarantee of failsafe operations, meantime between failure
   - Performance: response times, guaranteed capacity
   - Security: protection against system attacks
   - Support: hotline availability times, etc.

2. Specifications for the execution of operational activities are established by *operational guidelines* (e.g., in the form of work assignments); these guidelines therefore represent a certain target specification for the actions taking place in the operational processes.

... actual quality value

The actual value for quality is derived directly from the information accumulated in the components in the networked system or in the operational processes that provide the basis for statements on the quality of operations. A great deal of this information, also referred to as *quality indicators*, can be allocated to similar areas such as the content of the service level agreements. Other quality indicators relate to aspects such as customer satisfaction (number of complaints), corporate success (profitability, number of new customers), and employee skills (number and types of training programs conducted).

Description of the process through phases and actions

The process of operational quality monitoring and assurance is characterized by a cycle in which a comparison of actual information about quality (in the following referred to in brief as quality information) is run sequentially with the target specifications for quality and continuously repeated. The process therefore breaks down into phases, as shown in Figure 19.3. The actions that occur in these phases are clarified next.

⟨*Preparation*⟩ *Phase*

The actions in this phase provide the information required for the target performance comparison in a form usable for the analysis. The

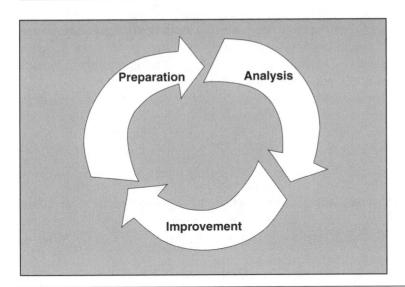

Figure 19.3
Cycle for operational quality monitoring and assurance

emphasis is clearly on the actual quality information that is collected, processed, and archived at the operational level. We will first begin with a description of the only action that relates to the target quality information.

The action ⟨*list target quality specifications*⟩ specifies the "measuring rod" applied to the operational quality information that is to be compiled. As we have already mentioned, the key sources for the quality targets are the operational guidelines that regulate the procedures within the operation as well as the service level agreements contracted with the customers. The object and purpose of the action is to process the information in these sources in such a way that it can be adopted as the target parameters for the analysis. For example, certain quality monitoring specifications for individual network components, computer systems, and the applications run on them should be derived from the service level agreement since this offers the only possibility for conducting a comparison with the quality information (actual values) supplied from these components.

The quality information that is extracted from the operational processes in the action ⟨*provide information about operational quality*⟩ is related to the quality targets and is necessary for checking the actual target values required. The information about quality required from operations depends on the type of analysis to be conducted. For instance, an analysis of the components of a networked system mainly relates to technical variables (e.g., system status information, response times), whereas an analysis of the variables of the operations deals with the operational processes (e.g., required processing time from receipt of problem notification to problem repair).

The action ⟨collect operational quality information⟩ is used to present the information on operational quality in a form that is appropriate for analysis. Certain important quality information can often be provided only through appropriate computation. Thus, for example, the runtime of an operational process consists of different partial times. Furthermore, possible deficiencies in the collected information may have to be clarified in this action. Examples of deficiences could be the lack of relevant supplementary information and the inaccuracy of collected information (e.g., due to time clock synchronization problems).

The information that is collected is stored and provided for analysis within the action ⟨archive operational quality information⟩. The archiving process is important because the operations of a networked system usually store the quality information only temporarily.

⟨Analysis⟩ Phase

The analysis phase consists of performance comparison of the quality targets compiled in the first phase and the operational quality information stored in an appropriate archive. To this extent, this phase comprises the core of the entire QMA process.

The core of the operational QMA process

The action ⟨initiate analysis⟩ comprises all the activities that have to be completed before a particular quality target can be checked. In a provider organization, specific analyses are initiated on a contract-related basis, as explained more precisely later. In this case, an estimation of the time required for the analysis can be desirable or necessary.

Target performance comparison

The action ⟨check quality information⟩ can be regarded as the core action of the quality process. It is in this action that the specifications for the quality targets are compared to the operational quality information collected during the first phase. The results obtained through the checking process identify the deviations from the existing targets.

The results achieved in the analysis are prepared for subsequent processing and forwarded to the location responsible for improvement within the action ⟨process and forward results⟩. Reports and reviews are typical examples of how the results are prepared.

⟨*Improvement*⟩ *Phase*

On the basis of the results achieved during the analysis phase, this phase defines the appropriate operational requirements and measures that are to be introduced to address any deviation from targets. The measures that could be considered encompass a broad spectrum of possibilities ranging from technical improvements and organizational changes to a modification of operational processes. These decisions are taken within the action ⟨*plan measures*⟩.

The defined measures are actually carried out in the action ⟨*execute measures*⟩. This also includes a notification of the locations responsible to ensure that the measures are accepted into operations.

19.2.2 Process-Oriented Management Means and Tool Requirements

As is the case with the operational processes, suitable resources are required for carrying out the quality processes. As Table 19.1 shows, these resources can also be allocated to the four types of process-oriented management means introduced in section 18.1.

The interaction between the (quality, Q) management means required for the process of operational quality monitoring and assurance is shown in Figure 19.4. The illustration indicates two ways in which a collection, archiving, and analysis of operational quality information (QI) can be initiated:

The following general description is put into a concrete form in an example in section 19.3

- A provider organization has certain requirements for the quality of operations defined by the management means ⟨Q-targets⟩, and the quality specified must constantly be monitored and guaranteed. To a certain extent, the ⟨Q-target⟩ serves as a "basic instruction" for this quality process.

- In addition, (authorized) customers can explicitly request the process to collect certain operational quality information (PoM ⟨Q-collection request⟩) or to analyze information that has already been collected and filed in the QI-archive (PoM ⟨Q-evaluation request⟩).

Explicit request

The management means that supports the execution of the quality process is ⟨QI-collection support⟩. It is closely associated with the ⟨Q-source base⟩ since this PoM provides it with the information needed for obtaining information about quality. This information can, for example, be the address of a component in a networked system that accumulates certain information about quality (see the example in

Management means for collection,...

Table 19.1 Support aspects in the process ⟨operational quality monitoring and assurance⟩

Support Aspects	PoM Type	PoM
For checking appropriate recording of targets for operation	Information Communication	Q-target
Documentation of sources that supply operational quality information	Information	Q-source base
Request for operational quality information being collected	Communication	QI-collection request
Support in compilation of operational quality information from respective sources of Q-source base being queried	Execution	QI-collection request
Storage of operational quality information	Information	QI-archive
Request for analysis (previously collected) operational quality information	Communication	Q-analysis request
Support in the analysis of collected and archived operational quality information	Execution	Q-assurance support
Specification and documentation of measures to be undertaken	Information	Q-measures catalog

section 19.3) or the identification of an organizational unit that stores quality information accumulated in the context of an operational process (e.g., operational statistics).

...analysis,...   The actual kernel of this process, namely, the execution of the target performance comparison, is supported by the process-oriented management means ⟨Q-assurance support⟩. The operational quality information needed for executing the comparison is provided by the PoM ⟨QI-archive⟩. The target being checked provides the ⟨Q-target⟩. If the target performance comparison is being initiated because of a contract-related reason, this information can also be a component part of ⟨Q-evaluation request⟩.

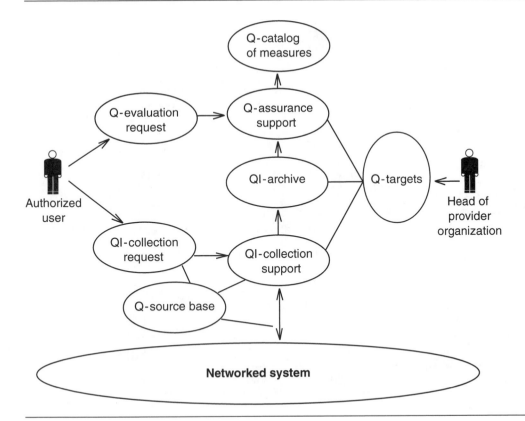

Figure 19.4
Interaction of process-oriented management means

The management means ⟨Q-catalog of measures⟩ is provided for the documentation of any identified deviations and the measures required to rectify these deviations.

...and documentation

The PoMs that have just been described relate to the most general case of operational quality monitoring and assurance. Consequently, the descriptions have been purposely kept as general as possible. The management means that were introduced will be examined more closely in the next section in the context of the pursuit of a concrete goal for security quality in the operation of networked systems.

As is shown in Figure 19.5, the types of tools required for computer-supported management means for the process ⟨operational quality monitoring and assurance⟩ are very similar to those for the operational processes. Some of the general requirements of the provider for these quality management tools are described next.

(Quality) management tools

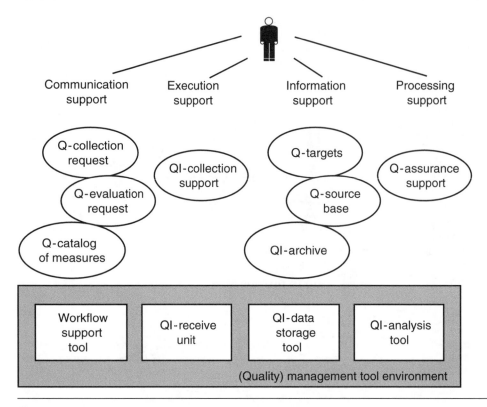

Figure 19.5
Tool support for operational quality monitoring and assurance

Accuracy of QI-Data Storage

This requirement concerns the computer-supported implementation of the management means ⟨Q-target⟩, ⟨Q-source base⟩, and ⟨QI-archive⟩. In particular, there must be a guarantee that the quality information derived from the components of a networked system and from the operational processes is stored on a reliable and supervised basis.

Automation of Collection Process

Operational QMA must be implemented efficiently

Complex networked systems have a large range of different sources that can be queried for operational quality information for the purposes of a competent operational quality monitoring and assurance process. Owing to the complexity of the process, and particularly for reasons of accuracy, it is important that the process be automated as far as possible by the tools that monitor the acceptance of the operational quality information.

Reduction of Additional Administrative Cost

The quality monitoring and assurance of operations necessitates an additional effort within the operational processes that, for the most part, relates to the documentation of the operational states of the networked system and of operational procedures. This creates additional administration, which should not be underestimated but can be reduced through the use of suitable workflow support and data storage tools.

This last point emphasizes the necessity of taking into account the *cost–benefit ratio* of operational quality monitoring and assurance. To a large degree, the costs are incurred through the provision of the quality information; there should be an aim to provide as much of the operational quality information on a tool-supported basis as possible:

- This requirement is already being addressed satisfactorily today through the use of efficient *network and system management tools* for the quality information directly supplied by the components of a networked system.

- However, the provision of quality information from the layer of the operational processes is more problematic (e.g., runtimes and turnaround times for requests). This type of operational quality information is available only in tools if workflow support tools or *workflow management systems* are used more intensively in the future for routine, problem, and change management, as was outlined in the example with CICC (section 18.6).

Quality information at the level of the networked system and operational processes

19.3   Case Study: Analysis of Security Data

This section closely examines the quality process ⟨operational quality monitoring and assurance⟩ on the basis of a concrete example and looks at how this process is applied to the problem of quality of security that has to be tackled in networked systems. The networked system used for the purposes of our study is a *telecommunications network* that is constructed from a partially intermeshed network of digital switching nodes (SNs). The SNs are very complex systems that can be effectively operated only with the support of special management tools and highly skilled personnel who use these tools. The EWSD systems from Siemens

The sample scenario being examined

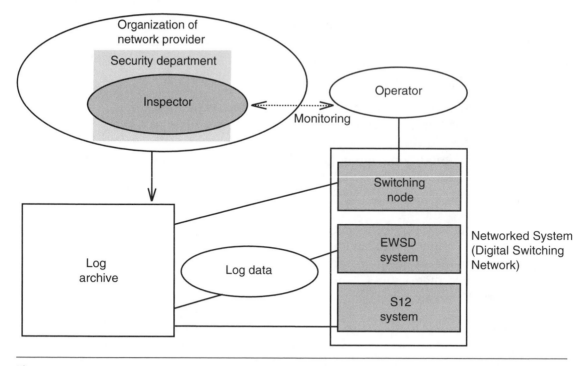

Figure 19.6
Digital switching network overview

and the S12 systems from Alcatel are concrete examples of these SN systems.

Restriction to a certain quality aspect

We will focus on one important aspect of the operation of the type of digital switching network illustrated in Figure 19.6. The provider has the responsibility of taking suitable measures to ensure that attacks that could pose a threat to the telecommunications network are detected and traced. An appropriate security department is set up for this purpose with so-called security inspectors who, using certain operational quality information, look for conspicuous signs of anything that could threaten the security of the networked system being monitored.

Quality goal: detection and tracing of security attacks

Although it may be desirable from the provider's view to have complete protection against any attacks to security, in practice, it is not possible to provide complete guarantees because of new threat scenarios that are constantly developing. For this reason, in addition to the security mechanisms integrated directly into the components of a digital switching network (e.g., for authentication and authorization), a higher-ranking control (a special kind of intrusion detection) is needed that specifically checks the network for potential security attacks.

The ISO 9000 standard described at the beginning of this chapter provides an important basis for the design of the QMA system used in this special scenario. In this context, the following two quality systems elements are of particular importance:

1. Auditing of the quality system: An extensive auditing process is necessary to ensure that the QMA measures established in connection with the switching nodes supply the desired quality.

2. Quality documentation and records: This quality element is used to specify how the quality information generated by the switching nodes in the given scenario is to be documented and circulated within the provider organization.

In the scenario examined here, the *log data* produced from the SNs is used to monitor the security quality of digital switching networks. The SN logs, described in more detail in section 19.3.1, also document all the administrative operations carried out by the operating personnel of these components. In the context being studied, the log data represents an important part of the process-oriented management means ⟨QI-source base⟩, which enables the identification of attacks to security or other security-critical wrong operation.

Identifying the PoMs in the sample scenario

The targets for security quality set by the provider can be described on the basis of *attack patterns*, which identify certain undesirable activities or sequences of activities at the switching nodes. In this scenario, therefore, the PoM ⟨Q-targets⟩ discussed in section 19.3.2 consist of a list of attack patterns that allow the provider to detect and follow up on potential attacks to security.

To check whether the attack patterns defined by ⟨Q-targets⟩ occur in the collected log data, a provider can use the management means ⟨Q-assurance support⟩, which simplifies the *attack pattern search*. Since the log data involves a massive quantity of data, suitable computer support in the form of a log evaluation tool is mandatory at this point (section 19.3.3).

Logfiles (section 19.3.4) from the separate switching nodes must be *transmitted* to a *central log archive* (section 19.3.5) to enable attack pattern searches to be carried out to all log data from a central location.

Sample *provider-accepted tool solutions* are indicated for all the PoMs needed for this concrete implementation of operational quality monitoring and assurance. An integrated approach that deals with cooperation of the tool user was incorporated into the development of these tools. The procedure used therefore corresponds to the CICC approach described in section 18.6. The interaction between all the

From PoMs to provider-accepted (quality) management tools

tools produces a generic solution of *cooperative IT log processing* (CILP) derived from the provider's requirements. The central CILP tools (log structure editor, log analyzer, log archive) have been designed so that they can be adapted for use with any operational QMA problems that are processed using log data. The following subsections look at how the provider's requirements for individual CILP tools have been taken into account.

19.3.1   QI-Source Base: SN Log Data

The key premise of this concrete form of the quality process ⟨operational quality monitoring and assurance⟩ is that security attacks are identified on the basis of SN log data. This data therefore forms the sole source for the quality process considered here. The PoM ⟨QI-source base⟩ contains two key component parts:

- A list of all SNs that supply log data that is to undergo an attack pattern analysis
- Information about the structure of the SN logfiles

Automation of updating

The requirement of the provider in the current scenario was that all SNs that build the digital switching network should be contained in the ⟨QI-source base⟩. An automatic comparison was required in the ⟨QI-source base⟩ to guarantee the completeness of the SN list when new SNs were added or existing SNs eliminated. The tool function used to implement the process-oriented management means ⟨QI-source base⟩ addressed the requirement of the provider for a continuous cross-check for agreement with the current configuration base.

Structure information for log data

In the quality process being examined, the provider requires a considerable amount of computer-based support in connection with the structure information contained in the QI-source base. The SN logfiles consist of a sequence of data sets in which the following information fields appear (see Figure 19.7):

- User name and unique user identifier
- Time and date
- Name of command executed at SN
- Details about SN
- Other plaintext

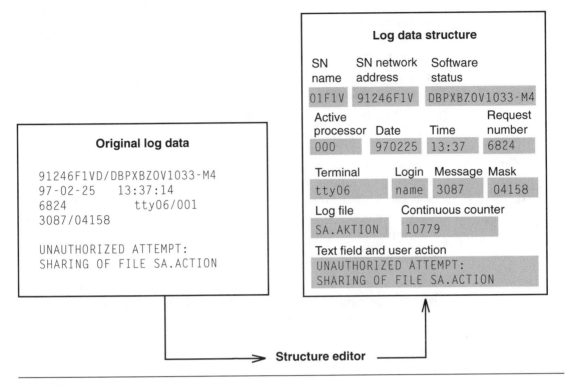

Figure 19.7
SN log data structure and structure editor

A knowledge of the structure of the data sets is essential if a computer-supported search for more complex attack patterns is to be carried out in the logfiles. Without the structure information, a logfile would be a pure (ASCII) character string, which can be searched only for conspicuous character patterns. In practice, an attack pattern used, for example, to check whether a user has initiated a command sequence (with specific parameter values, at a specific time interval, with a certain output result) cannot be supported by a computer-based tool at the character level unless knowledge of the structure of the log data set exists.

Close connection between structure information and attack patterns

Obtaining the necessary structure information for the switching network nodes described in the scenario is not an easy matter for the following reasons:

- Standardized specifications (e.g., those defined by [OEC91]) do not exist for the generation of the logfiles.

- Manufacturers of the switches used in this scenario supply neither formal nor informal specifications for the log data produced by their components.

- The content and structure of the log data varies from manufacturer to manufacturer.

- The content and structure of the log data depends on the software version that is run on the SN.

As a result of the circumstances outlined, the SN log data, which is important for the detection of attacks on security, is examined in provider organizations only on a spot-check basis by the respective experts who are (more or less) familiar with the structure of log data. Consequently, the structure information to be maintained in the PoM ⟨QI-source base⟩ exists either in the heads of the experts or in the form of informal notes.

Tool support for obtaining structure information

The computer-supported implementation of this aspect of the management means ⟨QI-source base⟩ leads to a tool called a *structure editor* in the CILP environment (see Figure 19.7). With this tool, the structure of any SN logfile can be gradually created in interaction with the appropriate expert and filed in a form suitable for computer-supported processing.

19.3.2 Q-Targets: Attack Pattern on Switching Network Nodes

The Q-target is contained in the attack pattern

In the case study examined, the ⟨Q-targets⟩ being monitored and guaranteed are defined through the specification of the kind of attack being prevented. The goal is to detect the attacks that threaten the security of the telecommunications network and, if possible, to prevent or rule them out in the future using suitable tracing measures. Attacks on security can be formulated at the SN logfile level in the form of suitable attack patterns.

Simple and complex attack patterns

A distinction is made in principle between two classes of attack patterns: single-command attack patterns and command sequence attack patterns.

Single-Command Attack Patterns

This class includes all the attack patterns that relate only to a single command type that is executed on the SN. The attack patterns in this class can be broken down further depending on whether the command type only or one or more parameters of the command are also included in the attack pattern. An example of an attack pattern that is based on only command type is switching off the log. As soon as this command is found in an SN log, the suspicion of an attack is aroused and should be pursued.

Command Sequence Attack Patterns

Complex attacks on a telecommunications network can be formulated only on the basis of these patterns that provide details about command sequences, although the sequence does not necessarily have to consist of directly consecutive commands. An example of this category of attack pattern is the multiple failed login attempts of a user on an SN.

In the environment of cooperative IT log processing, the process-oriented management means ⟨Q-targets⟩ is provided by an *(attack) pattern editor*. The general requirements formulated in the last subsection can be adapted as follows for the pattern editor.

(Quality) management tool: pattern editor

Simple Formulation of Attack Pattern

It was possible to keep the complex internal formalism (regular expressions) transparent to the user through the use of an appropriate graphical user interface developed in conjunction with users for entering patterns. A cryptographic formalism that is difficult to use and to learn was purposely avoided, which has contributed considerably toward increasing the acceptance of the CILP tool environment.

Structured and Secure Filing of Formulated Patterns

Previous patterns obtained by the security inspectors provide the knowledge base that serves as the foundation upon which the quality process being considered, operational quality monitoring and assurance, is based. The patterns must be filed in a structure prescribed by the provider organization to enable a systematic use and expansion of this knowledge base, and access to this base is controlled by a procedure that is part of security policy. The pattern editor provides suitable functions to meet these requirements that are in agreement with the functions of other tools in the CILP environment (especially log analyzer and log archive). The point being emphasized is that the pattern editor works in close association with the log analyzer.

19.3.3   Q-Assurance Support: Log Analyzer

Another (quality)
management tool
in connection with
attack patterns

The attack patterns described by the pattern editor are accepted by the log analyzer and applied to concrete SN log data. The log analyzer functions as a tool that is used to support quality assurance in the case study.

Design of
provider-accepted
user interface

A log analyzer can be used by security inspectors either for a fully automated search of attack patterns or on an interactive basis. The interactive user interface is roughly made up of the following areas:

- Display area. This is the main window in which the SN log data is displayed in the form required by the security inspector.

- Data field selection area. The individual fields of the log data records that are to be displayed can be selected in this area.

- Data record selection area. By moving the indicator that points to the data record currently being processed, the security inspector has the flexibility of quick access to a desired data record even in very large logfiles.

- Pattern selection functions. The attack patterns produced with the help of the pattern editor provide this tool with an overview of the selection available within a library. The currently active pattern is displayed in a specific area of the user interface.

A provider-accepted layout of the interface for the log analyzer and for all other tools in the CILP environment can be achieved only if a close cooperation exists between the security inspectors using these tools. The design of the interface described earlier resulted from a close dialog between developers and users, and this has led to a high acceptance of the tool in day-to-day use.

19.3.4   QI-Collection Support: Log Receive Unit

Goal: extensive
automation of
collection process

The operational quality information in the case study being examined is accumulated in the components of a networked system and is therefore automatically transported and processed on a computer-supported basis. As is shown in Figure 19.8, the process-oriented management means of QI-collection support is implemented by several so-called log receive units that receive the log data of the switching nodes over ISDN router components. The transmission volume can be reduced through data compression in the log receive units before the units transmit the (now compressed) SN log data to a central log archive (see next

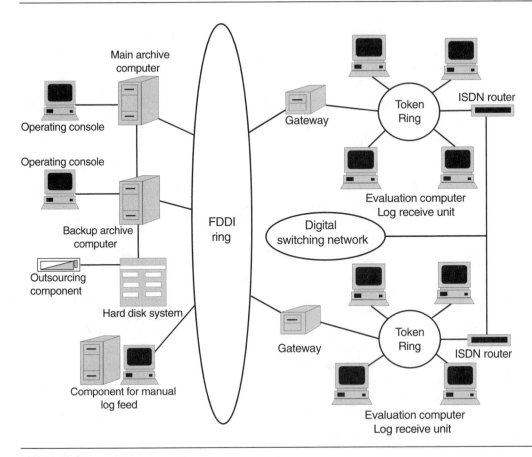

Figure 19.8
Implementation of PoMs ⟨QI-collection support⟩ and ⟨QI-archive⟩

section). In the actual case study, the log receive units that are part of a regional domain were combined through Token Rings. The log data from the local networks was consolidated over an FDDI ring.

As Figure 19.8 illustrates, the computer system on which the log receive unit is implemented can also be used to provide computer-supported parts of the PoM ⟨Q-assurance support⟩. Thus, in the actual scenario, for example, all those automated log analysis functions that relate to only one single logfile can be executed on this system. This procedure clearly reduces the burden on the analyses that are executed on the basis of the data in the central log archive.

19.3.5   QI-Archive: Central Log Archive

In addition to the components that provide QI-collection, the preceding illustration also shows all the systems that provide computer support

Problem of mass data

of the management means ⟨QI-archive⟩ in the case study. At the heart is a central archive processor that is designed with fault tolerance due to the special relevance of the operational quality information being archived by a backup archive processor. A hard disk storage system that stores data using RAID technology is linked to the archive processors. This is followed by external storage components that back up data on magnetic disks.

19.4   Future of Assistants for the Coordination of Operational Processes

Assistants merge provider-accepted individual solutions

Individual solutions that met the provider's requirements were created for each aspect being processed through the derivation of tools needed for the scenario from process-oriented management means (PoMs). The consolidation of these individual solutions to create a provider-accepted overall solution is the aim of the *log assistant*, which is also used in the coordination and cooperation of the roles involved in log processing. Figure 19.9 illustrates the different roles and the management means they require in order to carry out their activities.

These results provide the basis for an examination of the effective and efficient use of process-oriented management means. This requires a coordination of the tools used so that the roles receive maximum support in the implementation of their tasks. We will not pursue how the automated processing of the tasks is controlled and instead focus on how the roles should be initiated so that they execute their tasks in accordance with the goals.

For a detailed description of the actions of a process, the support aspects indicated in the PoMs provide an initial indication of which activities are the most important. What is noticeable is that the support aspects are linked to a number of work steps. These work steps are combined into a process according to logical criteria; the term *workflow* was introduced for this concept in Chapter 18.

Prerequisite for execution of a partial step

The fine granularity of the workflows allows a closer look at the content of the individual steps and the conditions attached to them—in other words, which conditions must be met to perform a single step. Each step is carried out by a role, and it is therefore evident which roles are involved in a workflow. An example is the workflow that is part of a support aspect: The storage of operational quality information (in the case study examined, this is the security data) is characterized by the fact that despite the use of automation, data is constantly filed

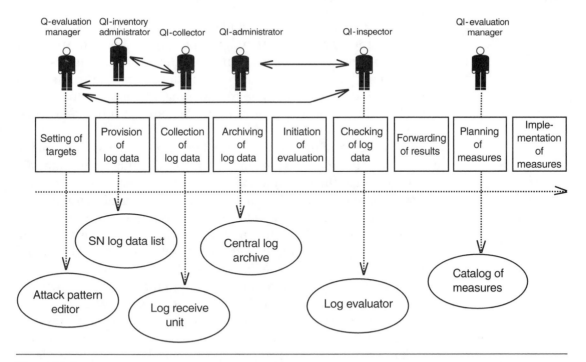

Figure 19.9
Cooperating roles

manually in an archive. The log administrator is responsible for this task that essentially comprises the identification of the file location, the actual filing process, and the conformance to archiving conditions.

The (management) tools that are actually operated and used by the roles during the processing of a workflow are defined by the PoMs. The workflow combines a number of management tools and determines from the operational situation which tool should be provided to the role. The information needed for this decision consists of the information to be processed (e.g., log data) and the individual workflow step.

A log assistant that initiates computer-supported processing must create a coordination between the workflows and the process-oriented management means. The log assistant uses a process description as a bracket over the tools. To those in operational personnel who work with the tools, this bracket is represented as a user interface that contains:

- The version of the process ⟨operational quality monitoring and assurance⟩ studied here

- The process-oriented management means provided for carrying out the actions of the process

Content of assistant interface

Operational personnel are guided through the process over the interface of the log assistant. At the appropriate locations in the process, the assistant supports the user in the utilization of the PoMs designed for handling the particular activity. This support can be in the form of warning indicators relating to frequent maloperation in the past or the call-up of a tool that is used to implement the process-oriented management means.

The approach of the log assistant offers a totally new kind of quality of provider-oriented management interface. The most important aspect is no longer the tool function but the operational process and the current operational situation in which access is available not only to management functions (depending on the computer-supported PoMs) but also to other noncomputer-supported means. The goal is to provide an efficient means for coping with the operational situation at hand. The log assistant does not replace the underlying management tools but instead is to be viewed as an extension to them that simplifies the use of existing process-oriented management means.

There isn't only one assistant approach in actual practice; instead, problem-oriented tools or individual functions for an operational assistant are available. For example, signaling facilities on the interfaces of management platforms provide an overview of an operational situation; these facilities display the status of network components and, for example, announce to roles in a graphically processed form that errors have occurred. Other functions that affect the overview are the display of different angles of the components (e.g., 2D/3D or attributes). Support functions that supply informal information about individual tool functions to the roles are also available.

In the decision sector, assisting tools are mainly used in problem management and repair. An attempt is made in this area to support the discovery of fault causes in networked systems so that roles receive pre-processed or consolidated information on faults and their causes. The tools contain diagnostic functions or decision trees that are based on knowledge banks and analyze these banks using dedicated guidelines.

Shortcomings of existing approaches

The assisting tools described here provide their support largely from a component-oriented point of view. Although support is provided to operational personnel, the cooperative aspects are for the most part not taken into account—in other words, guidelines on which tool should be used within an operational situation are lacking.

Requirements for Log Assistants

A log assistant must provide roles with the following attributes to deal with operational situations.

- *Process-oriented guidelines:* Operational procedures should be supported in each process. Owing to the large number of workflows, operational personnel do not have a clear overview of which steps are to be taken next. For the log assistant, this means that the user must be provided with an overview of his or her workflows and the subsequent steps mapped out for each workflow.

- *Diagnostic functions and view forming:* In operational situations, it often takes expert knowledge or a precise search to gain an accurate understanding of a situation. Roles must therefore be presented with different options that offer decisions or at least support the assessment of a situation. | Expert knowledge

- *Concealing technical specifics:* The heterogeneity of networked systems makes it difficult for operational personnel to develop a uniform knowledge and to implement an operational process efficiently. The log assistant carries out an abstraction of technical system specifics and provides only essential information and functions. | Knowledge of technical system specifics

- *Relieving administrative tasks:* A large part of working time is lost on administrative tasks (e.g., search and access to information or tools). Operating personnel already begin to lack an overview of storage locations after just a few work steps. Dynamic systems that file and provide information at strategically important locations in the process should be integrated into log assistants. | Routine knowledge

- *Learnability:* The operational situations that exist in a networked system are diverse and are always undergoing change. A log assistant must adjust to new situations to ensure that a role is initiated on an optimal basis, and it must accompany and guide the role in carrying out its activities with the current information base on the situation. | Independent structure of this knowledge

- *Flexibility:* Many operational situations are characterized by the fact that they cannot be carried out with uniformity—in other words, they have to be implemented according to the prevailing requirements. A log assistant must be prepared to deal with deviations from the mapped-out workflows and resynchronize itself with tools or users each time it enters or returns to a workflow, as well as support further procedures. | Deviation and …

- *Open workflows:* A characteristic of workflow processing is that sequential processing is not possible because interruptions and the | …interruption to workflow switchover to other workflows are part of the day-to-day operations of networked systems. The interlinked and irregular processing of workflows increases the complexity of a role's task area. The log assistant provides support to all workflows begun by role and also supplies the status that applied when the workflow was terminated.

Information from management tools is essential

These requirements can be fulfilled only by a log assistant if it cooperates with the management tools used so that it receives information that can be used for a statement on the status of the process. Moreover, the log assistant is constantly active in the background, accepts information, and if necessary, reacts to new situations.

Structure of the assistant

An architecture that specifies the principal structure of these systems is required if assistants are to be implemented to support concrete scenarios. The requirements that have been outlined give an indication that the design for a comprehensive architecture is divided into two parts. The *assistant platform* that provides a comprehensive infrastructure forms the first part. It is particularly responsible for transparent access to tools over different systems. Moreover, it takes into account the different physical conditions and provides uniform services.

The *applications* required for operational assistance are based on the assistant platform and provide users with functions over a graphical user interface. The functions break down into the categories of execution and initiation. The executing functions enable operating personnel to initiate active workflows using the associated tools, whereas methods used for the initiation map out the next step in the process.

The log assistant draws information from the process description identifying the operational situation in which a tool can be used by a certain role within the provider organization. To this extent, the process description represents a type of provider-oriented view on the tools, which is essential for an efficient implementation of the process.

The provider's requirements must always be taken into account during the development of assistants. The development, however, must be based on functions of existing management tools and must bundle these into an assistant so that existing modules can be used. As the following chapter shows, some provider-accepted modules are already being offered in management platforms.

Two Examples of Provider-Oriented Management Products

All the main manufacturers of management systems (such as CA, HP, IBM, Siemens, and Sun) have recognized the need to take greater account of provider requirements for management solutions. This is the only way to offer tools that will increase the efficiency of the operational processes described in previous chapters.

Increased requirement for provider-accepted tools

The two sample systems presented in this chapter represent only a small and incomplete segment of the type of management tools that integrate the view of the provider. The first system can be allocated to the area of *enterprise management systems* (also see section 14.1), whereas the second provider-oriented management system is an extension of the *trouble ticket system* (also see section 14.2). The chapter ends by highlighting how the two systems focus on entirely different aspects of provider orientation.

20.1 Tivoli Management Environment

With the IBM Tivoli Management Environment (TME), marketed under the product name TME10 (TIV97b), Tivoli is offering a comprehensive management concept that addresses the key task fields of the providers of networked systems. TME10 provides tool functions for the following four task fields identified as management disciplines: security, availability, deployment, and operations and administration.

Tivoli differentiates between four management disciplines

20.1.1 Security

In the security area, TME10 offers a management solution that allows the security policies formulated by a provider in a heterogeneous

Security poli-
cies and their
implementation

system environment to be implemented on an efficient automated basis. For example, the assignment of user identification is simplified through a policy that enables an automated provision of new identification with preset values (called *default policies*). It also allows a provider to define security policies for establishing and preventing intentional or unintentional changes to user identification (called *validation policies*).

TME10 offers providers a uniform security model that is superimposed over the security mechanisms offered by MVS, Unix, Windows, and OS/2 systems. A central aim is to automate routine tasks in the security area that are executed during operational procedures.

20.1.2   Availability

Connection
to problem
management

TME10 supplies a solution for problem management that is guided by the requirements of the provider. Monitors and event adapters that supply the status information for the network, system, and application components can be configured over a graphical user interface. The analysis of the status information is simplified for the provider through rule-based event management, which among other things:

- Consolidates events from any sources
- Eliminates messages or reports from monitors that are supplied in duplicate or are not important
- Escalates particularly important events

At the moment, TME10 allows the integration of more than 1000 different monitors that can be used to interrogate the entire spectrum of status information (e.g., the status of an application, number of users logged in, available disk space, network load) across the heterogeneous network and system landscape. The aim is to relieve the burden of this diversity of activity from operational personnel, for example, by standardizing the interrogation of the system load of a Windows NT server or of a Sun workstation.

The extensive options for event correlation offered by Tivoli merit mention in connection with the generation of provider-accepted management solutions. These options relieve a provider of the burden of dealing with a large number of less important individual events. Up to now, it has not been possible, however, to correlate these events to services. It is therefore also not possible to determine whether service level agreements with customers could be jeopardized by the events reported.

20.1.3 Deployment

All the management functions that affect the provision of applications, databases, systems, and communication software are combined by TME10 under deployment. The goal is to meet all the end users' requirements for this software. *Electronic software distribution* (ESD) resolves only one of the aspects. Other tasks allocated to "deployment" include applications management and the correction of configuration errors. The entire software process from development to bundling and packaging to installation is covered. The area referred to as deployment therefore comprises numerous tasks that were assigned to the change management of networked systems in Chapter 18.

Close reference to change management

TME10 supports the use of distributed applications software that extends across different operating system worlds. The individual software components are delivered and activated on the systems from a central location, with the management system taking responsibility for the necessary synchronization of the systems.

20.1.4 Operations and Administration

In this area, TME10 combines all those functions that make it easier and more efficient for a provider to carry out the tasks associated with routine management. Monitoring and controlling jobs, resetting printing queues, and controlling backups and data compression are examples of routine activities. The suggestion is that these tasks should for the most part be automated because the operational processes involved are familiar and constantly repeated.

Automation of routine tasks

Numerous management tools for individual network and systems components are used in the automation of processes and procedures. Operations and administration implemented within the framework of TME10 should offer the provider an additional possibility for executing routine tasks in a uniform and consistent way across all computer platforms.

Operational personnel have the option on all four management disciplines differentiated by TME10 to access uniformly designed management desktops, which to a certain degree, reduces the complexity of operation. However, a deep integration as described in earlier chapters cannot be achieved on this basis.

The tool kits used by Tivoli are relevant at this juncture. It already emerged from the foregoing description of the management disciplines that one of the main goals of TME10 is the integration of a broad spectrum of network, systems, and to a degree, applications

Tivoli tool kits ...

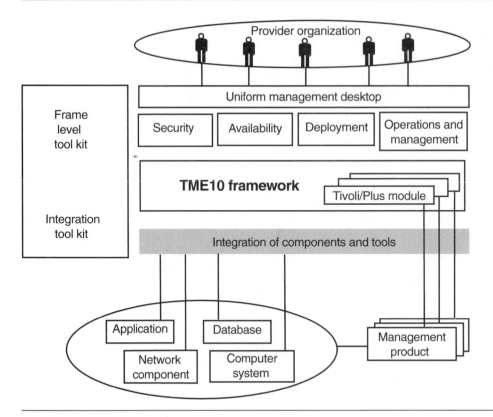

Figure 20.1
The Tivoli Management Environment approach

components. As illustrated in Figure 20.1, two *tool kits* are offered that enable components or management products of other vendors to be linked to the so-called *TME10 framework*. For example, the *integration tool kit* enables the integration of events of new resources that are transmitted to the *TME10 enterprise console* [TIV96] for comprehensive processing within the framework of rule-based event management (see management discipline "availability").

...allow the integration of other management tools

A link to the framework is already available for numerous management products, with the degree of closeness of this link dependent on the respective product; these management products are available in the form of *Tivoli/Plus modules*. These modules can be operated by operational personnel from a management desktop and therefore allow the uniform and synchronized use of a large number of management tools.

Brief evaluation

The framework and the associated tool kits help bridge the gap between provider-oriented management disciplines and existing management products. Through an open partnership that Tivoli developed with other manufacturers (e.g., Cabletron, Compaq, Hewlett-Packard, Peregrine, Remedy, SunSoft) in the *10/Plus Association,* interfaces could be defined that represent the technical prerequisite for integration into the framework. On the other hand, the Tivoli solution has not been developed satisfactorily to provide a systematic penetration of the provider view and the operational processes, although TME10 offers suitable functions for their support.

20.2　Mansys ExpertDesk

The *ExpertDesk* from Mansys Ltd. [MAN97] exemplifies a management system that explicitly and directly supports certain operational processes that exist in a provider organization. The product is oriented on the process descriptions for the ITIL standard from the CCTA described in Chapter 17. The process descriptions provide an important foundation for developing an understanding of operations—and consequently, the requirements of a provider organization for management tools. Different manufacturers have therefore begun to orientate their product development accordingly. The ExpertDesk is based on the *Action Request System* (ARS), a trouble ticket system from Remedy, and uses its flexible form-based functionality as well as the proprietary workflow engine to provide automated and provider-accepted support to certain parts of the mapped process descriptions.

Process-oriented management tool

The ExpertDesk system is designated as a *service desk application* (i.e., an extended help desk) with the additional following functionality:

Service desk and help desk

- Handling of change requests, thus the support of operations in change management
- Assistance in the search for error causes within the framework of problem management
- Provision of current configuration base and elementary monitoring functions for routine management

The ExpertDesk thus offers the provider a relatively simple tool for the support of certain parts of its operational process. As Figure 20.2 clarifies, the ExpertDesk is used by the operational personnel of the service desk to compile *incidents* from the customer side in a prescribed ExpertDesk *schema.* A *knowledge base* that contains the experience of previously processed incidents is available for use by the user processing the incident (known as a *call logger*) in the ExpertDesk. If a

Procedures in service desk

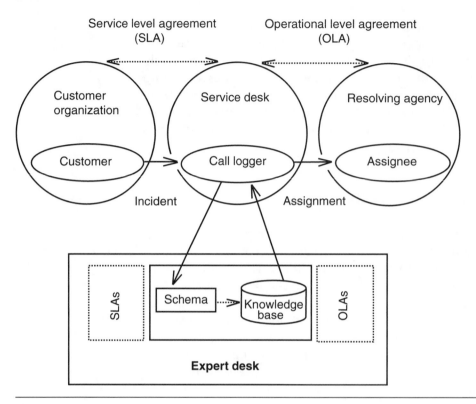

Figure 20.2
Mansys ExpertDesk

solution cannot be found in the service desk, the call logger turns to a so-called *resolving agency*. From the standpoint of the service desk, the resolving agency is a last-level support that forms an independent provider organization and has no direct access to the ExpertDesk.

Interface to customer

In addition to offering tool functions to the provider for the support of its internal procedures, the ExpertDesk also provides assistance to the provider with the specification of its interfaces to customers and to provider organizations (also see section 17.3). The *service level agreements* (SLAs) contracted with customers and the *operational level agreements* (OLAs) agreed on with resolving agencies (see Figure 20.2) both have a similar structure in the ExpertDesk and include the following information.

20.2.1   Defining Services

The *service schema* offered by the ExpertDesk enables the detailed definition of the service that is being agreed on with a customer or a resolving agency. Examples include general telephone support, advice on software being procured, advice on the operation of software applications, and hardware support (including repair and upgrades).

20.2.2   Targets

This comprises the compilation by the ExpertDesk of all time-related commitments that have been agreed on within a contract. The targets for each service in the SLA define the time within which a particular service is to be provided by the service desk. The resolving agency likewise makes a similar commitment to provide its services in accordance with the times stipulated in the targets defined in the OLA.

20.2.3   Alerts

Alerts are used in SLAs and OLAs to specify which alarms are to be produced within a workflow (used to supply the service in the service desk or in the resolving agency). The alerts document the service provided within the service desk or resolving agency, thereby enabling the service user to check that the service is being provided effectively.

The management *escalation procedures* supported in the Expert-Desk are closely linked to the targets and alerts. An appropriate escalation procedure is triggered if the tool establishes that certain alerts threaten the time guarantees agreed on through the targets. Through this procedure, those with the appropriate responsibility within the service-providing organization are informed about critical situations and instructed to initiate suitable countermeasures.

Availability of management escalation procedures

The service desk is able to maintain the SLA agreed on with the customer only if the participating resolving agencies do not violate the OLAs on their part. Through *SLA–OLA matching*, the service desk is supported by a tool that ensures that the contracts being concluded on both sides are in agreement with one another.

One of the strengths of the tool compared to many other management systems is the functions offered by the ExpertDesk for the agreement and monitoring of service level agreements and operational level agreements. The provider of a networked system is thereby in a position to introduce a *computer-supported service management*. The

Basis for service management

ExpertDesk offers only a small number of functions for a provider-accepted implementation of the agreed-on services. In particular, the system offers only inadequate possibilities for the integration of existing management tools that take over certain partial aspects of operation (refer to process-oriented management means introduced in the previous chapters). It is at this point that the TME10, with its framework that presents an approach to solving the difficult integration task of tools and IT components, has a contribution to make. There is no way of definitively establishing today what kind of acceptance this approach will find. Note that various other manufacturers, such as HP and CA, are also offering convincing solutions for dealing with the problems of integration (see Part III).

Although Tivoli has considered the needs and tasks of the provider, it has not yet been able to embed the tool functions successfully in the operational processes; this means that tools that are to be integrated into the framework should be seen more clearly against the background of the operational task involved.

Evaluation and comparison of both examples

These two management systems therefore deliver very different contributions to the challenge of integrated management to provide more provider-acceptable tool solutions in the future. ExpertDesk is an example of how requirements placed on the operation of networked systems (in the form of service level agreements) and the interfaces to other providing organizations (in the form of operational level agreements) can be addressed in a provider-accepted management system. Tivoli shows how these agreements concluded in the SLAs and OLAs can be monitored and guaranteed with provider acceptance by *one* management system into which a large number of specialized management tools have been integrated. The two management products singled out are not competitors but instead complement each other.

Part V

The Outlook

P arts I to IV described the state-of-the-art technology for network, systems, and applications management from the standpoint of concepts, architectures, and tools of management and their operational implementation. The material selected was essentially based on assured approaches. Of course, much more could be said about the subject of integrated management of networked systems, in particular about the many different application scenarios, but every book has its limits in terms of length.

Because of space constraints, we also were not able to delve into relevant research activities. Instead, we refer you to the proceedings of two international conferences that take place in alternating years: Integrated Management (IM, previously ISINM) from the IFIP/IEEE and Network Operations and Management Symposium (NOMS) from the IEEE/IFIP. The extensive bibliography at the end of the book also contains many helpful references.

The entire management world in IT is undergoing radical changes. New technologies and applications of networked systems are making new demands on management that are being reacted to with new solutions. We outline the recognizable trends in Chapter 21. Discussions are also continuing on management architectures and information models. Our assessment of the course of development in this area follows in Chapter 22. In the last chapter, Chapter 23, we conclude by asking how the problems of management will be affecting the future landscape of information processing.

Future Requirements and Solutions for IT Management

Various solutions to management in heterogeneous environments have been introduced comprehensively in the previous chapters. Yet certain topics and trends were mentioned but not dealt with in depth. These are topics that essentially are still in a state of flux. Either the requirement catalogs have not yet been analyzed, the underlying new technologies have not established themselves, or the relevant solutions are still at the discussion stage.

We made reference to some of these trends in Chapter 1, and now we want to refine some of the aspects mentioned. Since we will be discussing visions, current developments, and ongoing research, we are forced to remain subjective in our selection of topics as well as in our assessment of different aspects.

21.1 New Applications and Requirements

- A great number of public and private networks have emerged on the basis of Internet services and protocols. Cooperations between companies and dealer networks and chains of suppliers have led to *a linking of intranets to extranets*. There is a technical demand for the formation of groups through the creation of *virtual networks*, which are based on the existing network structures of companies and transit networks of service providers. These are supposed to offer new technological and cost-effective options for communication links to external business partners. On one hand, this means that new demands are being placed on the management of virtual private networks (VPNs) in the combined LAN–WAN environment (we covered this briefly for VLANs in section 16.1); on the other hand, there is a need for a definition of quality standards for the

Building virtual networks upon networks of intranets and extranets is becoming important different management functional areas and the ability to check that these standards are being adhered to, especially in the security and accounting areas. An example of this development is the *Automotive Network eXchange* (ANX) initiative of the automobile industry in the United States; a comparable counterpart to ANX in Europe is the *ANeT* extranet. Its aim is to enable closed user group networks (extranets) to be built on the basis of Internet standards. These networks will be demarcated from the Internet through controlled access mechanisms and a definition of special demands for quality with respect to data transfer rates, availability, and data authentication and privacy levels. A certification process guarantees that these specified management policies are implemented and enforced. The virtualization not only separates the groups but also guarantees a certain *homogenization of network services on the basis of heterogeneous structures.*

Paradigm shift from component-oriented management to service-oriented management

- In addition to general standard services (see, e.g., sections 2.4.1 and 2.4.2), there will be more and more of a tendency to offer *customized services for customers* with customer-specific QoS guarantees or service level agreements (SLAs). From the management view, this will substantially increase the importance of the areas of *service provisioning* and *customer networks* or *service management.* Service provisioning means offering flexibility in the configuration of quality of service features, service selection, and service concatenation. This not only affects the type of service access interface needed by users when services are used but also provides a guarantee that the customer-specific service type is available in the resources of the networked system, specifically in compliance with the agreed-on SLAs. This can even include preferential handling by a switch. Customer service management means that customer-oriented management information—therefore, not component-oriented MIB variables but service-oriented parameters—will be provided. Operations that enable a customer-controlled activation of the service provisioning functions are also conceivable; it is even worth considering workflow management front ends for customers in order to channel and automate the interaction interfaces between the customer's workflow and the IT processes of the provider. Examples of this can be seen in online activation of commercial services like Internet access accounts or even residential telephone service (available in some areas of the United States).

- Services such as email are gradually gaining in *company-critical significance,* thereby increasing the requirements for availability and verification. *Security-sensitive services (electronic commerce, home banking, online ordering)* are gaining acceptance. As a result, the entire functional area of security management is becoming important in the Internet environment in a way that did not exist before. This relates to management functions such as key management, trust center management for the certification of digital signatures (notaries, key escrow), authentication, authorization, user administration, and so forth. It should be mentioned that individual IT providers often do not have complete freedom in establishing security policies and implementing security measures because the legal frameworks of different countries can have a considerable bearing on how systems are used (data protection laws, signature laws, media laws, export limitations and restrictions).

■ There will be an increase in the *globalization of information.* This means that more careful planning will have to go into the placement of information servers and the building of cache hierarchies, along with the monitoring and control of load balancing. The need to set up and administer, for example, WWW proxies (for filtering unauthorized information) or to check the consistency of links will result in qualitative and quantitative management requirements of the likes never known before, especially against the backdrop of a rapid growth in the use of global information. The German scientific network B-WIN, which serves as the basis for scenario 1 in section 3.1, alone transports more than 120 TBytes per month with an (exponential) semiannual growth factor of 2.5. Yet the breakthrough of true multimedia (MM) communication as a mass service, especially interactive MM communication, is still ahead of us. Terminals are being produced with increased multimedia capability although not all customer requirements are yet being met. Voice over IP promises to further this expansion.

■ *Changes to configurations and topologies* (real as well as virtual) will be made with *greater frequency* since organizational structures will also have to react at short notice and with greater flexibility within the framework of the shorter response times required in service provisioning. Organizational units will be smaller and regrouped more frequently. Virtual IT infrastructures based on real structures will have to be managed for temporary virtual workgroups or companies that are formed. An exploration of the management services that will be needed is still the subject of research.

■ There will also be a change in user behavior. Attention should be given to the *mobility of users.* The use of mobile phones in the

Change in user behavior

telecommunications world is well dealt with from the standpoint of management. On the other hand, the use of complex services in the communications environment for nomadic end systems has hardly been addressed. *New types of users*, including those who previously had little contact with computers and networked systems, will be using the Internet technologies and services such as mobile IP or wireless data networks like GSM and CDPD. Open populations with nonfixed system access to a multitude of network services will trigger the creation of new management requirements.

- *Metacomputing* represents a new type of application of networked systems. This involves the formation of virtual processing structures on the basis of networked systems. An example is the use of a networked workstation farm as a massive parallel computer. This application has already been used successfully with homogeneous systems. One of the management requirements relates to *load balancing*. Metacomputing in heterogeneous environments is largely still a subject of research.

- It is becoming more and more complicated to *layer communications systems* (e.g., through multiple, iterated, tunneling layers). An example is SNA tunneling over IP in which IP as part of LAN coupling is transmitted via LANEmulation over ATM.

21.2   New Concepts and Trends in Management

In this chapter, we have described some of the changing conditions that are triggering the development of new requirements. How do we tackle these requirements? The main decision is to continue with the development of management architectures and related information models. Our assessment of the trends that are evident in these areas is presented in Chapter 22. Following are some of the new approaches and trends that we briefly outlined in earlier chapters:

Management by delegation and agent technology support scalability of management

- *Management by delegation.* We briefly mentioned this concept in section 4.5. It relates to the scalability of management when management requirements are constantly changing or networked systems are growing. An approach that is currently under discussion is one in which the usually static way of allocating management functionality to managers or agents is removed through the option of a dynamic delegation of functions [GOY95, MOU97, GOY98]. Though the idea has been around for some years now, management-relevant

issues related to this approach are currently still the subject of research (e.g. active and programmable networks, security issues of
mobile and intelligent agents, execution control of moving agents);
the first products and prototypes are already available (e.g., JDMK
from Sun). First, there must be a definition and description of
the delegatable management functionality, then of the control and
monitoring of the execution of delegated management tasks, and
finally, of the resulting security issues.

- *Modular agent structures.* Both the agentX approach (section 6.2)
  and SNMPv3 (section 6.5) revolved around modular agent structures, thus the issue of how agents can be extended dynamically or
  what a generic agent architecture should look like. Multiarchitectural agents (Chapter 10) also follow this track. What is still being
  sought is an agent structure that is suitable as a carrier system for
  management by delegation. A number of development activities are
  currently taking place internationally in this area under different
  names such as intelligent, mobile, autonomous, or flexible agents
  [MOU97, GOY98]. No general definitions have yet been established.

- *Distributed service management* is gaining in importance compared
  to the management of resources and hardware components. Some
  of the requirements in this area were mentioned earlier. These
  also include mapping component views to service views, such as
  through view building to a configuration or through developing
  customer-relevant parameters. Uniform concepts for solutions are
  not yet available, and existing approaches only touch upon certain
  aspects. On the other hand, service management is currently still a
  "hot" concept. Quite a few of the aspects covered in this book could
  be seen as building blocks for service management—for example,
  trouble ticket systems (section 14.2) and help desks (section 18.4);
  end-to-end management (section 16.2.5) and service quality monitoring (section 3.2.3); customer network management (section 3.1);
  SW distribution and deployment management (sections 14.1 and
  16.2); and subscriber administration (section 16.2.6). Service provisioning will be important in its own right through the extension
  of OAM nomenclature to OAM&P in the telecommunications area.
  However, this application is mostly being used only in a very narrow
  service section of telecommunications (e.g., the voice service with
  different service features).

- *Applications management* is, for the most part, currently being resolved on an applications-specific basis. General services for the
  managing of distributed services are still at the development stage

Convergence of communications and management architectures supports applications management

(e.g., see services, facilities, and domains in CORBA in Chapter 7). This actually also applies to general management models for distributed applications [KEN97a, NEU98]. An important question currently being debated is to what extent applications management should be interpreted as *deployment management*, thus as a function that covers the entire lifecycle of a distributed application, including version management (also see section 16.2).

- *Web-based management* (Chapters 9 and 22), in which Web browsers assume the role of management consoles, is another area considered to have not yet reached its full stage of development. However, the approaches that do exist are promising, especially for small (in particular, network-element) infrastructures.

- Other developments include the introduction of general *software engineering methods* for management (see Chapter 22). Another one involves the exploration of real event correlations instead of the simple event filtering that is mostly used today. This is especially relevant since event consolidation is a prerequisite for the integration of workflow management systems.

- Different sections of the book (e.g., Chapter 14 and Part IV) emphasized the fact that technical management tools (such as platforms) are not sufficient in themselves and that a network of integrating tools oriented to the IT processes of the provider of the IT infrastructure is required. The integrating *use of workflow management systems*, also in the context of the management of distributed systems, is still a subject of research (also see sections 14.1 and 19.4). This is an important topic of development; we are not aware of any current standardized solutions.

Tool integration and diversity of architectures are still challenges

- Lastly, the *integration of management tools* is an issue that still has not been resolved satisfactorily. This problem area is becoming more and more critical, first, because of new usages and resources in networked systems, and second, because of the diversity of management architectures. The first question that arises is at which level integration should take place (at the management architecture, platform, or tool level). Another question relates to what should be integrated (user interface, events, data, and so forth) and what the integration interface should look like. Integration is an extremely important issue for corporatewide integrated management. Until now, only partial solutions have been available for this area. We addressed the integration of tools and architectures in Chapters 10 and 14 (and will mention it briefly again in Chapter 22). The integration of tools in IT processes was also the subject of Part IV.

The lack of integration of management methods and tools in concrete company IT infrastructures is resulting in higher costs and personnel requirements. It is not only a system-oriented problem but, to a considerable degree, an organizational one as well.

Management Architectures and Information Models

The management trends outlined in the previous chapter raise issues that will have an important impact on the future management landscape:

- How will the existing *management architectures be positioned?*
- Which of these *architectures will be accepted* in the long term?
- Will the management area see a *concentration or a diversification*?
- Will one of the architectures crystallize into an *integrating architecture* for the other ones?

There still are no conclusive answers to these questions. We will home in on some of the central issues and address them as best we can with the knowledge available today:

- What has already been established in the area of management architectures in terms of the allocation of resources and disciplines, what is projected, and what is still not clear?
- How will the information models and standardized management information develop? Where will the emphases be?
- What kind of influence will software development processes and implementation languages have on management architectures and products?
- What will be the impact of architectural gateways? Which architectural gateways will realize their potential?

22.1   Positioning of Management Architectures

SNMP: well established for network devices

The *Internet management architecture* with *SNMP* (see Chapter 6) is the main architecture that has established itself in the area of network component management in data communications and, particularly, in the LAN world. This situation is not apt to change in the medium term. The only potential competition is Web-based management with Web servers embedded into network components. This could be an interesting solution for small environments in which complex SNMP-based platform solutions do not make economic sense.

Future of further SNMP development open

The future of *further SNMP development* is, however, still open. Owing to the unfavorable experience with SNMPv2 (see section 6.3.2), many manufacturers are taking a careful, wait-and-see approach with SNMPv3 (see section 6.5). Many manufacturers are announcing support of SNMP, but there is often no mention of concrete plans to introduce suitable products. It is a similar case with the work being carried out by the DISMAN group (see section 6.5); it still does not have a clear picture of which parts will be integrated by manufacturers into network components and which will be left up to midlevel managers and proxies.

SNMP for systems and applications management?

The future of *SNMP* in *systems and applications management* is another open issue. On the one hand, almost every system today is being supplied with an SNMP agent that often implements the end system-specific host resources MIB (RFC 1514) or parts thereof. On the other hand, it is hard to find well-developed support for other standardized system, service, or applications-related MIBs (see section 6.2.1) in the agents. Hence, manufacturers of management applications are less inclined to use these MIBs.

DMTF-DMI: well established in desktop management

The open management of *end systems* such as *desktops* is currently the domain of the desktop management interface of the Desktop Management Task Force (*DMTF-DMI*; see Chapter 8) and associated *MIF standard groups*. Along with diverse proprietary agents geared to specific platforms (Computer Associates Unicenter, IBM/Tivoli TME), the associated agent implementations represent the most important basis for end system management today. Intel's *Wired for Management Baseline* initiative for the definition of MIF profiles (see *http://www.intel.com*) and the first version of Tivoli's application management specification (AMS; see section 16.2.2), which is based on a standard MIF, should both have a positive impact on the future prospects for the DMI.

The DMTF's assumption of responsibility for the definition of the *common information model* (CIM) (see section 9.3.2) could prove to be very beneficial to the prospects for the DMI. CIM has every chance of becoming the management information model for end systems and applications. The question that arises overall is whether there is even room for a new standardized architecture alongside the architectures and agents of established manufacturers such as Computer Associates (Unicenter TNG) and IBM (TME10) in the area of end systems and applications.

Tivoli uses *common object request broker architecture* (CORBA; see Chapter 7) as the communication middleware for the management of end systems and applications. Yet the future of this architecture in this area is by no means assured; the problem is the overly strong market position of Microsoft and consequently the distributed component object model (DCOM). The eventual availability of CORBA/DCOM gateways could have a positive impact on the future of CORBA.

CORBA as a systems management architecture

An area that clearly does look promising for CORBA is *telecommunications network* management (see section 7.7). *OSI management* within *TMN* (see section 5.6) has firmly established itself for the management of components in telecommunications networks, and this situation will not change in the medium term. On the other hand, there seems to be a growing trend to use CORBA for the X interface of TMN or for the interfaces between OSF (operations system function) and mediation functions. CORBA could also be used for the communication between the components of a distributed application for telecommunications management. The work promoting a cooperation between CORBA and intelligent networks mentioned in section 7.7 is also important in this context. One possible solution would be as follows: OSI management with CMIP for element management and network management, thus the *lower layers* of TMN, and CORBA for service management and business management, thus the *upper layers* of TMN.

CORBA for the upper layers of TMN

The *Open Distributed Management Architecture* (ODMA; see ISO/ IEC 13244 or ITU-T X.703), now available, can be seen as promoting this kind of trend. This architecture uses the concepts and languages of the *reference model for open distributed processing* (RM-ODP; see ISO 10746 or ITU-T X.901, X.902, X.903) to define an open management architecture. CORBA is an obvious springboard for the implementation of ODMA. ODMA could therefore also be seen as an abstract specification for the CORBA-based management of telecommunications.

The trend toward *Web-based management solutions* (see section 9.1) is not dependent on specific resources. The question that remains unresolved today is whether a standard architecture for Web-based management has a chance of success since there is a difficulty in

Trend toward Web-based management solutions

projecting the future prospects for the original approaches in this direction (see sections 9.2 and 9.3).

Web browsers as management consoles

What can be counted on with certainty is that mainly *browser-based management consoles* will be used in the future. For providers, this means not only the use of uniform user interfaces but also far less dependence on location and architecture; it also means reducing the burden on hotlines because of the possibility offered to provide users with up-to-date information for self-help so that they can deal with problems themselves or track the processing status of TTs. The big advantage for users will be easy access to a large, perhaps even overwhelming, quantity of up-to-date information.

Embedded Web servers as management agents

Embedded Web servers (see section 9.1) in components on the agent side above all offer a basis for the cost-effective, platform-independent management of smaller information processing structures. However, these servers do not provide an integrated management for these environments; the management continues to be component oriented, and the individual applications are isolated.

It is still up to users of *complex platforms and frameworks* to make the decision on integrated management. These companies are, however, missing out on a high level of automation in management, high reliability (e.g., in diagnostics, fault detection), and improved tool integration.

22.2   Management Information Models

When it comes to management information models, the IT landscape today is divided into two parts:

- The complex object-oriented OSI information model (see section 5.2) is used in the telecommunications world.

- The simple data type–oriented models *Internet SMI* (*structure of management information*; see section 6.2) and *DMTF MIF* (*management information format*; see section 8.2), which are similar to each other, are being used in the data communications area and increasingly in the area of end systems and applications.

New approaches based on Internet SMI, such as *system-level MOs for applications* (RFC 2287), *application management MIB*, and *MOs for WWW services* (see *http://www.ietf.org*) prove that it is very *difficult to manage without object-oriented* methods and concepts such as specialization and inheritance. An awkward mechanism exists for emulating the latter using an information model that does not incorporate the appropriate provisions.

The introduction of CIM, which represents a further attempt to *establish an object-oriented* information model, can be interpreted as yet another reaction to these difficulties. Does CIM, which incorporates relationships between objects and relationship classes, represent the "renaissance of complex information models" now that the OSI model has been degraded to a niche model? The key difference between the two models is that the OSI information model is a model specific for management purposes, which can sometimes be very difficult to understand, whereas CIM is based on the universal *unified modeling language* (UML) (see section 9.3.2), which may be known to many software developers in the future.

A development that is also having an effect on information models is the trend away from pure component-oriented management to service management and the management of distributed applications. This trend is again raising the issue of an open basis for *cross-system* and *cross-component management information*. One obvious solution for static information is the use of *directory services*. Approaches like this that were previously found with OSI management and X.500 are now being resurrected. The *Directory Enabled Networks* initiative of Microsoft and CISCO (see *http://www.microsoft.com* or *http://www.cisco.com*) is attempting to establish data structures for management-relevant resources for LDAP-conformant directory services. In abstract terms, this is another attempt to standardize a management information model and the shared generic classes of managed objects based on it; the emphasis here is, above all, on services and users in addition to equipment and components.

Renaissance of complex information models?

Directory as management information base

22.3   Software Development Processes and Implementation Languages

If management information is specified through the use of the aforementioned methods, the issues that arise in the context of the development process relate to:

- The *binding* of the *models* used for the specification to the *implementation languages* (generation of stubs and skeletons, mapping and handling of data types, etc.)

- The related *open APIs* that facilitate easier programming of management products and tools

Development process unnecessarily management specific in some cases

The OSI information model and the Internet information model can use different approaches such as XMP/XOM and TMN C++ API (see section 15.3.1), which usually map to the previously dominant implementation languages C and C++. However, these tools and APIs produce a management orientation to large parts of the software development process (see, e.g., section 15.1.1). Moreover, some of the transitions between the specification languages for the management information and the models for the implementation languages are not trivial.

Two trends that are developing today can solve this problem:

Use of general software engineering methods for management

- Use of general *nonmanagement-specific software development methods* for management (see section 15.1.2). Thus, for example, CIM is based on UML, which allows the use of existing tools for modeling purposes. The possibility this provides for generating IDL interfaces and the related use of IDL compilers (see section 7.2.3) to generate programming language–specific interfaces and stubs and skeletons sets the stage for a comparatively smooth transition to the implementation languages and the use of CORBA middleware.

Bind the management information model to the implementation language

- The attempt to establish a *management information model* that is directly *linked* to a suitable *implementation language,* such as is the case with the MO concept of JMAPI (see section 9.2.2). The danger of data loss during the transition between models is then eliminated at the outset if Java is used as implementation language. Furthermore, it enables a linking of inheritance or specialization at the modeling level and the implementation levels. An existing implementation of a generic class can be used for the implementation of a refined class derived from it.

Another problem currently being addressed is the binding of the management information model to databases and access to MOs on platforms. Developers always used to claim that it was difficult to use the relevant platform-provided APIs. Recent developments in so-called object managers or managed object servers strive for uniform and easy-to-use interfaces for database access and integration. It is possible that these servers are providing the core infrastructures for future platforms.

The problem with all these is that they closely couple implementation and architecture. Although this naturally facilitates implementation in the target language, it does not allow flexibility for evolution of new languages and platforms. A balance between these two conflicting objectives is needed.

22.4   Architectural Gateways

As we mentioned at the beginning of the chapter, in addition to being beneficial to users, the existence of problem-free, more or less loss-free *gateways* between management architectures could also promote the establishment of new architectures—thus, for example, architectures that are more closely aligned to the usual software development methods than to the "classical" architectures.

Gateways could promote new management architectures

The work being conducted in this area (e.g., by the IIMC and the JIDM initiatives; see sections 10.3 and 10.4) has shown, however, that these types of management gateways can be highly complex. Gateways can usually be problem-free and simple only if they have been included as part of the planning process for the specifications for the architecture, as was the case with the gateway to SNMP or Internet SMI (see section 8.2.1) specified by the DMTF-DMI.

Gateways are complex and not loss-free

There is one thing that the different ongoing development and research work in this area has in common: In addition to protocol conversion, it is addressing the translation of management information at the *syntactical* level (see section 10.2.1). Yet truly transparent architectural gateways can be achieved only with translation at a *semantic* level. This would require a universal management information model and classes of MOs based on it—and this could partially be seen as a metamodel. The need for uniform, generally usable management information again surfaces; the importance of this need has been recognized for at least ten years, and it has taken that long to come up with a solution. And yet the perfect solution still has not been found. Time will show whether new approaches such as CIM make progress in this area or the quantity of existing competing information just continues to increase.

Management: Driving Force or Impediment?

We led into the problems of management in Chapter 1 by looking at the effect that changes in the information processing landscape have had on management. The obvious question to raise as we conclude is one that looks at the situation the other way around:

- What effect will the problems of management have on future information processing structures?
- What influence will it have on IT resources and services?

New publications and numerous studies by IT consultancies are dealing with this issue all the time. We will just single out and briefly address some of the interesting issues:

- Which *characteristics* of (new) resources are a direct result of management needs?
- What effect do management-related issues have on the *development process* of new resources and services?
- What is the effect of management on the *provisioning* of services?

The most obvious development that has been triggered in conjunction with management is the current trend in the client area. Following the replacement of "dumb" terminals from the mainframe area by "intelligent" PCs over the last few years, the cost of operating and maintaining these *fat clients* (total cost of ownership, TCO) is now dominating discussions. Catchwords and concepts like *thin clients, lean clients, network computers, network PCs*, and *Java stations* identify attempts to reduce these costs that were mainly incurred because of a lack of viable concepts and an inadequate degree of automation in the management of PCs. If the management of clients were relatively free of problems and largely automated, this development would not be of

Thin clients: a consequence of management problems

any major importance. Repeated past attempts at establishing *diskless clients* on a grand scale had the same motivation.

However, the problems of management do not stop with operating systems or the hardware equipment of end systems; the effect is so far-reaching that it can even affect the design of hardware. This is reflected in devices on PC main boards and network cards that enable the remote activation of PCs previously deactivated by users. Even if this same kind of automatic activation could be applied to facsimile reception, the development was essentially driven by management issues, such as the distribution of software to PCs outside normal office hours.

Management requirements even affect HW design

Management will generally have a greater effect on client PCs and end systems than we have experienced in the past. What we can anticipate is a *management instrumentation* of practically *all resources*, particularly also the diverse clients for applications that are seldom instrumented today. End-to-end management, quality of service management, and service level agreement monitoring will require that tests are carried out where the data being checked is actually located; for (measuring) transaction times, for example, this is frequently the client PC. The ARM specification is the first approach in this direction (see section 16.2.6). Even the trend toward the standardization of event and configuration interfaces for software components we are seeing with component-oriented software development approaches (e.g., Java beans, CORBA beans) can be interpreted as a management instrumentation of software—in this case, mainly for configuration management.

In the future: management instrumentation of all resources

These trends inevitably have an impact on the development process. Since an instrumentation of resources after the fact is complicated and expensive, there will be a move to enable *management requirements* to be reflected in the *development process* from the outset—in other words, to be taken into account at an earlier stage of resource development; this will particularly apply to applications development that heretofore has lagged behind, especially compared to protocol development (e.g., station management with FDDI).

Early reflection of management in the development process is necessary

Developers and users have recently become even more sensitive toward these management problems. The main reason for this is that the dynamic of some areas of modern information processing infrastructures with great revenue potential is being slowed down or delayed considerably due to a lack of management infrastructure or concepts:

Management problems may delay new technologies

- The state of the *integration* of *telecommunications* and *data communication* falls far short of what is technically possible of being achieved. Some of the reasons for this are the management problems with ATM and the slow progress of ATM standardization, which again, is partially caused by management problems.

- The *use* of Internet-based home banking applications, e-commerce, and other security-critical *Internet applications* is being held back by the lack of infrastructure for security management. Indeed, recent growth has been fostered by the use of ubiquitous browser tools and not standards for management.

- The progress of *Internet telephony* (see, e.g., *http://itel.mit.edu*), *videoconferencing* over the *Internet*, and similar services is partly being hindered because of the lack of mechanisms for quality of service management that are needed before business will consider voice over IP a serious alternative to the public switched telephone network.

- *Hypercomputing* and *metacomputing* are taking hold very slowly; the main problem is the lack of adequate management concepts to allow coordinated use of the enormous computing capacity available.

The addition of cost considerations to the equation, along with the technical aspects mentioned, contributes to the management problems on the DP landscape. Rising management costs has been one of the main reasons why *cost reductions* anticipated as the result of the *downsizing* of information processing infrastructures have not materialized. The effect has led to an increased *rehosting* of functions, such as backup and archiving, as well as a "renaissance" of mainframes as enterprise servers.

No cost reduction through downsizing as a result of management problems

The problems of management are promoting a *concentration* of *manufacturers involved in information technology* and leading to the formation of monopolies since providers are favoring the idea of using only a small cadre of manufacturers in their efforts to reduce operational costs.

Depending on the *point of view*, management can either be seen as a *driving force* or an *impediment* in the continued technical development of information processing infrastructures. On the one hand, a functioning management infrastructure is the prerequisite for offering customized services with flexible configurability, as available or being planned, for example, in the intelligent network environment. On the other hand, as was pointed out earlier, there can be a tremendous effect on the introduction of new technologies if management issues are not addressed carefully at the outset.

It takes functioning management infrastructures to achieve flexible information processing infrastructures. Management issues already have to be taken into account during the design phase of each new technology and resolved in tandem with the implementation and use of the technology. The same applies to the definition of IT processes in connection with the planning of IT infrastructures. Any disregard of these basic rules will produce an adverse effect on costs and even on the commercial viability of new technologies.

Bibliography

Note: ISO standards, ITU-T standards, and Internet RFCs are not listed in the following list of references. Information related to these documents can be found under *http://www.iso.ch/*, *http://www.itu.org/*, and *http://www.ietf.org/*.

[ABE96]   Abeck, S.: *Integrated Resource Management: A Process-Oriented Approach, Proceedings of European Summer School*. Eunice '96, Lausanne, September 1996.

[ABM97]   Abeck, S.; Mayerl, C.: Prozeßbeschreibungen als Basis für einen qualitätsgesicherten Betrieb von vernetzten Arbeitsplatzrechnern. *Proceedings der 4. Fachtagung über Arbeitsplatzrechensysteme* (APS'97), May 1997.

[ACH93]   Abeck, S.; Clemm, A.; Hollberg, U.: Simply Open Network Management—An Approach for the Integration of SNMP into OSI Management Concepts. *Proceedings of Third IFIP/IEEE International Symposium on Integrated Network Management*. North-Holland, 1993.

[AIP98]   Aidarous, S.; Plevyak, T.: *Telecommunications Network Management—Technologies and Implementations*. IEEE Press, 1998.

[ATM94a]   ATM Forum: Customer Network Management (CNM) for ATM Public Network Service, *http://www.atmforum.com*, 1994.

[ATM94b]   ATM Forum: M4 Interface Requirements and Logical MIB, *http://www.atmforum.com*, 1994.

[ATM94c]   ATM Forum: User–Network Interface Specification Version 3.1, *http://www.atmforum.com*, 1994.

[ATM95]   ATM Forum: BISDN Inter Carrier Interface (B-ICI) Specification, Version 2.0, *http://www.atmforum.com*, 1995.

[ATM96]   ATM Forum: Integrated Local Management Interface (ILMI) Specification, Version 4.0, *http://www.atmforum.com*, 1996.

[BDF97]   Barillaud, F.; Deri, L.; Feridun, M.: Network Management Using Internet Technologies. *Proceedings of Fifth IFIP/IEEE International Symposium on Integrated Network Management*. Chapman & Hall, 1997.

[BELL1]   Operations Technology Generic Requirements (OTGR)—Operations Application Messages— Network Maintenance—Network Element Transport and Surveillance Messages, TR-TSY-000833, Issue 5, Bellcore, Piscataway, NJ, 1993.

[BELL2]   Generic State Requirements for Network Elements, TR 1093, Issue 1, Bellcore, Piscataway, NJ, 1993.

[BLA95a]   Black, U.: *Frame Relay Networks*. McGraw-Hill, 1995.

[BLA95b]   Black, U.: *ATM, Vol. 1: Foundation for Broadband Networks, Vol. 2: Signaling in Broadband Networks, Vol. 3: Internetworking with ATM*. Prentice Hall, 1995.

[BLA97]   Black, U.: *Emerging Communications Technologies*. 2nd ed. Prentice Hall, 1997.

[BLS 97]   Blair, G.; Stefani, J. B.: *Open Distributed Processing and Multimedia*. Addison-Wesley, 1997.

[BOC96]   Bocker, P.: *ISDN, 4th ed.* Springer-Verlag. 1996.

[BRJ98]   Booch, G.; Rumbaugh, J.; Jacobson, I.: *Unified Modeling Language User Guide*. Addison-Wesley, 1998.

[BRU96]   Brunne, H.; Usländer, T.: *Design of a Monitoring System for CORBA-Based Applications*. Trends in Distributed Systems '96, Aachen, 1996.

[BUG95]   Buck-Emden, R.; Galimow, J.: *Die Client/Server-Technologie des SAP-Systems R/3*. Addison-Wesley, 1995.

[CAL97]   Calo, S. B.: Integrated Management in a Virtual World. *Proceedings of Fifth IFIP/IEEE International Symposium on Integrated Network Management*. Chapman & Hall, 1997.

[CAW98]   Campione, M.; Walrath, K.: *The Java Tutorial—Object-Oriented Programming for the Internet*. 2nd ed. Addison-Wesley, 1998.

[CCS97]   Chatt, T.; Curry, M.; Seppä, I; Hollberg, U.: TMN/C++—An Object-Oriented API for GDMO, CMIS, and ASN.1. *Proceedings of Fifth IFIP/IEEE International Symposium on Integrated Network Management*. Chapman & Hall, 1997.

[CCT94]   CCTA: The IT Infrastructure Library: An Introduction. HMSO, London, 1994.

[CCT97]   CCTA: The UK Central Computer and Telecommunications Agency, *http://open.gov.uk/ccza/cca-home.html* and *http://open.gov.uk/ccta/pubcat.html*, 1997.

[CHK97]   Chen, G.; Kong, Q.: Integrated TMN Service Provisioning and Management Environment. *Proceedings of Fifth IFIP/IEEE International Symposium on Integrated Network Management*. Chapman & Hall, 1997.

[CHW97]   Chadha, R.; Wuu, S.: Incorporating Manageability into Distributed Software. *Proceedings of Fifth IFIP/IEEE International Symposium on Integrated Network Management*. Chapman & Hall, 1997.

[CMK83]   Cash, J. I.; McFarlan, F. W.; Kenney, J. L.: *Corporate Information Systems Management: Text and Cases*. Irwin, Honewood, 1983.

[COM95]   Comer, D. E.: *Internetworking with TCP/IP. Vol. I: Principles, Protocols and Architecture*. 3rd ed. Prentice Hall, 1995.

[COR97]   Corsten, H.: *Management von Geschäftsprozessen: Theoretische Ansätze—Praktische Beispiele*. W. Kohlhammer GmbH, Stuttgart, 1997.

[COS97]   Comer, D. E.; Stevens, D. L.: *Internetworking with TCP/IP. Vol. III: Client Server Programming and Application*. Prentice Hall, 1997.

[COS98]   Comer, D. E.; Stevens, D. L.: *Internetworking with TCP/IP. Vol. II: Design, Implementation and Internals*. 3rd ed. Prentice Hall, 1998.

[CSS96]   Curtis, A.; Siller, J.; Shafi, M. (ed.): *Sonet/SDH—A Source Book of Synchronous Networking*. IEEE Comm. Soc., 1996.

[DAD97]   Dadam, P.: *Praxis-Seminar: Prozeßmodellierung und Workflow-Management.* Deutsche Informatik-Akademie, Ulm, 1997.

[DEV92]   Dev, R.: *Managing the Enterprise Network: Command and Control.* Cabletron Systems, 1992.

[DHM93]   Duff, J. B.; Hunter, J. D.; Matthews, D. C.: Process Management: The Vision of Integrated Management. *Proceedings of Third IFIP/IEEE International Symposium on Integrated Network Management.* North-Holland, 1993.

[DMN97]   Duarte, E. P.; Mansfield, G.; Nanya, T.; Noguchi, S.: Non-broadcast Network Fault-Monitoring Based on System-Level Diagnosis. *Proceedings of Fifth IFIP/IEEE International Symposium on Integrated Network Management.* Chapman & Hall, 1997.

[DRE95]   Dreo Rodosek, G.: *A Framework for Supporting Fault Diagnosis in Integrated Network and Systems Management.* Dissertation, TU München, 1995.

[DRK97]   Dreo Rodosek, G.; Kaiser, T.: Determining the Availability of Distributed Applications. *Proceedings of Fifth IFIP/IEEE International Symposium on Integrated Network Management.* Chapman & Hall, 1997.

[DRK98]   Dreo Rodosek, G.; Kaiser, Th.: Intelligent Assistant: A User-Guided Fault Localization. *Proceedings of Ninth IFIP/IEEE International Workshop on Distributed Systems: Operations and Management, DSOM '98.* Delaware, 1998.

[DRV95]   Dreo, G.; Valta, R.: Using Master Tickets as a Storage for Problem-Solving Expertise. *Proceedings of Fourth IFIP/IEEE International Symposium on Integrated Network Management.* Chapman & Hall, 1995.

[EMA94]   Emanuel, M.: Open Management—Addressing Real Business Needs. *Proceedings of IEEE/IFIP Network Operations and Management Symposium.* IEEE, 1994.

[ERP97]   Eriksson, H.; Penker, M.: *UML Toolkit.* John Wiley & Sons, 1997.

[FGK97]   Faynberg, I.; Gabuzda, L.; Kaplan, M.; Shah, N.: *Intelligent Network Standards: Their Application to Services.* McGraw-Hill, 1997.

[FHN95]   Feridun, M.; Heusler, L.; Nielsen, R.: Implementing OSI Agents for TMN. IBM Research Report RZ 2759, 1995.

[FHN96]   Feridun, M.; Heusler, L.; Nielsen, R.: Implementing OSI Agent/Managers for TMN. IEEE Communications Magazine, September 1996.

[FLA97]   Flanagan, D.: *Java in a Nutshell—A Desktop Quick Reference for Java Programmers.* 2nd ed. O'Reilly, 1997.

[FLO94]   Flojirin, G.: Workflow Management: A Limited View on Office Processes. *Proceedings of Workshop on Workflow Systems and Office Information Systems,* CSCW'94. 1994.

[FLY94]   Florissi, P.; Yemini, Y.: Management of Application Quality of Service. *Proceedings of Fifth IFIP/IEEE International Workshop on Distributed Systems: Operations and Management.* DSOM '94, 1994.

[FRW95]   Froitzheim, K.; Wolf, H.: Multimedia Application Sharing in a Heterogeneous Environment. *Proceedings of ACM Multimedia '95,* San Francisco 1995.

[GAS96]   Garfinkel, S.; Spafford, G.: *Practical Unix & Internet Security.* O'Reilly, 1996.

[GHE97]   Gheti, I. G.: *Networks and Systems Management—Platforms Analysis and Evaluation.* Kluwer, 1997.

[GIN98]   Ginsburg, D.: *ATM Networks,* 2nd ed. Addison-Wesley, 1998.

[GOR97]   Goralski, W. J.: *SONET—A Guide to Synchronous Optical Networks.* McGraw-Hill, 1997.

[GOY95]   Goldszmidt, G.; Yemini, Y.: Distributed Management by Delegation. *Proceedings of the 15th International Conference on Distributed Computing Systems.* June 1995.

[GOY98]   Goldszmidt, G.; Yemini, Y.: Delegated Agents for Network Management. *IEEE Comm. Magazine,* March 1998.

[GRA97]   Grimes, G.; Adley, B. P.: Intelligent Agents for Network Fault Diagnosis and Testing. *Proceedings of Fifth IFIP/IEEE International Symposium on Integrated Network Management.* Chapman & Hall, 1997.

[GRU98]   Gruschke, B.: A New Approach for Event Correlation Based on Dependency Graphs. *Proceedings of the Fifth Workshop of the Open View University Association,* OVUA '98, Rennes, France, April 1998.

[GUN95]   Gutschmidt, M.; Neumair, B.: Integration von Netz- und Systemmanagement. *Proceedings der 3. Fachtagung über Arbeitsplatzrechensysteme* (APS '95), Hannover, May 1995.

[HAL96]   Halsall, F.: Data Communications, *Computer Networks and Open Systems.* 4th ed. Addison-Wesley, 1996.

[HAW96]   Hegering, H.-G.; Abeck, S.; Wies, R.: Corporate Operation Frameworks for Network Service Management. *IEEE Communications Magazine Special Issue on Enterprise Networking,* April 1996.

[HEA94]   Hegering, H.-G.; Abeck, S.: *Integrated Network and System Management.* Addison-Wesley, 1994.

[HEB93]   Hebrawi, B.: *Open Systems Interconnection: Upper Layer Standards and Practices.* McGraw-Hill, 1993.

[HEI97]   Heiler, K.: *Eine Methodik zur Modellierung von Konfigurationsvorgängen für Szenarien im Netz- und Systemmanagement.* Dissertation. Technische Universität München 1997.

[HEW97]   Heilbronner, S.; Wies, R.: Managing PC Networks. *IEEE Communications Magazine,* Vol. 35, No. 10, Oct. 1997.

[HEY93]   Hegering, H.-G.; Yemini, Y. (eds.): *Proceedings of Third IFIP/IEEE International Symposium on Integrated Network Management.* North-Holland, 1993.

[HHS98]   Handel, R.; Huber, M.; Schroder, S.: *ATM Networks.* 3rd ed. Addison-Wesley, 1998.

[HKN96]   Heilbronner, S.; Keller, A.; Neumair, B.: Integriertes Netz- und Systemmanagement mit modularen Agenten. *Proceedings of SIWORK96.* pp. 275–286. Vdf-Hochschulverlag ETH Zürich, 1996.

[HOJ97]   Hood, C. S.; Ji, C.: Automated Proactive Anomaly Detection. *Proceedings of Fifth IFIP/IEEE International Symposium on Integrated Network Management.* Chapman & Hall, 1997.

[HOL94]   Hollingsworth, D.: *Workflow Management Coalition—The Workflow Reference Model.* Specification TC00- 1003, 1994.

[HOP95]   Hopkins, G. L.: *The ISDN Literacy Book.* Addison-Wesley, 1995.

[HUN98]   Huntingdon-Lee, J.: Network Management Functions. *Datapro Network Management 1510,* January 1998.

[HUP97]   Huber, H.; Poestges, A.: *Prinzipien und Werkzeuge für ein erfolgreiches Gestalten von Geschäftsprozessen.* In [COR97], 1997.

[IET98]   Kalbfleisch, C. (et al.): Application Management MIB. *http://www.ietf.org(html.charters/applmib-charter.html)*, 1998.

[INT97]   Intel Corporation: Wired for Management Baseline, Version 1.1, 1997.

[ISS98]   IEEE Communications Magazine. Special Issue on Global Network Evolution: Convergence or Collision. *Selected Papers from ISS '97.* Vol. 36, No. 1, January 1998.

[JAB95]   Jablonski, S.: Workflow-Management-Systeme: Motivation, Modellierung, Architektur. *Informatik-Spektrum* 18 (1), 1995.

[JAN96]   Jander, M.: Welcome to the Revolution—Web-Based Management. *Data Communications,* November 1996.

[JEN94]   Jennigs, N. R.: Cooperation in Industrial Multi-Agent Systems. *World Scientific Series in Computer Science,* Vol. 34, 1994.

[JEW98]   Jennings, N.: Woolridge, M. (eds.): *Agent Technology—Foundations, Applications, and Markets,* Springer, 1998.

[KAS93]   Kalyanasundaram, P.; Sethi, A.: An Application Gateway Design for OSI-Internet Management. *Proceedings of Third IFIP/IEEE International Symposium on Integrated Network Management.* North-Holland, 1993.

[KAS94]   Kalyanasundaram, P.; Sethi, A.: Interoperability Issues in Heterogeneous Network Management. *Journal of Network and Systems Management* 2(2), 1994.

[KEL98]   Keller, A.: Tool-Based Implementation of a Q-Adapter Function for the Seamless Integration of SNMP-Based Devices in TMN. *Proceedings of the Network Operations and Management Symposium NOMS '98,* IEEE, 1998.

[KEN97a]   Keller, A.; Neumair, B.: Using ODP as a Framework for CORBA-Based Distributed Applications Management. *Proceedings of the Joint International Conference on Open Distributed Processing (ICODP) and Distributed Platforms (ICDP).* Chapman & Hall, 1997.

[KEN97b]   Keller, A.; Neumair, B.: Interoperable Architekturen als Basis eines integrierten Managements. *Proceedings der GI-Fachtagung Kommunikation in verteilten Systemen KiVS '97.* Springer-Verlag, 1997.

[KER95]   Kerner, H.: *Rechnernetze nach OSI. 3. Auflage.* Addison-Wesley, 1995.

[KSC97]   Kephart, J.; Sorkin, G.; Chess, D.; White, S.: Fighting Computer Viruses, *Scientific American,* November 1997.

[KYA95]   Kyas, O.: *ATM Networks.* International Thomson Publishers, 1995.

[LEW93]   Lewis, L.: A Case-Based Reasoning Approach to the Resolution of Faults in Communication Networks. *Proceedings of Third IFIP/IEEE International Symposium on Integrated Network Management.* North-Holland, 1993.

[LLN98]   Langer, M.; Loidl, B.; Nerb, M.: Customer Service Management: A More Transparent View to Your Subscribed Services. *Proceedings of Ninth IFIP/IEEE International Workshop on Distributed Systems: Operations and Management,* DSOM '98, Delaware, 1998.

[LOC94]   Lockhardt, H.: *OSF DCE—Guide to Developing Distributed Applications.* IEEE Comp. Soc. Press, 1994.

[LSS97]   Lazar, A.; Saracco, R.; Stadler, R. (eds.): *Proceedings of Fifth IFIP/IEEE International Symposium on Integrated Network Management.* Chapman & Hall, 1997.

[MAN97]   *Mansys: Mansys ExpertDesk User Guide.* V1.0, 1997.

[MAP96]   Magedanz, T.; Popescu-Zeletin, R.: *Intelligent Networks: Basic Technology, Standards and Evolution.* International Thomson Computer Press, 1996.

[MAS97]   Maston, M.: Using the World Wide Web and Java for Network Service Management. *Proceedings of Fifth IFIP/IEEE International Symposium on Integrated Network Management.* Chapman & Hall, 1997.

[MBL93]   Mazumdar, S.; Brady, S.; Levine, D.: Design of Protocol Independent Management Agent to Support SNMP and CMIP Queries. *Proceedings of Third IFIP/IEEE International Symposium on Integrated Network Management.* North-Holland, 1993.

[MCC96]   McConnell, J.: *Managing Client–Server Environments: Tools and Strategies for Building Solutions.* Prentice Hall, 1996.

[MIL97]   Miller, M. A.: *Managing Internetworks with SNMP.* 2nd ed. M&T Books. MIS: Press, Inc., 1997.

[MOF94]   Moffet, J. D.: *Specification of Management and Discretionary Access Control.* In [SLO94], 1994.

[MOL94]   Moll, K. R.: *Informatik-Management.* Springer-Verlag, 1994.

[MOR97]   Mowbray T.; Ruh, W.: *Inside Corba—Distributed Object Standards and Applications.* Addison-Wesley, 1997.

[MOU97]   Mountzia, M.: *Flexible Agents in Integrated Network and Systems Management.* Dissertation, TU München, 1997.

[MUL97]   Muller, P.: *Instant UML.* Wrox Press, 1997.

[NEU98]   Neumair, B.: Distributed Applications Management Based on ODP Viewpoint Concepts and CORBA. *Proceedings of the IEEE/IFIP Network Operations and Management Symposium (NOMS 98).* IEEE, 1998.

[NMF26]   Network Management Forum: Forum 026, Translation of Internet MIBs to ISO/CCITT GDMO MIBs, *http://www.nmf.org*, 1993.

[NMF28]   Network Management Forum: Forum 028, ISO/CCITT to Internet Management Proxy, *http://www.nmf.org*, 1993.

[NMF30]   Network Management Forum: Forum 030, Translation of ISO/CCITT GDMO MIBs to Internet MIBs, *http://www.nmf.org*, 1993.

[OEC91]   Office for Official Publications of the European Communities: Information Technology Security Evaluation Criteria (IT-SEC), Luxemburg, 1991.

[OG306]   Open Group: Systems Management—Management Protocols API (XMP), CAE Specification 306, *http://www.opengroup.org*, 1994.

[OG509]   Open Group: Inter-Domain Management: Specification Translation, Document No. P509, *http://www.opengroup.org*, 1997.

[OG607]   Open Group: OSI-Abstract-Data Manipulation API (XOM), CAE Specification 607, *http://www.opengroup.org*, 1996.

[OHE96]   Orfali, R.; Harkey, D.; Edwards, J.: *The Essential Distributed Objects Survival Guide.* John Wiley & Sons, 1996.

[OHJ96]   O'Hare, G. M. P.; Jennings, N. R.: *Foundations of Distributed Artificial Intelligence.* John Wiley & Sons, 1996.

[OPR96]   Otte, R.; Patrick, P.; Roy, M.: *Understanding CORBA.* Prentice Hall, 1996.

[ORH98]   Orfali, R.; Harkey, D.: *Client/Server Programming with Java and Corba.* John Wiley & Sons, 1998.

[OSF92]   *Introduction to OSF DCE.* Prentice Hall, 1992.

[PAT98]   Pavón, J.; Tomás, J.; CORBA for Network and Service Management in the TINA Framework. *IEEE Communications Magazine,* March 1998.

[PEM97]   Perkins, D.; McGinnes, E.: *Understanding SNMP/MIBs.* Prentice Hall, 1997.

[PER92]   Perlman, R.: *Interconnections: Bridges and Routers.* Addison-Wesley, 1992.

[PLH97]   Park, J. T.; Lee, J. H.; Hong, J. W.; Kim, Y. M.; Kim, S. B.: A VPN Management Architecture for Supporting CNM Services. *Proceedings of Fifth IFIP/IEEE International Symposium on Integrated Network Management.* Chapman & Hall, 1997.

[POP98]   Pope, A.: *The CORBA Reference Guide.* Addison-Wesley, 1998.

[RAH94]   Rahm, E.: *Mehrrechner-Datenbanksysteme.* Addison-Wesley, 1994.

[RAS95]   Raynaud, Y.; Sethi, A. S.; Faure-Vincent, F. (eds.): *Proceedings of Fourth IFIP/IEEE International Symposium on Integrated Network Management.* Chapman & Hall, 1995.

[RBP91]   Rumbaugh, J.; Blaha, M.; Premerlani, W.; Eddy, F.; Lorensen, W.: *Object-Oriented Modeling and Design.* Prentice Hall, 1991.

[RJB98]   Rumbaugh, J.; Jacobson, I.; Booch, G.: *Unified Modeling Language Reference Manual.* Addison-Wesley, 1998.

[ROS96]   Rose, M.: *The Simple Book: An Introduction to Network Management.* 3rd ed. Prentice Hall, 1996.

[RPR97]   Reed, B.; Peercy, M.; Robinson, E.: Distributed Systems Management on the Web. *Proceedings of Fifth IFIP/IEEE International Symposium on Integrated Network Management.* Chapman & Hall, 1997.

[SCH96]   Schäl, T.: *Workflow Management Systems for Process Organisations.* Springer-Verlag, 1996.

[SID98]   Sidor, D. J.: TMN Standards: Satisfying Today's Needs While Preparing for Tomorrow. *IEEE Comm. Magazine,* March 1998.

[SIE96]   Siegel, J.: *CORBA Fundamentals and Programming.* John Wiley & Sons, 1996.

[SLO94]   Sloman, M. (ed.): *Network and Distributed Systems Management.* Addison-Wesley, 1994.

[SLT94]   Sloman, M.; Twiddle, K.: *Domains—A Framework for Structuring Management Policy.* In [SLO94], 1994.

[SMI93]   Smith, P.: *Frame Relay.* Addison-Wesley, 1993.

[SOH97]   Soukouti, N.; Hollberg, U.: Joint Inter Domain Management—CORBA, CMIP and SNMP. *Proceedings of Fifth IFIP/IEEE International Symposium on Integrated Network Management.* Chapman & Hall, 1997.

[SPI92]   Spivey, J.: *The Z Notation: A Reference Manual.* Prentice Hall, 1992.

[STA93]   Stallings, W.: *SNMP, SNMPv2, and CMIP.* Addison-Wesley, 1993

[STA95]   Stallings, W.: *ISDN and Broadband ISDN with Frame Relay and ATM.* 3rd ed. Prentice Hall, 1995.

[STA96]   Stallings, W.: *SNMP, SNMPv2 and RMON: Practical Network Management*. 2nd ed. Corporate and Professional Publishing Group, 1996.

[STA97]   Stallings, W.: *Data and Computer Communications*. 5th ed. Prentice Hall, 1997.

[STB98]   Sturm, R.; Bumpus, W.: *Managing Applications Using the IETF Application MIB*. John Wiley & Sons, 1998.

[STE94]   Stevens, W. R.: *TCP/IP Illustrated. Vol. I: The Protocols*. Addison-Wesley, 1994.

[STE96]   Stevens, W. R.: *TCP/IP Illustrated. Vol. III: TCP for Transactions, HTTP, NNTP and the Unix Domains Protocols*. Addison-Wesley, 1996.

[STI95]   Stiller, B.: *Quality-of-Service*. International Thomson Publishing, 1995.

[TAN95]   Tanenbaum, A. S.: *Distributed Operating Systems*. Prentice Hall 1995.

[TAN96]   Tanenbaum, A. S.: *Computer Networks*. 3rd ed. Prentice Hall, 1996.

[TAT97]   Tate, A.: WfMC: Coalition Overview. *http://www.aiai.ed.ac.uk/project/wfmc/overview.html*, 1997.

[TER92]   Terplan, K.: *Communications Network Management*. 2nd ed. Prentice Hall, 1992.

[TER95]   Terplan, K.: *Client/Server Management*. Datacom-Buchverlag Bergheim, 1995.

[TER97]   Terplan, K.: *Remote Monitoring*. International Thomson Publishing, 1997.

[TIV96]   Tivoli Systems: *Tivoli/Enterprise Console Training Guide*. Austin, Texas, 1996.

[TIV97a]   Tivoli Systems: *Application Management Specification Version 2.0*, 1997.

[TIV97b]   Tivoli Systems: *TME10 Product Information*. Austin, Texas, 1997.

[TIV97c]   Tivoli Systems: *TME2.0: Technology Concepts and Facilities*. Technology White Paper, Austin, Texas, 1997.

[VAD93]   Valta, R.; Dreo, G.: Einsatz eines integrierten Trouble-Ticket-Systems zur Verbesserung der Fehlerdiagnose. *Theorie und Praxis der Wirtschaftsinformatik*. HMD, Heft 171, 30. Jg., May 1993.

[VAR94]   Varley, B.: *User Administration and Accounting*. In [SLO 94] pp. 381–402

[VOB96]   Vossen, G.; Becker, G.: *Geschäftsprozeßmodellierung und Workflow-Management*. International Thomson Publishing, 1996.

[VOD97]   Vogel, A.; Duddy, K.: *Java Programming with CORBA*. John Wiley & Sons, 1997.

[WAL93]   Wall, D.: Rechner, Netze, Spezialisten: Leistungsangebot der GWDG. *Gesellschaft für wissenschaftliche Datenverarbeitung*. Göttingen, 1993.

[WIE95]   Wies, R.: *Policies in Integrated Network and Systems Management: Methodologies for the Definition, Transformation and Application of Management Policies*. Dissertation, University of Munich, 1995.

[WIL94]   Willetts, K.: Service Management—The Drive for Re-engineering. *Proceedings of IEEE/IFIP Network Operations and Management Symposium*. IEEE, 1994.

[WLA98]   Wies, R.; Lohrmann, J.; Abeck, S.; Eckardt, T.: Prozeßorientiertes Qualitätsmanagement für IV-Dienstleister—ein Erfahrungsbericht. Wirtschaftsinformatik, Heft 3/98, Vieweg-Verlag, 1998.

[WOR96]   Workflow Management Coalition: Terminology & Glossary. Specification TC00-1011, Issue 2.0, 1996.

[WRS95]   Wright, G. R.; Stevens, W. R.: *TCP/IP Illustrated. Vol. II: The Implementation*. Addison-Wesley, 1995.

Abbreviations

AAL	ATM Adaptation Layer	CDR	Common Data Representation
ACD	Automatic Call Distribution	CI	Component Interface
ACK	Acknowledgment	CICC	Corporate IT Change Control
ACSE	Association Control Service Elements (OSI)	CICS	Customer Information Control System
ADM	Add-Drop Multiplexer	CILP	Corporate IT Log Processing
ADMD	Administrative Management Domain	CIM	Common Information Model
		CIMOM	CIM Object Manager
ADSL	Asymmetric Digital Subscriber Line	CIT	Computer-Integrated Telephony
AFS	Andrew File System	CL	Connectionless
AMS	Application Management Specification	CMIP	Common Management Information Protocol
ANSI	American National Standards Institute	CMIS	Common Management Information Services
API	Application Programming Interface	CMOL	CMIP over LLC
ARM	Application Response Measurement	CMOT	CMIP over TCP
ARP	Address Resolution Protocol	CNM	Customer Network Management
ARS	Action Request System	CO	Connection-Oriented
ASE	Application Service Elements	CORBA	Common Object Request Broker Architecture
ASN.1	Abstract Syntax Notation One	COSS	Common Object Services Specification
ATM	Asynchronous Transfer Mode		
AUI	Attachment Unit Interface	CP	Control Point
AVM	Admin View Module	CP(E)	Convergence Protocol (Entity)
AWT	Abstract Windowing Toolkit	CQM	Circuit Quality Monitor
		CSMA/CD	Carrier Sense Multiple Access with Collision Detection
BER	Basic Encoding Rules		
BERT	Bit Error Rate Tester	CTI	Computer Telephony Integration
BGP	Border Gateway Protocol		
BLERT	Block Error Rate Tester	DBMS	Database Management System
		DCE	Data Circuit Terminating Equipment
CAD	Computer-Aided Design	DCE	Distributed Computing Environment
CATV	Community Antenna Television		
CBDS	Connectionless Broadband Data Service	DCOM	Distributed Component Object Model
CC	Cross-Connect	DCS	Digital Cross-Connect System
CCITT	Comité Consultatif International Télégraphique et Téléphonique	DEN	Directory-Enabled Networks
		DES	Data Encryption Standard
CCTA	Central Computer and Telecommunication Agency	DFS	Distributed File Service (DCE)

DHCP	Dynamic Host Configuration Protocol	HEMS	High-Level Entity Management System
DISMAN	Distributed Management Working Group	HMM	Hypermedia Management
		HMMP	Hypermedia Management Protocol
DLCI	Data Link Connection Identifier	HMOM	Hypermedia Object Manager
DME	Distributed Management Environment	HMP	Host Monitoring Protocol
		HTTP	Hypertext Transfer Protocol
DMI	Definition of Management Information	IAB	Internet Architecture Board
DMI	Desktop Management Interface	ICI	Interface Control Information
DMTF	Desktop Management Task Force	ICMP	Internet Control Message Protocol
DNS	Domain Name Service	ID	Identifier
DOD	Department of Defense	ID	Interface Data
DPI	Distributed Protocol Interface	IDL	Interface Definition Language
DQDB	Distributed Queue Dual Bus	IDU	Interface Data Unit
DS	Digital Line System	EIN	Internet Engineering Notes
DS0, 1, . . .	Digital Signal Level No. 0, 1, . . .	IETF	Internet Engineering Task Force
DTE	Data Terminal Equipment	IGMP	Internet Group Management Protocol
E0, 1, . . .	European Digital Signal Level No. 0, 1, . . .	IGP	Interior Gateway Protocol
		IIMC	ISO/CCITT and Internet Management Coexistence
ECMA	European Computer Manufacturers' Association	IIOP	Internet Inter-ORB Protocol
EFD	Event Forwarding Discriminator	ILMI	Interim Local Management Interface
EGP	Exterior Gateway Protocol	IMT	Inductive Modeling Technology
EMS	Element Management System	IN	Intelligent Network
ERMS	Entity-Relationship Management System	INMS	Integrated Network Management System
ESF	Extended Superframe Format	IP	Internet Protocol
ESIOP	Environment-Specific Inter-ORB Protocol	IRC	Internet Relay Chat
		IRTF	Internet Research Task Force
ETSI	European Telecommunications Standards Institute	ISDN	Integrated Services Digital Network
		ISO	International Standardization Organization
FCS	Frame Check Sequence	ISP	International Standardized Profiles
FDDI	Fiber Distributed Data Interface	ISP	Internet Service Provider
FDM	Frequency Division Multiplexing	IT	Information Technology
FDT	Formal Description Techniques	ITIL	Information Technology Infrastructure Library
FR	Frame Relay		
FRAD	Frame Relay Access Device	ITU	International Telecommunications Union
FTAM	File Transfer, Access, and Management		
FTP	File Transfer Protocol	JDMK	Java Dynamic Management Kit
		JIDM	Joint Inter-Domain Management
GDMO	Guidelines for the Definition of Managed Objects	JMAPI	Java Management API
GIOP	General Inter-ORB Protocol	LAN	Local Area Network
GMI	Generic Management Information	LANE	LAN Emulation over ATM
GMOC	Generic Managed Object Class (OSI)	LDAP	Lightweight Directory Access Protocol
GRM	General Relationship Model		
GUI	Graphical User Interface	LLC	Logical Link Control
		LOI	Letter of Intent
HDLC	Higher Data Link Control		
HDSL	High Bit Rate Digital Subscriber Line	MAC	Medium Access Control

MAC	Message Authentication Code	OAM	Operations, Administrations, Maintenance (TMN)
MAN	Metropolitan Area Network		
MBD	Management by Delegation	OAMP	Operation, Administration, Maintenance, Provisioning
Mbps	Megabit per Second		
MD	Mediation Device (TMN)	OC-1, 2	Optical Carrier Level 1, 2, . . .
MD	Message Digest	ODMA	Open Distributed Management Architecture
MF	Mediation Function (TMN)		
MHS	Message Handling System	ODP	Open Distributed Processing
MI	Management Interface	OI	Object Identifiers
MIB	Management Information Base	OIM	OSI Internet Management
MIF	Management Information Format	OIM	OSI Internet Management MIB
MIL	Management Information Library	OLA	Operational Level Agreement
MIS	Management Information Service	OMA	Object Management Architecture
MIT	Management Information Tree	OMG	Object Management Group
MMAC	Multimedia Access Center	OMT	Object Modeling Technique
MO	Managed Object	ORB	Object Request Broker
MOC	Managed Object Class	OS	Operating System
MOCS	Managed Objects Conformance Statements	OS	Operations System (TMN)
		OSA	Object Services Architecture
MOF	Managed Object Format	OSF	Open Software Foundation
MOM	Manager of Manager	OSF	Operations System Function (TMN)
MPOA	Multiprotocol over ATM	OSI	Open Systems Interconnection (ISO)
MR	Managed Resource	OSI-RM	OSI Reference Model
MS	Management System, Management Station	OSPFP	Open Shortest Path First Protocol
MTA	Message Transfer Agent	PAD	Packet Assembly Disassembly
MTP	Multicast Transport Protocol	PBX	Private Branch Exchange
MTS	Message Transfer System	PCI	Protocol Control Information
		PCM	Pulse Code Modulation
NAK	Negative Acknowledgment	PDU	Protocol Data Unit
NCP	Network Control Program	PICS	Protocol Implementation Conformance Statements
NDS	Novell Directory Service		
NE	Network Element (TMN)	PLP	Packet Layer Protocol
NETOU	Network Operator Utility	POTS	Plain Old Telephony Systems
NFS	Network File System	PPP	Point-to-Point Protocol
NIC	Network Information Center	PRMD	Private Management Domain
NIS	Network Information Service/System	PSE	Packet Switching Exchange
		PVC	Permanent Virtual Circuit
NIST	National Institute for Standards and Technology	QoS	Quality of Service
NM	Network Management		
NMC	Network Management Center	RAID	Redundant Array of Inexpensive Drives
NMF	Network Management Forum		
NMI	Network Management Interface	RARP	Reverse Address Resolution Protocol
NMP	Network Management Process	RDA	Remote Data Access
NMPE	Network Management Protocol Entity	RFC	Request for Change
		RFC	Request for Comments
NMS	Network Management Services	RFI	Request for Information
NMS	Network Management Station	RFP	Request for Proposal
NNI	Network–Node Interface (ATM)	RFS	Remote File Sharing
NNI	Network-to-Network Interface	RIP	Routing Information Protocol
NOC	Network Operations Center	RJE	Remote Job Entry
		RMI	Remote Method Invocation
		RMON	Remote Network Monitoring

ROC	Release of Change		TCP	Transmission Control Protocol
ROSE	Remote Operations Service Elements (OSI)		TDM	Time Division Multiplexing
			TDR	Time Domain Reflectometer
RPC	Remote Procedure Call		TINA	Telecommunications Information Network Architecture
RSVP	Resource Reservation Protocol			
			TME	Tivoli Management Envionment
SAP	Service Access Point		TMN	Telecommunications Management Network
SDH	Synchronous Digital Hierarchy			
SDL	Specification and Description Language		TN	Telecommunication Network
			TT	Trouble Ticket
SDSL	Symmetric Digital Subscriber Line		TTS	Trouble Ticket System
SDU	Service Data Unit			
SGMP	Simple Gateway Monitoring Protocol		UA	User Agent
			UDP	User Datagram Protocol
SHA	Secure Hash Algorithm		UML	Unified Modeling Language
SIOP	GIOP over SS7		UNI	User-to-Network Interface
SLA	Service Level Agreement		UPS	Uninterruptible Power Supply
SM	Systems Management		USM	User-based Security Model
SMA	Systems Management Application		UTP	Unshielded Twisted Pair
SMAE	Systems Management Application Entity			
			VC	Virtual Channel
SMAP	Systems Management Application Process		VCC	Virtual Channel Connection
			VCI	Virtual Channel Identifier
SMDS	Switched Multimegabit Data Service		VCI	Virtual Connection Identifier
SMF	Systems Management Function		VMTP	Versatile Message Transaction Protocol
SMFA	Systems Management Functional Area			
			VPC	Virtual Path Connection
SMI	Structure of Management Information		VPI	Virtual Path Identifier
			VPN	Virtual Private Network
SMP	Simple Management Protocol		VT	Virtual Terminal
SMTP	Simple Mail Transfer Protocol			
SNA	Systems Network Architecture (IBM)		WAIS	Wide Area Information Servers
SNMP	Simple Network Management Protocol		WAN	Wide Area Network
			WBEM	Web-Based Enterprise Management
SONET	Synchronous Optical Network		WfMC	Workflow Management Coalition
SP	Service Provider		WSF	Workstation Function
SQL	Structured Query Language		WWW	World Wide Web
S-STP	Screened Shielded Twisted Pair			
STM	Synchronous Transfer Mode		XMP	X/Open Management Protocol
STP	Shielded Twisted Pair		XOM	X/Open OSI Abstract Data Manipulation
STS	Synchronous Transfer Signal			
SVC	Switched Virtual Circuit		YP	Yellow Pages
TA	Terminal Adapter			

Index

A

Abstract Windowing Toolkit (AWT), 389
acceptance release form, 542
accept change in actual operations action, 527, 542–546
  acceptance in one step, 543
  change acceptance plan, 543, 544–545
  defined, 527, 542
  floating acceptance, 543
  ready message, 545–546
  support requirements, 544
  See also change management
access control, 81
accounting and billing applications, 333
  role in service costs, 453
accounting management, 89–91
  defined, 90
  functions of, 90
  importance of, 90
  See also management
accounting service, 66
action module, 350
Action Request System (ARS), 591
actions
  accept change in actual operations, 527, 542–546
  agree technical performance characteristics, 527, 531–532
  archive operational quality information, 568
  assign priority, 527, 536–537
  carry out data backup, 494, 496
  categorize problem notification, 515, 516–520
  check quality information, 568
  classify change, 527, 532–536
  collect operational quality information, 568
  compile operational statistics, 494, 495, 510–512
  defined, 126, 491

description, 491
escalate problem notification, 515, 516
execute changes in test operations, 527, 537–542
execute measures, 569
formulate change, 526, 528–531
handle detected exception, 494, 503–510
initiate analysis, 568
list target quality specifications, 567
monitor component status, 494, 496–503
plan measures, 569
PoMs selected for, 491
process and forward results, 568
process problem notification, 515, 520–524
provide information about operational quality, 567–568
release change, 528, 546–547
terminate problem processing, 516
undertake measures for service and maintenance, 494, 496
active information model, 316
adaptive routing, 55, 413
add-drop multiplexers (ADMs), 63
addressMap group, 189
administrative domains, 132
  defined, 132
  examples, 132
  illustrated, 133
administrative services, 450
admin view module (AVM), 249–251
  base, 250, 251
  help, 250, 251
  integration, 250
agent development tools, 378–384
  CORBA agents, 383
  DMTF-DMI, 382–383

interface specification approaches, 379
OSI management agents, 379–381
SNMP management agents, 381–382
See also development tools
agent extensibility (agentX) protocol, 171, 193
agent MIBs
  defined, 158
  example, 160
  MOs in, 162
  See also management information bases (MIBs)
agents
  ARM, 434
  basic management services, 263
  CMIP, 375
  CORBA, 383
  core, 263
  flexible, 118
  functionality of, 383
  implementation of, 373
  JDMK-developed, 383–384
  management, 251, 262–263
  management components, 263
  manager communication with, 171
  modular structures, 601
  OSI management, 379–381
  protocol adapters, 263
  RMON, 186, 189
  role, 131
  SNMP, 171–172, 251, 381–382
  software distribution, 428
  threshold monitoring, 175
  See also managers
agent technology, 262–263
  applying, to management, 262–263
  growth of, 262

About the Authors

Heinz-Gerd Hegering, born 1943, studied mathematics at the Universities of Muenster and Munich, where he received a diploma degree and Ph.D. in applied mathematics. Until 1984 he was head of the computer systems department of the Leibniz Supercomputing-Center in Munich. During that time he planned and installed several data communication networks for the universities in the state of Bavaria. From November 1984 until March 1989 he was associate professor of computer science at the Technical University of Munich. Since March 1989 he has been full professor of computer science at the University of Munich, director of the Institute for Informatik, and head of the board of directors of the Leibniz-Rechenzentrum of the Bavarian Academy of Sciences. He is also a member of several national advisory boards. His fields of active research are communication systems and management of IT infrastructures.

Sebastian Abeck received the diploma and doctorate degrees in computer science from the Technical University of Munich in 1987 and 1991, respectively. Until 1996 he worked as a senior researcher with the Munich Network Management Team. During that time he designed and implemented management solutions for big IT service providers. He is now a professor at the University of Karlsruhe, where he gives lectures on networking and distributed systems. Together with his team "Cooperation & Management," he works on provider-accepted IT management solutions. This work is tightly connected with demands from industrial partners. A second research interest concerns Web-based teaching and learning systems.

Bernhard Neumair received his diploma and Ph.D. in computer science from the Munich University of Technology. From 1993 to 1998, he was a senior researcher at the Ludwig-Maximilians University in Munich. His research interests included communication architectures and architectures and concepts for an integrated management of distributed computing environments. In 1998, he joined DeTeSystem GmbH, a subsidiary of German Telekom, as a group manager for communications solutions. He is responsible for design and realization of solutions in the areas of Internet and intranet, security, and e-commerce.